Lecture Notes in Computer Science 2406

Edited by G. Goos, J. Hartmanis, and J. van Leeuwen

Springer
Berlin
Heidelberg
New York
Barcelona
Hong Kong
London
Milan
Paris
Tokyo

Carol Peters   Martin Braschler
Julio Gonzalo   Michael Kluck (Eds.)

Evaluation of Cross-Language Information Retrieval Systems

Second Workshop of the
Cross-Language Evaluation Forum, CLEF 2001
Darmstadt, Germany, September 3-4, 2001
Revised Papers

Springer

Volume Editors

Carol Peters
Istituto di Scienza e Tecnologie
Consiglio Nazionale delle Ricerche
Via G. Moruzzi 1, 56124 Pisa, Italy
E-mail: carol@iei.pi.cnr.it

Martin Braschler
Eurospider Information Technology AG
Schaffhauserstrasse 18, 8006 Zürich, Switzerland
e-mail: martin.braschler@eurospider.com

Julio Gonzalo
Universidad Nacional de Educación a Distancia
E.T.S.I. Industriales, Ciudad Universitaria s/n
28040 Madrid, Spain
e-mail: julio@lsi.uned.es

Michael Kluck
InformationsZentrum Sozialwissenschaften
Lennestr. 30, 53113 Bonn, Germany
e-mail: Kluck@bonn.iz-soz.de

Cataloging-in-Publication Data applied for

Die Deutsche Bibliothek - CIP-Einheitsaufnahme

Evaluation of cross language information retrieval systems : revised papers
/ Second workshop of the Cross Language Evaluation Forum, CLEF 2001,
Darmstadt, Germany, September 3 - 4, 2001. Carol Peters ... (ed.). -
Berlin ; Heidelberg ; New York ; Barcelona ; Hong Kong ; London ; Milan ;
Paris ; Tokyo : Springer, 2002
    (Lecture notes in computer science ; Vol. 2406)
    ISBN 3-540-44042-9

CR Subject Classification (1998): H.3, I.2

ISSN 0302-9743
ISBN 3-540-44042-9 Springer-Verlag Berlin Heidelberg New York

Springer-Verlag Berlin Heidelberg New York,
a member of BertelsmannSpringer Science+Business Media GmbH

http://www.springer.de

© Springer-Verlag Berlin Heidelberg 2002
Printed in Germany

Typesetting: Camera-ready by author, data conversion by PTP-Berlin, Stefan Sossna e. K.
Printed on acid-free paper   SPIN: 10873667   06/3142   5 4 3 2 1 0

Preface

The second evaluation campaign of the Cross-Language Evaluation Forum (CLEF) for European languages was held from January to September 2001. This campaign proved a great success, and showed an increase in participation of around 70% compared with CLEF 2000. It culminated in a two-day workshop in Darmstadt, Germany, 3–4 September, in conjunction with the 5th European Conference on Digital Libraries (ECDL 2001). On the first day of the workshop, the results of the CLEF 2001 evaluation campaign were reported and discussed in paper and poster sessions. The second day focused on the current needs of cross-language systems and how evaluation campaigns in the future can best be designed to stimulate progress. The workshop was attended by nearly 50 researchers and system developers from both academia and industry. It provided an important opportunity for researchers working in the same area to get together and exchange ideas and experiences. Copies of all the presentations are available on the CLEF web site at http://www.clef-campaign.org. This volume contains thoroughly revised and expanded versions of the papers presented at the workshop and provides an exhaustive record of the CLEF 2001 campaign.

CLEF 2001 was conducted as an activity of the DELOS Network of Excellence for Digital Libraries, funded by the EC Information Society Technologies program to further research in digital library technologies. The activity was organized in collaboration with the US National Institute of Standards and Technology (NIST). The support of DELOS and NIST in the running of the evaluation campaign is gratefully acknow-ledged. We would also like to thank the other members of the Workshop Steering Committee for their assistance in the organization of this event.

April 2002

Carol Peters
Martin Braschler
Julio Gonzalo
Michael Kluck

CLEF 2001 Workshop Steering Committee

Martin Braschler, Eurospider Information Technology AG, Switzerland
Julio Gonzalo Arroyo, UNED, Madrid, Spain
Donna Harman, National Institute of Standards and Technology (NIST), USA
Djoerd Hiemstra, University of Twente, The Netherlands
Noriko Kando, National Institute of Informatics (NII), Japan
Michael Kluck, Informationszentrum Sozialwissenschaften (IZ), Bonn, Germany
Carol Peters, IEI-CNR, Pisa, Italy
Peter Schäuble, Eurospider Information Technology AG, Switzerland
Ellen Voorhees, National Institute of Standards and Technology (NIST), USA
Christa Womser-Hacker, University of Hildesheim, Germany

Table of Contents

Monolingual Experiments

Interactive Track

Part II. Evaluation Issues and Results

Appendix

Introduction

Carol Peters

IEI- CNR, Area di Ricerca, 56124 Pisa, Italy
carol@iei.pi.cnr.it

The objective of the Cross-Language Evaluation Forum (CLEF) is to develop and maintain an infrastructure for the testing and evaluation of information retrieval systems operating on European languages, and to create test-suites of reusable data that can be employed by system developers for benchmarking purposes. The second CLEF evaluation campaign was held from January to September 2001 and ended with a workshop held in Darmstadt, Germany, 3-4 September, in which the participants in the campaign reported their experiments and discussed their results.

These Proceedings consist of the revised, extended versions of the preliminary papers presented by the participants at the Workshop. In many cases, the participating groups not only describe and analyse their first results but report additional experiments made subsequent to the workshop. The volume consists of two parts and an appendix. The first part provides an exhaustive overview of the CLEF 2001 experiments whereas the second describes the framework against which these experiments were held. Readers who have never participated in CLEF or in similar evaluation campaigns may well prefer to begin with the second part in order to acquire the necessary background information on the organisation of this type of campaign, before entering into the details of the different cross-language and monolingual retrieval experiments. The appendix presents the results of all the participating groups for each track and task, run by run.

1 CLEF 2001 Experiments

Part I of this volume contains papers from the individual participating groups and provides a complete record of the CLEF 2001 experiments. The first paper by Martin Braschler introduces the experiments by giving a description of the various tracks and tasks and a summary of the main results. The remainder of Part I has been divided into three sections, reflecting to some extent the organisation of the Workshop.

In the first section, we have grouped all those papers that describe cross-language system testing activities: both multilingual, bilingual and domain-specific experiments are included here. The name of the section, "Mainly Cross-language" is determined by the fact that many of the authors also mention strategies implemented in monolingual runs; however, the main focus is on the cross-language aspect of their work. Twenty-two groups submitted runs for this kind of cross-language task, twenty of these groups have contributed a paper to these Proceedings.

Nine groups preferred to remain with the monolingual track at CLEF 2001; most of these were newcomers to CLEF activities. We expect many of them to move onto a

C.A. Peters et al. (Eds.): CLEF 2001, LNCS 2406, pp. 1-5, 2002.

cross-language task in the future. The work of seven of these groups is reported in the Monolingual section. CLEF 2001 provided the possibility to test monolingual systems on French, German, Dutch, Spanish and Italian collections. For most of these languages, CLEF offers the first opportunity for objective system evaluation under controlled conditions.

The final section of Part I is dedicated to the activities of another kind of cross-language task: interactive retrieval. The aim of the main cross-language and monolingual tracks was to measure system performance in terms of document rankings. However, this is not the only issue that interests the user. User satisfaction with an IR system is based on a number of factors, depending on the functionality of the particular system. An Interactive Track focusing on the interactive selection of documents that had been automatically translated from a language that the searcher would otherwise have been unable to read was experimented by a small group of three participants in CLEF 2001. The first paper in this section by Douglas Oard and Julio Gonzalo discusses the experimental design of this track, summarizes the results from the evaluation, and concludes with observations that can inform the design of subsequent evaluation activities for cross-language interactive systems. The other three papers describe the individual experiments conducted by the three groups.

Overall, the papers of Part I provide an important record of the state-of-the-art in the multilingual information access area, and of the main emerging research trends.

2   Evaluation Issues

Part II of the Proceedings consists of several papers which provide information concerning system evaluation activities not only for CLEF but also for the other two major international initiatives for system evaluation: the Text Retrieval Conferences (TREC) and the NACSIS Test Collection for Information Retrieval (NTCIR), both of which also organize tracks for cross-language system evaluation. Evaluation conferences such as TREC, NTCIR, and CLEF are all based on the evaluation methodology introduced in the Cranfield experiments. The first paper in this section by Ellen Voorhees reviews the fundamental assumptions and appropriate uses of the Cranfield paradigm, in particular as they apply in the context of today's evaluation conferences. The second paper by Noriko Kando introduces the NTCIR Workshop held in Japan for Asian languages, giving a brief history of the Workshop, and describing the tasks, test collections and evaluation methodology adopted.

The third paper in Part II is very much a CLEF-specific paper. Christa Womser-Hacker describes the topic generation process in a multilingual context. Topics are structured statements representing information needs from which the systems derive their queries and as such are an essential part of the test collection created for the campaign. Womser-Hacker discusses the various issues that have to be considered – linguistic and pragmatic - when constructing a standard set of topics in many different languages in a distributed framework.

The final paper in this section gives a complete overview of the organization of the CLEF 2001 evaluation campaign, describing the tasks and the test collection and explaining the techniques and measures used for result calculation and analysis. Readers who have no experience of CLEF are probably well-advised to look at this paper before beginning to read the details of the different experiments.

3 The Future

CLEF 2002 is now well under way. The CLEF 2000 and 2001 campaigns were sponsored by the DELOS Network of Excellence for Digital libraries; from October 2001, CLEF is funded mainly by the European Commission under the IST programme (IST-2000-31002). CLEF 2002 participants are able to build on and profit from the documented results of the first two campaigns. In particular, they have access to the test-suites that have been constructed as a result of the first two CLEF campaigns. It is our intention, in the future, to make this valuable data accessible to a wider research community.

Previous to the launching of the 2002 campaign, we conducted a survey in order to acquire input for the design of the tasks to be offered. Two types of users were considered: cross-language technology developers and cross-language technology deployers. The main recommendations made can be summed up in the following list:

- Increase the size and the number of languages in the multilingual test collection (both with respect to documents and topics);
- Provide the possibility to test on different text types (e.g. structured data);
- Provide more task variety (question-answering, web-style queries, text categorization);
- Study ways to test retrieval with multimedia data;
- Provide standard resources to permit objective comparison of individual system components (e.g. groups using a common retrieval system can compare the effect of their individual translation mechanisms);
- Focus more on user satisfaction issues (e.g. query formulation, results presentation).

As far as possible, the findings of this survey have been integrated into the definition of the CLEF 2002 campaign. Points that could not be taken up immediately will be considered for the future. As a first step, the size of the newspaper/newsagency collections and the number of languages covered have been increased. Language coverage in CLEF depends on two factors: the demand from potential participants and the existence of sufficient resources to handle the requirements of new languages. Our goal is to be able to cover not only the most widely used European languages but also some representative samples of less common languages, including members from each major group: e.g. Germanic, Romance, Slavic, and Ugro-Finnic languages. CLEF 2002 is seeing the addition of Finnish and Swedish to the multilingual corpus; hopefully, 2003 will see the inclusion of a Russian collection. Other languages will be considered in future years.

With respect to the demand for different types of texts and evaluation tasks, CLEF 2002 has seen the addition of the Amaryllis corpus of French bibliographic documents to the multilingual collection of scientific documents. We now have a specific track dedicated to testing systems operating on different types of domain-specific collections. For the future, we are considering the possibility of setting up a track for text categorization in multiple languages.

In order to meet the demand regarding end-user related issues, the interactive track has been extended in 2002 and will be testing both user-assisted query translation and also document selection.

Finally, as a first move towards handling multimedia, we are examining the feasibility of organising a spoken CLIR track in which systems would have to process and match spoken queries in more than one language against a spoken document collection. An experiment in this direction is being held this year within the framework of the DELOS Network of Excellence for Digital Libraries. The results will be presented at the annual CLEF Workshop in September 2002.

In conclusion, the results of the survey make it very clear that CLIR search functionality is perceived as just one component in a far more complex system cycle which goes from query formulation to results assimilation. In future years, we hope to go further in the extension of CLEF evaluation tasks, moving gradually from a focus on cross-language text retrieval and the measuring of document rankings to the provision of a comprehensive set of tasks covering all major aspects of multilingual, multimedia system performance with particular attention to the needs of the end-user.

More information on the activities of CLEF can be found on our Web site: http://www.clef-campaign.org/.

Acknowledgements. Many people and organizations must be thanked for their help in the running of CLEF 2001. First of all I should like to thank the other members of the CLEF Coordinating Group for all their efforts aimed at making both the campaign and workshop a great success. I should also like to express my gratitude to the ECDL 2001 Conference organisers for their assistance in the organisation of the CLEF Workshop.

It is not easy to set up an infrastructure that handles a large number of languages. The main topic sets (DE, EN, FR, IT, NL, SP) plus Russian were prepared by the project partners. Here, I should like to thank the following organisations that voluntarily engaged translators to provide topic sets in Chinese, Finnish, Japanese, Swedish and Thai, working on the basis of the set of source topics:

- Department of Information Studies, University of Tampere, Finland, which engaged the UTA Language Centre, for the Finnish topics;
- Human Computer Interaction and Language Engineering Laboratory, Swedish Institute of Computer Science (SICS), for the Swedish topics.
- National Institute of Informatics (NII), Tokyo, for the Japanese topics
- Natural Language Processing Lab, Department of Computer Science and Information Engineering, National Taiwan University, for the Chinese topics
- Kasetsart University, Thailand, for the Thai topics

I also gratefully acknowledge the support of all the data providers and copyright holders, and in particular:

- The Los Angeles Times, for the English data collection;
- Le Monde S.A. and ELDA: European Language Resources Distribution Agency, for the French data.
- Frankfurter Rundschau, Druck und Verlagshaus Frankfurt am Main; Der Spiegel, Spiegel Verlag, Hamburg, for the German newspaper collections.
- InformationsZentrum Sozialwissenschaften, Bonn, for the GIRT database.
- Hypersystems Srl, Torino and La Stampa, for the Italian newspaper data.
- Agencia EFE S.A., for the Spanish newswire data.
- NRC Handelsblad, Algemeen Dagblad and PCM Landelijke Dagbladen/Het Parool, for the Dutch newspaper data.
- Schweizerische Depeschenagentur, Switzerland, for the French, German and Italian Swiss news agency data.

Without their help, this evaluation activity would be impossible.

Last, but certainly not least, I should like to express my gratitude to Francesca Borri, IEI-CNR, for all her hard work in the editing and preparation of the final version of the texts. Much of the success of both the CLEF campaigns and the CLEF Workshops is a result of Francesca's valuable collaboration.

Part I

System Evaluation
Experiments at CLEF 2001

CLEF 2001 – Overview of Results

Martin Braschler

Eurospider Information Technology AG
Schaffhauserstr. 18
8006 Zürich, Switzerland
martin.braschler@eurospider.com

Abstract. CLEF, the Cross-Language Evaluation Forum, continued to grow substantially in the second year of its existence. Building on the success of the first CLEF campaign in 2000 and of its predecessors, the TREC cross-language tracks, CLEF 2001 attracted 34 participating groups which submitted nearly 200 different result sets. A description of the various tracks, and a summary of the main results and research directions are given in this overview. In addition, the CLEF multilingual test collection is examined with respect to the completeness of its relevance assessments. The analysis indicates that the test collection is stable and well suited for use in future evaluations.

1   Introduction

CLEF 2001 has built on the success of the first CLEF campaign in 2000 [3], which had already seen a substantial increase in the number of participating groups compared to the predecessors, the TREC cross-language (CLIR) tracks [7]. This trend continued in 2001, with the number of participants up by 70% and the number of experiments more than doubled. Contributing to this growth was the introduction of new tasks, resulting in an even more diverse set of experiments. This report aims to summarize and analyze the main results and research directions, as well as to compare the findings with those of the previous year.

The CLEF campaign is structured into several distinct tracks[1] (see also [15]). Some of these tracks are in turn structured into multiple tasks. The main focus of CLEF is the *multilingual retrieval track*, in which systems must use queries in one language to retrieve items from a test collection that contains documents written in a number of different languages (five for CLEF 2001). Participants are actively encouraged to work on this, the hardest task offered. Consequently, the multilingual track will be the main focus of this report. For those groups that do not want to handle this many languages, *bilingual* and *monolingual tasks* are offered. These smaller tasks serve important purposes, both in terms of helping to better understand the characteristics of

---

[1] While the cross-language activities in earlier TREC campaigns were organized as a single track (the TREC CLIR track), the larger CLEF campaigns are themselves structured into multiple tracks.

C.A. Peters et al. (Eds.): CLEF 2001, LNCS 2406, pp. 9-26, 2002.
© Springer-Verlag Berlin Heidelberg 2002

individual languages, as well as in attracting new participants. In addition, CLEF 2001 also featured a *domain-specific* and an *interactive track*.

In the following sections, details of the number of experiments for the individual tasks and different languages are given. The report then continues with a discussion of the methods employed and the results that were obtained, including a comparison with those of the previous year. Statistical significance testing provides indications of the validity of findings based on CLEF results. Finally, the CLEF 2001 test collection is investigated with respect to the completeness of its relevance assessments.

2   Tracks and Tasks

The tracks and tasks offered for the CLEF 2001 campaign were:
- *Multilingual Retrieval*. Retrieval of text documents in any of five languages (English, French, German, Italian, Spanish) using queries formulated in one language (choice of twelve different languages; see also Table 4). Result lists contain items from all five document languages.

- *Bilingual Retrieval*. Retrieval of text documents written in a language different from the query language. Participants could choose either English or Dutch as the target language, and from a selection of twelve different query languages.

- *Monolingual Retrieval*. Retrieval of text documents from a collection written in one of five languages: Dutch, French, German, Italian or Spanish. Query language identical to document language.

- *Domain-specific Retrieval*. Retrieval on a German document collection from the domain of social sciences. An accompanying thesaurus is available, queries were available in three languages (German, English, Russian).

- *Interactive*. Interactive experiments focused on selecting documents from a result list that contains items in a language different from the query language.

The results of the multilingual, bilingual, monolingual and interactive tasks are ranked lists containing those documents that best match a given query. Participants submitted one or several experiments ("runs") for an individual task.

In total, 34 groups from 15 different countries participated in one or more of the tasks that were offered for CLEF 2001 (see Table 1). Of these, 25 did some form of cross-language experiments, i.e. experiments that retrieve documents formulated in a language different from the query language (multilingual, bilingual, GIRT or interactive tracks). The remaining nine groups concentrated exclusively on monolingual retrieval. Just one group worked on the GIRT domain-specific track, and three groups participated in the new interactive track. Thirteen groups participated in more than one track, but no group tried more than three (Table 3).

Table 1. List of participants

Carnegie-Mellon Univ. (USA)	SINAI/Univ. Jaen (Spain)
Eidetica (Netherlands)	Thomson Legal (USA)*
Eurospider (Switzerland)*	TNO TPD (Netherlands)*
Greenwich Univ. (UK)	Univ. Alicante (Spain)
HKUST (Hong Kong)	Univ. Amsterdam (Netherlands)
Hummingbird (Canada)	Univ. Exeter (UK)
IAI (Germany)*	Univ. Glasgow (UK)*
IRIT (France)*	Univ. Maryland (USA)*
ITC-irst (Italy)*	Univ. Montreal/RALI (Canada)*
JHU-APL (USA)*	Univ. Neuchâtel (Switzerland)
Kasetsart Univ. (Thailand)	Univ. Salamanca (Spain)*
KCSL Inc. (Canada)	Univ. Sheffield (UK)*
Medialab (Netherlands)	Univ. Tampere (Finland)*
Nara Inst. of Tech. (Japan)	Univ. Twente (Netherlands)*
National Taiwan U (Taiwan)	UC Berkeley Group 1 (USA)*
OCE Tech. BV (Netherlands)	UC Berkeley Group 2 (USA)*
SICS/Conexor (Sweden)	UNED (Spain)

* also participant in 2000 (some as partners of other groups)

Table 2 compares the number of participants and experiments to those of earlier TREC CLIR tracks [7].

The first CLEF campaign in 2000 [3] was clearly a breakthrough in promoting larger participation. The growth trend was continued in this year's CLEF. Whereas the number of participants stayed more or less constant in the three years that the CLIR track was part of TREC, this number has nearly tripled after two years of CLEF as a stand-alone activity. A majority of last year's groups returned.

Table 2. Development in the number of participants and experiments

Year	# Participants	# Experiments
TREC6	13	$(95)^2$
TREC7	9	27
TREC8	12	45
CLEF 2000	20	95
CLEF 2001	34	198

A total of 198 experiments were submitted, more than double the number from last year. A breakdown into the individual tasks can be found in Table 3.

---

2 In TREC6, only bilingual retrieval was offered, which resulted in a large number of runs combining different pairs of languages [18]. Starting with TREC7, multilingual runs were introduced [4], which usually consist of multiple runs for the individual languages that are merged. The number of experiments for TREC6 is therefore not directly comparable to later years.

Table 3. Experiments listed by track/task

Task	# Participants	# Runs
Multilingual	8	26
Bilingual to EN	19	61
Bilingual to NL	3	3
Monolingual DE	12	25
Monolingual ES	10	22
Monolingual FR	9	18
Monolingual IT	8	14
Monolingual NL	9	19
Domain-specific GIRT	1	4
Interactive	3	6

All query languages were used for experiments, including the translations of the topics into Chinese, Finnish, Japanese, Russian, Swedish and Thai, which were provided by independent third parties. French, German and Spanish were the most popular query languages, with German being used the most. However, this is partly due to the fact that English was not an eligible query language for the bilingual and monolingual tasks. Table 4 shows a summary of the query languages and their use.

Table 4. Experiments listed by query language

Language	# Runs
Dutch	20
English	20
French	38
German	40
Italian	17
Spanish	33
Chinese*	9
Finnish*	1
Japanese*	2
Russian*	6
Swedish*	2
Thai*	4

* Query-only language

Queries were provided to participants in the form of "topics", which are textual formulations of statements of information need by hypothetical users. Such topics are structured into multiple fields, title, description and narrative, which provide increasingly more detailed representations of a search request. The title typically contains one to three words, whereas the description is usually one sentence long. The narrative, the longest representation, contains an elaborate formulation of several sentences. Participants construct queries for their systems either automatically or manually out of these topic statements.

A majority of runs (108 out of 192 non-interactive runs) used only the title and description fields of the topics for query construction, ignoring the narrative part. The reason for this was probably two-fold: First, the rules this year asked participants to submit at least one title+description run per task that they were tackling, and second, shorter queries were probably perceived as more "realistic" by some groups. Using all topic fields (longest possible queries) was the second most popular choice (63 runs). 13 runs used only the title field (resulting in very short queries). The remainder were more "exotic" combinations (description only, description+narrative). All tracks apart from the interactive used a distinction between "automatic" and "manual" runs, based on the methodology used for query construction. Only 12 manual experiments were submitted. Manual experiments are useful in establishing baselines and in improving the overall quality of relevance assessment pools. Therefore, an increase in the number of these experiments would be welcome; especially since they also tend to focus on interesting aspects of the retrieval process that are not usually covered by batch evaluations.

3   Characteristics of Experiments

Table 5 gives some key figures for the CLEF 2001 multilingual document collection. The collection was extended over the 2000 version by adding new documents in French, German and Italian, and by adding a new, fifth document language, Spanish. As can be seen from the table, the 2001 collection is very similar in characteristics to the widely used TREC7 and TREC8 ad-hoc retrieval test collections, both in terms of size and with regard to the amount of queries and relevance assessments.

Experiments ("runs") for the multilingual, bilingual and monolingual tasks were conducted by retrieving documents from all or part of this collection. Results were submitted in the form of ranked lists of those documents that best match a given query.

Table 5. Characteristics of the CLEF 2001 multilingual document collection.

Collection	# Part.	# Docs.	Size in MB	# Asses.	# Top.	# Ass. per topic
CLEF 2001	31	749,883	1982	80,624	50	1612
CLEF 2000	20	368,763	1158	43,566	40	1089
TREC8 CLIR	12	698,773	1620	23,156	28	827
TREC8 AdHoc	41	528,155	1904	86,830	50	1736
TREC7 AdHoc	42+4	528,155	1904	~80,000	50	~1600

In 2001, one general trend was a move towards corpus-based, statistical approaches. Many groups experimented with automatically constructed resources of this type, and used them either for query translation, or for resolving translation ambiguities (e.g. word sense disambiguation). Several groups used training data derived by mining the World Wide Web as input to their statistical models. Other groups used parallel or comparable corpora in several languages for a similar purpose. The statistical approaches were often combined with either machine-readable dictionaries or machine translation. As in 2000, the issues of stemming (morphological analysis) and decompounding (splitting of compound words in certain languages, such as Dutch and German) were explored extensively. However, conflicting results were reported for decompounding: while some groups reported substantial benefits (e.g. [12]), one group observed degradation of their retrieval results [5]. An encouraging sign was a clear trend of groups starting to adapt ideas that were presented in earlier campaigns. CLEF seems to accelerate the exchange of new methods in CLIR. Further evidence of this is the increased use of combination approaches, adding additional components to systems that were originally based on one particular method.

Some additional noteworthy characteristics include (in no particular order):

- Use of HMMs by ITC-IRST for query translation [1]
- Use of Chinese-English Wordnet by NTU [10]
- Web mining by Univ. Montreal [13]
- Random Indexing by SICS [17]
- Pseudo relevance feedback on passages by Univ. Exeter [9]
- Language-independent methods and the use of untranslated queries for cross-language retrieval by JHU/APL [11]

For a detailed discussion of these and more characteristics, please refer to the individual participants' papers in this volume.

4   Results

The following sections describe the results for the multilingual, bilingual, monolingual and domain-specific tracks. Results from the interactive track are described in a separate paper [14].

4.1   Multilingual Track

Eight groups submitted results for the multilingual track. Most of these groups submitted more than one result set. The multilingual track is the main focus of the CLEF campaign, and participants are actively encouraged to tackle it. Therefore, it was somewhat disappointing to see the number of groups for this track drop from eleven in the previous year. This may be partly due to the addition of a fifth language (Spanish), and the enlargement of the test collection, which meant additional effort for participants, and which may have seemed daunting to some newcomers. The experience gained this year in the simpler bilingual and monolingual tracks should allow more groups to move up to the multilingual experiments next year. Fig. 1 shows the best experiments of the five top groups in the automatic category for this track.

Four of the five top groups were participants in last year's campaign (the two Berkeley groups participated jointly in 2000), but not the group that submitted the top entry, Université de Neuchâtel. However, Univ. Neuchâtel has participated in TREC before, and therefore is no stranger to this sort of evaluation. The small number of

CLEF newcomers taking part in the multilingual track is another indication that the task was challenging.

Many of the top performing entries (Neuchâtel, Eurospider, Berkeley) used combination approaches: they translated the queries and/or documents with the help of more than one translation system or method (different forms of machine translation, machine-readable dictionaries, several corpus-based approaches).

CLEF 2001 Multilingual Track - Automatic

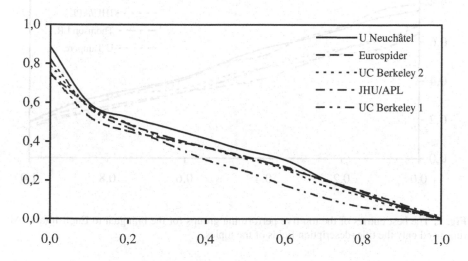

Fig. 1. The best entries of the top five performing groups for the multilingual track. All runs used only the title+description fields of the topics.

4.2 Bilingual Track

The bilingual track was split into two different tasks, search on the English (already offered in 2000) or on the Dutch documents (new for 2001). Fig. 2 shows the best entries for the top five performing groups in the bilingual to English task (experiments using title+description fields of the topics). Two groups have results that are substantially above the rest: University of Exeter and TNO. Exeter concentrated exclusively on bilingual retrieval. They used French, German, Chinese and Japanese as topic languages to search the English collection. TNO participated in the multilingual, bilingual and monolingual tracks. For their bilingual runs on the English documents, they used French as the topic language. The best entries from both groups used some form of query expansion combined with French-English Systran machine translation output. Systran translation for the bilingual track was also used by JHU/APL with good results. The other two groups in the top five used machine-readable dictionaries (Thomson Legal, Spanish-English using a dictionary combined with a similarity thesaurus, and University of Tampere, Finnish-English using a dictionary only). Only three groups submitted bilingual runs for the Dutch target language task.

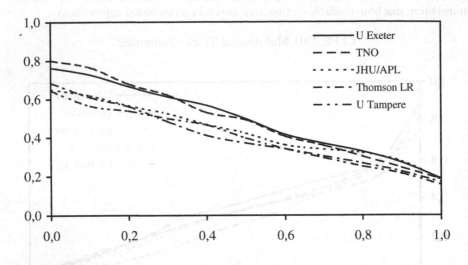

CLEF 2001 Bilingual to English Task - Automatic

Fig. 2. The best entries of the top five performing groups for the bilingual to English task. All runs used only the title+description fields of the topics.

4.3   Monolingual Track

Some of the best performing entries in the monolingual track came from groups that did not conduct cross-language experiments and instead concentrated on monolingual retrieval (Hummingbird, Univ. of Amsterdam). The five monolingual collections (Dutch, French, German, Italian, Spanish) were used by at least eight (Italian) and at most twelve (German) groups. Between fourteen (Italian) and twenty-five (German) experiments were submitted for the individual tasks.

Dutch Monolingual. The Dutch monolingual task was new in CLEF 2001. Six of the nine groups that participated came from the Netherlands, with the majority of them being newcomers. The group that submitted the top performing entry was TNO, one of the groups from the Netherlands. Their entry used a morphological analyzer and "fuzzy expansion" to match out-of-vocabulary terms. Unlike four of the five top performing groups that used a linguistically motivated stemming and/or decompounding process, JHU/APL submitted a run that performed well even though it used exclusively language-independent indexing methods (combination of words and n-grams).

CLEF2001 Dutch Monolingual Task - Automatic

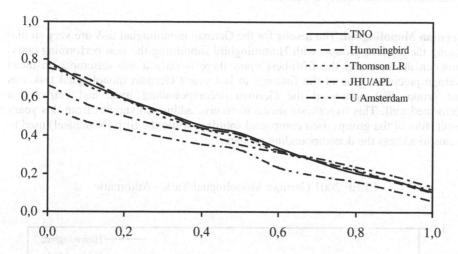

Fig. 3. The best entries of the top five performing groups for the Dutch monolingual task

French Monolingual. Four of the five groups that submitted good entries for the Dutch monolingual task were also among the top five groups for the French task.

CLEF 2001 French Monolingual Task - Automatic

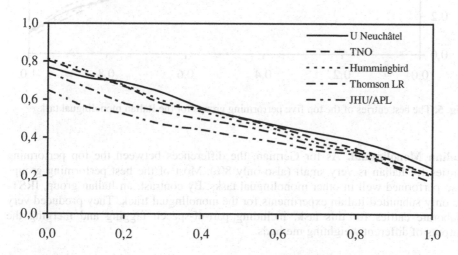

Fig. 4. The best entries of the top five performing groups for the French monolingual task.

However, the best performing entry came from Université de Neuchâtel, which did not participate in the Dutch task. This entry used a comparatively simple stemmer, combined with blind query expansion.

German Monolingual. The results for the German monolingual task are very similar among the top five groups, with Hummingbird submitting the best performing entry. Between the best and the fifth-best entry there is only a 8% difference in mean average precision. One of the findings in last year's German monolingual task was that groups that addressed the German decompounding issue had entries that performed well. This hypothesis seems to receive additional support from this year's result: four of the groups used compound splitting, while the fifth (Neuchâtel) used n-grams to address the decompounding problem.

CLEF 2001 German Monolingual Task - Automatic

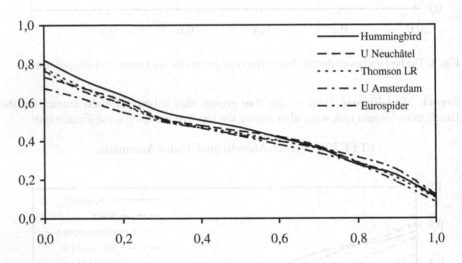

Fig. 5. The best entries of the top five performing groups for the Italian monolingual task

Italian Monolingual. As for German, the differences between the top performing entries for Italian is very small (also only 8%). Most of the best performing groups also performed well in other monolingual tasks. By contrast, an Italian group, IRST-itc only submitted Italian experiments for the monolingual track. They produced very elaborate entries for this task, including part-of-speech tagging and merging the outputs of different weighting methods.

CLEF 2001 Italian Monolingual Task - Automatic

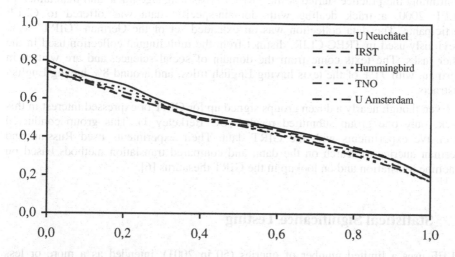

Fig. 6. The best entries of the top five performing groups for the Italian monolingual task.

Spanish Monolingual. For Spanish, one group (Neuchâtel) clearly outperformed the rest, which were in turn very close in performance.

CLEF 2001 Spanish Monolingual Task - Automatic

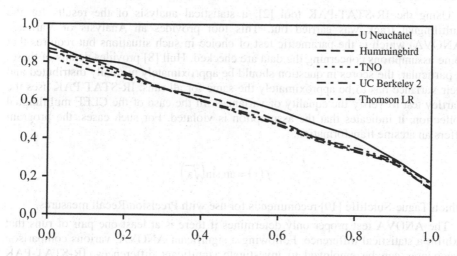

Fig. 7. The best entries of the top five performing groups for the Spanish monolingual task.

4.4   GIRT

Continuing the practice started at the TREC7 cross-language track, and maintained in CLEF 2000, a track dealing with domain-specific data was offered to CLEF participants. The data collection was an extended set of the German "GIRT" texts previously used in TREC-CLIR, distinct from the multilingual collection used in the other tasks. The texts come from the domain of social science, and are written in German, with 71% of the texts having English titles, and around 8% having English abstracts.

Even though nearly a dozen groups signed up for GIRT or expressed interest in this track, only one group submitted results (UC Berkeley 1). This group conducted extensive experiments with the GIRT data. Their experiments used Russian and German queries to search on the data, and compared translation methods based on machine translation and on lookup in the GIRT thesaurus [6].

5   Statistical Significance Testing

CLEF uses a limited number of queries (50 in 2001), intended as a more or less appropriate sample of the population of all possible queries that user would want to ask from the collection. When the goal is to validate how well results can be expected to hold beyond this particular set of queries, statistical testing can help. This way it is possible to determine what differences between runs appear to be real as opposed to differences that are due to sampling variation. As with all statistical testing, conclusions will be qualified by an error probability, which was chosen to be 0.05 in the following.

Using the IR-STAT-PAK tool [2], a statistical analysis of the results for the multilingual track was carried out. This tool provides an Analysis of Variance (ANOVA) which is the parametric test of choice in such situations but requires that some assumptions concerning the data are checked. Hull [8] provides details of these; in particular, the scores in question should be approximately normally distributed and their variance has to be approximately the same for all runs. IR-STAT-PAK uses the Hartley test to verify the equality of variances. In the case of the CLEF multilingual collection, it indicates that the assumption is violated. For such cases, the program offers an arcsine transformation,

$$f(x) = \arcsin\left(\sqrt{x}\right)$$

which Tague-Sutcliffe [19] recommends for use with Precision/Recall measures.

The ANOVA test proper only determines if there is at least one pair of runs that exhibit a statistical difference. Following a significant ANOVA, various comparison procedures can be employed to investigate significant differences. IR-STAT-PAK uses the Tukey T test for grouping the runs.

Run Name	Participant Name	
UniNEmum	Univ. Neuchâtel	
UniNEmuL	Univ. Neuchâtel	
BK2MUEAA1	UC Berkeley Group 2	
EIT01M3N	Eurospider	
UniNEmu	Univ. Neuchâtel	
EIT01M3D	Eurospider	
BKMUEAA2	UC Berkeley Group 1	
EIT01M1N	Eurospider	
BK2MUEAA2	UC Berkeley Group 2	
aplmuenb	JHU-APL	
aplmuend	JHU-APL	
BKMUGAM1	UC Berkeley Group 1	
aplmuena	JHU-APL	
EIT01M2N	Eurospider	
BKMUEAA1	UC Berkeley Group 1	
tnoex3	TNO TPD	
tnonx3	TNO TPD	
tnoex4	TNO TPD	
BK2MUCAA1	UC Berkeley Group 2	
BK2MUCAA2	UC Berkeley Group 2	

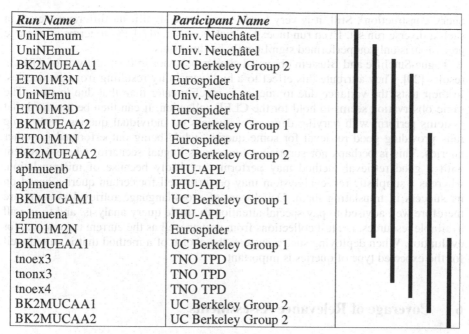

Fig. 8. Table of the top 20 runs for the multilingual track, sorted by descending performance in terms of average precision. The vertical bars indicate groups of runs that have performance differences which are not statistically significant.

Looking at the result for the top 20 multilingual runs (Fig. 8), according to the test all runs that are included in the same group (denoted by the black vertical bars) do not have significantly different performance. All runs scoring below a certain group perform significantly worse than at least the top entry of that group. Likewise, all runs scoring above a certain group perform significantly better than at least the bottom entry in that group. To determine all runs that perform significantly worse than a certain run, determine the rightmost group that includes the run. All runs scoring below the bottom entry of that group are significantly worse. Conversely, to determine all runs that perform significantly better than a given run, determine the leftmost group that includes the run. All those runs that score better than the top entry of that group perform significantly better.

Examples:

The run EIT01M1N significantly outperforms run BK2MUCAA2 (plus all runs that perform below the top 20).

The run tnoex4 is significantly outperformed by runs UniNEmum, UniNEmuL, BK2MUEAA1.

The second example is especially interesting. In the table, all types of multilingual runs have been mixed – regardless of topic fields, topic language or automatic/manual query construction[3]. Still, it is very hard to find large significant differences even in such a diverse run set. Even run tnoex4, which is only ranked 18th in terms of average precision, is only outperformed significantly by three runs.

Tague-Sutcliffe and Blustein observed similar behavior in their analysis of TREC3 results [20]. They attribute this effect to a high variability resulting from the queries. In their tests, the variance due to queries is much greater than that due to runs. The same observation seems to hold for the CLEF collection. It can then be assumed that systems perform with varying degrees of success on individual queries, with some runs providing good retrieval for some queries, while being outperformed for other queries. This is perhaps not surprising for a cross-lingual scenario, where a system with a good retrieval method may perform very badly because of mistranslation, whereas a simplistic retrieval system may perform well for certain queries based on its success in translating them. Developers of cross-language retrieval systems are therefore well advised to pay special attention to single query analysis, and to use all available resources, i.e. test collections from past as well as the current campaigns, for evaluation. When deploying such a system, the choice of a method that is suited well for the expected type of queries is important.

6   Coverage of Relevance Assessments

The results reported in this paper rely heavily on the concept of judging the relevance of documents with respect to given topics. The relevance of a document is usually judged by one or more human assessors, making this a costly undertaking. These relevance assessments are then used for the calculation of the recall/precision figures that underlie the graphs and figures presented in this report.

Their central importance for the calculation of many popular evaluation measures means that relevance assessments are not without critics. Generally, concerns mentioned focus mostly on two aspects: the "quality" and the "coverage" ("completeness") of the assessments. The first concern stems from the subjective nature of relevance, which can lead to disagreements between different assessors or even when the same assessor judges a document twice. Such disagreements can emerge from, among other things, personal bias of the judge, or a lack of understanding of the topics and documents. There is no "solution" for obtaining universal relevance judgments. Rather, researchers that rely upon the results from an evaluation campaign such as CLEF have to be aware of this issue and its implications. Numerous studies have analyzed the impact of disagreement in judging on the validity of evaluation results. These studies generally conclude that as long as sufficient consistency is maintained during judging, the ranking and comparison of systems is stable even if the absolute performance values calculated on the basis of the assessments change. The quality and consistency of the assessments in CLEF is ensured by following a well-proven methodology based on TREC experience. More details of relevance assessment processes can be found in [16].

The problem of coverage arises from practical considerations in the production of the relevance assessments. While it is comparatively easy to judge a substantial part

---

[3] This diversity of runs included in the table means that it is only intended for comparison of pairs of runs, not for a global ranking of all multilingual runs.

of the top-ranked results submitted by participants, it is much harder to judge the documents that were not part of any of the submitted result sets, since the number of such documents is usually far greater than that of the documents retrieved in result sets. This is especially the case with today's large test collections. Judging the non-retrieved documents is necessary to calculate some evaluation measures such as recall.

In order to keep costs manageable, only documents included and highly ranked in at least one result set are judged for relevance (with the union of all judged result sets forming a "document pool"). This implies that some relevant documents potentially go undetected if they are not retrieved by any of the participating systems. The assertion is that a sufficient number of diverse systems will turn up most relevant documents this way. Figures calculated based on these "limited" assessments are then a good approximation of theoretical figures based on complete assessments. A potential problem is the usability of the resulting test collection for the evaluation of a system that did not contribute to this "pool of judged documents". If such a system retrieves a substantial number of unjudged documents that are relevant, but went undetected, it is unfairly penalized when calculating the evaluation measures. An investigation into whether the assessments for the CLEF multilingual collection provide sufficient coverage follows below.

One way to analyze the coverage of the relevance judgments is by focusing on the "unique relevant documents" [22]. For this purpose, a unique relevant document is defined as a document that was judged relevant with respect to a specific topic, but that would not have been part of the pool of judged documents had a certain group not participated in the evaluation, i.e., only one group retrieved the document with a score high enough to have it included in the judgment pool. This addresses the concern that systems not directly participating in the evaluation are unfairly penalized. Subtracting relevant documents only found by a certain group, and then reevaluating the results for this group, simulates the scenario that this group was a non-participant. The smaller the change in performance that is observed, the higher is the probability that the relevance assessments are sufficiently complete.

For CLEF 2000, this kind of analysis was run for the experiments that were submitted to the multilingual track. In 2001, the same analysis was again run for the new, enlarged multilingual document collection and the new topics. A total of nine sets of relevance assessments were used: the original set, and eight sets that were built by taking away the relevant documents uniquely found by one specific participant. The results for every multilingual experiment were then recomputed using the set without the group-specific relevant documents. Fig. 9 shows the number of unique relevant documents per group participating in CLEF. The key figures obtained after rerunning the evaluations can be found in Table 6 and Fig. 10.

The ranking of the systems is also very stable: the only systems that switch ranks have an original performance difference of less than 0.008 in average precision, a difference that is well below any meaningful statistical significance. The differences reported here are slightly higher than the ones observed for the CLEF 2000 campaign [3], probably due to the larger overall number of relevant documents, which makes it harder to achieve complete coverage. Still, the figures indicate that the relevance assessments for the CLEF test collection are well suited for evaluating systems that did not directly participate in the original evaluation campaign.

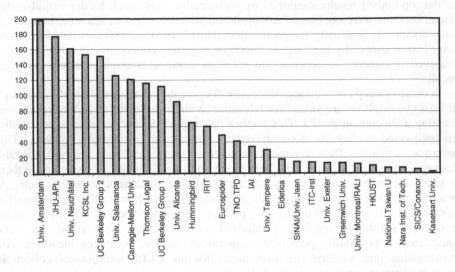

Fig. 9. Number of unique relevant documents contributed by each CLEF participant for the multilingual document collection.

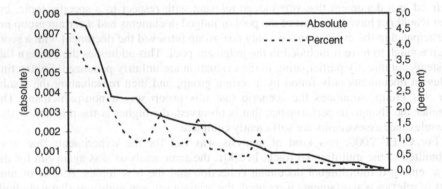

Fig. 10. Changes in mean average precision (absolute values and percentages) for all multilingual runs submitted to CLEF. The majority of runs experienced a change of less than 0.002.

7   Conclusions

Compared to the CLEF 2000 campaign, CLEF 2001 experienced growth in nearly all areas: more participants, more experiments, more tasks, larger collections and more topics and relevance assessments. Experiments show a clear trend towards more sophisticated combination approaches, and towards the adopting of ideas that were introduced in the previous evaluation campaign. This can be considered as a sign of maturity of this kind of evaluation campaigns. The best performing experiments often came from "veteran" participants, showing that returning groups successfully use the experiences that they gained to improve their systems.

This report gives an overview of the results of the participating systems for the different tracks/tasks and also provides a statistical analysis of the runs for the multilingual track. It turns out to be difficult to detect significant differences between runs, probably due to a high variability over queries. It will be interesting to see if adoption and exchange of translation methods will have an impact on query variability in future campaigns.

Table 6. Key figures[4] for investigation into the effect of "unique relevant documents" on the recall and precision measures. Presented are the observed changes in mean average precision.

Mean absolute diff.	0.0023	Mean diff. in percent	1.02%
Max absolute diff.	0.0076	Max diff. in percent	4.50%
Standard deviation	0.0051	Standard deviation	2.37%

Finally, the multilingual collection has been investigated for the coverage of its relevance assessments. The CLEF 2001 multilingual collection has key characteristics (size, topic set, number of assessments) very similar to the well-respected TREC-7/8 ad-hoc retrieval collections. Analysis of uniquely found relevant documents indicates that their coverage is also comparable to those collections, and that evaluation figures calculated on the basis of the CLEF collection are likely to be stable even for systems that have not participated in the official evaluation.

Acknowledgements. The author would like to thank Carol Peters for corrections and suggestions that helped improve the paper.

References

1. Bertoldi, N., Federico, M.: ITC-irst at CLEF 2001: Monolingual and Bilingual Tracks. In this volume.
2. Blustein, J.: IR STAT PAK. URL: http://www.csd.uwo.ca/~jamie/IRSP-overview.html
3. Braschler, M.: CLEF 2000 – Overview of Results. In Peters, C. (Ed.) Cross-Language Information Retrieval and Evaluation. Workshop of the Cross-Language Evaluation Forum, CLEF 2000, Revised Papers. Pages 89-101
4. Braschler, M., Krause, J., Peters, C., Schäuble, P.: Cross-Language Information Retrieval (CLIR) Track Overview. In: Proceedings of the Seventh Text REtrieval Conference (TREC-7), NIST Special Publicatio 500-242, Pages 25-32.
5. Chen, A.: Multilingual Information Retrieval using English and Chinese Queries. In this volume.
6. Gey, F. C., Jiang, H., Perelman, N.: Working with Russian Queries for the GIRT, Bilingual and Multilingual CLEF Tasks. In this volume.

---

[4] These numbers were calculated based on the absolute values of the differences. Note that even though relevant documents are removed from the evaluation, mean average precision can actually increase after recalculation due to interpolation effects. The figures reported for TREC in [21] are based on signed numbers, and therefore not directly comparable. Still, calculating the CLEF way produces larger differences, which means that the figures compares favorably with an observed mean difference of -0.0019 (-0.78%) for TREC8 ad hoc and -0.0018 (-1.43%) for TREC9 Chinese CLIR.

7. Harman, D., Braschler, M., Hess, M., Kluck, M., Peters, C., Schäuble, P., Sheridan P.: CLIR Evaluation at TREC. In Peters, C. (Ed.) Cross-Language Information Retrieval and Evaluation. Workshop of the Cross-Language Evaluation Forum, CLEF 2000, Revised Papers. Pages 7-23.
8. Hull, D. A: Using Statistical Testing in the Evaluation of Retrieval Experiments. In Proceedings of the 16th Annual International ACM SIGIR Conference on Research and Development in Information Retrieval, Pittsburg, USA, 1993.
9. Jones, G. J. F., Lam-Adesina, A. M.: Experiments with Machine Translation for Bilingual Retrieval. In this volume.
10. Lin, W. C., Chen, H.-H.: Using Co-Occurrence, Augmented Restrictions, and C-E WordNet for Chinese-English Cross-Language Information Retrieval at CLEF 2001. In this volume.
11. McNamee, P., Mayfield, J.: JHU/APL Experiments at CLEF: Translation Resources and Score Normalization. In this volume.
12. Monz, C., de Rijke, M.: Shallow Morphological Analysis in Monolingual Information Retrieval for Dutch, German and Italian. In this volume
13. Nie, J.-Y., Simard, M.: Using Statistical Translation Models for Bilingual IR. In this volume.
14. Oard, D., Gonzalo, J.: The CLEF 2001 Interactive Track. In this volume.
15. Peters, C.: Introduction. In this volume.
16. Peters, C., Braschler, M.: European research letter: Cross-language system evaluation: The CLEF campaigns, In Journal of the American Society for Information Science and Technology, Volume 52, Issue 12, pages 1067-1072
17. Sahlgren, M., Karlgren, J.: Vector-based Semantic Analysis using Random Indexing for Cross-lingual Query Expansion. In this volume.
18. Schäuble, P. Sheridan, P.: Cross-Language Information Retrieval (CLIR) Track Overview. In *Proceedings of the Sixth Text Retrieval Conference (TREC6)* (1997)
19. Tague-Sutcliffe, J.: The Pragmatics of Information Retrieval Experimentation, Revisited. In Sparck-Jones, K. and Willett, P. (Eds.): Readings in Information Retrieval, Morgan Kaufmann Publishers, San Francisco, CA, USA, 1997.
20. Tague-Sutcliffe, J., Blustein, J.: A Statistical Analysis of the TREC-3 Data. In Proceedings of the Third Text REtrieval Conference (TREC-3), NIST Special Publication 500-226. Page 385ff.
21. Voorhees, E. M., Harman, D.: Overview of the Eighth Text REtrieval Conference (TREC-8). In *Proceedings of the Eighth Text Retrieval Conference (TREC8)* (1999)
22. Zobel, J.: How reliable are the results of large-scale information retrieval experiments? In *Proceedings of the 21st Annual International ACM SIGIR Conference on Research and Development in Information Retrieval* (1998)

Report on CLEF-2001 Experiments: Effective Combined Query-Translation Approach

Jacques Savoy

Institut interfacultaire d'informatique, Université de Neuchâtel,
Pierre-à-Mazel 7, 2000 Neuchâtel, Switzerland
Jacques.Savoy@unine.ch http://www.unine.ch/info/clef/

Abstract. In our first participation in CLEF retrieval tasks, the primary objective was to define a general stopword list for various European languages (namely, French, Italian, German and Spanish) and also to suggest simple and efficient stemming procedures for these languages. Our second aim was to suggest a combined approach that could facilitate effective access to multilingual collections.

1 Monolingual Indexing and Searching

Most European languages (including French, Italian, Spanish, German) share many of the same characteristics as does the language of Shakespeare (e.g., word boundaries marked in a conventional manner, variant word forms generated generally by adding suffixes to the end of roots, etc.). Any adaptation of indexing or searching strategies thus means the elaboration of general stopword lists and fast stemming procedures. Stopword lists contain non-significant words that are removed from a document or a request before the indexing process is begun. Stemming procedures try to remove inflectional and derivational suffixes in order to conflate word variants into the same stem or root.

This first part will deal with these issues and is organized as follows: Section 1.1 contains an overview of our five test collections while Section 1.2 describes our general approach to building stopword lists and stemmers to be used with languages other than English. Section 1.3 depicts the Okapi probabilistic model together with various vector-space models and also evaluates them using the five test collections written in five different languages (monolingual track).

1.1 Overview of the Test Collections

The corpora used in our experiments included newspapers such as the *Los Angeles Times*, *Le Monde* (French), *La Stampa* (Italian), *Der Spiegel*, *Frankfurter Rundschau* (German) together with various articles edited by news agencies such as *EFE* (Spanish) and the Swiss news agency (available in French, German and Italian but without parallel translation). As shown in Table 1, these corpora are of various sizes, with the English, German and Spanish collections being twice the volume of the French and Italian sources. On the other hand, the mean

C.A. Peters et al. (Eds.): CLEF 2001, LNCS 2406, pp. 27–43, 2002.
© Springer-Verlag Berlin Heidelberg 2002

number of distinct indexing terms per document is relatively similar across the corpora (around 130), while this number is a little bit higher for the English collection (167.33). From those original documents, during the indexing process we only retained the following logical sections in our automatic runs: <TITLE>, <HEADLINE>, <TEXT>, <LEAD>, <LEAD1>, <TX>, <LD>, <TI>, and <ST>, On the other hand, we conducted two experiments (indicated as manual runs), one on the French collection and another on the Italian corpora within which we retained the following tags: for the French collections: <DE>, <KW>, <TB>, <SUBJECTS>, <CHA1>, <NAMES>, <NOM1>, <NOTE>, <GENRE>, <ORT1>, <SU11>, <SU21>, <GO11>, <GO12>, <GO13>, <GO14>, <GO24>, <TI01>, <TI02>, <TI03>, <TI04>, <TI05>, <TI06>, <TI07>, <TI08>, <PEOPLE>, <TI09>, <SOT1>, <SYE1>, and <SYF1>; while for the Italian corpora, and for one experiment, we used the following tags: <DE>, <KW>, <TB>, <NAMES>, <ARGUMENTS>, <LOCATIONS>, <TABLE>, <PEOPLE>, <ORGANISATIONS>, and <NOTE>.

From topic descriptions, we automatically removed certain phrases such as "Relevant document report ...", "Find documents that give ...", "Trouver des documents qui parlent ...", "Sono valide le discussioni e le decisioni ...", "Relevante Dokumente berichten ..." or "Los documentos relevantes proporcionan información ...".

In order to evaluate our approaches, we used the SMART system as a test bed for implementing the Okapi probabilistic model [1] and other vector-space strategies. This year our experiments were conducted on an Intel Pentium III/600 (memory: 1 GB, swap: 2 GB, disk: 6 x 35 GB).

Table 1. Test collection statistics

	English	French	Italian	German	Spanish
Size (in MB)	425 MB	243 MB	278 MB	527 MB	509 MB
# of documents	113,005	87,191	108,578	225,371	215,738
Number of distinct indexing terms / document					
Mean	167.33	140.48	129.91	129.26	120.25
Standard deviation	126.3	118.6	97.6	119.8	60.1
Median	138	102	92	96	107
Maximum	1,812	1,723	1,394	2,593	682
Minimum	2	3	1	1	5
Number of queries	47	49	47	49	49
Number of rel. items	856	1,212	1,246	2,130	2,694
Mean rel. items / request	18.21	24.73	26.51	43.47	54.97
Standard error	3.29	3.47	3.56	6.97	9.09
Median	10	17	18	27	26
Maximum	107	90	95	212	261
Minimum	1	1	2	1	1
With 5- rel. docs	18	10	9	4	4
With 10- rel. docs	28	15	16	13	10

1.2 Stopword Lists and Stemming Procedures

When defining general stopword lists, we knew that such lists were already available for the English [2] and French languages [3]. For the other three languages, we established general stopword lists by following the guidelines described in [2]. Firstly, we sorted all word forms appearing in our corpora according to frequency of occurrence and extracted the 200 most frequently occurring words. Secondly, we inspected this list to remove all numbers (e.g., "1994", "1"), plus all nouns and adjectives more or less directly related to the main subjects of the underlying collections. For example, the German word "Prozent" (ranking 69), the Italian noun "Italia" (ranking 87) or from the Spanish corpora the term "política" (ranking 131) was removed from the final list. From our point of view, such words can be useful as indexing terms in other circumstances. Thirdly, we included some non-information-bearing words, even if they did not appear in the first 200 most frequent words. For example, we added various personal or possessive pronouns (such as "meine", "my" in German), prepositions ("nello", "in the" in Italian), conjunctions ("où", "where" in French) or verbs ("estar", "to be" in Spanish). Another debatable issue was the presence of homographs and to some extent, we had to make arbitrary decisions relative to their inclusion in stopword lists. For example, the French word "son" can be translated as "sound" or "his".

The resulting stopword lists thus contained a large number of pronouns, articles, prepositions and conjunctions. As in various English stopword lists, there were also some verbal forms ("sein", "to be" in German; "essere", "to be" in Italian; "sono", "I am" in Italian). In our experiments we used the stoplist provided by the SMART system (571 English words) along with our 217 French words, 431 Italian words, 294 German words and 272 Spanish terms (these stopword lists are available at http://www.unine.ch/info/clef/).

After removing high frequency words, as an indexing procedure we used a stemming algorithm that tries to conflate word variants into the same stem or root. In developing this procedure for the French, Italian, German and Spanish languages, it is important to remember that these languages have more complex morphologies than does the English language [4]. As a first stage we decided to remove only inflectional suffixes such that singular and plural word forms or feminine and masculine forms conflate to the same root. More sophisticated schemes have already been proposed for the removal of derivational suffixes (e.g., "-ize", "-ably", "-ship" in the English language), such as the stemmer developed by Lovins [5], based on a list of over 260 suffixes, while that of Porter [6] looks for about 60 suffixes. For the Spanish language for example, Figuerola [7] described two different ones and their experiments showed that removing only inflectional suffixes (88 different inflectional suffixes were defined) seemed to provide better retrieval levels, compared with removing both inflectional and derivational suffixes (this extended stemmer included 230 suffixes).

A "quick and efficient" stemming procedure had already been developed for the French language [3]. Based on this same concept, we implemented a stemming algorithm for the Italian, Spanish and German languages (the C code for these stemmers can be found at http://www.unine.ch/info/clef/). In our approach, we only tried to remove inflectional suffixes attached to nouns or adjectives. In this context, the main inflectional rule in Italian is to modify the final character (e.g., "-o", "-a" or "-e") into another (e.g., "-i", "-e"). As a second rule, Italian morphology may also alter the final two letters (e.g., "-io" in "-i", "-co" in "-chi", "-ga" in "-ghe"). In Spanish, the main inflectional rule is to add one or two characters to denote the plural form of nouns or adjectives (e.g., "-s", "-es" like in "amigo" and "amigos" (friend) or "rey" and "reyes" (king)) or to modify the final character (e.g., "-z" in "-ces" in "voz" and "voces" (voice)). In German, a few rules may be applied to obtain the plural form of words (e.g., "Sängerin" into "Sängerinnen" (singer), "Boot" into "Boote" (boat), "Gott" into "Götter" (god)). However, our suggested algorithms cannot handle person and tense variations found in verbs or other derivational constructions.

Most European languages contain other morphological characteristics that our approach does not consider, with just one example being compound word constructions (e.g., handgun, worldwide). In German, compound words are widely used and hence causes many more difficulties than in English. For example, a life insurance company employee would be "Lebensversicherungsgesellschaftsangeteller" (Leben + s + versicherung + s + gesellschaft + s + angeteller for life + insurance + company + employee). Also morphological markers ("s") are not always present (e.g., "Bankangetellenlohn" built as Bank + angetellen + lohn (salary)). According to Monz & de Rijke [8] or Chen [9], including both compounds and their composite parts (only noun-noun decompositions in [8]) in queries and documents can provide better performance. However, according to Molina-Salgado [10], decomposition of German words causes the average precision to be reduced.

Finally, diacritic characters are usually not present in English collections (with some exceptions, such as "à la carte" or "résumé"); and these characters are replaced by their corresponding non-accented letter in the Italian, German and Spanish language.

Given that French, Italian and Spanish morphology is comparable to that of English, we decided to index French, Italian and Spanish documents based on word stems. For the German language and its more complex compounding morphology, we decided to use a 5-gram approach [11], [12]. However, and contrary to [11], our generation of 5-grams indexing terms does not span word boundaries. This value of 5 was chosen for two reasons; it results in better performance when using the CLEF-2000 corpora [13], and it is also close to the mean word length of our German corpora (mean word length: 5.87; standard error: 3.7). Using this indexing scheme, the compound "das Hausdach" (the roof of the house) will generate the following indexing terms: "das", "hausd", "ausda", "usdac" and "sdach".

1.3 Indexing and Searching Strategy

In order to obtain a broader view of the relative merit of various retrieval models [14], we first adopted a binary indexing scheme where each document (or request) is represented by a set of keywords without any weights. To measure the similarity between documents and requests we counted the number of common terms, computed from the inner product (retrieval model denoted "doc=bnn, query=bnn" or "bnn-bnn"). Binary logical restrictions are however often too limiting for document and query indexing. In order to weight the presence of each indexing term in a document surrogate (or in a query), we might take the term occurrence frequency into account, thus providing better term distinction and increasing indexing flexibility (retrieval model notation: "doc=nnn, query=nnn" or "nnn-nnn").

Those terms that do occur very frequently in the collection are not however believed to be very helpful in discriminating between relevant and non-relevant items. Thus we might count their frequency in the collection, or more precisely the inverse document frequency (denoted by idf), resulting in larger weights for sparse words and smaller weights for more frequent ones. Moreover, a cosine normalization could prove beneficial and each indexing weight might vary within the range of 0 to 1 (retrieval model notation: "ntc-ntc", Table 2 depicts the exact weighting formulation).

Table 2. Weighting schemes

bnn	$w_{ij} = 1$	npn	$w_{ij} = tf_{ij} \cdot ln\left[\dfrac{n - df_j}{df_j}\right]$
nnn	$w_{ij} = tf_{ij}$		
ntc	$w_{ij} = \dfrac{tf_{ij} \cdot idf_j}{\sqrt{\sum_{k=1}^{t}(tf_{ik} \cdot idf_k)^2}}$	atn	$w_{ij} = idf_j \cdot \left[\dfrac{0.5 + 0.5 \cdot tf_{ij}}{max\ tf_{i\cdot}}\right]$
Okapi	$w_{ij} = \dfrac{(k_1+1) \cdot tf_{ij}}{K + tf_{ij}}$ with $K = k_1 \cdot \left[(1-b) + b \cdot \dfrac{l_i}{advl}\right]$		
dtu	$w_{ij} = \dfrac{(ln(ln(tf_{ij})+1)+1) \cdot idf_j}{(1-slope) \cdot pivot + (slope \cdot nt_i)}$		
dtc	$w_{ij} = \dfrac{(ln(ln(tf_{ij})+1)+1) \cdot idf_j}{\sqrt{\sum_{k=1}^{t}[(ln(ln(tf_{ik})+1)+1) \cdot idf_k]^2}}$		
Lnu	$w_{ij} = \dfrac{\frac{ln(tf_{ij})+1}{pivot + 1}}{(1-slope) \cdot pivot + (slope \cdot nt_i)}$		

Other variants could also be created, especially in situations when the occurrence of a given term in a document is a rare event. Thus, it may be a good practice to give more importance to the first occurrence of this word as compared to any successive, repeated occurrences. Therefore, the tf component may be computed as 0.5 + 0.5 • [tf / max tf in a document] (retrieval model denoted "doc=atn").

Finally we should assume that a term's presence in a shorter document provides stronger evidence than in a longer document. To account for this, we integrated document length within the weighting formula, leading to more complex IR models; those denoted for example by "doc=Lnu" [15] and "doc=dtu" [16]. Finally for CLEF-2001, we also conducted various experiments using the Okapi probabilistic model [1]. In our experiments, the constants b, k_1, advl, pivot and slope shown in Table 2 are fixed at b = 0.75, k_1 = 1.2, advl = 900, pivot = 125, and slope = 0.1. To measure the length of document i, we used the notation l_i corresponding to the sum of tf_{ij}.

Table 3. Average precision of various indexing and searching strategies based on monolingual requests and documents

	Average precision				
	English	French	Italian	German	Spanish
Title only	47 queries	49 queries	47 queries	49 queries	49 queries
Okapi–npn	**48.50**	**43.79**	**39.60**	**32.62**	**48.87**
Lnu–ltc	44.36	40.35	38.18	29.23	45.13
atn–ntc	44.30	40.99	36.81	31.56	45.38
dtu–dtc	46.47	41.88	39.00	31.22	45.68
ntc–ntc	23.65	28.76	26.32	24.31	32.90
bnn–bnn	22.98	21.90	23.31	20.95	25.48
nnn–nnn	13.33	16.00	19.04	11.62	21.71
Title-Desc					
Okapi–npn	**54.17**	**49.88**	**45.88**	**39.51**	**54.71**
Lnu–ltc	51.05	47.43	43.60	36.71	51.37
atn–ntc	51.09	47.97	41.62	37.54	51.31
dtu–dtc	53.26	48.97	43.49	36.72	50.59
ntc–ntc	31.25	32.21	30.01	30.08	36.83
bnn–bnn	25.51	17.91	25.66	18.79	28.68
nnn–nnn	12.06	14.13	20.78	9.83	24.74
Title-Desc-Narr					
Okapi–npn	**58.13**	**51.16**	**48.92**	**42.71**	**55.85**
Lnu–ltc	57.35	50.43	47.21	40.07	52.28
atn–ntc	54.52	50.78	45.21	39.26	54.82
dtu–dtc	54.49	51.49	46.47	36.79	51.90
ntc–ntc	36.13	36.69	32.74	31.10	40.17
bnn–bnn	20.36	11.71	19.90	5.75	21.86
nnn–nnn	13.28	16.58	22.52	5.38	25.10

To evaluate the retrieval performance of these various IR models, we adopted non-interpolated average precision (computed on the basis of 1,000 retrieved items per request by the TREC-EVAL program), thus allowing a single number to represent both precision and recall. Our evaluation results in Table 3 show that the Okapi probabilistic model provides the best performance when considering five different languages and three different query formulations. In the second position, we cannot see any clear distinction between three vector-space models, namely "doc=Lnu, query=ltc", "doc=atn, query=ntc" or "doc=dtu, query=dtc". For example, for the French corpus the second best approach is always "doc=dtu, query=dtc". For the Spanish collection, however, the IR model "doc=dtu, query=dtc" reveals the second best performance when using a query based on only the Title section, the "doc=Lnu, query=ltc" when using a query based on Title and Descriptive logical sections and "doc=atn, query=ntc" when using the longest query formulation. Finally, the traditional tf-idf weighting scheme ("ntc-ntc") does not provide very satisfactory results, and the simple term-frequency weighting scheme ("nnn-nnn") or the simple coordinate match ("bnn-bnn") results in poor retrieval performance.

Table 4. Average precision using blind query expansion

Title-Desc	Average precision				
	English 47 queries	French 49 queries	Italian 47 queries	German 49 queries	Spanish 49 queries
Okapi–npn	54.17	49.88	45.88	39.51	54.71
10 terms / 5 docs	**54.81**	**50.21**	48.65	41.36	**58.00**
15 terms / 5 docs	52.81	49.91	48.85	41.87	57.85
20 terms / 5 docs	52.18	48.70	48.79	**42.29**	57.59
10 terms / 10 docs	51.91	50.00	48.54	40.99	57.17
15 terms / 10 docs	51.39	49.86	48.86	41.42	57.41
20 terms / 10 docs	50.27	49.28	**49.25**	41.81	57.24

It has been observed that pseudo-relevance feedback (blind expansion) seems to be a useful technique for enhancing retrieval effectiveness. In this study, we adopted Rocchio's approach [15] with $\alpha = 0.75$, $\beta = 0.75$ where the system was allowed to add to the original query m terms extracted from the n best ranked documents. To evaluate this proposition, we used the Okapi probabilistic model and enlarged the query by 10 to 20 terms, provided by the best 5 or 10 articles retrieved. The results depicted in Table 4 indicate that the optimal parameter setting seems to be collection-dependant, with a slight preference for extracting 10 terms from the best 5 ranked documents. Moreover, performance improvement also seems to be collection-dependant (or language-dependant), with an increase of only 1.18% for the English corpus (average precision increased from 54.17 to 54.81) while for the Spanish language, enhancement is around 6% (average precision increased from 54.71 to 58.00).

In the monolingual track, we submitted six runs along with their corresponding descriptions, as listed in Table 5. Four of them were fully automatic using the request's Title and Descriptive logical sections, while the last two used more of the document's logical sections and were based on the request's Title, Descriptive and Narrative sections. These last two runs were labeled "manual" because we used logical sections containing manually assigned index terms. For all runs, we did not use any manual interventions during the indexing and retrieval procedures.

Table 5. Official monolingual run descriptions

Run name	Language	Query	Form	Query expansion	Average pr.
UniNEmofr	French	T-D	automatic	10 terms / 5 docs	50.21
UniNEmoit	Italian	T-D	automatic	10 terms / 5 docs	48.65
UniNEmoge	German	T-D	automatic	30 terms / 5 docs	43.09
UniNEmoes	Spanish	T-D	automatic	10 terms / 5 docs	58.00
UniNEmofrM	French	T-D-N	manual	no expansion	51.88
UniNEmoitM	Italian	T-D-N	manual	10 terms / 5 docs	54.18

2   Multilingual Information Retrieval

In order to overcome language barriers [17], [18], [19], we based our approach on free and readily available translation resources that automatically provide translations of queries in the desired target language. More precisely, the original queries were written in English and we did not use any parallel or aligned corpora to derive statistically or semantically related words in the target language. The first section of this chapter describes our combined strategy for cross-lingual retrieval while Section 2.2 provides some examples of translation errors. Finally, Section 2.3 presents different merging strategies along with their evaluations (multilingual track).

2.1   Query Translation

In order to develop a fully automatic approach, we chose to translate requests using the SYSTRAN system [20] (available at http://babel.altavista.com) and to translate query terms word-by-word using the BABYLON bilingual dictionary (available at http://www.babylon.com). The bilingual dictionary is able to provide not only one but several options for the translation of each word [21]. In our experiments, we decide to pick the first translation available (listed under "BABYLON 1") or the first two terms (listed under "BABYLON 2").

In order to obtain a quantitative picture of term ambiguity, we analyzed the number of translation alternatives generated by BABYLON's bilingual dictionaries. This study did not take determinants into account (e.g., "the"), conjunctions and prepositions (e.g., "and", "in", "of") or words appearing in our English stopword list (e.g., "new", "use"), and terms generally having a larger number of translations. Based on the Title section of the English requests, we found 137 search keywords to be translated.

The data in Table 6 shows how the mean number of translations provided by BABYLON dictionaries can vary depending on language, for example from 2.94 for German to 5.64 for Spanish. We found the maximum number of translation alternatives for the word "fall" in French and German (the word "fall" can be viewed as a noun or a verb), for the term "court" in Italian and for the word "attacks" in Spanish. The median value of their distributions is rather small, varying from 2 for German to 4 for Spanish. Thus for the first two translation alternatives, we covered around 54% of the keywords to be translated in German, 40.9% in French, 42.3% in Italian and 36.5% for Spanish.

Table 6. Number of translations provided by the BABYLON system for English keywords appearing in the Title section of our queries

	Number of translation alternatives			
	French	Italian	German	Spanish
Mean number of translations	3.63	5.48	2.94	5.64
Standard deviation	3.15	5.48	2.41	5.69
Median	3	3	2	4
Maximum	17	19	12	24
with word	"fall"	"court"	"fall"	"attacks"
No translation	8	9	9	8
Only one alternative	27	36	40	28
Two alternatives	21	13	25	14
Three alternatives	31	15	21	15

In order to improve search performance, we tried combining the SYSTRAN system's machine translation with a bilingual dictionary. In this case, we translated a query using the SYSTRAN system and for each English search term we added the first or the first two translated words obtained from a bilingual dictionary look-up.

Table 7 provides an overview of the relative performance of our three automatic query translation approaches, depicting average precision achieved by manually translated queries (labeled "monolingual") in Column 2. Column 3 lists the retrieval performance achieved by the machine translation SYSTRAN system and Column 4 the mean precision obtained using only the first translation candidate provided by BABYLON's bilingual dictionary. Column 5 accounts for the first two translations alternatives provided by the bilingual dictionary, and finally Column 6 shows our combined approach, where a query is translated automatically by the machine translation system and the first translation candidate for each search keyword is added to the translated request.

For each language, Table 7 lists the mean difference between manually translated queries and our various automatic translation strategies. These values indicate that the manual approach always performs better than the four automatic schemes, while the machine translation approach provides better retrieval performance when compared to the bilingual dictionary. For this latter approach, choosing only the first translation candidate seems to provide better results than choosing the first two. As shown in the last column, the retrieval effectiveness of our combined translation strategy usually provides the best automatic performance. However, the average difference between the manual translation approach and our combined scheme is usually around 14%, except for the French collection, where the difference is only 3.43%. Moreover, for the French corpus and

Table 7. Average precision using different query translation strategies (Title-Desc)

French	Average precision				
	monolingual	SYSTRAN	BABYLON 1	BABYLON 2	combined
Okapi–npn	49.88	44.79	35.06	31.07	**48.62**
Lnu–ltc	47.43	42.74	34.81	34.32	**45.83**
atn–ntc	47.97	41.52	29.50	27.17	**45.65**
dtu–dtc	48.97	43.01	29.47	28.67	**46.39**
ntc–ntc	32.21	27.92	24.49	24.10	**31.04**
Mean difference		-11.81%	-31.72%	-35.07%	-3.93%
Italian					
Okapi–npn	45.88	33.10	31.41	27.11	**37.00**
Lnu–ltc	43.60	31.94	33.28	28.95	**38.27**
atn–ntc	41.62	28.44	28.65	25.26	**33.29**
dtu–dtc	43.49	29.93	33.58	29.90	**37.37**
ntc–ntc	30.01	23.26	24.11	22.98	**27.64**
Mean difference		-27.99%	-25.76%	-33.70%	-14.71%
German					
Okapi–npn	39.51	29.64	27.74	27.86	**35.06**
Lnu–ltc	36.71	25.80	25.61	28.49	**32.75**
atn–ntc	37.54	25.96	25.39	23.53	**31.47**
dtu–dtc	36.72	27.24	25.72	27.12	**31.53**
ntc–ntc	30.08	23.46	19.93	20.07	**27.65**
Mean difference		-26.67%	-31.22%	-29.72%	-12.09%
Spanish					
Okapi–npn	54.71	41.56	35.94	32.59	**45.77**
Lnu–ltc	51.37	39.92	36.51	34.13	**43.49**
atn–ntc	51.31	37.25	35.65	30.49	**43.39**
dtu–dtc	50.59	38.03	36.86	31.98	**44.09**
ntc–ntc	36.83	25.99	24.90	24.54	**29.81**
Mean difference		-25.60%	-30.66%	-36.94%	-15.80%

the Okapi model, the average precision for our combined solution is 48.62, only -2.5% below the retrieval performance of manually translated queries (average precision of 49.88).

2.2   Examples of Translation Failures

In order to obtain a preliminary picture of the difficulties underlying our automatic translation approaches, we analyzed some queries by comparing the translations produced by our two machine-based tools with those written by a humans being (see Table 8 for examples). As a first example, the title of Query #70 is "Death of Kim Il Sung" (in which the number "II" is written as the letter "i" followed by the letter "l"). This couple of letters "IL" is interpreted as the chemical symbol for illinium (chemical element #61 "found" by two University of Illinois researchers in 1926; a discovery not confirmed until the chemical element #61 was finally found in 1947, and named promethium). Moreover, the proper name "Sung" was interpreted as the past participle of the verb "to sing".

As another example, we analyzed Query #54 "Final four results" translated as "demi-finales" in French or "Halbfinale" in German. This request resulted in the incorrect identification of a multi-word concept (namely "final four") both by our two automatic translation tools and by the manual translation provided in Italian and Spanish (where a more appropriate translation might be "semifinali" in Italian or "semifinales" in Spanish).

Table 8. Examples of unsucessful query translations

C070 (query translations failed in French, Italian, German and Spanish)
<EN-TITLE> Death of Kim Il Sung
<FR-TITLE manually translated> Mort de Kim Il Sung
<FR-TITLE SYSTRAN> La mort de Kim Il chantée
<FR-TITLE BABYLON> mort de Kim Il chanter
<IT-TITLE manually translated> Morte di Kim Il Sung
<IT-TITLE SYSTRAN> Morte di Kim Il cantata
<IT-TITLE BABYLON> morte di Kim ilinio cantare
<GE-TITLE manually translated> Tod von Kim Il Sung
<GE-TITLE SYSTRAN> Tod von Kim Il gesungen
<GE-TITLE BABYLON> Tod von Kim Ilinium singen
<SP-TITLE manually translated> Muerte de Kim Il Sung
<SP-TITLE SYSTRAN> Muerte de Kim Il cantada
<SP-TITLE BABYLON> muerte de Kim ilinio cantar
C047 (both query translations failed in French)
<EN-TITLE> Russian Intervention in Chechnya
<FR-TITLE manually translated> L'intervention russe en Tchéchénie
<FR-TITLE SYSTRAN> Interposition russe dans Chechnya
<FR-TITLE BABYLON> Russe intervention dans Chechnya
C054 (query translations failed in French, Italian, German and Spanish)
<EN-TITLE> Final Four Results
<FR-TITLE manually translated> Résultats des demi-finales
<FR-TITLE SYSTRAN> Résultats De la Finale Quatre
<FR-TITLE BABYLON> final quatre résultat
<IT-TITLE manually translated> Risultati della "Final Four"
<IT-TITLE SYSTRAN> Risultati Di Finale Quattro
<IT-TITLE BABYLON> ultimo quattro risultato
<GE-TITLE manually translated> Ergebnisse im Halbfinale
<GE-TITLE SYSTRAN> Resultate Der Endrunde Vier
<GE-TITLE BABYLON> abschliessend Vier Ergebnis
<SP-TITLE manually translated> Resultados de la Final Four
<SP-TITLE SYSTRAN> Resultados Del Final Cuatro
<SP-TITLE BABYLON> final cuatro resultado

In Query #48 "Peace-keeping forces in Bosnia" or in Query #57 "Tainted-blood trial", our automatic system was unable to decipher compound word constructions using the "-" symbol and thus failed to translate the term "peace-keeping" or "tainted-blood".

In Query #74 "Inauguration of Channel Tunnel", the term "Channel Tunnel" was translated into French as "Eurotunnel". In the Spanish news test there were various translations for this proper name, including "Eurotúnel" (which appears in the manually translated request), as well as the term "Eurotunel" or "Eurotunnel".

2.3   Merging Strategies

Using our combined approach to automatically translate a query, we were able to search a document collection for a request written in English. However, this represents only the first stage our proposed cross-language information retrieval systems. We also needed to investigate situations where users write requests in English in order to retrieve pertinent documents in English, French, Italian, German and Spanish. To deal with this multi-language barrier, we divided our document sources according to language and thus formed five different collections. After searching in each corpora and the five result lists, they had to be merged so that users would be provided with a single list of retrieved articles.

Recent works suggested various solutions to merge separate results list obtained from separate collections or distributed information services. As a preliminary approach, we will assume that each collection contains approximately the same number of pertinent items and that the distribution of the relevant documents is similar across the result lists. We could interleave the results in a round-robin fashion, based solely on the rank of the retrieved records. According to previous studies [22], [23], the retrieval effectiveness of such interleaving schemes is around 40% below that of single retrieval schemes working with a single huge collection representing the entire set of documents. However, this decrease was found to diminish (around -20%) when using other collections [24].

To account for the document score computed for each retrieved item (or the similarity value between the retrieved record and the request denoted score rsv_j), we might formulate the hypothesis that each collection is searched by the same or a very similar search engine and that similarity values are therefore directly comparable [25], [26]. Such a strategy, called raw-score merging, produces a final list sorted by the document score computed by each collection. However, as demonstrated by Dumais [27], collection-dependent statistics in document or query weights may vary widely among collections, and therefore this phenomenon may invalidate the raw-score merging hypothesis.

To account for this fact, we might normalize document scores within each collection by dividing them by the maximum score (i.e. the document score of the retrieved record in the first position). As a variant of this normalized score merging scheme, Powell et al. [28] suggest normalizing the document score rsv_j according to the following formula:

Table 9. Average precision using different merging strategies, based on manually translated queries (top half) or automatically translated queries (bottom half)

Title-Desc Original	round-robin baseline	Average precision (% change)		
		raw-score	CORI	normalized score
Okapi–npn	34.23	15.87 (-53.6%)	13.00 (-62.0%)	**38.02** (+11.1%)
Lnu–ltc	32.09	31.41 (-2.1%)	21.23 (-33.8%)	**34.36** (+7.1%)
atn–ntc	31.31	23.03 (-26.4%)	17.15 (-45.2%)	**33.81** (+8.0%)
dtu–dtc	31.80	32.72 (+2.9%)	23.77 (-25.3%)	**34.60** (+8.8%)
ntc–ntc	20.97	17.30 (-17.5%)	15.37 (-26.7%)	**22.77** (+8.6%)
Mean difference		-19.36%	-38.61%	+8.70%
Translated queries				
Okapi–npn	29.59	13.08 (-55.8%)	11.19 (-62.2%)	**31.27** (+5.7%)
Lnu–ltc	28.84	25.41 (-11.9%)	17.30 (-40.0%)	**29.80** (+3.3%)
atn–ntc	27.32	17.56 (-35.7%)	13.49 (-50.6%)	**28.78** (+5.3%)
dtu–dtc	28.25	26.59 (-5.9%)	18.58 (-34.2%)	**30.21** (+6.9%)
ntc–ntc	19.16	13.14 (-31.4%)	11.60 (-39.5%)	**20.23** (+5.6%)
Mean difference		-28.14%	-45.30%	+5.37%

$$rsv'_j \;=\; (rsv_j - rsv_{min}) \;/\; (rsv_{max} - rsv_{min})$$

in which rsv_j is the original retrieval status value (or document score), and rsv_{max} and rsv_{min} are the maximum and minimum document score values that a collection could achieve for the current request. In this study, rsv_{max} is provided by the document score obtained by the first retrieved item and the retrieval status value obtained by the 1000th retrieved record becomes the value of rsv_{min}.

Finally, we might use the CORI approach [23] within which each collection is viewed as a single gigantic document. In a first step, this system computes a collection score for each corpus in a manner similar to that used by an IR system to define a document score, according to a given request. In a second step, instead of using document scores directly as in the raw-score merging strategy, each document score is multiplied by the corresponding collection score and the system uses the value of this product as a key to sort the merged lists.

Table 9 provides an overview of retrieval performances for these various merging strategies by depicting average precision for the round-robin, raw-score and normalized score merging strategies, together with the performance achieved by the CORI approach. From studying this table, it seems that the best merging approach is the normalized score merging strategy. However, we must recall that in our experiments we used whole words when indexing English, French, Italian and Spanish collections and 5-grams when indexing German documents. Document scores are not really comparable across collections, thus penalizing both the raw-score merging and CORI approaches.

We used the normalized score merging strategy for our three official runs of the multilingual track, using the manually translated requests in the "UniNE-mum" and "UniNEmuLm" runs as a baseline for comparison. In order to retrieve more relevant items from the various corpora, the "UniNEmuL" and "UniNEmuLm" runs were based on long requests (using the Title, Descriptive and Narrative sections) while the "UniNEmu" and "UniNEmum" runs were based on queries built with the Title and Descriptive logical sections.

Table 10. Descriptions of our official multilingual runs

Run name	English	French	Italian	German	Spanish
UniNEmum	original	original	original	original	original
expand	5 doc/10 ter	5 doc/10 ter	5 doc/10 ter	5 doc/30 ter	5 doc/10 ter
UniNEmu	original	syst+baby1	syst+baby2	syst+baby2	syst+baby2
expand	5 doc/10 ter	10 doc/15 ter	5 doc/50 ter	10 doc/40 ter	10 doc/15 ter
UniNEmuLm	original	original	original	original	original
expand	5 doc/10 ter	no	10 doc/15 ter	10 doc/100 ter	5 doc/10 ter
UniNEmuL	original	syst+baby1	syst+baby2	syst+baby1	syst+baby1
expand	5 doc/10 ter	10 doc/10 ter	5 doc/50 ter	10 doc/30 ter	10 doc/15 ter

As indicated in Table 10, our automatic "UniNEmu" and "UniNEmuL" runs used both the query translation furnished by the SYSTRAN system and one or two translation alternatives given by the BABYLON bilingual dictionary. The average precision achieved by these runs is depicted in Table 11.

Table 11. Average precision of our official multilingual runs

Run name	average prec.	% change	prec@5	prec@10	prec@20
UniNEmum	40.50	-	66.00	61.60	59.70
UniNEmu	33.73	-16.72%	61.20	60.40	55.60
UniNEmuLm	42.11	-	71.20	67.00	60.50
UniNEmuL	37.32	-11.37%	70.00	63.40	59.40

3   Conclusion

As our first participation in the CLEF retrieval tasks, we would suggest a general stopword list for the Italian, German and Spanish languages. Based on our experiments with the French language [3], we suggest a simple and efficient stemming procedure be used for these three languages. In this case and after comparing our approach with those used by others, removing inflectional suffixes attached only to nouns or adjectives seems to be worthwhile.

For the German language and its high frequency of compound word constructions, it might still be worthwhile to determine whether n-gram indexing approaches might produce higher levels of retrieval performance relative to an

Table 12. Title of the queries of the CLEF-2001 test collection

C041 <EN-TITLE> Pesticides in Baby Food
C042 <EN-TITLE> U.N./US Invasion of Haiti
C043 <EN-TITLE> El Niño and the Weather
C044 <EN-TITLE> Indurain Wins Tour
C045 <EN-TITLE> Israel/Jordan Peace Treaty
C046 <EN-TITLE> Embargo on Iraq
C047 <EN-TITLE> Russian Intervention in Chechnya
C048 <EN-TITLE> Peace-Keeping Forces in Bosnia
C049 <EN-TITLE> Fall in Japanese Car Exports
C050 <EN-TITLE> Revolt in Chiapas
C051 <EN-TITLE> World Soccer Championship
C052 <EN-TITLE> Chinese Currency Devaluation
C053 <EN-TITLE> Genes and Diseases
C054 <EN-TITLE> Final Four Results
C055 <EN-TITLE> Swiss Initiative for the Alps
C056 <EN-TITLE> European Campaigns against Racism
C057 <EN-TITLE> Tainted-Blood Trial
C058 <EN-TITLE> Euthanasia
C059 <EN-TITLE> Computer Viruses
C060 <EN-TITLE> Corruption in French Politics
C061 <EN-TITLE> Siberian Oil Catastrophe
C062 <EN-TITLE> Northern Japan Earthquake
C063 <EN-TITLE> Whale Reserve
C064 <EN-TITLE> Computer Mouse RSI
C065 <EN-TITLE> Treasure Hunting
C066 <EN-TITLE> Russian Withdrawal from Latvia
C067 <EN-TITLE> Ship Collisions
C068 <EN-TITLE> Attacks on European Synagogues
C069 <EN-TITLE> Cloning and Ethics
C070 <EN-TITLE> Death of Kim Il Sung
C071 <EN-TITLE> Vegetables, Fruit and Cancer
C072 <EN-TITLE> G7 Summit in Naples
C073 <EN-TITLE> Norwegian Referendum on EU
C074 <EN-TITLE> Inauguration of Channel Tunnel
C075 <EN-TITLE> Euskirchen Court Massacre
C076 <EN-TITLE> Solar Energy
C077 <EN-TITLE> Teenage Suicides
C078 <EN-TITLE> Venice Film Festival
C079 <EN-TITLE> Ulysses Space Probe
C080 <EN-TITLE> Hunger Strikes
C081 <EN-TITLE> French Airbus Hijacking
C082 <EN-TITLE> IRA Attacks in Airports
C083 <EN-TITLE> Auction of Lennon Memorabilia
C084 <EN-TITLE> Shark Attacks
C085 <EN-TITLE> Turquoise Program in Rwanda
C086 <EN-TITLE> Renewable Power
C087 <EN-TITLE> Inflation and Brazilian Elections
C088 <EN-TITLE> Mad Cow in Europe
C089 <EN-TITLE> Schneider Bankruptcy
C090 <EN-TITLE> Vegetable Exporters

enhanced word segmentation heuristic, where a German dictionary is not required.

Moreover, we might also consider additional evidence sources when translating a request (e.g., based on statistical translation models [29] or on the EuroWordNet [30]) or logical approaches that could appropriately weight translation alternatives. Finally, when searching in multiple collections containing documents written in various languages, it might be worthwhile to look into those merging strategies that provide better results or include intelligent selection procedures in order to avoid searching in a collection or in a language that does not contain any relevant documents.

Acknowledgments. The author would like to thank C. Buckley from SabIR for giving us the opportunity to use the SMART system, without which this study could not have been conducted. This research was supported in part by the SNF (grant 21-58 813.99).

References

1. Robertson, S.E., Walker, S., Beaulieu, M.: Experimentation as a Way of Life: Okapi at TREC. Information Processing & Management **36** (2000) 95–108
2. Fox, C.: A Stop List for General Text. ACM-SIGIR Forum **24** (1999) 19–35
3. Savoy, J.: A Stemming Procedure and Stopword List for General French Corpora. Journal of the American Society for Information Science **50** (1999) 944–952
4. Sproat, R.: Morphology and Computation. The MIT Press, Cambridge (1988)
5. Lovins, J.B.: Development of a Stemming Algorithm. Mechanical Translation and Computational Linguistics **11** (1968) 22–31
6. Porter, M.F.: An Algorithm for Suffix Stripping. Program **14** (1980) 130–137
7. Figuerola, C.G., Gómez, R., Zazo Rodríguez, A.F.: Stemming in Spanish: A First Approach to its Impact on Information Retrieval. In *this volume*
8. Monz, C., de Rijke, M.: The University of Amsterdam at CLEF 2001. In *this volume*
9. Chen, A.: Multilingual Information Retrieval using English and Chinese Queries. In *this volume*
10. Molina-Salgado, H., Moulinier, I., Knutson, M., Lund, E., Sekhon, K.: Thomson Legal and Regulatory at CLEF 2001: Monolingual and Bilingual Experiments. In *this volume*
11. McNamee, P., Mayfield, J.: A Language-Independent Approach to European Text Retrieval. In: Peters, C. (ed.): Cross-Language Information Retrieval and Evaluation. Lecture Notes in Computer Science, Vol. 2069. Springer-Verlag, Berlin Heidelberg New York (2001) 131–139
12. McNamee, P., Mayfield, J.: JHU/APL Experiments at CLEF: Translation Resources and Score Normalization. In *this volume*
13. Savoy, J.: Bilingual Information Retrieval: CLEF-2000 Experiments. In Proceedings ECSQARU-2001 Workshop. IRIT, Toulouse (2001) 53–63
14. Salton, G.: Automatic Text Processing: The Transformation, Analysis, and Retrieval of Information by Computer. Addison-Wesley, Reading (1989)
15. Buckley, C., Singhal, A., Mitra, M., Salton, G.: New Retrieval Approaches Using SMART. In Proceedings TREC-4. NIST, Gaithersburg (1996) 25–48

16. Singhal, A., Choi, J., Hindle, D., Lewis, D.D., Pereira, F.: AT&T at TREC-7. In Proceedings TREC-7. NIST, Gaithersburg (1999) 239–251
17. Oard, D., Dorr, B.J.: A Survey of Multilingual Text Retrieval. Institute for Advanced Computer Studies and Computer Science Department, University of Maryland (1996), http://www.clis.umd.edu/dlrg/filter/papers/mlir.ps
18. Grefenstette, G. (ed.): Cross-Language Information Retrieval. Kluwer, Amsterdam (1998)
19. Peters, C. (ed.): Cross-Language Information Retrieval and Evaluation. Lecture Notes in Computer Science, Vol. 2069. Springer-Verlag, Berlin Heidelberg New York (2001)
20. Gachot, D.A., Lange, E., Yang, J.: The SYSTRAN NLP Browser: An Application of Machine Translation Technology. In: Grefenstette, G. (ed.): Cross-Language Information Retrieval. Kluwer, Boston (1998) 105–118.
21. Hull, D., Grefenstette, G.: Querying Across Languages. In Proceedings of the ACM-SIGIR'1996. The ACM Press, New York (1996) 49–57
22. Voorhees, E.M., Gupta, N.K., Johnson-Laird, B.: The Collection Fusion Problem. In Proceedings of TREC-3. NIST, Gaithersburg (1995) 95–104
23. Callan, J.P., Lu, Z., Croft, W.B.: Searching Distributed Collections with Inference Networks. In Proceedings of the ACM-SIGIR'1995. The ACM Press, New York (1995) 21–28
24. Savoy, J., Rasolofo, Y.: Report on the TREC-9 Experiment: Link-Based Retrieval and Distributed Collections. In Proceedings TREC-9. NIST, Gaithersburg (2001)
25. Kwok, K.L., Grunfeld L., Lewis, D.D.: TREC-3 Ad-hoc, Routing Retrieval and Thresholding Experiments Using PIRCS. In Proceedings of TREC-3. NIST, Gaithersburg (1995) 247–255
26. Moffat, A., Zobel, J.: Information Retrieval Systems for Large Document Collections. In Proceedings of TREC-3. Gaithersburg, NIST (1995) 85–93
27. Dumais, S.T.: Latent Semantic Indexing (LSI) and TREC-2. In Proceedings of TREC-2. NIST, Gaithersburg (1994) 105–115
28. Powell, A.L., French, J.C., Callan, J., Connell, M., Viles, C.L.: The Impact of Database Selection on Distributed Searching. In Proceedings of ACM-SIGIR'2000. The ACM Press, New York (2000) 232-239
29. Nie, J.Y., Simard, M.: Using Statistical Translation Models for Bilingual IR. In this volume
30. Vossen, P.: EuroWordNet: A Multilingual Database with Lexical Semantic Networks. Kluwer, Dordrecht (1998)

Multilingual Information Retrieval Using English and Chinese Queries

Aitao Chen

School of Information Management and Systems
University of California at Berkeley, CA 94720, USA
aitao@sims.berkeley.edu

Abstract. The University of California at Berkeley group two participated in the CLEF 2001 monolingual, bilingual, and multilingual retrieval tasks. In this paper, we present a German decompounding procedure and a method of combining multiple translation resources for
translating Chinese into English. We also report on our experiments with
three different approaches to multilingual retrieval.

1 Introduction

At CLEF 2001, we participated in the monolingual, bilingual, and multilingual
tasks. Our main interest in the monolingual task is to test the idea of treating the German decompounding problem in the same way as that of Chinese
word segmentation and applying Chinese word segmentation algorithms to split
German compounds into their component words. Our interest in cross-lingual
retrieval is to experiment with techniques for combining translations from diverse translation resources. We are also interested in different approaches to the
multilingual retrieval task and various strategies for merging intermediate results
to produce a final ranked list of documents for a multilingual retrieval run. For
our experiments we used English and Chinese topics. In translating the topics
into the document languages which are English, French, German, Italian, and
Spanish, we used two machine translators, one bilingual dictionary, two parallel
text corpora, and one Internet search engine.

Several official runs were submitted for the monolingual, bilingual, and multilingual tasks, and more unoffical runs were performed and evaluated locally. To
differentiate the unofficial runs from the official ones, the IDs of the official runs
are all in uppercase while the IDs of the unofficial runs are all in lowercase. The
unofficial runs are those evaluated locally using the official relevance judgments
for CLEF 2001.

2 Test Collection

The document collection for the multilingual IR task consists of documents in
five languages: English, French, German, Italian, and Spanish. The collection
has about 750,000 documents which are newspaper articles published in 1994

C.A. Peters et al. (Eds.): CLEF 2001, LNCS 2406, pp. 44–58, 2002.
© Springer-Verlag Berlin Heidelberg 2002

Table 1. Document collection for the multilingual task.

Name	Language	No. of Documents	Size (MB)	Year(s)
Los Angeles Times	English	113,005	425	1994
Le Monde	French	44,013	157	1994
SDA French	French	43,178	86	1994
Frankfurter Rundschau	German	139,715	320	1994
Der Spiegel	German	13,979	63	1994/95
SDA German	German	71,677	144	1994
La Stampa	Italian	58,051	193	1994
SDA Italian	Italian	50,527	85	1994
EFE	Spanish	215,738	509	1994

except that part of the *Der Spiegel* was published in 1995. The distribution of documents among the five document languages is presented in Table 1. A set of 50 topics was developed initially in Dutch, English, French, German, Italian, and Spanish. Then the topics were translated into Chinese, Finnish, Japanese, Swedish, Thai, and Russian. A topic has three parts: 1) *title*, a short description of information need; 2) *description*, a sentence-long description of information need; and 3) *narrative*, specifying document relevance criteria. The multilingual IR task at CLEF 2001 was concerned with searching the collection consisting of English, French, German, Italian, and Spanish documents for relevant documents, and returning a combined, ranked list of documents in any document language in response to a query. The bilingual IR task was concerned with searching a collection of documents using queries in a different language. We used the English and Chinese topic sets in our participation in the multilingual IR task; Chinese topics in the bilingual IR task; and German and Spanish topic sets in the monolingual IR task.

3   Document Ranking

We used a logistic regression-based document ranking formula developed at Berkeley [1] to rank documents in response to a query. The log odds of relevance of document D with respect to query Q , denoted by $\log O(R|D,Q)$, is given by

$$\log O(R|D,Q) = \log \frac{P(R|D,Q)}{P(\overline{R}|D,Q)} \tag{1}$$

$$= -3.51 + 37.4 * x_1 + 0.330 * x_2 - 0.1937 * x_3 + 0.0929 * x_4 \tag{2}$$

where $P(R|D,Q)$ is the probability that document D is relevant to query Q, $P(\overline{R}|D,Q)$ the probability that document D is irrelevant to query Q. The four composite variables x_1, x_2, x_3, and x_4 are defined as follows:

$$x_1 = \frac{1}{\sqrt{n}+1} \sum_{i=1}^{n} \frac{qtf_i}{ql+35}$$

$$x_2 = \frac{1}{\sqrt{n+1}} \sum_{i=1}^{n} \log \frac{dtf_i}{dl+80}$$

$$x_3 = \frac{1}{\sqrt{n+1}} \sum_{i=1}^{n} \log \frac{ctf_i}{cl}$$

$$x_4 = n$$

where n is the number of matching terms between a document and a query, qtf_i is the within-query frequency of the ith matching term, dtf_i is the within-document frequency of the ith matching term, ctf_i is the occurrence frequency in a collection of the ith matching term, ql is query length (i.e., number of terms in a query), dl is document length (i.e., number of terms in a document), and cl is collection length (i.e., number of terms in a test collection). The relevance probability of document D with respect to query Q can be written as follows, given the log odds of relevance.

$$P(R|D,Q) = \frac{1}{1 + e^{-logO(R|D,Q)}}$$

The documents are ranked in decreasing order by their relevance probability $P(R|D,Q)$ with respect to a query. The coefficients were determined by fitting the logistic regression model specified in Eqn. 2 to training data using a statistical software package. We refer readers to reference [1] for more details. All retrieval runs were performed without query expansion using a blind (also called pseudo) relevance feedback technique.

4   Monolingual Retrieval Experiments

4.1   German Decompounding

We chose German topics for the monolingual task to study the effect of decomposing German compounds into their component words on the retrieval performance. We present an algorithm to break up German compounds into their component words. We treat the German decompounding problem in the same way as the Chinese word segmentation problem which is to segment a string of characters into words. We applied the Chinese segmentation algorithm as described in section 5.1 to decompose German compound words. The German decompounding procedure consists of three steps. First, we create a German lexicon consisting of all the words, including compounds, found in the CLEF 2001 German collection for the multilingual task. The uppercase letters are changed to lower case. Second, we identify all possible ways to break up a compound into its component words found in the German lexicon. Third, we compute the probabilities for all possible ways to break up a compound into its component words, and choose the decomposition of the highest probability. For example, the German compound *Mittagessenzeit* has three decompositions: 1) *Mittag, Essen,*

Zeit; 2) *Mittagessen, Zeit*; and 3) *Mittag, Essenzeit.* The probability of the first decomposition is computed as p(*Mittag*)*p(*Essen*)*p(*Zeit*), the probability of the second decomposition is p(*Mittagessen*)*p(*Zeit*), and the probability of the third decomposition is p(*Mittag*)*p(*Essenzeit*). If the second decomposition has the highest probability, then the compound is decomposed into *Mittagessen, Zeit.* As in Chinese word segmentation, the probability of a word is estimated by its relative frequency in the German document collection. That is,

$$p(w_i) = \frac{tf(w_i)}{\sum_{k=1}^{n} tf(w_k)},$$

where $tf(w_i)$ is the number of times word w_i occurs in the collection, including the cases where w_i is a component word in compounds; and n is the number of unique words, including compounds, in the collection. When computing the occurrence frequency of a word in the collection for the purpose of decompounding, we not only count the cases where the word occurs alone, but also the cases where the word occurs as a component word of some compounds. Consider the example *Mittagessenzeit* again. It is considered that all of its component words, *Mittagessen, Mittag, Essen, Zeit, Essenzeit,* occur once in the compound. In decompounding, the component words consisting of three or fewer letters were not considered.

We submitted two German monolingual runs labeled BK2GGA1 and BK2GGA2, respectively, and two Spanish monolingual runs labeled BK2SSA1 and BK2SSA2, respectively. The first run for both languages used title, description, and narrative fields in the topics, while the second run for both languages used title and description only. The stopwords were removed from both documents and topics, compounds were split into their component words using the decompounding procedure described above, then words were stemmed using the Muscat German stemmer[1]. The compounds and their component words were kept in both documents and topics indexing. The Spanish words were stemmed using the Muscat Spanish stemmer. The monolingual retrieval evaluation results for the official runs and additional unofficial runs for other languages are presented in Table 2. The monolingual runs were performed using the original, untranslated topics. There are 50 topics for each document language. There are in total 856 relevant English documents, 1,212 relevant French documents, 1,246 relevant Italian documents, 2,130 relevant German documents, and 2,694 relevant Spanish documents. To provide a baseline for comparison, four additional German monolingual retrieval runs with different features were carried out. The results for the four unofficial runs whose IDs are in lower case together with one official run are presented in Table 3. For the three unofficial runs, bk2gga3,bk2gga4,bk2gga5, and our two official runs, BK2GGA1, BK2GGA2, the German compounds and their component words were retained in both query and document indexing. But for the run labeled bk2gga6, only the component words of German compounds were retained in the topic indexing while both compounds and their component words were retained in document indexing.

---

[1] http://open.muscat.com

Table 2. Monolingual IR performance.

Run ID	Language	Topic Fields	Average Precision	Overall Recall
BK2GGA1	German	T,D,N	0.4050	1973/2130
BK2GGA2	German	T,D	0.3551	1881/2130
BK2SSA1	Spanish	T,D,N	0.5302	2561/2694
BK2SSA2	Spanish	T,D	0.5225	2526/2694
bk2eea1	English	T,D,N	0.5553	816/856
bk2eea2	English	T,D	0.5229	820/856
bk2ffa1	French	T,D,N	0.4743	1198/1212
bk2ffa2	French	T,D	0.4676	1190/1212
bk2iia1	Italian	T,D,N	0.4370	1194/1246
bk2iia2	Italian	T,D	0.4527	1200/1246

Table 3. German monolingual retrieval performance. Both compounds and their component words were retained in topic indexing for BK2GGA1, but only the component words of the compounds were retained in topic indexing for bk2gga6.

Run ID	Topic Fields	Features	Overall Recall	Average Precision
BK2GGA1	T,D,N	+stemming, +decompounding, −expansion	92.63%	0.4050
bk2gga3	T,D,N	+stemming, −decompounding, −expansion	90.94%	0.4074
bk2gga4	T,D,N	−stemming, +decompounding, −expansion	89.81%	0.3594
bk2gga5	T,D,N	−stemming, −decompounding, −expansion	88.12%	0.3673
bk2gga6	T,D,N	+stemming, +decompounding, −expansion	94.60%	0.4436

The results in Table 3 shows that decompounding degraded slightly the German monolingual retrieval performance when both the compounds and their component words were retained in topic indexing. However, when only the component words of the compounds were kept in topic indexing, decompounding improved the average precision by 8.88%.

4.2   More Experiments with German Decompounding

We present another German decompounding procedure which is a variant of the decompounding procedure described in section 4.1. The procedure is described as follows:

1. Create a German base dictionary consisting of single words only (compounds are excluded).
2. Decompose a compound into its components words found in the German base dictionary.
3. Choose the decomposition with the smallest number of component words. If there are two or more decompositions having the smallest number of component words, then choose the decomposition of the highest probability.

For example, when the German base dictionary contains *film, fest, fests, fest-spiele, piele, s* and others, the German compound *filmfestspiele* can be decomposed into component words with respect to the base dictionary in four different ways as shown in Table 4. The last decomposition has the smallest number of

Table 4. Decompositions of compound *filmfestspiele*.

	Decompositions			
1	film	fest	s	piele
2	film	fest	spiele	
3	film	fests	piele	
4	film	festspiele		

component words, so the German compound *filmfestspiele* is split into *film* and *festspiele*. Table 5 presents another example which shows the decompositions of German compound *hungerstreiks* with respect to a base dictionary containing *erst, hung, hunger, hungers, hungerst, reik, reiks, s, streik, streiks,* and other words. The compound *hungerstreiks* has six decompositions with respect to the

Table 5. Decompositions of compound *hungerstreiks*.

	Decompositions				log p(D)
1	hung	erst	reik	s	-55.2
2	hung	erst	reiks		-38.0
3	hunger	streik	s		-38.7
4	hunger	streiks			-21.4
5	hungerst	reik	s		-52.1
6	hungerst	reiks			-34.9

base dictionary. Because two decompositions have the smallest number of component words, the rule of selecting the decomposition with the smallest number of component words cannot be applied here. We have to compute the probability of the decomposition for the decompositions with the smallest number of component words. The last column in Table 5 shows the log of the decomposition probability for all six decompositions. According to the rule of selecting the decomposition of the highest probability, the fourth decomposition should be chosen as the decomposition of the compound *hungerstreiks*. That is, the compound *hungerstreiks* should be split into *hunger* and *streiks*. Consider the decomposition of compound c into n component words, $c = w_1 w_2 \ldots w_n$. The probability of a decomposition is computed as follows:

$$p(c) = p(w_1)p(w_2)\ldots p(w_n) = \prod_{i=1}^{n} p(w_i)$$

where the probability of component word w is computed as follows:

$$p(w_i) = \frac{tfc(w_i)}{\sum_{j=1}^{N} tfc(w_j)}$$

where $tfc(w_i)$ is the number of occurrences of word w_i in a collection, N is the number of unique words, including compounds, in the collection. The occurrence frequency of a word is the number of times the word occurs alone in the collection. The frequency count of a word does not include the cases where the word is a component word of some compounds. Also, the base dictionary does not contain any words of three letters or less except for the letter s. We created a German base dictionary of about 780,000 words by combining a lexicon extracted from Morphy, a german morphological analyzer [2], German wordlists found on the Internet, and German words in the CLEF-2001 German collection. In our implementation, we considered only the case where a compound is the concatenation of component words, including the single-letter word s. A component word may change its form when it is combined with other component words to create a compound word. For example, when the word *Erde* is combined with the word *Atmoshpäre* to create a compound, the compound is not *Erdeatmoshpäre*, but *Erdatmoshpäre*. The final letter e of the word *Erde* is removed from the compound. Note that the number of possible decompositions of a compound is determined by what is in the base dictionary. For example, when the word *mittagessen* is not in the base dictionary, the compound *mittagessenzeit* would be split into three component words *mittag*, *essen*, and *zeit*. We

Table 6. German decompounding and monolingual retrieval performance. Both compounds and their component words were retained in document indexing, but only the component words were retained in query indexing. The numbers given in parenthesis are overall recall values.

Test collections	-decompounding -stemming -query expansion	+decompounding -stemming -query expansion	Change
CLEF-2001	.3673 (1877/2130)	.4314 (1949/2130)	+17.45%
CLEF-2000	.3189 (673/821)	.4112 (770/821)	+28.94%
TREC-6/7/8	.2993 (1907/2626)	.3368 (2172/2626)	+12.53%

performed six German monolingual retrieval runs using three German test collections, CLEF-2001, CLEF-2000, and combined TREC-6/7/8. The CLEF-2001 test collection consists of 50 topics and about 225,000 documents, CLEF-2000 consists of 40 topics and about 154,000 documents, and combined TREC-6/7/8 consists of 73 topics with at least one relevant document and about 252,000 documents. Three of the runs were performed without German decompounding and the other three with German decompounding. All three topic fields were used in all six runs. Both the compounds and their component words were retained in document indexing, but only the component words of the compounds found in the topics were retained in topic indexing. The evaluation results for all six runs were presented in Table 6. German decompounding brought an improvement in overall precision of 17.45% for CLEF-2001 collection, 28.94% for CLEF-2000 collection, and 12.53% for combined TREC-6/7/8 collection.

The decompounding procedure differs from the one described in section 4.1 in two aspects. First, the base dictionary in the new procedure contains German words only (the compounds are excluded), while the base dictionary for the previous procedure contains both German words and German compounds. Second, the occurrence frequency of a word includes only the cases where the word occurs alone in the new procedure, while the occurrence frequency for the previous procedure considers both the cases where the word occurs alone and the cases where the word occurs as a component word of some compounds. The results presented in this and previous sections show that the new procedure is more effective.

5   Bilingual Retrieval Experiments

In this section we will describe the pre-processing of the Chinese topics and translation of the Chinese topics into English.

5.1   Chinese Topics Preprocessing

We first break up a Chinese sentence into text fragments consisting of only Chinese characters. Generally there are many ways to segment a fragment of Chinese text into words. We segment Chinese texts in two steps. First, we examine all the possible ways to segment a Chinese text into words found in a Chinese dictionary. Second, we compute the probabilities of all the segmentations and choose the segmentation with the highest probability. The probability of a segmentation is the product of the probabilities of the words making up the segmentation. For example, let $s = c_1 c_2 \ldots c_n$ be a fragment of Chinese text consisting of n Chinese characters. Suppose one of the segmentation for the Chinese text is $s_i = w_1 w_2 \ldots w_m$, where m is the number of words resulted from the segmentation, then the probability of this segmentation is computed as follows:

$$p(s_i) = p(w_1 w_2 \ldots w_m) = \sum_{j=1}^{m} p(w_j) \qquad (3)$$

and

$$p(w_j) = \frac{tf(w_j)}{\sum_{k=1}^{N} tf(w_k)} \qquad (4)$$

where $tf(w_j)$ is the number of times the word w_j occurs in a Chinese corpus, and N is the number of unique words in the corpus. $p(w_j)$ is just the maximum likelihood estimate of the probability that the word w_j occurs in the corpus. For a Chinese text, we first enumerate all the possible segmentations with respect to a Chinese dictionary, then we compute the probability for each segmentation. The segmentation of the highest probability is chosen as the final segmentation for the Chinese text. We used the Chinese corpus of the English-Chinese CLIR track at TREC-9 for estimating word probabilities. The Chinese corpus is about 213 MB in size and consists of about 130,000 newspaper articles.

A commonly used Chinese segmentation algorithm is the longest-matching method which repeatedly chops off the longest initial string of characters that appears in the segmentation dictionary until the end of the sentence. A major problem with the longest-matching method is that a mistake often leads to multiple mistakes immediately after the point where the mistake is made. All dictionary-based segmentation methods suffer from the out-of-vocabulary problem. When a new word is missing in the segmentation dictionary, it is often segmented into a sequence of single or two-character words. Based on this observation, we combine the consecutive single-character terms into one word after removing the stopwords from the segmented Chinese topics. We will call this process the de-segmentation of the segmented text.

5.2   Chinese Topics Translation

The segmentation and de-segmentation of the Chinese topics result in a list of Chinese words for each topic. We translate the Chinese topic words into English using three resources: 1) a Chinese/English bilingual dictionary, 2) two Chinese/English parallel corpora, and 3) a Chinese Internet search engine. First, we look up each Chinese word in a Chinese-English bilingual wordlist prepared by the Linguistic Data Consortium.[2] The wordlist has about 128,000 Chinese words, each paired with a set of English words. If a Chinese word has three or fewer English translations, we retain them all, otherwise we choose the three translations that occur most frequently in the *Los Angeles Times* collection which is part of the document collection for the CLEF 2001 multilingual task.

We created a Chinese-English bilingual lexicon from two Chinese/English parallel corpora, the *Hong Kong News corpus* and the *FBIS corpus*. The Hong Kong News corpus consists of the daily Press Release of the Hong Kong Government in both Chinese and English during the period from April, 1998 through March, 2001. The source Chinese documents and English documents are not paired. So for each Chinese document, we have to identify the corresponding English document. We first aligned the Hong Kong News corpus at the document level using the LDC bilingual wordlist. Then we aligned the documents at the sentence level. Unlike the Hong Kong News corpus, the Chinese documents and their English translations are paired in the FBIS corpus. The documents in the FBIS corpus are usually long, so we first aligned the parallel documents at the paragraph level, then at the sentence level. We adapted the

---

[2] The wordlist is publicly available at http://morph.ldc.upenn.edu/Projects/Chinese/.

length-based alignment algorithm proposed by Gale and Church [4] to align parallel English/Chinese text. We refer readers to the paper in [5] for more details.

From the aligned Chinese/English sentence pairs, we created a Chinese/English bilingual lexicon based on co-occurrence of word pairs in the aligned sentences. We used the maximum likelihood ratio measure proposed by Dunning [6] to compute the association score between a Chinese word and an English word. The bilingual lexicon takes as input a Chinese word and returns a ranked list of English words. We looked up each Chinese topic word in this bilingual Chinese/English lexicon, and retained the top two English words.

For the Chinese words that are missing in the two bilingual lexicons, we submitted them one by one to Yahoo!China, a Chinese Internet search engine publicly accessible at http://chinese.yahoo.com. Each entry in the search result pages has one or two sentences that contain the Chinese word searched. For each Chinese word, we downloaded all the search result pages if there are fewer than 20 result pages, or the first 20 pages if there are more than 20 result pages. Each result page contains 20 entries. From the downloaded result pages for a Chinese word, we extracted the English words in parentheses that follow immediately after the Chinese word. If there are English words found in the first step, we keep all the English words as the translations of the Chinese word. And if the first step failed to extract any English words, we extracted the English words appearing after the Chinese words. If there are more than 5 different English translations extracted from the result pages, we keep the top three most frequent words in the translations. Otherwise we keep all English translations. We refer readers to the paper in [3] for more details. This technique is based on the observation that the original English proper nouns sometimes appear in parentheses immediately after the Chinese translation. This technique should work well for proper nouns which are often missing in dictionaries. For many of the proper nouns in the CLEF 2001 Chinese topics missing in both the LDC bilingual dictionary and the bilingual dictionary created from parallel Chinese/English corpora, we extracted their English translations from the Yahoo!China search results. The last step in translating Chinese words into English is to merge the English translations obtained from the three resources mentioned above and weight the English translation terms. We give an example to illustrate the merging and weighting of the English translation terms. If a Chinese word has three English translation terms e_1, e_2, and e_3 from the LDC bilingual dictionary; and two English translation terms e_2 and e_4 from the bilingual dictionary created from the parallel texts. Then the set of words e_1, e_2, e_3, e_2, e_4 constitutes the translation of the Chinese word. There is no translation term from the third resource because we submit a Chinese word to the search engine only when the Chinese word is not found in both bilingual dictionaries. Next we normalize the weight of the translation terms so that the sum of their weights is one unit. For the above example, the weights are distributed among the four unique translation terms as follows: $e_1 = .2$, $e_2 = .4$, $e_3 = .2$, and $e_4 = .2$. Note that the weight for the term e_2 is twice of that for the other three terms because it came from both dictionaries. We believe a translation term appearing in both dictionaries is more likely to be the appropriate translation than one appearing in only one of the dictionaries. Finally we multiply the weight by the frequency of the Chinese word in the original topic. So if the Chinese word occurs three times in the topic, the final weights assigned to the English translation terms of the Chinese word are $e_1 = .6$, $e_2 = 1.2$, $e_3 = .6$, and $e_4 = .6$.

The English translations of the Chinese topics were indexed and searched against the LA Times collection. We submitted two Chinese-to-English bilingual runs, one using all three topic fields, and the other using title and description only. Both runs were carried out without pre-translation or post-translation query expansion. The documents and English translations were stemmed using the Muscat English stemmer. The performance of these two runs are summarized in Table 7. The results of the cross-language runs from English to the other four languages are presented in Table 8, and the results of the cross-language runs from Chinese to all five document languages are in table 9. The translations of both the English topics and the Chinese topics into French, German, Italian, and Spanish are described in the next section.

Table 7. Chinese to English bilingual retrieval performance.

Run ID	Topic Fields	Translation Resources	Overall Recall	Average Precision
BK2CEA1	T,D,N	dictionary, parallel texts, search engine	755/856	0.4122
BK2CEA2	T,D	dictionary, parallel texts, search engine	738/856	0.3683

Table 8. Bilingual IR performance.

Run ID	Topic Fields	Topic Language	Document Language	Translation Resources	Overall Recall	Average Precision	% Mono Performance
bk2efa1	T,D,N	English	French	Systran+L&H	1186/1212	0.4776	100.7%
bk2ega1	T,D,N	English	German	Systran+L&H	1892/2130	0.3789	93.56%
bk2eia1	T,D,N	English	Italian	Systran+L&H	1162/1246	0.3934	90.02%
bk2esa1	T,D,N	English	Spanish	Systran+L&H	2468/2694	0.4703	88.70%

6   Multilingual Retrieval

We participated in the multilingual task using both English and Chinese topics. Our main approach was to translate the source topics into the document languages which are English, French, German, Italian, and Spanish, perform retrieval runs separately for each language, then merge the individual results for

Table 9. Bilingual IR performance.

Run ID	Topic Fields	Topic Language	Document Language	Overall Recall	Average Precision	%Monolingual Performance
BK2CEA1	T,D,N	Chinese	English	755/856	0.4122	74.23%
bk2cfa1	T,D,N	Chinese	French	1040/1212	0.2874	60.59%
bk2cga1	T,D,N	Chinese	German	1605/2130	0.2619	64.67%
bk2cia1	T,D,N	Chinese	Italian	1004/1246	0.2509	57.41%
bk2csa1	T,D,N	Chinese	Spanish	2211/2694	0.2942	55.49%

all five document languages into one ranked list of documents. We created a separate index for each of the five document collections by language. The stopwords were removed, words were stemmed using Muscat stemmers, and all uppercase letters were changed to lower case. The topics were processed in the same way.

For the multilingual retrieval experiments using English topics, we translated the English topics directly into French, German, Italian, and Spanish using both the Systran translator and the L&H Power translator. The topic translations of the same language from both translators were combined by topic, and then the combined topics were searched against the document collection of the same language. So for each multilingual retrieval run, we had five ranked lists of documents, one for each document language. The five ranked lists of documents were merged by topic to produce the final ranked list of documents for each multilingual run.

The documents in the intermediate runs were ranked by their relevance probability estimated using Eqn. 2. Our merging strategy is to combine all five intermediate runs and rank the documents by adjusted relevance probability. Before we merge the intermediate runs, we made two adjustments to the estimated probability of relevance in the intermediate runs. First, we reduced the estimated probability of relevance by 20% (i.e, multiplying the original probability by .8) for the English documents retrieved using the original English source topics. Then we added a value of 1.0 to the estimated probability of relevance for the top-ranked 50 documents in all monolingual runs. After these two adjustments to the estimated probability, we combined all five intermediate runs by topic, sorted the combined results by adjusted probability of relevance, then took the top-ranked 1000 documents for each topic to create the final ranked list of documents. The aim of making the first adjustment is to make the estimated probability of relevance for all document languages closely comparable. Since translating topics from the source language to a target language probably introduces information loss to some degree, the estimated probability of relevance for the same topic may be slightly underestimated for the target language. In order to make the estimated probabilities for the documents retrieved using the original topics and using the translated topics comparable, the estimated probabilities for the documents retrieved using the original topics should be slightly lowered. The intention of making the second adjustment is to make sure that the top-ranked 50 documents in each of the intermediate results will be among the top-ranked 250 documents in the final ranked list.

For the multilingual retrieval experiments using Chinese topics, we translated the Chinese topics word by word into French, German, Italian, and Spanish in two stages. First, we translated the Chinese topics into English using three resources: 1) a bilingual dictionary, 2) two parallel corpora, and 3) one Chinese search engine. The procedure of translating Chinese topics into English was described in section 5. The English translations from the source Chinese topics consist of not sentences but words. Second, we translated the English words into French, German, Italian, and Spanish using both Systran translator and L&H power translator for lack of resources to directly translate the Chinese topics into these languages. The merging strategy was the same as the one in multilingual experiments using English topics.

We submitted four official multilingual runs, two using English topics and two using Chinese topics. The official runs are summarized in Table 10. The

Table 10. Multilingual retrieval performance. The document languages are English, French, German, Italian, and Spanish.

Run ID	Topic Language	Topic Fields	Overall Recall	Average Precision
BK2MUEAA1	English	T,D,N	5953/8138	0.3424
BK2MUEAA2	English	T,D	5686/8138	0.3029
BK2MUCAA1	Chinese	T,D,N	4738/8138	0.2217
BK2MUCAA2	Chinese	T,D	4609/8138	0.1980

multilingual run labeled BK2MUEAA1 was produced by combining the monolingual run bk2eea1 (.5553), and four cross-language runs bk2efa1 (.4776), bk2ega1 (.3789), bk2eia1 (.3934), bk2esa1 (.4703). The multilingual run labeled BK2MUCAA1 was produced by combining five cross-language runs, BK2CEA1, bk2cfa1, bk2cga1, bk2cia1, and bk2csa1. The performance of these five cross-language runs using Chinese topics is presented in Table 9.

The problem of merging multiple runs into one is closely related to the problem of calibrating the estimated probability of relevance and the problem of estimating the number of relevant documents with respect to a given query in a collection. If the estimated probability of relevance is well calibrated, that is, the estimated probability is close to the true probability of relevance, then it would be trivial to combine multiple runs into one, since all one needs to do is to combine the multiple runs and re-rank the documents by the estimated probability of relevance. If the number of relevant documents with respect to a given query could be well estimated, then one could take the number of documents from each individual run that is proportional to the number of estimated relevant documents in each collection. Unfortunately, neither one of the problems is easy to solve.

Since merging multiple runs is not an easy task, an alternative approach to this problem is to work on it indirectly, that is, transform it into another problem that does not involve merging documents and so may be easier to solve. We describe two alternative approaches to the problem of multilingual information retrieval. The first method works by translating the source topics into all document languages, combining the source topics and their translations in document languages, and then searching the combined, multilingual topics against a single index of documents in all languages. The second method works by translating all documents into the query language, then performing monolingual retrieval against the translated documents which are all in the same language as that of the query.

We applied the first alternative method to the multilingual IR task. We translated the source English topics directly into French, German, Italian, and Spanish using both Systran translator and L&H Power translator. Then we combined the English topics with the other four translations of both translators into one set of topics. The within-query term frequency was reduced by half. We used the multilingual topics for retrieval against a single index of all documents. The performance of this run labeled bk2eaa3 is shown in Table 11. For lack of

Table 11. Multilingual IR performance.

Run ID	Topic Language	Topic Fields	Overall Recall	Average Precision
bk2eaa3	English	T,D,N	5551/8138	0.3126
bk2eaa4	English	T,D,N	5697/8138	0.3648

resources, we were not able to apply the second alternative method. Instead, we experimented with the method of translating the French, Italian, German, and Spanish documents retrieved in the intermediate runs back into English, and then carring out a monolingual retrieval run. We did not use Systran translator or L&H Power translator to translate the retrieved documents into English. We compiled a wordlist from the documents retrieved, then submitted the wordlist into Systran translator and L&H Power translator. The translation results of the wordlist were used to translate word by word the retrieved documents in the intermediate runs into English. The overall precision is .3648 for this run labeled bk2eaa4.

7 Conclusions

We have presented a German decompounding procedure in two different versions. German decompounding did not improve overall precision when both the compounds and their component words were retained in topic indexing. However, when only the component words of the compounds found in the topics were retained in topic indexing, the German monolingual retrieval performance on the CLEF 2001 German collection improved 8.88% using the first version of the German decompounding procedure. The second version of the German decompounding improved the overall precision on the CLEF 2001 German collection by 17.45%. A German base dictionary of words, but not compounds, is required for applying the second version. We also presented a method for translating Chinese topics into English by combining translations from three different translation resources which seems to work well. We experimented with three approaches to multilingual retrieval. The method of translating the documents retrieved in the intermediate runs back into the language of the source topics, and then carring out monolingual retrieval achieved the best precision.

Acknowledgements. This research was supported by DARPA under research contract N66001-97-8541; AO# F477: Search Support for Unfamiliar Metadata Vocabularies, PI: Michael Buckland. The author would like to thank Fred Gey for translating the English topics into other document languages using L&H Power Translator, Hailing Jiang for downloading the Muscat stemmers, and Michael Buckland for helpful comments.

References

1. Cooper, W. S., Chen, A., Gey, F.: Full Text Retrieval based on Probabilistic Equations with Coefficients fitted by Logistic Regression. In: Harman, D. K. (ed.): The Second Text REtrieval Conference (TREC-2) (1994) 57-66.
2. Lezius, W., Rapp R., Wettler M.: A Freely Available Morphological Analyzer, Disambiguator and Context Sensitive Lemmatizer for German. In: Proceedings of the 36th Annual Meeting of the Association for Computational Linguistics and 17th International Conference on Computational Linguistics (COLING-ACL'98), Montreal, Canada, August 10-14, 1998. pp.743-748.
3. Chen, A., Jiang H., Gey, F.: Combining Multiple Sources for Short Query Translation in Chinese-English Cross-Language Information Retrieval. In: Proceedings of the Fifth International Workshop on Information Retrieval with Asian Languages, Hong Kong, Sept. 30-Otc 1, 2000. pp.17-23.
4. Gale, W. A., Church, K. W.: A Program for Aligning Sentences in Bilingual Corpora. In: Computational linguistics. **19** (1993) 75-102.
5. Chen, A., Gey, F., Jiang H.: Alignment of English-Chinese Parallel Corpora and its Use in Cross-Language Information Retrieval. In: 19th International Conference on Computer Processing of Oriental Languages, Seoul, Korean, May 14-16, 2001. pp. 251-257.
6. Dunning, T.: Accurate Methods for the Statistics of Surprise and Coincidence. In: Computational linguistics. **19** (1993) 61-74.

Exeter at CLEF 2001: Experiments with Machine Translation for Bilingual Retrieval

Gareth J.F. Jones and Adenike M. Lam-Adesina

Department of Computer Science, University of Exeter, EX4 4PT, U.K.
{G.J.F.Jones,A.M.Lam-Adesina}@exeter.ac.uk

Abstract. The University of Exeter participated in the CLEF 2001 bilingual task. The main objectives of our experiments were to compare retrieval performance for different topic languages with similar easily available machine translation resources and to explore the application of new pseudo relevance feedback techniques recently developed at Exeter to Cross-Language Information Retrieval (CLIR). This paper also describes more recent experimental results from our investigations of the combination of results from alternative machine translation outputs; specifically we look at the use of data fusion of the output from individual retrieval runs and the combination of alternative topic translations.

1 Introduction

The CLEF 2001 bilingual task is the first standardised evaluation to enable comparison of Cross-Language Information Retrieval (CLIR) behaviour for European and Asian language pairings. The primary objective of our participation in the bilingual task was to explore retrieval behaviour with the English language document collection with as many of the translated topic sets as possible. Our official submissions covered French, German, Chinese and Japanese topics. In this paper for comparison, we also report results for English, Italian and Spanish topics. In order to compare results for different language pairings fairly we wished to use similar translation resources for each pair; to this end we chose to use commercially developed machine translation (MT) systems. For our official submissions we used the online Babelfish translation system (available at http://babelfish.altavista.com) based on *SYSTRAN*. In this paper we also report comparative results for French, German, Italian and Spanish using *Globalink Power Translator Pro Version: 6.4*. There is an underlying assumption with this approach that the translation resources for each language pair have been subject to an amount of development which makes such comparisons meaningful. Since we do not have detailed information about MT system development, we can only comment on performance achieved and sources of failure, but not the scope for improvement in the MT systems with its associated possible cost implications. In addition, we report more recent results combining the outputs of these MT resources using data fusion and query combination [1]. Our general approach was to use a topic translation strategy for CLIR. Topic statements were submitted to the selected MT system, the output collected and then applied to the information retrieval system.

Pseudo relevance feedback (PRF) has been shown to be effective in many retrieval applications including CLIR [3] [4]. We have recently conducted experimental work with the Okapi BM25 probabilistic retrieval model and a new PRF query-expansion method using document summaries [5]. This work also investigated a novel approach to term-selection that separates the choice of relevant documents from the selection of a pool of potential expansion terms. These techniques have been shown to be considerably more effective than using full-document expansion on the TREC-8 ad hoc retrieval task. Our CLEF 2001 submission investigated the application of this technique to CLIR.

The remainder of this paper is organised as follows: Sect. 2 reviews the information retrieval methods used, Sect. 3 outlines the features of our summarisation system for PRF, Sect. 4 describes our data combination methods, Sect. 5 gives the experimental results and analysis, and Sect. 6 concludes the paper.

2   Information Retrieval Approach

The experiments were carried out using the City University research distribution version of the Okapi system. The documents and search topics were processed to remove stop words from a list of around 260 words, suffix stripped using the Okapi implementation of Porter stemming [6] and terms were further indexed using a small set of synonyms.

Document terms are weighted using the Okapi *combined weight* (cw), often known as BM25, originally developed in [7] and further elaborated in [8]. The BM25 cw for a term is calculated as follows,

$$cw(i,j) = \frac{cfw(i) \times tf(i,j) \times (K1+1)}{K1 \times ((1-b) + (b \times ndl(j))) + tf(i,j)} \tag{1}$$

where $cw(i,j)$ represents the weight of term i in document j, $cfw(i)$ is the standard collection frequency (inverse document frequency) weight, $tf(i,j)$ is the document term frequency, and $ndl(j)$ is the normalized document length. $ndl(j)$ is calculated as,

$$ndl(j) = \frac{dl(j)}{\text{Average } dl \text{ for all documents}},$$

where $dl(j)$ is the length of j. $K1$ and b are empirically selected tuning constants for a particular collection. $K1$ is designed to modify the degree of effect of $tf(i,j)$, while constant b modifies the effect of document length. High values of b imply that documents are long because they are verbose, while low values imply that they are long because they are multi-topic.

2.1   Relevance Feedback

Assuming that relevant documents are available within a collection, the main reason that they may not be retrieved is the query-document match problem. Short and imprecise queries often result in relevant documents being retrieved at low rank or not being retrieved at all, and retrieval of non-relevant documents at high rank. Relevance feedback (RF) using query expansion, where additional terms are added to the original query based on the user's assessment of document relevance, is one method which seeks to overcome the query-document match problem. PRF methods, in which a number of topic ranked documents from an initial retrieval run are assumed to be relevant, are on average found to give improvement in retrieval performance, although this is usually smaller than that observed for true user based RF. Application of PRF in retrieval post translation of the search query has been shown to be effective in CLIR in various studies including [3] [4].

The main implementational issue for PRF is the selection of appropriate expansion terms. In PRF problems can arise when terms taken from assumed relevant documents that are actually non-relevant, are added to the query causing a drift in the focus of the query. However, if the initial retrieval results are good and a large proportion of the documents retrieved at high rank are relevant, feedback is likely to improve retrieval performance. A further problem can arise since many documents are multi-topic, i.e. they deal with several different topics. This means that only a portion of a document retrieved in response to a given query may actually be relevant. Nevertheless standard RF treats the whole document as relevant, the implication of this being that using terms from non-relevant sections of these documents for expansion may also cause query drift. The exclusion of terms from non-relevant sections of documents, or those present in non-relevant documents which are not closely related to the concepts expressed in the initial query, could thus be beneficial to PRF and potentially in true RF as well.

These issues have led to several attempts to develop automatic systems that can concentrate a user's attention on the parts of the text that possess a high density of relevant information. This method known as passage retrieval [9] [10] has the advantage of being able to provide an overview of the distribution of the relevant pieces of information within the retrieved documents. However, passage retrieval has not been found to provide significant improvement in retrieval performance. We have developed a novel approach to the exclusion of terms from consideration based on document summarization. In this method only terms present in the summarized documents are considered for query expansion. Earlier experiments [11] [12] demonstrated that selecting best passages from documents for query expansion is very effective in reducing the number of inappropriate possible feedback terms taken from multi-topic or non-relevant documents. In [13] Tombros showed that query-biased summaries are more effective than using simple leading sentence summaries for user relevance decisions; thus in our summaries we also make use of query-biased summaries. A related approach to the one reported here is described by Strzalkowski in [14] where an

RF procedure using summaries of retrieved relevant documents is used. A weakness of this approach is that all terms from the summaries were added to the query. We prefer to adopt the approach taken in the Okapi TREC submissions [2] [15] [16] which expand queries conservatively using only a small number of terms.

In the Okapi approach potential expansion terms are ranked using the Robertson selection value (rsv) [17], defined as,

$$rsv(i) = r(i) \times rw(i)$$

where $r(i)$ is again the number of relevant documents containing term i, and $rw(i)$ is the standard Robertson/Sparck Jones relevance weight [18] defined as,

$$rw(i) = \log \frac{(r(i) + 0.5)(N - n(i) - R + r(i) + 0.5)}{(n(i) - r(i) + 0.5)(R - r(i) + 0.5)}$$

where $n(i)$ is the total number of documents containing term i, R is the total number of relevant documents for this query, and N is the total number of documents in the collection. The top ranking terms are then added to the query.

The rsv has generally been based on taking an equal number of relevant (or assumed relevant) documents for both the available expansion terms and term ranking. In our experiments we have explored the use of an alternative approach which takes a smaller number of relevant documents to determine the pool of potential expansion terms than the number of documents used to determine the rsv ranking. In effect we assume that higher ranked documents are more likely to contain useful expansion terms. The use of further documents for evaluation of $r(i)$ should give better estimates of $rsv(i)$ and hopefully more reliable selection of expansion terms from those available. It should be noted that the $r(i)$ value for each term i in our method is calculated based on its occurrence in the entire document rather than in the summary alone.

3   Summary Generation

Summary generation methods seek to identify document contents that convey the most "important" information within a document, where importance may depend on the use to which the summary is to be put. Since we require a very robust summarizer for the different text types likely to be encountered within a retrieval system we adopt a summarisation method based on sentence extraction. Sentence extracted summaries are formed by scoring the sentences in the document using various criteria, ranking the sentences, and then taking a number of the top ranking sentences as the summary.

Each sentence score is computed as the sum of its constituent words and other scores. The following section outlines the summary generation methods used in this investigation.

3.1 Luhn's Keyword Cluster Method

The first component of our summaries uses Luhn's classic cluster measure [19]. In order to determine the sentences of a document that should be used as the summary, a measure is required by which the information content of all the sentences can be analysed and graded. Luhn concluded that the frequency of a word occurrence in an article, as well as its relative position, determines its significance in that article. Following the work of Tombros [13], which studied summarization of TREC documents, the required minimum occurrence count for significant terms in a medium-sized TREC document was taken to be 7; where a medium sized document is defined as one containing no more than 40 sentences and not less than 25 sentences. For documents outside this range, the limit for significance is computed as,

$$ms = 7 + (0.1(L - NS))$$

for documents with NS < 25, and

$$ms = 7 + (0.1(NS - L))$$

for documents with NS > 40,

where ms = the measure of significance
  L = Limit (25 for NS < 25 and 40 for NS > 40)
  NS = number of sentences in the document

In order to score sentences based on the number of significant words contained in them, Luhn reasoned that whatever the topic under consideration the closer certain words are, the more specifically an aspect of the subject is being treated. Hence, wherever clusters of significant words are found, the probability is very high that the information being conveyed is most representative of the article. Luhn specified that two significant words are considered significantly related if they are separated by not more than five insignificant words. Thus, a cluster of significant words is created whereby significant words are separated by not more than five non-significant words as illustrated below.

"The sentence [**scoring** process utilises **information** both from the **structural**] organization."

The cluster of significant words is given by the words in the brackets ([—]), where significant words are shown in bold. The cluster significance score factor for a sentence is given by the following formula

$$SS1 = \frac{SW^2}{TW}$$

where $SS1$ = Luhn score for a sentence
  SW = the number of bracketed significant words (in this case 3)
  TW = the total number of bracketed words (in this case 8)

Thus $SS1$ for the above sentence is 1.125. If two or more clusters of significant words appear in a given sentence, the one with the highest score is chosen as the sentence score.

3.2   Title Terms Frequency Method

The title of an article often reveals the major subject of that document. In a sample study the title of TREC documents was found to convey the general idea of its contents. Thus, a factor in the overall sentence score is the presence of title words within the sentence. Each constituent term in the title section is looked up in the body of the text. For each sentence a title score is computed as follows,

$$SS2 = \frac{TTS}{TTT}$$

where $SS2$ = the title score for a sentence
  TTS = the total number of title terms found in a sentence
  TTT = the total number of terms in a title

TTT is used as a normalization factor to ensure that this method does not have an excessive sentence score factor contribution relative to the overall sentence score.

3.3   Location/Header Method

Edmundson [20] noted that the position of a sentence within a document is often useful in determining its importance to the document. Based on this observation, Edmundson defined a location method for scoring each sentence based on whether it occurs at the beginning or end of a paragraph or document.

To determine the effect of this sentence scoring method on the test collection a further sample study was conducted. This confirmed that the first sentences of a TREC document often provide important information about the content of the document. Thus the first two sentences of an article are assigned a location score computed as follows,

$$SS3 = \frac{1}{NS}$$

where $SS3$ = the location score for a sentence
  NS = the number of sentences in the document

Furthermore, section headings within the documents were found to provide information about the different sections discussed in the documents. Thus, marked section headings were given a similar location score.

3.4   Query-Bias Method

The addition of a sentence score factor bias to score sentences containing query terms more highly can reduce the query drift caused by the use of bad feedback terms taken from parts of a document not associated with its relevance. Thus, whether a relevant or non-relevant document is used, the feedback terms are taken from the most relevant section identified in the document, in relation to the submitted query. In order to generate a query biased summary in this work we adopt the technique described in [13]. In this method each constituent sentence of a document being processed is scored based on the number of query terms it contains. The following situation gives an example of this method. For a query "falkland petroleum exploration" and a sentence "The british minister has decided to continue the ongoing petroleum exploration talks in the falkland area". The query score $SS4$ is computed as follows,

$$SS4 = \frac{TQ^2}{NQ}$$

where $SS4$ = query-bias score for a sentence
       TQ = the number of query terms present in a sentence
       NQ = the number of terms in a query

Therefore the query-bias score factor $SS4$ for the above sentence is 3. This score is assigned based on the belief that the number of query terms contained in a sentence, the more likely it is that this sentence conveys a large amount of information related to the query.

3.5 Combining the Scores

The previous sections outlined the components used in scoring sentences to generate the summaries used in this work. The overall score for each sentence is calculated by summing the individual score factors obtained for each method used. Thus the final score for each sentence is

$$SSS = SS1 + SS2 + SS3 + SS4$$

where SSS = Sentence Significance Score.

In order to generate an appropriate summary it is essential to place a limit on the number of sentences to be used as the summary content. To do this however it is important to take into consideration the length of the original document and the amount of information that is needed. The objective of the summary generation system is to provide terms to be used for query expansion, and not to act as a stand alone summary that can be used to replace the entire documents. Hence the optimal summary length is a compromise between maintaining terms that can be beneficial to the retrieval process, while ensuring that the length is such that non relevant terms are kept to the barest minimum if they cannot be removed totally.

Experiments were performed with various maximum summary lengths to find the best one for term-selection. The lower limit of the summary length was set at 15% of the original document length because the document collection also consisted of very short documents. Thus high ranked sentences, up to the maximum summary length and not less than the set minimum summary length, are presented as the content for each document summarized. Inspection of our example summaries showed them to be reasonable representations of the original documents. However, in our case an objective measure of summary quality is their overall effect on retrieval performance. Experiments with the TREC-8 ad hoc test collection showed an improvement over baseline average precision of around 15% using summary-based query expansion with expansion terms selected only from the test collection as a source of term distribution information [5]. The summarisation system was implemented so that the relative weight of each component of *SSS* could be varied. Development experiments were performed to vary the component weights to optimise performance for the CLEF bilingual task.

4   Combination Methods

The combination of evidence from multiple information sources has been shown to be useful for text retrieval in TREC tasks. In our experiments we examine two forms of index combination defined in [1]: *data fusion* and *query combination*. This section briefly describes these methods and then analyses their operation.

4.1   Data Fusion

In data fusion ranked lists of retrieved documents from multiple retrieval systems are merged to form a single list. In our experiments with data fusion the ranked document lists produced independently by topics translated using Babelfish and Power Translator Pro were combined by adding the corresponding query-document matching scores from the two lists and forming a new re-ranked list using the composite scores. We investigated both simple summing of the matching scores and summation after the scores had separately been normalised with respect to the highest score in each list.

4.2   Query Combination

In query combination multiple statements of a user information need are merged into a single query statement for application to a retrieval system. One of the important issues in query translation for CLIR is the choice of the best translation(s) of the search terms. The output of an individual MT system gives the best overall translation available for the input given its rules and dictionary. Thus different MT systems often give different translated outputs for the same input. In query combination the translated queries produced by the two MT systems were combined into a single representation to score against the document archive. A set of combined queries was formed by taking the unique items from each query and forming them into a single topic statement.

4.3   Analysis of Data Fusion and Query Combination

While data fusion and query combination are both conceptually simple and easy to implement, it is useful to consider how they are actually operating in the retrieval process. This section analyses the effect of these techniques on the retrieval score of each document and the relationship between them.

Let the query generated by the Babelfish MT system be denoted as Q_b and the query produced by Power Translator Pro be denoted as Q_p. Let the complete indexing vocabulary of the retrieval system be denoted as v. As an aid to describing the situation, describe each query as a binary vector $Q = (q(1), q(2), \ldots, q(v))$ where $q(i) = 0$ or 1 indicates the presence or absence of a term from the vocabulary v within the query.

Denote the matching score for each document d_j as $ms_b(d_j)$ and $ms_p(d_j)$ for the Babelfish and Power Translator Pro translations respectively. The computation of each of these scores can now be represented as,

$$ms_b(j) = \sum_{i=0}^{v} q(i)_b . cw(i,j) \tag{2}$$

$$ms_p(j) = \sum_{i=0}^{v} q(i)_p . cw(i,j) \tag{3}$$

where $cw(i,j)$ is the combined weight described in (1).

The overall data fusion $ms_{df}(j)$ for each document without score normalisation is formed by summing $ms_b(j)$ and $ms_p(j)$.

$$ms_{df}(j) = \sum_{i=0}^{v} q(i)_b . cw(i,j) + \sum_{i=0}^{v} q(i)_p . cw(i,j)$$

which can be simply rearranged as,

$$ms_{df}(j) = 2 \sum_{i=0}^{v} q(i)_b q(i)_p . cw(i,j) + \sum_{i=0}^{v} q(i)_b (1 - q(i)_p) cw(i,j)$$

$$+ \sum_{i=0}^{v} (1 - q(i)_p) q(i)_p . cw(i,j)$$

Stated with reference to Q_b and Q_p the overall $ms_{qm}(j)$ for query combination is as follows,

$$ms_{qc}(j) = \sum_{i=0}^{v} q(i)_b q(i)_p . cw(i,j) + \sum_{i=0}^{v} q(i)_b (1 - q(i)_p) cw(i,j)$$

$$+ \sum_{i=0}^{v} (1 - q(i)_p) q(i)_p . cw(i,j)$$

Thus, the only difference between these two techniques is that data fusion provides a boost of a factor of 2 to terms that are common to both queries.

When PRF is applied 2 and 3 are expanded as follows,

$$ms_{be}(j) = C \sum_{i=0}^{v} q(i)_b . cw(i,j) + \sum_{i=0}^{v} q(i)_{be} . cw(i,j)$$

$$ms_{pe}(j) = C \sum_{i=0}^{v} q(i)_p.cw(i,j) + \sum_{i=0}^{v} q(i)_{pe}.cw(i,j)$$

where C is a scalar multiplier to control the relative weight of original query terms versus expansion terms, and Q_{be} and Q_{pe} are the vectors of expansion terms for Babelfish and Power Translator Pro translations respectively. Note that by definition $Q_b \wedge Q_{be} = \phi$ and $Q_p \wedge Q_{pe} = \phi$.

The data fusion matching score for each document with the expanded query can thus be expressed as,

$$ms_{dfe}(j) = Cms_{df}(j) + \sum_{i=0}^{v} q(i)_{be}.cw(i,j) + \sum_{i=0}^{v} q(i)_{pe}.cw(i,j)$$

which can be rearranged to give,

$$ms_{dfe}(j) = Cms_{df}(j) + 2 \sum_{i=0}^{v} q(i)_{be}q(i)_{pe}.cw(i,j)$$

$$+ \sum_{i=0}^{v} q(i)_{be}(1 - q(i)_{pe}).cw(i,j) + \sum_{i=0}^{v} (1 - q(i)_{be})q(i)_{pe}.cw(i,j)$$

Thus data fusion effectively forms a combined query from the two translations and the selected expansion terms, with terms appearing in the final query with a number of different upweighting values. Four different potential scalar multiplier weighting values are clearly visible here, but to these different weightings should be added further possibilities to allow for the fact that, $Q_b \wedge Q_{pe}$ and $Q_p \wedge Q_{be}$ may not be ϕ.

In the case of query combination the matching score $ms_{qce}(j)$ after PRF has been applied is calculated as,

$$ms_{qce}(j) = Cms_{qc}(j) + \sum_{i=0}^{v} q(i)_{qce}.cw(i,j)$$

which is somewhat simpler than the query effectively used for data fusion matching score computation with terms only having two scalar weightings associated with them. The number of expansion terms added for each method will obviously depend on the number selected, but if the individual runs add the same number, the data fusion method will tend to add more different terms since its individual topic runs will compute different expansion sets prior to list fusion. However, any retrieval effects resulting from this can be compensated for to some extent by adding more expansion terms in the query combination search.

The analysis of data fusion with score normalisation leads to a slightly more complex equation which effectively gives an upweight towards the document list with the lower maximum matching score. This may be undesirable for the CLEF task considered here since a higher $ms(j)$ is likely to be associated with a good query translation.

Table 1. Baseline retrieval results for topic translation using Babelfish.

		Topic Language						
		English	French	German	Italian	Spanish	Chinese	Japanese
Prec.	5 docs	0.494	0.477	0.392	0.383	0.417	0.336	0.434
	10 docs	0.406	0.366	0.330	0.298	0.353	0.287	0.332
	15 docs	0.353	0.326	0.288	0.257	0.312	0.253	0.268
	20 docs	0.317	0.289	0.263	0.231	0.284	0.231	0.245
Av Precision		0.484	0.473	0.398	0.375	0.389	0.341	0.411
% change CLIR		—	-2.3%	-17.8%	-22.5%	-19.6%	-29.5%	-15.1%

Table 2. Baseline retrieval results for topic translation using Power Translator Pro.

		Topic Language				
		English	French	German	Italian	Spanish
Prec.	5 docs	0.494	0.438	0.438	0.472	0.464
	10 docs	0.406	0.368	0.349	0.364	0.383
	15 docs	0.353	0.332	0.302	0.321	0.340
	20 docs	0.317	0.296	0.271	0.288	0.303
Av Precision		0.484	0.438	0.439	0.427	0.417
% change CLIR		—	-9.5%	-9.3%	-11.8%	-13.8%

5   Experimental Results

This section describes the establishment of the parameters of our experimental system and gives results from our investigations for the CLEF 2001 bilingual task. We report procedures for the selection of system parameters, baseline retrieval results for different language pairs and translation systems without application of feedback, corresponding results with use of feedback, and results for our data combination experiments. In all cases the results use the mandatory Title and Description fields from the CLEF search topics.

5.1   Selection of System Parameters

Various parameters had to be selected for our experimental system. In order to do this we carried out a series of development runs using the CLEF 2000 bilingual test collection. This data consisted of the CLEF 2000 English document set, which is actually the same document set as used for the CLEF 2001 task, and corresponding CLEF 2000 topic sets in French, German, Italian and Spanish.

The Okapi parameters were set as follows: $K1 = 1.0$ and $b = 0.5$. In the PRF runs 5 documents were assumed to be relevant in each case for term selection, document summaries comprised the best scoring 4 sentences in each case. Following experimentation with the sentence scoring components it was found that the best retrieval results were achieved when the Luhn and Title were given twice the relative weight compared to the Location and Query-Bias methods. The top 20 ranked expansion terms taken from these summaries were added to the original topic in each case. The rsv values to rank the potential expansion terms were selected by assuming the top 20 ranked documents were relevant. The original topic terms are upweighted by a factor of 3.5 relative to terms introduced by PRF.

5.2   Baseline Results

Tables 1 and 2 show baseline retrieval precision results for topic translation using Babelfish and Power Translator Pro respectively. From these results it can be seen that both the MT systems give reasonable CLIR performance, although there is considerable variability. The result for French topics using Babelfish translation is particularly good with a degradation relative to the monolingual baseline of only 2.3%. Performance for Chinese topic translation using Babelfish is by far the worst with a degradation of almost 30%; this contrasts with Japanese topic translation where performance is reduced by only 15%. While French topic translation using Babelfish is by far the best overall, retrieval after topic translation using Power Translator Pro generally shows more consistent behaviour.

5.3   Feedback Results

Tables 3 and 4 show retrieval results after the application of our summary-based PRF method. The results for French, German, Chinese and Japanese in Table 3 are revised versions of our official submissions for the CLEF 2001 bilingual task. These runs use identical system parameters settings to our official submissions with a change to the Okapi operational settings to correctly set the score cutoff above which documents are returned. This increases the likelihood that at least some documents will be returned in response to a search query. The effect on results is to increase the number of topics for which documents are returned, and gives a consequent small improvement in average precision over our official submissions in each case.

It can be seen from the results that in all cases feedback improves the absolute average precision over the baseline figures. In general the average precision relative to the monolingual baseline is similar to that observed without feedback, although in some cases it is rather worse. The average improvement in performance for each language pair is around 5%. This is somewhat less than the 15% improvement that we observed in our previous experiments with the TREC-8 ad hoc task. Further investigation is needed to establish the reasons for this. One reason may be that in our previous work we worked only with the topic Title fields, meaning that there is often significant room for improvement in retrieval performance for individual topics by adding additional terms to the request. In the case of the CLEF runs here we are using both the Title and Description fields meaning that there may be less room for improvement from adding additional terms. Further experimental work will be carried out to explore this possibility. Figures 1 and 2 again show corresponding recall-precision graphs. These show similar trends to the precision results with respect to the behaviour of individual languages pairs.

Table 3. Retrieval results for topic translation using Babelfish with summary-based expansion term selection. (* indicates revised CLEF 2001 submitted results.)

			Topic Language					
		English	**French***	**German***	Italian	Spanish	**Chinese***	**Japanese***
Prec.	5 docs	0.498	0.477	0.421	0.400	0.477	0.340	0.438
	10 docs	0.400	0.366	0.336	0.320	0.394	0.292	0.362
	15 docs	0.362	0.326	0.301	0.286	0.342	0.253	0.311
	20 docs	0.329	0.289	0.275	0.252	0.299	0.227	0.268
Av Precision		0.517	0.489	0.415	0.395	0.423	0.342	0.451
% change no FB.		+6.8%	+3.4%	+4.3%	+5.3%	+8.7%	+0.3%	+9.7%
% change CLIR		—	-5.4%	-19.7%	-23.6%	-18.1%	-33.8%	-12.8%

Table 4. Retrieval results for topic translation using Power Translator Pro with summary-based expansion term selection.

			Topic Language			
		English	French	German	Italian	Spanish
Prec.	5 docs	0.498	0.464	0.472	0.481	0.481
	10 docs	0.400	0.402	0.381	0.396	0.411
	15 docs	0.362	0.346	0.318	0.233	0.355
	20 docs	0.329	0.316	0.284	0.295	0.313
Av Precision		0.517	0.466	0.456	0.432	0.419
% change no FB		+6.8%	+6.4%	+3.9%	+1.2%	+0.5%
% change CLIR		—	-9.9%	-11.8%	-16.4%	-18.9%

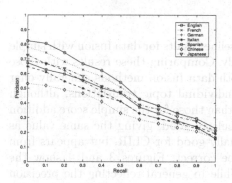 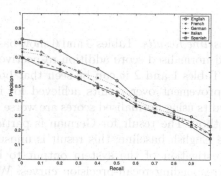

Fig. 1. Recall-Precision curves for retrieval with summary-based feedback with translation using Babelfish.

Fig. 2. Recall-Precision curves for retrieval with summary-based feedback with translation using Power Translator Pro.

5.4 Combination Results

Data Fusion. The following sections gives data fusion results. The first results show performance for the combination of the single translation baseline docu-

Table 5. Baseline retrieval results for Data Fusion.

		Topic Language				
		English	French	German	Italian	Spanish
Prec.	5 docs	0.494	0.477	0.494	0.485	0.464
	10 docs	0.406	0.385	0.394	0.387	0.385
	15 docs	0.353	0.342	0.352	0.333	0.342
	20 docs	0.317	0.303	0.305	0.296	0.301
Av Precision		0.484	0.479	0.484	0.426	0.423
% change		—	-1.0%	-0.0%	-12.0%	-12.6%

Table 6. Baseline retrieval results for Data Fusion with score normalisation.

		Topic Language				
		English	French	German	Italian	Spanish
Prec.	5 docs	0.494	0.477	0.481	0.481	0.451
	10 docs	0.406	0.379	0.379	0.377	0.368
	15 docs	0.353	0.333	0.326	0.322	0.326
	20 docs	0.317	0.296	0.287	0.283	0.289
Av Precision		0.484	0.463	0.467	0.417	0.420
% change		—	-4.3%	-3.5%	-13.8%	-13.2%

ment lists, and the latter results the combination of single translation lists with summary-based PRF.

Baseline Results. Tables 5 and 6 show baseline results for data fusion with simple and normalised score addition respectively. Comparing these results with those in Tables 1 and 2 it can be seen that both data fusion methods generally offer improvement over results achieved for individual topic translations, although results using normalised scores are worse than those for the simple score addition method. The result for German is particularly good, giving the same value as the English baseline; this result is unusually good for CLIR, but appears from investigation of the system output to be correct. Figures 3 and 4 show the corresponding recall-precision curves. While in general reflecting the precision results shown in Tables 5 and 6, these curves show some interesting behaviour; in particular there are a large number of crossing points. One observation of note is that the CLIR precision levels at low recall are actually on average higher than for the monolingual baseline whose overall average precision is considerably higher. As illustrated in Sect. 4 the data fusion lists are effectively merged queries with common terms having their weight boosted by a factor of two. In retrieval terms this may be considered similar to limited thesaurus based expansion. This appears to be useful for relevant documents with many matching terms, but less effective where there are less matching terms and the expansion can lead to increased retrieval of non-relevant documents.

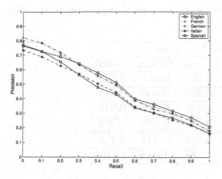

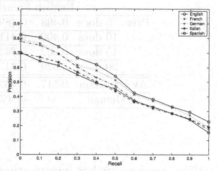

Fig. 3. Baseline retrieval Recall-Precision curves for Data Fusion.

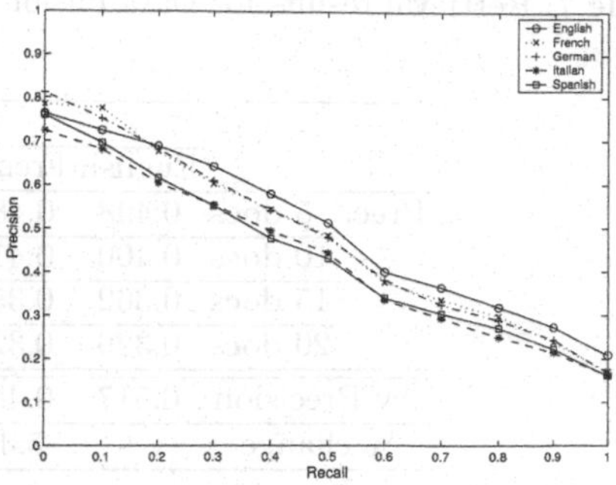

Fig. 4. Baseline retrieval Recall-Precision curves for Data Fusion with score normalisation.

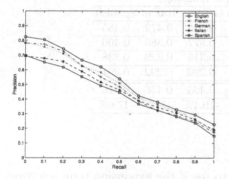

Fig. 5. Recall-Precision curves for Data Fusion retrieval with summary-based expansion term selection.

Fig. 6. Recall-Precision curves for Data Fusion retrieval with score normalisation with summary-based expansion term selection.

Feedback Results. Tables 7 and 8 show results for data fusion with summary-based PRF applied. Feedback again generally results in an improvement in average precision over the data fusion baseline, except for the case of German, where as noted previously the baseline data fusion result was unusually good. Simple score addition is again superior to addition of score normalisation. Average precision results are better in all cases compared to the feedback results for the individual topic translations shown in Tables 3 and 4. Figures 5 and 6 show the corresponding recall-precision curves. Contrasting these with the baseline data fusion curves shown in Figures 3 and 4, it can be seen that the improvement in performance shown in the precision results is reflected in the levels of the recall-precision results. One interesting result is that the monolingual results are now superior to the CLIR results at all recall levels. This suggests that the selection of expansion terms from the monolingual baseline lists is more effective than that for CLIR resulting in better retrieval performance in the feedback run.

Table 7. Retrieval results for Data Fusion with summary-based expansion term selection.

		Topic Language				
		English	French	German	Italian	Spanish
Prec.	5 docs	0.498	0.489	0.502	0.481	0.506
	10 docs	0.400	0.415	0.396	0.400	0.413
	15 docs	0.362	0.352	0.338	0.335	0.345
	20 docs	0.329	0.322	0.313	0.305	0.303
Av Precision		0.517	0.489	0.476	0.451	0.426
% change		—	-5.4%	-7.9%	-12.8%	-17.6%

Table 8. Retrieval results for Data Fusion with score normalisation with summary-based expansion term selection.

		Topic Language				
		English	French	German	Italian	Spanish
Prec.	5 docs	0.498	0.489	0.494	0.472	0.485
	10 docs	0.400	0.411	0.377	0.389	0.400
	15 docs	0.362	0.343	0.316	0.329	0.338
	20 docs	0.329	0.317	0.292	0.292	0.297
Av Precision		0.517	0.489	0.463	0.436	0.426
% change		—	-5.4%	-10.4%	-15.7%	-17.6%

This effect requires further investigation to see if the expansion term selection methods can be enhanced for the CLIR case.

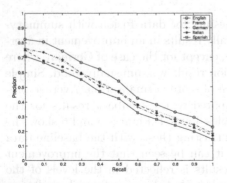

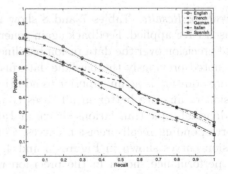

Fig. 7. Baseline Recall-Precision retrieval curves for Query Combination.

Fig. 8. Recall-Precision retrieval curves for Query Combination with summary-based expansion term selection.

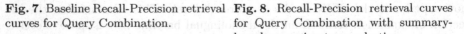

Table 9. Baseline retrieval results for Query Combination.

		Topic Language				
		English	French	German	Italian	Spanish
Prec.	5 docs	0.494	0.464	0.447	0.472	0.451
	10 docs	0.406	0.372	0.375	0.372	0.375
	15 docs	0.353	0.323	0.331	0.331	0.339
	20 docs	0.317	0.290	0.301	0.294	0.303
Av Precision		0.484	0.455	0.457	0.440	0.403
% change		—	-6.0%	-5.6%	-9.1%	-16.7%

Table 10. Retrieval results for Query Combination with summary-based expansion term selection.

		Topic Language				
		English	French	German	Italian	Spanish
Prec.	5 docs	0.498	0.519	0.443	0.472	0.477
	10 docs	0.400	0.404	0.394	0.385	0.409
	15 docs	0.362	0.339	0.333	0.338	0.346
	20 docs	0.329	0.309	0.303	0.304	0.318
Av Precision		0.517	0.498	0.406	0.469	0.421
% change		—	-3.7%	-21.5%	-9.3%	-18.6%

Query Combination. Tables 9 and 10 show baseline and feedback retrieval results respectively for query combination, with corresponding recall-precision graphs in Figures 7 and 8. Feedback generally results in an improvement in performance, except in the case of German where average precision is reduced dramatically. Baseline recall-precision behaviour shown in Figure 7 is fairly predictable reflecting the precision results, however behaviour after feedback shown in Figure 8 is very varied with many line crossings.

Overall Observations. The combination results are overall encouraging for CLIR suggesting combining evidence from multiple topic translations generated using machine translation can be effective. It is not clear from the results presented here whether data fusion or query combination is in general better, although in the former case data fusion without score normalisation looks to be the better choice. Perhaps this area of work would benefit from further development of the analysis ofSect. 4 to form a more general theory of evidence combination.

6   Concluding Remarks and Further Work

This paper has presented our results for the CLEF 2001 bilingual English language retrieval task. The results indicate that good retrieval results are achieved using different commercial MT systems. In particular the results for French CLIR with Babelfish translation show that MT can provide very effective retrieval.

SYSTRAN translation for English-French is one of the most longstanding and best developed MT systems. This retrieval result suggests that investment in improving an MT system can be valuable in improving CLIR performance, and further that the choice of MT for query translation in CLIR should depend on the resourcing of the MT system and probable consequent quality of translation. Results for six different query-document pairs indicate that similar performance can be achieved for CLIR for Asian and European language topics for retrieval of English documents despite the greater difference between the languages in the former case. However, the result for Chinese topics is the worst, and further investigation is required to better understand the reason for this. In addition, we intend to do query by query analysis of retrieval performance across the different languages pairs to investigate the effect of individual translation effects on retrieval behaviour. The application of our summary-based PRF method was generally shown to be effective, although the improvement was less than hoped for; and also some improvement in retrieval performance can often be gained from application of data fusion and query combination methods with alternative topic translations.

Acknowledgment. The analysis of the Data Fusion and Query Combination methods was suggested by a conversation with Wassel Kraaji.

References

1. N. J. Belkin, P. Kantor, E. A. Fox, and J. A. Shaw. Combining the evidence of multiple query representations for information retrieval. *Information Processing and Management*, 31:431–448, 1995.
2. S. E. Robertson, S. Walker, and M. M. Beaulieu. Okapi at TREC-7: automatic ad hoc, filtering, VLS and interactive track. In E. Voorhees and D. K. Harman, editors, *Overview of the Seventh Text REtrieval Conference (TREC-7)*, pages 253–264. NIST, 1999.
3. G. J. F. Jones, T. Sakai, N. H. Collier, A. Kumano, and K. Sumita. A Comparison of Query Translation Methods for English-Japanese Cross-Language Information Retrieval. In *Proceedings of the 22nd Annual International ACM SIGIR Conference on Research and Development in Information Retrieval*, pages 269–270, San Francisco, 1999. ACM.
4. L. Ballesteros and W. B. Croft. Phrasal Translation and Query Expansion Techniques for Cross-Language Information Retrieval. In *Proceedings of the 20th Annual International ACM SIGIR Conference on Research and Development in Information Retrieval*, pages 84–91, Philadelphia, 1997. ACM.
5. A. M. Lam-Adesina and G. J. F. Jones. Applying Summarization Techniques for Term Selection in Relevance Feedback. In *Proceedings of the 24th Annual International ACM SIGIR Conference on Research and Development in Information Retrieval*, pages 1–9, New Orleans, 2001. ACM.
6. M. F. Porter. An algorithm for suffix stripping. *Program*, 14:130–137, 1980.
7. S. E. Robertson and S. Walker. Some simple effective approximations to the 2-Poisson model for probabilistic weighted retrieval. In *Proceedings of the 17th Annual International ACM SIGIR Conference on Research and Development in Information Retrieval*, pages 232–241, Dublin, 1994. ACM.

8. S. E. Robertson, S. Walker, M. M. Beaulieu, M. Gatford, and A. Payne. Okapi at TREC-4. In D. K. Harman, editor, *Overview of the Fourth Text REtrieval Conference (TREC-4)*, pages 73–96. NIST, 1996.

9. J. P. Callan. Passage-Level Evidence in Document Retrieval. In *Proceedings of the 17th Annual International ACM SIGIR Conference on Research and Development in Information Retrieval*, pages 302–310, Dublin, 1994. ACM.

10. D. Knaus, E. Mittendorf, P. Schauble, and P. Sheridan. Highlighting Relevant Passages for users of the Interactive SPIDER Retrieval System. In *Proceedings of the Fourth Text REetrieval Conference (TREC-4)*, pages 233–238. NIST, 1996.

11. J. Xu and W. B. Croft. Query Expansion Using Local and Global Document Analysis. In *Proceedings of the 19th Annual International ACM SIGIR Conference on Research and Development in Information Retrieval*, pages 4–10, Zurich, 1996. ACM.

12. J. Allan. Relevance Feedback with too much Data. In *Proceedings of the 18th Annual International ACM SIGIR Conference on Research and Development in Information Retrieval*, pages 337–343, Seattle, 1995. ACM.

13. A. Tombros and M. Sanderson. The advantages of query-biased summaries in Information Retrieval. In *Proceedings of the 21st Annual International ACM SIGIR Conference on Research and Development in Information Retrieval*, pages 2–10, Melbourne, 1998. ACM.

14. T. Strzalkowski, J. Wang, and B. Wise. Summarization-based query expansion in information retrieval. In *Proceedings of 17th COLING-ACL'98*, pages 1–21, Montreal, 1998. ACL.

15. S. E. Robertson, S. Walker, S. Jones, M. M. Hancock-Beaulieu, and M. Gatford. Okapi at TREC-3. In D. K. Harman, editor, *Overview of the Third Text REtrieval Conference (TREC-3)*, pages 109–126. NIST, 1995.

16. S. E. Robertson and S. Walker. Okapi/Keenbow. In E. Voorhees and D. K. Harman, editors, *Overview of the Eighth Text REtrieval Conference (TREC-8)*, pages 151–162. NIST, 2000.

17. S. E. Robertson. On term selection for query expansion. *Journal of Documentation*, 46:359–364, 1990.

18. S. E. Robertson and K. Sparck Jones. Relevance weighting of search terms. *Journal of the American Society for Information Science*, 27(3):129–146, 1976.

19. H. P. Luhn. The Automatic Creation of Literature Abstracts. *IBM Journal of Research and Development*, 2(2):159–165, 1958.

20. H. P. Edmundson. New Methods in Automatic Astracting. *Journal of the ACM*, 16(2):264–285, 1969.

TNO at CLEF-2001: Comparing Translation Resources

Wessel Kraaij

TNO-TPD, P.O. Box 155, 2600 AD Delft, The Netherlands
kraaij@tpd.tno.nl

Abstract. This paper describes the official runs of TNO TPD for
CLEF-2001. We participated in the monolingual, bilingual and multilingual tasks. The main contribution of this paper is a systematic comparison of three types of translation resources for bilingual retrieval based
on query translation. We compared several techniques based on machine
readable dictionaries, statistical dictionaries generated from parallel corpora with a baseline of the Babelfish MT service, which is available on
the web. The study showed that the topic set is too small to draw reliable conclusions. All three methods have the potential to reach about
90% of the monolingual baseline performance, but the effectiveness is
not consistent across language pairs and topic collections. Because each
of the individual methods are quite sensitive to missing translations, we
tested a combination approach, which yielded consistent improvements
up to 98% of the monolingual baseline.

1   Introduction

Research on Cross Language Information Retrieval has been on the agenda of
TNO TPD since 1997. TNO TPD participated in the CLIR tracks of TREC
and CLEF, usually together with the University of Twente under the flag of the
"Twenty-One" project, a EU project focusing on cross language dissemination of
information. University of Twente and TNO still cooperate in various research
domains in the DRUID project. For CLEF 2001, we did not change our basic
approach to CLIR, but experimented with different translation resources and
the best way to integrate them. Therefore we will restrict ourselves to a rather
concise description of the basic retrieval model and concentrate on this year's
experiments.

2   The CLIR Model

The basic approach for our CLIR experiments is query translation. The major advantage of query translation is its scalability. Some groups have shown
however that document translation can yield competitive results, especially in
combination with query translation [1,2]. At this point we have chosen to refine
our approach instead of testing all kinds of combination strategies, which could
suffer from collection dependency.

C.A. Peters et al. (Eds.): CLEF 2001, LNCS 2406, pp. 78–93, 2002.

All runs were carried out with an information retrieval system based on a model developed by Hiemstra [3]. The basic idea is that documents can be represented by simple statistical language models. Now, if a query is more probable given a language model based on document d_1, than given a language model based on document d_2, then we hypothesise that the document d_1 is more relevant to the query than document d_2. Thus the probability of generating a certain query given a document-based language model can serve as a score to rank documents with respect to relevance.

$$P(T_1, T_2, \cdots, T_n | D_k) P(D_k) = P(D_k) \prod_{i=1}^{n} (1 - \lambda) P(T_i) + \lambda P(T_i | D_k) \quad (1)$$

Formula 1 shows the basic idea of this approach to information retrieval, where the document-based language model is interpolated with a background language model to compensate for sparseness. In the formula, T_i is a random variable for the query term on position i in the query ($1 \leq i \leq n$, where n is the query length), which sample space is the set $\{t^{(0)}, t^{(1)}, \cdots, t^{(m)}\}$ of all terms in the collection. The probability measure $P(T_i)$ defines the probability of drawing a term at random from the collection, $P(T_i | D_k)$ defines the probability of drawing a term at random from the document; and λ is the smoothing coefficient. The optimal λ (0.3) was found by tuning on earlier CLIR collections. The a-priori probability of relevance $P(D_k)$ is usually taken to be a linear function of the document length, modelling the empirical fact that longer documents have a higher probability of relevance.

The retrieval model has been extended for the CLIR task, by integrating a statistical translation step into the model [5]. The CLIR extension is presented in the following formula:

$$P(D_k, S_1, S_2, \cdots, S_n) =$$
$$P(D_k) \prod_{i=1}^{n} \sum_{j=1}^{m} P(S_i | T_i = t^{(j)})((1 - \lambda) P(T_i = t^{(j)}) + \lambda P(T_i = t^{(j)} | D_k)) \quad (2)$$

Here S_i refers to terms in the source (query) language and T_i refers to terms in the target (document) language, $P(S_i | T_i = t^{(j)})$ represents the probability of translating a term from the target language T_i in a source language term S_i. Note that the notions of source and target language are a bit confusing here, because the CLIR retrieval model contains a translation component, which translates target language terms in source language terms.

An informal paraphrase of the extension is: the relevance of a document in a target language with respect to a query in a different source language can be modelled by the probability that the document generates the query. We know that several words $t^{(j)}$ in the target language can be translated into the query term S_i, we also assume for the moment that we know their respective translation probabilities. The calculation of the probability of the query involves an extra step: the probability of generating a certain query term is the sum of the probabilities that a document in the target language generates a word which in turn is translated to the query term. These probabilities are defined as the product of the probability $P(T_i|D)$ (as in Formula 1) and the translation probability $P(S_i|T_i)$. We refer to [4] and [5] for a technical description of the model. A crucial aspect of the approach is that the model treats alternative translations as a probabilistic disjunction resulting in highly structured queries.

3   Integrating Prior Knowledge

In previous years (CLEF2000) we have seen that adding a so-called document prior conditioned on the document length results in a significant improvement of retrieval performance especially for short queries. The document prior was simply integrated into the model as a multiplication, assuming independence.

The approach has some problems:

1. The approach assumes that both sources of information are independent.
2. It is hard to normalise scores.
3. Its effect on short (title) queries is much larger than on longer queries.

Especially problem (2) is important for CLIR, because for the multilingual task, we want to normalise scores. Document scores in the original model are linearly related to the query length. Now suppose, we translate the query into different languages using Systran. It could very well be the case that a translation into a compounding language results in a shorter query, thus the translated queries will not have a homogeneous length. An easy strategy is to divide the document scores by the query length. But this division would also affect the "document prior". We propose to model the a-priori probability of relevance conditioned on the document length and the normalised generative probability of the query based on the document unigram model as separate models.

$$RSV_{final} = \mu \log(P(D_k|len(D_k) = d)) + (1 - \mu) \log(P(T_1, T_2, \cdots, T_n|D_k))/n \tag{3}$$

The scores of these models are subsequently interpolated via linear interpolation, in formula (3) the final retrieval status value (RSV) is composed of two components, the first addend is the a-priori probability of relevance of a document conditioned on its length, the second component is the unigram component. It is difficult to estimate $P(D_k|len(D_k) = d)$ on a test corpus, since we do not have many data points for each individual document length. One could approximate this by using a binning approach on a training collection, but we assumed a simple linear function.

In studies on other collections we found that the optimal value for the interpolation parameter is relatively stable across collections, but is dependent on the query characteristics. The optimal value of the interpolation parameter is inversely related to the query length. This can be explained as follows: for short queries, the probability of relevance is not dependent on the document length because of the document normalisation which comes with the maximum likelihood estimates for $P(T_i|D_k)$. However, there is empirical evidence that longer documents have a higher probability to be relevant [6], because longer documents often contain more information. Robertson calls this the "scope hypothesis" [7]. Therefore it is beneficial to have a rather high value of μ for title queries, which give the hybrid retrieval model a slight bias to longer documents. For longer queries, the generative model will have an increasing bias for longer documents, because of the "soft" coordination effect, thus it is important to use a small (or even zero) value of μ. For our CLEF experiments, we used formula (3) with $\mu = 0.2$, which was found to give optimal results on title+description queries from the CLEF2000 topic collection.

4   Lemmatisation

The major part of the experiments was based on an indexing procedure which involves morphological lemmatisation. The lemmatiser is based on the Xelda morphological toolkit[1], developed by XRCE Grenoble, which supports a wide range of European languages. The lemmatiser removes inflectional suffixes, performs case normalisation (proper nouns and German nouns keep their capitalisation) and can segment compounds. This year, we tested whether keeping the capitalisation would improve precision (cf. Section 6.1). For German and Dutch, the basic procedure for handling compounds was to add both the full compound (inflection removed) and the recognised compound segments to the set of index terms (at indexing and retrieval time). This approach has proved to work well [8], but is a very ad-hoc plugin to the probabilistic retrieval framework that we apply for term weighting [3]. Several runs were done based on a Porter like stemming procedure [9]. The Dutch version of Porter [10] cannot split compounds but removes also some derivational suffixes, which is sometimes beneficial [8,11].

5   Translation Resources

While the development of a theoretical framework for CLIR is extremely important, a more practical but not less important issue is the acquisition or development of translation resources. CLEF 2000 showed that there are several classes or resources that can be used for successful CLIR.

1. High quality machine readable dictionaries are available for the major European languages [5].
2. Commercial MT systems with different levels of quality can be used at no or relatively small costs. CLEF 2000 showed successful use of the Babelfish translation service based on Systran, the Powertranslator system from L&H and several other systems [12,2].

---

[1] cf. http://www.xrce.xerox.com/ats/xelda/overview.html

3. Some groups exploited parallel or comparable corpora for CLIR: parallel corpora can be used to train probabilistic bilingual translation dictionaries [13], comparable corpora can be used to generate similarity thesauri [2].

In this paper we will compare these three types of resources in a quantitative and qualitative way. For the machine readable dictionaries we used the VLIS lexical database of lexicon publisher Van Dale. For a description of the structure and contents of the VLIS database we refer to our CLEF 2000 paper [5]. We estimated the "reverse" translation probabilities $P(S_i|T_j)$ (the translation probability of a term in the source language given a term in the target language) using some very sparse pseudo frequency information extracted from the lexical database (cf. [5]).

We contrasted query translation using VLIS with query translation based on the Babelfish MT service and word by word translation based on dictionaries derived from a collection of parallel web documents.

For CLEF 2000, we had already developed three parallel corpora based on web pages in close cooperation with RALI, Université de Montréal. We used the PTMiner tool [13] to locate web pages which have a high probability to be translations of each other. The mining process consisted of the following steps:

1. Query a web search engine for web pages with a hyperlink anchor text "English version" and respective variants.
2. (For each web site) Query a web search engine for all web pages on a particular site.
3. (For each web site) Try to find pairs of path names that match certain patterns, e.g.:
   /department/tt/english/home.html and
   /department/tt/italian/home.html.
4. (For each pair) download web pages, perform a language check using a probabilistic language classifier, remove pages which are not positively identified as being written in a particular language.

The mining process was repeated for three language pairs (EN-IT, EN-DE and EN-NL) and resulted in three modestly sized parallel corpora. RALI had already mined a parallel web corpus for English-French. Table 1 lists some quantitative data about these corpora.

Table 1. Intermediate sizes during corpus construction

language	nr of web sites	nr of candidate pages	nr of candidate pairs	retrieved + cleaned pairs
EN-IT	3651	1053649	23447	8504
EN-DE	3817	1828906	33577	10200
EN-NL	3004	1170082	24738	2907
EN-FR	n.a.	n.a.	n.a.	18807

The parallel corpora were subsequently used to train simple translation models (IBM model 1, [14]) for both translation directions. For CLEF 2000 we did some preliminary runs with encouraging results. This year we decided to do some more extensive tests with the translation models for two language pairs: EN-IT and EN-FR. We chose these language pairs because the translation models are trained on lemmatised/stemmed corpora. The IR indexes are also based on lemmatised documents, thus both lemmatisation/ stemming schemes have to be sufficiently equal. For the pairs EN-IT and EN-FR we were able to synchronise the lemmatisation/stemming schemes of the translation models and the IR indexes. The translation models were built at RALI (Université de Montréal) and used a RALI lemmatiser for English and French and the Porter stemmer from MUSCAT[2] for Italian. All IR indexes were built using the Xelda lemmatisation tools. For our bilingual EN-IT corpus runs, we built an index using the Porter stemmer for Italian. We tested several alternatives to include the translation probabilities into the model on the CLEF 2000 collection. Strangely enough, the use of forward probabilities $P(T_j|S_i)$ proved to be more effective than using reverse probabilities, the most probable translation or using equal translation probabilities. Pruning the translation model proved to be a key issue. We will elaborate on these aspects in a later publication. For CLEF 2001, we decided to use the best performing estimates i.e. the forward probabilities, neglecting the fact that the theoretical model calls for reverse translation probabilities.

6   Experiments

Although our focus this year was on the bilingual task, we also participated in the monolingual and multilingual tasks. All reported runs used only the title and description fields for the automatic construction of queries.

6.1   Monolingual Results

Our main goal for the monolingual runs was to improve the pool and to provide a baseline for bilingual experiments. We also did a minor experiment with case sensitivity and fuzzy query term expansion.

Table 2 shows the results of our monolingual runs. We added some unofficial runs to complete the picture. Since case insensitivity had deteriorated the performance of some topics in previous years (when a proper name and a normal noun are homonyms e.g. Turkey and turkey) we decided to test the proper name recognition function of the Xelda morphological analyser. We did not apply any case normalisation after the Xelda lemmatisation step. Xelda can often correctly disambiguate homonyms, but when the context is not sufficient, our indexer chose the proper noun reading.

As in previous years, we also tested the effectiveness of a fuzzy lookup scheme. If a query term does not match with a term in the index vocabulary, a fuzzy lookup procedure (based on n-grams) substitutes the nearest matching term. This function is practical for misspellings in queries. The same fuzzy matching

---

[2] http://open.muscat.com

Table 2. Monolingual results (italic=unofficial run)

run tag	language	m.a.p.	judged@100	description
tnodd1	DE	0.3946	81	baseline
tnodd2	DE	0.3945	81	fuzzy lookup
tnodd3	DE	0.4111	87	fuzzy expansion
tnoee1	EN	0.5144	75	baseline
tnoee2	EN	0.5130	75	fuzzy lookup
tnoee3	EN	0.5289	75	fuzzy expand
tnoff1	FR	0.4877	90	baseline
tnoff2	FR	0.4883	90	fuzzy lookup
tnoff3	FR	0.4796	90	fuzzy expansion
tnoff4	FR	0.4904	91	case normalisation
tnoii1	IT	0.4411	87	baseline
tnoii2	IT	0.4449	87	fuzzy lookup
tnoii3	IT	0.4534	88	fuzzy expansion
tnoii4	IT	0.4508	88	case normalisation
tnonn1	NL	0.3795	84	baseline
tnonn1p	NL	0.3643	74	Porter stemmer (case insensitive)
tnonn2	NL	0.3720	84	fuzzy lookup
tnonn3	NL	0.3917	86	fuzzy expansion
tnonn5	NL	0.3071	72	no stemming
tnonn6	NL	0.3977	84	Xelda, case insensitive
tnoss1	ES	0.5181	88	baseline
tnoss2	ES	0.5182	88	fuzzy lookup
tnoss3	ES	0.5234	90	fuzzy expansion

procedure can also be used to expand the query with near matches of all query terms. This function can be practical for queries that contain diacritics or such as accents, or spelling variants like the German ß/ss. The CLEF 2001 monolingual runs showed some modest improvements for the fuzzy expand option. We suspect however, that this is mostly due to undoing the case sensitivity, which is a side-effect of the expansion operation. For most languages, fuzzy conflation increases average precision by about 1% (absolute scale), the only exception being French. We will look at two languages (French and Dutch) in some more detail.

For French, mean average precision is hurt by the expansion operation. Looking closer at runs tnoff1 and tnoff3 shows that the main differences occur at topic 70 an 75. Topic 70 is about *Kim Il Sung* while Le Monde almost invariably spells his name as *Kim Il-sung*. The tokeniser converts dashes into spaces, a strategy which is necessary here, but it is clear also that case normalisation is necessary for proper matches. Omitting case normalisation (tnoff1) is 0.14 % less effective than doing case normalisation (tnoff3). Topic 75 is an odd topic because it only contains one relevant document; run tnoff3 has the relevant document on the first position, whereas run tnoff1 retrieves the document in third position. The key point here is that the topic mentions *tuerie*. The baseline run retrieves the single relevant document in first position, the fuzzy expansion run conflates *tuerie* with *tuer* which has the effect that two other marginally relevant documents have an increased score and the single relevant document has rank 3, decreasing the map for this topic with 0.666. We did a control run (tnoff4) which was similar to the baseline (no fuzzy expansion) but which did apply case normalisation. The run performed marginally better at 0.4904, confirming our conjecture that our sub-optimal proper noun recognition module effectively hurts average precision.

For Italian, we also have conclusive evidence that case sensitivity deteriorated retrieval performance slightly instead of an expected improvement. There are marked differences only for a small number of topics. E.g. topic 88 talks about *Spongiforme Encefalopatia*. The Italian Xelda lexicon does not contain these words, and thus the capitalisation is left in place, which hurts performance here, because in most documents these terms are used in lowercase. A possible strategy could be to lowercase unknown words, but this information is not available for all languages.

For Dutch the fuzzy expansion run increases mean average precision w.r.t the baseline run. The increase is mainly due to topic 52 (0.0165 versus 0.5000). Here, the effect is merely due to case normalisation: Xelda sometimes assigns the lemma *Chinese* and sometimes *chinese*, which causes a great loss of recall in the baseline (case sensitive) run. The control run (tnonn6) confirms again that case sensitivity hurts average precision in the current set-up.

Our conclusion is that in principle it is good to do proper noun recognition (which we implemented by capitalisation) because sometimes a proper noun is homonymous with another word (e.g. in English: (Kim Il) *Sung* and *sung*). However, if the proper noun recognition is not perfect, e.g. it cannot deal with spelling variation (Kim Il-sung versus Kim Il Sung) it might hurt recall more than it improves precision. In practice, an imperfect proper name recognition module will yield inconclusive results which depend on the specific topic set. Our conjecture is that a proper name recognition module in combination with a proper name normalisation module (which conflates spelling variants of proper nouns) could improve retrieval effectiveness in a convincing way. The fuzzy matching technique as a means to find spelling variants other than case alternatives can help to improve retrieval performance as a fall-back option (i.e. when a query term is not found in the indexing vocabulary). Expanding every query term to find spelling variants is probably only useful when it is constrained to special word classes:

1. Languages with accentuated words: sometimes accents are left out or diacritics like the umlaut are mapped to a different form: $\ddot{u} \rightarrow ue$.
2. Spelling variants of proper nouns: transliteration of non-Latin script names into a Latin script is usually done in different ways.

A principled approach would be to recognise these word classes (which are language dependent!) and build tailored normalisation/conflation modules for each of them. Our non-principled fuzzy conflation procedure does the job, but often also hurts precision because it is not constrained to these word classes.

The second experiment was a comparison between Xelda inflectional lemmatisation and a Dutch variant of the Porter stemming algorithm [8]. We did an unofficial case insensitive run based on Xelda lemmatisation (tnonn6) in order to do a clean comparison. The Xelda based run performs noticeably better than the Porter based run (+0.03) Big performance gains by the lemmatisation based approach can be seen in topic 68 (+0.50), where dictionary based approach correctly removes the inflectional suffix of the query term *synagogen* whereas the Dutch Porter fails to conflate *synagogen* and *synagoge* and in topic 55 (+0.55), where it is crucial to split the compound *alpeninitiatief*. The latter example confirms our earlier conclusions that splitting of compound terms is essential [8]. The Xelda compound splitter is based on a lexicon of segmented compounds. This approach is not optimal, since compounding is a highly productive process (e.g. the terms *gekkekoeienziekte, schatzoekactiviteiten* from the CLEF 2001 topic collection). Unfortunately, we lacked the time to test existing better compound splitting algorithms, like the one we used for our experiments with the UPLIFT collection [15].

The 4th column of Table 2 shows the percentage of documents of the top 100 which is judged. In comparison with last year, this percentage has increased slightly, possibly due to the increased pool depth (60 instead of 50) and/or the increased number of participants. Only the English pool is of a slightly lower quality, questioning again why monolingual English runs are excluded from the pool.

6.2 Bilingual Results

Table 3 shows the results of our official and unofficial (italic) bilingual runs, complemented with monolingual baselines.

FR-EN: Babelfish versus corpus. A striking result is that the web corpus runs perform at the same level as the Systran based Babelfish service. Again we looked at some topics with marked differences in average precision. First, the topics where the web corpus run performs better: in topic 47 (+0.55), Systran lacks the translation of Tchétchénie (Chechnya); topic 58 (+0.46), Systran translates *mort* and *mourir* with *died* and *die*, whereas the web corpus has the additional concepts of *death* and *dead*; topic 82 (about IRA attacks, +0.4) Systran translates *l'IRA* erroneously by *WILL GO*, the corpus based translation brings in the related term *bomb* as a translation of attack. Secondly, the topics where Systran performs much better: topic 65 (-0.39) the corpus translations of *trésor* are *treasury* and *board*, which would be a fine phrase translation. In this context however, *trésor* does not have the financial meaning and because our system does not recognise phrases, *treasury* and *board* are used as separate query terms, which has the effect that the much more frequent term *board*, brings in a lot of irrelevant documents. Topic 75 (-0.98) suffers from a wrong interpretation of the word *sept*, which is translated to *sept (September)* and *7*, the latter term is discarded by the indexer. The month abbreviation retrieves a lot of irrelevant documents, resulting in a low position of the single relevant document; in topic 80 (about hunger strikes) *faim* is translated both by *hunger* and *death*. *Death* might be a related term in some cases, but it also retrieves documents about strikes and death, hurting precision; topic 89 talks about an *agent immobilier*, Systran produces the correct translation *real estate agent*, but the corpus based translation has *officer* and *agent* as additional translation. Here, the phrase translation of Systran is clearly superior.

Table 3. Bilingual results CLEF 2001

run tag	language pair	m.a.p.	% of baseline	description
tnoee1	EN-EN	0.5144	100	baseline
tnoee3	EN-EN	0.5289	103	fuzzy expand
tnofe1	FR-EN	0.4637	90	RALI parallel web corpus, forward probabilities, fuzzy expansion
tnofe1a	FR-EN	0.4320	84	RALI parallel web corpus, forward probabilities, no fuzzy expansion
tnofe2	FR-EN	**0.4735**	92	Babelfish MT, fuzzy expansion
tnofe3	FR-EN	0.3711	73	VLIS MRD, inverse probabilities, fuzzy expansion
tnonn1	NL-NL	0.3795	100	baseline
tnoen1	EN-NL	0.3336	87	VLIS MRD, inverse probabilities, fuzzy expansion
tnoff1	FR-FR	0.4877	100	baseline
tnoef3	EN-FR	**0.4051**	83	VLIS MRD, inverse probabilities, fuzzy expansion
tnoef4	EN-FR	0.4039	82	Babelfish MT, fuzzy expansion
tnoef5	EN-FR	0.3642	76	RALI parallel web corpus, forward probabilities, fuzzy expansion
tnoii1	IT-IT	0.4411	100	baseline
tnoei3	EN-IT	**0.3549**	80	VLIS MRD, inverse probabilities, fuzzy expansion
tnoei4	EN-IT	0.2824	64	Babelfish MT, fuzzy expansion
tnoei5	EN-IT	0.3137	70	RALI parallel web corpus, forward probabilities

FR-EN: Babelfish versus VLIS. We also looked at some topics that revealed marked differences between the Systran run and the VLIS run. Topic 58 is a clear example where VLIS gives the best results (+0.44) , it correctly translates the key term *euthanasie* by *euthanasia* instead of the non standard translation *euthanasy* by Systran. In most cases however, Systran gives better results, some examples: topic 79 (-1.00), here VLIS fails to translate *Ulysse* into *Ulysses*, the word by word translation strategy also fails for *sonde spatiale*, VLIS translates sonde into *sampler;sound;probe;catheter;gauge;plumb;sink;auger* and spatiale into *spatial;dimensional*. Probably the fact that the query terms *Ulysses* and *space* are missing is more detrimental then the fact that VLIS generates some irrelevant translations for *sonde*, since the correct translation (*probe*) is found. In topic 62 (-0.50) both *Japon* is not found in VLIS and the multi-word unit *tremblement de terre* is not recognised as the French translation of *earthquake*. In topic 66 (-0.50) the seminal proper noun *Lettonie* is not found in VLIS, but is successfully translated by Systran. The proper nouns are probably not found in VLIS because in French, country names are usually denoted in combination with a determiner *La France, Le Québec,...*, our lexical lookup routine was not aware of this fact. In topic 80 (-0.65) the seminal query term *faim* is translated to *appetite;lust* instead of hunger (Systran). In topic 83 (-0.40), VLIS translates *enchère* by *raise;bid*, whereas Systran gives the contextual better translation *auction*. Finally, the low effectiveness of the VLIS based translation for topic 86 (-0.50) is due to a combination of factors, the dictionary based translation is rather fertile (e.g *usage* is translated in *currency;commonness;use;custom;habit;way;practice;usage;word*) and also the fuzzy expansion process is active, to correct for the case sensitivity of the index, which brings in more unwanted terms. Summarising, the Systran based Babelfish service outperforms the VLIS based run, because i) VLIS lacks translations of some proper nouns, ii) the word by word based translation fails for some topics (we currently have not accessed the phrasal translations in VLIS) and iii) VLIS has no method for sense disambiguation. Babelfish most probably uses phrase translations as a form of contextual sense disambiguation: the translation in isolation of *enchères* is *bidding, ventes aux enchères* gives *auction sales* and *ventes enchères* gives *sales biddings*.

EN-IT and EN-FR. We do not want to base our judgement of the effectiveness of translation resources on one language pair and one topic set. Therefore we included two other languages pairs: EN-IT and EN-FR. For these language pairs, the VLIS based runs is clearly superior, which is not trivial, since these translations use Dutch as a pivot language. The EN-IT web based run performs surprisingly good (better than Systran), given its relatively small size and the fact that the corpus is hardly cleaned.

CLEF 2000 topic collection. For an even better perspective, Table 4 shows the results for the same language pairs based on the CLEF 2000 topics.

When we make a comparison of CLEF 2000 and CLEF 2001 results, we hardly see any consistent results, this confirms experiences we had with the various CLIR tracks at TREC6/7/8. The bilingual results depend strongly on lexical coverage. When a resource misses a few important concepts in the topic collection, its performance is seriously affected. In other words the mean average precision of a run is proportional to the lexical coverage. Unfortunately a set of 50 topics proves to be too small to measure the retrieval performance of a system based on a particular translation resource and its inherent lexical coverage in a reliable way. We could do a few things to remedy this problem:

- Devise a special test for lexical coverage.
- Remove topics from the collection, for which one of the methods has serious lexical gaps. This might very well introduce a bias, but has the advantage that we can concentrate on some interesting research questions:

Table 4. Bilingual results CLEF 2000

method	language pair	m.a.p.	% of baseline
mono	FR-FR	0.4529	100
web corpus	EN-FR	**0.3680**	82
Babelfish	EN-FR	0.3321	73
VLIS	EN-FR	0.2773	62
mono	EN-EN	0.4164	100
web corpus	FR-EN	0.3995	95
Babelfish	FR-EN	**0.4007**	95
VLIS	FR-EN	0.2971	71
mono	IT-IT	0.4808	100
web corpus	EN-IT	**0.3771**	79
Babelfish	EN-IT	0.3564	75
VLIS	EN-IT	0.3266	69

- How well do the different methods deal with the translation of phrases?
- Is query term disambiguation really necessary?
- Can we exploit synonym translations?

Combination of translation resources. If we are merely interested in a strategy yielding "the best" result, it is fairly obvious that a combination of lexical resources could help to remedy the gaps of the individual translation resources. Some groups experimented with this idea, but with mixed results [2,16]. We took a very straightforward approach and simply concatenated the (structured) translations of the different methods, which indeed improved upon the results of the individual runs. Results are presented in Table 5. This simple approach proved consistently effective: every combination of runs is more effective than the individual composing runs. The fact that combining a good and a bad translation resource does not degrade the performance is another indication that (at least for t+d queries) it is much more important to have at least one good translation and that the retrieval model is fairly robust against "noise" translations.

Table 5. Combination runs CLEF 2001

method	language pair	m.a.p.	% of baseline
mono	EN-EN	0.5144	100
web corpus	FR-EN	0.4637	90
Babelfish	FR-EN	0.4735	92
VLIS	FR-EN	0.3711	73
corpus&Babelfish	FR-EN	0.4895	96
corpus&VLIS	FR-EN	0.4672	92
VLIS&Babelfish	FR-EN	0.4783	94
VLIS&Babelfish&corpus	FR-EN	**0.5032**	98

6.3 Multilingual Results

Our strategy for the multilingual task was identical to previous years. First we ran retrieval runs for each of the sub-collections, involving a translation step for most of these runs (the only exception is the EN-EN run). Subsequently we merged results using a naive merging strategy based on raw scores. The main difference with last year was that the VLIS lexical database was extended with translations from Dutch to Italian. Spanish did not pose any problem, because it was supported both by VLIS and Xelda. This gave us the opportunity to compare two set-ups: one based on the Babelfish service and one based on the VLIS lexical database. We did not have time to run a multilingual experiment based on the parallel web corpora.

Table 6. Multilingual results CLEF 2001

run tag	language pair	mean average precision	description
tnoex3	EN-X	0.2634	VLIS
tnoex3P	EN-X	**0.3082**	VLIS (bugfix)
tnoex4	EN-X	0.2413	Babelfish
tnonx3	NL-X	0.2513	VLIS
tnonx3P	NL-X	0.2699	VLIS (bugfix)

Table 6 presents the results of our official multilingual runs. Unfortunately, the VLIS based runs contained a bug, which had a negative effect on our scoring strategy which is based on raw scores. We fixed the bug (runs with suffix P), which especially helped the EN-X run. We can make several observations. The VLIS based run (bugfixed) performs much better than the Babelfish based run based on English topics. This is a bit surprising since Babelfish had a better performance for the CLEF2000 EN-X task and also showed superior performance on the FR-EN bilingual task. A possible explanation could be that the translation quality of the various language pairs offered by Babelfish and/or Systran is not homogeneous. We will assess this shortly. Secondly, the VLIS run based on Dutch topics performs worse than the VLIS run based on English topics. This is not surprising, since the NL-X run does not contain a monolingual EN-EN run, which is easier than a bilingual run.

We have computed the mean average precision of the partial runs which make up the multilingual runs, results are shown in table 7. The number of topics on which the mean average precision is based is shown between brackets. We discovered that something went wrong with the Babelfish translations for some of the topics from English into Spanish (hence 47 instead of 49).

Rerunning the Babelfish EN-X multilingual run yielded a mean average precision of 0.2465, which does not really change the picture.

When we compare the Babelfish bilingual EN-X translation runs with the official FR-EN run (90%), we see that these runs compare less favourable with respect to the corresponding monolingual run: EN-FR:86%, EN-DE: 72%, EN-IT:

Table 7. mean average precision of intermediate runs

run tag	languages	English	French	German	Italian	Spanish
tnoex3	EN-X	0.5289(47)	0.4051(49)	0.3184(49)	0.3549(47)	0.3990(49)
tnoex3P	EN-X	0.5289(47)	0.4148(49)	0.3271(49)	0.3671(47)	0.4074(49)
tnoex4	EN-X	0.5289(47)	0.4039(49)	0.2827(49)	0.2824(47)	0.3910(47)/**fix:**0.4135(49)
tnonx3	NL-X	0.4196(47)	0.4189(49)	0.3419(49)	0.3359(47)	0.3422(49)
tnonx3P	NL-X	0.4148(47)	0.4170(49)	0.3405(49)	0.3358(47)	0.3453(49)
mono run		0.5289	0.4877	0.3946	0.4411	0.5181

64%, EN-ES: 80%. Indeed, the translation quality of Babelfish is not homogeneous across languages for this set of topics.

7   Conclusions

At CLEF 2001, we concentrated on monolingual and bilingual experiments. Our hypothesis was that proper noun recognition could improve precision, because proper nouns are sometimes homonymous with other words. Our implementation of a proper noun aware indexing strategy turned out to hurt average precision. This is probably caused by a sub-optimal way to deal with the sometimes sill ambiguous output of the Xelda lemmatiser. We also experimented with a fuzzy query expansion method, in other to deal with spelling variation of especially proper nouns. A control experiment showed that the effectiveness of this algorithm is largely due to the conflation of capitalised/uncapitalised forms. We suggest a class based expansion scheme instead. Further we compared two different lemmatisation schemes for Dutch: the morphological lemmatisation (which includes the decomposition of compounds) proved to be markedly more effective than the Dutch variant of the Porter suffix stripper. For the bilingual task, we compared three different translation resources: a bilingual MRD (VLIS), a statistical dictionary based on a parallel web corpus and the Babelfish MT service. For the translation pair French-English, the web based and the MT based run reach a quite impressive level of 90 and 92% of the monolingual EN-EN run. The VLIS based run reached a level of 73%, which is due to several factors: deficiencies in the lexical lookup of proper names, lack of phrase handling and translation via a pivot language. For the translation pair English-Dutch, the VLIS based run scored better at 87% of the monolingual baseline, but failure analysis showed that phrase translation could improve results substantially. We think that the good results of the Babelfish based runs are mostly due to its ability to translate phrases. We consider the competitive results of the runs based on a web corpus based dictionary as a breakthrough in CLIR, because parallel web corpora for EN-* language pairs are relatively easy to acquire. We hope to improve upon these results by training more complex models which allow for phrase translations. We also looked at several other bilingual tasks and did a comparison with CLEF 2000 topics. Our conclusion is that the topic sets are too small to really compare techniques to integrate translation resources into the retrieval model.

Retrieval performance is proportional to lexical coverage. The set of 50 topics is too small to estimate lexical coverage, thus results are highly dependent on the particular topic set. We tested a combination approach, which merely concatenates the translated queries and proved to be consistently effective. Finally, in the multilingual task, our best result was achieved by a run based on the English topic set and the VLIS lexical database. In comparison with the other participants in CLEF 2001, our runs were competitive in all tasks.

Acknowledgements. We thank XRCE Grenoble for making the Xelda morphological toolkit available to us. We thank Van Dale Data to make an extended version of VLIS available which includes translations into Italian. Furthermore we would like to thank Michel Simard (RALI, Université de Montréal) for helping with the construction of aligned corpora and building translation models. We also thank George Foster and Jian-Yun Nie (also RALI) for general discussions about the application of statistical translation models for CLIR.

References

1. Franz, M., McCarley, J.S., Roukos, S.: Ad hoc and multilingual information retrieval at IBM. Ellen Voorhees and Donna Harman, editors, The Seventh Text REtrieval Conference (TREC-7). National Institute for Standards and Technology, 1999. Special Publication 500-242.
2. Braschler, M., Schäuble, P.: Carol Peters, editor, Cross-Language Information Retrieval and Evaluation, number 2069 in Lecture Notes in Computer Science. Springer Verlag, 2001.
3. Hiemstra, D. A linguistically motivated probabilistic model of information retrieval. Christos Nicolaou and Constantine Stephanides, editors, Research and Advanced Technology for Digital Libraries - Second European Conference, ECDL'98, Proceedings, number 1513 in Lecture Notes in Computer Science, pages 569–584 Springer Verlag, September 1998.
4. Kraaij, W., Pohlmann, R., Hiemstra, D.: Twenty-one at TREC-8: using language technology for information retrieval. The Eighth Text Retrieval Conference (TREC-8). National Institute for Standards and Technology, 2000.
5. Hiemstra, D., Kraaij, W., Pohlmann, R., Westerveld, T.: Twenty-one at clef-2000: Translation resources, merging strategies and relevance feedback. Carol Peters, editor, Cross-Language Information Retrieval and Evaluation, number 2069 in Lecture Notes in Computer Science. Springer Verlag, 2001.
6. Amit Singhal, Chris Buckley, and Mandar Mitra. Pivoted document length normalization. Proceedings of the 19th Annual International ACM SIGIR Conference on Research and Development in Information Retrieval, pages 21–29, 1996.
7. Robertson, S.E.: and Walker, S.: Some simple effective approximations to the 2-poisson model for probabilistic weighted retrieval. Proceedings of the Seventeenth Annual International ACM SIGIR Conference on Research and Development in Information Retrieval, pages 232–241, 1994.
8. Kraaij, W., and Pohlmann, R.: Viewing stemming as recall enhancement. Hans-Peter Frei, Donna Harman, Peter Schäuble, and Ross Wilkinson, editors, Proceedings of the 19th ACM-SIGIR Conference on Research and Development in Information Retrieval (SIGIR96), pages 40–48, 1996.

9. Porter, M.F.:, An algorithm for suffix stripping. Program, **14**(3):130–137, 1980.
10. Kraaij, W.,and Pohlmann, R.: Porter's stemming algorithm for Dutch. In L.G.M. Noordman and W.A.M. de Vroomen, editors, Informatiewetenschap 1994: Wetenschappelijke bijdragen aan de derde STINFON Conferentie, pages 167–180, 1994.
11. Hull, D.: Stemming algorithms – a case study for detailed evaluation. Journal of the American Society for Information Science, **47**(1), 1996.
12. McNamee, P. and Mayfield, J.: A language-independent approach to european text retrieval. Carol Peters, editor, Cross-Language Information Retrieval and Evaluation, number 2069 in Lecture Notes in Computer Science. Springer Verlag, 2001.
13. Nie, J.Y., Simard, M., Isabelle, P., Durand, R.: Cross-language information retrieval based on parallel texts an d automatic mining of parallel texts in the web. Proceedings of the 22nd ACM-SIGIR Conference on Research and Development in Information Retrieval (SIGIR99), pages 74–81, 1999.
14. Brown, P.F., Della Pietra, S.A., Della Pietra, V.J., and Mercer, R.L.,: The mathematics of statistical machine translation: Parameter estimation. Computational Linguistics, **19**(2):263–311, June 1993.
15. Vosse, T. G.: The Word Connection. PhD thesis, Rijksuniversiteit Leiden, Neslia Paniculata Uitgeverij, Enschede, 1994.
16. Nie, J.Y., Simard, M., Foster, G.,: Using parallel web pages for multi-lingual ir. Carol Peters, editor, Cross-Language Information Retrieval and Evaluation, number 2069 in Lecture Notes in Computer Science. Springer Verlag, 2001.

ITC-irst at CLEF 2001: Monolingual and Bilingual Tracks

Nicola Bertoldi and Marcello Federico

ITC-irst - Centro per la Ricerca Scientifica e Tecnologica
I-38050 Povo, Trento, Italy
{bertoldi, federico}@itc.it

Abstract. This paper reports on the participation of ITC-irst in the Cross Language Evaluation Forum (CLEF) of 2001. ITC-irst took part in two tracks: the monolingual retrieval task, and the bilingual retrieval task. In both cases, Italian was chosen as the query language, while English was chosen as the document language of the bilingual task. The retrieval engine that was used combines scores computed by an Okapi model and a statistical language model. The cross language system used a statistical query translation model, which is estimated on the target document collection and on a translation dictionary.

1 Introduction

This paper reports on the participation of ITC-irst in two Information Retrieval (IR) tracks of the Cross Language Evaluation Forum (CLEF) 2001: the monolingual retrieval task, and the bilingual retrieval task. The language for the queries was always Italian, and English documents were searched in the bilingual task. With respect to the 2000 CLEF evaluation [1], the monolingual IR system was just slightly refined, while most of the effort was dedicated to develop an original cross-language IR system.

The basic IR engine, used for both evaluations, combines scores of a standard Okapi model and of a statistical language model. For cross-language IR, a lightweight statistical model for translating queries was developed, which does not need any parallel or comparable corpora to be trained, but just the target document collection and a bilingual dictionary.

This paper is organized as follows. In Section 2, the text pre-processing modules that were used are presented. Section 3 describes the IR models, Section 4 introduces the cross-language specific models, namely the query translation model and the retrieval model. Section 5 presents the official evaluation results. Finally, Section 6 gives some conclusions.

2 Text Pre-processing

Text pre-processing is performed in several stages, which may differ according to the task and language. In the following a list of modules used to pre-process documents and queries is given, including information as to which languages they have been applied.

C.A. Peters et al. (Eds.): CLEF 2001, LNCS 2406, pp. 94–101, 2002.

Table 1. List of often used symbols.

Q, T, D	random variables of query, translation, and document
q, t, d	instances of query, query translation, and document
w, i, e	generic term, Italian term, English term
$\mathcal{D}$	collection of documents
$\mathcal{V}, \mathcal{V}(d)$	set of terms occurring in $\mathcal{D}$, and in document d
$N, N(d)$	number of term occurrences in $\mathcal{D}$, and in a document d
$N(w), N(d, w), N(q, w)$	frequency of term w in $\mathcal{D}$, in document d, and in query q
N_w	number of documents in $\mathcal{D}$ which contain term w
$|\cdot|$	size of a set

2.1 Tokenization – IT+EN

Text tokenization is performed in order to isolate words from punctuation marks, recognize abbreviations and acronyms, correct possible word splits across lines, and distinguish between accents and quotation marks.

2.2 Morphological Analysis – IT

A morphological analyzer decomposes each Italian inflected word into its morphemes, and suggests all possible POSs and base forms of each valid decomposition. By base forms we mean the not inflected entries of a dictionary.

2.3 POS Tagging – IT

Words in a text are tagged with parts-of-speech (POS) by computing the best text-POS alignment through a statistical model. The tagger that was used works with 57 tag classes and has an accuracy around 96%.

2.4 Base Form Extraction – IT

Once the POS and the morphological analysis of each word in the text is computed, a base form can be assigned to each word.

2.5 Stemming – EN

Word stemming is only performed on English words using the Porter's algorithm.

2.6 Stop-Word Removal – IT+EN

Words that are not considered relevant for IR are discarded in order to save index space. Words are filtered out on the basis either of their POS (if available) or their inverted document frequency.

2.7   Multi-word Recognition – EN

Multi-words are just used for the sake of the query translation. Hence, the statistics used by the translation models do contain multi-words. After translation, multi-words are split into single words.

3   Information Retrieval Models

3.1   Okapi Model

To score the relevance of a document d versus a query q, the following Okapi weighting function is applied:

$$s(d) = \sum_{w \in q \cap d} N(q, w) \, W_d(w) \, idf(w) \tag{1}$$

where:

$$W_d(w) = \frac{N(d, w)(k_1 + 1)}{k_1(1 - b) + k_1 b \frac{N(d)}{l} + N(d, w)} \tag{2}$$

scores the relevance of w in d, and the inverted document frequency:

$$idf(w) = \log \frac{N - N_w + 0.5}{N_w + 0.5} \tag{3}$$

evaluates the relevance of term w inside the collection. The model implies two parameters k_1 and b to be empirically estimated over a development sample. As in previous work, the settings $k_1 = 1.5$ and $b = 0.4$ were used. An explanation of the terms involved can be found in [7] and other papers referenced there.

3.2   Language Model

According to this model, the match between a query random variable Q and a document random variable D is expressed through the following conditional probability distribution:

$$Pr(D \mid Q) = \frac{Pr(Q \mid D)Pr(D)}{Pr(Q)} \tag{4}$$

where $Pr(Q \mid D)$ represents the likelihood of Q, given D, $Pr(D)$ represents the a-priori probability of D, and $Pr(Q)$ is a normalization term. By assuming a uniform a-priori probability distribution among the documents, and disregarding the normalization factor, documents can be ranked, with respect to Q, just by the likelihood term $Pr(Q \mid D)$. If we assume an order-free multinomial model, the likelihood is:

$$Pr(Q = w_1, \ldots, w_n \mid D = d) = \prod_{k=1}^{n} Pr(w_k \mid d) \tag{5}$$

The probability that a term w is generated by d can be estimated by a statistical language model (LM). Previous work on statistical information retrieval [3,5] proposed to interpolate relative frequencies in each document with those of the whole collection, with interpolation weights empirically estimated from the data. In this work we use an interpolation formula which applies the smoothing method proposed by [8]. This method linearly smoothes word frequencies of a document, and the amount of probability assigned to never observed terms is proportional to the number of different words contained in the document, i.e.:

$$Pr(w \mid d) = \frac{N(d, w)}{N(d) + |\mathcal{V}(d)|} + \frac{|\mathcal{V}(d)|}{N(d) + |\mathcal{V}(d)|} P(w) \tag{6}$$

where $Pr(w)$, the word probability over the collection, is estimated by interpolating the smoothed relative frequency with the uniform distribution over the vocabulary $\mathcal{V}$:

$$Pr(w) = \frac{N(w)}{N + |\mathcal{V}|} + \frac{|\mathcal{V}|}{N + |\mathcal{V}|} \frac{1}{|\mathcal{V}|} \tag{7}$$

3.3 Combined Model

Previous work [1] showed that Okapi and the statistical model rank documents almost independently. Hence, information about the relevant documents can be gained by integrating the scores of both methods. Combination of the two models is implemented by taking the sum of scores. Actually, in order to adjust to scale differences, scores of each model are normalized in the range $[0, 1]$ before summation.

3.4 Blind Relevance Feedback

Blind relevance feedback (BRF) is a well-known technique that allows to improve retrieval performance. The basic idea is to perform retrieval in two steps. First, the documents matching the original query q are ranked; then the B best ranked documents are taken and the R most relevant terms contained in them are added to the query. Finally, the retrieval phase is repeated with the augmented query. In this work, new search terms are extracted by sorting all the terms of the B top documents according to [2]:

$$r_w \frac{(r_w + 0.5)(N - N_w - B + r_w + 0.5)}{(N_w - r_w + 0.5)(B - r_w + 0.5)} \tag{8}$$

where r_w is the number of documents, among the top B documents, which contain word w. In all the experiments performed the values $B = 5$ and $R = 15$ were used.

4   Cross-Language IR Model

4.1   Query Translation Model

Query translation is based on a *hidden Markov model* (HMM) [6], in which the observable part is the query Q in the source language (Italian), and the hidden part is the corresponding query T in the target language (English). Hence, the joint probability of a pair Q, T can be decomposed as follows:

$$Pr(Q = i_1, \ldots, i_n, T = e_1, \ldots, e_n) =$$
$$= \prod_{k=1}^{n} Pr(i_k \mid e_k) Pr(e_k \mid e_{k-1}) \tag{9}$$

Given a query $Q = i_1, \ldots, i_n$ and estimates of the discrete distributions in the right side of equation (9), the most probable translation $T^* = e_1^*, \ldots, e_n^*$ can be determined through the well-known Viterbi algorithm [6]. Probabilities $Pr(i \mid e)$ are estimated from a translation dictionary as follows:

$$Pr(i \mid e) = \frac{\delta(i, e)}{\sum_{i'} \delta(i', e)} \tag{10}$$

where $\delta(i, e) = 1$ if the English term e is one of the translations of Italian term i and $\delta(i, e) = 0$ otherwise. For the CLEF evaluation an Italian-English dictionary of about 45K entries was used.

Probabilities $Pr(e \mid e')$ are estimated on the target document collection, through the following bigram LM, that tries to compensate for different word orderings induced by the source and target languages:

$$Pr(e \mid e') = \frac{Pr(e, e')}{\sum_{e''} Pr(e, e'')} \tag{11}$$

where $Pr(e, e')$ is the probability of e co-occurring with e', regardless of the order, within a text window of fixed size. Smoothing of the probability is performed through absolute discounting and interpolation as follows:

$$Pr(e, e') = \max\{\frac{C(e, e') - \beta}{N}, 0\} + \beta Pr(e) Pr(e') \tag{12}$$

$C(e, e')$ is the number of co-occurrences appearing in the corpus, $Pr(e)$ is estimated according to equation (7), and the absolute discounting term β is equal to the estimate proposed in [4]:

$$\beta = \frac{n_1}{n_1 + 2n_2} \tag{13}$$

with n_k representing the number of term pairs occurring exactly k times in the corpus.

4.2   IR Model

As a first method to perform cross-language retrieval, a simple plug-in method was devised, which decouples the translation and retrieval phases. Hence, given a query Q in the source language, the Viterbi decoding algorithm is applied to compute the most probable translation T^* in the target language, according to the statistical query translation model explained above. Then, the document collection is searched by applying a conventional monolingual IR method.

Table 2. Plug-in method for cross-language IR.

1. Find the best translation of query Q: $\quad T^* = \arg\max_T Pr(Q, T)$ 2. Order documents by using the translation T^*

5   Evaluation

5.1   Monolingual Track

Two monolingual runs were submitted to the Italian monolingual track. The first run used all the information available for the topics, while the second run used just the title and description parts. The Italian collection consisted of 108,578 documents with 1,246 instances of a document being relevant to one of the 47 topics.

A detailed description of the used system follows now:

- Document/query pre-processing: tokenization, POS tagging, base form extraction, stop-term removal.
- Retrieval step 1: separate Okapi and LM runs.
- BRF: performed on each model output.
- Retrieval step 2: same as step 1 with the expanded query.
- Final rank: sum of Okapi and LM normalized scores.

Results of the submitted runs are given in Table 3.

5.2   Bilingual IR Evaluation

Two runs were submitted to the Italian-to-English bilingual track, with the same modalities of the monolingual track. The bilingual collection consisted of 110,282 documents, with 856 instances of a document being relevant to one of the 47 topics. A detailed description of the system follows:

- Document pre-processing: tokenization, stemming, stop-word removal.
- Query pre-processing: tokenization, POS tagging, base form extraction, stop term removal, translation, multi-words split, stemming.

Table 3. Results for the Italian monolingual tracks.

Retrieval Mode	Official Run	mAvPr
title+desc+narr	IRSTit1	48.59
title+desc	IRSTit2	46.44

Table 4. Results for the Italian-English bilingual tracks.

Retrieval Mode	Official Runs	mAvPr
title+desc+narr	IRSTit2en1	42.51
title+desc	IRSTit2en2	34.11

Retrieval Mode	Non Official Runs	mAvPr
title+desc+narr	Babelfish	44.53
title+desc	Babelfish	37.99

- Retrieval step 1: separate Okapi and LM runs.
- BRF: performed on each model output.
- Retrieval step 2: same as step 1 with the expanded query.
- Final rank: sum of Okapi and LM normalized scores.

An important issue concerns the use of multi-words. Multi-words were only used for the target language, i.e. English, and just for the translation process. After translation, multi-words in the query are split again into single words.

For comparison, our statistical query translation model was replaced with the Babelfish text translation service powered by Systran and available on the Internet[1]. Cross-language retrieval performance was measured by keeping all the other components of the system fixed. Results obtained by the submitted runs and by the Babelfish translator are shown in Table 4. The mean average precision achieved with the commercial translation system shows is about 5%-10% higher, depending on the retrieval mode. Detailed results of the experiments are shown in Table 4.

6 Conclusion

In this paper we have presented the monolingual and cross-language information retrieval systems developed at ITC-irst and evaluated in the CLEF 2001 campaign. The cross-language system uses a statistical query translation algorithm that requires minimal language resources: a bilingual dictionary and the target document collection. Results on the CLEF 2001 evaluation data show that satisfactory performance can be achieved with this simple translation model. However, experience gained from the many experiments that we performed suggests that a fair comparison between different systems would require a much

---

[1] http://world.altavista.com

larger set of queries. The retrieval performance of our system has shown to be very sensitive to the translation step.

Current work aims at further developing the statistical model proposed here for cross-language IR. In particular, significant improvements have been achieved by closely integrating the translation and retrieval models.

Acknowledgements. The authors would like to thank their colleagues at ITC-irst, Bernardo Magnini and Emanuele Pianta, for putting an electronic Italian-English dictionary at our disposal.

References

1. Bertoldi, N. and M. Federico, 2000. Italian text retrieval for CLEF 2000 at ITC-irst. In *Working notes of CLEF 2000*. Lisbon, Portugal.
2. Johnson, S.E., P. Jourlin, K. Spark Jones, and P.C. Woodland, 1999. Spoken document retrieval for TREC-8 at Cambridge University. In *Proc. of 8th TREC*. Gaithersburg, MD.
3. Miller, David R. H., Tim Leek, and Richard M. Schwartz, 1998. BBN at TREC-7: Using hidden Markov models for information retrieval. In *Proc. of 7th TREC*. Gaithersburg, MD.
4. Ney, Herman, Ute Essen, and Reinhard Kneser, 1994. On structuring probabilistic dependences in stochastic language modelling. *Computer Speech and Language*, 8:1–38.
5. Ng, Kenney, 1999. A maximum likelihood ratio information retrieval model. In *Proc. of 8th TREC*. Gaithersburg, MD.
6. Rabiner, Lawrence R., 1990. A tutorial on hidden Markov models and selected applications in speech recognition. In Alex Weibel and Kay-Fu Lee (eds.), *Readings in Speech Recognition*. Los Altos, CA: Morgan Kaufmann, pages 267–296.
7. Robertson, S. E., S. Walker, S. Jones, M. M. Hancock-Beaulieu, and M. Gatford, 1994. Okapi at TREC-3. In *Proc. of 3rd TREC*. Gaithersburg, MD.
8. Witten, Ian H. and Timothy C. Bell, 1991. The zero-frequency problem: Estimating the probabilities of novel events in adaptive text compression. *IEEE Trans. Inform. Theory*, IT-37(4):1085–1094.

Experiments with the Eurospider Retrieval System for CLEF 2001

Martin Braschler, Bärbel Ripplinger, and Peter Schäuble

Eurospider Information Technology AG
Schaffhauserstr. 18, 8006 Zürich, Switzerland
{braschler|ripplinger|schauble}@eurospider.com

Abstract. Eurospider participated in both the multilingual and monolingual retrieval tasks for CLEF 2001. Our multilingual experiments, the main focus of this year's work, combine multiple approaches to cross-language retrieval: machine translation, similarity thesauri, and machine-readable dictionaries. We experimented with both query translation and document translation. The monolingual experiments focused on the use of two fundamentally different stemming components: a stemmer based on commercial considerations, and a linguistically motivated stemmer.

1 Introduction

This paper describes the experiments we conducted for CLEF 2001. Much of the work for this year builds directly on ideas we already applied to last year's experiments [1]. Eurospider participated in the multilingual and German and French monolingual retrieval tasks. In multilingual retrieval we tried to combine as many approaches to translation as possible in order to obtain a robust system. We used similarity thesauri (a corpus-based method), machine-readable dictionaries and a machine translation system. We also tried both document and query translation. The focus of the monolingual experiments was on investigating various aspects of stemming.

The remainder of the paper is structured as follows: First, we present our system setup, and outline some details of the collection and indexing. This is followed by a description of the particular characteristics of the individual experiments (including a comparison with last year) and a preliminary analysis of our results. The paper closes with a discussion of our findings.

2 System Setup

In the following, we provide details about the system setup, indexing method, weighting scheme and the parts of the CLEF test collection that were used for our experiments.

C.A. Peters et al. (Eds.): CLEF 2001, LNCS 2406, pp. 102–110, 2002.

System: For our runs, we used the standard Eurospider retrieval system, a core part of all of Eurospider's commercial products, enhanced by some experimental multilingual information access (MLIA) components.

Indexing: Indexing of German documents and queries for the multilingual task used the German Spider stemmer, which is based on a dictionary coupled with a set of rules for decompounding of German nouns. German umlauts were mapped to their corresponding two-letter representations.

Indexing of French documents for the multilingual task used the French Spider stemmer. French accents were retained.

For the German and French monolingual task, we carried out a more in-depth analysis on stemming, and therefore used different stemming methods. These differences are discussed in section 4.

Indexing of Italian documents used the Spider Italian rule-based stemmer. For the La Stampa documents, there was a simple preprocessing that replaced the combination "vowel + quote" with an accented vowel, to normalize the alternative way of representation for accented characters in this subcollection. This simple rule produces some errors if a word was intentionally quoted, but the error rate was considered too small to justify the development of a more sophisticated replacement process. This heuristic was not necessary for the AGZ/SDA Italian texts.

Indexing of English documents used an adapted version of the Porter rule-based stemmer.

Indexing of the Spanish documents used a new experimental stemmer specifically developed for this task.

Weighting: The Spider system was configured to use a straight Lnu.ltn weighting scheme for retrieval, as described in [5].

Test Collection: The CLEF multilingual test collection consists of newspaper and newswire articles for German (Frankfurter Rundschau, Der Spiegel, SDA), French (Le Monde, ATS), Italian (La Stampa, AGZ), English (LA Times) and, new in 2001, Spanish (EFE). There are additional documents in Dutch and German, which are used for special subtasks that we did not participate in.

3   Multilingual Retrieval

We spent our main effort on experiments for the multilingual task. The goal of this task in CLEF is to pick a topic language, and use the queries to retrieve documents independent of their language. This means a mixed result list has to be returned, potentially containing documents in all five languages (English, French, German, Italian and Spanish).

We submitted four runs for this task, labeled EIT01M1N, EIT01M2N, and EIT01M3D/EIT01M3N. They represent increasingly complex experiments. All runs use the German topics; the "N" runs use all topic fields, whereas the "D" run uses title+description only.

We investigated both query translation (abbreviated "QT" in the following) and document translation ("DT"). We used multiple methods for query translation, since it is our belief that merging input from multiple translation resources enhances the quality and robustness of a cross-language IR system. All queries were therefore translated using similarity thesauri ("ST"), machine-readable dictionaries ("MRD") and a commercially available machine translation ("MT") system. Due to performance considerations, only the MT system was used for document translation.

A description of these key technologies follows.

Similarity Thesaurus: A similarity thesaurus is an automatically calculated data structure, which is built on suitable training data. It links terms to lists of their statistically most similar counterparts [2]. If multilingual training data is used, the resulting thesaurus is also multilingual. Terms in the source language are then linked to the most similar terms in the target language [4]. Such a thesaurus can be used to produce a "pseudo-translation" of the query by substituting the source language terms with those terms from the thesaurus that are most similar to the query as a whole.

Because some of the data that was newly added to the CLEF collections overlaps with the training data of the thesauri we used for our 2000 CLEF experiments, we rebuilt all thesauri to make sure that the training data is completely disjoint from the CLEF collection.

For German/French and German/Italian, we used training data provided by the Schweizerische Depeschenagentur (SDA), which is from a different time period than the SDA data in CLEF. For German/Spanish, we aligned German SDA with Spanish texts from Reuters and Agence France Presse (AFP). Since this thesaurus is only used to search the Spanish subcollection (EFE), the use of all SDA data was acceptable. For German/English, we used German SDA data aligned to English data from the Associated Press (AP).

There was a considerable difference in the amount of training data available to build the thesauri for the different language pairs. While the training data for German/French and German/Italian was substantial (roughly 10 and 9 years of newswire articles, respectively), we started from scratch for German/English (we used no German/English ST in 2000) and German/Spanish. Therefore, the resulting thesauri for these latter language combinations were not as well refined as for the earlier language pairs. As expected, this had a significant impact on retrieval quality.

In all cases, training used comparable corpora, not parallel corpora that contain real translations.

Machine Translation System: For a limited number of language pairs, commercial end-user machine translation products are available. Since some of these systems are inexpensive and run on standard PC hardware, we decided to loosely combine such a product with both our translation component and our retrieval software. We used MT to translate both the document collection and the queries. There was no direct German/Spanish machine translation available to us, so we used a two-step German/English/Spanish translation in this case.

Machine-Readable Dictionaries: This year, we added general-purpose MRDs to our experiments. These dictionaries were used for query translation outside the system, without a proper integration into the system's weighting mechanism. In case of translation ambiguity, we used a heuristic to decide on the number of potential translations to be generated. This lack of integration limited the control over terms left untranslated due to gaps in the dictionary.

Table 1. Size of the machine-readable dictionaries used for the multilingual experiments

Language Pair	# of Entries
German - English	486,851
German – French	70,161
German – Italian	7,953
German - Spanish	36,636

Using these three translation methods, the ranked lists for the four multilingual runs were obtained as follows:

EIT01M1N: This run is based on one large, unified index containing all German documents plus the MT-translations of all English, French, Italian and Spanish documents. We then performed straight German monolingual retrieval on this index. An added benefit of using the combined index is the avoidance of the merging problem that typically arises when results are calculated one language at a time. Since only one search needs to be performed on one index, a single ranked list is obtained. We used all topic fields (title, description and narrative) for this run.

EIT01M2N: This is an experiment based on query translation. The final, multilingual ranked lists are obtained through merging of four bilingual retrieval runs (one for each language pair – German/French, German/Italian, German/Spanish, and German/-English) and one monolingual German retrieval run. The bilingual runs were in turn produced by combining results from three different translation strategies: similarity thesaurus, machine translation, and machine-readable dictionaries. All topic fields were used for this run.

EIT01M3D/EIT01M3N: The two runs are related: for EIT01M3D, we used only the title and description fields, and for EIT01M3N, we used all topic fields. The two experiments combine all elements described for the EIT01M1N (DT-based) and EIT01M2N (QT-based) runs. EIT01M3N is the result of merging EIT01M1N and EIT01M2N, and EIT01M3D is the result of merging the two corresponding title+description runs (EIT01M1D and EIT01M2D, which were not submitted as official experiments).

4 Monolingual Retrieval

Our interest in the monolingual track was to investigate the effects of stemming for German and French. We had the opportunity this year to use the MPRO morpho-syntactic analysis for some research experiments. This analysis component provides elaborate linguistic information, among them base forms and compound analysis for German [3].

By standard, the Eurospider system uses stemming procedures that have been adapted over the years specifically to the needs communicated by customers of Eurospider's commercial retrieval systems. We were now interested to see how such a "commercial" approach compares to a more linguistically motivated approach.

We submitted three runs for the German monolingual task: EIT01GGSSN, an all-topic-fields run using the original Spider stemmer; EIT01GGLUN, a run using the MPRO morpho-syntactic analysis (all topic fields), and EIT01GGLUD, a variant of the second run, using topic+description fields only.

For French monolingual, we also submitted three runs, EIT01FFFN, a run using a new experimental variant of the French Spider stemmer, and EIT01FFLUN, a run using the MPRO analysis, both using all topic fields. Our third run, EIT01FFFD, a title+description run, was mistakenly lost during the submission process, and therefore had to be disqualified from the official evaluation.

While analyzing our results, we found a bug in EIT01FFFN. After fixing this bug (missing accents in queries), performance improved significantly.

The concentration on stemming means that we did not use some "enhancements", such as blind feedback, that probably would have increased overall performance, but would have made it harder to investigate the impact of stemming. The runs therefore are simplistic: removal of stopwords, stemming, and then straight retrieval.

5   Results

Multilingual Retrieval

Problems: We begin by listing some of the major problems we identified when analyzing this year's performance results.

One of the major obstacles was a lack of suitable training data to build the German/English and German/Spanish similarity thesauri. We built the thesauri for these two language pairs even though we expected their quality to be inadequate. The reason was two-fold: one, to investigate the effects of using (too) little training data, and two, to build a system that treats all languages in the same way.

Analysis of the QT-based run (EIT01M2N) shows that both the German/English and German/Spanish components performed poorly, and therefore hurt overall performance. Unfortunately, the German/French and German/Italian thesauri also did not perform as well as last year. Probably, this is due to the exclusion of the SDA data from 1994 (which was used in the CLEF document collection). However, the German/French and German/Italian thesauri performed much better than their English and Spanish counterparts due to much larger training sets.

All multilingual runs also suffered from the lack of a direct German/Spanish machine translation component. The use of English as an intermediate language (first translating German to English, and then English to Spanish) resulted in decreased performance due to accumulation of errors.

The dictionary-based components we introduced into the QT-based run experienced a similar problem, with the Italian dictionary being very small. Again, we expected this to hurt overall performance, but the Italian dictionary was used to allow consistent handling of the languages.

Comparison: Comparing the three translation methods used for each language pair (MT, ST, MRD), machine translation generally performed best. There are, however, big performance differences between more "popular" language combinations (German/English) and less "popular" ones (German/Italian).

The similarity thesaurus did significantly worse. Like last year, we observe that a sizable part of the difference is caused by a subset of queries that completely fail to retrieve any relevant documents. The remaining queries perform well, but average performance suffers from the outliers.

We observed last year that the combination of machine translation with similarity thesauri substantially outperformed the use of a single strategy. This year, the combination of three methods generally gives only performance comparable to machine translation alone, probably due to the less appropriate quality of the thesauri. However, the combination approach led to an increase in recall, and also better performance in the high precision range.

The dictionary-based translations in general performed similarly to the similarity thesaurus-based translations. When combined with machine translation, the dictionary gave no advantage, but instead affected retrieval performance negatively.

Table 2. Average precision numbers for the multilingual experiments

Runs against Multilingual Collection	Average Precision
EIT01M1N (DT; TDN)	0.3099
EIT01M2N (QT; TDN)	0.2773
EIT01M3D (Combination; TD)	0.3128
EIT01M3N (Combination; TDN)	0.3416

The combined run produces the best results, and does so on a consistent basis. As shown in table 3, the majority of queries improves, often substantially, in terms of average precision when compared to the DT-only or QT-only run. The picture is less conclusive for the comparison between DT-only and QT-only. This seems to indicate that the combination works well and boosts performance.

Analysis by Language: For the French runs, we observed good performance of the MT translations. The similarity thesaurus performed appropriately, but not as well as last year, probably due to the mismatch between the time period covered by the training data and the CLEF test set. The performance of dictionary-based translations was adequate, thanks to a sufficiently sized dictionary for French.

Combining MT with ST benefited mainly long queries, since the number of queries failing completely was higher for the short queries. In both cases, long and short, combination helped in high precision situations. Further combination with MRD brought no additional improvement.

Table 3. Comparison of average precision numbers for individual queries

Comparison Avg. Prec. per Query	better; diff.>10%	better; diff.<10%	worse; diff.<10%	worse; diff.>10%
EIT01M3N (comb.) vs. EIT01M1N (DT)	20	21	9	0
EIT01M3N (comb.) vs. EIT01M2N (QT)	20	16	9	5
EIT01M1N (DT) vs. EIT01M2N (QT)	17	8	9	16

For the English runs, MT performed well, as expected. The similarity thesaurus performed poorly, because the English/German thesaurus had the least appropriate training data available (time shift and too little volume). This means that the combination with a ST negatively affected the English component.

The Italian ST outperformed the thesauri for other languages. While not as good as the Italian MT translations, a full 13 queries performed at least 10% better based on the ST translations than using the MT system. Combining MT with ST outperformed MT alone, especially in high precision situations. The Italian dictionary was the smallest, and consequently of no additional benefit.

Our work in Spanish was started specifically for CLEF. The performance of the German/Spanish thesaurus was adequate. Having training data from the same time period as the CLEF test data proved to be an advantage, even though the pool of training data was not as big as necessary to achieve quality similar to the French or Italian thesauri. The Spanish dictionary did not lead to an overall gain for the German/Spanish component run.

Overall Performance: We are pleased to see that our runs compare favorably with other entries in CLEF. Table 4 shows an analysis of per-query performance compared to the median performance of all participants. All runs are above a "theoretical median", defined as the average of the median average precision values. The combined runs performed especially strongly and were among the best entries for CLEF 2001.

Table 4. Officially submitted runs (multilingual task) compared to median of all submitted runs (on individual query basis)

Run	Best	Above	Median	Below	Worst	Avg. Prec vs. Theor. Median
EIT01M1N	1	23	0	25	1	+0.0351
EIT01M2N	1	21	6	22	0	+0.0024
EIT01M3D	1	28	1	20	0	+0.0379
EIT01M3N	1	36	1	12	0	+0.0667

Monolingual Retrieval

For German, the elaborate morpho-syntactic analysis of MPRO seems to bring a slight improvement over the more conventional Spider stemmer. However, the number of queries affected positively and negatively by over 10% in average precision is equal. We therefore intend to further investigate the difference of the two approaches to stemming in the future. All German runs performed well compared to median performance.

For French, the broken run EIT01FFFN performs poorly. When fixed, performance improves substantially, and outperforms the MPRO analysis component. The fixed French run topped median performance

Table 5. Average precision numbers for the monolingual experiments

Runs against Multilingual Collection	Average Precision
EIT01GGSN (German; TDN)	0.4285
EIT01GGLUN (German; TDN)	0.4408
EIT01GGLUD (German; TD)	0.4132
EIT01FFFN (French; TDN) (official/broken)	0.3848
EIT01FFFN (French; TDN) (unofficial/fixed)	0.4712
EIT01FFLUN (French; TDN)	0.4471

Taking into account the simplicity of the monolingual experiments, we consider the performance to be satisfactory.

Table 6. Comparison of average precision numbers for individual queries

Comparison Avg. Prec. per Query	better; diff.>10%	better; diff.<10%	worse; diff.<10%	worse; diff.>10%
EIT01GGLUN vs. EIT01GGSN	8	19	14	8
EIT0FFLUN vs. EIT01FFFN (official/broken)	19	10	14	4
EIT01FFLUN vs. EIT01FFFN (unofficial/fixed)	4	14	20	8

Table 7. Officially submitted runs compared to median of all submitted runs (on individual query basis)

Run	Best	Above	Median	Below	Worst	Avg. Prec vs. Theor. Median
EIT01GGSN	3	27	4	15	0	+0.0625
EIT01GGLUN	1	30	6	12	0	+0.0748
EIT01GGLUD	1	28	4	16	0	+0.0472
EIT01FFFN (brk)	1	13	5	28	2	-0.0787
EIT01FFFN (cor)	(2)	(23)	(4)	(20)	(0)	+0.0076
EIT01FFLUN	4	17	7	21	0	-0.0164

6   Summary

This year, we tried a combination of three different translation strategies: machine translation, similarity thesauri and machine-readable dictionaries. The results using similarity thesauri were not as remarkable as last year, because of the lack of appropriate training data for some language pairs. Combining similarity thesauri with machine translation showed potential in the same areas already identified last year, i.e. substantial benefit in recall and the high precision range for a number of queries. The general-purpose dictionaries we introduced this year did not improve the performance of our experiments. This is partly due to the small size of the dictionaries for some of the language pairs.

The monolingual experiments concentrated on an investigation into stemming behavior. We tested both the standard Spider stemmer, which is commercially motivated, and stemming based on the MPRO morpho-syntactic component. Based on our CLEF 2001 results, we plan more experiments and an in-depth analysis.

Acknowledgements. We thank IAI Saarbrücken for the opportunity to use MPRO. Anne Göhring worked on the French and Spanish Spider stemmers, and Ron Caneel updated the similarity thesaurus components. Some of the tools for converting result lists were originally written by Min-Yen Kan for the Eurospider TREC-8 experiments.

References

1. Braschler, M., Schäuble, P.: Experiments with the Eurospider Retrieval System for CLEF 2000. In Proceedings of CLEF 2000. Lecture Notes in Computer Science, Springer Verlag, 2001.
2. Qiu, Y., Frei, H.: Concept Based Query Expansion. In Proceedings of the 16th ACM SIGIR Conference on Research and Development in Information Retrieval, Pittsburgh, PA, pages 160 - 169, 1993.
3. Ripplinger, B.: The Use of NLP Techniques in CLIR. In Proceedings of CLEF 2000. Lecture Notes in Computer Science, Springer Verlag, 2001.
4. Sheridan, P., Braschler, M., Schäuble, P.: Cross-language information retrieval in a multilingual legal domain. In Proceedings of the First European Conference on Research and Advanced Technology for Digital Libraries, pages 253 - 268, 1997.
5. Singhal, A., Buckley, C., Mitra, M.: Pivoted Document Length Normalization. In Proceedings of the 19th ACM SIGIR Conference on Research and Development in Information Retrieval, pages 21 - 29, 1996.

Using Co-occurrence, Augmented Restrictions, and C-E WordNet for Chinese-English Cross-Language Information Retrieval at CLEF 2001

Wen-Cheng Lin and Hsin-Hsi Chen

Department of Computer Science and Information Engineering,
National Taiwan University,
Taipei, TAIWAN, R.O.C.
denislin@nlg2.csie.ntu.edu.tw, hh_chen@csie.ntu.edu.tw

Abstract. This paper reports the work of NTU in the bilingual-retrieval task at CLEF 2001. In this experiment, we compared the effectiveness of several approaches in Chinese-English cross-language information retrieval. Five models were proposed. Model 1 used co-occurrence information in the target language to disambiguate translation equivalents; Model 2 augmented restriction terms to the original queries to restrict the use of query terms in the target language; Model 3 used a Chinese-English WordNet to translate queries; Model 4 combined Model 3 with Model 2; Model 5 merged the queries constructed by Model 2 and 3.

1 Introduction

The Natural Language Processing Laboratory (NLPL), National Taiwan University (NTU) participated in the bilingual-retrieval task at CLEF 2001. Cross language information retrieval (CLIR) [1][2] deals with the use of queries in one language to access documents in another. Since the languages of queries and documents are different, the performance of using source language queries directly is usually very poor. In order to cross the language barrier, we can translate queries into the language that documents are written in or translate documents into the language that queries are described in or translate both queries and documents into an intermediate language. Query translation is usually employed for efficiency. In this experiment, we used Chinese queries to retrieve English documents and query translation was adopted to unify the language of queries and documents.

In our previous work, several approaches were proposed. Bian and Chen [3] proposed a hybrid approach that integrated both lexical and corpus knowledge to translate queries. A bilingual dictionary provides the translation equivalents of each query term, and the word co-occurrence information derived from a target language text collection is used to disambiguate the translation. Mutual information (MI) [4] is used to measure the co-occurrence strength. For a query term, the translation equivalent with the highest MI value is selected. Target polysemy is another problem in CLIR. Chen, Bian and Lin [5] augmented a pseudo context to a query term to restrict its use in the target language. The contextual information is derived from a

C.A. Peters et al. (Eds.): CLEF 2001, LNCS 2406, pp. 111-117, 2002.

source language text collection. Chen, Lin and Lin [6] proposed a method to construct a Chinese-English WordNet automatically. We used this C-E WordNet and a bilingual dictionary to translate queries. In this paper, we experiment with the approaches described above. In addition, we propose a combined approach using the C-E WordNet and the augmented restrictions to construct target queries.

2   Resources

In this work, we used four linguistic resources:

(1) Chinese-English dictionary
     The bilingual dictionary is integrated from four sources, including LDC Chinese-English dictionary, Denisowski's CEDICT, BDC Chinese-English dictionary v2.2 and a dictionary used in query translation in the MTIR project [7]. The dictionary gathers 200,037 words, where a word may have more than one translation.

(2) ASBC [8]
     Academic Sinica Balanced Corpus (abbreviated as the ASBC corpus) is a POS-tagged Chinese balanced corpus. The major topics include philosophy (10%), science (10%), society (35%), art (5%), life (20%), and literary (20%). This corpus is composed of five million words.

(3) TREC6 text collection [9]
     The text collection contains 556,077 English documents, and is about 2.2G bytes.

(4) Chinese-English WordNet
     In our previous work [6], we proposed a method to construct a Chinese-English WordNet automatically. Chinese words in a Chinese thesaurus tong2yi4ci2ci2lin2 ("同義詞詞林") [10] are mapped into WordNet [11]. Following the structures of WordNet, a Chinese WordNet and a Chinese-English WordNet are derived.

When translating queries and selecting augmented restriction terms, the co-occurrence information between words is used to select best translation and appropriate restriction terms. The co-occurrence information for Chinese and English words was derived from the ASBC corpus and TREC6 text collection respectively. We adopted the mutual information formula to measure its strength. For each word, we collected its mutual information value with other words within a window of size 3.

3   Query Translation

We adopted query translation to unify the language of queries and documents. The Chinese queries were translated into English. The translated English queries were used to retrieve English documents using a monolingual information retrieval system. We proposed four models to translate queries. Model 1 uses co-occurrence information derived from a text collection in the target language to select the best translation equivalents of source language query terms. Model 2 tries to resolve the target polysemy problem by augmenting some restriction words. Model 3 uses an automatically constructed C-E WordNet to translate queries. Model 4 combines Models 2 and 3.

3.1   Model 1 – CO Model

When translating queries, a query term may have more than one sense. If all translations of a polysemous word are included in the target query, the incorrect senses are also included and may reduce performance. Therefore, a selection operation should be adopted to select appropriate translations. Bian and Chen [3] proposed a hybrid approach that integrated both lexical and corpus knowledge to translate queries. First, the Chinese queries were segmented. For each Chinese word, we collected the translation equivalents by looking up a Chinese-English bilingual dictionary. Then the best translation equivalents were selected by using the co-occurrence information. The mutual information was derived from a text collection in the target language, i.e. TREC6 text collection. For a query term, we compare the MI values of all the translation equivalent pairs (x, y), where x is the translation equivalent of this term, and y is the translation equivalent of another query term within a sentence. The word pair (x_i, y_j) with the highest MI value is extracted, and the translation equivalent x_i is regarded as the best translation equivalent of this query term. Selection is carried out based on the order of the query terms.

3.2   Model 2 – Resolving the Target Polysemy Problem

In order to resolve the target polysemy problem, we augmented some words to restrict the use of a translated query term in the target language. In this model, the Chinese queries were translated by the CO model, and the translation equivalents of augmented words were added to target language queries. The augmented restriction words of a source language query term are those words that frequently co-occur with it within a window. The co-occurrence information was derived from the ASBC corpus, and the mutual information formula was used to measure the strength. We collected the co-occurring terms that have only one translation as candidates. Then we applied the CO model to the translations of these candidates and select one term for each original query term.

The translations of the original query terms and augmented restriction terms were assigned different weights. They were determined by the following formulas:

$$\text{weight}(E_i) = \sum_{k=1}^{n} m_k . \tag{1}$$

$$\text{weight}(EW_{ij}) = 1 . \tag{2}$$

where n is the number of words in a query Q; E_i is the translation of query term C_i; EW_{ij} is the translation of the augmented restriction term CW_{ij} and m_k is the number of words in a restriction for C_k.

3.3   Model 3 – Using Chinese-English WordNet

In this model, the Chinese-English WordNet was used to construct English queries. First, a Chinese query was tagged by a POS tagger. After removing stop words, we looked up the Chinese-English WordNet for the remaining Chinese words. A set of synsets was retrieved for each Chinese query term. A synset is a set of synonyms that can be used to express a concept. We computed the mutual information for the sets of synsets, and selected a synset for each Chinese query term. The mutual information of two synsets is defined as follows. Let $synset_1$ and $synset_2$ be synsets for two query terms. Assume $synset_1$ and $synset_2$ are composed of m and n English words, respectively:

$$MI(synset_1, synset_2) = \sum_{i=1}^{m} \sum_{j=1}^{n} MI(t_{1i}, t_{2j}) /(m \times n) \cdot \tag{3}$$

where t_{ik} is the kth English word in $synset_i$. The MI values of any two English words are derived from the TREC6 corpus. All English words in the selected synsets were used to construct the target query. The translation equivalents in the selected synsets were assigned larger weights. The weights of translation equivalents in the selected synsets were 3 and that of other words were 1.

When looked up in the Chinese-English WordNet, some query terms were not found. For these query terms, we added their translation equivalents to the English query. The weights of these translation equivalents were 1.

3.4   Model 4 – Combined Approach

In Model 3, we used all translation equivalents for those terms that cannot be found in the Chinese-English WordNet. If a term is polysemous, using all its translation equivalents will introduce noise. In this model, we used translations and restriction terms obtained in Model 2 instead of all translation equivalents retrieved from our bilingual dictionary. The weights of these translations were 3 and that of the restriction terms were 1.

4   The IR System

Our Information Retrieval system is based on the vector space model. The index terms are English words, and the term weighting function is tf*idf. When a query is submitted to this IR system, it computes the similarities of this query and all documents, then returns top rank documents. We adopt the cosine vector similarity formula to measure the similarity of a query and a document. A higher score means that the query and the document are more similar.

5   Results

We submitted four runs: NTUco, NTUa1wco, NTUaswtw and NTUtpwn. The English queries of these four runs were constructed by using Models 1, 2, 3 and 4, respectively. In our experiments, only the Title and Description fields were used to generate queries. The results are shown in Table 1. There were some bugs in our IR system. Only the documents in January, February and March were indexed. We re-indexed all documents and did four new runs: CO, A1WCO, ASWTW and TPWN. We also did an unofficial run: MONO, a monolingual run. The results are shown in Table 2.

Table 1. Results of official runs

Run	Average precision	R-Precision	Rel_ret
NTUco	0.0254	0.0292	134
NTUa1wco	0.0255	0.0297	135
NTUaswtw	0.0224	0.0328	149
NTUtpwn	0.0195	0.0301	141

Table 2. Results of new runs

Run	Average precision	R-Precision	Rel_ret
MONO	0.2139	0.2039	611
CO	0.1108 (51.80%)	0.1214 (59.54%)	482
A1WCO	0.1107 (51.75%)	0.1198 (58.75%)	485
ASWTW	0.0816 (38.15%)	0.0814 (39.92%)	472
TPWN	0.1080 (50.49%)	0.1172 (57.48%)	491
ASWTW2	0.1011(47.27%)	0.1051(51.54%)	522
TPWN2	0.1135 (53.06%)	0.1201 (58.90%)	512

The average precision of run CO is 0.1108, which is 51.8% of monolingual information retrieval. The performances of some queries were very bad. Word segmentation errors may be one of the reasons. Take "史特加" as an example. The word "史特加" (Schneider) was segmented into "史", "特" and "加", which were translated into "history", "unusual" and "recruit" respectively. Dictionary coverage is another problem. Some proper nouns are not included in our bilingual dictionary. For example, "歐斯基爾肯" (Euskirchen) is not included in the dictionary. Because of the lack of the translation of "歐斯基爾肯", the relevant document of query 75 cannot be retrieved.

The performance of run A1WCO is almost the same as run CO. In Model 2, we add some restriction terms to the original queries. The augmented restriction terms help us to retrieve more relevant documents, but the average precision decrease. When we add words to the original queries, we may also introduce noise. Some augmented restriction terms are related to the query terms that the restriction terms are augmented to, but are not relevant to the queries. Thus, these terms become noise.

When we used C-E WordNet, the performance was not good. While constructing C-E WordNet, some Chinese words may have been mapped to wrong synsets. For example, "中國" (China) was mapped to the synset that only contain "Kyushu". Thus we cannot find any document that is relevant to "Chinese Currency Devaluation". In run ASWTW, the weights of translation equivalents obtained from the dictionary are lower than those of translations in selected synsets. The reason is that we try to reduce the interference of inappropriate translations. But this also reduces the importance of correct translations. We adjusted the weights of these translations equivalents in a new run ASWTW2. The translations obtained from dictionary and synsets are assigned the same weight, i.e. 3. The average precision is 0.1011.

In Model 3, we used all translation equivalents of the words that are not included in C-E WordNet. In this way, some inappropriate translations were also added to the target queries. In Model 4, we used the translations and restriction terms that obtained from Model 2. The result shows that performance is improved. The average precision of run TPWN is 0.1080, which is 50.49% of monolingual information retrieval. It is better than run ASWTW, but still worse than other runs. We tried another combination method. We simply merged the target queries that are constructed by Model 2 and 3. The last row of Table 2 shows the result. The average precision of run TPWN2 is 0.1135.

In the paper [5], we tried to resolve the target polysemy problem by augmenting a pseudo context to a query term to restrict its use in the target language. We experimented on the TREC6 text collection and the result showed that the performance of this method is slightly better than the CO model (0.0918 vs. 0.0831). Chen, Lin and Lin [6] proposed a method to construct a Chinese-English WordNet automatically. We used this C-E WordNet and a bilingual dictionary to translate queries. The average precision was increased to 0.1010. We participated in the TREC9 Cross-Language track last year [12]. We used English queries to retrieve Chinese documents. The performances of the CO model and the A1W model were very close. In the A1W model, an original query term was augmented by all unambiguous terms that frequently co-occur with it. In CLEF 2001, the performance of the CO model is slightly better than that of A1WCO model and ASWTW model. Reviewing the results of these experiments, the performance of augmenting restriction terms is close to the CO model. But it takes more time to select restriction terms. The Chinese-English WordNet is a useful resource, but it still contains errors. If the Chinese-English WordNet is revised by humans, the performance obtained by using this C-E WordNet to translate query should improve.

6   Conclusions

At CLEF 2001, we proposed five models. Model 1 used a hybrid approach that integrated both lexical and corpus knowledge to translate queries. The word co-occurrence information is used to disambiguate translation equivalents; Model 2 augmented some restriction terms to the original queries to deal with target polysemy problem; Model 3 used the C-E WordNet to translate queries; Model 4 combined Model 3 with Model 2; Model 5 merged the queries constructed by Model 2 and 3. The best one is Model 5. The average precision of Model 5 is 0.1135, which is 53.06% of monolingual information retrieval.

Dictionary coverage is a problem while translating queries. Since the important words of some queries are not included in our bilingual dictionary, the performances of these queries were bad. Word segmentation error is another problem. If a word is not segmented correctly, we cannot find its correct translation. In Model 3, we found that the C-E WordNet has errors. Some Chinese words may have been mapped to wrong synsets. In the future, we will refine the bilingual dictionary and C-E WordNet.

References

1.   Oard, D.W.: Alternative Approaches for Cross-Language Text Retrieval. In: Working Notes of AAAI-97 Spring Symposiums on Cross-Language Text and Speech Retrieval, (1997) 131-139.
2.   Oard, D.W. and Dorr, B.J.: A Survey of Multilingual Text Retrieval. Technical Report UMIACS-TR-96-19, University of Maryland, Institute for Advanced Computer Studies. http://www.ee.umd.edu/medlab/filter/papers/mlir.ps. (1996).
3.   Bian, G.W. and Chen, H.H.: Integrating Query Translation and Document Translation in a Cross-Language Information Retrieval System. Machine Translation and Information Soup. Lecture Notes in Computer Science, No. 1529. Spring-Verlag (1998) 250-265.
4.   Church, K.W., et al.: Parsing, Word Associations and Typical Predicate-Argument Relations. In: Proceedings of International Workshop on Parsing Technologies (1989) 389-398.
5.   Chen, H.H., Bian, G.W. and Lin, W.C.: Resolving Translation Ambiguity and Target Polysemy in Cross-Language Information Retrieval. In: Proceedings of 37th Annual Meeting of the Association for Computational Linguistics (1999) 215-222.
6.   Chen, H.H., Lin, C.C., and Lin, W.C.: Construction of a Chinese-English WordNet and Its Application to CLIR. In: Proceedings of the Fifth International Workshop on Information Retrieval with Asian Languages. Hong Kong: ACM (2000) 189-196.
7.   Bian, G.W. and Chen, H.H.: Cross language information access to multilingual collections on the Internet. Journal of American Society for Information Science, 51(3) (2000) 281-296.
8.   Huang, C.R., et al.: Introduction to Academia Sinica Balanced Corpus. In: Proceedings of ROCLING VIII. Taiwan, (1995) 81-99.
9.   Harman, D.K.: TREC-6 Proceedings. Gaithersburg, Maryland, (1997).
10.   Mei, J., et al.: tong2yi4ci2ci2lin2. Shanghai Dictionary Press (1982).
11.   Fellbaum, C. (ed.): WordNet: An Electronic Lexical Database. Cambridge, MA: MIT Press (1998).
12.   Lin, C.J., Lin, W.C. and Chen, H.H.: Description of NTU QA and CLIR Systems in TREC-9. In: Proceedings of The Ninth Text REtrieval Conference (TREC 9). NIST Special Publication 500-249, Gaithersburg, Maryland, (2000) 389-398.

Utaclir @ CLEF 2001 – Effects of Compound Splitting and N-Gram Techniques

Turid Hedlund, Heikki Keskustalo, Ari Pirkola, Eija Airio, and Kalervo Järvelin

Department of Information Studies, University of Tampere, 33014 Tampere, Finland
turid.hedlund@shh.fi, heikki.keskustalo@uta.fi,
ari.pirkola@tukki.jyu.fi, eija.airio@uta.fi,
kalervo.jarvelin@uta.fi

Abstract. The Tampere University CLEF research group participated in CLEF2001 with four automated bilingual runs. Our cross-lingual software, UTACLIR, uses an automated method for query construction for cross-language information retrieval (CLIR). This method seeks to automatically extract topical information from request sentences written in one of the source languages and to create a target language query, based on translations given by a translation dictionary. The new features for the CLIR process from Finnish, Swedish and German to English focus on translating and matching compound words, and a new n-gram based technique for translating and matching proper names and other non-translatable words. Non-translatable words can also be components in compounds. The n-gram based method is clearly efficient in matching inflected proper names and spelling variants. However, using it for all non-identified and non-translatable words adds noise to the query. For German – English we have tested two types of dictionaries (two runs). The first included all translations from the standard dictionary. The second contained the same data, except that all direct translations of compounds were excluded. The test with two dictionaries for the German runs gives an indication that the new features for compound processing work well even with a limited dictionary.

1   Introduction

The study of the formation of compound words and their combinatorial behavior in general language and the proper handling of them for CLIR translation is an extensive linguistic as well as an IR task [8], [13]. In this study, by a compound we mean two or more adjacent words (compound components). All the source languages we use are rich in this type of compound, and thus, one of our main efforts is the morphological decomposition of compounds into constituents and their proper translation. In languages rich in compounds the right translation of compounds (or their components) is a factor that affects retrieval results. The new features and the approach for our automated method for query construction are intentionally designed to be as source language independent as possible [2].

In the query construction phase, the right use of windowing techniques and phrase construction have been emphasized [3], [7], [14]. This is necessary especially for CLIR-queries where compound splitting and translation of components is performed. In our method for handling compounds we have experimented with the window size

C.A. Peters et al. (Eds.): CLEF 2001, LNCS 2406, pp. 118–136, 2002.

and the phrase operator. In last year's CLEF tests we used an operator requiring strict word order and a fairly small window size. This year we also allow for a free word order and a broader window size in the phrase construction for compounds.

Proper names often are prime keys in requests, and if not translated by dictionaries, query performance may be ruined. However, the fact that proper names in different languages are often form variants suggests the use of approximate string matching techniques to find the target language correspondents for the source language names. Approximate matching techniques include *Soundex* and *Phonix*, which compare words on the basis of their phonetic similarity [1] and *n-gram based matching* [9], [12], [15]. N-gram matching is a language independent matching technique. It thus seems to be an ideal approximate matching technique for CLIR systems processing different languages. Moreover, n-gram matching has been reported to be an effective technique among various approximate matching techniques [9], [15].

2   The New Process

We will present the new features of the UTACLIR research process in this year's CLEF. The old process that is used as a base in the development process is described in detail in the Working Notes and Proceedings of the last year's CLEF [4], [5]. The old process is used for the Finnish – English test run, except that for compounds we use a more flexible proximity operator and a broader window size. The n-gram matching technique is also in use.

Our approach to solve the general problems for bilingual CLIR is based on 1) word normalization during indexing, 2) stop-word lists, 3) normalization of topic words, 4) splitting of compounds, 5) normalization and a grouping strategy for components, 6) handling of non-translated words 7) phrase composition of compounds in the target language, 8) bilingual dictionaries and 9) structured queries. For structuring of queries see Pirkola [10]. The language pairs used in the bilingual tests are Finnish – English (FIN-ENG), Swedish – English (SWE-ENG) and German – English (GER-ENG). An overview of the new UTACLIR process is shown in Figure 1.

The new features are as follows:

- A new process for dictionary look-up and translation of compound words
- A new process for matching proper names and other non-translatable words
- New ways of using stop word lists
- Normalization of dictionary output

Dictionary look-up and translation of compound words. In the present process, normalized compound words, if they are not stop words, are first looked up in the dictionary (see Figure 2a). If a translation, or a set of translations, is available, it is likely to be the best alternative for the source word (a compound or non-compound). Such compounds often are non-compositional, i.e., the meaning of a compound meaning may be quite different from the meanings of its components (e.g., strawberry). If the translation is a phrase, it will be handled as a phrase in the subsequent phases.

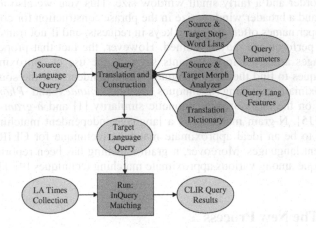

Fig. 1. UTACLIR process overview

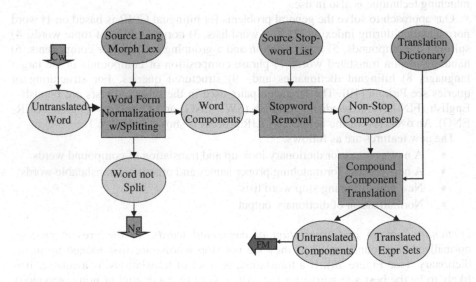

Fig. 2a. Direct translation of compounds

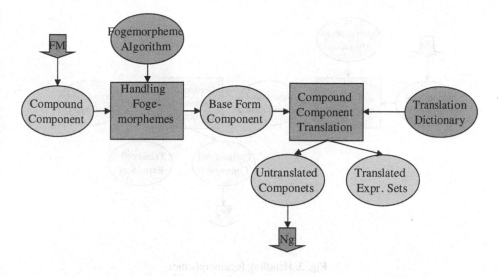

Fig. 2b. Splitting of compounds

Figs. 2 a and b Compound word translation

Compound words that do not translate are split into their components (see Figure 2b). For Swedish and German, all consecutive component pairs are formed and translated (if possible). For example, for a four-component compound a-b-c-d, the component pairs of a-b, b-c, and c-d are formed. Then the pairs are looked up in the dictionary. In the case of several translations, the equivalents are used as synonyms. If the normalized component did not translate, due to the use of "fogemorphemes" (joining morphemes) it was modified by using a fogemorpheme algorithm before a new translation attempt. Fogemorphemes (or Fuge-elements in German) are elements joining compound components in Germanic languages, e.g. "s" in the Swedish word *rättsfall* (legal case). If it still did not translate, then the n-gram method (described below) was used for retrieving the set of six most similar index terms with respect to the component. All combinations of the translation equivalents are formed for the query. The rationale behind this method is that for a multi-component compound word it is hard to know which consecutive components form common established compounds contained in the dictionary.

For German and Swedish compounds, we applied the fogemorpheme algorithm as in CLEF2000 (see Figure 3). For fogemorphemes in Swedish see Hedlund et al. [6]. Finnish compound processing differed from the earlier process used in CLEF2000 in that this year we used a more flexible proximity operator and a broader window size. That is, the proximity operator was changed from OD (ordered window) to UW (unordered window) which allows for free word order in the target phrases. The window size was set to 5 + n, where n = the number of spaces between words in the phrase.

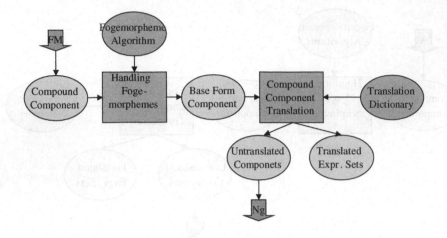

Fig. 3. Handling fogemorphemes

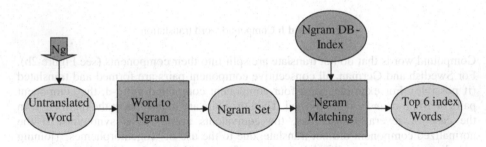

Fig. 4. N-gram processing

In the present process, proper names and other untranslatable words are handled by an advanced n-gram method (see Figure 4). The method is language independent and is described in detail in (Pirkola & al., 2001). The method is able to find target language spelling variants for source language proper names. Correspondents may be found despite slight variations in characters and/or the number of characters. Proper name translation and matching in CLIR is complicated by the fact that proper names may be inflected similarly to common nouns (particularly in Finnish), and may have suffixes (representing different case and number features, and other grammatical categories). The n-gram technique was used for all source languages. It was applied for each untranslatable source language word. The six most similar words (the degree of similarity based on similarity calculations associated with the n-gram technique) from the target database index were included into the final query. For German, the n-gram technique was also applied for untranslatable components of compounds.

In the new process, stop-word lists are used in a different way than last year. The new stop lists are used after the normalization of words to base forms. Thus we do not have to include inflected word forms onto the lists. Some modifications were applied to last year's lists. Owing to the change in the process, only base form words were added to the lists. This is important when dealing with highly inflectional source languages. Stop lists are not used for the target language query in the Swedish-English and the German-English process.

Dictionary output can include phrases and words in inflected forms. These do not match the normalized index terms. Therefore, because index terms were normalized, dictionary output was also normalized.

3   Runs and Results

The runs. We participated in CLEF2001 with four automated bilingual runs (three language pairs), Finnish – English, Swedish – English and German – English. For all runs, queries were constructed on the basis of the title and description field of the topics.

The main resources used in the translation process were:

- Motcom Swedish – English translation dictionary (60.000 entries) by Kielikone plc, Finland

- Motcom Finnish – English translation dictionary (110.000 entries) by Kielikone plc, Finland

- Oxford Duden German – English translation dictionary (260.000 entries)

- Morphological analyzers: SWETWOL, FINTWOL, GERTWOL and ENGTWOL by Lingsoft plc, Finland

- Inquery retrieval system. Center for Intelligent Information Retrieval (CIIR), University of Massachusetts.

German – English translation processes. For German – English we have tested two types of dictionaries (two runs). Using the Duden German-English dictionary (260.000 words), two translation tables for the 50 CLEF topics were created. The first included all translations from the dictionary. The second translation table contained the same data, except that all direct translations of compounds were excluded. The construction of the German-English translation table was a separate process analyzed by a human, following strict syntactic rules for selecting strings from the PC screen. The German – English process could not be automated because of interface problems and color fonts used in the Duden dictionary. However, the translation tables were used automatically.

The results. The results of the four UTACLIR runs for the CLEF campaign are presented in Table 1 and in Figure 5.

Table 1. Results for the official CLEF testruns

Testrun code	Explanation	Average precision
TAYfinstr	Finnish structured	0,3894
TAYswestr	Swedish structured	0,3769
TAYgerstr	German structured	0,3474
TAYgershort	German / short structured	0,3054

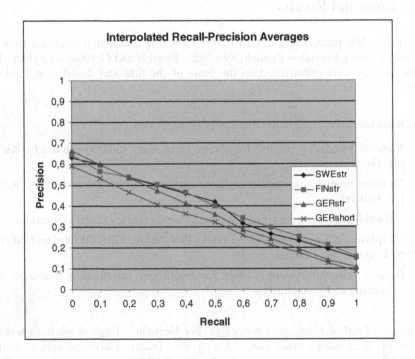

Fig. 5. Results: Interpolated Recall – Precision Averages for the official test runs with n-gram algorithm.

Generally the results for all the four runs are good. Average precision for all the queries shows clear improvements, but there still is great variation in the performance of single queries. Some queries perform exceedingly well getting high scores, but some fail to retrieve relevant documents. This holds for all language pairs.

Additional runs. As additional runs we have performed test runs eliminating the n-gram algorithm from the process. The results are presented in Table 2 and in Figure 6.

Table 2. Effects of the n-gram algorithm

Test run name	Original run	Run without n-grams	Difference
FINstr Finnish structured	0,3894	0,3443	+0,0451
SWEstr Swedish structured	0,3769	0,3465	+0,0304
GERstr German structured	0,3476	0,3830	-0,0354
GERshort German with short dict.	0,3054	0,3547	-0,0493

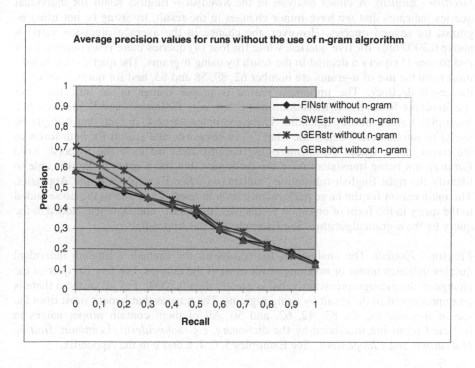

Average precision values for runs without the use of n-gram algrorithm

Legend:
- FINstr without n-gram
- SWEstr without n-gram
- GERstr without n-gram
- GERshort without n-gram

(x-axis: Recall, y-axis: Precision)

Fig. 6. Results: Average precision values for additional runs without the n-gram algorithm

Eliminating the n-gram algorithm from the automated process results in a decline in performance (average precision value for all the 47 queries) for the Finnish – English and the Swedish – English runs. On the other hand, both German runs perform better without the n-gram algorithm. For individual queries the result varies, as can be seen in Table 3.

Table 3. N-gram effects at individual query level

Total queries =47	Swe - Eng	FIN - Eng	Ger - Eng	Ger -Eng short
	No. of queries	No. of queries	No. of queries	No. of queries
Results improving using n-grams	16	9	8	8
Results improving without n-grams	14	11	12	16
Equally good results	17	27	27	23

Swedish - English. A closer analysis of the Swedish – English result for individual queries indicates that we have minor changes in the result, by using or not using n-grams, for several queries. However, the change in the average precision value is above 0,2000 only for five queries, while for four (4) queries there is an improvement and for one (1) query a decline in the result by using n-grams. The queries that benefit most from the use of n-grams are number 62, 89, 58 and 83, and for query number 75 the result declines. The important reason is proper names in an inflected form (genitive) not found in the translation dictionary, e.g., *Hokkaidos* and *Schneiders*. See Examples 1 and 2 in the Appendix. These examples suggest, in fact, that it might be useful to automatically delete the final "s" in keywords and search for both forms in the target index. Query 58 is interesting because here we have the Swedish word *Eutanasi* not being translated using the dictionary, but the n-gram method is able to identify the right English translation "euthanasia". See Example 4 in the Appendix. The main reason for the large performance drop in query 75 is due to the noise added to the query in the form of common words like "miniskirt" and "kitchen" added to the query by the n-gram algorithm. See Example 3 in the Appendix.

Finnish – English. The analysis of the results for the Finnish – English individual queries indicates minor or no changes for most of the queries. For five (5) queries the change in the average precision value is greater than 0,2000. For all of them there is an improvement in the result by using n-grams. The queries that benefit most from the use of n-grams are 89, 83, 42, 62, and 50. All of them contain proper names in inflected forms not translated by the dictionary, e.g. *Schneiderin, Lennonin, Haitiin, Hokkaidon,* and *Chiapasissa* . See Examples 5, 6, 7, 8 and 9 in the Appendix.

German – English. For both the German - English runs (with a comphrehensive dictionary and a limited dictionary) the effect of the use of the n-gram algorithm is similar. The results decline when using the n-gram algorithm. For six (6) individual queries of the run with a limited dictionary and five (5) of the run with a comprehensive dictionary the change in the average precision result is greater than 0,2000.

Query 48 is an exception, the German "Bosnien" is matched by the n-gram algorithm to the English "Bosnia". This has a positive effect on the result, the average precision rises from 0,0239 to 0,2902 for the comprehensive dictionary, while the result for the limited dictionary improves from 0,0007 to 0,1347 (not reaching the 0,2000 limit). See Example 10 in the appendix. The reason for the decline in the result seems to be that the noise is added to the queries by the use of the n-gram algorithm. Query 75, about the massacre in Euskirchen, and Query 64, about computer mouse disease, can illustrate this. Even though the algorithm matches the right index words "Euskirchen" and "rsi", very common words as "kitchen and crisis" are added to the queries See Examples 11 and 12 in the Appendix. For longer queries, where n-grams are used for untranslated components in compounds, the effect on the result is smaller. See Example 13 in the Appendix.

4   Discussion and Conclusion

After last year's CLEF evaluation we identified 1) problems with the translation of proper names (especially true for Finnish), 2) problems with untranslated components in the compound handling process, 3) that the handling of compounds containing more than two components was not satisfactory, and 4) that normalization is needed for the dictionary translation in order to match the normalized index of the database.

This year we focused on compound words and proper names. Both are important and common in the source languages and in this year's topics. Therefore, the way they are handled affects the results.

The choice of using the n-gram technique for all unidentified words was successful for identifying proper names especially for Finnish, a language where proper names quite often appear in inflected forms. However, the use of the n-gram technique also increased noise in the form of many nonsense words that were added to the final query. For German, the test results did not show an improvement. The reason for this seems to be twofold: 1) proper names in German that need the n-gram algorithm are few in this test sample; 2) additional noise is added to the queries in the form of nonsense words. This is especially crucial if the query is short. For German untranslated compound components were also handled by the n-gram technique. However, this is not affecting the result to the same extent as long as the query text contains other content bearing words.

The new compound process was effective for some topics but failed for some topics. The Finnish process can still be improved for compounds. In several queries, compound components are not translated. An untranslated component in a combination using phrase structure has negative effects.

The fogemorpheme algorithm improved the translations of compound components for both Swedish and German.

The test with two dictionaries for the German runs gives an indication that the new features in the UTACLIR process work well also with a limited dictionary. On the other hand, the advantage of a direct translation of compounds is inevitable. Our method for handling compounds works as a good and necessary complement, since no dictionary, not even a comprehensive one, holds entries for all compounds. Compound splitting is needed in several queries in the TAYgerstr-run where a comprehensive dictionary is used. The queries in the TAYgershort-run become very long since all compounds were split into their components. When all the alternative translations for the components are combined to a phrase in the target language query, the number of combinations may be high. Nonsense combinations also occurred quite frequently. On the other hand, generally the process can be said to work as expected because of the existing relevant combinations.

All the processes tested, with exception to the German/short process, yield performance within a fairly narrow bandwidth. We consider this as a good sign regarding the robustness of the process since the three source languages have quite different morphological properties. In particular, Swedish and German have the fogemorpheme problem, while Finnish does not. Finnish is highly inflectional, while Swedish and German are only moderately so. Swedish is rich in homographs (60% of words in running text being homographic), while the two other languages are not.

Acknowledgements. The *Inquery* search engine was provided by the Center for Intelligent Information Retrieval at the University of Massachusetts.

ENGTWOL (Morphological Transducer Lexicon Description of English): Copyright (c) 1989-1992 Arto Voutilainen and Juha Heikkilä.
FINTWOL (Morphological Description of Finnish): Copyright (c) Kimmo Koskenniemi and Lingsoft plc. 1983-1993.
GERTWOL (Morphological Transducer Lexicon Description of German): Copyright (c) 1997 Kimmo Koskenniemi and Lingsoft plc.
SWETWOL (Morphological Transducer Lexicon Description of Swedish): Copyright (c) 1998 Fred Karlsson and Lingsoft plc.
TWOL-R (Run-time Two-Level Program): Copyright (c) Kimmo Koskenniemi and Lingsoft plc. 1983-1992.
MOT Dictionary Software was used for automatic word-by-word translations. Copyright (c) 1998 Kielikone plc, Finland.

This research is part of the research project *Query structures and dictionaries as tools in concept-based and cross-lingual information retrieval* funded by the Academy of Finland (Research Projects 44703; 49157).

References

1. Gadd, T. 1990. Phonix: The algorithm. *Program*, 24(4), 363-369.
2. Grefenstette, G., Segond, F. (1997) Multilingual natural language procesing. *International Journal of Corpus Linguistics* 2(1), 153-162.
3. Haas, S. W., Losee, R. M. Jr (1994) Looking in text windows: Their size and composition. *Information Processing and Management* 30(5), 619-629.
4. Hedlund, T., Keskustalo, H., Pirkola, A., Seppänen, M., Järvelin, K. (2000) Bilingual tests with Swedish, Finnish and German queries. Working Notes for CLEF Workshop http://www.iei.pi.cnr.it/DELOS/CLEF/Notes.html
5. Hedlund, T., Keskustalo, H., Pirkola, A., Seppänen, M., Järvelin, K. (2001a) Bilingual tests with Swedish, Finnish and German queries: Dealing with morphology, compound words and query structuring. In Carol Peters (ed). *Cross-Language Information Retrieval and Evaluation*: Proceedings of the CLEF 2000 Workshop, Lecture Notes in Computer Science 2069, Springer 2001, pp 211-225.

6.   Hedlund, T., Pirkola, A. and Järvelin, K. (2001b). Aspects of Swedish Morphology and Semantics from the Perspective of Mono- and Cross-language Information Retrieval. *Information Processing & Management* vol. 37/1 pp.147-161.

7.   Jacquemin, C. (1996) What is the three that we see through the window: A linguistic approach to windowing and term variation. *Information Processing & Management* 32(4), 445-458.

8.   Levi, J. N. (1978) The syntax and semantics of complex nominals. London: Academic Press.

9.   Pfeifer, U., Poersch, T., and Fuhr, N. 1996. Retrieval effectiveness of proper name search methods. *Information Processing & Management,* 32(6), 667-679.

10. Pirkola, A., Keskustalo, H., Leppänen, E., and Järvelin, K. 2001. Targeted s-gram matching: a novel n-gram matching technique for cross- and monolingual word form variants. Manuscript, submitted to Information Research

11. Pirkola, A. (1998). The Effects of Query Structure and Dictionary Setups in Dictionary-Based Cross-language Information Retrieval. In *Proceedings of the 21ˢᵗ ACM/SIGIR Conference, pp. 55-63.*

12. Robertson, A.M. and Willett, P. 1998. Applications of n-grams in textual information systems. *Journal of Documentation,* 54(1), 48-69.

13. Spyns, P., De Wachter, L. (1995) Morphological analysis of Dutch medical compounds and derivations. *ITL review of applied linguistics Institute of applied linguistics* 109-110, 19-35.

14. Zhou, J. (1999) Phrasal terms in real-word applications. In Thomek Strzalkowski (ed). *Natural language informations retrieval.* Dordrecht: Kluwer 1999.

15. Zobel, J. and Dart, P. 1995. Finding approximate matches in large lexicons. *Software - practice and experience,* 25(3), 331-345.

Appendix

Example 1.

Swedish – English query no. 62 with n-grams   Average precision 1
#sum(earthquake #6(the north) #syn(japan japanese lika) earthquake #syn(hokkaido adios naidoo @nikaido @kaid @gaidor) #6(east coast) #6(the north) #syn(japan japanese lika) #syn(1994 @1994))
Swedish – English query no. 62 without n-grams   Average precision 0,2500
#sum(earthquake   #6(the   north)   #syn(japan   japanese   lika)   earthquake #syn(@hokkaidos hokkaidos) #6(east coast) #6(east coast) #6(the north) #syn(japan japanese lika) #syn(@1994 1994))

Example 2.

Swedish – English query no. 89 with n-grams   Average precision 0,7361
#sum(#syn(schneider   schneiderman   wiedersehen   @schnieders   @bergschneider @schnieder) bankruptcy #syn(german german) #6(estate agent) #syn(schneider schneiderman wiedersehen @schnieders @bergschneider @schnieder) bankruptcy)
Swedish – English query no. 89 without n-grams   Average precision 0, 0031
#sum(#syn(@schneiders schneiders) bankruptcy bankruptcy #syn(german german) #6(estate agent) #syn(@schneiders schneiders) bankruptcy bankruptcy) ;

Example 3.
Swedish – English query no. 75 with n-grams   Average precision 0,0064
#sum(#syn(mass massa masse @massy @masse @massathing object matter thing business mass massa masse @massy @masse @massasakthing object matter thing business saker) #6(court house) #syn(kitchen bircher besmirch @euskirchen @kirchen @neunkirchen) #syn(7 @7) #syn(miniskirt ennis annis @anisko @yiskor @skor) kill #6(court house) #syn(kitchen bircher besmirch @euskirchen @kirchen @neunkirchen));
Swedish – English query no. 75 without n-grams   Average precision 0,5
#sum(#syn(@mass mass) sakthing object matter thing business saker) #6(court house) #6(court house) #syn(@euskirchen euskirchen) #syn(@7 7) #syn(@människor människor) kill kill #6(court house) #syn(@euskirchen euskirchen)) ;

Example 4.
Swedish – English query no. 58 with n-grams   Average precision 0,3466
#sum(#syn(euthanasia atanas anastasi @utans @attanasio @tortanasi) #syn(eutanasi euthanasia atanas anastasi @utans @attanasio @tortanasifall case eutanasi euthanasia atanas anastasi @utans @attanasio @tortanasifall #6(be killed) drop tumble) #syn(interpret #7(give expression to)) worthy #syn(dead death) #syn(dish course right rightful true court reda rightly correctly right straight rather quite) #syn(die av #6(be killed)))
Swedish – English query no. 58 without n-grams   Average precision 0,0223
#sum(#syn(@eutanasi eutanasi) #syn(e#syn(@eutanasi eutanasi) fall case e#syn(@eutanasi eutanasi) fall #6(be killed) drop tumble) #syn(@eutanasi eutanasi) fall #6(be killed) drop tumble) #syn(interpret #7(give expression to)) worthy #syn(dead death) #syn(dish course right rightful true court reda rightly correctly right straight rather quite) #syn(die av #6(be killed))) ;

Example 5.
Finnish – English query no. 89 with n-grams   Average precision 0,8611
#sum(#syn(schneider schneiderman sherine @schneiderhan @schnieder @hofschneider) bankruptcy german #syn(#uw7(kiinteistl sijoittaja investor)) #syn(jurgen gergen bergen @jorgen @regen @jergens) #syn(schneider schneiderman sherine @schneiderhan @schnieder @hofschneider) bankruptcy) ;
Finnish – English query no. 89 without n-grams   Average precision 0,0159
#sum(#syn(@schneiderin schneiderin) bankruptcy german #syn(#uw7(kiinteistl sijoittaja investor)) #syn(@j~rgen j~rgen) #syn(@schneiderin schneiderin) bankruptcy) ;

Example 6.
Finnish – English query no. 83 with n-grams   Average precision 0,4894
#sum(#syn(lennon lenin leonine @lennnon @lenonis @lennonist) #syn(feistiness sistine insensitive @niesi @histine @dennistine) auction #syn(john johnny joh @john @johna @johni) #syn(lennon lenin leonine @lennnon @lenonis @lennonist) #syn(feistiness sistine insensitive @niesi @histine @dennistine) #syn(avowed general open professed public) auction) ;
Finnish – English query no. 83 without n-grams   Average precision 0,0159
#sum(#syn(@lennonin lennonin) #syn(@esineistln esineistln) auction #syn(@john john) #syn(@lennonin lennonin) #syn(@esineistln esineistln) #syn(avowed general open professed public) auction) ;

Example 7.
Finnish – English query no. 42 with n-grams   Average precision 0,3679
#sum(un #syn(musa tusa hausa @usa @usaa @cusa) #syn(disembarkation landing) #syn(haiti haitian hait @haiti @haitien @chaitin) un #syn(n @n) #syn(musa tusa hausa   @usa   @usaa   @cusa)   #syn(n   @n)   #syn(serviceman   soldier) #syn(disembarkation landing) #syn(haiti haitian hait @haiti @haitien @chaitin)) ;
Finnish – English query no. 42 without n-grams   Average precision 0,0012
#sum(un #syn(@usa usa) #syn(disembarkation landing) #syn(@haitiin haitiin) un #syn(@n   n)   #syn(@usa   usa)   #syn(@n   n)   #syn(serviceman   soldier) #syn(disembarkation landing) #syn(@haitiin haitiin)) ;

Example 8.
Finnish – English query no. 62 with n-grams   Average precision 0,5000
#sum(#syn(joist   hojo   hoist   @shoji   @hojin   @joiseph)   #syn(japan   japanese) earthquake #syn(joist hojo hoist @shoji @hojin @joiseph) #syn(japan japanese) #uw6(east   coast)   #syn(hokkaido   sidon   naidoo   @gidon   @nikaido   @phaidon) #syn(1994 @1994) earthquake) ;
Finnish – English query no. 62 without n-grams   Average precision 0,1429
#sum(#syn(@pohjois   pohjois)   #syn(japan   japanese)   earthquake   #syn(@pohjois pohjois) #syn(japan japanese) #uw6(east coast) #syn(@hokkaidon hokkaidon) #syn(@1994 1994) earthquake) ;

Example 9.
Finnish – English query no. 50 with n-grams   Average precision 0,9107
#sum(#syn(insurrection mutiny rebellion revolt rising uprising) #syn(chiapas chiapas-like aphasia @chiapis @chiapans @chiapan) #syn(#uw6(american indian) indian) #syn(#uw6(national   revolt)   rising)   #syn(chiapas   chiapas-like   aphasia   @chiapis @chiapans @chiapan) mexico) ;
Finnish – English query no. 50 without n-grams   Average precision 0,6869
#sum(#syn(insurrection mutiny rebellion revolt rising uprising) #syn(@chiapasissa chiapasissa) #syn(#uw6(american indian) indian) #syn(#uw6(national revolt) rising) #syn(@chiapasissa chiapasissa) mexico) ;

Example 10.
German – English with comprehensive dictionary, query no. 48 with n-grams
Average precision 0,2902
#sum(#uw7(peace keep force) #syn(bossiness bosnian bosnia @bosnic @blonien @nbissine)#syn(find set establish organization start base) #syn(reason bottom grind ground land soil valley)   retreat #syn(dun bun fun @un @aun @duun)#syn(#uw6(blue helmet) #uw6(blue conical roof)) #syn(#uw6(helmet unit) #uw6(helmet troops) #uw6(helmet forces) #uw6(helmet army) #uw6(helmet troupe) #uw6(helmet company) #uw6(helmet   squad) #uw6(helmet   team) #uw6(conical roof   unit) #uw6(conical roof troops) #uw6(conical roof forces) #uw6(conical roof army) #uw6(conical roof troupe) #uw6(conical roof company) #uw6(conical roof squad) #uw6(conical roof   team)) #syn(bossiness bosnian bosnia @bosnic @blonien @nbissine)) ;

German – English with comprehensive dictionary, query no. 48 without n-grams
Average precision 0,0239
#sum(#uw7(peace keep force) #syn(@bosnien bosnien) #syn(find set establish organization start base) #syn(reason bottom grind ground land soil valley) retreat #syn(@un un) #syn(#uw6(blue helmet) #uw6(blue conical roof)) #syn(#uw6(helmet unit) #uw6(helmet troops) #uw6(helmet forces) #uw6(helmet army) #uw6(helmet troupe) #uw6(helmet company) #uw6(helmet squad) #uw6(helmet team) #uw6(conical roof unit) #uw6(conical roof troops) #uw6(conical roof forces) #uw6(conical roof army) #uw6(conical roof troupe) #uw6(conical roof company) #uw6(conical roof squad) #uw6(conical roof team)) #syn(@bosnien bosnien)) ;

German – English with short dictionary, query no. 48 with n-grams   Average precision 0,1347
#sum(#syn(#uw6(frieden unit) #uw6(frieden troops) #uw6(frieden forces) #uw6(frieden army) #uw6(frieden troupe) #uw6(frieden company) #uw6(frieden squad) #uw6(frieden team) #uw6(fried unit) #uw6(fried troops) #uw6(fried forces) #uw6(fried army) #uw6(fried troupe) #uw6(fried company) #uw6(fried squad) #uw6(fried team) #uw6(deep-fried unit) #uw6(deep-fried troops) #uw6(deep-fried forces) #uw6(deep-fried army) #uw6(deep-fried troupe) #uw6(deep-fried company) #uw6(deep-fried squad) #uw6(deep-fried team) #uw6(@friedgen unit) #uw6(@friedgen troops) #uw6(@friedgen forces) #uw6(@friedgen army) #uw6(@friedgen troupe) #uw6(@friedgen company) #uw6(@friedgen squad) #uw6(@friedgen team) #uw6(@freiden unit) #uw6(@freiden troops) #uw6(@freiden forces) #uw6(@freiden army) #uw6(@freiden troupe) #uw6(@freiden company) #uw6(@freiden squad) #uw6(@freiden team) #uw6(@frieder unit) #uw6(@frieder troops) #uw6(@frieder forces) #uw6(@frieder army) #uw6(@frieder troupe) #uw6(@frieder company) #uw6(@frieder squad) #uw6(@frieder team)) #syn(bossiness bosnian bosnia @bosnic @blonien @nbissine) #syn(find set establish organization start base) #syn(reason bottom grind ground land soil valley) #syn(#uw6(rick train) #uw6(rick tram) #uw6(rick streetcar) #uw6(rick truck) #uw6(rick lorry and trailer) #uw6(rick team) #uw6(rack train) #uw6(rack tram) #uw6(rack streetcar) #uw6(rack truck) #uw6(rack lorry and trailer) #uw6(rack team) #uw6(reck train) #uw6(reck tram) #uw6(reck streetcar) #uw6(reck truck) #uw6(reck lorry and trailer) #uw6(reck team) #uw6(@rc train) #uw6(@rc tram) #uw6(@rc streetcar) #uw6(@rc truck) #uw6(@rc lorry and trailer) #uw6(@rc team) #uw6(@ck train) #uw6(@ck tram) #uw6(@ck streetcar) #uw6(@ck truck) #uw6(@ck lorry and trailer) #uw6(@ck team) #uw6(@rock train) #uw6(@rock tram) #uw6(@rock streetcar) #uw6(@rock truck) #uw6(@rock lorry and trailer) #uw6(@rock team)) #syn(dun bun fun @un @aun @duun)#syn(#uw6(blue helmet) #uw6(blue conical roof))
#syn(#uw6(helmet unit) #uw6(helmet troops) #uw6(helmet forces) #uw6(helmet army) #uw6(helmet troupe) #uw6(helmet company) #uw6(helmet squad) #uw6(helmet team) #uw6(conical roof unit) #uw6(conical roof troops) #uw6(conical roof forces) #uw6(conical roof army) #uw6(conical roof troupe) #uw6(conical roof company) #uw6(conical roof squad) #uw6(conical roof team)) #syn(bossiness bosnian bosnia @bosnic @blonien @nbissine)) ;

German – English with short dictionary, query no. 48 without n-grams Average precision 0,0007

#sum(#syn(#uw6(@fried~e\ns unit) #uw6(@fried~e\ns troops) #uw6(@fried~e\ns forces) #uw6(@fried~e\ns army) #uw6(@fried~e\ns troupe) #uw6(@fried~e\ns company) #uw6(@fried~e\ns squad) #uw6(@fried~e\ns team) #uw6(fried~e\ns unit) #uw6(fried~e\ns troops) #uw6(fried~e\ns forces) #uw6(fried~e\ns army) #uw6(fried~e\ns troupe) #uw6(fried~e\ns company) #uw6(fried~e\ns squad) #uw6(fried~e\ns team))

#syn(@bosnien bosnien) #syn(find set establish organization start base) #syn(reason bottom grind ground land soil valley) #syn(#uw6(@r~ck train) #uw6(@r~ck tram) #uw6(@r~ck streetcar) #uw6(@r~ck truck) #uw6(@r~ck lorry and trailer) #uw6(@r~ck team) #uw6(r~ck train) #uw6(r~ck tram) #uw6(r~ck streetcar) #uw6(r~ck truck) #uw6(r~ck lorry and trailer) #uw6(r~ck team)) #syn(@un un) #syn(#uw6(blue helmet) #uw6(blue conical roof)) #syn(#uw6(helmet unit) #uw6(helmet troops) #uw6(helmet forces) #uw6(helmet army) #uw6(helmet troupe) #uw6(helmet company) #uw6(helmet squad) #uw6(helmet team) #uw6(conical roof unit) #uw6(conical roof troops) #uw6(conical roof forces) #uw6(conical roof army) #uw6(conical roof troupe) #uw6(conical roof company) #uw6(conical roof squad) #uw6(conical roof team)) #syn(@bosnien bosnien)) ;

Example 11
German – English, comprehensive dictionary without n-grams   Average precision for query 75: 1

#sum(massacre #syn(#uw6(local court) #uw6(district court)) #syn(@euskirchen euskirchen) #syn(@7 7) #syn(man human person woman people no mankind wow good for slut trollop) #syn(local district) #uw6(court house) #syn(@euskirchen euskirchen) #syn(murder assassinate))

German – English, comprehensive dictionary with n-grams   Average precision for query 75: 0,0016

#sum(massacre #syn(#local court) #uw6(district court)) #syn(**kitchen** bircher besmirch @euskirchen @kirchen @neunkirchen)) #syn(@7 7) #syn(man human person woman people no mankind wow good for slut trollop) #syn(local district) #uw6(court house) #syn(**kitchen** bircher besmirch @euskirchen @kirchen @neunkirchen) #syn(murder assassinate))

German – English, short dictionary without n-grams   Average precision for query 75: 1

#sum(massacre #syn(#uw6(post court) #uw6(post bench) #uw6(post your honour) #uw6(position court) #uw6(position bench) #uw6(position your honour) #uw6(office court) #uw6(office bench) #uw6(office your honour) #uw6(task court) #uw6(task bench) #uw6(task your honour) #uw6(job court) #uw6(job bench) #uw6(job your honour) #uw6(duty court) #uw6(duty bench) #uw6(duty your honour) #uw6(department court) #uw6(department bench) #uw6(department your honour) #uw6(exchange court) #uw6(exchange bench) #uw6(exchange your honour) #uw6(mass court) #uw6(mass bench) #uw6(mass your honour)) #syn(@euskirchen euskirchen) #syn(@7 7) #syn(man human person woman people no mankind wow good for slut trollop) #syn(#uw6(post court) #uw6(post bench) #uw6(post your honour) #uw6(position court) #uw6(position bench)

#uw6(position your honour) #uw6(office court) #uw6(office bench) #uw6(office your honour) #uw6(task   court) #uw6(task   bench) #uw6(task your honour) #uw6(job court) #uw6(job bench) #uw6(job your honour) #uw6(duty court) #uw6(duty   bench) #uw6(duty   your honour) #uw6(department   court) #uw6(department bench) #uw6(department your honour) #uw6(exchange court) #uw6(exchange   bench) #uw6(exchange   your honour) #uw6(mass   court) #uw6(mass   bench) #uw6(mass   your honour)) #syn(#uw6(court   building) #uw6(court structure) #uw6(court edifice) #uw6(bench building) #uw6(bench structure) #uw6(bench edifice) #uw6(your honour   building) #uw6(your honour structure) #uw6(your honour edifice)) #syn(@euskirchen euskirchen) #syn(murder assassinate)) ;

German – English, short dictionary with n-grams
Average precision for query 75: 0,0015
#sum(massacre #syn(#uw6(post court) #uw6(post bench) #uw6(post your honour) #uw6(position   court) #uw6(position   bench) #uw6(position   your honour) #uw6(office court) #uw6(office bench) #uw6(office your honour) #uw6(task court) #uw6(task bench) #uw6(task your honour) #uw6(job court) #uw6(job bench) #uw6(job your honour) #uw6(duty court) #uw6(duty bench) #uw6(duty your honour)#uw6(department court) #uw6(department bench) #uw6(department your honour) #uw6(exchange court) #uw6(exchange bench) #uw6(exchange your honour) #uw6(mass   court) #uw6(mass   bench) #uw6(mass   your honour)) #syn(kitchen bircher besmirch @euskirchen @kirchen @neunkirchen)
#syn(7 @7) #syn(man human person woman people no mankind wow good for slut trollop) #syn(#uw6(post court) #uw6(post bench) #uw6(post your honour) #uw6(position   court) #uw6(position   bench) #uw6(position   your honour) #uw6(office court) #uw6(office bench) #uw6(office your honour) #uw6(task court) #uw6(task bench) #uw6(task your honour) #uw6(job court) #uw6(job bench) #uw6(job your honour) #uw6(duty court) #uw6(duty bench) #uw6(duty your honour) #uw6(department court) #uw6(department bench) #uw6(department your honour) #uw6(exchange court) #uw6(exchange bench) #uw6(exchange your honour) #uw6(mass court) #uw6(mass bench) #uw6(mass your honour)) #syn(#uw6(court building) #uw6(court structure) #uw6(court edifice) #uw6(bench building) #uw6(bench structure) #uw6(bench edifice) #uw6(your honour building) #uw6(your honour structure) #uw6(your honour edifice))
#syn(kitchen bircher besmirch @euskirchen @kirchen @neunkirchen) #syn(murder assassinate)) ;

Example 12
German – English, comprehensive dictionary without n-grams   Average precision for query 64: 0,2041
#sum(#syn(#uw6(computer mouse) #uw6(computer bread) #uw6(computer dough)) #syn(sri parsi **crisis** @rsi @ersi @orsi) #syn(illness disease) #syn(sri parsi **crisis** @rsi @ersi @orsi)
German – English, short dictionary with n-grams   Average precision for query 64: 0,0021
#sum(#syn(#uw6(computer mouse) #uw6(computer bread) #uw6(computer dough)) #syn(@rsi rsi) #syn(illness disease) #syn(@rsi rsi))

German – English, short dictionary without n-grams   Average precision for query 64: 0,2041
#sum(#syn(#uw6(computer   mouse) #uw6(computer   bread) #uw6(computer dough)) #syn(@rsi rsi) #syn(illness disease illness disease) #syn(@rsi rsi)) ;
German – English, short dictionary with n-grams   Average precision for query 64: 0,0021
#sum(#syn(#uw6(computer   mouse) #uw6(computer   bread) #uw6(computer dough)) #syn(sri parsi crisis @rsi @ersi @orsi) #syn(illness disease illness disease) #syn(sri parsi crisis @rsi @ersi @orsi)) ;

Example 13
German – English with short dictionary, query no. 86 with n-grams   Average precision 0,3977
#sum(#syn(bareness cerebrate raeburn @neuerberg @neuerburg @arenenberg) #syn(energy energy vigour)   #syn(cultivation exploitation harness use utilization) #syn(#uw6(welt   freund) #uw6(welt   gutfreund) #uw6(welt   freud) #uw6(welt @freundlich) #uw6(welt @freundt) #uw6(welt @endlich) #uw6(welty freund) #uw6(welty gutfreund) #uw6(welty freud) #uw6(welty @freundlich) #uw6(welty @freundt) #uw6(welty @endlich) #uw6(welter freund) #uw6(welter gutfreund) #uw6(welter freud) #uw6(welter @freundlich) #uw6(welter @freundt) #uw6(welter @endlich) #uw6(@welte freund) #uw6(@welte gutfreund) #uw6(@welte freud) #uw6(@welte @freundlich) #uw6(@welte @freundt) #uw6(@welte @endlich) #uw6(@elt   freund) #uw6(@elt   gutfreund) #uw6(@elt   freud) #uw6(@elt @freundlich) #uw6(@elt @freundt) #uw6(@elt @endlich) #uw6(@cawelti freund)   #uw6(@cawelti   gutfreund) #uw6(@cawelti   freud) #uw6(@cawelti @freundlich) #uw6(@cawelti @freundt) #uw6(@cawelti @endlich)) #syn(energy energy vigour)   #syn(richter bichette etheric @richtet @vongerichten @detterich) #syn(policy politics tactic) #syn(concern affect befall hurt apprehend) #syn(d @d) #syn(h @h) #syn(energy energy vigour)   #syn(bareness cerebrate raeburn @neuerberg @neuerburg @arenenberg) #syn(#uw6(energy quell) #uw6(energy ellen) #uw6(energy   queen) #uw6(energy   @quelle)#uw6(energy @quella) #uw6(energy @quello) #uw6(energy quell) #uw6(energy ellen) #uw6(energy queen) #uw6(energy @quelle) #uw6(energy @quella) #uw6(energy @quello) #uw6(vigour quell) #uw6(vigour ellen) #uw6(vigour queen) #uw6(vigour @quelle) #uw6(vigour @quella) #uw6(vigour @quello)) #syn(#uw6(energy source) #uw6(energy spring) #uw6(energy source) #uw6(energy spring)#uw6(vigour source) #uw6(vigour spring)) #syn(#uw6(energy quell) #uw6(energy que) #uw6(energy raquel) #uw6(energy @quello) #uw6(energy @quella) #uw6(energy @quelle)#uw6(energy quell) #uw6(energy que) #uw6(energy raquel) #uw6(energy @quello) #uw6(energy @quella) #uw6(energy @quelle) #uw6(vigour quell) #uw6(vigour que) #uw6(vigour raquel) #uw6(vigour @quello) #uw6(vigour @quella) #uw6(vigour @quelle)) #syn(produce generate manufacture produce))

German – English with short dictionary, query no. 86 without n-grams Average precision 0,4214
#sum(#syn(@erneuerbare erneuerbare)#syn(energy energy vigour) #syn(cultivation exploitation harness use utilization)   #syn(#uw6(@m|welt @freund~lich) #uw6(@m|welt freund~lich) #uw6(m|welt @freund~lich) #uw6(m|welt freund~lich))

#syn(energy energy vigour)   #syn(@ausgerichtete ausgerichtete)   #syn(policy politics
tactic)   #syn(concern affect befall hurt apprehend)   #syn(@d d) #syn(@h h)
#syn(energy energy vigour)   #syn(@erneuerbaren erneuerbaren) #syn(#uw6(energy
@quell~en) #uw6(energy quell~en) #uw6(energy @quell~en) #uw6(energy quell~en)
#uw6(vigour @quell~en) #uw6(vigour quell~en)) #syn(#uw6(energy source)
#uw6(energy spring) #uw6(energy source) #uw6(energy spring) #uw6(vigour
source) #uw6(vigour spring)) #syn(#uw6(energy @quell) #uw6(energy quell)
#uw6(energy @quell) #uw6(energy quell) #uw6(vigour @quell) #uw6(vigour quell))
#syn(produce generate manufacture produce)) ;

Using Statistical Translation Models for Bilingual IR

Jian-Yun Nie and Michel Simard

Laboratoire RALI,
Département d'Informatique et Recherche Opérationnelle,
Université de Montréal
C.P. 6128, succursale Centre-ville
Montréal, Québec, H3C 3J7 Canada
{nie, simardm}@iro.umontreal.ca

Abstract. This report describes our tests on applying statistical translation models for bilingual IR tasks in CLEF-2001. These translation models have been trained on a set of parallel web pages automatically mined from the Web. Our previous studies have shown the utility of such corpora for cross-language information retrieval. The goal of the current tests is to see how we can improve the quality of the translation models and make best uses of them. Several questions are considered: Is it useful to consider the IDF factor in addition to the translation probabilities? Is it useful to further clean the training corpora before model training or the translation models themselves? How could we combine the translation models with bilingual dictionaries? Although our tests do not allow us to answer all these questions, they provide useful indication to several further research directions.

1 Introduction

In addition to the problems of monolingual IR, CLIR has some additional aspects to be considered, in particular, the selection of the appropriate translation terms/words, and the proper weighting of these terms [1]. The selection of translation words can be done either through a bilingual dictionary prepared manually, or through the use of a parallel corpus. A bilingual dictionary can be exploited directly by a translation process in a more or less complex manner (e.g. select all the possible translation words, or select some of them and assign a weight to them according to statistical information). It can also be incorporated in a machine translation system. In this case, the selection of translation words is usually done by using rules prepared manually. Whatever the manner, the translation by a dictionary is always limited to those words stored in the dictionary. The question that we can ask is whether a dictionary can contain all the appropriate translations. In many cases, the answer is no for several reasons.

1. A dictionary of general domains often covers the most frequently used meanings of words. They usually contain few meanings in specialized domains.
2. Languages are evolving. A word may be associated with new meanings. The terminology used in computer science is a typical example (e.g. the word "web"). A manually prepared dictionary cannot be up-to-date to cover these new words or new meanings.

C.A. Peters et al. (Eds.): CLEF 2001, LNCS 2406, pp. 137–150, 2002.

A possible alternative to a dictionary is a statistical translation model. A statistical translation model (TM) is a probability function that is trained on a large set of parallel texts. It observes the uses of words and their co-occurrences in the corresponding sentences in two languages in order to extract the translation relationships between them. Using a TM has several advantages over the use of a dictionary (either in a simple way or within a machine translation system):

1. The training of a TM can be completely automatic. No (or little) manual preparation is required.
2. The resulting TM reflects well the word usage in the training corpus. This offers the possibility to train specialized and up-to-date TMs.

There have been several experiments on using statistical translation models for Cross-Language Information Retrieval (CLIR) [2, 3]. It has been shown that with a proper use of the translation models, we can obtain effectiveness comparable to that using a good machine translation system.

However, a critical aspect of using TM is the availability of the training corpora. For a few languages, there are parallel corpora ready for use (e.g. for English-French). However, such corpora are not available to many other language pairs. Therefore, we conducted a project on automatically mining parallel web pages on the Web [3, 4]. This has been very successful: using some heuristic criteria, we were able to gather several large sets of parallel web pages for the following language pairs: Chinese-English, French-English, German-English, Italian-English[1]. In our previous research, several approaches have been tested on the use of these parallel corpora for CLIR. However, a number of questions remain unanswered. In our tests in CLEF2001, we conducted several new alternatives in order to see how these corpora can be better used for CLIR. The following problems will be addressed in our tests:

- the combination of translation probabilities with IDF to improve term weighting;
- the clean up of the parallel corpora in order to create neater corpora;
- the cut-off of translation models in order to eliminate unreliable translations;
- the use of two-directional query translation;
- and the combination of translation models with bilingual dictionaries to improve the coverage.

In the following sections, let us first recall briefly the corpora and the training of translation models. Then we will report each of the above experiments.

2   Parallel Text Mining and Translation Model Building

For our bilingual IR tasks, the parallel corpora of French, Italian and German with English are used. Their sizes are shown in the following table (where raw data contain HTML markups, while these are removed from the cleaned data).

---

[1] The mining of parallel corpora for German-English and Italian-English has been done in collaboration with Wessel Kraaij of TNO.

Table 1. Sizes of the training corpora

	fr-en		de-en		it-en	
# Text Pairs	18 807		10 200		8 504	
Raw data (MB)	198	174	100	77	68	50
Cleaned data (MB)	155	145	66	50	50	35

(Note: Through out this report, we will use fr, de, it, en to designate French, German, Italian and English.)

Let us briefly describe the model training process.

2.1. Sentence Alignment

Given a set of parallel texts in two languages, it is first aligned into parallel sentences. The goal of this process is to limit the translation relationships between words within the corresponding sentence. The criteria used in sentence alignment are basically the order of the sentence in the text (parallel sentences are in similar orders in two parallel texts) and the length of the sentence (their length ratio is comparable with the standard length ratio of the two languages) [5]. In [6], it is proposed that cognates may be used as an additional criterion. Cognates denote the words (e.g. proper names or words that share a common stem) or symbols (e.g. numbers) that are identical or very similar in form in two languages. If two sentences contain such cognates, it provides additional evidence that they are parallel. It has been shown that the approach using cognates performs better than the one without cognates.

2.2. Model Training with EM

Once a set of parallel sentences is obtained, word translation relations are estimated. First, it is assumed that every word in a sentence may be a translation of every word in its corresponding sentence. Therefore, the more often two words co-occur in parallel sentences, the more they are thought of to be translations of one another. In this way, we obtain the initial probabilities of word translation.

At the second step, the probabilities are submitted to a process of Expectation Maximization (EM) in order to maximize iteratively the expectation of probability with respect to the aligned sentences. The details of EM algorithm are described in [7]. The final result is a probability function $P(t|s)$ which gives the probability that a source word s is translated to a target word t. In our work, we only use the IBM model 1 [7].

Using this function, we can determine a set of probable word translations in the target language for each source word of the query, or for a complete query in the source language. In our tests reported here, we use the second approach.

Our previous research has tested the number of translation words per query to be retained. It turned out that a number between 20-50 is reasonable for queries in

TREC and CLEF. In our current tests, we use 50 translation words (or less, if there are less than 50 translation words). A threshold of 0.0001 on the translation probabilities is also used: translations with a probability lower than this threshold are not retained. These turned out to be quite an effective way to remove unreliable translations.

3   Translation Probabilities Alone vs. prob*idf?

The translation models provide a set of most probable words and their probabilities. A straightforward use would be to consider this list as a new query without further treatment.

However, the probability $P(t|s)$ provided by a TM only tells how probable t is as a translation of s with respect to the training corpus. It does not tell how this translation fits the text collection searched, or how specific a translation word is with respect to the text collection. This second factor is important in IR. In fact, in the weighting scheme tf*idf, we explicitly incorporate the specificity (i.e. IDF) of index terms to some documents. We need to proceed in a similar way in weighting translation words, i.e. to combine the original probabilities with the IDF of the translation words in the document collection.

The following comparison was made: using only the translation probabilities as the weights of translation words in the new query, or combining them with the IDF factor. Our tests are made with the SMART system. The two weightings correspond respectively to "nnn" and "ntn" in SMART.

The following table and the figure on the next page show the comparison of two weightings for Clef2000 and Clef2001 queries.

Table 2. Comparison of weighting of translation words

	de-en		fr-en		it-en	
	nnn	ntn	nnn	ntn	nnn	ntn
Clef 2000	0.1589	0.1613	0.2534	0.2463	0.2349	0.2201
Clef 2001	0.2097	0.2360	0.2572	0.2635	0.3301	0.3577

We can see that the impact of adding IDF is not always the same. For Clef2000 queries, we observe decreases in retrieval effectiveness (average precision), while for Clef2001, there are improvements. Note that the two sets of queries are evaluated against the same set of documents. So the impact of IDF only depends on the queries.

A possible factor is the correspondence between the queries and the document collection. A hypothesis is that, if the queries correspond well to the document collection (i.e. there are more relevant documents for them), then the IDF factor seems to have a positive impact. This hypothesis seems to correspond well to the results we have: we have better retrieval effectiveness for Clef2001 queries than for Clef2000 queries. Therefore, the IDF factors may be more reasonable for the words in the translations of Clef2001. However, this hypothesis has to be further tested and examined with more tests.

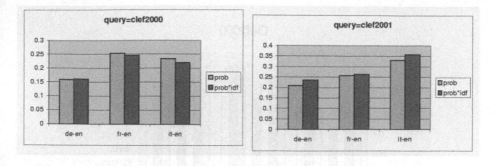

Fig. 1. Comparison of weighting of translation words.

4 Cut-Off of Translation Models

A TM contains translations for every lexical item encountered in a training corpus, even if the item appeared only once. In the case where an item does not appear often, its translation is often sparse, i.e. it is translated by many different words with low probabilities. In fact, if a source word occurs only once in the training corpus, it may be translated by every word in the target sentence with quite comparable probabilities. Such low-probability translations are usually not reliable. Although we used the number of translation words retained (50) and the probability threshold (0.0001) as means of filtering out some unreliable translation words, this is not enough. Many inaccurate translation words still appear in the translations. Therefore, a stricter filtering is necessary.

In addition, the storage of a huge translation model requires a large space. It is not always practical to use such a translation model in a real application. For example, the original French-English model contains more than 13 millions entries. Therefore, we exploited the possibility of reducing the translation models by cutting off the translations that we judge unreliable.

Two ways to cut off a model are investigated:

- keep a fixed number of lexical items in the model;
- remove all the translations below a certain threshold of translation probability.

Using the first strategy, we created models of the following sizes: 1 million (1M), 100 thousands (100K), 10 thousands (10K), 5 thousands (5K) and 1 thousand (1K). The thresholds 0.05, 0.1 and 0.25 are used in the second strategy. The impacts of these cutoffs are shown in Figure 2.

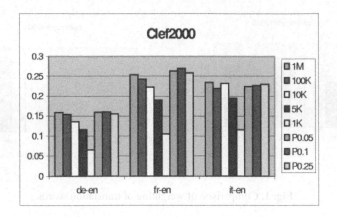

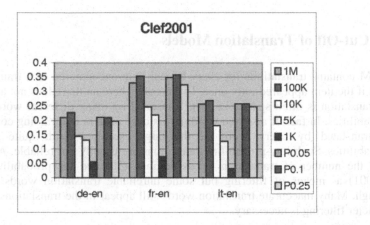

Fig. 2. Effects of model cutoffs

We can see that the cutoff by probability is a better solution. Cutting with model size, except for the size 100K in Clef2001, leads to decreases in effectiveness in the other cases. When using a cutoff with a probability threshold, in several cases, an improvement is observed. In particular, the threshold 0.1 (P0.1) seems to be a reasonable value that produces the highest improvements. The cutoffs by size have variable effects for large sizes (1M and 100K), but when the size is too small (10K or less), the effectiveness decreases. Clearly, a size of 10K or less is not enough to cover many words correctly.

5   Cleaning-Up of Parallel Corpora

The parallel corpora gathered from the Web contain a certain proportion of non-parallel texts. If we can filter out this part of non-parallel texts, the translation models, and the CLIR effectiveness, could be improved. However, it is impossible to eliminate all the non-parallel texts in such a corpus automatically. While we remove some non-parallel texts, there will also be some truly parallel texts removed. In addition, the filtering process could also result in a smaller corpus, maybe too small for model training. So the question we raise is whether it is helpful to filter the corpora in some manner.

In our sentence alignment process, we observed that a non-parallel text pair usually has more difficulty to be aligned. In particular, there will be likely a large proportion of empty alignments, i.e. sentences that failed to get aligned with anything. Therefore, the principle we use for the filtering is essentially to test the proportion of the empty alignments. If the proportion of empty alignments is higher than a certain threshold, then we consider the text pair to be non-parallel, and it is removed from the corpus [8].

In addition, we also notice that sentence alignment relies only on sentence length. Even in the case where two sentences have very different lengths, the length-based alignment algorithm would always end up with an alignment which is the best among all the possible ones. This does not mean that the alignments are always reasonable. In our analysis, we observed that a certain number of sentences of very different lengths have been unduly forced to get aligned. To deal with this problem, we try to favor alignment of sentences of truly comparable lengths. That is, if two sentences have a length ratio very similar to the standard length ratio of the two languages, then a bonus value is added to the alignment score of the sentences. This score is the one used in the sentence alignment algorithm.

Furthermore, we also observe that "known translation" is another useful criterion for sentence alignment. By known translation, we mean the translations that are known by the machine, e.g. those translations stored in a bilingual dictionary. This factor is used by human beings when judging if two sentences can be aligned. In fact, for a human being who does not know every word in a pair of sentences, but only part of them, one possible approach to judge if they are parallel is to see how many of the known words can be translated mutually. In other words, he would use the translations known to him in his judgment. We exploit the same principle in our alignment process. The score of sentence alignment is again increased by another factor that is proportional to the number of known translations we can find in the sentences.

The above approach has been recently tested on a Chinese-English corpus [8] of web pages, mined with the same mining tool. We tested both the quality of resulting translation models (with 200 randomly selected words) and CLIR performance. The following tables describe the results we obtained.

Table 3. Accuracy of translation models and improvements with the filtered corpora for ch-en.

Translation accuracy	Combination	
	No filter	Best filtering
E-C	80.50%	91.50% (+13.66%)
C-E	77.00%	86.50% (+12.34%)

Table 4. CLIR effectiveness on two sets of TREC documents

Direction	Combination	
	No filter	Best filtering
E-C	0.1843	0.2013 (+9.22%)
C-E	0.1898	0.2063 (+8.69%)

For the de-en, fr-en and it-en corpora, we applied the same filtering criteria as for ch-en. The sizes of corpora have been reduced after the filtering, as shown in Table 5:

Table 5. Sizes of original and filtered corpora

	de-en		fr-en		it-en	
	de	en	fr	en	it	en
Original	66M	50M	155M	145M	50M	35M
Filtered	42M	42M	147M	139M	34M	33M

Despite the differences between the languages, we still expected to have some degree of improvement after the filtering. However, as shown in the figure on the next page, the effectiveness is generally reduced in every case (except for Clef2000, fr-en case).

This counter-performance may be due to several factors:

- The parameters determined for the Chinese-English corpus (that are used during the filtering) are not necessarily suited to the corpora of European languages;

- In particular, the filtering process may rely too much on the comparable-length factor. In fact, if we observe the sizes of the resulting corpora after the filtering, we see that the sizes for two languages become surprisingly similar. Even in the case of manually constructed high-quality parallel corpora, there is a much larger difference in size. This means that the filtering process is not perfect, although it worked well for Chinese-English.

- A certain number of researchers in computational linguistics believe that "more data is better data" whatever the quality of it is. It is too early to say that our decreased results with smaller (and possibly better) corpora confirm this belief, but this is another possibility to be examined more closely.

We will investigate other filtering methods in order to obtain better results. For the following test, we will only use the unfiltered corpora.

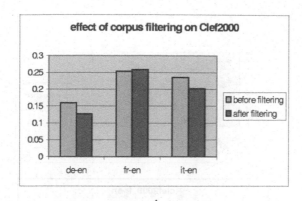

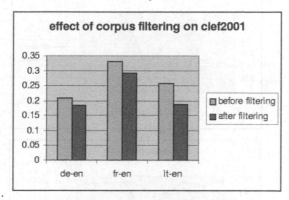

Fig. 3. Effect of corpus filtering for 1M model

6   Two-Direction Translation of Queries

It is observed that certain common English words often appear as one of the top-ranked translations of queries (e.g. make, provide, due, etc.). This is because these words frequently appear in the training corpora, and they are not considered as stopwords. So they are considered to be highly probable translations for many words in French, German and Italian. However, if we also consider translations of these English words back to the source languages, they would likely be translated to many different words, i.e. their translations would not be concentrated on the same source words for which they have been suggested as translations. Therefore, a combination of both directions in translation could eliminate such common words in query translations. This is the intuition of using the two-direction translation of queries.

In our implementation, the translation probabilities of both directions are multiplied, i.e. for a pair (e, f) of English and French, the probability of $P(e|f)$ is multiplied by the probabilities of $\Sigma_{f'} P(f'|e)$ where f' is all the words in the original French query, then normalized.

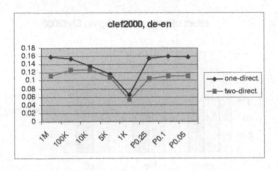

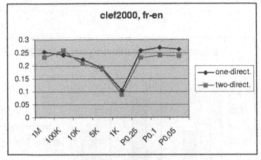

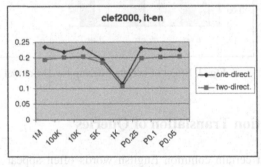

Fig. 4. Comparison of one-direction and two-direction translations

However, our test did not show that this idea or this implementation works well. Figure 4 shows the results with Clef2000. The effect on Clef2001 is very similar. We observe a large decrease in performance when two-direction translation is used.

A possible reason is the filtering of the translations: after the translation of each query, we only keep the translations whose probability is higher than a certain threshold (0.0001). So in many cases, we want to retain much less than 50 translation words. As a matter of fact, there are less translation words per query with the two-direction translation, as we can see in Table 6 which compares the number of translation words in the two translation results.

Table 6. Number of translation words per query.

	Clef2000			Clef2001		
	de-en	fr-en	it-en	de-en	fr-en	it-en
One-direct.	28.4	43.3	39.2	30.2	43.7	38.9
Two-direct.	23.0	36.7	35.7	22.4	36.5	35.5

Another fact that we observe is that, although there is a relative concentration of probability value to the top-ranked translation words in the two-direction translation (i.e. the top-ranked words have a higher probability), many undesirable translation words still remain in the query translation. Their probability values are often less, but their rank in the translation is not necessarily decreased. As an example, we can examine the translations of the first Italian query in Clef2001("reconstruction of Berlin") in Figure 5.

We observe that some good translation words (e.g. berlin, architecture, and rebuild) have been enhanced; but some undesirable words (e.g. cad, part, general, and documentation) have also been enhanced. So the enhancement is not only for the desired words. This shows that the two-direction translation may not be as effective as we expected (at least in the way we implemented it).

Another phenomenon we observe is that there are more untranslated words (e.g. generali, trovato) in the two-direction translation and they are ranked higher. This is expectable: These words only appear in some untranslated sentences in the training corpus. So their translation by themselves is strong in both directions. They are thus enhanced in the two-direction translations. The inclusion of these untranslated words is harmful (the untranslated words shown in Figure 5 do appear in some of the English documents used in CLEF experiments!).

These problems point us to some possible improvement directions of the two-direction translation in the future.

7   Combination with Dictionaries

In our previous research, we found that we can greatly improve CLIR effectiveness by combining a translation model with a bilingual dictionary. The method we used is to assign a fixed value to those translations that are found in the dictionary. In other words, if a translation is stored in the dictionary, then the weight of this translation will be increased by a fixed value (0.01 seemed to be a good value).

We observed that common words often have more translations than specialized words. As a result, common words will be represented by more translations, and indirectly, their importance in the query is increased unduly. In order to take into account the commonness of a translation word, we combine the translation probabilities with the *idf* value of the translation word. The intuition is to increase the probabilities of the uncommon translation words and to lower the probabilities of common translation words. Figure 6 shows the experiments of combining TMs with bilingual dictionaries. The dictionaries are FreeDict that we found on the Web (http://www.freedict.com/ dictionary/index.html). In particular, we used the dictionaries of French, German and Italian to English.

One-direction translation:	Two-direction translation
0.10420 berlin	0.13189 berlin
0.08136 architecture	0.11845 architecture
0.05469 wall	0.07879 cad
0.04925 part	0.05806 part
0.04849 cad	0.05322 general
0.04206 find	0.04290 rebuild
0.03932 general	0.04267 city
0.03665 aspect	0.04002 documentation
0.03635 city	0.03464 find
0.03364 architectural	0.03423 wall
0.02988 rebuild	0.03319 aspect
0.02512 documentation	0.02720 architectural
0.02395 sedan	0.02080 reconstruction
0.02060 relate	0.01464 town
0.01870 town	0.01242 sedan
0.01773 reconstruction	0.00862 generali
0.01694 detail	0.00772 trovato
0.01268 wait	0.00646 relate
0.01218 trovato	0.00584 reconstruct
0.00981 special	0.00564 parte
0.00873 saloon	0.00471 trova
0.00829 regard	0.00462 architectures
0.00780 fall	0.00429 wait
0.00683 reconstruct	0.00363 regard
0.00672 library	0.00326 detail
0.00647 architectures	0.00212 architectonic
0.00577 generali	0.00161 expect
0.00483 parte	0.00129 library
0.00480 muro	0.00123 fall
0.00468 expect	0.00111 murano
0.00422 architectonic	0.00109 special
0.00410 compartment	0.00088 start

Fig. 5. Example of query translation (Reconstruction of Berlin)

Globally, we see that the combination with a dictionary leads to some improvements. For de-en, a combination with dictionary is generally helpful. In particular, when the dictionary translations are weighted with tf*idf scheme, we obtain the best results.

For fr-en, the results are more variable. The combinations with fixed weighting do not seem to help in Clef2000, while these combinations have little impact on Clef2001. However, again, the combination with tf*idf weighting leads to some improvements in both Clef2000 and Clef2001.

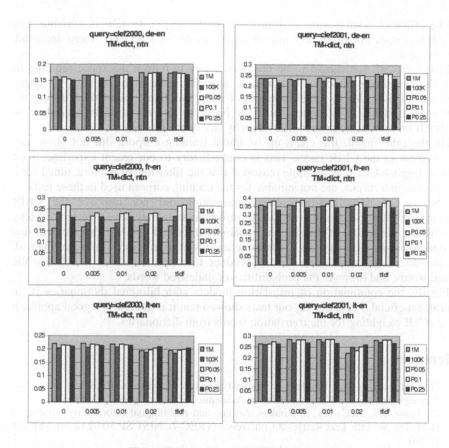

Fig. 6. Combination of TM with dictionaries.

For it-en, the best combinations are those with fixed values 0.05 and 0.1. These combinations bring higher improvements in Clef2001 than in Clef2000.

Considering the TM filtering and dictionary combination together, it seems that the best model filtering is with a threshold of 0.1 on translation probability. The dictionary combination with tf*idf weighting seems to be a good choice in most cases.

8 Final Remarks

In this series of tests on bilingual IR in CLEF, we tested several approaches to using translation models for bilingual IR:
- the combination of translation probability with IDF,
- the use of cutoff of statistical translation models,
- the clean-up of the training corpora,
- the use of two-directional query translation,
- and the combinations of translation models with bilingual dictionaries.

The effect of combination of translation probability with IDF is variable. For Clef2000, it does not bring any improvement, while for Clef2001, there are some improvements.

Model cut-off was shown to be not only a way to reduce the space required to store the translation models, but also a way to increase the quality of query translation. This is due to the elimination of many unreliable translations during the cutoffs. In addition, we found that it is better to cut off models according to thresholds on translation probabilities than by size of the model.

On the other hand, the clean up of initial training corpora did not show any improvement in the CLIR tasks. This is contradictory to our recent experiments on Chinese-English CLIR. A possible reason is that the filtering parameters, tuned for a Chinese-English corpus, are not suitable for the training corpora used in these tests.

The use of two-directional query translation did not improve the CLIR performance either. Several factors in our implementation may have affected this test, in particular, the setting of translation probability threshold of 0.001 that leads to few translation words per query. As a consequence, fewer translation words are retained. The two-directional translation did not produce the expected effect to enhance the desired words, and to lower the probabilities of undesired words.

Finally, the combination of translation models with bilingual dictionaries is, in general, beneficial. In particular, our tests showed that it is generally a good approach to use tf*idf weighting for the translation words from dictionaries.

References

1. G. Grefenstette. The Problem of Cross-Language Information Retrieval. In Cross-language Information Retrieval. Kluwer Academic Publishers. pages 1-9, 1998
2. M. Franz, J.S. McCarley, S. Roukos, Ad hoc and multilingual information retrieval at IBM, The Seventh Text Retrieval Conference (TREC-7), NIST SP 500-242, pp. 157-168 (1998)
3. J.Y. Nie, P. Isabelle, M. Simard, R. Durand, Cross-language information retrieval based on parallel texts and automatic mining of parallel texts from the Web, ACM-SIGIR conference, Berkeley, CA, pp. 74-81(1999).
4. J. Chen, J.Y. Nie. Automatic construction of parallel English-Chinese corpus for cross-language information retrieval. Proc. ANLP, pp. 21-28, Seattle (2000).
5. W. A. Gale, K.W. Church, A program for aligning sentences in bilingual corpora, Computational Linguistics, 19: 1, 75-102 (1993).
6. M. Simard, G. Foster, P. Isabelle, Using Cognates to Align Sentences in Parallel Corpora, Proceedings of the 4th International Conference on Theoretical and Methodological Issues in Machine Translation, Montreal (1992).
7. P. F. Brown, S. A. D. Pietra, V. D. J. Pietra, and R. L. Mercer, The mathematics of machine translation: Parameter estimation. Computational Linguistics, vol. 19, pp. 263-312 (1993).
8. J.Y. Nie, J. Cai, Filtering noisy parallel corpora of web pages, IEEE symposium on NLP and Knowledge Engineering, pp. 453-458, (2001).

Cross-Lingual Pseudo-Relevance Feedback Using a Comparable Corpus

Monica Rogati and Yiming Yang

Computer Science Department, Carnegie Mellon University
{mrogati, yiming}@cs.cmu.edu

Abstract. We applied a Cross-Lingual PRF (Pseudo-Relevance Feedback) system to both the monolingual task and the German->English task. We focused on the effects of extracting a comparable corpus from the given newspaper data; our corpus doubled the average precision when used together with a parallel corpus made available to participants. The PRF performance was lower for the queries with few relevant documents. We also examined the effects of the PRF first-step retrieval in the parallel corpus vs. the entire document collection.

1 Introduction

For its first year at CLEF, the CMU group applied a Cross-Lingual PRF (Pseudo-Relevance Feedback) system to both the monolingual task and the German->English task. We focused on the effects of extracting a comparable corpus from the given newspaper data; our corpus doubled the average precision when used together with the parallel corpus made available to CLEF participants. The PRF performance was lower for the queries with few relevant documents. We also examined the effects of the PRF first-step retrieval in the source language half of the parallel corpus (submitted runs), when compared to the entire document collection (unofficial runs). This provides a relative upper bound for the bilingual PRF method, since the entire collection is not available as bilingual text.

Section 2 briefly presents the PRF system; section 3 discusses the comparable corpus, and section 4 details the experimental setup and results.

2 The CMU Pseudo-Relevance Feedback System

The Pseudo-Relevance Feedback procedure is a well known approach to query expansion in Information Retrieval. Its uses for both monolingual and translingual IR have been previously explored [3]. For the monolingual case, the algorithm assumes the top K retrieved documents are relevant and expands the original query using words selected from these documents. To cross the language barrier using PRF, a parallel bilingual collection is used for retrieval in the query (source) language, followed by query expansion/substitution using the corresponding documents in the target language.

C.A. Peters et al. (Eds.): CLEF 2001, LNCS 2406, pp. 151–157, 2002.
© Springer-Verlag Berlin Heidelberg 2002

A good parallel collection that closely matches the statistical profile of the target collection is essential for the success of this method. Given such a collection, the parameters that need to be tuned are the number of top relevant document used (K) , the number of words in the new query (E) and the weighting scheme for the retrieval engine (in our case, SMART). Section 4 contains more details about the experimental setup and the parameter values.

3   The Comparable Corpus

Intrigued by the IBM success in TREC 7 & 8 in the CLIR track [1], we adapted their approach to the extraction of a comparable corpus.

A web-based parallel collection was provided by the CLEF organizers; however, we believed that a parallel corpus that closely matched the document collection would be beneficial to the PRF performance. In the absence of such corpus, a comparable corpus that is derived from the given German and English newspapers could still be a useful resource. To obtain such a corpus, we used the statistical machine translation-based methodologies from IBM [1], adapted to our own resources and goals. As our results section shows, the comparable corpus doubled the 11-pt. average precision on the 2001 CLEF queries.

The fundamental assumption that underlines the generation of the comparable corpus is that the data itself is "comparable"; more specifically, that the articles in the newspapers contain the same events and ideas. This proved to be somehow difficult with the CLEF data, where the articles come from newspapers with very different characteristics. A similar mismatch has been previously observed when using the SDA data; we believe the LA Times/German newspapers mismatch to be more pronounced. The results are even more encouraging when this mismatch is taken into account.

3.1   The Algorithm for Generating the Comparable Corpus

1.) Divide the German and English newspaper articles into time-overlapping windows .

2.) Initialize a dictionary (similarity thesaurus)

3.) While the results are improving,
        a.   For each window,
                i.   Break the articles into fixed-size (P) paragraphs
                ii.   Do a word-by-word translation of the paragraphs, using dictionary D and fertility F[1]
                iii. Use each paragraph in one language as a query, and retrieve the top matching paragraph among the ones in the other language

---

[1] The fertility is the number of words used to translate one word in the other language. This is different for every language pair.

        iv. Repeat, switching languages
        v. If two paragraphs retrieved each other with a score above
           a certain threshold S, consider them "mates" and add them
           to the comparable corpus C
    b. Extract a dictionary D' from C using CHI-SQUARED (see below)
       as a similarity measure between words
    c. D = D'

The CHI-SQUARED statistic is measure we found useful in several contexts, which captures the crosslingual lexical associations based on co-occurrence in the training corpus.

$$CHI\text{-}SQUARED\ (t,s) = N(AD\text{-}BC)^2/[(A+C)(A+B)(D+B)(D+C)]$$

where
    t = term in the target language
    s = term in the source language
    N = number of document pairs
    A = number of documents where t occurs in the target language document and s occurs in the corresponding source language document
    B = number of documents where t occurs in the target language document and s DOES NOT occur in the corresponding source language document
    C = number of documents where t DOES NOT occur in the target language document and s occurs in the corresponding source language document
    D = N-A-B-C

4   Experimental Setup and Results

We used the Porter stemmer and the SMART stopword list for the English collection. For the German collection, we used Morphix [2] as a German stemmer / compound analysis tool. We also used a short corpus-derived German stopword list. Morphix significantly improved the performance in the early stages of system development, and was used in all subsequent experiments.

The PRF parameters were tuned using the CLEF-200 data. Good empirical values were 15-25 for K (number of top documents considered relevant), 200-300 for E (number of query words after expansion), and the standard SMART tf*idf (ntc) and logtf*idf (ltc) term weighting schemes The same values proved to be best for the CLEF-2001 queries, with the exception of the term weighting scheme (ntc performed significantly worse than ltc on the new queries).

We used one week windows overlapping by half when generating the comparable corpus, because some of the newspapers were published weekly and a more fine-grained distinction was not needed. The best results were obtained when the starting dictionary was not initialized (i.e. the first retrieval step was based on names and cognates). The resulting corpus had ca. 20000 paragraph pairs. A paragraph size of 250 bytes (plus the bytes necessary to keep the entire last word) worked best.

The quality of the comparable corpus was fairly low (most paragraphs were far from being translations of each other). This is understandable given that the only thing linking the German and English articles was the time period; the culture, continent and the newspapers' political goals and interpretations were different.

4.1   Official Runs and Results

There were 6 runs: 3 monolingual (DE->DE) and 3 bilingual (DE->EN). The results varied widely, and the term weighting was critical for the bilingual runs.

The monolingual runs were obtained by using the German (source language) half of the parallel corpus for the first retrieval step, in order to be consistent with the bilingual runs and provide a collection-dependent upper bound for them. Subsequent experiments revealed a significant difference between this procedure and the one using the entire collection (see Figure 1).

Run Name	Task (DE)	Avg Precision	Weighting scheme	K	E	Query
CMUmll15e200td	ML	0.2467	ltc	5	2000	Title+desc
CMUmll5e300td	ML	0.2397	ltc	5	300	Title+desc
CMUmll15e300tdn	ML	0.3057	ltc	15	300	Title+desc+narr
CMUbnn25e2td15	BL	0.1007	ntc	25	200	Title+desc
CMUbll25e3tdn25	BL	0.2013	ltc	25	300	Title+desc+narr
CMUbnn25e2tdn15	BL	0.1041	ntc	25	200	Title+desc+narr

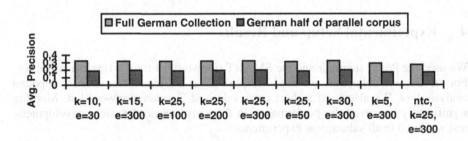

Fig. 1. Monolingual Performance Using the Entire Collection

Another important factor that affected our performance was the number of relevant documents. When a query only has one or two relevant documents, the basic assumption of the PRF idea is violated. Specifically, PRF assumes the first K documents to be relevant, which is false for at least 75% of the CLEF-2001 queries (if K>=20), even with a perfect search engine.

Our method's sensitivity to the low number of relevant documents is illustrated in the figure above, where PRF is compared to the best method for each query. The correlation between the fictional "best" method and the number of relevant documents was practically non-existent (-0.07), while CMU-PRF was comparatively more affected by the low number of relevant documents (the correlation is 0.26). We do not know how the individual runs from which the best result was selected were affected by the low number of relevant documents.

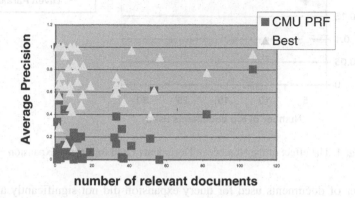

number of relevant documents

Fig. 2. Correlations between avg. precision and the number of relevant documents

4.2 Unofficial Results and Experiments

After the release of the relevance judgments, we conducted several experiments to examine the effect different parameters had on the bilingual PRF system. The most impressive was the gain obtained from using the comparable corpus in addition to the given parallel corpus (the performance was doubled).

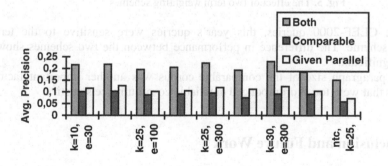

Fig. 3. The Comparable Corpus Doubles the Performance

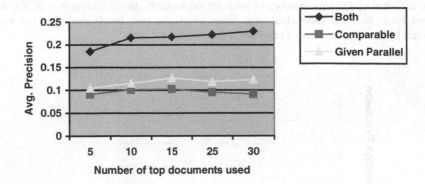

Fig. 4. The effect of the Number of Documents Used for Query Expansion

The number of documents used for query expansion did not significantly affect the average precision, although the effects on individual queries remain to be examined.

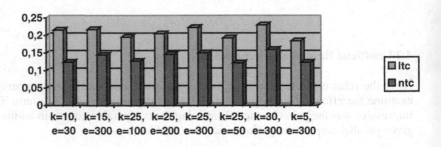

Fig. 5. The effect of two term weighting schemes

Unlike the CLEF-2000 queries, this year's queries were sensitive to the term weighting scheme. The difference in performance between the two schemes shown above is significant.

The fixed paragraph size of the comparable corpus was another important factor. Paragraphs that were too short produced unreliable co-occurrence statistics.

5   Conclusion and Future Work

The most important finding in our experiments was the effect of the comparable corpus had on the average performance of the PRF method. Since the quality and quantity of parallel or comparable text is crucial to this method, we plan to gather more such data from the web. Preliminary results showed improvements over the official and unofficial CLEF runs and will be discussed elsewhere.

We are also planning to expand our CLEF toolkit to other methods previously implemented at CMU, such as GVSM, LSI, EBT and LLSF [3].

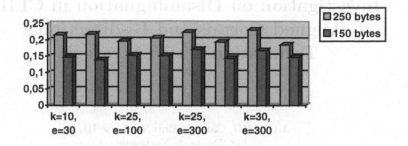

Fig. 6. The effect of two comparable corpus paragraph sizes

References

1. M. Franz et al. Ad hoc and Multilingual Information Retrieval at IBM. In The Seventh Text REtrieval Conference (TREC-8)
2. G. Neumann. Morphix Software Package. http://www.dfki.de/~neumann/morphix/morphix.html
3. Y. Yang et al. Translingual Information Retrieval: Learning from Bilingual Corpora. In AI Journal Special Issue: Best of IJCAI 1997
4. J. Xu and W.B. Croft. Query Expansion Using Local and Global Document Analysis. In Proceedings of the Nineteenth Annual International ACM SIGIR Conference on Research and Development in Information Retrieval

Investigation on Disambiguation in CLIR: Aligned Corpus and Bi-directional Translation-Based Strategies

M. Boughanem, C. Chrisment, and N. Nassr

IRIT/SIG, Campus Univ.Toulouse III,
118, Route de Narbonne
F-31062 Toulouse Cedex 4
{boughane, chrisme, nassr}@irit.fr

Abstract. One of the main problems in Cross-Language Information Retrieval (CLIR) is how to cross languages. This report describes the work done by the IRIT team in the multilingual, bilingual and monolingual tasks at Cross-Language Evaluation Forum (CLEF). Our approach to CLIR is based on query translation. The queries were translated using free dictionaries and then two disambiguation strategies were compared. The first is based on aligned corpora and the second on bi-directional translation. The experiments were performed using the Mercure system [4].

1 Introduction

One of the most important functions of Cross-Language Information Retrieval (CLIR) systems is to help users to retrieve documents written in a language different to the query language. In CLIR we deal with a query in one language and documents to be retrieved in other languages.

Several methods have been proposed to address the language barrier in CLIR [7],[9]: machine translation, machine-readable dictionaries and corpus-based approaches. These methods are mainly based on query translation because document translation is impractical [8], and try to solve the following two main problems of CLIR: firstly, how a term expressed in one language could be written in another (translation problem) and, secondly, deciding which of the possible translations should be retained when multiple translations exist for a given term (disambiguation problem).

Most work in CLIR uses dictionaries for query translation and tries to reduce the ambiguity problem that is induced by dictionaries.

Davis[5], and Gachot et al [6] have used probabilistic methods on parallel corpora in order to build the relationship between terms.

Ballesteros and Croft [2] use term co-occurrence data and part-of-speech tagging to reduce ambiguity of dictionaries.

Pirkola [10] reduces the effect of the ambiguity problem by structuring the queries and translating them using a general and a domain-specific dictionary.

C.A. Peters et al. (Eds.): CLEF 2001, LNCS 2406, pp. 158–168, 2002.
© Springer-Verlag Berlin Heidelberg 2002

Our CLIR approach is also based on query translation. Our investigations for this year in the CLEF campaign concern disambiguation problems in the bilingual track. Two techniques for disambiguation are compared and applied to select the right translation: the first technique is based on aligned corpora and the second is based on bi-directional translation. We use all source languages: French, English, German, Italian and Spanish.

All experiments were done using the Mercure system [4] which is presented in Section 2 of this paper. Section 3 defines our disambiguation strategies of disambiguation and finally, section 4 describes the experiments and results obtained through CLEF.

2   Mercure Model

Mercure is an information retrieval system based on a connectionist approach and modelled by a three-layered network (as shown in Figure 1). The network is composed of a query layer (set of query terms), a term layer representing the indexing terms and a document layer [3],[4].
Mercure includes the implementation of a retrieval process based on spreading activation forward and backward through weighted links. Queries and documents can be either inputs or outputs of the network. The links between two layers are symmetric and their weights are based on the $tf * idf$ measure inspired by the OKAPI [11] term weighting formula.

– the term-document link weights are expressed by:

$$d_{ij} = \frac{tf_{ij} * (h_1 + h_2 * log(\frac{N}{n_i}))}{h_3 + h_4 * \frac{dl_j}{\Delta d} + h_5 * tf_{ij}} \tag{1}$$

– the query-term links (at stage s) are weighted as follows:

$$q_{ui}^{(s)} = \begin{cases} \frac{nq_u * qtf_{ui}}{nq_u - qtf_{ui}} & si \ (nq_u > qtf_{ui}) \\ qtf_{ui} \ otherwise \end{cases} \tag{2}$$

The query weights are based on spreading activation: Each neural node computes an input and spreads an output signal:

1. The query k is the input of the network. $Input_K = 1$. Then, each neuron from the term layer computes an input value from this initial query:
$$In(N_{ti}) = Input_k * q_{ki}^s$$
The output value is computed as follows:

$$Out(N_{ti}) = g(In(N_{ti})) \text{ where g is the identity function.}$$

2. These signals are propagated forward through the network from the term layer to the document layer. Each neuron computes an input and output value :

$$In(N_{dj}) = \sum_{i=1}^{T} Out(N_{ti}) * w_{ij}$$

and,

$$Out(N_{dj}) = g(In(N_{dj}))$$

the system output is:

$$Output_k(Out(N_{D1}), Out(N_{D2}), ..., Out(N_{DN}))$$

These output values are then ranked to build the corresponding ranked document list.

Notations :
T: the total number of indexing terms,
N: the total number of documents,
q_{ui}: the weight of the term t_i in the query u,
t_i: the term t_i,
d_j: the document d_j,
w_{ij}: the weight of the link between the term t_i and the document d_j,
dl_j: document length in words (without stop words),
Δd: average document length, tf_{ij}: the term frequency of t_i in the document d_j,
n_i: the number of documents containing term t_i,
nq_u: the query length (number of unique terms)
qtf_{ui}: query term frequency.

3   Disambiguation Strategies

The word-sense ambiguity problem occurs in the process of translating queries from one language to another using the bilingual dictionary. Generally, before translating queries, a separate index is built for the documents in each language. English words are stemmed using the Porter algorithm, French words are stemmed using truncation (7 first characters), no stemming is used for the German, Italian and Spanish words. The German, Italian and Spanish stoplists were downloaded from the Internet. Then each term of the source query is translated via bilingual dictionaries into another language by replacing it with all senses of that term in the dictionary. For the CLEF 2001 experiments, five bilingual dictionaries were downloaded from the Internet at http://www.freedict.com, all of which were actually simply lists of terms in language $L1$ that were paired with some equivalent terms in language $L2$.

Our aim at CLEF 2001 was to reduce the ambiguity problem induced from the bilingual dictionary. If multiple translations exist for a given term, the disambiguation process is applied to select the most probable query term in the target language. Two disambiguation strategies have been compared:

1. The first one is based on aligned corpora.
2. The second one is based on bi-directional translation.

More details on our strategies are described below.

3.1   Disambiguation Based on Aligned Corpora

The principle of this disambiguation method (see Fig. 1) is that, if one translation is better than another, then this translation should appear in documents which are translations of documents where the original word expression appears. This approach compares the ranking of documents induced by different translations to the ranking of documents induced by the initial term. The idea is that one ranking $R(t1)$ is preferred to another ranking $R(t2)$ if the documents in $t1$ have a rank lower than that of documents in $t2$.

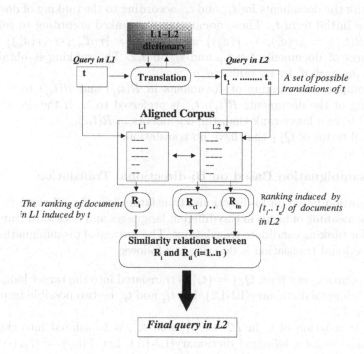

Fig. 1. Disambiguation based on an aligned corpus

The disambiguation process is described as follows:

1. Let $Q_{L1} = \{t_i\}$, be a query in $L1$ to be translated, and $Q_{L2} = \{t_{i_1}, t_{i_2}\}$ two possible translations of t_i in $L2$.

2. For each term t_i of the source query Q_{L1} we evaluate t_i on the documents from the aligned corpus expressed in $L1$,

3. Select the top ($X = 50$) documents containing the term t_i, let $D(t_i) = \{d_1, \cdots, d_{50}\}$ be the set of documents in $L1$ for t_i retrieved from the aligned corpus.

4. We rank all documents retrieved for t_i. This ranking is obtained by simply considering the relevance of each document in the language $L1$ with respect to the initial query t_i. The most relevant document gets rank 1, while the least relevant document gets rank n. The number n is a threshold which depends on the number of relevant documents in the aligned corpus.

5. Evaluate each translation of t_i, ie t_{i_1} and t_{i_2} on the documents of the aligned corpus in $L2$.

6. For each translation term, (i.e. t_{i_1} and t_{i_2}), we retrieve the ($X = 50$) best documents. Let $D(t_{i_1}) = \{d'_i, \cdots, d'_j\}$ be the set of documents in $L2$ for t_{i_1} retrieved in the aligned corpus and $D(t_{i_2}) = \{d'_m, \cdots, d'_k\}$ be the set of documents in $L2$ for t_{i_2} retrieved in the aligned corpus.

7. We rank the documents for t_{i_1} and t_{i_2} according to the ranking of documents for the initial term t_i. These documents are ranked according to relevance. Let: $R(t_{i_1}) = \{r(d'_i), \cdots, r(d'_j)\}$ and $R(t_{i_2}) = \{r(d'_m), \cdots, r(d'_k)\}$ be two rankings of documents for t_{i_1} and t_{i_2} in $L2$. The ranking is obtained by replacing each d'_i by its rank $r(d'_i)$.

8. We compare the ranking of documents in $R(t_{i_1})$ and $R(t_{i_2})$ to the initial ranking of the documents $R(t_i)$. t_{i_1} is preferred to t_{i_2} if the documents in $R(t_{i_1})$ have a lower rank than the documents in $R(t_{i_2})$.

9. Add all terms of Q_{L1} that have no translation.

3.2   Disambiguation Based on Bi-directional Translation

Disambiguation based on bi-directional translation (see Fig. 2) consists of comparing the meaning of terms in two different languages and backward translations are used for ranking candidate translations. The process of disambiguation based on bi-directional translation is described as follows:

1. Each source query term $Q_{L1} = \{t_i\}$ is translated into the target language using a bilingual dictionary(L1-L2). Let t_{i_1} and t_{i_2} be two possible translations of t_i in $L2$

2. Each translation of t_i in $L2$, i.e. t_{i_1} and t_{i_2}, is translated into the source language using a bilingual dictionary(L2-L1). Let $T(t_{i_1}) = \{t_1, \cdots, t_n\}$ be the set of translated terms of t_{i_1} in $L1$, and $T(t_{i_2}) = \{t_1, \cdots, t_n\}$ the set of terms for t_{i_1} in $L1$.

3. We compare the sets of terms $T(t_{i_1})$ and $T(t_{i_2})$ with the initial term t_i in $L1$.

    a) If t_i exists in the set $T(t_{i_1})$ and not in the set $T(t_{i_2})$, then t_{i_1} is preferred to t_{i_2}.

    b) If t_i exists in the set $T(t_{i_2})$ and not in the set $T(t_{i_1})$, then t_{i_2} is preferred to t_{i_1}.

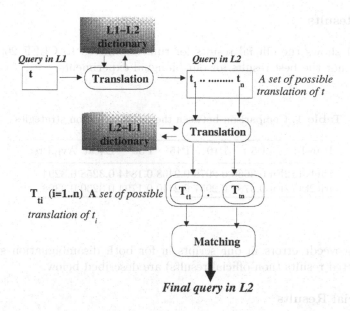

Fig. 2. Disambiguation based on bi-directional translation

c) If t_i exists in neither or in both sets $T(t_{i_1})$ and $T(t_{i_1})$, then both t_{i_2} and t_{i_1} are selected as translations of t_i.

4. Add all terms of Q_{L1} that have no translation.

4   Experiments and Results

4.1   Bilingual Experiments

Our aim for the bilingual task was to evaluate two strategies for disambiguation: a bi-directional translation and an aligned corpus strategy. Two runs irit1bFr2En and irit2bFr2En, using French topics and retrieving documents from the pool of documents in English, were submitted.

These runs were compared to a dictionary experiment (Dico) where queries are translated via a (French-English) bilingual dictionary without disambiguation. In this case, we use all translations.

Both runs irit1bFr2En and irit2bFr2En used this dictionary to translate the queries and when there were multiple translations for a given term, the run irit1bFr2En was based on bi-directional translation and irit2bFr2En on the aligned corpus to reduce the problem of ambiguity.

Disambiguation based on an aligned corpus was performed using the WAC (Word-wide-web Aligned Corpus) parallel corpus built by RALI Lab (http://www-rali.iro.umontreal.ca/wac/).

Official Results

Table 1 shows the official results for runs submitted to CLEF 2001. These results are not the best results for our bilingual experiments.

Table 1. Comparison between the disambiguation strategies

Run-Id	P5	P10	P15	P30	Excat	Avg.Prec.
irit1bFr2En	0.3660	0.2979	0.2468	0.1844	0.3258	0.3294.
irit2bFr2En	0.3787	0.2957	0.2440	0.1794	0.3250	0.3398.

We discoveedr errors in our scripts in for both disambiguation strategies. The corrected results (non-official results) are described below.

Non-official Results

1-Effect of Disambiguation Based on Bi-directional Translation:

Table 2 compares the results between the dictionary experiment (Dico) and the run irit1bFr2En (dictionary with disambiguation based on bi-directional translation). It can be seen that at different document cut-off values (P5, P10, P15, P30) the precision improves. And, in particular, the average precision improves more than 5%. These results show that the disambiguation based on bi-directional translation is better than the dictionary alone.

Table 2. Impact of the disambiguation based on bi-directional translation

Run-id (50 queries)	P5	P10	P15	P30	Exact	Avg.Prec
irit1bFr2En	0.38727	0.2979	0.2468	0.1823	0.3295	0.3472
Dico	0.3660	0.2936	0.2397	0.1809	0.3161	0.3305
Impr (%)	5.79	1.46	2.96	0.77	4.23	5.05

Table 3 shows which queries have been disambiguated and which queries improve in average precision. This table also compares the value for average precision of each query obtained with disambiguation (Dico+Disambiguation) and without disambiguation (Dico). 21 of the 50 queries have been disambiguated: 9 queries improved their average precision and 11 queries experienced degradation. When we look at these results, we see that the disambiguation based on bi-directional translation is not effective and should be improved.

Table 3. Queries disambiguated by the bi-directional translation strategy

Queries	Dico(Avg.pre)	irit1bFr2En (Avg.pre)	Improvement.(%)
45	0.4804	0.4294	-10.61 %
47	0.4412	0.2990	-32.23%
48	0.1293	0.1529	18.25%
49	0.3025	0.2747	-9.19%
56	0.0026	0.0024	-7.69%
58	0.0347	0.0339	-2.3%
63	0.0278	0.0312	12.23%
65	0.0023	0.3686	15926.08%
66	0.7621	0.7464	-2.06%
68	0.3030	0.3655	20.62%
69	0.0016	0.0015	-6.25%
70	0.4629	0.4639	0.21%
71	0.4894	0.4853	-0.83%
76	0.0000	0.0809	$+\infty$%
78	0.0032	0.5000	15525%
79	0.0061	0.0038	-37.70%
82	0.7011	0.7024	0.18%
83	0.0216	0.0053	-75.46%
87	0.4106	0.5975	45.51%
89	0.73211	0.5611	-23.35%
90	0.3302	0.3246	-1.69%

2-Effect of Disambiguation Based on an Aligned Corpus:

Table 4 compares the results between the dictionary-only run (Dico) and the run irit2bFr2En (dictionary with disambiguation based on an aligned corpus). It can be seen that the results obtained with disambiguation are slightly better than those obtained with the dictionary only. This disambiguation improves the average precision by 4%.

Table 4. Impact of the disambiguation based on an aligned corpus

Run-id (50 queries)	P5	P10	P15	P30	Exact	Avg.Prec
irit2bFr2En	0.3787	0.3043	0.2496	0.1851	0.3249	0.3436
Dico	0.3660	0.2936	0.2397	0.1809	0.3161	0.3305
Impr (%)	3.46	3.64	4.13	2.32	2.78	4

To really demonstrate the effectiveness of this disambiguation, the detailed analysis (see table 5) shows which queries have been disambiguated and how many improve their average precions. Table 5 compares the values for average precision for each query before and after disambiguation. We show that 9 of the 50 queries have been disambiguated, 8 queries were improved and 1 was degraded.

Table 5. Queries disambiguated by an aligned corpus

Queries	Dictionary (Dico)	irit2bFr2En (Dico+Disambiguation)	Improvement.(%)
48	0.1293	0.1557	20.41 %
51	0.0082	0.0018	-78.04%
53	0.0172	0.0628	265.11%
66	0.7621	0.7683	0.81%
69	0.0016	0.0065	306.25%
71	0.4894	0.4933	0.796%
78	0.0032	0.3333	10315.62%
87	0.4106	0.5975	45.51%
89	0.7321	0.7500	2.44%

4.2 Multilingual Experiments

We did not focus our efforts on the multilingual task. We used English topics to retrieve documents from the pool of documents in all four languages (German, French, Italian, Spanish and English). In these experiments, we followed these three steps:

- Translate English queries to German, French, Italian and Spanish.
- Retrieve documents from document sets.
- Merge the retrieval results.

English queries were translated using the downloaded bilingual dictionaries. No disambiguation took place, all the translated words were retained in the target queries and a merged document list was returned. We submitted one run irit-muEn2A for this task.

Table 6. Comparison of pair-wise search and the merged multilingual list

Run-Id	P5	P10	P15	P30	Exact	Avg. Prec.
iritmuEn2A(50 queries)	0.4040	0.3520	0.3173	0.2760	0.1509	0.1039
Language pair	P5	P10	P15	P30	Exact	Avg. Prec.
E2F (49 queries)	0.2204	0.2102	0.1823	0.1415	0.2005	0.2044
E2S (49 queries)	0.3633	0.3265	0.3116	0.2537	0.2589	0.2281
E2I (47 queries)	0.1872	0.1596	0.1475	0.1255	0.1320	0.1321
E2E (47 queries)	0.5149	0.4085	0.3518	0.2716	0.4564	0.4863

Table 6 describes the results of different pair-wise runs (e.g. E2F means English queries translated to French and run against French documents, etc.). We can easily see that the monolingual (E2E) search performs much better than all the pair-wise (E2F, E2G, E2I, E2S) searches. Moreover, all the pair-wise searches have an average precision that is better than the multilingual search. The merging strategy caused the loss of relevant documents.

4.3 Monolingual Experiments

Monolingual IR results have been submitted for the following languages: French, Italian, German and Spanish. Four runs were submitted for the monolingual tasks : iritmonoFR, iritmonoIT, iritmonoGE and iritmonoSP.

Table 7. Figures for the monolingual searches

Run-id (50 queries)	P5	P10	P15	P30	Exact	Avg. Prec.
iritmonoFR FR (49 queries)	0.4286	0.3898	0.3483	0.2830	0.3565	0.3700
iritmonoIT IT (47 queries)	0.4723	0.3894	0.3574	0.2730	0.3568	0.3491
iritmonoGE GE (49 queries)	0.4327	0.3816	0.3442	0.2884	0.2736	0.2632
iritmonoSP SP (49 queries)	0.4694	0.4347	0.4082	0.3626	0.3356	0.3459

Table 7 summarizes our results. The French monolingual results seems to be better than the Italian, Spanish and German. Italian results are better than Spanish and German.

5 Conclusion

In CLEF 2001, our efforts were focused mainly on the bilingual task. Our goal was to compare our two disambiguation techniques: the aligned corpus and the bi-directional translation technique. Summarizing our experiments, we conclude that in bilingual IR, the disambiguation technique based on bi-directional translation is better than the one based on aligned corpus. In multilingual IR we showed that the merging strategy caused the loss of relevant documents and a decrease in precision at all different cut-off points for documents.

Acknowledgements. This work was in part supported by the Electronic Court: judicial IT-based management (e-Court Project, IST-2000-28199, http://laplace.intrasoft-intl.com/e-court/).

References

1. Ballesteros L, Croft W. (1998). Resolving Ambiguity for Cross-Language Retrieval. in Proceedings of the 21st ACM SIGIR'98, pages:64-71.

2. Ballesteros L., Croft W. (1998). Statistical Methods for Cross-Language Information Retrieval in Grefenstette (Ed.) Cross language information retrieval, Kluwer Academic Publisher Boston, pages:23-40
3. M.Boughanem, C.Chrisment, C.Soule-Dupuy.(1999) Query modification based on relevance backpropagation in adhoc environment. Information Processing and Managment, pages:121-139
4. M.Boughanem, T.Dkaki, J.Mothe, C.Soule-Dupuy.(1997) Mercure at trec7. Proceedings of the 7th International Conference on Text REtrieval TREC7, E. M. Voorhees and Harman D.K. (Ed.),NIST SP 500-236, Nov, pages:413-418
5. M.Davis. (1998) On the effective use of large parallel corpora in cross-language text retrieval in Grefenstette (Ed.) Cross language information retrieval, Kluwer Academic Publisher Boston: pages:11-22
6. D.Gachot,S.Yang, E.lang.(1998) The Systran NLP browser: An application of machine translation technique in multilingual information retrieval in Grefenstette (Ed.) Cross language information retrieval, Kluwer Academic Publisher Boston, pages:105-117
7. G.Grefenstette. (1998) Cross language information retrieval. Edited by Gregory Grefenstette, Kluwer Academic Publisher Boston, pages:1-9
8. Oard, D.W., Diekema, A.R.(1998) Cross language information retrieval. Annual Review of Information Science and Technology, 33
9. Oard, D, Dorr, B.J.(1996): A survey of multilingual text retrieval. Institute for Advanced Computer Studies and Computer Science Department, University of Maryland, http://www.clis.umd.edu/dlrg/filter/papers/mlir.ps.
10. A.Pirkola. (1998) The effect of query structure and dictionary setups in dictionary-based cross-language information retrieval. In Proceedings of 21st International ACM SIGIR conference on Research and Development in Information Retrieval, pages:55-63
11. S.Robertson and al.(1997) Okapi at TREC-6, Proceedings of the 6th International Conference on Text REtrieval TREC6, Harman D.K. (Ed.), NIST SP 500-236, pages:125-136

Vector-Based Semantic Analysis Using Random Indexing for Cross-Lingual Query Expansion

Magnus Sahlgren and Jussi Karlgren

Swedish Institute of Computer Science, SICS,
Box 1263, SE-164 29 Kista, Sweden
{mange, jussi}@sics.se
http://www.sics.se/humle/homeosemy

Abstract. Random Indexing is a vector-based technique for extracting semantically similar words from the co-occurrence statistics of words in large text data. We have applied the technique on aligned bilingual corpora, producing French-English and Swedish-English thesauri that we have used for cross-lingual query expansion. In this paper, we report on our CLEF 2001 experiments on French-to-English and Swedish-to-English query expansion.

1 Meaning in Information Access

Meaning, the arguably most important theoretical object of study in information access, is decidedly situation-dependent. While much of meaning appears to achieve consistency across usage situations – a term will seem to mean much the same thing in many of its contexts – most everything *can* be negotiated on the go. Human processing appears to be flexible in this respect, and oriented towards learning from prototypes rather than learning by definition: learning new words and adding new meanings or shades of meaning to an existing word does not need a formal re-training process. And, in fact, natural use of human languages does not make use of definitions or semantic delimitations; finding an explicit definition in natural discourse is a symptom of communicative malfunction, not of laudable explicitness.

We would like to build a text model that would invite processing in a human-oriented way. To do this we need to understand language better. But not any knowledge of language will do: a text model should model language *use* rather than language in the abstract. We need a better understanding of how meaning is negotiated in human language usage: fixed representations do not seem practical, and do not reflect observed human language usage. We need more exact study of inexact expression, of the *homeosemy* (homeo- from Greek *homoios* similar) or near and close synonymy of expressions of human language. This means we need to understand the temporality, saliency, and topicality of terms, relations, and grammatical elements – it means modeling the life cycle of terms in language, the life cycle of referents in discourse, and the connection between the two.

This is a tall order but the present experiments are intended to be a first step in the direction of a flexible text model. Our hope is that if we can show that

C.A. Peters et al. (Eds.): CLEF 2001, LNCS 2406, pp. 169–176, 2002.

information retrieval experiments – especially cross-lingual ones – can benefit from associative and dynamic modeling of meaning and text, we are on the right track.

2   Overview

We have built a query expansion and translation tool. When used in one single language it will expand the terms of a query with synonyms and near synonyms; when used across languages it will provide numerous translations and near translations for the source language terms.

The underlying technology we are testing is that of Random Indexing [2], [3], a vector-based semantic analysis method based on stochastic pattern computing. The method is related to Latent Semantic Analysis (LSA)/Latent Semantic Indexing (LSI) [1], [4].

Our tool is built for people who want to formulate a query in another language, and is designed for interactive use. In this year's CLEF we have used it automatically with no human intervention to produce queries for cross-lingual retrieval, but we have also designed a pleasing window-based interface for experimentation. The queries we produced were tested on a standard InQuery installation at another site.

Our approach, as a data-intensive method, relies on the availability of reasonably large amounts of relevant training data and on the adequate preprocessing of the training material. This paper briefly describes how we acquired training data, aligned it, analyzed it using morphological analysis tools, and finally built a thesaurus using the data. The main focus of the paper is to provide an overview of vector-based semantic analysis, and to describe how Random Indexing differs from Latent Semantic Analysis in its current form.

3   Vector-Based Semantic Analysis Using Random Indexing

Vector-based semantic analysis is a term that we use to describe the practice of extracting semantically similar terms from textual data by observing the distribution and collocation of terms in text. The result of running a vector-based semantic analysis on a text collection is in effect a thesaurus: an associative model of term meaning. This can be used to build a synonym tool for application e.g. in query expansion. Similarly, the vector-based semantic analysis can be used to find correspondences across languages. If multi-lingual data are used, correspondences from them are as easy to establish as within a language.

We have been experimenting with vector-based semantic analysis using stochastic pattern computing in a technique we call Random Indexing. The initial step is to use sparse, high-dimensional random *index vectors* to represent documents (or context regions or textual units of any size). Given that each document has been assigned a random index vector, semantic term vectors can be calculated by computing a terms-by-contexts co-occurrence matrix where each row represents a unique term. Each time a term is found in a document, that document's random index vector is added to the row for the term in question. In this way, terms are represented in the matrix by high-dimensional semantic *context vectors* that contain traces of each document the term has been observed in. The context vectors have the same dimensionality as the random index vectors assigned to documents.

The context vectors can be used to extract semantically similar terms. The idea is that semantically similar terms occur in similar contexts, and that their context vectors therefore to some extent will be similar. So by extracting, for any given term, the terms with the most similar context vectors (mathematically, similarity between context vectors is established by calculating the cosine of the angles between them), we may produce an automatically generated thesaurus.

This technique is akin to Latent Semantic Analysis, which also uses document-based co-occurrence statistics to accumulate a terms-by-contexts matrix from which semantic term vectors can be extracted. However, LSA uses local representations – each position in the term vectors indicate the frequency of the term in a given document. This means that each column in the matrix of LSA represents a unique document, which is not the case in Random Indexing. Furthermore, LSA applies singular value decomposition to the matrix in order to reduce its dimensionality, making the representations more compact and improving on the generalization.

This dimension reduction step is superfluous in Random Indexing, since the dimensionality of the random index vectors is smaller than the number of documents in the text data, and this lack of a dimension reduction phase makes Random Indexing more efficient than methods using the computationally demanding singular value decomposition. Random Indexing is also more flexible as regards unexpected data than are methods which rely on dimension reduction: a new document does not require a larger matrix but will simply be assigned a new random index vector of the same dimensionality as the preceding ones and a new term requires no more than a new row in the matrix. Also, the technique is scalable: random index vectors of a dimension on the order of 1,000 may be used to cover a wide range of vocabulary.

In the present experiment, we have used Random Indexing to index aligned bilingual corpora and extract semantically similar terms across languages.

3.1 Training Data

The training data used in these experiments consisted of 77 documents of a few hundred sentences each in Swedish, English and French. The documents were downloaded from the Eur-Lex website (http://europa.eu.int/eur-lex) by using keywords in the CLEF queries as search terms. The keywords were extracted from the queries by filtering out stop words and query specific terms (such as "relevant", "documents", "discuss" etc.). The documents were concatenated language by language to produce corresponding training corpora consisting of roughly 2 million words in each language.

This amount of training data is probably near the absolute minimum for the technique to be able to provide any reasonable semblance of thesaurus functionality. It should also be pointed out that, due to the somewhat narrow topical spread of the Eur-Lex database (which consists of legislation texts from the European Union), not every CLEF query returned satisfying search results. Indeed, a few CLEF queries did not return one single relevant document, such as for example keywords (in italics) to the query:

C044: Indurain Wins Tour. Reactions to the fourth Tour de France won by Miguel Indurain. Relevant documents comment on the *reactions* to the *fourth consecutive victory* of *Miguel Indurain* in the *Tour de France*. Also relevant are documents discussing the *importance* of *Indurain* in *world cycling* after this *victory*.

Such a topically uneven distribution will be immediately reflected in the consistency of results across topics, and considering the already somewhat meager amount of training data available to us, this lack of topically pertinent vocabulary presents a serious impediment for the technique.

3.2 Alignment Algorithm

The training corpora were aligned bilingually using a dynamic weighting algorithm written in SICStus Prolog. The algorithm gave high weight to headings and subheadings, anchoring the alignment, and then aligned sentences between anchor points using a matching function based on word overlap and relative length of clauses. An example of the alignment process can be seen in Table 1. This step was much aided by the fact that European legislation is written to match clause by clause between the various official languages: the alignment algorithm could assume that a perfect match was attainable. In fact, this principle is not always adhered to, and the alignment continues to be a non-trivial problem.

Unfortunately, processing constraints of various sorts proved problematic for the alignment algorithm. Only about half of the available data were actually processed through the aligner and this, after the data collection itself, proved the most crucial bottleneck for our query processing.

3.3 Morphological Analysis

For some of the runs, the texts were also morphologically analyzed using tools from Conexor (http://www.conexoroy.com). Conexor's tools provided morphological base forms and, for Swedish, compound splitting. In future experiments, we intend to try making use of more text-oriented analyses as provided by syntactic components of the tools.

Table 1. Example of alignment using headings and subheadings as anchor points

article premier	Match!	article 1
section 1	Match!	section 1
objectif de ensemble de la législation alimentaire général la présent proposition avoir notamment pour objectif de mettre en place une base global commun pour la législation alimentaire . elle établir de es principe commun régir la législation alimentaire , définir de es terme commun et créer un cadre général pour la législation alimentaire	?	overall aim of general food law one of the aim of this proposal be to provide a common comprehensive basis for food law
...	?	...
article 2	Match!	article 2

4   Thesaurus Tool for Cross-Lingual Query Expansion

Having aligned the training data, the actual thesaurus can be constructed. This was done bilingually since, for every run, we used English as the target language and altered the source language between Swedish and French. This means that we in effect produced two separate bilingual thesauri: one Swedish-English, and one French-English.

The first step in constructing a bilingual thesaurus using Random Indexing and the aligned bilingual training corpora is to assign a 1,000-dimensional sparse random index vector to each aligned paragraph. These 1,000-dimensional random index vectors consist of 6 randomly distributed -1s and $+1$s (3 of each), with the rest of the elements in the vector set to zero. The random index vectors are then used to accumulate a terms-by-contexts co-occurrence matrix by, as previously described, adding a paragraph's index vector to the row for a given term every time the term occurs in that paragraph. Terms are thus represented in the terms-by-contexts matrix by 1,000-dimensional context vectors.

As above, if two terms have similar meanings, they are assumed to occur in similar paragraphs, and if two terms occur in similar paragraphs, they will get similar context vectors. So by comparing the context vectors across languages it is possible to extract for each term its nearest neighbors in the other language. Presumably, the nearest neighbor will be a translation, or a near translation, of the term in question.

To perform the cross-lingual query expansion and thereby constructing our CLEF queries, we extracted the five highest correlated terms in English for each content word (i.e. those words that were left after having filtered out stop words and query specific terms) in the Swedish and French queries, respectively. We also used a threshold for the correlations to avoid extracting terms with very low correlation to the focus word (since terms with low correlation are assumed to be semantically unrelated, or at least not comparatively similar). Such cases may appear for example when the focus word has a low frequency of occurrence in the training data. The threshold was set to exclude words with a correlation less than 0.2 to the target word. A correlation of 1 could be thought of as a complete match – i.e. two words that have occurred in exactly the same documents, and a correlation of 0 as a complete disaster – i.e. two words that have not co-occurred in a single document (although the randomness of the index vectors makes it possible for even distributionally unrelated words to get a correlation higher than 0).

4.1   Retrieval and CLEF Results

The retrieval itself was done using an InQuery system set up by the Information Sciences department at Tampere University[1]. The expanded English queries were re-edited to InQuery query syntax (we used the synonym operator for the expanded terms) and retrieved from the CLEF database. We submitted four runs to CLEF: three French-English bilingual runs: description (sicsfed), narrative (sicsfen), narrative+morphological analysis (sicsfenf), and one Swedish-English run: narrative+morphological analysis (sicssen). The results can be seen in Table 2. Using the narrative rather than the description gave about double the number of query terms (more than 20 terms per query rather than about ten); using the morphological analysis almost doubled the number of terms again. The Swedish run provided rather fewer query terms than did the French runs, owing to better aligned training data as far as we can determine.

The retrieval results by CLEF standards can fairly be characterized as underwhelming. For most queries in our submitted runs our results are well under the median.

Table 2. Results from bilingual runs

Run name	Average precision	Relevant returned	Terms/query
SICSFED	0,1646	390	12
SICSFEN	0,2216	433	26
SICSFENF	0,0864	342	48
SICSSEN	0,0139	211	34

4.2   Interactive Interface and Web Service Availability

The thesaurus is quite demanding with regards to memory, since we store the entire co-occurrence matrix in working memory. This is done in order to en-

[1] We are very grateful to Heikki Keskitalo for helping us gain access to the InQuery system used at his department.

sure the flexibility of the thesaurus tool – if new information is added, it can be immediately incorporated into the matrix, and the context vectors updated accordingly. This means that adding new meanings or shades of meaning to an existing word does not need a formal re-training process, which is not the case in other vector-based semantic analysis methods, such as LSA, where the supply of new information means that the entire matrix has to be rebuilt from scratch. Since we do not want the thesaurus to be fixed and rigid, we do not explicitly store the correlations between terms. Rather, we compute them on the fly. A flexible text model is a better reflection of observed human language usage than a model using fixed and rigid representations.

Due to the somewhat demanding memory requirements, the thesaurus will naturally run on some server. We should add that it has been built with no regard to usability issues. Should such issues become a concern, or in the case of commercial interest, the thesaurus could be compiled into a very compact form.

For experimentation and demonstration purposes, we have designed and built Synkop, an interface for accessing the thesaurus tool over the WWW. Synkop, written entirely in Java using the Swing package, should be able to run on most platforms as a client to a thesaurus server on our site, which has been made network accessible through CGI. Synkop may be downloaded from our web site (http://www.sics.se/humle/homeosemy).

5   Lessons Learnt and Proposals for Future CLEFs

Our approach is based on constructing useful queries, not on more effective retrieval as such. We used InQuery for testing our queries. A standard system for this purpose would be useful – and we suspect other groups might be interested in the same. Could we somehow organize a set-up where some site that experiments with retrieval systems sets up some such service over the net?

We have several query-oriented problems to work on for future CLEFs. This year we paid no attention to interaction between query terms, but translated them one by one. Next year we intend to address the likely collocations between synonym candidates to weed out unlikely combinations. In addition, we made little use of the language analysis tools at our disposal; the syntactic processing may well be crucial for improving understanding of context similarity and we plan to experiment with including syntactic information into the Random Indexing scheme during next year. Both query analysis and syntax should help us improve precision somewhat.

But recall is the major problem. Training data and its preprocessing are the major bottlenecks for our approach. Our results will vary with query topic and the availability of training data for that specific topic and domain. This year we only used one information source for the training data and used an experimental and not very satisfactory alignment tool; for future CLEFs we intend to add sources and partially automate the training data acquisition process.

In a real-life retrieval situation the queries will have to be inspected by the person performing the search: we have built a demonstration interface to illustrate a likely retrieval process where someone searches data in a language they know but do not know well. We will most likely not attempt interactive experimentation, but the interface demonstration will serve as an example of what functionality we can provide. The main aim will continue to be to understand textuality and text understanding – information access is an excellent testing ground for the hypotheses we are working on.

References

1. Deerwester, S., Dumais, S. T., Furnas, G. W., Landauer, T. K., Harshman, R.: Indexing by Latent Semantic Analysis. Journal of the Society for Information Science, 41(6) (1990) 391–407
2. Kanerva, P., Kristofersson, J., Holst, A.: Random Indexing of Text Samples for Latent Semantic Analysis. In: Gleitman, L.R., Josh, A.K. (eds.): Proceedings of the 22nd Annual Conference of the Cognitive Science Society. Erlbaum, New Jersey (2000) 1036
3. Karlgren, J., Sahlgren, M.: From Words to Understanding. In: Kanerva et al. (eds.): Foundations of Real World Intelligence. CSLI publications, Stanford (2001) 294–308
4. Landauer, T. K., Dumais, S. T.: A Solution to Plato's Problem: The Latent Semantic Analysis Theory of Acquisition, Induction and Representation of Knowledge. Psychological Review, 104(2) (1997) 211–240

Query Expansion Techniques for the CLEF Bilingual Track

Fatiha Sadat[1], Akira Maeda[1,2], Masatoshi Yoshikawa[1,3], and Shunsuke Uemura[1]

[1] Graduate School of Information Science, Nara Institute of Science and Technology
(NAIST) 8916-5 Takayama, Ikoma, Nara, 630 0101. Japan.
[2] CREST, Japan Science and Technology Corporation (JST)
[3] National Institute of Informatics (NII)
{fatia-s, aki-mae, yosikawa, uemura}@is.aist-nara.ac.jp

Abstract. This paper evaluates the effectiveness of query translation and disambiguation as well as expansion techniques on the CLEF Collections, using the SMART Information Retrieval System. We focus on the query translation, disambiguation and methods used to improve the effectiveness of information retrieval. A dictionary-based method in combination with a statistics-based method is used to avoid the problem of translation ambiguity. In addition, two expansion strategies are tested to see whether they improve the effectiveness of information retrieval: expansion via relevance feedback before and after translation as well as expansion via domain feedback after translation. This method achieved 85.30% of the monolingual counterpart, in terms of average precision.

1 Introduction

This first participation in the Cross-Language Evaluation Forum (CLEF 2001) is considered as an opportunity to better understand issues in Cross-Language Information Retrieval (CLIR) and to evaluate the effectiveness of our approach and techniques. We worked on the bilingual track for French queries to English runs, with a comparison to the monolingual French and English tasks.

In this paper, we focus on query translation, disambiguation and expansion techniques, to improve the effectiveness of information retrieval through different combinations. A bilingual Machine Readable Dictionary (MRD) approach is considered as a prevalent method in Cross-Language Information Retrieval. However, simple translations tend to be ambiguous and give poor results. A combination with a statistics-based approach for disambiguation can significantly reduce the error associated with polysemy in dictionary translation. Query expansion is our second interest [1]. As a main hypothesis, a combination of query expansion methods before and after query translation will improve the precision of information retrieval as well as the recall. Two sorts of query expansion were evaluated: relevance feedback and domain feedback, which is an original part of this study. These expansion techniques did not show the expected improvement with respect to the translation method.

C.A. Peters et al. (Eds.): CLEF 2001, LNCS 2406, pp. 177-184, 2002.
© Springer-Verlag Berlin Heidelberg 2002

We have evaluated our system by using the SMART Information Retrieval System (version 11.0), which is based on a vector space model, as this is considered to be more efficient than Boolean or probabilistic model.

The rest of this paper is organized as follows. Section 2 gives a brief overview of the dictionary-based method and the disambiguation method. The proposed query expansion and its effectiveness in information retrieval are described in Section 3. The results of our experiments are described and evaluated in section 4. Section 5 concludes the paper.

2   Query Translation via a Dictionary-Based Method

A dictionary-based method, where each term or phrase in the query is replaced by a list of all its possible translations, represents a simple and acceptable first pass for a query translation in Cross-Language Information Retrieval.

In our approach [1], we used a *stop-word list* on the French queries in order to remove stop words and stop phrases and to avoid the undesired effect of some terms, such as pronouns, ... etc.

A simple *stemming* of the query terms was performed before query translation, to replace each term with its inflectional root, to remove most plural word forms, to replace each verb with its infinitive form and to reduce headwords to their inflectional roots. The next step was a term-by-term *translation* using a bilingual machine-readable dictionary. An overview of the Query Translation and Disambiguation Module is shown in Fig. 1.

2.1   Query Term Disambiguation Using a Statistics-Based Method

A word is *polysemous,* if it has senses that are different but closely related; as a noun, for example, right can mean something that is morally approved, or something that is factually correct, or something that is due to one. In the proposed system, a disambiguation of the English translation candidates is performed; the best English term equivalent to each French query term is selected by applying a statistical method based on the co-occurrence frequency. For the purpose of this study, we decided to use the mutual information measure [2], which is defined as follows:

$$MI\ (W_1,\ W_2) = \ Log_2 \left(\frac{N\ f(w_1,w_2)}{f(w_1)\ f(w_2)} \right) \tag{1}$$

where N is the size of the corpus, f (w) is the number of times the word w occurs in the corpus and f (w_1, w_2) is the number of times both w_1 and w_2 occur together in a given context window.

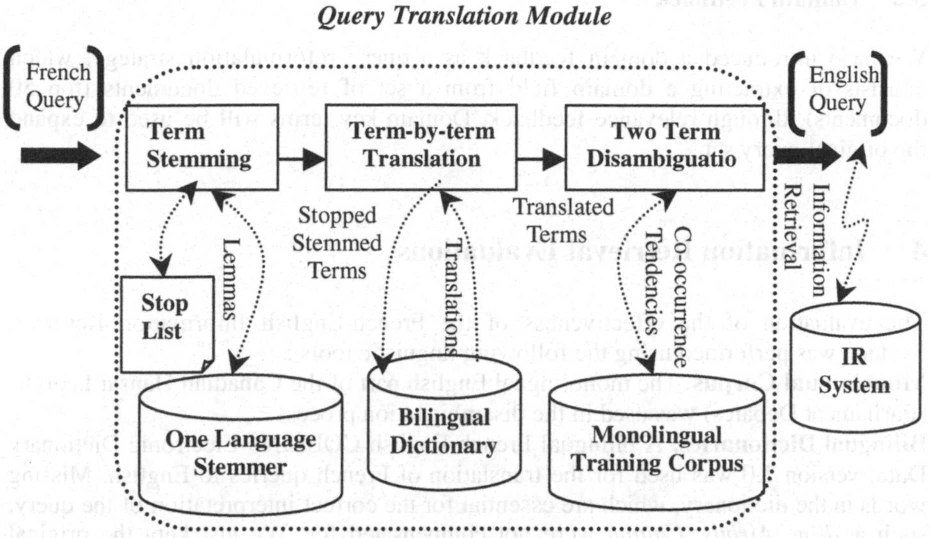

Query Translation Module

Fig. 1. Query Translation and Disambiguation Module Phases

3   Query Expansion in Cross-Language Information Retrieval

Query expansion, which modifies queries using judgments of the relevance of a few highly ranked documents, has been an important method in increasing the performance of information retrieval systems.

In this study, we have tested two sorts of query expansion: a relevance feedback before and after the translation and disambiguation of query terms, and a domain feedback after the translation and disambiguation of query terms.

3.1   Relevance Feedback before and after Translation

We apply an automatic relevance feedback, by fixing the number of retrieved documents and assuming the top–ranking documents obtained in an initial retrieval as relevant. This approach consists of adding some term concepts, about 10 terms from a fixed number of the top retrieved documents (about 50 top documents), which occur frequently in conjunction with the query terms. The presumption is that these documents are relevant for a new query. One advantage of the use of a query expansion method, such as automatic relevance feedback, is to create a stronger base for short queries in the disambiguation process, when using co-occurrence frequency approach.

3.2   Domain Feedback

We have introduced a domain feedback as a query reformulation strategy, which consists of extracting a domain field from a set of retrieved documents (top 50 documents), through relevance feedback. Domain key terms will be used to expand the original query set.

4   Information Retrieval Evaluations

The evaluation of the effectiveness of the French-English Information Retrieval System, was performed using the following linguistic tools :

Monolingual Corpus. The monolingual English part of the Canadian Hansard corpus (Parliament Debates) was used in the disambiguation process.

Bilingual Dictionaries. A bilingual French-English COLLINS Electronic Dictionary Data, version 1.0 was used for the translation of French queries to English. Missing words in the dictionary, which are essential for the correct interpretation of the query, such as *Kim, Airbus, Chiapa* were not compensated for. We just kept the original source words as target translations, by assuming that missing words could be proper names, such as *Lennon, Kim*, etc...

Stemmer and Stop Words. The stemming part was performed by the English *Porter[1] Stemmer*.

Retrieval System. The SMART Information Retrieval System[2] was used to retrieve English and French documents. SMART is a vector model, which has been used in many studies on Cross-Language Information Retrieval.

4.1   Submission for the CLEF 2001 Main Tasks

We submitted 4 runs for the bilingual (non-English) task with French as the topic language, and one run for the Monolingual French task, as shown in Table 1.

Table 1. The Submitted CLEF Bilingual and Monolingual Runs

Bilingual task	Language	Run Type	Priority
RindexTR	French	Manual	1
RindexDOM	French	Manual	2
RindexFEED	French	Manual	3
RindexORG	English	Manual	4
Monolingual Task			
RindexFR	French	Manual	1

---

[1] http://bogart.sip.ucm.es/cgi-bin/webstem/ stem
[2] ftp://ftp.cs.cornell.edu/pub/smart

RindexORG The original English query topics are searched against the English Collection (Los Angeles Times 1994 : 113,005 documents , 425 MB).

RindexTR The original French query topics are translated to English, disambiguated by the proposed strategy and then searched against the English collection.

RindexFEED The original French query topics are expanded by relevance feedback, translated and disambiguated by the proposed method and again expanded, before the search against the English data collection.

RindexDOM The translated disambiguated query topics are expanded by a domain feedback, after translation and searched against the English collection.

RindexFR The original French query topics are searched against the French Collection (Le Monde 1994 : 44,013 documents, 157 MB and SDA French 1994 : 43,178 documents , 86 MB).

Query topics were constructed manually by selecting terms from fields <title> and <description> of the original set of queries.

4.2   Results and Performance Analysis

Our participation in CLEF 2001 showed two runs, which contributed to the relevance assessment pool: **RindexTR**, the translation and disambiguation method, and **RindexFR**, the monolingual French retrieval. Because of limited evaluation resources, the result files of our other bilingual runs did not directly contribute to the relevance assessment pool. However, the runs were subject to all other standard processing, and are still scored as official runs. Table 2 shows the average precision for each run.

4.3   Discussion

In our previous research [1], we tested and evaluated two types of feedback loops: a combined relevance feedback before and after translation and a domain feedback after translation. In terms of average precision, we noticed a great improvement in performance with the two methods with comparison to the translation-disambiguation method. In addition, the proposed translation-disambiguation method showed an improvement, comparing to a simple dictionary translation method. As a conclusion, the disambiguation method improved the average precision. Moreover, query expansion via the two types of feedback loops, gave greater improvement [1].

However, in this study, the submitted bilingual runs did not show any improvement in terms of average precision for a query expansion via a relevance feedback before and after translation or a domain feedback after translation. The proposed translation and disambiguation method RindexTR, achieved 85.30% accuracy of the monolingual performance RindexORG (English information retrieval) and 77.23% of the monolingual performance RindexFR (French Information Retrieval).

Table 2. Results of the Submitted CLEF Bilingual and Monolingual Runs

Recall	Precision				
	RindexORG	RindexTR	RindexFEED	RindexDOM	RindexFR
0.00	0.3233	0.3262	0.3242	0.3304	0.2952
0.10	0.2328	0.2002	0.1843	0.1956	0.2234
0.20	0.1606	0.1361	0.1317	0.1219	0.1695
0.30	0.1292	0.1066	0.1059	0.0974	0.1432
0.40	0.1074	0.0925	0.0864	0.0764	0.1240
0.50	0.0881	0.0731	0.0653	0.0593	0.1059
0.60	0.0714	0.0586	0.0497	0.0481	0.0867
0.70	0.0572	0.0448	0.0373	0.0376	0.0696
0.80	0.0357	0.0295	0.0203	0.0244	0.0590
0.90	0.0250	0.0164	0.0104	0.0117	0.0401
1.00	0.0126	0.0092	0.0063	0.0066	0.0166
Avg. Prec	0.1014	0.0865	0.0798	0.0780	0.1120
% Eng Mono	100	85.30	78.69	76.92	--
% Fr Mono	--	77.23	71.25	69.64	100

This accuracy is higher than that of relevance feedback or domain feedback, as shown in Table 2. The relevance feedback before and after translation with RunindexFEED, showed a second best result in terms of average precision, 78.69% and 71.25% of the monolingual English and French retrieval, respectively. RindexDOM, the domain feedback showed a less effective result in terms of average precision, with 76.92% and 69.64% of the monolingual English and French retrieval, respectively. Fig 2 shows the precision-recall curves for the submitted runs to CLEF 2001.

These results were less effective than we expected. This is because: first the bilingual dictionary does not cover technical terms and proper nouns, which are the most useful in improving the overall IR accuracy. In this study, the French query set contains 11 untranslated English terms. Using the Collins French-English Bilingual dictionary as the only resource for term translations does not help much in discovering the right translation of proper nouns, which are used in CLEF query set.

When a word is not found in the dictionary, we just kept the original source word as the target translation one. This method is successful for some proper names, such as *Lennon, Kim*, etc...but not for others, such as *Chiapas*. Missing words in the bilingual dictionary is one major cause of the introduction of noise into our results. The second reason is due to the selection of terms to expand the original queries, domain keywords for a domain feedback or terms that occur most often with the original query terms. This made the expansion methods ineffective, comparing to our previous work [1]. We hope to be able to improve the effectiveness of an information retrieval, as explained below:

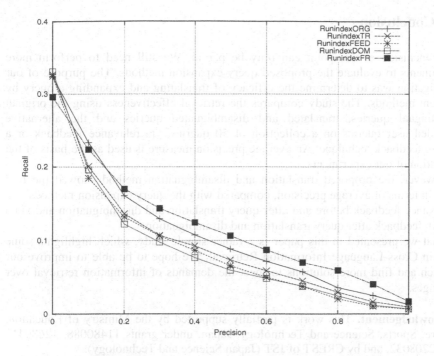

Fig. 2. Precision-Recall Curves for the Submitted Bilingual and Monolingual Runs

Bilingual Translation. The bilingual dictionary should be improved to cover all terms described in the original queries. One solution to this problem is to extract terms and their translations through parallel or comparable corpora, and extend the existing dictionary with that terminology for Cross-Language Information Retrieval.

Term Extraction for a Feedback Loop. According to previous research work [3] [1], query expansion before and after translation improves the effectiveness of the information retrieval. In our case, we used the mutual information [2] to select and add those terms, which occur most often with the original query terms. Previous results showed that results based on mutual information are significantly worse than those based on the log-likelihood-ratio or chi-square test or modified dice coefficient [4]. For an efficient use of the term co-occurrence frequency in the relevance feedback process, we will select the log-likelihood-ratio for further experiments.

Domain Feedback. A combination of the proposed domain feedback method with a relevance feedback before or after translation could help to improve the effectiveness of an information retrieval system.

5   Conclusion

Our conclusion at this point can only be partial. We still need to perform more experiments to evaluate the proposed query expansion methods. The purpose of our investigation was to determine the efficacy of translating and expanding a query by different methods. The study compares the retrieval effectiveness using the original monolingual queries, translated and disambiguated queries and the alternative expanded user queries on a collection of 50 queries, via relevance feedback or a domain feedback technique. An average precision measure is used as the basis of the evaluation of our experiments.

However, the proposed translation and disambiguation method showed the best result in terms of average precision, compared with the query expansion methods: via a relevance feedback before and after query translation and disambiguation and via a domain feedback after query translation and disambiguation.

What we presented in this paper is a rather simple study, which highlights some areas in Cross-Language Information Retrieval. We hope to be able to improve our research and find more solutions to meet the demands of information retrieval over languages.

Acknowledgement. This work is partially supported by the Ministry of Education, Culture, Sports, Science and Technology, Japan, under grants 11480088, 12680417 and 12208032, and by CREST of JST (Japan Science and Technology).

References

1. Sadat, F., Maeda, A., Yoshikawa, M. and Uemura, S.: Cross-Language Information Retrieval via Dictionary-based and Statistical-based Methods. Proceedings of the 2001 IEEE Pacific Rim Conference on Communications, Computers and Signal Processing (PACRIM'01), (August 2001).
2. Gale, W. A. and Church, K.: Identifying word correspondences in parallel texts. Proceedings of the 4th DARPA Speech and Natural Language Workshop, (1991). P.152-157.
3. Ballesteros, L. and Croft, W. B.: Phrasal Translation and Query Expansion Techniques for Cross-Language Information Retrieval. Proceedings of the 20th ACM SIGIR Conference, (1997). P 84-91.
4. Maeda, A., Sadat, F., Yoshikawa, M. and Uemura, S.: Query Term Disambiguation for Web Cross-Language Information Retrieval using a Search Engine. Proceedings of the 5th International Workshop on Information Retrieval with Asian Languages, (Oct 2000). P 25-32.

Intelligent Information Access Systems (SINAI) at CLEF 2001: Calculating Translation Probabilities with SemCor

Fernando Martínez-Santiago, L. Alfonso Ureña-López, M. Carlos Díaz-Galiano, Maite Martín-Valdivia, and Manuel García-Vega

Dpto. Computer Science. University of Jaén. Avda. Madrid 35. 23071 Jaén, Spain
{dofer,laurena,mcdiaz,maite,mgarcia}@ujaen.es

Abstract. The aim of this paper is to present an approach for bilingual Spanish-English information retrieval based on EuroWordNet but also using another linguistic source known as SemCor. SemCor is used to calculate the translation probabilities of words that share the same meaning in EuroWordNet. The focus of the paper is thus on evaluating the performance of SEMCOR, previously used with success in traditional IR, in a bilingual context.

1   Introduction

CLIR (Cross Language Information Retrieval) is a particular application of Information Retrieval, which aims at building systems capable of retrieving relevant documents in a language that is not necessarily that of the query. This requirement creates a lot of additional problems to those of monolingual IR [1, 2], almost all stemming from the need to overcome the existing linguistic barrier. In our case, the barrier is that between English and Spanish. Namely, we are retrieving texts in English from queries in Spanish. The approach we used is an electronic dictionary (ED) based system. Thus, we start with a query in Spanish and translate it word by word through the ED into English, and use this new query with a traditional IR system. We have used EuroWordNet [3] as if it were an ED. The choice of EuroWordNet has been determined by the main purpose of this study, which is not so much to test a new method for CLIR but rather to highlight the quality of the SemCor linguistic resource in calculating translation probabilities. Whilst there are studies that propose the implementation of CLIR systems using EuroWordNet [4,3], we have focused in this paper on the specific study of the calculation of translation probabilities.

2   SemCor

SemCor [5] is a subset of the Brown Corpus [6] containing documents dealing with several topics such as politics, sports, music, films, philosophy, etc. SemCor is tagged at different syntactic and semantic levels. Every word in SemCor

C.A. Peters et al. (Eds.): CLEF 2001, LNCS 2406, pp. 185–192, 2002.
© Springer-Verlag Berlin Heidelberg 2002

186   F. Martínez-Santiago et al.

```
<contextfile concordance=brown>
<context filename=br-a01 paras=yes>
<p pnum=1>
<s snum=1>
<wf cmd=ignore pos=DT>The</wf>
<wf cmd=done rdf=group pos=NNP lemma=group wnsn=1
lexsn=1:03:00:: pn=group>Fulton_County_Grand_Jury</wf>
<wf cmd=done pos=VB lemma=say wnsn=1
lexsn=2:32:00::>said</wf>
<wf cmd=done pos=NN lemma=friday wnsn=1
lexsn=1:28:00::>Friday</wf>
<wf cmd=ignore pos=DT>an</wf>
<wf cmd=done pos=NN lemma=investigation wnsn=1
lexsn=1:09:00::>investigation</wf>
<wf cmd=ignore pos=IN>of</wf>
<wf cmd=done pos=NN lemma=atlanta wnsn=1
lexsn=1:15:00::>Atlanta</wf>
<wf cmd=ignore pos=POS>'s</wf>
<wf cmd=done pos=JJ lemma=recent wnsn=2
lexsn=5:00:00:past:00>recent</wf>
<wf cmd=done pos=NN lemma=primary_election wnsn=1
lexsn=1:04:00::>primary_election</wf>
<wf cmd=done pos=VB lemma=produce wnsn=4
lexsn=2:39:01::>produced</wf>
<punc>``</punc>
<wf cmd=ignore pos=DT>no</wf>
<wf cmd=done pos=NN lemma=evidence wnsn=1
lexsn=1:09:00::>evidence</wf>
<punc>''</punc>
<wf cmd=ignore pos=IN>that</wf>
<wf cmd=ignore pos=DT>any</wf>
<wf cmd=done pos=NN lemma=irregularity wnsn=1
lexsn=1:04:00::>irregularities</wf>
<wf cmd=done pos=VB lemma=take_place wnsn=1
lexsn=2:30:00::>took_place</wf>
<punc>.</punc>
</s>
</P>
```

Fig. 1. Fragment of a document in SEMCOR

(nouns, verbs, adjectives and adverbs), is annotated with its correct sense in the WORDNET lexical database, when possible.

Figure 1 shows a text fragment of SEMCOR, corresponding to the following sentence from the Brown Corpus:

The Fulton County Grand Jury said Friday an investigation of Atlanta's recent primary election produced "no evidence" that any irregularities took place.

The figure shows the labels used to indicate the sense of every term that composes the sentence. For example, the term *investigation* appears labelled under the first sense in WORDNET (wnsn=1).

3   EuroWordNet

The EUROWORDNET project implemented a multilingual database, in which the languages present are represented and structured in the style of WORDNET 1.5 [7]. The languages are linked cross-linguistically through English, which acts as an "inter-language" or pivot language, for want of a better word. As in WORD-NET, in EUROWORDNET the words are linked by meaning in sets of synonyms (*synsets*). Thus, within one *synset* we will find all those words from a particular language that share a common sense. The *synsets* are linked by a number of relations such as hypernym, holonym, etc. In addition, *synsets* of different languages are also linked by relationships of synonymy or of near synonymy, what we could call "words with close meaning", i.e. words which, without being synonymous over languages, do share a similarity in meaning.

Table 1. Query Translation using EUROWORDNET as ED

Original Spanish	Consequences of Chernobil	
Lematized With MACO+ RELAX	Consecuencias de Chernobil	
No empty words	Consecuencia Chernobil	
Word and meaning, translated according to the relationship of synonym from EUROWORDNET	Consequence (3 meanings)	implication#1 entailment#1 deduction#4
		consequence#2 aftermath#1
		upshot#1 result#3 outcome#2 effect#4 consequence#3
	chernobil (No translation)	chernobil#1

In our experiments with EUROWORDNET we have used the relationship of synonymy for the translation of the words. There are other studies which also make use of the "similar meaning" relationship in the translation [8]. We have preferred to use only the synonymy relationship in a more restrictive approach. Once the query is constructed in this way in Spanish, we eliminate stop words, and lemmatize each word using MACO + RELAX [9] and, for each meaning of the lemma, extract the set of words that make up the corresponding *synsets* in the target language - English in this particular case.

4   Filtering of Queries

This simple approach evidences several problems, already manifest in WORD-NET: the great amount of "noise" that the *synsets* introduce due to the fine distinction of meanings existing for each word. For instance, the word "capacidad" (capacity) has up to twelve possible translations into English, shared among the five meanings of the source word.

Table 2. Weights for the 3 meanings of the word *absolute*

Word	Meaning	Frequency	Weight
absolute	1	10	0,6665
	2	4	0,2667
	3	1	0,0667

One way of solving this problem may be by classifying, i.e. identifying where the difference is irrelevant to the needs of Information Retrieval [10]. The difficulty of this approach lies in knowing when two or more meanings must be joined into just one. Our approach differs considerably from the idea of grouping according to meaning, although the two methods are not incompatible. The method suggested here attempts to filter the query obtained through a word by word translation using EUROWORDNET, disposing of those words we consider to be very rare translations of the Spanish word. It is important to point out that no disambiguation of the original word in Spanish is being made as all the possible meanings of the word are taken into account. All we are trying to achieve is to get rid of all those words in English which are highly unlikely as translations of the original word in Spanish. In short, what we are tying to establish is, for a given word T in Spanish and its corresponding translation into English $\{S1,....Sn\}$., how probable it is that Si be a translation of T. Although there are lexical databases, such as VLIS [11,12], that make this calculation of translation probabilities process easier, we have decided to calculate this fact from the SEMCOR corpus.

The idea is simple: SEMCOR labels every word with its sense, so it is possible to calulate how many times a term is used with a given sense. Thus the probability or weight of every sense for a given term is known automatically: this way, it is easy to build up a frequency table of senses which shows how often a particular sense is assigned to each term. Table 2 shows an example of this process corresponding to the word "absolute". This term receives three senses in SEMCOR, the third one being the most unusual.

For the translation, we make use of the frequency table of senses as follows: EUROWORDNET gives us the translation of every term into different languages by means of the synonymy relationship. For instance, the Spanish word "sanatorio" may be translated into English as *"sanatorium"* or *"home"* because, both pairs < *sanatorio, sanatorium* > and < *sanatorium, home* > share a particular meaning. However the problem is: should we translate the term "sanatorio" with both meanings?

The solution to this problem depends on the strength of the synonymy relationship. The second sense of "home" is synonymous with the first sense of "sanatorio". So, we conclude that the probability of translating "sanatorio" by "home" is exactly that of when "home" is used in its second sense. This frequency information is that stored in our table of senses. Moreover, according to this table, we see that the word "home" usually appears with its first sense rather than the sense shared with "sanatorio". So we consider "home" with the meaning of "sanatorio" as irrelevant.

The use of this method, in addition to its availability, shows another clear advantage of an ED with translation probabilities, that of being readily gradable in word-pairs. It provides information on the probability of translating the words $T1$ and $T2$ by $S1$ and $S2$, assuming we find $S1$, $S2$ in the text, each with its specific meaning. The relationship between $S1$ and $S2$ can be calculated through SEMCOR according to criteria such as co-relation indexes [2] and more complex techniques such as the use of trees of dependence in micro-contexts [13].

Another feature of this approach is that it is very appropriate for the application of disambiguation techniques over the original query, written in Spanish in this instance. Since we are translating T by S, due to the fact that they share a certain meaning, it would be important to know whether T is really acting with the same meaning that it shares with S. Although this approach could almost certainly improve our levels of precision, its use is beyond the scope of this current study.

However, SEMCOR has two serious drawbacks. The first is its relatively small size (SEMCOR 1.6 has approximately 31.600 word, meaning pairs)and the second is that it is only available for English.

5 Description of the Experiment

In our experiment we used the ZPrise [14] Information Retrieval System. This choice was determined by its availability and because this system has been recommended in the evaluation of linguistic resources in CLIR tasks such as the one presented here [15]. For our corpus, we used the "Los Angeles Times, 1994" made available by CLEF. This collection has 113.005 documents from the 1994 editions of the "Los Angeles Times". The title, heading and article text were extracted. The official experiments carried out were as follows:

1. *sinai_org* run: original set of queries in English. This is taken as the best case and used as reference for the rest of runs. For our runs, we used the set of queries provided in Spanish and translated them word by word, using the relationship of cross-language synonymy in EUROWORDNET. We then performed three different experiments using this translation:

2. *sinai-ewn* run: using the query obtained through the word by word EUROWORDNET translation.

3. *sinai-ewn2* run: a filtering was applied, based on the probabilities of translation obtained with SEMCOR, to the set of queries obtained in 1. The aim was to eliminate all those target term candidates below a threshold of 0,25 in their probability of translation. It is important to point out that those words that do not appear in SEMCOR in any of it meanings are retained in the original query, as we have no information for them.

6 Results Obtained

The 11-pt precision we obtained for each of the following experiments is shown in Figure 2, together with the average precision.

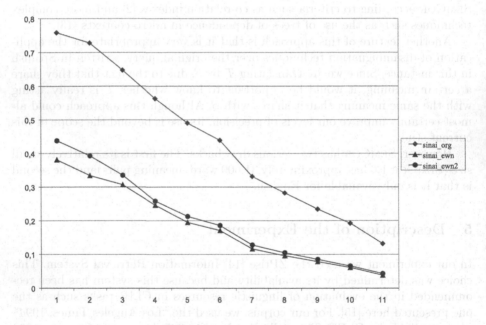

Fig. 2. 11 pt-precision obtained

Table 3. Avg precision obtained

Official run	Average Precision
sinai_org	0,4208
sinai_ewn	0,1701
sinai_ewn2	0,1941

If we take *sinai-org*, as the reference experiment we notice that the loss of precision in the *sinai-ewn* experiment is 59,5% compared with a 53,8% loss in the *sinai-ewn2* (EUROWORDNET+SEMCOR) run. Therefore the use of translation probabilities calculated on SEMCOR reduces the lack of precision by 6,3% compared to that obtained using EUROWORDNET without filtering (*sinai-ewn* experiment). It is likely this percentage would improve if we had a corpus containing all the meanings from EUROWORDNET with a number of words far superior to that of SEMCOR.

Table 4. Breakdown of words in the queries translated from EUROWORDNET. PT = Probability of Translation

	cons_exp		cons_exp+multiwords	
Appear in SEMCOR	PT> 0, 25	344	PT> 0, 25	42
	PT< 0, 25	295	PT< 0, 25	12
	Sum:	639	Sum:	54
Do not appear in SEMCOR	196		137	
Sum	735		191	

Table 4 shows how many times SEMCOR provided information that helped to eliminate noise. Thus, we note that of a total of 735 words, which is the sum of words in the *cons-exp* queries, on 196 occasions we do not obtain any information from SEMCOR. This means that 27% of times we cannot decide whether the word is a good translation or not. This situation becomes considerably worse when we consider the multi-words. The percentage of indecision in this case rises to 72%. However, for those multi-words not found in SEMCOR, we note that 77,8% are assigned a probability of translation, PT, superior to 0,25 compared to 53,8% of simple words. This could be read as meaning that multi-words tend to be a more precise translation of the original word, as in general a multi-word tends to be monosemous or have very few meanings.

7   Conclusions and Future Work

We have presented a CLIR system based on an ED. In future work, we will study the effect of multi-words in indexes that can handle these lexical units, rather than just simple words.

Along these lines, in the search for evidence that could indicate the existence of multi-words not registered in EUROWORDNET, studies of the queries as well as of the text retrieved appear promising.

In addition, we have also mentioned a possible solution to the excessively fine granularity of the EUROWORDNET sense disambiguation for Information Retrieval. This solution is based on using the translation probabilities calculated from the frequency of meanings of the words listed in SEMCOR. However, although this approach shows a gain in terms of precision and appears useful it is far from being completely satisfactory. Our next steps must be directed towards improving the calculation of translation probabilities, through the use of linguistic resources of larger dimensions than SemCor, such as large parallel corpus or similar. Another strategy that could be worth studying is the combination of the approach proposed with techniques for lexical disambiguation [16]; we consider these approaches as two sides of the same coin.

References

1. G. Grefenstette. *Cross-Language Information Retrieval.* E. by G. Grefenstette Kluwer Academic Publishers, 1998.
2. D. Hull and G. Grefenstette. Querying across languages: A dictionary-based approach to multilingual information retrieval. In *The 19th Annual International ACM/SIGIR Conference on Research and Development in Information Retrieval,* 1996.
3. P. Vossen. EuroWordNet: A multilingual database for information retrieval query expansion using lexical-semantic relations. In *THIRD DELOS WORKSHOP Cross-Language Information Retrieval,* 1997.
4. J. Gonzalo, F. Verdejo, C. Peters, and N. Calzolari. Applying EuroWordNet to cross-language text retrieval. *Computers and the Humanities,* (2/3), 1998.
5. C. Fellbaum. WORDNET: *An Electronic Lexical Database.* The MIT Press, 1998.
6. W. Francis. *Problems of Assembling and Computerizing Large Corpora.* 1982.
7. G. Miller. WORDNET: An on-line lexical database. In *An International Journal of Lexicography,* 1990.
8. T. Gollins and M. Sanderson. CLEF 2000 submission(bilingual track - German to English). In *Working Notes for CLEF 2000 Workshop,* 2000.
9. S. Acebo, A. Ageno, S. Climent, J. Farreres, L. Padró, F. Ribas, H. Rodríguez, and O. Soler. EMACO: Morphological analyzer corpus-oriented. In *In ESPRIT BRA-7315 Acquilex II,* 1994.
10. J. Gonzalo, I. Chugur, and F. Verdejo. Sense clusters for information retrieval: Evidence from SemCor and the interlingual index. In *Proceedings of the ACL'2000 workshop on Word Senses and Multilinguality,* 2000.
11. D. Hiemstra, W. Kraaij, R. Pohlmann, and T. Westerveld. Twenty-one at CLEF-2000: Translation resources, merging strategies and relevance feedback. In *Working Notes for CLEF 2000 Workshop,* 2000.
12. D. Hiemstra and W. Kraaij. Twenty-one at TREC-7: Ad-hoc and cross-language track. In *Proceedings of the seventh Text Retrieval Conference TREC-7,* 2000.
13. M. Holub and A. Böhmová. Use of dependency tree structures for the microcontext extraction. In *ACL'2000 workshop on Recent Advances in Natural Language Processing and Information Retrieval,* 2000.
14. D. Dimmick. ZPrise NIST. *Available on demand at* http://www.itl.nist.gov/iaui/894.02/works/papers/zp2/zp2.html [2/6/2001], 2000.
15. J. Gonzalo. Language resources in cross-language information retrieval: a CLEF perspective. In *Cross-Language Information Retrieval and Evaluation: Proceedings of the First Cross-Language Evaluation Forum,* 2001.
16. L.A. Ureña, M. Buenaga, and J.M. Gómez. Integrating linguistic resources in TC through WSD. *Computers and the Humanities,* 35(2):215–230, May 2001.

JHU/APL Experiments at CLEF: Translation Resources and Score Normalization

Paul McNamee and James Mayfield

Johns Hopkins University Applied Physics Lab
11100 Johns Hopkins Road, Laurel, MD 20723-6099 USA
{mcnamee, mayfield}@jhuapl.edu

Abstract. The Johns Hopkins University Applied Physics Laboratory participated in three of the five tasks of the CLEF-2001 evaluation, monolingual
retrieval, bilingual retrieval, and multilingual retrieval. In this paper we describe
the fundamental methods we used and we present initial results from three
experiments. The first investigation examines whether residual inverse
document frequency can improve the term weighting methods used with a
linguistically-motivated probabilistic model. The second experi-ment attempts
to assess the benefit of various translation resources for cross-language
retrieval. Our last effort aims to improve cross-collection score normalization, a
task essential for the multilingual problem.

1   Introduction

The Hopkins Automated Information Retriever for Combing Unstructured Text
(HAIRCUT) is a research retrieval system developed at the Johns Hopkins University
Applied Physics Laboratory (APL). The design of HAIRCUT was influenced by a
desire to compare various methods for lexical analysis and tokenization; thus the
system has no commitment to any particular method. With western European
languages we typically use both unstemmed words and overlapping character n-grams
as indexing terms, and previous experimentation has led us to believe that a
combination of both approaches enhances performance [8].

We participated in three tasks at this year's workshop, monolingual, cross-
language, and multilingual retrieval. All of our official submissions were automated
runs and our official cross-language runs relied on query translation using one of two
machine translation systems. In the sections that follow, we first describe our standard
methodology and we then present initial results from three experiments. The first
investigation examines whether residual inverse document frequency can improve the
term weighting methods used with a linguistically-motivated probabilistic model. The
second experiment attempts to assess the benefit of various translation resources for
cross-language retrieval. Our last effort aims to improve cross-collection score
normalization, a task essential for the multilingual problem.

C.A. Peters et al. (Eds.): CLEF 2001, LNCS 2406, pp. 193–208, 2002.
© Springer-Verlag Berlin Heidelberg 2002

2   Methodology

For the monolingual tasks we used twelve indices, a word and an n-gram (n=6) index for each of the six languages. For the bilingual and multilingual tasks we used the same indices with translated topic statements. Information about each index is provided in Table 1.

Table 1. Index statistics for the CLEF-2001 test collection

	# docs	collection size (MB gzipped)	name	# terms	index size (MB)
Dutch	190,604	203	words	692,745	162
			6-grams	4,154,405	1144
English	110,282	163	words	235,710	99
			6-grams	3,118,973	901
French	87,191	93	words	479,682	84
			6-grams	2,966,390	554
German	225,371	207	words	1,670,316	254
			6-grams	5,028,002	1387
Italian	108,578	108	words	1,323,283	146
			6-grams	3,333,537	694
Spanish	215,737	185	words	382,664	150
			6-grams	3,339,343	1101

2.1   Index Construction

Documents were processed using only the permitted tags specified in the workshop guidelines. First SGML macros were expanded to their appropriate Unicode character. Then punctuation was eliminated, letters were downcased, and only the first four of a sequence of digits were preserved (e.g., 010394 became 0103##). Diacritical marks were preserved. The result is a stream of words separated by spaces. Exceedingly long words were truncated; the limit was 35 characters in the Dutch and German languages and 20 otherwise. When using n-grams we extract indexing terms from the same stream of words; thus, the n-grams may span word boundaries, but sentence boundaries are noted so that n-grams spanning sentence boundaries are not recorded. N-grams with leading, central, or trailing spaces are formed at word boundaries. For example, given the phrase, "the prime minister," the 6-grams in Table 2 are produced.

The use of overlapping character n-grams provides a surrogate form of morphological normalization. For example, the n-gram "minist" could have been generated from several different forms like *administer, administrative, minister, ministers, ministerial,* or *ministry*. It could also come from an unrelated word like *feminist*. Another advantage of n-gram indexing comes from the fact that n-grams containing spaces can convey phrasal information. In the table below, 6-grams such as "rime-m", "ime-mi", and "me-min" may act much like the phrase "prime minister" in a word-based index using multiple word phrases.

Table 2. Example 6-grams produced for the input "the prime minister." Term statistics are based on the LA Times subset of the CLEF-2001 collection. Dashes indicate whitespace characters.

Term	Document Frequency	Collection Frequency	IDF	RIDF
-the-p	72,489	241,648	0.605	0.434
the-pr	41,729	86,923	1.402	0.527
he-pri	8,701	11,812	3.663	0.364
e-prim	2,827	3,441	5.286	0.261
-prime	3,685	5,635	4.903	0.576
prime-	3,515	5,452	4.971	0.597
rime-m	1,835	2,992	5.910	0.689
ime-mi	1,731	2,871	5.993	0.711
me-min	1,764	2,919	5.966	0.707
e-mini	3,797	5,975	4.860	0.615
-minis	4,243	8,863	4.699	1.005
minist	15,428	33,731	2.838	0.914
iniste	4,525	8,299	4.607	0.821
nister	4,686	8,577	4.557	0.816
ister-	7,727	12,860	3.835	0.651

At last year's workshop we explored language-neutral retrieval and avoided the use of stopword lists, lexicons, decompounders, stemmers, lists of phrases, or manually-built thesauri [7]. Such resources are seldom in a standard format, may be of varying quality, and worst of all, necessitate additional software development to utilize. Although we are open to the possibility that such linguistic resources may improve retrieval performance, we are interested in how far we can push performance without them. We followed the same approach this year.

We conducted our work on four Sun Microsystems workstations shared with about 30 other researchers. Each machine has at least 1GB of physical memory and we have access to dedicated disk space of about 200GB. Using character n-grams increases the size of both dictionaries and inverted files, typically by a factor of five or six, over those of comparable word-based indices. Furthermore, when we use pseudo-relevance feedback we use a large number of expansion n-grams. As a consequence, runtime performance became an issue that we needed to address. Over the last year we made a number of improvements to HAIRCUT to reduce the impact of large data structures, and to allow the system to run in less memory-rich environments.

To minimize the memory consumption needed for a dictionary in a large term-space, we developed a multi-tiered cache backed by a B-tree. If sufficient memory is available, term/term-id pairs are stored in a hash table; if the hash table grows too large, entries are removed from the table, but still stored in memory as compressed B-tree nodes; if the system then runs out of memory data are written to disk.

To reduce the size of our inverted files we applied gamma compression [10] and saw our disk usage shrink to about 1/3 of its former size. HAIRCUT also generates dual files, an analogous structure to inverted files that are document-referenced vectors of terms; the dual files also compress rather nicely.

2.2   Query Processing

HAIRCUT performs rudimentary preprocessing on topic statements to remove stop structure, *e.g.*, phrases such as "... would be relevant" or "relevant documents should....". We have constructed a list of about 1000 such English phrases from previous topic sets (mainly TREC topics) and these have been translated into other languages using commercial machine translation. Other than this preprocessing, queries are parsed in the same fashion as documents in the collection.

In all of our experiments we used a linguistically-motivated probabilistic model for retrieval. Our official runs all used blind relevance feedback, though it did not improve retrieval performance in every instance. To perform relevance feedback we first retrieved the top 1000 documents. We then used the top 20 documents for positive feedback and the bottom 75 documents for negative feedback; however, we removed any duplicate or near duplicate documents from these sets. We then selected terms for the expanded query based on three factors, a term's initial query term frequency (if any); the cube root of the (α=3, β=2, γ=2) Rocchio score; and a term similarity metric that incorporates IDF weighting. The 60 top ranked terms were then used as the revised query with words as indexing terms; 400 terms were used with 6-grams. In previous work we penalized documents containing only a fraction of the query terms; we are no longer convinced that this technique adds much benefit and have discontinued its use. As a general trend we observe a decrease in precision at very low recall levels when blind relevance feedback is used, but both overall recall and mean average precision are improved.

3   Monolingual Experiments

Once again our approach to monolingual retrieval focused on language-independent methods. We submitted two official runs for each target language, one using the mandated <title> and <desc> fields (TD runs) and one that added the <narr> field as well (TDN runs), for a total of 10 submissions. These official runs were automated runs formed by combining results from two base runs, one using words and one using n-grams.

In all our experiments we used a linguistically-motivated probabilistic model. This model has been described in a report by Hiemstra and de Vries [6], which compares the method to traditional retrieval models. This is essentially the same approach that was used by BBN in TREC-7 [9] which was billed as a Hidden Markov Model. The similarity calculation that is performed is:

$$Sim(q,d) = \prod_{t=terms}(\alpha \cdot f(t,d) + (1-\alpha) \cdot mrdf(t))^{f(t,q)} \qquad (1)$$

where $f(t,d)$ is the relative frequency of term t in document d (or query q) and $mrdf(t)$ denotes the mean relative document frequency of t. The parameter α is a tunable parameter that can be used to ascribe a degree of importance to a term. For our baseline system we simply fix the value of α at 0.3 when words are used as indexing terms. Since individual n-grams tend to have a lower semantic value than words a lower α is indicated; we use a value of 0.15 for 6-grams. In unpublished training experiments using the TREC-8 test collection we found performance remained acceptable across a wide range of values. When blind relevance feedback is applied we do not adjust this importance value on a term by term basis; instead we just expand the initial query.

Table 3. Official results for monolingual task. The shaded rows contain results for comparable, unofficial English runs.

	topic fields	average precision	recall	# topics	# ≥ median	# = best	# = worst
aplmodea	TDN	0.4596	2086 / 2130	49	36	11	0
aplmodeb	TD	0.4116	2060 / 2130	49	40	6	0
aplmoena	TDN	0.4896	838 / 856	47	unofficial English run		
aplmoenb	TD	0.4471	840 / 856	47	unofficial English run		
aplmoesa	TDN	0.5518	2618 / 2694	49	36	16	1
aplmoesb	TD	0.5176	2597 / 2694	49	31	6	0
aplmofra	TDN	0.4210	1202 / 1212	49	24	11	0
aplmofrb	TD	0.3919	1195 / 1212	49	19	4	2
aplmoita	TDN	0.4346	1213 / 1246	47	32	8	1
aplmoitb	TD	0.4049	1210 / 1246	47	26	6	1
aplmonla	TDN	0.4002	1167 / 1224	50	40	12	0
aplmonlb	TD	0.3497	1149 / 1224	50	37	3	0

We were interested in performing an experiment to see if baseline performance could be improved by adjusting the importance parameter α for each query term. Residual inverse document frequency (RIDF) [3] is a statistic that represents the burstiness of a term in the documents in which it occurs (see Equation 2 below). Terms with high RIDF tend to be distinctive, so when they are present, they occur more frequently within a document than might otherwise be expected; terms with low RIDF tend to occur indiscriminately. Numerals and adverbs, and to some extent adjectives all tend to have low RIDF. For example, the English words *briefly* and *computer* both occur in just over 5000 LA Times articles, yet computer appears 2.18 times per occurrence, on average, while briefly almost always appears just once (1.01 times on average). By taking this into account, we hope to minimize the influence that a word like briefly has on document scores (aside: Yamamoto and Church have recently published an efficient method for computing RIDF for all substrings in a collection [11]).

$$RIDF(t) = IDF(t) - \log\left(\frac{1}{1 - e^{-cf(t)}}\right) \tag{2}$$

Equation 2 is the computation of residual inverse document frequency for a term. The log term in the equation represents the expected IDF if the term had a Poisson distribution.

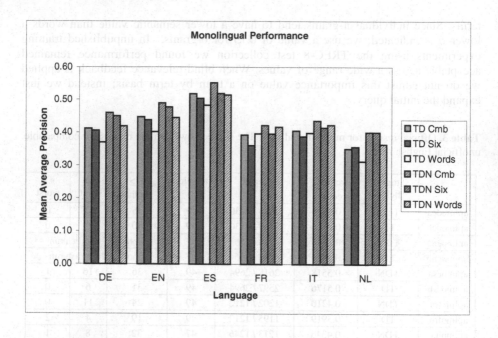

Fig. 1. Comparison of retrieval performance across target languages. For each language, results using both TD and TDN queries are shown when words, 6-grams, or a combination of the two is used. Unsurprisingly, longer queries were more effective. 6-gram runs most often had better performance than words, but this was not the case in French or Italian. Combination of the two methods yielded a slight improvement.

Our approach to incorporate term-specific weighting in our language model is as follows. For each query term, we adjust the importance value, α, for each term depending on RIDF. We linearly interpolate the RIDF value based on the minimum and maximum values observed in the collection and multiply by a constant k to determine the adjusted α. For these initial experiments we only consider $k=0.2$.

$$\alpha(t) = \alpha_{baseline} + k \cdot \frac{RIDF(t) - RIDF_{min}}{RIDF_{max} - RIDF_{min}} \quad (3)$$

We are still analyzing these results, however the preliminary indications are promising. Figure 2 shows the change in average precision when applying this rudimentary method.

We observe a small positive effect, particularly with intermediate-length queries. One possible explanation for why the improvement does not occur with very short queries (e.g., title-only) is because these queries are unlikely to contain low-RIDF terms (being short and to the point), and the adjustment in importance value is unwarranted. As yet, we have no explanation for why long queries (TDN or those with expanded queries) do not seem to gain much with this method. As time permits an analysis of individual topics may reveal what is happening.

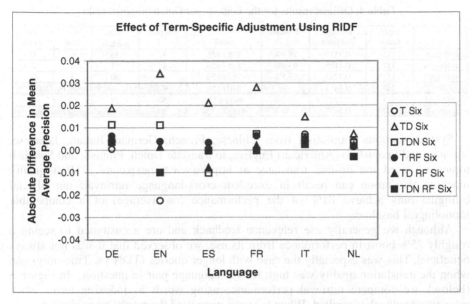

Fig. 2. Impact on mean average precision when term-specific adjustments are made. 6-gram indexing shown for six query types (different topic fields and use of pseudo-relevance feedback) in each language.

4   Bilingual Experiments

Our goal for the bilingual task was to assess retrieval performance when four approaches to query translation are used: commercial machine translation software; publicly available bilingual wordlists; parallel corpora mined from the Web; and untranslated queries. The last is only likely to succeed when languages share word roots. We wanted to attempt as many of the topic languages as possible, and managed to use all available query languages except Thai. At the time of the workshop, we had not finished developing the software and resources needed to use bilingual wordlists or aligned corpora for translation; however, we now have some preliminary post hoc experiments using such resources that we report on in section 4.3 below.

4.1   Experiments Using Machine Translation

In the past we have observed good performance when commercial machine translation is used, and so all of our official runs used MT. Since only four official runs were permitted, we had a hard time choosing which topic languages to use. We attempted the Dutch bilingual task as well as the English task, and ended up submitting runs using French, German, and Japanese topics against English documents, and using English topics for the Dutch documents.

Table 4. Official results for the English and Dutch bilingual tasks

	topic fields	average precision	% mono	recall	# topics	# ≥ median	# = best	#= worst
aplbifren	TD	0.3519	78.7%	778 / 856	47	36	6	0
aplbideen	TD	0.4195	93.8%	835 / 856	47	31	4	2
aplbijpen	TD	0.3285	73.5%	782 / 856	47	30	3	1
aplmoenb	TD	0.4471	--	840 / 856	47	monolingual baseline		
aplbiennl	TD	0.2707	77.4%	963 / 1224	50	38	14	13
aplmonlb	TD	0.3497	--	1149 / 1224	50	monolingual baseline		

Systran supports translation from Chinese, French, German, Italian, Japanese, Russian, and Spanish to (American) English; to translate Dutch, Finnish, and Swedish topics we used the on-line translator at http://www.tranexp.com/. High quality machine translation can result in excellent cross-language retrieval; our official bilingual runs achieve 81% of the performance (on average) of a comparable monolingual baseline.

Although we generally use relevance feedback and are accustomed to seeing a roughly 25% boost in performance from its use, we observed that it was not always beneficial. This was especially the case with longer queries (TDN vs. Title-only) and when the translation quality was high for the language pair in question. In Figure 3 (below), we compare retrieval performance using words as indexing terms when relevance feedback is applied. When 6-grams were used the results were similar.

Translations of Topic 41 into English

German   <DE-title> pestizide in baby food
            <DE-desc> reports on pestizide in baby food are looked for.

English   <EN-title> Pesticides in Baby Food
            <EN-desc> Find reports on pesticides in baby food.

Spanish   <ES-title> Pesticidas in foods for you drink
            <ES-desc> Encontrar the news on pesticidas in foods stops you drink.

Finnish   <FI-title> Suppression-compositions lasten valmisruuassa
            <FI-desc> Etsi raportteja suppression-aineista lasten valmisruuassa.

French   <FR-title> Of the pesticides in food for babies
            <FR-desc> To seek documents on the pesticides in food for babies.

Italian   <IT-title> Pesticidi in the alimony for children
            <IT-desc> Trova documents that they speak about the pesticidi in the alimony for children.

Japanese   <JP-title>Damage by disease and pest control medicine in baby hood
            <JP-desc>The article regarding the damage by disease and pest pest control medicine in the baby hood was searched to be.

Dutch	<NL-title> Pesticide within babyvoeding <NL-desc> Missing unpleasant documents via pesticide within babyvoeding.
Russian	<RU-title> pesticides in the children's nourishment of <RU-desc> to find articles about the pesticides in the children's nourishment of
Swedish	<SV-title> Bekdmpningsmedel a baby <SV-desc> Svk report a bekdmpningsmedel a baby.
Chinese	<ZH-title> In baby food includes report which in pesticide <ZH-desc> inquiry concerned baby food includes pesticide.

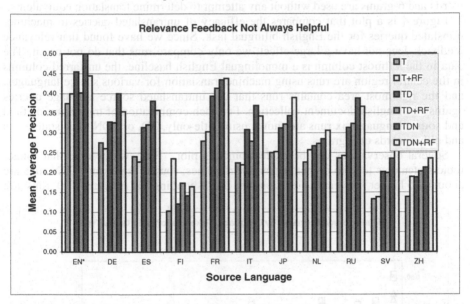

Fig. 3. Bilingual performance using words as indexing terms, examining the effect of relevance feedback. Results using English topics are shown at the left.

4.2   Using Untranslated Queries

The Finnish translations are poor in quality, which explains the rather low relative performance when those topics were used. However, looking over the translated topics we observe that many untranslated terms are near cognates to the proper English word. For example, *pestizide* (German), *pesticidas* (Spanish), and *pesticidi* (Italian) are easily recognizable. Similarly, 'baby hood' is phonetically similar to 'baby food', an easy to understand mistake when Japanese phonetic characters are used to transliterate a term.

In TREC-6, Buckley et al. explored cross-language English to French retrieval using cognate matches [1]. They took an 'English is misspelled French' approach and attempted to 'correct' English terms into their proper French equivalents, projecting that 30% or so of non-stopwords could be transformed automatically. Their results were unpredictably good, and they reported bilingual performance of 60% of their monolingual baseline. Although this approach is non-intuitive, it can be used as a worst-case approach when few or no translation resources are available, so long as the source and target languages are compatible. Furthermore, it can certainly be used as a lower bound on CLIR performance that can serve as a minimal standard by which to assess the added benefit of additional translation resources.

While Buckley et al. manually developed rules to spell-correct English into French, this work may be entirely unnecessary when n-gram indexing is used, since n-grams provide a form of morphological normalization. Thus we consider a more radical hypothesis than 'English is misspelled French', namely, 'other languages are English.' We now examine more closely the relative performance observed when words and 6-grams are used without any attempt to determine translation equivalents.

Figure 4 is a plot that compares the efficacy of untranslated queries to machine-translated queries for the English bilingual task. Since we have found that relevance feedback does not have a large effect, we only compare runs that do not use it. The data in the leftmost column is a monolingual English baseline, the unstarred columns in the central region are runs using machine translation for various source languages, and the rightmost area contains runs that use untranslated source language queries against the English document collection. For each combination of translation method and source language six runs are shown using title-only, TD, or TDN topic statements and either words or 6-grams.

Several observations can be made from this plot. First, we observe that longer topic statements tend to do better than shorter ones; roughly speaking, TDN runs are about 0.05 higher in average precision than corresponding TD runs, and TD runs are

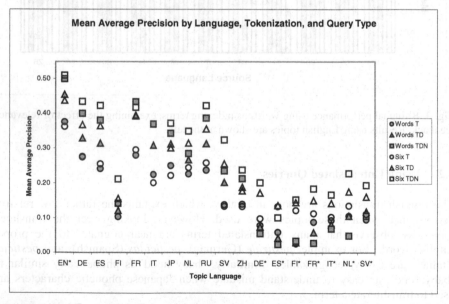

Fig. 4. Comparing word and n-gram indexing on machine-translated, and untranslated topics. Untranslated topics are indicated with a star.

about the same amount better than title-only runs. Second, we note that 6-grams tend to outperform words; the mean relative difference among comparable MT runs is 5.95%. Looking at the various source languages we note that as a group, the Systran translated runs (DE, ES, FR, IT, JP, RU, and ZH) outperform the InterTran translated queries (FI, NL, and SV); this may reveal an underlying difference in product quality, however a better comparison would be to use languages they translate in common. Translation quality is rather poor for the Finnish and Swedish topics (InterTran) and also with the Chinese topics (Systran). Averaging across all source languages, the translated runs have performance between 41- 63% of the top monolingual English run when words are used, and 41-70% when 6-grams are used.

The untranslated queries plotted on the right clearly do worse than their translated equivalents. Averaging across the seven languages encoded in ISO-8859-1, word runs achieve performance between 9-15% of the top monolingual English run, but 6-gram runs do much better and get performance between 22-34% depending on the topic fields used.   The mean relative advantage when n-grams are used on these unstranslated topics is 183%, almost a doubling in efficacy over words. The 6-grams achieve 54% of the performance of the machine-translated runs (on average); this approaches the 60% figure reported by Buckley et al. Though not shown in the plot, relevance feedback actually does enhance these untranslated 6-gram runs even though we have shown that relevance feedback did not significantly affect the translated topics.   One final observation is that shorter queries are actually better when words are used; we suspect that this is because longer topics may contain more matching words, but not necessarily the key words for the topic.

One concern we have with this analysis is that it compares runs using an aggregate measure, mean average precision. For untranslated topics, we imagine the variance in performance is greater over many topics since some topics will have almost no cognate matches. We hope to examine individual topic behavior in the future.

We looked for this effect in other measures besides average precision. Recall at 1000 documents was effectively doubled when 6-grams were used instead of words; roughly 70% of the monolingual recall was observed. Averaged across language, precision at 5 documents was 0.1921 when 6-grams were used with TDN topics with blind relevance feedback. Thus even this rudimentary approach finds one relevant document on average in the top five.

4.3   Experiments Using Translation Resources Mined from the Web

Since the workshop in September, our group has been able to exploit some translation resources derived from the World Wide Web for query-translation. Both bilingual wordlists and a parallel corpus have been created. These resources are not validated and numerous errors may exist. We hope to publish more details about these resources in the near future and would like to make them available to the community. For now, we describe the essentials and show how preliminary attempts to use them for retrieval compare to the use of high quality machine translation software.

We collected a variety of bilingual wordlists in which English was one of the languages. Currently translation equivalents for over 94 thousand English words are available in at least one of 46 languages. No attempt was made to normalize words based on spelling variations or diacritical marks. We did not attempt to utilize or reverse engineer web-based interfaces to dictionaries, but only sought wordlists in the public domain, or whose use appeared unrestricted; the Ergane dictionaries are the largest single source [12]. The size of several individual wordlists is shown below.

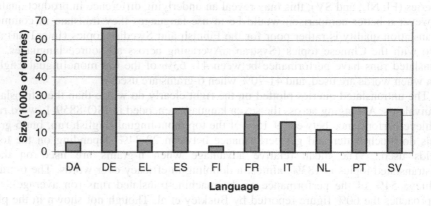

Bilingual Wordlist Size by Language

Fig. 5. Size of bilingual wordlists for various European languages measured by the number of corresponding English words.

We also built a set of aligned corpora using text mined from the Europa site [13]; specifically, we downloaded about eight months of the Official Journal of the European Union. The Journal is published in eleven languages in PDF format. We converted the PDF text to ISO-8859-1 (giving up on Greek), aligned the documents using simple rules for whitespace and punctuation, and with Church's char_align program[2], and then indexed the data. Our approach to alignment made it easier for us to make a separate aligned corpus for each language other than English, rather than to make a single ten language, multiply-aligned collection; if char_align supports the latter we did not know it. Roughly 8 GB of data were downloaded, but the PDF source is roughly ten times larger than the unformatted text. We ended up with slightly less than 100MB of text in each language. Lexical equivalences were extracted from this parallel collection as follows. Up to 10,000 passages containing the source language word of interest are identified, and the corresponding passages in the target language collection are examined. The top-ranked term from the target language passages is deemed a translation; terms are ranked by a term selection function using local and global term frequencies that is similar to mutual information.

Results comparing all four translation resources to translate German queries for the English bilingual tasks are shown in Figure 6; very similar results were obtained with other source languages. Three different conditions are shown, when title-only, TD, or TDN topic statements are used. From left to right, the methods are (1) Monolingual Baseline; (2) Using the Europa parallel collection with pretranslation query expansion; (3) Using the bilingual wordlists with pretranslation expansion; (4) Using the Systran translation product to translate the topics; (5) Using the Europa corpus for translation without pretranslation expansion; (6) Using the bilingual wordlist without expansion; and (7) No attempt at translation whatsoever. Observe that the top title-only runs using the parallel corpus outperform the monolingual baseline.

We are encouraged to find that the use of freely available resources, in particular resources mined from the Web and not curated, can outperform approaches to CLIR using commercial translation software for query translation. At the present time, we have not had an opportunity to combine multiple methods for query translation.

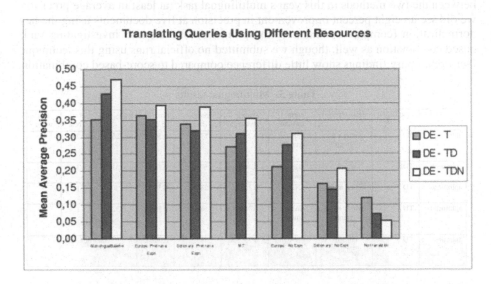

Fig. 6. Comparing several methods for query translation for the English bilingual task. Here German topics were translated, but results were very similar with other source languages. Words were used as indexing terms and no pseudo-relevance feedback was used.

5   Multilingual Experiments

When combining several runs, one must either use document rank as a measure of the importance of a document, or try to make some sense out of system-generated scores. Using rank is problematic when the two runs cover different documents.   For example, if a different index is built for each language in a multilingual retrieval task, there is no way to distinguish a language that has many relevant documents from one that has few or no relevant documents using rank alone.   On the other hand, raw scores are not typically comparable. For example, the scores produced by our statistical language model are products, with one factor per query term. Even if the individual factors were somehow comparable (which they are not), there is no guarantee that a query will have the same number of terms when translated into two or more different languages. Other similarity metrics suffer from similar difficulties. Thus, score normalization is crucial if scores are to be used for run combination.

We tried a new score normalization technique this year. We viewed scores as masses, and normalized by dividing each individual score by the sum of the masses of the top 1000 documents. (Because our probabilistic calculations are typically performed in log space, and scores are therefore negative, we achieved the desired effect by using the reciprocal of a document's score as its mass.) Our previous method of score normalization was to interpolate scores for a topic within a run onto [0,1]. We were concerned that this would cause documents in languages with few or no relevant documents for a topic to appear comparable to top-ranked documents in a language with many relevant documents. While there was no appreciable difference between the two methods in this year's multilingual task (at least in average precision) we did see an eight percent improvement in precision at five documents using the new normalization (compare *aplmuena* with *aplmuend*). We are still investigating rank-based combination as well, though we submitted no official runs using this technique. Our preliminary findings show little difference compared to score-based combination.

Table 5. Multilingual results

	topic fields	index type(s)	norm. method	average precision	recall (8138)	prec. @ 5 docs	# ≥ median	# = best	# = worst
aplmuena	TD	words + 6-grams	mass contrib.	0.2979	5739	0.5600	25	2	0
aplmuenb	TDN	words	mass contrib.	0.3033	5707	0.5800	31	3	0
aplmuenc	TD	unified words	NA	0.1688	2395	0.5600	9	1	9
aplmuend	TD	words + 6-grams	linear interp.	0.3025	5897	0.5240	32	1	0
aplmuene	TD	unified 5-grams	NA	0.2593	4079	0.5960	unofficial run		

We were intrigued by a method that the U.C. Berkeley team used for multilingual merging in TREC-7 [5] and in last year's CLEF workshop [4], where documents from all languages were indexed as a common collection. Queries were translated into all target languages and the resulting collective query was run against the collection. Berkeley's results using this approach in last year's multilingual task (run BKMUEAA1) were comparable to runs that used a merging strategy. We were inspired to try this method ourselves and built two unified indices, one using words and one using 5-grams. Using unstemmed words as indexing terms, our performance with this method was poor (run *aplmuenc*); however, we did see a significant improvement using 5-grams instead (see Table 5). Still, our attempts using a unified term space have not resulted in better scores than approaches combining separate retrievals in each target language. We will continue to examine this method because of its desirable property of not requiring cross-collection score normalization.

6   Conclusions

The second Cross-Language Evaluation Forum workshop has offered a unique opportunity to investigate multilingual retrieval issues for European languages. We participated in three of the five tasks and were able to conduct several interesting experiments. Our first investigation into the use of term-specific adjustments using a statistical language model showed that a small improvement can be obtained when residual inverse document frequency is utilized. However, this conclusion is preliminary and we do not feel we understand the mechanism involved.

Our second experiment compared bilingual retrieval performance when various query translation methods were used. The first method using extant commercial machine translation gives very good results that approach a monolingual baseline. We also showed that reasonable performance can be obtained when no attempt whatsoever is made at query translation, and we have demonstrated that overlapping character n-grams have a strong advantage over word-based retrieval in this scenario. The method is of course only practicable when related languages are involved. We think this result is significant for several reasons. First, it quantifies a lower bound for bilingual performance that other approaches may be measured against. Secondly, it implies that translation to a related language, when translation to the target language of interest is infeasible, may form the basis of a rudimentary retrieval system.

We also reported on preliminary work using parallel corpora and publicly available bilingual wordlists mined from the Web. These unrefined resources were extracted automatically, but still required significant effort to construct. Despite the lack of human processing to identify and remove errors they appear to outperform leading machine translation software for query translation-based CLIR and to rival monolingual performance.

Multilingual retrieval, where a single source language query is used to search for documents in multiple target languages, remains a critical challenge. Our attempt to improve cross-collection score normalization was not successful. We will continue to investigate this problem, which will only grow more difficult as a greater number of target languages is considered.

Acknowledgements. We are grateful to the various providers who allow their linguistic resources such as bilingual dictionaries to be used without constraint. The freely available parallel texts produced by the European Union appear to be quite valuable for mining translation equivalents and we appreciate their electronic publication which serves both the citizens of the E.U. and linguistic researchers. Mr. Alex Chin's assistance with our efforts to mine the Europa site, and to align the parallel data during an internship during the 2000-2001 academic year, proved invaluable.

References

[1] C. Buckley, M. Mitra, J. Walz, and C. Cardie, 'Using Clustering and Super Concepts within SMART: TREC-6'. In E. Voorhees and D. Harman (eds.), *Proceedings of the Sixth Text REtrieval Conference (TREC-6),* NIST Special Publication 500-240, 1998.

[2] K. W. Church, 'Char_align: A program for aligning parallel texts at the character level.' In the *Proceedings of the 31ˢᵗ Annual Meeting of the Association for Computational Linguistics,* pp. 1-8, 1993.

[3] K. W. Church, 'One Term or Two?', In the *Proceedings of the 18ᵗʰ International Conference on Research and Development in Information Retrieval (SIGIR-95),* pp. 310-318, 1995.

[4] F. Gey, H. Jiang, V. Petras, and A. Chen, 'Cross-Language Retrieval for the CLEF Collections – Comparing Multiple Methods of Retrieval.' In Carol Peters (ed.), *Cross-Language Information Retrieval and Evaluation: Proceedings of the CLEF 2000 Workshop, Lecture Notes in Computer Science 2069,* Springer, pp. 116-128, 2001.

[5] F. Gey, H. Jiang, A. Chen, and R. Larson, 'Manual Queries and Machine Translation in Cross-language Retrieval and Interactive Retrieval with Cheshire II at TREC-7'. In E. M. Voorhees and D. K. Harman, eds., *Proceedings of the Seventh Text REtrieval Conference (TREC-7)*, pp. 527-540, 1999.

[6] D. Hiemstra and A. de Vries, 'Relating the new language models of information retrieval to the traditional retrieval models.' *CTIT Technical Report TR-CTIT-00-09*, May 2000.

[7] P. McNamee, J. Mayfield, and C. Piatko, 'A Language-Independent Approach to European Text Retrieval.' In Carol Peters (ed.), *Cross-Language Information Retrieval and Evaluation: Proceedings of the CLEF 2000 Workshop, Lecture Notes in Computer Science 2069*, Springer, pp. 129-139, 2001.

[8] J. Mayfield, P. McNamee, and C. Piatko, 'The JHU/APL HAIRCUT System at TREC-8.' In E. M. Voorhees and D. K. Harman, eds., *Proceedings of the Eighth Text REtrieval Conference (TREC-8)*, pp. 445-451, 2000.

[9] D. R. H. Miller, T. Leek, and R. M. Schwartz, 'A Hidden Markov Model Information Retrieval System.' In the *Proceedings of the 22nd International Conference on Research and Development in Information Retrieval (SIGIR-99)*, pp. 214-221, August 1999.

[10] Witten, A. Moffat, and T. Bell, 'Managing Gigabytes', Chapter 3, Morgan Kaufmann, 1999.

[11] M. Yamamoto and K. Church, 'Using Suffix Arrays to Compute Term Frequency and Document Frequency for all Substrings in a Corpus'. In *Computational Linguistics,* vol 27(1), pp. 1-30, 2001.

[12] http://dictionaries.travlang.com/

[13] http://europa.eu.int/

Dictionary-Based Thai CLIR: An Experimental Survey of Thai CLIR

Jaruskulchai Chuleerat

Department of Computer Science, Faculty of Science
Kasetsart University, Bangkok, Thailand
fscichj@ku.ac.th

Abstract. This paper describes our participation in the Cross-Language Evaluation Forum. Our objectives for this experiment were three-fold. Firstly, the coverage of the Thai bilingual dictionary was evaluated when translating queries. Secondly, we investigated whether the segmentation process affected the CLIR. Lastly, this research examines query formation techniques. Since this is our first international experimental in CLIR, our approach used dictionary-based techniques to translate Thai queries into English queries. Four runs were submitted to CLEF: (a) single mapping translation with manual segmentation, (b) multiple mapping translation with manual segmentation, (c) single mapping translation with automatic segmentation and (d) single mapping with query enhancement using words from our Thai thesaurus. The retrieval effectiveness was worse than we expected. The simple dictionary mapping technique is unable to achieve retrieval effectiveness, although the dictionary lookup gave a very high percentage of mapping words. The words from the dictionary lookup are not specific terms but each is mapped to a definition or meaning of that term. Furthermore, Thai stopwords, stemmed words and word separation have reduced the effectiveness of Thai CLIR.

1   Introduction

Most of the CLIR research community believes that CLIR would be useful for people who do not speak a foreign language well. Unfortunately, the results of some Thai CLIR research work have not been evaluated with appropriate data. Thus, we viewed our participation in the Cross-Language Evaluation Forum (CLEF) as an opportunity to better understand the issues in Cross-Language Information Retrieval (CLIR) research. We performed four Thai-English cross language retrieval runs. Our approach to CLIR was to translate the Thai topics into English by using dictionary mapping techniques. The bilingual dictionaries used are LEXiTRON [1], and Seasite [2]. These two dictionaries were compiled by the Software and Language Engineering Laboratory, the National Electronics and Computer Technology Center (NECTEC) [3] and Northern Illinois University [2].

The objectives of these four runs were as follows: to test the effectiveness of a Machine Readable Dictionary (MRD) and the coverage of its vocabulary, to investigate query formation techniques, to explore the possibility of automatic translation, and to enhance query formulation by using a Thai thesaurus.

C.A. Peters et al. (Eds.): CLEF 2001, LNCS 2406, pp. 209–218, 2002.

In accordance with these objectives, our four official runs were a single dictionary mapping, multiple dictionary mapping, manual and automatic segmentation, query expansion using a Thai thesaurus.

We used shareable or public MRDs in our experiments.

The rest of this paper is as follows. Section 2 briefly reports related work in Thai text information retrieval. Summaries of relevant Thai CLIR resources are given in Section 3.. Our experimental design is described inSsection 4. Experimental results are presented in the last section.

2   Related Work

In this section, the state of the art of Thai computer processing and Thai Natural Language Processing is briefly discussed to help understand current available technology, which plays an important role in the CLIR.

2.1   Computer Processing of Thai

Attempts to work with the Thai language on the computer started when computers were first introduced into the country more than four decades ago. There are no special characters to separate words from phrases and sentences in the Thai writing system. To overcome this problem, artificial intelligence, natural language processing, and computational linguistics techniques have been exhaustively studied. These studies resulted in the establishment of the machine translation project by the National Electronics and Computer Technology Center (NECTEC) in 1980 [4]. Additionally, some research has been promoted commercially, for example, hand-held electronic dictionaries and translators from English to Thai (Pasit) [5], Thai spelling checker software and word segmentation programs.

2.2   Thai Text Retrieval

Most Thai text retrieval systems use segmentation algorithms. Automatic extraction of keywords from documents is a nontrivial task. Trie Structure, along with dictionary based word segmentation, is proposed in [6] to solve the problem of unknown words. However, only the indexing process is presented, there is no report on retrieval effectiveness. The work done in [7] contributed more to research in information retrieval. The paper presented a number of comparisons of methods for segmentation, indexing techniques and the term weighting systems for Thai text retrieval. Three indexing methods were proposed, ngram-based, word-based and rule-based. When applying the term weight system, the segmentation process has little effect on retrieval performances. All the performance metrics have been tested on Thai news documents. The collection size is about 8 MB with 4800 documents. Additionally, the SMART text retrieval system [8] was used. Another indexing technique, the signature file, has been proposed for indexing Thai Text in [9]. This paper studied the number of bits for representing each document signature; the test collection used was the Thai Holy Bible.

2.3   Research in CLIR for Thai

Some Thai research papers [10-12] present work in the area of CLIR. All the techniques reported are based on the use of transliterated words. The paper in [10] presented transliterated word encoding algorithms and created 5000 Thai-English personal names. Retrieval effectiveness was evaluated using this database. This paper claimed CLIR effectiveness of 69% and 73% for precision and recall. The second paper [11] is from the same research lab, and aimed at achieving better precision and recall of over 80% for CLIR. Their CLIR model retrieved documents containing either English or Thai transliterated words using phonetic codes for keywords. The phonetic coding is based on the Soundex coding of Odell and Russell. The result of their experiment was evaluated with Thai-English transliterated words taken from the Royal Academy transliteration Guidelines, Science Dictionary, Mathematics Dictionary, Chemistry Book1: High School Level. Most of the words are proper nouns, and technical terms. The last paper [12] also presented transliteration from Thai to English to solve the problem of loan words. This paper focuses more on solving loan word problems such as non-native accents, information loss and orthographic translation. Two processes are used to identify loan words. First, explicit unknown words are recognized by mapping against the Thai dictionary. Secondly, hidden unknown words, which are composed of one or more known words, are identified by frequency checking. However, it is unclear how these algorithms can be applied to work with CLIR.

In Asian CLIR research, the best-known methods are dictionary-based and query translation strategies are employed [13-14]. The work done in [13], also employed a dictionary-based method for Indonesian-English Cross-Language Text Retrieval. Local-feedback techniques are applied to expand the query terms to improve retrieval effectiveness. Chen and his colleagues [14] worked on Japanese English cross language. They examined the segmentation problem for Japanese, including a number of technical terms in their study. To increase the size of the vocabulary, a parallel corpus is employed. They stated that CLIR retrieval effectiveness was affected by the coverage of terms in the dictionary

3   Resources Available for Thai CLIR

The most important resource for CLIR is a bilingual dictionary. In our survey of bilingual electronic dictionaries, a number of Thai-English bilingual electronic dictionaries were found, for example:- the Thai internet education project [15], an Online Thai Dictionary (Seasite) [2], and LEXiTRON [1]. Only the last two dictionaries provide a complete electronic form. However, the Seasite dictionary needs to be re-encoded since the original encoding system is different from the current system. The total number of words in each dictionary is 16,060 and 11,188 for LEXiTRON and Seasite respectively. A machine-readable Thai thesaurus is not publicly available. We prepared our own Thai thesaurus from [16]. Around 20,000 Thai thesaurus words were collected and used in this research.

Another important resource is a Thai segmentation program. Processing of the Thai language has been ongoing for more than three decades. The free resource for breaking phrases or sentences into words is Wordbreak from NECTEC [3] and from

University of Massachusetts [7]. In [7], Wordbreak, from NECTEC, was shown to be most effective in the segmentation process.

Therefore, in our CLIR research, we used LEXiTRON, and Seasite to check the coverage of the vocabulary used in the automatic query translation. Additionally, for automatic translation, the segmentation process needs to be verified and Wordbreak (Swath) from the NECTEC was used for this.

4   Experimental Design

The Thai CLEF experiment was for the bilingual task. English documents were retrieved from Thai topics. Since Thai is not an official language in the CLEF, no topic is provided by CLEF. Thus, the CLEF's English topics were chosen and translated manually into two types of Thai queries. One is segmented Thai queries by human and the other is like the normal Thai writing system. The Swath's NECTEC is used to break phrases or sentences of the unsegmented Thai queries into words. The disadvantage of manual translation is that it relies on human judgment and may be biased. Then we apply the dictionary mapping techniques to translate the Thai queries back to English queries. In the dictionary lookup process, if any words are unable to be looked up, the process will leave that word from the topic. Thus, the concept terms or relevant terms may not be included. The four official runs, which rely on the query formation, are as follows.

(a) Single Mapping: The bilingual Thai-English definition trend to give several senses or meanings. Thus, English queries are translated by using single dictionary mapping, and only the first map is selected for translation.

(b) Multiple Mapping: Since the first map did not always give the right translation. This second run, English queries are replaced with all meanings found in the dictionary.

(c) Single Mapping and Segmentation: The unsegmented Thai queries are segmented using the NECTEC wordbreak program and single mapping is applied for the query translation.

(d) Query Expansion: Thai thesaurus words are added to the queries created using single mapping. The expansion of query terms is done before translation.

In order to test the coverage of terms in a electronic dictionary, the SEASITE dictionary is used to translate English queries. Figure 1 shows our experimental design. The SMART system from Cornell University [8] is used to measure the retrieval effectiveness of our Thai CLIR. In all runs, stop words and stemming were applied to the queries and to the text collection. Term weights were applied to the document collection.

The documents collection, the Los Angeles Times for 1994, was indexed using the SMART vector model. The English queries were indexed based on the long query format, or on the descriptions, identified by the <DESC> marked tag. Although SMART is based on the vector model, we did not modify the original topics. When a query was sent to the system, the 1,000 highest-ranked records were returned.

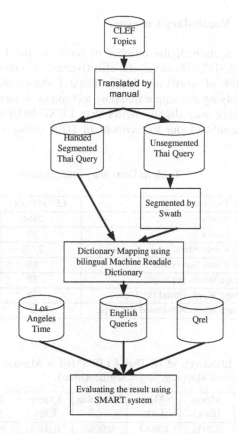

Fig. 1. The Thai CLIR Experiment

The dictionary terms of the dictionary mapping algorithms were loaded into the MySQL database. The mapping algorithm was deployed using Java technology and running in a Linux Environment.

5   Results

We have learned from [17-18], that retrieval effectiveness of CLIR based on dictionary mapping, will drop by about a half.. The retrieval results were below this worse when we tested our Thai-CLIR system on the CLEF text collection. Previously, this method for Thai CLIR was experimented with ZIFF TREC collection. The retrieval results dropped by about 40% [18]. The following subsections report our Thai CLIR results in detail.

5.1   Dictionary Vocabulary Coverage

As mentioned in Section 3, the number of terms in the LEXiTRON dictionary is greater than in SEASITE. However, the effectiveness of both dictionaries is almost the same and over 90% of words are found. Table 1 shows the characteristics of Thai queries. When applying the single mapping technique, it turns out that the SEASITE retrieval performance was slightly better than LEXiTRON (See Table 2.), which is contrary to the results of our experiment in [18]. However, this difference is not significant.

Table 1. Dictionary Effectiveness

Using Dictionary	LEXiTRON	SEASITE
Total Words	2864	2864
Total Topics	50	50
Total Words Found	2778	2746
Total Words Not-Found	86	118
Average Words Per Topic	58	58
Average Words Found Per Topic	55	54
Average Words Not-Found Per Topic	2	3

Table 2. Retrieval Effectiveness of Thai CLIR (Man = Manual, Lex = LEXiTRON, Sea= SEASIE, Mul = Multiple Mapping, Seg = Segmentation)

Recall Level	Mono (Eng)	Man Lex.	Man. Sea	Query Exp.	Mul. Lex.	Seg.
at 0.00	0.2932	0.0041	0.0065	0.0015	0.0014	0.0120
at 0.10	0.2111	0.0016	0.0054	0.0007	0.0004	0.0054
at 0.20	0.1583	0.0012	0.0040	0.0004	0.0002	0.0016
at 0.30	0.1207	0.0011	0.0039	0.0003	0.0000	0.0014
at 0.40	0.1035	0.0010	0.0034	0.0000	0.0000	0.0014
at 0.50	0.0864	0.0008	0.0032	0.0000	0.0000	0.0012
at 0.60	0.0680	0.0008	0.0031	0.0000	0.0000	0.0007
at 0.70	0.0574	0.0005	0.0031	0.0000	0.0000	0.0007
at 0.80	0.0422	0.0005	0.0031	0.0000	0.0000	0.0007
at 0.90	0.0335	0.0005	0.0031	0.0000	0.0000	0.0007
at 1.00	0.0294	0.0005	0.0031	0.0000	0.0000	0.0007
Rel_ret	589	41	54	26	24	46
Avg:	0.1094	0.0012	0.0038	0.0003	0.0002	0.0026

5.2   The Effect of the Segmentation Algorithm in CLIR

As mentioned in Section 3 for automatic query translation, the effectiveness of the current technology for segmenting phrases or sentences into words needs to be verified. In our experiment, it is not clear whether the segmentation has affected the CLIR results. Though it has been reported in [18] that segmentation is effective in CLIR, we were unable to prove in this in our experiment. In our discussion, we focus on topic translation techniques from English to Thai. In our first experiment, the researcher used a dictionary to translate from English to Thai and to try to break words according to the mapping of the word in the dictionary. Some unofficial reports state that the terms given in the Thai-bilingual electronic dictionary are the smallest terms with meaning. Thus, some manually segmented words cannot be found in the dictionary. However, the percentage of words found was quite high. Therefore, when we compared the original query with the translated query, we found that only 15 percent of words match. This means words, which are found in the dictionary, are not relevant to the search terms.

Table 3 shows the significant differences in retrieval between manual and automatic segmentation after modifying Thai topics. The modifying of Thai topics was done by deleting Thai stopwords from the Thai queries (see discussion in next section).

Table 3. Retrieval Effectiveness after Modifying Thai Topics.

Recall Level	Mono (Eng)	Man Lex.	Man. Sea	Query Exp	Mul. Lex.	Seg.
at 0.00	0.2932	0.0471	0.0163	0.0111	0.0381	0.0153
at 0.10	0.2111	0.0294	0.0142	0.0048	0.0246	0.0061
at 0.20	0.1583	0.0202	0.0127	0.0037	0.0155	0.0055
at 0.30	0.1207	0.0156	0.0118	0.0030	0.0119	0.0039
at 0.40	0.1035	0.0110	0.0112	0.0018	0.0094	0.0024
at 0.50	0.0864	0.0083	0.0110	0.0015	0.0063	0.0023
at 0.60	0.0680	0.0060	0.0107	0.0015	0.0046	0.0010
at 0.70	0.0574	0.0039	0.0107	0.0015	0.0039	0.0009
at 0.80	0.0422	0.0025	0.0107	0.0015	0.0026	0.0009
at 0.90	0.0335	0.0014	0.0107	0.0015	0.0026	0.0009
at 1.00	0.0294	0.0014	0.0107	0.0015	0.0026	0.0009
Rel_ret	589	278	70	76	230	119
Avg:	0.1094	0.0133	0.0119	0.0030	0.0026	0.0036

5.3   CLIR Effectiveness

Table 2 shows the results of our techniques. Not all techniques achieve retrieval effectiveness. Query expansion by adding Thai thesaurus terms does not only decrease the recall/precision but the retrieval effectiveness also drops.

Compared to our previous results [18], in which the retrieval effectiveness is around 40% of the monolingual retrieval, there are many differences in the design process which can be summarized as fellows:

1. The manual translation techniques from English to Thai: As mention in section 4.2, our previous translation technique is based on the vocabulary in the dictionary terms.

2. Query length: Our previous query topics are translated from the <TITLE> tag. The Thai keywords from the <TITLE> tag are more relevant to the retrieval system since the translation process was biased. In this experiment, the query topics are translated from <DESC> tag and avoid consulting the dictionary. Although, there are more terms, most of the terms are not specific to the query or are more general. As we learned from expanding the query topics with Thai thesaurus, this does not increase the retrieval effectiveness.

3. Thai stopword and Thai stemming: Relatively few intensive studies in Thai stopword and stemming have been reported. Some Thai stopwords are reported in [7]. It is not clear whether the Thai language has stemming properties. The words 'การ:kan:when prefixed to a noun, indicate action and 'ความ:kwam:when prefixed to an adjunctive indicates state, condition. Removing or not removing can impact retrieval effectiveness, language knowledge is needed to assess this. When a Thai prefix is removed, the meaning of the stem word may not relate to the original meaning. Therefore, adding these stem words will degrade retrieval effectiveness.

To prove the above claims, Thai topics were modified using human judgment; some Thai stopwords were removed from the topics, and search terms were selected which can be found in the dictionary. Using these modified topics, the retrieval effectiveness improved by 1.5 of the queries in which no Thai stopwords had been removed (see Table 3). Retrieval performance increases to 40% of a monolingual retrieval. However, the retrieval effectiveness still does not achieve the level of CLIR, which deployed dictionary mapping techniques.

The results in Table 3 restored our confidence. They showed that the number of terms in the LEXiTRON has more coverage than SEASITE, that the segmentation process still is a critical issue in CLIR for Thai, and that adding Thai thesaurus terms does not improve retrieval effectiveness. There are some variations in average precision for individual queries.

5.4   Implementation of Thai CLIR

The algorithm for Thai CLIR has been implemented and has been made publicly accessible at http://www.cs.sci.ku.ac.th/~ThaiIr/CLIR/demo. The web demo receives Thai keywords from users and translates them using single dictionary mapping. The results of the translation are sent back and the user can select the English keywords. The query is sent to Google or Altavista to search English web pages. Furthermore, the results of cross language retrieval can be translated from English to Thai by Pasit. This part of the demonstration program was supported by NECTEC.

6   Discussion

The Thai CLIR experiments faced the same problems as other MRD-based CLIR work. The fundamental problems in MRD-based CLIR are as follows: phrase translation, handling polysemy and dictionary coverage. Phrase translation is very critical for Thai CLIR. Some Thai words may be classified as sentences or phrases. Therefore, phrase translation is dependent on the segmentation process. Research on segmentation algorithms in Thailand can be classified into two types. The first (and preferable) segmentation is based on the longest matching word. The second research direction segments text into the smallest possible words. Theoretically, these smallest words can form new words. Electronic dictionaries are based on the first approach.

We also have learned that research in the area of CLIR, not only requires knowledge from the information retrieval field but also requires knowledge and resources from Machine Translation. Although the Machine Translation project has been activated for more than 4 decades, the resources from the MRD are still very limited and are not yet ready for public dissemination. Thus, there exists a need to accelerate research in this area.

The feed-back from our Web demonstration shows that Thai-CLIR users are quite satisfied the Thai-CLIR system. Unfortunately, in research experiments, not all query translation techniques can achieve their objectives. This raises awareness in the Thai-CLIR area. The basic infrastructure for CLIR in Thai needs urgently needs further development.

7   Future Work

In this CLIR research experiment, the fundamentals of CLIR research have been established. A number of research techniques will enhance Thai-CLIR performance by solving term disambiguation problems, detecting transliterated words, and using local feedback. The most important point is that the MRDs must make data in electronic form availablefor the research community.

References

1. LEXiTRON, Thai<->English Dictionary, Software and Language Engineering Laboratory, National Electronics and Computer Technology Center, http://www.links.nectec.or.th/lexit/lex_t.html (downloaded in June, 2001)
2. Online Thai English Dictionary, Northern Illinois University, www.seasite.niu.edu/Thai/home_page/online_thai_dictionaries.htm (download in June 2001)
3. Thai Wordbreak Insertion Services, National Electronics and Computer Technology Center, URL:http://ntl.nectec.or.th/services/wordbreak/ (downloaded in June, 2001)
4. Sophonpanich Kalaya, The R&D Activities of MT in Thailand, The National Electronics and Computer Technology Center, Bangkok, Thailand.
5. Parsit, Information Research and Development Division, National Electronics and Computer Technology Center, http://www.links.nectec.or.th/services/parsit/index2.html (downloaded in June, 2001)
6. Kanlayanawat W., and Prasitjutrakul S., Automatic Indexing for Thai Text with Unknown Words using Trie Structure, Department of Computer Engineering, Chulalongkorn University.
7. Jaruskulchai C., An Automatic Indexing for Thai Text Retrieval, Ph.D. Thesis, George Washington University, U.S.A., Aug 1998.
8. SMART, ftp.cs.cornell.edu/pub/smart/smart.11.0.tar.z
9. Charoenkitkarn, N., and Udomporntawee, R. Optimal Text Signature Length for Word Searching on Thai Holy Bible(in Thai). Proceeding of Electrical Engineering Conference, KMUTT, Bangkok, November 1998, 549-552.
10. Suwanvisat Prayut and Prasitjutrakul Somchai, Transliterated Word Encoding and Retrieval Algorithms for Thai-English Cross-Language Retrieval.
11. Suwanvisat P. and Prasijutrakul S., Thai-English Cross-Language Transliterated Word Retrieval Soundex Technique, NCSEC2000.

12. Kawtrakul A., Deemagarn A., Thumkanon C., Khantonthong N and McFetridge Paul., Backward Transliteration for Thai Document Retrieval, Natural Language Processing and Intelligent Information System Technology, Research Laboratory, Dept. of Computer Engineering, Kasetsart University, Bangkok, Thailand.
13. Adriani M., and Croft Bruce, The Effectiveness of a Dictionary-Based Technique for Indonesian-English Cross-Language Text Retrieval, Center for Intelligent Information Retrieval, Computer Science Department, University of Massachusetts, USA.
14. Chen, Gey, Kishida, Jiang and Liang, Comparing multiple methods for Japanese and Japanese-English text retrieval, Working Notes of the Cross-Language Evaluation Forum 2000, http://www.clef-campaign.org
15. The Thai Internet Education Project, http://www.cyberc.com/crcl/ehelp/base.htm (doug@crcl.chula.edu: Contract person, downloaded in June, 2001)
16. Yuen Phuwarawan and team, Thai Thesaurus, in Thai, Ed publisher.
17. Pirkola Ari, The Effects of Query Structure and Dictionary Setups in Dictionary-Based Cross-language Information Retrieval, SIGIR'98
18. Sripimonwan V. and Jaruskulchai C., Cross-Language Retrieval from Thai to English (in Thai), submitted to The Fifth National Computer Science and Engineering Conference, Thailand.

English-Dutch CLIR Using Query Translation Techniques

Mirna Adriani

Department of Computing Science
University of Glasgow
Glasgow G12 8QQ, Scotland
mirna@dcs.gla.ac.uk

Abstract. We present a report on our participation in the English-Dutch bilingual task of the 2001 Cross-Language Evaluation Forum (CLEF). We attempted to demonstrate that good cross-language query translation results can be obtained by combining dictionary based and parallel corpus based approaches. A parallel corpus based technique was used to choose the best sense from all possible senses found in the dictionary. However, our results demonstrate that a pure dictionary based technique produces the best query translation as compared to a pure parallel corpus based and the combined techniques. We also show that improvement in retrieval effectiveness can be obtained using a query expansion technique.

1 Introduction

This year the University of Glasgow IR-group participated in the bilingual task of the 2001 Cross Language Evaluation Forum (CLEF), i.e., the English-Dutch Cross-Language Information Retrieval (CLIR). Our work was focused on the bilingual task using English queries to retrieve documents from the Dutch collections. We employed a dictionary based query translation technique using a publicly available dictionary from the Internet. From the previous year's work, we were aware of the fact that the quality of the free dictionary was not as good as a complete dictionary, especially, in terms of the size of vocabulary and senses. We hope that we will be able to improve on our results using other resources in the future.

We also used a parallel corpus that was made available for this forum to create a glossary table, i.e., a table of cross-language term co-occurrence. The parallel corpus is available from RALI, a research laboratory at the University of Montreal, that collected parallel (in multiple languages) web-pages from the Internet automatically. A set of linguistic tools was used to automatically identify the language of the pages and extract parallel sentences from pairs of parallel documents. Nie et.al. [6] reported good CLIR results from applying statistical methods to the parallel corpus.

CLIR work on an Dutch-English corpus was done in CLEF 2000. Since no Dutch collection was provided in that year, groups who participated in the task used the

C.A. Peters et al. (Eds.): CLEF 2001, LNCS 2406, pp. 219–225, 2002.
© Springer-Verlag Berlin Heidelberg 2002

Dutch queries to retrieve documents in the English collection. Similar to German, Dutch has many compound terms consisting of several words each. We found a large number of Dutch compound terms that are not very common and, thus, rarely found in dictionaries. This is one of the major challenges in CLIR involving Dutch and other similar languages. De Vries [8] and Hiemstra et.al [5] showed that by applying a compound word splitter to Dutch compound query terms and translating the individual words separately, better retrieval performance can be obtained.

2   The Query Translation Process

In this section, we describe how our query translation process operates using the dictionary and the parallel corpus, and how we improve the retrieval performance using a query expansion technique

Our dictionary-based query translation technique translates each term in a given query to another language by replacing it with the translation senses of that term in the dictionary. Obviously, there are problems with such a simple translation technique, mainly, the ambiguity of the term, the difficulty of translating phrases, and problems with terms that are not found in the dictionary such as acronyms or technical terms. These problems result in very poor retrieval performance of the translation queries.

First, we translate each of the English query terms using the dictionary. Then we use a glossary table created from the Dutch-English parallel corpus to select the best translation terms. Finally, we expand the resulting query by adding more terms into the query to improve its performance.

2.1   The Glossary Table

We use the RALI Dutch-English parallel corpus that has been aligned at sentence level to create a glossary table. The glossary table contains lists of possible Dutch translations for each English term, weighted by their degree of parallel co-location in the corpus. The weights are computed using a statistical method.

First, we make sure that the parallel sentences from the corpus do not contain any noise. Due to some inaccuracy in the automatic parallel corpus creation, there are many misclassified documents where Dutch documents are classified as English and vice versa. Also, there are English documents that contain Dutch words and vice versa. We filtered out misclassified sentences using stopword lists. If a Dutch sentence contains at least one English stopword then it is discarded, as is an English sentence that contains at least one Dutch stopword. Although this technique may exclude correctly classified source sentences that happen to contain one or two terms of the target (opposite) language, the detrimental effect of using a misclassified sentence is much worse than incorrectly excluding a sentence. After this filtering process, the resulting parallel corpus contains 62,536 sentences.

The weights of English-Dutch term pairs in the glossary table entry are computed using the following Jaccard's coefficient formula:

$$PT = tf_{ED} / (tf_E + tf_D - tf_{ED})$$

where

PT = the probability that an English term is a translation of a Dutch term

tf_{ED} = the frequency of English and the Dutch terms occurring together

tf_E = the occurrence frequency of the English term

tf_D = the occurrence frequency of the Dutch term

For each English term in the sentence, we obtain the Dutch translation term from the parallel sentences with the highest PT. Below are some sample entries in the glossary table and their PT values:

4.5946 *find-vind*
5.5946 *human-humaan*
6.6868 *indian-indisch*
6.7637 *russia-rusland*

2.2 Choosing the Best Translation Term

The dictionary based query translation technique produces one or more translation terms in the target language for each term in the source language. A sense disambiguation technique is used to choose the best possible translation term. Given an English query term, we perform the sense disambiguation process as follows:

1. Obtain the Dutch translation terms of the English term from the dictionary.
2. Obtain entries in the glossary table for the English term.
3. Select the Dutch translation term from terms obtained in step 1 that has the highest PT value in the entries obtained in step 2.
4. If the English term is not found in the dictionary but has entries in the glossary table then select the Dutch term from the glossary entry that has the highest *PT* value.
5. If the English term is not found in either the dictionary or the glossary table then it is taken without translation.

2.3 Query Expansion Technique

Expanding translation queries has been shown to improve CLIR effectiveness by many researchers. One of the query expansion techniques is called *pseudo relevance feedback* [3]. This technique is based on the assumption that the top few documents retrieved in the initial query are indeed relevant to the query, and so they must contain other terms that are also relevant to the query. The query expansion technique adds such terms to the original queries. We employ this technique in this work. In choosing the good terms from the top ranked documents, we use the $tf*idf$ term weighting formula [7]. We add a number of terms that have the highest weight values into the query.

3 Experiment

In the experiments we used the Dutch document collection containing 190,604 documents from two Dutch newspapers, the *Algemeen Dagblad* and the *NRC Handelsblad*. We opted to use the combination of the query title and description as our query for all of the 50 topics provided. In addition to the combined dictionary and parallel corpus based technique we also conducted experiments using pure dictionary based and pure parallel corpus based query translation techniques.

All the query translation process was performed fully automatically. Stopwords were removed from the English queries and the remaining terms were stemmed using the Porter word stemmer. For the pure dictionary based translation technique, we simply included all possible translation terms found in the dictionary, i.e., without any sense disambiguation. If phrases in the queries were not found in the dictionary, they were translated by translating the individual constituent terms. For the pure parallel corpus based translation technique, we simply selected the translation term in the glossary entry that has the highest *PT* value. In these two techniques, English terms that were not found in the dictionary or in the glossary table were taken as-is without translation.

We used a machine-readable dictionary downloaded from the Internet at http://www.freedict.com. This dictionary contains short translations of English words in a number of languages. We realized that the dictionary was not ideal for our purpose, as most of its entries contain only one or two senses. However, its free availability outweighs its limitation. We reformatted the dictionary files so that our query translator program can read them. The dictionary contains 9,972 entries.

Finally, we applied the pseudo relevance feedback query expansion technique to the result of the combined dictionary and parallel corpus based technique. We used the top 20 and 30 documents to extract the expansion terms. Any Dutch stopwords in the translation queries and pseudo relevance feedback documents were removed.

In these experiments, we used the INQUERY information retrieval system [4] to index and retrieve the documents. Terms in the Dutch queries and documents were stemmed using the Dutch stemmer from Muscat (see http://open.muscat.com).

4 Results

The result that we submitted (code-named *glaenl*) is from the combined dictionary and parallel corpus based technique. Table 1 shows the result of our experiments. The retrieval performance of the translation queries obtained using the dictionary based technique falls 34.55% below that of the equivalent monolingual query (see Table 1). The performance of the pure parallel corpus based query translation technique is the worst, i.e., 60.46% below that of the monolingual query. The retrieval performance of the combined method is 40.80% below the monolingual performance. This suggests that the parallel corpus based sense disambiguation technique worsened the performance of the dictionary based translation queries by 5.25%.

Table 1. The average retrieval precision of the monolingual runs and the bilingual runs using English queries translated into Dutch using dictionary only, parallel corpus only, and combined dictionary and parallel corpus techniques.

Task	P/R	% Change
Monolingual	0.3238	-
Dictionary	0.2119	-34.55
Parallel corpus	0.1280	-60.46
Dictionary & P corpus	0.1917	-40.80

Table 2. The average retrieval precision of the translation queries expanded using the top 30-document method.

Query translated using Dict & PC	5 terms	10 terms	20 terms	30 terms
0.1917	0.2002 (+4.43%)	0.2003 (+4.49%)	0.2048 (+6.86%)	0.2074 (+8.20%)

Table 3. The average retrieval precision of the translation queries expanded using the top 20-document method.

Query translated using Dict & PC	5 terms	10 terms	20 terms	30 terms
0.1917	0.2123 (+10.72%)	0.2111 (+10.13%)	0.2116 (+10.39%)	0.2205 (+15.01%)

The performance of the translation queries using the pure dictionary-based technique is better than that of using only the glossary table. This correlates with the number of terms in the queries that are not found the dictionary and the glossary table.

Out of 569 English terms, there are 135 terms that are not found in the dictionary and 260 terms that are not found in the glossary table.

As we assumed that translating the queries using the combined dictionary and glossary technique would perform better than the other techniques, we applied the query expansion only to the queries obtained using the combined technique. We used the top 20 and 30 documents in the pseudo relevance feedback to get the list of best terms. Then we added the top 5, 10, 20, and 30 terms to the translated queries. The result shows that the query expansion can improve the retrieval performance by 4% to 15% (see Table 2 and 3). The best retrieval performance was achieved by adding 30 terms from the top 20 documents into the queries. It increased the average retrieval performance of the translated queries by 15.01% (see Table 3).

Dutch is one of the languages that use compound words. It has been shown that applying a compound-word splitter can result in better retrieval performance [3]. Unfortunately, we do not have any Dutch compound-word splitter that could have improved the entries of our glossary table. In our previous work [1, 2], we showed that German queries can be better translated into English than Spanish queries because German compound words have non-ambiguous meanings in English as compared to Spanish phrases which have to be translated word by word using a dictionary. In other words, the degree of ambiguity of the German queries is less than that of the Spanish queries or queries in other languages that do not use compound terms. Hence, translating queries from English to Dutch is a more difficult task as it involves translating multi-word terms into single-word compound terms.

5 Summary

Our results demonstrate that using freely available bilingual dictionaries can produce a cross-language retrieval performance which is somewhat superior to that obtained using more expensive parallel corpora. However, it also depends on the breadth of the topic coverage of the dictionary and the parallel corpus used. Given more sophisticated linguistic tools such as compound-word splitters and part of speech taggers, a parallel corpus based technique is likely to perform as effective, if not more, than the dictionary based approach. Our future research will study the use of such linguistics tools and knowledge in improving CLIR query translation techniques.

References

1. Adriani, M. and C.J. van Rijsbergen. Term Similarity Based Query Expansion for Cross Language Information Retrieval. In *Proceedings of Research and Advanced Technology for Digital Libraries*, ECDL'99, p. 311-322. Springer Verlag: Paris, September 1999.
2. Adriani, M. Ambiguity Problem in Multilingual Information Retrieval. . In *CLEF 2000 Proceedings, Lecture Notes in Computer Science* 2069, Springer 2001, 156-165.
3. Attar, R. and A. S. Fraenkel. *Local Feedback in Full-Text Retrieval Systems*. Journal of the Association for Computing Machinery, 24: 397-417, 1977.

4.   Callan, J. P., Croft, W.B., Harding, S.M.. The Inquery Retrieval System. In *Proceedings of Third International Conference on Database and Expert Systems Applications*, 1992.
5.   Hiemstra, Djoerd, Wessel Kraaij, Renee Pohlmann, and Thijs Westerveld. Twenty-One at CLEF-2000: Translation resources, merging strategies and relevance feedback. In *CLEF 2000 Proceedings, Lecture Notes in Computer Science* 2069, 102-115.
6.   Nie, J. Y., P. Isabelle, M. Simard, and R. Durand. Cross-language Information Retrieval Based on Parallel Texts and Automatic Mining of Parallel Texts From the Web. In *Proceedings of the SIGIR 1999 Conference*, p. 74-81. Berkeley, 1999.
7.   Salton, Gerard, and McGill, Michael J. *Introduction to Modern Information Retrieval*, New York: McGraw-Hill, 1983.
8.   De Vries, Arjen P. A Poor Man's Approach to CLEF. In *CLEF 2000 Proceedings, Lecture Notes in Computer Science* 2069, Springer 2001, 149-155.

Thomson Legal and Regulatory at CLEF 2001: Monolingual and Bilingual Experiments

Hugo Molina-Salgado, Isabelle Moulinier, Mark Knudson, Elizabeth Lund, and Kirat Sekhon

Thomson Legal & Regulatory
610 Opperman Drive, Eagan MN 55123, USA,
Isabelle.Moulinier@westgroup.com

Abstract. Thomson Legal and Regulatory participated in the monolingual track for all five languages and in the bilingual track with Spanish-English runs. Our monolingual runs for Dutch, Spanish and Italian use settings and rules derived from our runs in French and German last year. Our bilingual runs compared merging strategies for query translation resources.

1 Introduction

Thomson Legal and Regulatory (TLR) participated in CLEF-2001 with two goals: to verify reuse of rules and settings inside a family of languages for monolingual retrieval, and to start our effort on bilingual retrieval.

In our monolingual runs, we considered Dutch and German as being one family of languages, while French, Spanish and Italian formed another. We used the parameters we derived from our runs at CLEF-2000 for German and French for each language in their respective family. In addition, we investigated the use of phrases for French and Spanish document retrieval.

Our first attempt at the bilingual track was from Spanish queries to English documents. In that task, we experimented with combining various resources for query translation. Our submitted runs used similarity thesauri and a machine-readable dictionary to translate a Spanish query into a single English query. We also compared our official runs with the merging of individual runs, one per translation resource. While we also conducted experiments using French and English, we did not submit any official runs.

In this paper, we briefly present our search engine and the settings common to all experiments in Section 2. Section 3 discusses our bilingual effort, while Section 4 describes our participation in the monolingual track.

2 General System Description

The WIN system is a full-text natural language search engine, and corresponds to TLR/West Group's implementation of the inference network retrieval model. While based on the same retrieval model as the INQUERY system [1], WIN

C.A. Peters et al. (Eds.): CLEF 2001, LNCS 2406, pp. 226–234, 2002.
© Springer-Verlag Berlin Heidelberg 2002

has evolved separately and focused on the retrieval of legal material in large collections in a commercial environment that supports both Boolean and natural language searches [6].

WIN has also been modified to support non-English document retrieval. This included localization of tokenization rules (for instance, handling elision for French and Italian) and stemming. Stemming of non-English terms is performed using a third-party toolkit, the LinguistX platform commercialized by Inxight. A variant of the Porter stemmer is used for English.

The WIN engine supports various strategies for computing term beliefs and document scores. We used a standard tf-idf for computing term beliefs in all our runs. Among all the variants, we retained document scoring and portion scoring. Document scoring assigns a score to the document as a whole. This was used in our bilingual runs. Portion scoring finds the best dynamic portion in a document and combines the score of the best portion to the score of the whole document. Portion scoring can be considered as an approximation of paragraph scoring (we used this setting last year for French), when documents have no paragraph. We used portion scoring in our monolingual runs.

A WIN query consists of concepts extracted from natural language text. Normal WIN query processing eliminates stopwords and noise phrases (or introductory phrases), recognizes phrases or other important concepts for special handling, and detects misspellings. Many of the concepts ordinarily recognized by WIN are specific to English documents, in particular within the legal domain. Query processing in WIN usually relies on various resources: a stopword list, a list of noise phrases ("Find cases about...", "A relevant document describes...") , a dictionary of (legal) phrases, and a list of common misspelled terms.

We used stopword and noise phrases lists for all languages, while for French and monolingual Spanish, we also used a phrase dictionary. We used our French and German stopword lists from last year, the Dutch list given on the CLEF homepage, and compiled Spanish and Italian stopword lists from various sources on the Web. For all languages, we extracted introductory phrases from the query sets of previous CLEF and TREC conferences. As we had no Italian speaker in our team, our introductory list in Italian is very limited and simple.

Finally, we submitted two sets of runs: runs including only the title and description fields from the CLEF topic, and runs including the whole topic. The former runs are labeled with 'td' and doubled weighted the title fields. The latter are labeled with 'tdn' and used a weight of 4 for the title field, 2 for the description field, and 1 for the narrative.

3   Bilingual Retrieval Experiments and Results

In our bilingual runs, we concentrated on query translation and more specifically the combination of various translation resources. We used three main resources, a machine-readable dictionary (MRD) that we downloaded from the Internet[1]

---

[1] We downloaded dictionaries from http://www.freedict.com.

and two different similarity thesauri. Coverage of these resources is reported in Table 1.

Table 1. Coverage of the translation resources used

	Dictionary	Unigram Thesaurus	Bigram Thesaurus
Spanish	19,466 terms	33,674 terms	42,081 bigrams
French	35,273 terms	43,644 terms	66,099 bigrams

We implemented a variant of the similarity thesaurus approach described in [3] for multilingual retrieval. We used a parallel corpus to generate two different thesauri: a unigram thesaurus and a bigram thesaurus. Our intent with the bigram thesaurus was to capture some phrase translations. For instance, the bigram *south pacific* is found as a translation of the French *pacifique sud* or the Spanish *pacífico sur*, and *iraq peopl* as a translation of French *peuple iraquien* or *population iraquien*. We limited the number of bigrams by constraining bigrams to not contain stopwords, and by frequency thresholding. We used at most 15 translations from each thesaurus, and also used a threshold on the similarity to filter out translations that we thought would not be helpful. This threshold was determined on training data from CLEF 2000. We used all translations from the MRD. In all cases, multiple translations of the same source term were grouped as the same concept given a translation source.

We investigated two main approaches to combine our translation resources: a priori merging, i.e. combining translations during query construction, and a posteriori merging, i.e. merging runs produced by queries translated from a single resource. For a posteriori merging, we used a score-based and a rank-based technique to generate the merged score. The score-based technique relies on a feature of the WIN engine. WIN computes the best score a document can achieve for a given query. We used that maximum score to normalize individual runs. Normalized runs are merged in a straightforward manner. The rank-based technique is also fairly simple. The score in the merged result list is a function of the ranks in the original lists. Here, we report experiments using the sum of the logarithms of the document rank in each run.

3.1   Spanish-English Bilingual Runs

We submitted official runs from Spanish queries to English documents, although we also ran experiments from French to English. Our official runs relied on the a priori approach, combining translations during construction. Runs tlres2entdw and tlres2entdnw combined only the unigram thesaurus to the dictionary, while runs tlres2entdb and tlres2entdb combined both thesauri with the dictionary. In Table 2, we also report a posteriori merging using the following conversion: b refers to the bigram thesaurus, u to the unigram thesaurus and d to the dictionary. The different scoring methods are indicated by an s for score and r for rank. Thus, the run labeled es_b+u+d_r_tdn refers to combining both thesauri and the MRD using rank-based merging for a Spanish-English run. In all cases, terms not found in any resource were left intact in the query. Both similarity thesauri were trained on the same parallel corpus, the UN parallel text corpus produced by the Linguistic Data Consortium.

Table 2. Results from our bilingual Spanish to English experiments.

Official runs (a priori merging)

Run	Avg. Prec.	R-Prec.	Performance of individual queries				
			Best	Above	Median	Below	Worst
Tlres2entdw	0.3846	0.3914	5	26	1	13	2
Tlres2entdb	0.3909	0.3914	6	26	1	12	2
Tlres2entdnw	0.4264	0.4234	6	29	1	9	2
Tlres2entdnb	0.4338	0.4291	6	30	1	8	2

Unofficial runs (a posteriori merging)

Run	Avg. Prec.	R-Prec.	Run	Avg. Prec.	R-Prec.
es_u+d_s_td	0.3164	0.3198	es_u+d_s_tdn	0.3875	0.3918
es_b+u+d_s_td	0.2921	0.3008	es_b+u+d_s_tdn	0.3813	0.3833
es_u+d_r_td	0.3210	0.3107	es_u+d_r_tdn	0.3636	0.3656
es_b+u+d_r_td	0.2862	0.2841	es_b+u+d_r_tdn	0.3197	0.3138

Figure 1 summarizes the impact of combining resources, as it shows runs using individual resources as well as our official runs using all fields in the CLEF topics. Run es_b_tdn used only the bigram thesaurus, run es_u_tdn the unigram thesaurus, while run es_d_tdn used the MRD. We did not report runs using only the title and description fields from the CLEF topics, as they showed the same behavior.

Table 2 shows that our official runs performed well in this year's evaluation. The results show a slight advantage in using the bigram thesaurus in combination with the other resources. However, the bigram thesaurus on its own shows very poor performance. There are two main reasons for that behavior. First, the coverage of the bigram thesaurus was poor: only a limited number of bigrams were found in the queries, some queries having no bigram. Second, English bigrams[2] sometimes were not present in the retrieval collection, as thesauri were constructed on a non-related corpus. This resulted in some queries returning very few or no documents.

The poor performance of the bigram thesaurus also impacted our a posteriori merging. Indeed, runs using the bigram thesaurus show lower average precision

---

[2] We represented bigrams as phrase nodes in our structured queries. Two terms satisfy a phrase if they are within a window of 3 of one another.

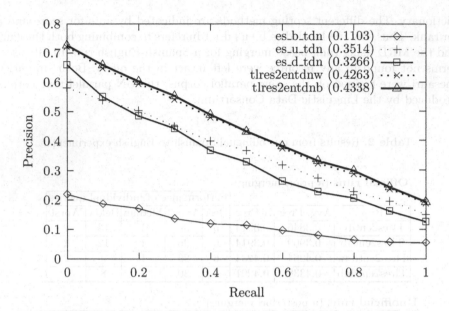

Fig. 1. Summary of the Spanish to English bilingual runs

than runs only using the unigram thesaurus and the MRD. The score-based technique performed better than the rank-based technique. The rank-based technique reported here is based on the product of the ranks. As a result, documents with very different ranks in the individual runs are penalized.

Finally, a priori merging performed better than both techniques for a posteriori merging. One reason is that the number of non-translated terms diminished when resources are combined a priori. Further analysis is needed to better understand the difference in behaviors.

3.2 French-English Bilingual Runs

We adopted a similar strategy for processing French queries. We constructed both bigram and unigram similarity thesauri using the French-English parallel documents from UN parallel text corpus. We used the same threshold and number of translations as our Spanish runs. Results are reported in Table 3.

While satisfactory for a first attempt, our French-English runs do not perform as well as our Spanish-English runs. This may be explained by several factors. First we used parameters tuned on the training set for Spanish, not for French. Further experiments will determine whether the optimal number of translated terms retained from the thesauri is language dependent. Next, we observed that, on average, there are more stems (morphological roots) per term in French than in Spanish. As a result, structured queries in the French-English run are longer and include more general English terms.

Table 3. Results from our unofficial, bilingual French to English experiments

Run	Avg. Prec.	R-Prec.	Run	Avg. Prec.	R-Prec.
fr_b+u+d_td	0.3765	0.3472	fr_b+u+d_tdn	0.4106	0.3866
fr_u+d_td	0.3820	0.3502	fr_u+d_tdn	0.4169	0.3866
fr_b_td	0.0991	0.1203	fr_b_tdn	0.1135	0.1318
fr_u_td	0.3597	0.3469	fr_u_tdn	0.4109	0.3833
fr_d_td	0.2643	0.2503	fr_d_tdn	0.2855	0.2891

One common assumption is that a dictionary with wider coverage should help improve performance of the retrieval system. Since the French-English dictionary is one and a half times larger than the Spanish-English dictionary, we expected runs fr_d_td and fr_d_tdn to have better performance. After analyzing the translated queries, we found that the main problem related to our use of the dictionary, rather than the dictionary itself. Specifically, we did not process phrases in the dictionary correctly, which generated a fair amount of noise in the translation. We believe that the poor individual behavior of the MRD is also the reason why our a priori combined runs do not noticeably outperform the runs using the unigram thesaurus only. This was a main difference between our Spanish and French bilingual runs.

4 Monolingual Retrieval Experiments and Results

In our monolingual runs, we considered two aspects: families of languages, and the use of a phrase dictionary. We used the same rules for Dutch and German on the one hand, and French, Spanish and Italian on the other. In addition, we introduce a phrase dictionary in some of our Spanish and French runs.

German and Dutch were considered as compounding languages. Using the LinguistX morphological analyzer allowed us to detect compound words and break them at indexing and search time. We used a structured query and loose noun phrases to represent compounds.

For French, Spanish and Italian, we allowed the LinguistX morphological analyzer to generate several stems (we did not disambiguate using part-of-speech tags). Multiple stems were grouped as a single concept (using an OR/SYN or a SUM node for instance) in the structured query. For French and Spanish, we generated a dictionary of roughly 1000 noun phrases. We extracted noun phrases from the French and Spanish document collections, we then derived some rules to filter out proper nouns like "Bill Clinton" and phrases we thought non-content bearing such as "année dernière" or "premier trimestre". Finally, we manually filtered the 1500 most frequent noun phrases to remove noisy phrases not captured by our simple rules. Examples of phrases are "unión europea" and "casque bleu".

Table 4 summarizes our results. Runs marked with the sign † are unofficial runs; for these runs the comparison to the median is indicative. We have also included a corrected value for all our official runs. During the analysis of our results, we realized that while our documents were ranked correctly according to the scores in the engine, some of the scores reported were incorrect due to a conversion error in Java. This influenced our performance, since the evaluation program trec_eval resorts documents based on their score. Finally, we also include results using the new implementation of our search engine as it stands now[3].

Using a phrase dictionary was neither harmful, nor helpful. We observed that phrases from the dictionary were found in only one fifth of the queries. For those queries, there is no clear emerging behavior: some perform better using phrases, while others do not. The difference in precision per query between the two runs is usually very small.

Our results for the compounding languages are in the better half of the participants for these runs. Dutch benefited from German. So did our Spanish results benefit from French. We believe that reuse of settings in a family of languages is indeed helpful. We need to perform some further analysis to confirm that belief.

Our Italian run was hindered by the lack of a good noise phrase list, as some of our structured queries still contained terms like "information" or "document".

While we used last year's settings for French, we did not achieve the performance we were aiming for. So far, we have identified two reasons. First, our noise phrase list for French missed capturing some of the patterns used in this year's topics. When we manually cleaned the topics, we observed an improvement in the average precision. Some topics, however, benefited from non-content bearing terms that were not very frequent in the collection (for instance "énumérant" in queries 59 and 71). Next, while we originally intended to consider a term with multiple stems as a single concept, we realized that our scoring was overweighing such a term. Changing the behaviour, the runs labelled French, did show a larger improvement for our French runs than for our Spanish runs. This can be explained by a higher number of terms with multiple stems in French queries than in Spanish queries, as we already observed in Section 3.

5   Final Remarks

One of the problems in our bilingual runs was the coverage of the translation resources. For Spanish, many translated queries still included original terms. In order to solve that problem, we can either use an MRD with a wider coverage (20,000 entries is a rather limited dictionary), or try to get a better coverage from the similarity thesauri. Better coverage may be achieved by using a parallel/comparable corpus in the same domain as the retrieval collections, if not the retrieval collections themselves (see [3]). We will be investigating alignments of documents in related collections in the future. For French, we have identified some issues in our use of the MRD. We will first resolve these issues, before attempting to enrich the dictionary or the thesauri.

---

[3] During our participation at CLEF, we uncovered some implementation issues and we have since then corrected them.

Table 4. Summary of all monolingual runs

Run	Avg. Prec.	R-Prec.	Performance of individual queries				
			Best	Above	Median	Below	Worst
German and Dutch							
Tlrdetd	0.4205	0.4151	1	33	1	14	0
(corrected)	(0.4418)	(0.4269)					
Tlrdetdn	0.4581	0.4570	4	38	3	5	0
(corrected)	(0.4701)	(0.4606)					
German (td) †	0.4491	0.4377					
German (tdn) †	0.4723	0.4546					
Tlrnltd	0.3775	0.3731	6	31	2	11	0
(corrected)	(0.3797)	(0.3756)					
Dutch (td)†	0.3877	0.3804					
Dutch (tdn)†	0.4052	0.3882					
French, Spanish and Italian							
Tlrfrtd	0.4339	0.4386	4	17	4	23	1
(corrected)	(0.4557)	(0.4531)					
Tlrfrtdn	0.4516	0.4436	7	15	10	16	1
(corrected)	(0.4684)	(0.4638)					
Tlrfrtdnpc	0.4503	0.4388	6	18	10	14	1
(corrected)	(0.4698)	(0.4596)					
French (td)†	0.4697	0.4717					
French (tdn)†	0.4817	0.4777					
Tlrestd	0.5195	0.5132	3	26	10	10	0
(corrected)	(0.5302)	(0.5175)					
Tlrestdpc	0.5180	0.5095	3	25	11	10	0
(corrected)	(0.5299)	(0.5169)					
Tlrestdnpc	0.5347	0.5280	5	33	2	8	1
(corrected)	(0.5559)	(0.5361)					
Spanish (td)†	0.5319	0.5248					
Spanish (tdn)†	0.5643	0.5387					
Tlrittd	0.4306	0.4325	3	13	4	25	2
(corrected)	(0.4375)	(0.4292)					

Our monolingual runs contain no query expansion or pseudo-relevance feedback. Once we have refined the list used in query processing, for instance adding a list for misspelled terms, we will focus on automatic query expansion to try and enhance our searches.

References

[1] W. B. Croft, J. Callan, and J. Broglio. The inquery retrieval system. In *Proceedings of the 3rd International Conference on Database and Expert Systems Applications*, Spain, 1992.

[2] D. A. Hull. Stemming algorithms: A case study for detailed evaluation. *Journal of The American Society For Information Science*, 47(1):70–84, 1996.

[3] P. Sheridan, M. Braschler, and P. Schäuble. Cross-lingual information retrieval in a multilingual legal domain. In *Proceedings of the First European Conference on Research and Advanced Technology for Digital Libraries*, 1997.

[4] P. Thompson, H. Turtle, B. Yang, and J. Flood. Trec-3 ad hoc retrieval and routing experiments using the win system. In *Overview of the 3rd Text Retrieval Conference (TREC-3)*, Gaithersburg, MD, April 1995. NIST Special Publication 500-225.

[5] H. Turtle. *Inference Networks for Document Retrieval.* PhD thesis, Computer and Information Science Department, University of Massachussetts, October 1990.

[6] H. Turtle. Natural language vs. boolean query evaluation: a comparison of retrieval performance. In *Proceedings of the 17th Annual International Conference on Research and Development in Information Retrieval*, Dublin, 1994.

Working with Russian Queries for the GIRT, Bilingual, and Multilingual CLEF Tasks

Fredric C. Gey[1], Hailing Jiang[2], and Natalia Perelman[2]

[1] UC Data Archive & Technical Assistance,
[2] School of Information Management and Systems
University of California
Berkeley, CA 94720 USA

Abstract. For our activities within the CLEF 2001 evaluation, Berkeley Group One participated in the bilingual, multilingual and GIRT tasks focussing on the use of Russian queries. Performance on the Russian queries—→English documents bilingual task was excellent, comparable to performance using German queries. For the multilingual task we utilized English as a pivot language between Russian and German and the English/French/German/Italian/Spanish document collections. Performance here was merely average. The GIRT task performed Russian —→ German Cross-Language IR by comparing web-available machine translation with lookup techniques on the GIRT thesaurus.

1 Introduction

Successful cross-language information retrieval (CLIR) combines linguistic techniques (phrase discovery, machine translation, bilingual dictionary lookup) with robust monolingual information retrieval. For monolingual retrieval the Berkeley group has used the technique of logistic regression from the beginning of the TREC series of conferences. In TREC-2 [3] we derived a statistical formula for predicting probability of relevance based upon statistical clues contained within documents, queries and collections as a whole. This formula was used for document retrieval in Chinese [2] and Spanish in TREC-4 through TREC-6. We utilized the identical formula for English and German queries against the English/French/German/Italian document collections in the CLEF 2000 evaluation [7]. During the past two years, the formula has proven well-suited for Japanese and Japanese-English cross-language information retrieval as well as English-Chinese CLIR [1], even when only trained on English document collections. Participation in the NTCIR Workshops in Tokoyo (http://research.nii.ac.jp/ñtcadm/ workshop/work-en.html) led to different techniques for cross-language retrieval, ones which utilised the power of human indexing of documents to improve retrieval. Alignments of parallel texts were used to create large-scale bilingual lexicons between English and Japanese and between English and Chinese. Such lexicons were well-suited to the technical nature of the NTCIR collections of scientific and engineering articles.

C.A. Peters et al. (Eds.): CLEF 2001, LNCS 2406, pp. 235–243, 2002.

2   Logistic Regression for Document Ranking

The document ranking formula used by Berkeley in all of our CLEF retrieval runs was the TREC-2 formula [3]. The ad hoc retrieval results on the TREC test collections have shown that the formula is robust for long queries and manually reformulated queries. Applying the same formula (trained on English TREC collections) to other languages has performed well, as on the TREC-4 Spanish collections, the TREC-5 Chinese collection and the TREC-6 and TREC-7 European languages (French, German, Italian) [5,6]. Thus the algorithm has demonstrated its robustness independent of language as long as appropriate word boundary detection (segmentation) can be achieved. The logodds of relevance of document D to query Q is given by

$$\log O(R|D,Q) = log\frac{P(R|D,Q)}{P(\overline{R}|D,Q)} \tag{1}$$

$$= -3.51 + \frac{1}{\sqrt{N}+1}\Phi + .0929 * N \tag{2}$$

$$\Phi = 37.4 \sum_{i=1}^{N} \frac{qtf_i}{ql+35} + 0.330 \sum_{i=1}^{N} \log\frac{dtf_i}{dl+80}$$

$$-0.1937 \sum_{i=1}^{N} \log\frac{ctf_i}{cl} \tag{3}$$

where $P(R|D,Q)$ is the probability of relevance of document D with respect to query Q, $P(\overline{R}|D,Q)$ is the probability of irrelevance of document D with respect to query Q. Details about the derivation of these formulae may be found in our TREC paper [3]. It is to be emphasized that training has taken place exclusively on English documents but the matching has proven robust over seven other languages in monolingual retrieval, including Japanese and Chinese where word boundaries form an additional step in the discovery process.

3   Submissions for the CLEF Main Tasks

CLEF has three main tasks: monolingual (non-English) retrieval, bilingual (where non-English queries are run against the CLEF sub-collection of English language documents), and multilingual, where queries in any language are run against a multilingual collection of documents comprised of the union of subcollections in English, French, German, Italian and Spanish. We chose this year to participate in the bilingual and multilingual main tasks. In addition, whereas our focus last year was on English and German source queries, this year we wished to explore the interesting question of whether a less-used query language (in this case Russian) could achieve performance comparable to the more mainstream Western European languages.

For CLEF main tasks we submitted 7 runs, 3 for the bilingual (German/Russian-English) task and 4 for the multilingual task. Table 1 summarizes these runs which are described in the next sections.

Table 1. Summary of seven official CLEF runs.

For the Bilingual task we submitted:			
Run Name	Language	Run type	Priority
BKBIGEM1	German	Manual	1
BKBIREM1	Russian	Manual	2
BKBIREA1	Russian	Automatic	3
For the Multilingual task we submitted:			
BKMUGAM1	German	Manual	1
BKMUEAA1	English	Automatic	2
BKMUEAA2	English	Automatic	3
BKMUREA1	Russian	Automatic	4

3.1   Bilingual Retrieval of the CLEF Collections

Bilingual retrieval is performed by running queries in another language against the English collection of CLEF. We chose to focus on Russian but to do German for a baseline comparison. The run BKBIGEM1 was obtained by translating the German queries to English using the L&H Power Translator and then manually adjusting the resulting queries by searching for the untranslated terms in our own special association dictionary created from a library catalog. An example of words not found comes from Topic 88 about 'mad cow disease'. In the German version, the words Spongiformer and Enzephalopathie were not translated by the commercial system, but our association dictionary obtained the words 'hepatic encephalopathy' associated with the inquery Enzephalopathie. Further details about our methodology can be found in [4]. The run BKBIREA1 was obtained by using the PROMPT web-based translator (http://www.translate.ru/). As with the German translation, certain words were not translated. Our methodology to deal with this was twofold – first we transliterated the Russian queries to their romanized alphabetic equivalent, and then we added untranslated terms to the English query in their transliterated form. For example Topic 50 on 'uprising of Indians in Chiapas', the Russian word чиапас was not translated, It can, however, be transliterated as 'chiapas'.

3.2   Bilingual Performance

Our bilingual performance can be found in Table 2. The final line of the table, labeled "CLEF Prec" is computed as an average of each CLEF median precision among all submitted runs. The average is performed over the 47 queries for which the English collection had relevant documents. While an average of medians cannot be considered a statistic from which rigorous inference can be made, we have found it useful to average the medians of all queries as sent by CLEF organizers. Comparing our overall precision to this average of medians yields some fuzzy gauge of whether our performance is better, poorer, or about the same as the median performance.

Table 2. Results of three official Berkeley CLEF bilingual runs.

Run ID	BKBIGEM1	BKBIREM1	BKBIREA1
Retrieved	47000	47000	47000
Relevant	856	856	856
Rel. Ret	812	737	733
Precision			
at 0.00	0.7797	0.6545	0.6420
at 0.10	0.7390	0.6451	0.6303
at 0.20	0.6912	0.5877	0.5691
at 0.30	0.6306	0.5354	0.5187
at 0.40	0.5944	0.4987	0.4806
at 0.50	0.5529	0.4397	0.4167
at 0.60	0.4693	0.3695	0.3605
at 0.70	0.3952	0.3331	0.3218
at 0.80	0.3494	0.2881	0.2747
at 0.90	0.2869	0.2398	0.2339
at 1.00	0.2375	0.1762	0.1743
Brk. Prec.	0.5088	0.4204	0.4077
CLEF Prec.	0.2423	0.2423	0.2423

Using this measure we can find that all our bilingual runs performed significantly better than the median for CLEF bilingual runs.

3.3   Multilingual Retrieval of the CLEF Collections

Our non-English multilingual retrieval runs were based upon our bilingual experiments, extended to French/Italian/Spanish using English as a pivot language and (again) the L&H Power Tranlator as the MT system to translate queries from one language to another. Run BKMURAA1 takes the English translated queries of the bilingual run BKBIREA1 and again translates them to French/German/Italian/Spanish. Run BKMUGAM1 takes the German queries of bilingual run BKBIGEM1 as well as the translation of their English equivalents into French/Italian/Spanish. For comparison we did direct translation from the English queries in runs BKMUEAA1 and BKMUEAA2. The difference between these two runs is that BKMUEAA1 used Title and Description fields only.

The results show that with Russian queries we are about one third lower in average precision than with either English or German queries. We are currently studying why this is so. In addition our overall performance seems only slightly above the CLEF-2001 median performance. This seemed puzzling when compared to our excellent bilingual performance and our above average performance at CLEF-2000. For comparison we also inserted the average of median precisons for last year (Row 2000 Prec. at the bottom of Table 3). As can be seen, the median performance in terms of query precision for CLEF-2001 of 0.2749 is about 50 percent better than the median multilingual performance of

0.1843 of CLEF-2000. This argues that significant progress has been made by the CLEF community in terms of European cross-language retrieval performance.

Table 3. Results of four official CLEF-2001 multilingual runs.

Run ID	BKMUEAA2	BKMUEAA1	BKMUGAM1	BKMURAA1
Retrieved	50000	50000	50000	50000
Relevant	8138	8138	8138	8138
Rel. Ret	5520	5190	5223	4202
Precision				
at 0.00	0.8890	0.8198	0.8522	0.7698
at 0.10	0.6315	0.5708	0.6058	0.4525
at 0.20	0.5141	0.4703	0.5143	0.3381
at 0.30	0.4441	0.3892	0.4137	0.2643
at 0.40	0.3653	0.3061	0.3324	0.1796
at 0.50	0.2950	0.2476	0.2697	0.1443
at 0.60	0.2244	0.1736	0.2033	0.0933
at 0.70	0.1502	0.1110	0.1281	0.0556
at 0.80	0.0894	0.0620	0.0806	0.0319
at 0.90	0.0457	0.0440	0.0315	0.0058
at 1.00	0.0022	0.0029	0.0026	0.0005
Brk. Prec.	0.3101	0.2674	0.2902	0.1838
CLEF Prec.	0.2749	0.2749	0.2749	0.2749
2000 Prec.	0.1843	0.1843	0.1843	0.1843

4   GIRT Retrieval

The special emphasis of our current funding has focussed upon retrieval of specialized domain documents which have been assigned individual classification identifiers by human indexers. These classification identifiers can come from thesauri. Since many millions of dollars are expended on developing such classification schemes and using them to index documents, it is natural to attempt to exploit the resources to the fullest extent possible to improve retrieval. In some cases such thesauri are developed with identifiers translated (or provided) in multiple languages, and can thus be used to transfer words across the language barrier.

The GIRT collection consists of reports and papers (grey literature) in the social science domain. The collection is managed and indexed by the GESIS organization (http://www.social-science-gesis.de). GIRT is an excellent example of a collection indexed by a multilingual thesaurus, originally German-English, recently translated into Russian. The GIRT multilingual thesaurus (German-English), which is based on the Thesaurus for the Social Sciences [10], provides the vocabulary source for the indexing terms within the GIRT collection of

CLEF. Further information about GIRT can be found in [8] There are 76,128 German documents in the GIRT subtask collection. Almost all the documents contain manually assigned thesaurus terms. On average, there are about 10 thesaurus terms assigned to each document. Figure 1 is an example of a thesaurus entry. Since transliteration of the Cyrillic alphabet is a key part of our retrieval strategy, we have transliterated all Russian thesaurus entries.

```
- <entry>
    <german>regionale Wirtschaftspolitik</german>
    <russian>региональная экономическая политика</russian>
    <translit>regional'naia ekonomicheskaia politika</translit>
  </entry>
```

Fig. 1. GIRT German-Russian Thesaurus Entry with Transliteration

In our experiments, we indexed the TITLE and TEXT sections in each document (not the E-TITLE or E-TEXT). The CLEF rules specified that indexing any other field would need to be declared a manual run. For our CLEF runs this year we again used the Muscat stemmer, which is similar to the Porter stemmer but for the German language.

4.1   Query Translation from Russian to German

In order to prepare for query translation, we first extracted all the single words and bigrams from the Russian topic fields. Since we do not have a Russian POS tagger, we took any two adjacent words (overlapping word bigram) to be considered a potential phrase. The single words and bigrams in each Russian query were then compared against the Russian-German thesaurus. If a word or bigram was found in the thesaurus, its German translation was added to the new German query being created. The resulting German query was then run against the German collection to retrieve relevant documents.

For comparison, we also used an online MT system to translate the Russian queries to German (Promt-Reverso: http://translation2.paralink.com/).

Fuzzy Matching for the Thesaurus. The first approach to thesaurus-based translation was exact matching for thesaurus lookup. From the 25 GIRT topics we obtain about 1300 Russian query terms (words and bigrams). Only 50 of them were directly found in the thesaurus, and these were all single words. Two problems contribute to the low matching rate:

First, a Russian word may have several forms or variations. Usually only the base form or general form appears in the thesaurus. For example, "evropa" (Europe in English) is in the thesaurus, but "evrope" and "evropu" are not. In this case, a Russian morphological analyzer would be helpful. Since we do not have a Russian morphological analyzer, we used fuzzy matching to address this problem.

Original Russian word	Russian word in the thesaurus	German translation
migratsiiu	migratsiia	wanderung
migratsii	migratsiia	wanderung
bezrabotitsei	bezrabotitsa	arbeitslosigkeit
televideniia	televidenie	fernsehen
kul'turu	kul'tura	kultur
kul'turoi	kul'tura	kultur
tekhnologiei	tekhnologiia	technologie
tekhnologii	tekhnologiia	technologie

There are different kinds of algorithms for fuzzy matching, such as Levenshtein distance, common n-grams, longest common subsequence, etc [9]. We found that the simple common bigram algorithm to be very efficient and effective for matching different word forms. The two strings are divided into their constituent bigrams and Dice's coefficient is used to compute the similarity between the two strings.

Above are some examples of Russian words that do not occur in the thesaurus but whose different forms were found in the thesaurus by fuzzy matching (the Russian characters in the examples are transliterated for easy reading).

The second problem lies in finding query bigrams which do not match exactly to thesaurus entries. Fuzzy matching was also useful for finding different forms of bigrams, even in cases where word order is changed, examples are:

Original Russian bigram	Bigram found in the thesaurus	German translation
tekhnologicheskogo razvitiia	tekhnologicheskoe razvitie	technologische entwicklung
razvitie i organizatsiia	organizatsionnoe razvitie	organisationsentwicklung
upravlenie organizatsiia	organizatsiia upravleniia	verwaltungsorganisation
rabochem meste	rabochee mesto	arbeitsplatz
rukovodiashchikh rabotnikov	rukovodiashchie rabotniki	führungskraft

The way bigram 'phrases' were created had two problems: first, many of the bigrams were simply not meaningful; second, even though most genuine phrases contain two words (bigrams), approximately 25 percent of Russian terms in the thesaurus contain 3 or more words. A Russian POS tagger would be very helpful for finding meaningful or long phrases.

4.2   GIRT Results and Analysis

Our GIRT results are summarized in Table 4. The runs can be described as follows: BKGRGGA is a monolingual run using the German version of the topics run against the German GIRT document collection. BKGRRGA1 is a Russian-German bilingual run using an MT system for query translation. BKGRRGA2 is a Russian-German bilingual run using thesaurus lookup and fuzzy matching.

Table 4. Results of official GIRT Russian-German runs.

Run ID	BKGRGGA	BKGRRGA1	BKGRRGA2	BKGRRGA3
Retrieved	25000	25000	25000	25000
Relevant	1111	1111	1111	1111
Rel. Ret	1054	774	781	813
Precision				
at 0.00	0.9390	0.4408	0.4032	0.3793
at 0.10	0.8225	0.3461	0.3018	0.2640
at 0.20	0.7501	0.2993	0.2441	0.2381
at 0.30	0.6282	0.2671	0.2257	0.1984
at 0.40	0.5676	0.2381	0.1790	0.1782
at 0.50	0.5166	0.1999	0.1341	0.1609
at 0.60	0.4604	0.1400	0.0993	0.1323
at 0.70	0.4002	0.1045	0.0712	0.1125
at 0.80	0.3038	0.0693	0.0502	0.0765
at 0.90	0.2097	0.0454	0.0232	0.0273
at 1.00	0.0620	0.0051	0.0013	0.0000
Brk. Prec.	0.5002	0.1845	0.1448	0.1461

BKGRRGA3 is a Russian-German bilingual run which is identical in methodology to BKGRRGA2 except that only title and description sections of the topic were used for matching. As we can see, our Russian runs achieve only about 1/3 of the precision of the German-German monolingual run, with a significant edge to the machine translation version. While the full narrative run BKGRRGA3 retrieved more relevant documents, this did not translate into higher overall precision.

5 Summary and Acknowlegments

The participation of Berkeley's Group One in CLEF-2001 has enabled us to explore the difficulties in extending cross-language information retrieval to a non-Roman alphabet language, Russian, for which limited resources are available. Specifically we have explored a comparison of bilingual and multilingual retrieval where original queries were in Russian when compared against German as a query language or English as a query language for multilingual retrieval. For the GIRT task we compared various forms of Russian⟶German retrieval. We have determined that there is significant work to be done before cross-language information retrieval from the Russian language will become competitive to other European languages.

This research was supported by DARPA (Department of Defense Advanced Research Projects Agency) under contract N66001-97-8541; AO# F477: Search Support for Unfamiliar Metadata Vocabularies within the DARPA Information Technology Office. We thank Aitao Chen for indexing the main CLEF collections.

References

1. Chen, A., Jiang, H. and Gey, F.: Berkeley at NTCIR-2: Chinese, Japanese and English IR Experiments. In: N. Kando (ed): Proceedings of the Second NTCIR Workshop on Evaluation of Chinese and Japanese Text Retrieval and Summarization, Tokoyo, Japan, (2001) 32-39
2. Chen, A., He, J., Xu, L., Gey, F., Meggs, J.: Chinese Text Retrieval Without Using a Dictionary. In: Nicholas J. Belkin, A. Desai Narasimhalu and Peter Willett (eds.): Proceedings of the 20th Annual International ACM SIGIR Conference on Research and Development in Information Retrieval, Philadelphia, (1997) 42-49
3. Cooper, W., Chen, A., Gey, F.: Full Text Retrieval based on Probabilistic Equations with Coefficients fitted by Logistic Regression. In: D. K. Harman (ed.): The Second Text REtrieval Conference (TREC-2) (1994) 57-66
4. Gey, F., Buckland, M., Larson, R., Chen, A.: Entry Vocabulary – A Technology to Enhance Digital Search. In: Proceedings of the First International Conference on Human Language Technology (2001)
5. Gey, F.C., Chen, A.: Phrase Discovery for English and Cross-language Retrieval at TREC-6. In: D. K. Harman and Ellen Voorhees (eds.): The Sixth Text REtrieval Conference (TREC-6), NIST Special Publication 500-240 (1998) 637-647
6. Gey, F. C., Jiang, H.: English-German Cross-Language Retrieval for the GIRT Collection – Exploiting a Multilingual Thesaurus. In: Ellen Voorhees (ed.): The Eighth Text REtrieval Conference (TREC-8), draft notebook proceedings (1999) 219-234
7. Gey, F., Jiang, H., Petras, V., Chen, A.: Cross-Language Retrieval for the CLEF Collections – Comparing Multiple Methods of Retrieval. In: Carol Peters (ed.): Cross Language Retrieval Evaluation, Proceedings of the CLEF 2000 Workshop. Lecture Notes in Computer Science, Vol. 2069. Springer (2001) 116-128
8. Kluck, M., Gey, F.: The Domain-Specific Task of CLEF - Specific Evaluation Strategies in Cross-Language Information Retrieval. In: Carol Peters (ed.): Cross Language Retrieval Evaluation, Proceedings of the CLEF 2000 Workshop. Lecture Notes in Computer Science, Vol. 2069. Springer (2001) 48-56
9. Oakes, M.: Statistics for Corpus Linguistics. Edinburgh University Press (1998)
10. Schott, Hannelore (ed.): Thesaurus for the Social Sciences. [Vol. 1:] German-English. [Vol. 2:] English-German. [Edition] 1999, InformationsZentrum Sozialwissenschaften Bonn (2000)

IR-n: A Passage Retrieval System at CLEF-2001

Fernando Llopis and José L. Vicedo

Grupo de investigación en Procesamiento del Lenguaje y Sistemas de Información
Departamento de Lenguajes y Sistemas Informáticos
Universidad de Alicante
Alicante, Spain {llopis,vicedo}@dlsi.ua.es

Abstract. Previous work demonstrates that information retrieval system performance is sensibly improved when using document passages as the basic unit of information. However, the IR community has not yet arrived at consensus about the best way of defining text passages for retrieval purposes. This paper reports on experiments with the IR-n system, an information retrieval system that applies a new method for passage selection. Passages are defined as a fixed number of adjoining sentences in a document. This approach has been tested for the monolingual (Spanish) and bilingual (Spanish-English) tasks at CLEF-2001 with different success rates.

1 Introduction

Information retrieval (IR) is the term conventionally applied to the task of giving information on the existence of documents relevant to a given request. Given a collection of documents and a user's query, the purpose of an automatic retrieval strategy is to obtain all and only the set of documents relevant to the query. IR approaches usually measure the level of similarity between a document and a query by analysing the frequency of appearance of query terms in the document collection. Particularly in texts of considerable size, this fact can mean that a document can be considered relevant without really being so.

An alternative to this model is represented by IR systems that use contiguous text fragments (or passages), instead of full documents, as the basic unit of information. This approach, called passage retrieval (PR), means that similarity results are not affected excessively by the size of the documents. In this case, the similarity value assigned to a document depends on the most relevant passages of the document.

Passage retrieval systems are more complex than document retrieval ones. First, they need to store a larger quantity of information for each term appearing in the document, and usually its position in every document. Second, the computational effort needed to evaluate the relevance of each one of the passages is higher than when using documents as the unit of information. Nevertheless, previous studies [1] [3] [2] show that this high complexity is rewarded with better performance results.

The main discussion with respect to PR is nowadays centred on finding the best way of splitting documents into passages. Passages can be classified in three

C.A. Peters et al. (Eds.): CLEF 2001, LNCS 2406, pp. 244–252, 2002.

types [2] depending on the techniques used for selecting them from documents: *discourse, semantic* and *window*. Discourse passages are obtained by splitting documents into textual discourse units (e.g. sentences or paragraphs). The use of techniques based on the subject or content of the text generates semantic passages. Finally, window passages are extracted from text by selecting a fixed or variable number of contiguous words.

IR-n proposes a new discourse-based method for passage selection. IR-n uses passages of variable size that are consist of a fixed number of sentences. Passages overlap through the document. This means that, if a passage is N long, the first paragraph will be made up of sentences from *1* to N the second, from *2* to $N+1$ and so on. The relevance of a document to a query will depend on the similarity values computed for all the passages it contains.

This paper is structured as follows. The following section presents IR-n system architecture and components. The third section describes the different runs performed for this campaign and discusses the results obtained. Finally, the last section extracts initial conclusions and opens directions for future work.

2   System Overview

The IR-n system is consists of three modules: *Indexing module, Query processing module* and *Retrieval module*. The first module processes the document collection and builds indexes. The query module processes the query by expanding and translating it when necessary. Finally, the retrieval module ranks the documents according to several similarity measures. Figure 1 shows the system architecture.

2.1   Indexing Module

This process generates the dictionaries providing the necessary information for retrieval. Indexing terms consist of character strings that are made up of letters and symbols whose length is less than 21 characters, and numbers with less than five digits. Before indexing, documents are pre-processed to detect sentence boundaries and terms are normalized. This normalization is achieved by stemming English terms and lemmatising Spanish words. Non-content terms are eliminated using a stop-word list.

Passage indexing requires storing diverse data items. The system stores the number of documents a term appears in, the number of appearances of a term in a document and its position in the document (determined by the number of the sentence in which it appears and its position within the sentence). This results in an increase in the information to be stored in comparison to document-oriented retrieval systems.

2.2   Query Processing Module

The query processing task consists in translating the topics into the language of the document collection. As our main objective is to test our passage re-

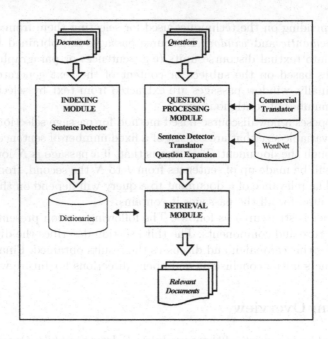

Fig. 1. System architecture

trieval approach to cross-lingual retrieval, this step has been accomplished using a commercial translator.

Once the query has been translated, the system performs term normalisation (stemming for English and lemmatising for Spanish) and stop-word removal. Finally, query expansion is applied by adding semantic information to the query. This expansion is accomplished by adding all the synonyms of query terms. The synonyms have been extracted from the WordNet lexical thesaurus [4].

2.3   Retrieval Module

This module retrieves a ranked list containing the most relevant documents to the query. This process is accomplished as follows:

1. Query terms are ordered depending on the number of documents of the collection in which they appear.
2. Documents that contain at least one term are selected.
3. Similarity between the query and all the passages of these documents is computed (*Passage similarity*).
4. Each document is assigned a score depending on the similarity values obtained for the passages appearing in it (*Document score*).
5. Documents are ranked depending on their score.
6. Results are presented in an ordered list.

The similarity value between a topic and a passage is computed as follows:

$$Passagesimilarity = \sum_{t \in p \wedge q} W_{p,t} * W_{q,t} \tag{1}$$

Where $W_{p,t} = log_e(f_{p,t} + 1)$, $f_{p,t}$ the number of appearances of term t in passage p, $W_{q,t} = log_e(f_{q,t} + 1) * idf$, $f_{q,t}$ the number of appearances of term t in query q, $idf = log_e(N/f_t + 1)$, N the number of documents of the collection and f_t the number of documents term t appears in.

As can be observed, this formula is similar to the cosine measure defined in [5]. The main difference is that length normalisation is omitted. Instead, our proposal normalises length by defining passage size as a fixed number of textual discourse units. In this case, the discourse unit selected is the sentence and a passage is defined as a fixed number N of sentences. In this way, although the number of terms of each passage may vary, the number of sentences is constant. The optimal number N of sentences pertaining to a passage was derived using the CLEF-2000 document collection and topics for the monolingual English task. Figure 2 shows the results obtained with passage lengths from 5 to 30 sentences. The best results were obtained for passages of 20 sentences. Therefore, we chose this size for our CLEF-2001 experiments.

Recall	Precision on passage length (number of sentences)					
	5	10	15	20	25	30
0.00	0,64	0,65	0,70	0,73	0,68	0,68
0.10	0,53	0,55	0,54	0,55	0,53	0,53
0.20	0,42	0,46	0,47	0,49	0,46	0,44
0.30	0,34	0,37	0,38	0,40	0,35	0,36
0.40	0,28	0,30	0,30	0,30	0,28	0,28
0.50	0,26	0,28	0,27	0,26	0,25	0,25
0.60	0,18	0,19	0,18	0,19	0,19	0,19
0.70	0,15	0,16	0,15	0,15	0,15	0,15
0.80	0,12	0,12	0,12	0,13	0,12	0,13
0.90	0,08	0,09	0,09	0,09	0,09	0,09
1.00	0,07	0,07	0,08	0,08	0,07	0,07

Fig. 2. Passage length training results

After computing the similarity between the query and the relevant passages, documents are scored (*document score*). This value is obtained by combining the similarity values of the passages pertaining to each document. In this case, the system assigns the highest similarity value obtained by the passages contained in a document.

3   Experiments and Results

In CLEF 2001, we participated in two tasks: bilingual (Spanish-English) and monolingual (Spanish). The bilingual task uses Spanish queries on a document collection of English texts. The monolingual task queries a Spanish collection in Spanish.

The test collection was made up by 50 topics written in Spanish that were used for querying the "Agencia EFE S.A. Spanish news agency 1994" document collection for the monolingual task and the "Los Angeles Times 1994" newspaper collection for the bilingual task.

3.1   Runs Description

We carried out three runs for the monolingual task and four runs for the bilingual task. The characteristics of these runs are described below:

- **EI** run obtains baseline results. This run uses the topic title and the standard cosine similarity measure (based on whole documents) for document ranking [5]. This run allows us to compare document retrieval and passage retrieval approaches.
- **PR** run performs passage retrieval by measuring similarity between the topic title and the passages contained in each document. The similarity score assigned to a document is the highest similarity value obtained for the passages it contains.
- **EXP** run is similar to PR run but applies query expansion to the topic title. This expansion consists in adding synonyms of query terms to the query. Synonyms were obtained from the WordNet lexical database. Query expansion was only used for the bilingual task.
- **PRM** run is more complex. This run manages all the information in a topic: title, description and narrative. First, the topic is processed by detecting sentence boundaries. The PR run is then applied for each of these sentences. In this way, a ranked list of relevant documents is obtained for each sentence in the topic. Finally, the system computes the document score by adding the similarity values obtained for each document in these relevance lists and dividing this value by the number of sentences in the topic. Documents are then ranked on this final score.

The runs described were used for both monolingual and bilingual tasks. The only difference is that the queries were previously translated for the bilingual task.

3.2   Bilingual Task

We carried out four tests for the bilingual Spanish-English task (EXP, EI, PR and PRM). Figure 3 depicts the results obtained for each of these runs. It can be observed that all passage retrieval techniques improve the results obtained by the baseline system except for the EXP run. The PRM run achieves the best result. This run, unlike the remaining runs that only use the title, uses all the information in the topic (title, description and narrative). Another important aspect to be taken into account is the poor results obtained when query was expanded with query term synonyms. Comparison between applied passage retrieval techniques leads us to conclude that this kind of query expansion introduces too much noise into the retrieval system. In fact, the EXP run performance was worse than the baseline (EI).

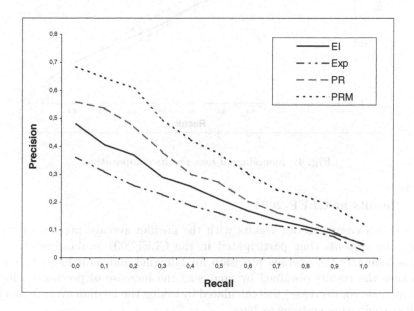

Fig. 3. Bilingual task results comparative

3.3   Monolingual Task

Three runs were carried out for the monolingual task (EI, PR and PRM). As comparative results show (see figure 4), using passage retrieval (PR and PRM runs) gives no significant improvement over standard document retrieval approaches (EI). Furthermore, the short query results (PR run) are similar to the long query results (PRM run).

The following question arises when our bilingual and monolingual results are compared: Why are the performance differences between passage retrieval techniques and the baseline not similar for the bilingual and monolingual tasks? The explanation is now clear. In general, passage retrieval approaches obtain considerably better results that document retrieval ones. The poor results for monolingual passage retrieval task are due to the use of a really bad Spanish lemmatizer.

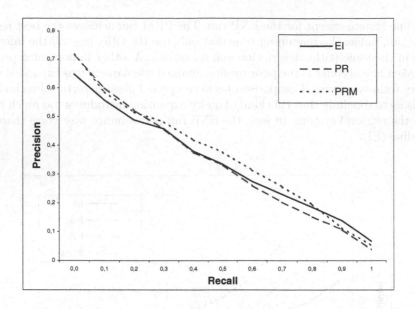

Fig. 4. monolingual task results comparative

3.4   Results at CLEF-2001

This section compares our results with the median average precision obtained by all the systems that participated in the CLEF2001 evaluation campaign. Figure 5 depicts the average precision for bilingual and monolingual runs and compares the results obtained by analysing the increase of precision achieved. This increase (or decrease) was calculated by taking the median average precision of all participating systems as base.

	Bilingual Task		Monolingual Task	
	Average precision	Increment	Average precision	Increment
Median	0,2422	0,00%	0,4976	0,00%
PRM	0,3759	55,20%	0,3528	-29,10%
PR	0,2725	12,51%	0,3287	-33,94%
EXP	0,1672	-30,97%		
EI	0,2197	-9,29%	0,3297	-33,74%

Fig. 5. Bilingual and Monolingual tasks at CLEF-2001

The second and third columns show a bilingual results comparison. For this task, the IR-n system results are above the CLEF-2001 median. As can be observed, the PRM and PR runs improve median results by 55,20% and 12,5% respectively. This fact demonstrates that our passage retrieval approach is very effective for cross-language retrieval purposes. It is interesting to note that the EXP run performed 30.96% worse than median results. This fact confirms that the query expansion technique applied has not been as effective as could have been expected.

The fourth and fifth columns show a monolingual results comparison. As we can observe, the results achieved are worse than the median. As we have stated above, this was due to an incorrect choice of the Spanish lemmatizer. We have since detected many errors in the lemma selection process by this system.

4 Conclusions and Future Work

As our results demonstrate, using groups of sentences as basic text units for measuring the similarity between queries and documents in the environment of IR systems is shown to be a very effective technique. For the bilingual task we obtained a considerable improvement when we used passage retrieval techniques. However, this improvement was small when we worked with the Spanish document collection for the monolingual task (mainly due to the wrong choice of the Spanish lemmatizer).

We have also observed that the selection of the appropriate size of passage depends on the size of the documents contained in the collection. For these tasks, the optimal number of sentences was 20. Nevertheless, this number needs to be recalculated for collections containing mainly small documents.

Again, some considerations need to be made concerning whether to use all the information contained in a topic or not. Using the title, description and narrative was more effective for passage retrieval (PRM run) than using only title. Even though our results for monolingual tasks are not relevant, they are very significant for bilingual tasks.

The query expansion technique applied achieved the poorest results. Adding query term synonyms, extracted from a thesaurus such as WordNet, has been shown to be a very bad choice. The huge granularity of WordNet introduced a lot of strange synonyms and therefore, the expanded query meaning differed too much from the original one. As a result, this technique seriously harmed system performance.

Another objective was to test whether the use of a commercial translator without manual supervision could be effective for bilingual tasks. The results show that these translators can be used without affecting too much system performance. In fact, our results for bilingual task were over the median.

After this first experience, we are examining several lines of future work. We want to analyse the optimal number of sentences that should form a paragraph, depending on the median size of the documents contained in a collection. In addition, in spite of the bad results obtained using query expansion, we want to continue studying the advantages of a query expansion process. In particular, we are already investigating the application of domain labeling techniques for reducing WordNet granularity and testing query expansion by applying these labels.

Acknowledgements. This work has been supported by the Spanish Government (CICYT) with grant TIC2000-0664-C02-02.

References

1. J. Callan, B. Croft, and J. Broglio. Trec and tipster experiments with inquery. *Information Processing and Management*, 31(3):327–343, 1994.
2. Marcin Kaszkiel and Justin Zobel. Passage retrieval revisited. In *Proceedings of the 20th Annual International ACM SIGIR Conference on Research and Development in Information Retrieval*, Text Structures, pages 178–185, 1997.
3. Marcin Kaszkiel, Justin Zobel, and Ron Sacks-Davis. Efficient passage ranking for document databases. *ACM Transactions on Information Systems*, 17(4):406–439, October 1999.
4. G. Miller. Wordnet: A Lexical Database for English. In *Communications of the ACM 38(11))*, pages 39–41, 1995.
5. G. Salton. *Automatic Text Processing: The Transformation, Analysis, and Retrieval of Information by Computer*. Addison Wesley, New York, 1998.

Spanish Monolingual Track: The Impact of Stemming on Retrieval

Carlos G. Figuerola, Raquel Gómez, Angel F. Zazo Rodríguez, and
José Luis Alonso Berrocal

Universidad de Salamanca
c/ Francisco de Vitoria, 6-16, 37008 Salamanca, Spain
[figue|afzazo|berrocal|rgomez]@usal.es

Abstract. Most of the techniques used in Information Retrieval rely
on the identification of terms from queries and documents, as much to
carry out calculations based on the frequencies of these terms as to carry
out comparisons between documents and queries. Terms coming from
the same stem, either by morphological inflection or through derivation,
can be presumed to have semantic proximity. The conflation of these
words to a common form can produce improvements in retrieval. The
stemming mechanisms used depend directly on each language. In this
paper, a stemmer for Spanish and the tests conducted by applying it to
the CLEF Spanish document collection are described, and the results are
discussed.

1 Introduction

At one time or another, most of the models and techniques employed in Information Retrieval use frequency counts of the terms appearing in documents and
queries. The concept of term in this context, however, is not exactly the same
as that of word. Leaving to one side the matter of so-called stop words, which
cannot be considered terms as such, we have the case of words derived from the
same stem, to which can be attributed a very close semantic content [1]. The
possible variations of the derivatives, together with their inflections, alterations
in gender and number, etc., make it advisable to group these variants under one
term. If this is not done, a dispersion in the calculation of the frequency of such
terms occurs and difficulty ensues in the comparison of queries and documents
[2].

Programs that process queries must be able to identify inflections and derivatives - which may be different in the query and the documents - as similar and
as corresponding to the same stem. Stemming, as a way of standardising the
representation of the terms with which Information Retrieval systems operate,
is an attempt to solve these problems.

However, the effectiveness of stemming has been the object of discussion,
probably beginning with the work of Harman [3], who, after trying several algorithms (for English), concluded that none of them increased effectiveness in

C.A. Peters et al. (Eds.): CLEF 2001, LNCS 2406, pp. 253–261, 2002.
© Springer-Verlag Berlin Heidelberg 2002

retrieval. Subsequent work [4] pointed out that stemming is effective as a function of the morphological complexity of the language being used, while Krovetz [5] found that stemming improves recall and even precision when documents and queries are short.

2   Previous Work

Stemming applied to Information Retrieval has been tried in several ways, from succinct stripping to the application of far more sophisticated algorithms. Studies began in the 1960s with the aim of reducing the size of indices [6] and, apart from being a way of standardising terms, stemming can also be seen as a means to expand queries by adding inflections or derivatives of the words to documents and queries.

One of the best known contributions is the algorithm proposed by Lovin in 1968 [7], which is in some sense the basis of subsequent algorithms and proposals, such as those of Dawson [8], Porter [2] and Paice [9]. Although much of the work reported is directed towards use with documents in English, it is possible to find proposals and algorithms for other languages, among them Latin, in spite of its being a dead language [10], Malaysian [11], French [12], [13], Arabic [14], Dutch [15], [16], Slovene [4] and Greek [17].

Various stemming mechanisms have been applied to Information Retrieval operations on Spanish texts in some of the TREC conferences (Text Retrieval Conference) [18]. In general, these applications consisted in using the same algorithms as for English, but with suffixes and rules for Spanish. Regardless of the algorithms applied, and of their adaptation to Spanish, the linguistic knowledge used (lists of suffixes, rules of application, etc.), was quite poor [19].

From the language processing perspective, in recent years several stemmers and morphological analysers for Spanish have been developed, including the COES tools [20], made available to the public at *http://www.datsi.fi.upm.es/ ~coes/* under GNU licensing; the morpho-syntax analyser MACO+ [21] (*http:// nipadio.lsi.upc.es/cgi-bin/demo/demo.pl*) or the FLANOM / FLAVER stemmers [22], [23] (*http://protos.dis.ulpgc.es/*). However, we are unaware of any experimental results of the application of these tools to Information Retrieval.

On the other hand, on several occasions the use of n-grams has been proposed to obviate the problem posed by inflectional and derivational variation [24]. In previous work, however, we were able to verify the scant effectiveness of this mechanism from the Information Retrieval viewpoint [25], as well as the inadequacy of the well-known Porter algorithm for languages such as Spanish.

3   The Stemmer

The basis of our stemmer consists of a finite state machine that attempts to represent the modifications undergone by a stem when a certain suffix is attached or added to it. There is thus an instance of this automaton for each suffix contemplated: each of these implies a series of rules expressing how that suffix is incorporated into the stem. Since, for the same suffix, at times there may be a large number of variants and exceptions, the resulting automaton can be quite complex.

Thus, in order to stem a word, the longest suffix coinciding with the end of this word is sought and the corresponding automaton is formed with the rules for that suffix. The network of this automaton is searched with the word to be stemmed and the string obtained in the terminal node of the automaton is contrasted with a dictionary of stems. If the chain obtained is found in the dictionary the stem is considered to be correct.

Taking into account that the transformations may occasionally overlap, adding more than one suffix, the process is repeated recursively until the correct stem is found. If, once the possibilities are exhausted, none of the terminal strings obtained are found in the dictionary of stems, it is deduced that either the word can be considered as standardised in itself, or else it is a case not foreseen by the stemmer.

This last instance may mean the following:

1. the word has a suffix that is not included in the list of suffixes of the stemmer
2. the suffix is added in a way that was not predicted by the rules incorporated in the knowledge base
3. the stem is not in the dictionary of stems.

Thus, the stemmer is to be subjected to a training process in which the results of stemming the words of a corpus are examined manually and the knowledge base of the stemmer is corrected when necessary.

We can distinguish between two classes of stemming: inflectional and derivative. Whereas the former has clear and defined limits, this does not occur with the latter. Moreover, the semantic distance between two different inflections of the same stem can in general be considered of little importance (for example, *libro* and *libros*), whereas the semantic difference between a stem and its derivatives may be great; for example, *sombra* (shade), *sombrilla* (parasol, sunshade), and even *sombrero* (hat).

Inflectional stemming should heed changes in gender and/or number for nouns and adjectives and changes in person, number, tense and mode for verbs. Treatment of nouns and adjectives is simple, since both changes in gender and in number follow simple rules. Exceptions to these rules exist but they are few and can be treated individually. Verbs, however, are another case. Besides the great number of forms a verb can take, the main problem lies in the large amount of irregular verbs in Spanish. There may be more than 40,000 irregular verbs and any basic course of Spanish includes lists of 8 or 10 thousand irregular verbs. Fortunately, these can be grouped into approximately 80 different models, although they do not always strictly follow a given model and there are many exceptions.

In inflectional stemming there is another complex problem to be solved: the grammatical ambiguity of many words. A certain word ending in a certain suffix may pertain to different grammatical categories and, depending on which it

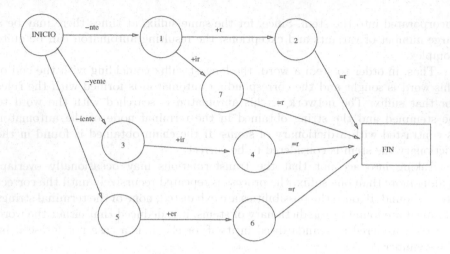

Fig. 1. Automaton for the suffix -*ente*

pertains to, the inflectional transformations it has undergone will be different and will in consequence have come from different stems. A simple example would be the word *colecciones*: it could be the plural of the noun *colección* (collection) or else the second person singular present subjunctive of *coleccionar* (to collect), and would thus give rise to two different stems.

The way to solve this ambiguity could lie in resorting to the specific context of the word and determining its grammatical category, in order to then choose the right stem. Our stemmer cannot yet resolve this ambiguity. However, one should take into account that some forms are more frequent than others; a verb in subjunctive mode is much more infrequent than a noun, and even more so in journalistic texts such as the ones we have dealt with.

For the moment, until we manage to solve this ambiguity, our stemmer chooses the most frequent stems; this necessarily introduces an element of error, but since it always applies the same stem, the error is always less than it would be without stemming. Furthermore, derivation produces a much higher number of forms based on one stem. Inflectional transformations can occur on any of these forms and therefore derivative stemming should be carried out after flexional stemming; for example, *libreros* (book-sellers) is a plural noun that should be reduced to singular in order to eliminate the suffix and end up with the stem *libro* (book).

4   The Impact of Stemming on Information Retrieval

The 50 queries of the CLEF Spanish monolingual collection were processed in three modalities: without stemming, applying inflectional stemming and applying inflectional plus derivational stemming. Obviously, the stemming was applied both to documents and queries, and in all three cases stop words were eliminated previously, based on a standard list of 538 (articles, conjunctions, prepositions, etc.).

The algorithm is the same for both inflectional and derivative stemming. What changes, obviously, are the suffixes and rules of application, as well as the dictionary or list of stems to be used. For inflectional stemming the number of suffixes considered was 88, with a total of 2,700 rules of application. The dictionary of stems consists of 80,000 entries. For derivative stemming the number of suffixes is higher (since it is actually a matter of inflection plus derivatives): 230 with 3,692 rules of application. The dictionary or list of stems is much shorter: approximately 15,000 stems.

After eliminating stop words, the document collection produced a total of 36,573,577 words, with 353,868 unique words. Inflectional stemming reduced these 353,868 unique words to 284,645 stems; nevertheless, of these, 141,539 (almost half) were stems that appeared only once in the document collection. A simple glance shows that a good part of them correspond to typographical errors (which cannot be stemmed without previous detection and correction), as well as to proper names, acronyms, etc. Derivative stemming reduced the number of stems: the 353,868 unique words produced 252,494 single stems. Of these, 127,739 appeared only once in the document collection; most of them are typographical errors.

4.1   The Retrieval Model

To execute or solve the queries we used our own retrieval engine, Karpanta, [26], which is based on the well known vectorial model, defined by Salton some time ago [27]. The weights of the terms were calculated according to the usual scheme of *Frequency of term in the document* x *IDF*. IDF (Inverse Document Frequency) is an inverse function of the frequency of a term in the entire collection (understood as the number of documents in which it appears) [28]. The similarity between each document and each query was calculated using the formula of the cosine, as is usual in these cases [29].

Taking into account that our objective was to evaluate the effect of stemming, we did not consider it necessary to apply additional techniques such as feedback of queries [30], although the Karpanta retrieval system permits this. Actually, our intention was not so much to achieve the best results, but to measure the differences among the results obtained with each of the three modalities mentioned above.

5   Results

The results can be seen in the attached plot, and they are somewhat disappointing. The differences among the cases are scarce. Inflectional stemming produces about 7 % of improvement over unstemming. Derivative stemming is even a little bit worse than no stemming.

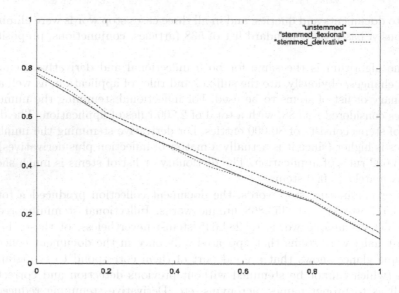

Fig. 2. Results of the official runs

This is somewhat surprising because it differs considerably from the results obtained in previous tests with another document collection. In effect, both stemmers, inflectional and derivative, were tested with the Datathéke collection, obtaining significantly better results. Datathéke is a small homogeneous collection of 1074 documents in Spanish, consisting of scientific paper abstracts in Information and Library Science. Additionally, it has a set of 15 queries with corresponding relevance assessments.

The test results with this small collection can be seen in Figure 3, and they show a significant improvement using both stemmers, especially the inflectional one. Certainly, Datathéke is not a very representative collection, fundamentally due to its small size, but even so the difference in results is surprising.

There are, nevertheless, some important differences between two collections, in addition to the size, that can help to understand the difference between the results obtained. First, the document collection used in CLEF consists of agency news. It is known that journalistic texts are especially flat with regard to morphology and syntax; thus, less morphological complexity could attenuate the effects of stemming. Additionally, agency newswires are typically even poorer in stylistic complexity, since they are not written to be published such as, but in the hope that newspapers editors of each newspaper process the news that finally gets published from them.

A second difference is the use of proper nouns in the queries. The queries of Datathéke hardly contain proper nouns in their formulation. Proper nouns cannot be stemmed, and several CLEF queries for Spanish are based on proper nouns. So, they can largely be processed on the basis of these proper nouns. In

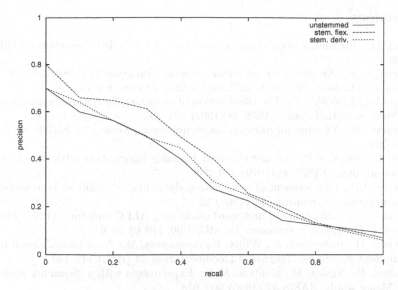

Fig. 3. Results of the *Datathéke* collection

fact, there are some queries in which results are practically obtained just using a simple substring search only with the proper nouns. For these queries the impact of stemming is, obviously, none. This happens with queries 46, 47, 48, 49, 50, 51, 66, 73, 79, 83, 88 and 89, and specially with 66 and 89. In these, for example, the same documents were retrieved by means of our Karpanta system (based on the vectorial model) and by means of a substring search with the terms *Letonia* and *Rusia* for query 66 and *Schneider* for 89.

6   Conclusions and Future Work

The stemming of terms from queries and documents in Spanish can be a means to improve the results in retrieval. This improvement depends on the morphological complexity of queries and documents. Inflectional stemming seems to produce better results than derivational stemming, since the latter introduces excesive ambiguity in the stems.

We must now complete the stemmer, in particular with regards to the resolution of the ambiguity in the inflectional stems. This could be achieved by means of an examination of the context in which each term appears. In addition, we must decide whether derivative stemming must be discarded definitively, or if a careful selection of the suffixes could be useful, discarding those that produce very semantically distant terms. Another possibility could be the use of thesauri or other linguistic resources to determine the relation between the stem and the derivative.

References

1. Hull, D.: Stemming algorithms: a case study for detailed evaluation. JASIS 47 (1996)
2. Porter, M.F.: An algorithm for suffix stripping. Program 14 (1980) 130–137
3. Harman, D.: How effective is suffixing? JASIS 42 (1991) 7–15
4. Popovic, M., Willet, P.: The effectiveness of stemming for natural-language access to Slovene textual data. JASIS 43 (1992) 384–390
5. Krovetz, R.: Viewing morphology as an inference process. In: SIGIR 93. (1993) 191–203
6. Bell, C., Jones, K.P.: Toward everyday languaje information retrieval system via minicomputer. JASIS 30 (1979) 334–338
7. Lovins, J.B.: Development of a stemming algorithm. Mechanical Translation and Computational Linguistics 11 (1968) 22–31
8. Dawson, J.: Suffix removal and word conflation. ALLC bulletin 2 (1974) 33–46
9. Paice, C.D.: Another stemmer. In: SIGIR 90. (1990) 56–61
10. Schinke, R., Robertson, A., Willet, P., Greengrass, M.: A stemming algorithm for Latin text databases. Journal of Documentation 52 (1996) 172–187
11. Ahmad, F., Yussof, M., Sembok, M.T.: Experiments with a stemming algorithm for Malay words. JASIS 47 (1996) 909–918
12. Savoy, J.: Effectiveness of information retrieval systems used in a hypertext environment. Hypermedia 5 (1993) 23–46
13. Savoy, J.: A stemming procedure and stopword list for general French corpora. JASIS 50 (1999) 944–952
14. Abu-Salem, H., Al-Omari, M., Evens, M.W.: Stemming methodologies over individual queries words for an Arabian information retrieval system. JASIS 50 (1999) 524–529
15. Kraaij, W., Pohlmann, R.: Porter's stemming algorithm for Dutch. In Noordman, L.G.M., de Vroomen, W.A.M., eds.: Informatiewetenschap, Tilburg, STINFON (1994)
16. Kraaij, W., Pohlmann, R.: Viewing stemming as recall enhancement. In: SIGIR 96. (1996) 40–48
17. Kalamboukis, T.Z.: Suffix stripping with moderm Greek. Program 29 (1995) 313–321
18. Harman, D.: The TREC conferences. In: Proceedings of the HIM'95 (Hypertext-Information Retrieval-Multimedia). (1995) 9–23
19. Figuerola, C.G.: La investigación sobre recuparación de la información en español. In Gonzalo García, C. y García Yebra, V., ed.: Documentación, Terminología y Traducción, Madrid, Síntesis (2000) 73–82
20. Rodríguez, S., Carretero, J.: A formal approach to Spanish morphology: the Coes tools. In: XII Congreso de la SEPLN, Sevilla (1996) 118–126
21. Carmona, J., Cervell, S., Márquez, L., Martí, M., Padrón, L., Placer, R., Rodríguez, H., Taulé, M., Turmo, J.: An environment for morphosyntactic processing of unrestricted Spanish text. In: Proceedings of the First International Conference on Language Resources and Evaluation (LREC'98), Granada, Spain (1998)
22. Santana, O., Pérez, J., Hernández, Z., Carreras, F., Rodríguez, G.: Flaver: Flexionador y lematizador automático de formas verbales. Lingüística Española Actual XIX (1997) 229–282
23. Santana, O., Pérez, J., Carreras, F., Duque, J., Hernández, Z., Rodríguez, G.: Flanom: Flexionador y lematizador automático de formas nominales. Lingüística Española Actual XXI (1999) 253–297

24. Robertson, A., Willet, P.: Applications of n-grams in textual information systems. Journal of Documentation 54 (1999) 28–47
25. Figuerola, C.G., Gómez, R., de San Román, E.L.: Stemming and n-grams in spanish: an evaluation of their impact on information retrieval. Journal of Information Science 26 (2000) 461–467
26. Figuerola, C.G., Berrocal, J.L.A., Rodríguez, A.F.Z.: Disseny d'un motor de recuperació d'informació per a ús experimental i educatiú = diseño de un motor de recuperación de información para uso experimental y educativo. BiD. textos universitaris de biblioteconomia i documentació 4 (2000)
27. Salton, G., McGill, M.: Introduction to Modern Information Retrieval. McGraw-Hill, New York (1983)
28. Harman, D.: Ranking algorithms. In: Information retrieval: data structures and algorithms, Upple Saddle River, NJ, Prentice-Hall (1992) 363–392
29. Salton, G.: Automatic Text Processing. Adisson-Wesley, Reading, MA (1989)
30. Harman, D. In: Relevance Feedback and Others Query Modification Techniques. Prentice-Hall, Upple Saddle River, NJ (1992)

Shallow Morphological Analysis in Monolingual Information Retrieval for Dutch, German, and Italian

Christof Monz* and Maarten de Rijke**

Language & Inference Technology, University of Amsterdam,
Nieuwe Achtergracht 166, 1018 WV Amsterdam, The Netherlands.
{christof,mdr}@science.uva.nl
www.science.uva.nl/~{christof,mdr}

Abstract. This paper describes the experiments of our team for CLEF 2001, which include both official and post-submission runs. We took part in the monolingual task for Dutch, German, and Italian. The focus of our experiments was on the effects of morphological analyses, such as stemming and compound splitting, on retrieval effectiveness. Confirming earlier reports on retrieval in compound splitting languages such as Dutch and German, we found improvements to be around 25% for German and as much as 69% for Dutch. For Italian, lexicon-based stemming resulted in gains of up to 25%.

1 Introduction

This is the first year that the University of Amsterdam is participating in the CLEF conference and retrieval comparison. We took part in three monolingual tracks: Dutch, German, and Italian. Each of these languages is morphologically richer than English, and we were particularly interested in the effects of shallow morphological analysis for these languages: stemming or lemmatization, and compound splitting. In languages such as Dutch and German, compound building is a very common issue. For instance, the Dutch noun *zonnecel* (English: *solar cell*) is a compound built from *zon* (English: *sun*) and *cel* (English: *cell*). Previous work has indicated that it may help to enhance retrieval effectiveness for Dutch and German if compounds in queries or documents are split, and their parts added to the query or document. Below, we report on monolingual experiments for Dutch and German that confirm and refine these results using the CLEF data collection. All our experiments were performed using the FlexIR system.

The paper is organized as follows. In Section 2 we describe the FlexIR system as well as our basic retrieval approach. Section 3 is devoted to a detailed description of our techniques for compound splitting, for both Dutch and German. Section 4 describes our official runs for CLEF 2001 and the results we obtained. In Section 5 we discuss the results we have obtained for a small number of post-submission experiments, mainly

---

* Supported by the Physical Sciences Council with financial support from the Netherlands Organization for Scientific Research (NWO), project 612-13-001.
** Supported by the Spinoza project 'Logic in Action' and by grants from the Netherlands Organization for Scientific Research (NWO), under project numbers 612-13-001, 365-20-005, 612.069.006, 612.000.106, and 220-80-001.

concerning the interaction between blind feedback and compound splitting. Finally, in Section 6 we offer some conclusions and outline plans regarding research within our group in the area of document retrieval.

2 System Description

All our runs used FlexIR, an information retrieval system developed by the first author. The main goal underlying FlexIR's design is to facilitate flexible experimentation with a wide variety of retrieval components and techniques. FlexIR is implemented in Perl; it is built around the standard UNIX pipeline architecture, and supports many types of preprocessing, scoring, indexing, and retrieval tools.

2.1 Approach

The retrieval model underlying FlexIR is the standard vector space model. All our official (and post-hoc) runs for CLEF 2001 used the Lnu.ltc weighting scheme [3] to compute the similarity between a query (q) and a document (d):

$$
sim(q,d) = \sum_{i \in q \cap d} \frac{\frac{1+\log(\mathrm{freq}_{i,d})}{1+\log(\mathrm{avg}_{j \in d}\mathrm{freq}_{j,d})} \cdot \frac{\mathrm{freq}_{i,q}}{\max_{j \in q}\mathrm{freq}_{j,q}} \cdot \log\left(\frac{N}{n_i}\right)}{((1-sl) \cdot pv + sl \cdot \mathrm{uw}_d) \cdot \sqrt{\sum_{i \in q}\left(\frac{\mathrm{freq}_{i,q}}{\max_{j \in q}\mathrm{freq}_{j,q}} \cdot \log\left(\frac{N}{n_i}\right)\right)^2}}
$$

For the experiments on which we report in this paper, we fixed *slope* at 0.2; the pivot was set to the average number of unique words per document.

In addition, blind feedback was applied to expand the original query with related terms. Term weights were recomputed by using the standard Rocchio method [15], where we considered the top 10 documents to be relevant and the bottom 250 documents to be non-relevant. We allowed at most 20 terms to be added to the original query. We did not carry out any filtering [11] before applying Rocchio, since some experiments that we carried out on the CLEF 2000 data set indicated a decrease in retrieval effectiveness.

2.2 Inflectional Morphology

Previous retrieval experimentation [6] in English did not show consistent significant improvements by applying morphological normalization such as rule-based stemming [14] or lexical stemming [8].

With respect to the effect of stemming on retrieval performance for languages that are morphologically richer than English, such as Dutch, German, Italian or Spanish, we have a similar mixed picture from CLEF 2000 and other experiments. Kraaij and Pohlmann [9] report that for Dutch the effect of stemming is limited; it tends to help as many queries as it hurts. Likewise, for German and French, reports seem to indicate results similar to those for English [12].

In our participation in this year's edition of CLEF, we focused on Dutch, German and Italian. Although versions of Porter's stemmer are available for each of these languages, we decided to use a lexical-based stemmer, or lemmatizer, where available, because it tends to be less aggressive than rule-based stemmers, and we conjectured that this might benefit further morphological analyses such as compound splitting (see below). For Dutch we used a Porter stemmer developed within the Uplift project [20]. The lemmatizer that we used for German and Italian is part of the TreeTagger part-of-speech tagger [16]. Each word is assigned its syntactic root by lexical look-up. Mainly number, case, and tense information is removed, leaving other morphological processes such as nominalization intact. As an example in German, *Vereinbarung* (English: agreement) and German: *vereinbaren* (English: agree) are not conflated.

3   Compound Splitting

Compound splitting (sometimes referred to as decompounding) is not an issue in English since almost all compounds, such as *Computer Science*, *peace agreement*, etc. are separated by a white space, disregarding some exceptions such as *database* or *bookshelf*. In Dutch and German, compounds are not separated and compound building is a very common phenomenon. Kraaij and Pohlmann [10] show that compound splitting leads to significant improvement of retrieval performance for Dutch, and Moulinier et al. [12] obtain similar results for German.

In some of our official runs for Dutch and German we used a compound splitter. Our compound splitter for Dutch was built using the Dutch lexicon provided by Celex [2], while our German compound splitter used the part-of-speech information provided by TreeTagger. There are several forms of compounds in German, based on different parts-of-speech, including noun-noun (e.g., German: *Straßenbahn*, English: *tram*), verb-noun (e.g., German: *Tankstelle*, English: *gas station*), verb-verb (e.g., German: *spazierengehen*, English: *taking a walk*), noun-adjective (e.g., German: *arbeitslos*, English: *unemployed*), adjective-verb (e.g., German: *sicherstellen*, English: *to secure*); etc., see [4] for a more detailed overview. We decided to limit our compound splitter to noun-noun compounds, since this is the most frequent form of compounding.

To estimate the impact of compound splitting, we first analyzed how frequent the compounding phenomenon is in Dutch and German. We compiled a list of arbitrarily chosen nouns and annotated each noun with its compound parts; Table 3 provides some details on the distribution of compounds.

Table 1. Distribution of compounds.

# compound parts	# distinct words			
	Dutch		German	
1	410	(76.6%)	2156	(75.5%)
2	118	(22.1%)	635	(22.3%)
3	7	(1.3%)	60	(2.1%)
4	0	(0.0%)	2	(0.1%)
Total	535	(100%)	2853	(100%)

Nouns that cannot be further split up, i.e., having one compound part, form the vast majority of nouns, approximately 75% in both languages. On the other hand, approximately

25% of all nouns are complex and can be decompounded into two or more parts. The differences between Dutch and German are relatively small. The most notable difference is that German contains more compounds of higher complexity, i.e., having more than two compound parts. Of course, the samples we investigated here are far too small to make a strong claim about the distribution of compounds in both languages, nevertheless, we think that they reveal a reasonable approximation of the distribution of compounds.

Since nouns are valuable information carriers, and assuming that, indeed, around 25% of the nouns are complex, decompounding seems to be an essential component of any information retrieval system for Dutch or German.

3.1   Implementation of a Compound Splitter

Our compound splitter works by recursively analyzing each noun to see whether it can be split into a sequence of concatenated nouns. We do allow for a glueing-*s*; e.g., the German compound *Friedensvertrag* (English: *peace agreement*) is split into *Frieden*+s *Vertrag*. Figure 1 shows the pseudo-code for the recursive compound splitting function split.

```
1 string split(string s)
2 {
3   int length = strlen(s);
4   string r;
5   for(int char_pos=1; char_pos<=length; char_pos++)
6   {
7     if(substr(1,char_pos,s)∈noun_lex
8        && !strcmp(split(substr(char_pos+1,length,s)),''))
9     {
10       r = split(substr(char_pos+1,length,s));
11       return concat(substr(1,char_pos,s),+,r);
12     } else if(substr(1,char_pos,s)∈noun_lex
13        && strcmp(substr(char_pos+1,char_pos+1,s),'s')
14        && !strcmp(split(substr(char_pos+2,length,s)),''))
15     {
16       r = split(substr(char_pos+2,length,s));
17       return concat(substr(1,char_pos,s),+,r);
18     };
19   };
20   if(s∈noun_lex)
21     return s;
22   else
23     return '';
24 }
```

Fig. 1. The algorithm underlying the compound splitter.

The function split takes a string, i.e., a potentially complex noun, as argument and it returns a string where the compound boundaries are indicated by a plus sign. For instance, split(bahnhof) returns bahn+hof. If it cannot split up a string into smaller components it returns the same string, and if it fails to analyze a string at all, it returns the empty string.

A number of things within the pseudo-code in Figure 1 might require further explanation, and we will now discuss the basic components of the function. The for-loop in lines 5–19 tries to split the input string at every character position proceeding from left to right. If a noun has been identified as the prefix of the string (line 7), split is called again, with the remaining part to the right of the prefix (line 8). If split did not fail to analyze this remaining string, the prefix and the analysis of the right part as it was returned by the nested call to split is returned as the value of the first call to split (line 11). The else if block in lines 12–18 is similar to the first if-condition, but allows for a glueing-*s* to separate the prefix from the remaining string (line 13). If no further split up was found during the for-loop, the input string itself is returned if it could be looked up in a noun lexicon (line 20–21), otherwise, the empty string is returned.

Note that split works from left to right, implying that the resulting analysis will be strictly right-branching (or left-branching, depending on how you look at it). For many compounds this is inappropriate from a linguistic point of view. For instance, consider the noun *Autobahnraststätte* (English: *highway restaurant*), among the theoretically possible analyses are (a) and (b) in Figure 2.

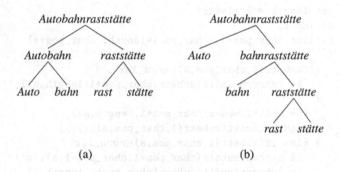

Fig. 2. Morphological analyses for the compound *Autobahnraststätte*.

From a linguistic point of view, (a) is clearly preferred over (b), since the intermediate compound *bahnraststätte* in (b), although syntactically correct, is semantically very awkward. However, since we focus on the leaves of a tree for retrieval purposes, and therefore do not exploit intermediate levels, the difference between (a) and (b) disappears, as both trees have the same set of leaves.

3.2 Evaluating the Compound Splitter

Before evaluating the effect of compound splitting in the context of retrieval, in Sections 4 and 5, we consider the quality of the compound splitter itself. To this end we compiled a set of nouns taken from the document collection, and annotated the compound parts of each compound. For each noun, there is a set S_c containing pairs of the form (p_b, p_e), indicating the character position at which a compound part begins and ends. If a noun cannot be further split up, p_b is 1 and p_e is the length of the noun. This set of annotated nouns constitutes our gold standard or reference corpus. In addition to the set of correct compound parts, there is a set S_g of compound parts produced by the compound splitter.

The bracketed match B is the number of pairs that S_c and S_g have in common, i.e., $B = \#(S_c \cap S_g)$. Analogous to the evaluation of syntactic parsers [7] and retrieval systems, the quality of the compound splitter is measured in terms of precision and recall. Both measures are further divided into micro-average precision/recall and macro-average precision/recall, depending on the way the average is computed, see Figure 3, where N_c and N_g are the size of S_c and S_g, respectively.

$$micro\text{-}avg.\ precision = \frac{\sum\limits_{Nouns} B/N_c}{\#Nouns} \qquad micro\text{-}avg.\ recall = \frac{\sum\limits_{Nouns} B/N_g}{\#Nouns}$$

$$macro\text{-}avg.\ precision = \frac{\sum\limits_{Nouns} B}{\sum\limits_{Nouns} N_c} \qquad macro\text{-}avg.\ recall = \frac{\sum\limits_{Nouns} B}{\sum\limits_{Nouns} N_g}$$

Fig. 3. Evaluation measures for compound splitting.

Precision is the percentage of compound parts returned by the compound splitter that are correct, and recall is the percentage of correct compound parts which have been identified by the compound splitter. For micro-averaging, precision and recall are computed for each noun and then they are averaged over the number of nouns. For macro-averaging, precision and recall are computed with respect to the union of all brackets of all nouns. For example, consider two nouns A and B with compound parts (a_1) and $(b_1)(b_2)(b_3)$, where the compound splitter returns (a_1) and $(b_1)(b_2b_3)$. Precision and recall for A are 1, precision for B is 0.5, and recall for B is $0.\overline{3}$. Then, micro-average precision is $(1 + 0.5)/2 = .75$, and micro-average recall is $(1 + 0.\overline{3})/2 = 0.\overline{6}$. Macro-average precision is $2/3 = 0.\overline{6}$, since 3 brackets have been assigned in total, of which two were correct, and macro-average recall is $2/4 = 0.5$, because 4 brackets were to be found in total, of which 2 were actually found by the compound splitter.

We decided to use macro-averaging in addition to the more commonly used micro-averaging, because it is more susceptible to small differences in precision and recall.

Table 3.2 shows the results of the compound splitter for Dutch and German.

Table 2. Evaluation of the compound splitter.

		Dutch		German	
		micro-avg.	macro-avg.	micro-avg.	macro-avg.
# all nouns	precision	79.7%	77.4%	86.1%	84.9%
	recall	79.7%	70.2%	86.0%	79.1%
# complex nouns	precision	27.1%	37.6%	49.3%	60.5%
	recall	27.3%	29.3%	49.0%	50.6%

The compound splitter was evaluated with respect to two kinds of sets, first all nouns, i.e., 553 Dutch nouns and 2853 German nouns, cf. Table 3, and second, only nouns which were classified as complex during manual annotation or by the compound splitter. The second set is used to deemphasize the effect of simple nouns and to focus on the complex cases, where compound splitting actually matters. It is worth noting that there is basically no difference between precision and recall when using micro-averaging. This is mainly due to the small number of partially correct decompoundings. In most cases a noun is either correctly or incorrectly split up, which is again due to the small number of nouns with a higher number of compound parts; only 1.3% of the Dutch nouns and 2.2% of the German nouns can be split into more than two components, cf. Table 3. Since macro-averaging averages over the total number of brackets instead of the number of nouns, it is more susceptible to smaller differences, and indeed reveals a better distinction between precision and recall. In both languages, precision is considerably higher than recall, which can be explained by the conservative splitting strategy used. For instance, nouns having *es* as a gluing infix, such as *Landesregierung* (English: *state government*) are not identified by the splitting algorithm as it was described in Figure 1, but it should be trivial to enhance the current algorithm to do so. Of course, there are also non-trivial cases such as *Augapfel* (English: *eyeball*) whose correct splitting is *Auge+Apfel*, where the letter *e* has been removed during compound building and during decompounding has to be added again in order to recognize *Auge* as an existing noun; see [1] for more heuristics in German decompounding. Since these rules for compound splitting are not considered in the algorithm, recall decreases.

Also to be noted in Table 3.2 is the difference in precision and recall for Dutch and German. The compound splitter performs much worse for Dutch than for German. Although we do not have a clear explanation for this, it could be the different lexicons used for recognizing simple nouns. As mentioned above, the lexicon for German is compiled by tagging the input text and simply storing all lemmas of words which have been tagged as noun. Since we did not have access to a part-of-speech tagger for Dutch, we used Celex as a lexicon, which is somewhat smaller than the tagger-based lexicon used for German, and it is also not based on the terminology used in the actual document collection. The major problem for Dutch decompounding is that the lexicon does not contain plurals, e.g. *klantenservice* (English: *customers service*) is to be split into *klanten+service*, where *klanten* is the plural of *klant*. Unfortunately, plurals are not mentioned in Celex, and therefore not recognized as nouns. One solution is to apply stemming to the potential compound parts, but again, stemming is often too aggressive, resulting in non-words. What is needed is either a lexicon containing plurals, or a lemmatizer which returns the morphological stem of a word.

3.3   Exploiting Decompounding during Retrieval

For retrieval purposes, each document in the collection is analyzed and if a compound is identified, all of its parts are added to the document. In some cases, compound splitting can give rather awkward results, e.g., German: *Bahnhof* (English: train station) is split into *Bahn* (rail) and *Hof* (court/yard). Whereas 'rail' is semantically related to 'train station,' this is less obvious for 'court' or 'yard.' Hence, it can happen that compound splitting adds some rather unrelated words to a document causing a slight topic drift.

The current versions of our compound splitters are not tuned for retrieval purposes; for instance, we made no attempt to avoid the addition of unrelated compound parts.

Compounds occurring in a query are analyzed in a similar way: the parts are simply added to the query. Since we also expand the documents with compound parts, there is no need for compound formation [13].

Currently, as mentioned above, only the minimal parts of a compound (i.e., the leaves in a tree, as shown in Figure 2) and the compound itself are considered. If a compound is more complex, containing more than two compound parts, intermediate compound parts could also be considered. Although less specific than the compound itself, they are more specific than the minimal compounds. In the current setting we refrained from using intermediate compound parts, because it raises the issue of ambiguity, as explained above, but we think that, given a well-performing compound splitter, it might also be worth adding intermediate compound parts to increase precision.

The approach of adding compound parts to the document itself has some side effects whose impact is not clear yet. For example, what is an appropriate matching strategy for compounds? In our implementation, compounds and their parts are treated independently of each other, i.e., the term weight (tf.idf score) is computed independently for the compound and its parts. If a query contains a compound A, split into $(a_1)(a_2)$, and a document also contains compound A, computing the similarity score considers all three matches: A, a_1, and a_2. This seems to be inappropriate as the compound parts are conceptually not independent of the compound itself. However, this approach rewards compound matching in contrast to simple term matching, which again seems appropriate since compounds are more specific their compound parts. This issue of compound matching and assigning weights to compounds is very similar to the problem of phrase matching and phrase weighting in English [5,19].

Another problem with simply adding the compound parts to the document itself concerns document length. Table 3.3 shows the differences in average document length before and after adding compound parts to the documents in the collection that was used for the CLEF 2001 evaluation exercise.

Table 3. Effect of adding compounds on document length and weight.

document length/weight	Dutch		German	
	orig.	+ comp. parts	orig.	+ comp. parts
avg. length in byte	1587	2116 (+33.3%)	1567	1420 (+10.4%)
avg. no. unique words	171	203 (+18.7%)	142	156 (+9.9%)
avg. cosine document weight	11.01	11.74 (+6.6%)	10.73	11.25 (+4.8%)

The three measures listed above are the most commonly used measures for pivoted document normalization, cf. [17]. Adding compound parts has a significant effect on the document length, but it is unclear to what extent this affects retrieval effectiveness.

Finally, some figures about the topics that were used in the CLEF 2001 evaluation exercise. For Dutch 50 topics were used, for German 49. The average number of (non-unique) nouns in the (combined) title and description fields was 6.62 for Dutch and 6.42 for German, with an average of 1.3 (non-unique) compounds for Dutch and 1.46 for German. The average number of (non-unique) parts added per topic by a human compound splitter was 2.66 for Dutch and 3.22 for German.

4 Official Runs

At CLEF 2001, the University of Amsterdam participated in the monolingual task only, covering retrieval in Dutch, German, and Italian. For each language we submitted three types of runs:

Type M (Morphological) The title and the description field of the topic are used to generate the retrieval query (this was a mandatory requirement to be met by at least one of the runs). Words are morphologically normalized and compounds are split (Dutch and German). Blind feedback is applied to the top 10 documents adding at most 20 terms to the original query. This includes the runs AmsNlM, AmsDeM, and AmsItM.

Type Nv (Naïve) The title and the description field of the topic are used to generate the retrieval query. Blind feedback is applied to the top 10 documents adding at most 20 terms to the original query. In contrast to runs of type M, no morphological normalization or compound splitting are applied. This includes the runs AmsNlNv, AmsDeNv, and AmsItNv.

Type T (Title only) The same retrieval and document processing techniques are used as for runs of type M, but query formulation is restricted to the title field of the topic. This includes the runs AmsNlT, AmsDeT, and AmsItT.

Our motivations for these runs were as follows. Type M runs were intended to be the most effective runs, using techniques which are considered to improve retrieval effectiveness, such as blind feedback. Type T runs use the same techniques, but queries are much shorter and, therefore, more closely resemble queries posed by non-experts. In contrast to type M runs, type Nv runs apply no language specific techniques such as stemming/lemmatization or compound splitting.

After our submissions had been evaluated and our scores returned, we discovered that the compound splitter malfunctioned for a large number of Dutch nouns due to a bug in the interface between the stemmer and the compound splitter. This affected our type M and type T runs for Dutch submitted to CLEF 2001. Below we report on both the official (submitted) runs and the corrected ones. To start, Figure 4 displays the interpolated precision-recall curves for the three languages, with two plots for Dutch (not corrected and corrected).

Next, considering the non-interpolated avg. precisions for type M and type Nv runs in Table 4, one can see that morphological normalization does result in significant improvements[1] in effectiveness: $\approx 25\%$ for German and Italian and even $\approx 54\%$ ($\approx 69\%$) for Dutch (Dutch corrected).

The improvements were consistent across all topics, as is witnessed by the histograms in Figure 5, where we have plotted the improvements in average precision of type M runs over type Nv runs for each of the individual topics.

It is not obvious why the improvement for Dutch (whether corrected or not) is so much bigger than for the other two languages. One reason could be that our precision scores for Dutch are, in general, considerably lower than the precision scores for German and

---

[1] Note that significant improvement here refers to the definition in [18], where changes of more than 5% are considered significant.

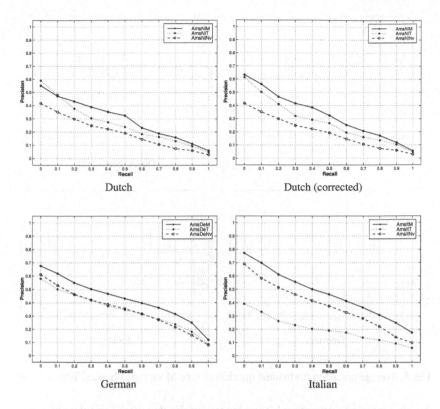

Dutch   Dutch (corrected)

German   Italian

Fig. 4. 11pt interpolated avg. precision for all submitted runs.

Italian. Our results seem to suggest that the improvements brought about by compound splitting (plus stemming) are independent from the underlying retrieval engine. Observe that there are some topics for which the type M run performs worse than the type Nv run. A closer inspection of the topics showed that this was due to topic drift resulting from blind feedback.

Table 4. Non-interpolated avg. precisions of type M runs vs. type Nv runs.

	Dutch	Dutch (corrected)	German	Italian
Naïve (Nv)	0.1833	0.1833	0.3342	0.3580
+ Morph. Anal. (M)	0.2833	0.3114	0.4172	0.4485
	+54.6%	+69.9%	+24.8%	+25.3%

Table 5. Non-interpolated avg. precisions of TD-queries vs. T-queries.

	Dutch	Dutch (corrected)	German	Italian
Morph. Analysis (M)	0.2833	0.3114	0.4172	0.4485
Title only (T)	0.2418	0.2582	0.3342	0.1895
	-14.6%	-17.1%	-19.9%	-57.7%

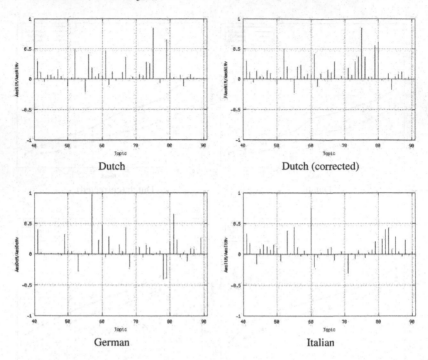

Dutch   Dutch (corrected)

German   Italian

Fig. 5. Average precision (individual queries) of type M vs. type Nv runs, Topics 41–90.

Another interesting question is to compare queries that were formulated by using the title and the description field of the topic to queries that were formulated by using the title of the topic only. Queries based on title information only are much shorter and more closely resemble queries a non-expert would formulate. Table 1 shows that for Dutch and German the decrease in effectiveness is certainly significant but not too dramatic. On the other hand, for Italian, using the title field only has a drastic impact on effectiveness, decreasing it by $\approx 57\%$. What causes this dramatic decrease, particularly in comparison to Dutch and German, is not obvious at this stage.

Finally, Table 1 shows the average precisions at a set of fixed ranks. This is again interesting from a regular user's point of view, who will hardly ever consider more than the top 20 documents returned by a retrieval system.

5   Post-submission Experiments

Following the release of the results of our submitted runs and of the evaluation scripts, we conducted a number of post-submission experiments. These were aimed at exploring the interaction between compound splitting and the various other techniques that we used to enhance retrieval effectiveness. In particular, we wanted to understand the interaction between blind feedback and compound splitting. As compound splitting is not an issue for Italian, we restricted ourselves to Dutch and German.

Table 6. Avg. precision at rank n.

	Dutch (corrected)			German			Italian		
	PAmsN1M	AmsN1Nv	PAmsN1T	AmsDeM	AmsDeNv	AmsDeT	AmsItM	AmsItNv	AmsItT
p@5	0.4160	0.2760	0.3510	0.5102	0.4490	0.4286	0.5660	0.4255	0.2426
p@10	0.3480	0.2280	0.2714	0.5102	0.4163	0.4082	0.5170	0.4000	0.2106
p@15	0.3067	0.2027	0.2408	0.4721	0.4122	0.3878	0.4638	0.3645	0.1957
p@20	0.2840	0.1840	0.2306	0.4582	0.3878	0.3582	0.4330	0.3340	0.1766
p@30	0.2520	0.1667	0.2027	0.4102	0.3503	0.3218	0.3695	0.3007	0.1539
p@100	0.1412	0.0890	0.1231	0.2504	0.2143	0.1980	0.1970	0.1572	0.0898
p@200	0.0884	0.0552	0.0815	0.1669	0.1441	0.1288	0.1147	0.0951	0.0618
p@500	0.0402	0.0264	0.0393	0.0793	0.0715	0.0669	0.0502	0.0457	0.0338
p@1000	0.0211	0.0140	0.0209	0.0410	0.0380	0.0381	0.0255	0.0240	0.0202

For both Dutch and German, we considered four types of runs: with or without blind feedback (F/NoF) and with or without compound splitting (C/NoC); all runs used stemming. Observe that runs of type FC coincide with the earlier type M runs; the difference between type Nv runs and type FNoC runs is that the latter use stemming. We use the suffix 'Nl' to indicate Dutch runs, and 'D' to indicate German runs.

5.1 Dutch

For Dutch, adding compound splitting in the absence of feeedback leads to an improvement in average precision of slightly more than 6%; in the presence of feedback it gives a slightly bigger improvement of 8.5%. Adding relevance feedback in the presence or absence of decompounding did not evidence any significant changes: with compound splitting switched off, feedback gave a 1.5% improvement, and otherwise it gave a 3.8% improvement. The combination of feedback and compound splitting resulted in an improvement of 10.1% in average precision over no feedback and no compound splitting; see Table 5.1 for a summary.

Table 7. Non-interpolated avg. precision for Dutch without/with relevance feedback and without/with compound splitting.

Dutch	No feedback (NoF)	+ Feedback (F)	
No compound splitting (NoC)	0.2828	0.2871	+1.5%
+ Compound splitting (C)	0.3001	0.3114	+3.8%
	+6.1%	+8.5%	+10.1%

It is instructive to look at the histograms comparing the various runs on a topic-by-topic basis; see Figure 6. The top row illustrates the impact of adding blind feedback. As was to be expected (based on reports in the literature), in some cases the addition of feedback hurts precision; this is largely independent of compound splitting being switched on, see e.g., Topics 84 and 85.

The addition of compound splitting leads to some decrease in precision for some topics (e.g., Topic 56), while it leads to more substantial improvements in others (e.g., Topics 76 and 80), even on top of blind feedback (see FCN1/FNoCN1). Note that there is no topic-by-topic correlation between the effects of compound splitting and the effects

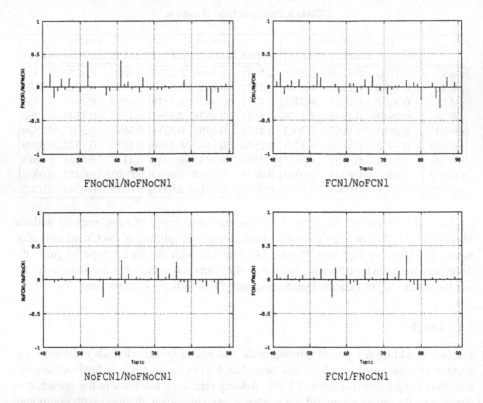

Fig. 6. Comparisons of avg. precision (individual queries) for four Dutch runs. (Top): Adding relevance feedback. (Bottom): Adding compound splitting.

of blind feedback, but one can observe similar *kinds* of improvements (degradations) across all topics.

5.2   German

The phenomena that we observed for German were similar to those observed for Dutch, with the main differences being that the overall improvements — whether caused by blind feedback or by compound splitting — tend to be more significant (as witnessed by Table 5.2), while some local changes were more dramatic than for Dutch (as witnessed by Figure 7).

Table 8. Non-interpolated avg. precision without/with relevance feedback and without/with compound splitting.

German	No feedback (NoF)	+ Feedback (F)
No compound splitting (NoC)	0.3551	0.3961 +11.5%
+ Compound splitting (C)	0.3892	0.4172 +7.2%
	+9.6%	+5.3% +17.5%

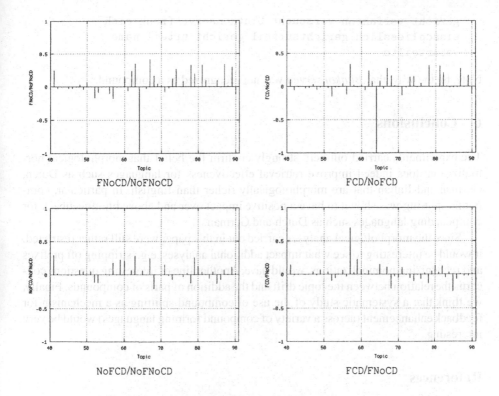

FNoCD/NoFNoCD

FCD/NoFCD

NoFCD/NoFNoCD

FCD/FNoCD

Fig. 7. Comparisons of avg. precision (individual queries) for four German runs. (Top): Adding relevance feedback. (Bottom): Adding compound splitting.

To make matters more concrete, let us take a closer look at one of the topics. In particular, feedback caused a serious drop in precision for topic 64:

```
<DE-title>Computermäuse und RSI </DE-title>
<DE-desc>Suche Dokumente, die über Erkrankungen an RSI
berichten.
</DE-desc>
```

One of the examples in which splitting worked particularly well on top of blind feedback was topic 57:

```
<DE-title>Strafprozess über verseuchte
Blutkonserven</DE-title>
<DE-desc>Suche alle Informationen über Gerichtsverfahren zu
verseuchten Blutkonserven in Frankreich, einschließlich der
Gerichtsurteile und der Namen der Verurteilten.</DE-desc>
```

The split (and stopped and lemmatized) reformulation of this topic was

```
strafprozess verseucht blutkonserve alle en
gerichtsverfahren
```

    gericht verfahren verseucht blutkonserve frankreich
    einschliesslich gerichtsurteil gericht urteil name
    verurteilte

Note, by the way, that *Blutkonserven* was not recognized as a compound.

6 Conclusions

The experiments carried out here strongly confirm the belief that morphological normalization does indeed improve retrieval effectiveness for languages such as Dutch,
German and Italian that are morphologically richer than English. In particular, compound splitting was shown to have a positive impact over and above blind feedback for
compounding languages such as Dutch and German.

Since the morphological analyses carried out in this paper were still rather restricted,
it would be interesting to see what impact additional analyses, e.g., stripping off prefixes
and recognizing nominalizations, would have. Another line of interesting questions concerns the relation between the topic drift and the addition of parts of compounds. Finally,
we think that a systematic study of the use of compound splitting as a mechanism for
feedback enhancement (across a variety of compound forming languages) would be very
interesting.

References

1. M. Adda-Decker and G. Adda. Morphological decomposition for ASR in German. In *Work-shop on Phonetics and Phonology in Automatic Speech Recognition*, 2000.
2. R. Baayen, R. Piepenbrock, and L. Gulikers. The CELEX lexical database (release 2). Dis-tributed by the Linguistic Data Consortium, University of Pennsylvania, 1995.
3. C. Buckley, A. Singhal, and M. Mitra. New retrieval approaches using SMART: TREC 4. In D. Harman, editor, *Proceedings of the Fourth Text REtrieval Conference (TREC-4)*, pages 25–48. NIST Special Publication 500-236, 1995.
4. G. Drosdowski, editor. *Duden: Grammatik der deutschen Gegenwartssprache*. Dudenverlag, fourth edition, 1984.
5. J. Fagan. *Experiments in Automatic Phrase Indexing for Document Retrieval: A Comparison of Syntactic and Non-Syntactic Methods*. PhD thesis, Department of Computer Science, Cornell University, 1987.
6. W. Frakes. Stemming algorithms. In W. Frakes and R. Baeza-Yates, editors, *Information Retrieval: Data Structures & Algorithms*, pages 131–160. Prentice Hall, 1992.
7. J. Goodman. Parsing algorithms and metrics. In *Proceedings of the 34th Annual Meeting of the Association for Computational Linguistics (ACL'96)*, pages 177–183, 1996.
8. D. Harman. How effective is suffixing? *Journal of the American Society for Information Science*, 42:7–15, 1991.
9. W. Kraaij and R. Pohlmann. Viewing stemming as recall enhancement. In *Proceedings of the 19th Annual International ACM SIGIR Conference on Research and Development in Information Retrieval*, pages 40–48, 1996.
10. W. Kraaij and R. Pohlmann. Comparing the effect of syntactic vs. statistical phrase index strategies for Dutch. In *Proceedings ECDL'98*, pages 605–617, 1998.

11. M. Mitra, A. Singhal, and C. Buckley. Improving automatic query expansion. In *Proceedings of the 21st Annual International ACM SIGIR Conference on Research and Development in Information Retrieval*, pages 206–214, 1998.
12. I. Moulinier, J. McCulloh, and E. Lund. West Group at 2001: Non-English monolingual retrieval. In *Proceedings CLEF-2000*, 2000.
13. R. Pohlmann and W. Kraaij. Improving the precision of a text retrieval system with compound analysis. In J. Landsbergen, J. Odijk, K. van Deemter, and G. Veldhuijzen van Zanten, editors, *Proceedings of the 7th Computational Linguistics in the Netherlands Meeting (CLIN 1996)*, pages 115–129, 1996.
14. M. Porter. An algorithm for suffix stripping. *Program*, 14(3):130–137, 1980.
15. J. Rocchio. Relevance feedback in information retrieval. In G. Salton, editor, *The SMART Retrieval System — Experiments in Automatic Document Processing*. Prentice Hall, 1971.
16. H. Schmid. Probabilistic part-of-speech tagging using decision trees. In *Proceedings of International Conference on New Methods in Language Processing*, 1994.
17. A. Singhal, G. Salton, M. Mitra, and C. Buckley. Document length normalization. *Information Processing & Management*, 32(5):619–633, 1996.
18. K. Sparck Jones. Automatic indexing. *Journal of Documentation*, 30(4):393–432, 1974.
19. T. Strzalkowski. Natural language information retrieval. *Information Processing & Management*, 31(3):397–417, 1995.
20. UPLIFT: Utrecht project: Linguistic information for free text retrieval. http://www-uilots.let.uu.nl/~uplift/.

Stemming Evaluated in 6 Languages by Hummingbird SearchServer™ at CLEF 2001

Stephen Tomlinson

Hummingbird
Ottawa, Ontario, Canada
stephen.tomlinson@hummingbird.com
http://www.hummingbird.com/

Abstract. Hummingbird submitted ranked result sets for all 5 Monolingual Information Retrieval tasks (German, French, Italian, Spanish and Dutch) of the Cross-Language Evaluation Forum (CLEF) 2001. SearchServer's Intuitive Searching™ produced the highest average precision score in the German task of the 12 groups submitting automatic, Title+Description runs. Enabling stemming in SearchServer increased average precision by 43% in German, 30% in Dutch, 18% in French, 16% in Italian, 12% in Spanish and 12% in English. All points in the 95% confidence interval for the impact of stemming on average precision in German (based on the two-sided Wilcoxon signed rank test) were greater than all points in the corresponding intervals for French, English and Italian, evidence that stemming is more beneficial in German than in French, English or Italian.

1   Introduction

Hummingbird SearchServer[1] is an indexing, search and retrieval engine for embedding in Windows and UNIX information applications. SearchServer, originally a product of Fulcrum Technologies, was acquired by Hummingbird in 1999. Founded in 1983 in Ottawa, Canada, Fulcrum produced the first commercial application program interface (API) for writing information retrieval applications, Fulcrum® Ful/Text™. The SearchServer kernel is embedded in many Hummingbird products, including SearchServer, an application toolkit used for knowledge-intensive applications that require fast access to unstructured information.

SearchServer supports a variation of the Structured Query Language (SQL), called SearchSQL™, which has extensions for text retrieval. SearchServer conforms to subsets of the Open Database Connectivity (ODBC) interface for C programming language applications and the Java Database Connectivity (JDBC) interface for Java applications. Almost 200 document formats are supported,

---

[1] Fulcrum® is a registered trademark, and SearchServer™, SearchSQL™, Intuitive Searching™ and Ful/Text™ are trademarks of Hummingbird Ltd. All other copyrights, trademarks and tradenames are the property of their respective owners.

C.A. Peters et al. (Eds.): CLEF 2001, LNCS 2406, pp. 278–287, 2002.
© Springer-Verlag Berlin Heidelberg 2002

such as Word, WordPerfect, Excel, PowerPoint, PDF and HTML. Many character sets and languages are supported. SearchServer's Intuitive Searching algorithms were updated for version 4.0 which shipped in Fall 1999, and in subsequent releases of other products. SearchServer 5.0, which shipped in Spring 2001, works in Unicode internally [2] and contains improved natural language processing technology, particularly for languages with many compound words, such as German, Dutch and Finnish.

2   Setup

For the official CLEF runs, internal development builds of SearchServer 5.0 were used (5.0.501.115 plus some experimental changes motivated by tests on the CLEF 2000 collections). For the diagnostic runs used to evaluate stemming, internal build 5.0.504.157 was used.

2.1   Data

The CLEF 2001 collections consisted of tagged (SGML-formatted) news articles (mostly from 1994) in 6 different languages: German, French, Italian, Spanish, Dutch and English. Table 1 gives their sizes. For more information on the CLEF collections, see the CLEF web site [1].

Table 1. Sizes of CLEF 2001 Collections

Language	Text Size (uncompressed)	Number of Documents
German	555,285,140 bytes (530 MB)	225,371
French	253,528,734 bytes (242 MB)	87,191
Italian	290,771,116 bytes (277 MB)	108,578
Spanish	544,347,121 bytes (519 MB)	215,738
Dutch	558,560,087 bytes (533 MB)	190,604
English	441,048,231 bytes (421 MB)	113,005

2.2   Text Reader

The custom text reader called cTREC, originally written for handling TREC collections [7], handled expansion of the library files of the CLEF collections and was extended to support the CLEF guidelines of only indexing specific fields of specific documents. The entities described in the DTD files were also converted, e.g. "=" was converted to the equal sign "=".

The documents were assumed to be in the Latin-1 character set, the code page which, for example, assigns e-acute (é) hexadecimal 0xe9 or decimal 233. cTREC passes through the Latin-1 characters, i.e. does not convert them to

Unicode. SearchServer's Translation Text Reader (nti), was chained on top of cTREC and the Win_1252_UCS2 translation was specified via its /t option to translate from Latin-1 to the Unicode character set desired by SearchServer.

2.3 Indexing

A separate SearchServer table was created for each language, created with a SearchSQL statement such as the following:

```
CREATE SCHEMA CLEF01DE CREATE TABLE CLEF01DE
(DOCNO VARCHAR(256) 128)
TABLE_LANGUAGE 'GERMAN'
STOPFILE 'GER_AW.STP'
PERIODIC
BASEPATH 'e:\data\clef';
```

The TABLE_LANGUAGE parameter specifies which language to use when performing stemming operations at index time. The STOPFILE parameter specifies a stop file containing typically a couple hundred stop words to not index; the stop file also contains instructions on changes to the default indexing rules, for example, to enable accent-indexing, or to change the apostrophe to a word separator. Here are the first few lines of the stop file used for the French task:

```
IAC = "\u0300-\u0345"
PST = "'‘"
STOPLIST =
a
à
afin
# 112 stop words not shown
```

The IAC line enables indexing of the specified accents (Unicode combining diacritical marks 0x0300-0x0345). Accent indexing was enabled for all runs except the Italian and English runs. Accents were known to be specified in the Italian queries but were not consistently used in the Italian documents. The PST line adds the specified characters (apostrophes in this case) to the list of word separators. The apostrophes were changed to word separators for all submitted runs except the German and English runs. Probably it would have made no difference to have also included it in the German runs. Note that the IAC syntax is new to SearchServer 5.0, and the interpretation of the PST line may differ from previous versions.

Into each table, we just needed to insert one row, specifying the top directory of the library files for the language, using an Insert statement such as the following:

```
INSERT INTO CLEF01DE ( FT_SFNAME, FT_FLIST ) VALUES
('German','cTREC/E/d=128:s!nti/t=Win_1252_UCS2:cTREC/C/@:s');
```

To index each table, we just executed a Validate Index statement such as the following:

```
VALIDATE INDEX CLEF01DE VALIDATE TABLE
TEMP_FILE_SIZE 2000000000 BUFFER 256000000;
```

By default, the index supports both exact matching (after some Unicode-based normalizations, such as converting to upper-case and decomposed form) and matching on stems.

3   Search Techniques

The CLEF organizers created 50 "topics" and translated them into many languages. Each topic contained a "Title" (subject of the topic), "Description" (a one-sentence specification of the information need) and "Narrative" (more detailed guidelines for what a relevant document should or should not contain). The participants were asked to use the Title and Description fields for at least one automatic submission per task this year to facilitate comparison of results.

We created an ODBC application, called QueryToRankings.c, based on the example stsample.c program included with SearchServer, to parse the CLEF topics files, construct and execute corresponding SearchSQL queries, fetch the top 1000 rows, and write out the rows in the results format requested by CLEF. SELECT statements were issued with the SQLExecDirect api call. Fetches were done with SQLFetch (typically 1000 SQLFetch calls per query).

3.1   Intuitive Searching

For all runs, we used SearchServer's Intuitive Searching, i.e. the IS_ABOUT predicate of SearchSQL, which accepts unstructured text. For example, for the German version of topic C041, the Title was "Pestizide in Babykost" (Pesticides in Baby Food), and the Description was "Berichte über Pestizide in Babynahrung sind gesucht" (Find reports on pesticides in baby food). A corresponding SearchSQL query would be:

```
SELECT RELEVANCE('V2:3') AS REL, DOCNO
FROM CLEF01DE
WHERE FT_TEXT IS_ABOUT 'Pestizide in Babykost Berichte über
Pestizide in Babynahrung sind gesucht'
ORDER BY REL DESC;
```

This query would create a working table with the 2 columns named in the SELECT clause, a REL column containing the relevance value of the row for the query, and a DOCNO column containing the document's identifier. The ORDER BY clause specifies that the most relevant rows should be listed first. The statement "SET MAX_SEARCH_ROWS 1000" was previously executed so that the working table would contain at most 1000 rows.

3.2   Stemming

SearchServer "stems" each distinct word to one or more base forms, called stems, using lexicon-based natural language processing technology. For example, in English, "baby", "babied", "babies", "baby's" and "babying" all have "baby" as a stem. Compound words in languages such as German, Dutch and Finnish produce multiple stems; e.g., in German, "babykost" has "baby" and "kost" as stems. SearchServer 5.0 uses Inxight LinguistX Platform 3.2 for stemming operations.

By default, Intuitive Searching stems each word in the query, counts the number of occurrences of each stem, and creates a vector. Optionally some stems are discarded (secondary term selection) if they have a high document frequency or to enforce a maximum number of stems, but we didn't discard any stems for our CLEF runs. The index is searched for documents containing terms which stem to any of the stems of the vector.

The VECTOR_GENERATOR set option controls which stemming operations are performed by Intuitive Searching. Table 2 lists the settings used for our submitted runs.

Table 2. VECTOR_GENERATOR Settings

Language	Recommended VECTOR_GENERATOR (SearchServer 5.0)
German	word!ftelp/lang=german/base|*|word!ftelp/lang=german/expand
French	word!ftelp/lang=french/base/single|*|word!ftelp/lang=french/expand
Italian	word!ftelp/lang=italian/base/single|*|word!ftelp/lang=italian/expand
Spanish	word!ftelp/lang=spanish/base/single|*|word!ftelp/lang=spanish/expand
Dutch	word!ftelp/lang=dutch/base|*|word!ftelp/lang=dutch/expand
English	word!ftelp/lang=english/base/single|*|word!ftelp/lang=english/expand

Besides linguistic expansion from stemming, we did not do any other kinds of query expansion. For example, we did not use approximate text searching for spell-correction because the queries were believed to be spelled correctly. We did not use row expansion or any other kind of blind feedback technique.

3.3   Statistical Relevance Ranking

SearchServer calculates a relevance value for a row of a table with respect to a vector of stems based on several statistics. The inverse document frequency of the stem is estimated from information in the dictionary. The term frequency (number of occurrences of the stem in the row (including any term that stems to it)) is determined from the reference file. The length of the row (based on the number of indexed characters in all columns of the row, which is typically dominated by the external document), is optionally incorporated. The already-mentioned count of the stem in the vector is also used. To synthesize this information into a relevance value, SearchServer dampens the term frequency and adjusts for document length in a manner similar to Okapi [4] and dampens the inverse document frequency in a manner similar to [5]. SearchServer's relevance values are always an integer in the range 0 to 1000.

SearchServer's RELEVANCE_METHOD setting can be used to optionally square the importance of the inverse document frequency (by choosing a RELEVANCE_METHOD of 'V2:4' instead of 'V2:3'). The importance of document length to the ranking is controlled by SearchServer's RELEVANCE_DLEN_IMP setting (scale of 0 to 1000).

3.4 Query Stop Words

Our QueryToRankings program removed words such as "find", "relevant" and "document" from the topics before presenting them to SearchServer, i.e. words which are not stop words in general but were commonly used in the topics as general instructions. The lists for the CLEF languages were developed by examining the CLEF 2000 topics (not this year's topics). After receiving the relevance assessments this year, we did an experiment, and this step had only a minor benefit; the average precision increased just 1% or 2% in all languages (in absolute terms, from 0.0031 in Italian to 0.0107 in French). It doesn't appear to be important to comb the old topics files for potential query stop words.

4 Results

The evaluation measures are explained in a paper at the end of this volume. Briefly: *Precision* is the percentage of retrieved documents which are relevant. *Precision@n* is the precision after n documents have been retrieved. *Average precision* for a topic is the average of the precision after each relevant document is retrieved (using zero as the precision for relevant documents which are not retrieved). *Recall* is the percentage of relevant documents which have been retrieved. *Interpolated precision* at a particular recall level for a topic is the maximum precision achieved for the topic at that or any higher recall level. For a set of topics, the measure is the average of the measure for each topic (i.e. all topics are weighted equally).

The Monolingual Information Retrieval tasks were to run 50 queries against document collections in the same language and submit a list of the top-1000 ranked documents to CLEF for judging (in June 2001). The 5 languages were German, French, Italian, Spanish and Dutch. CLEF produced a "qrels" file for each of the 5 tasks: a list of documents judged to be relevant or not relevant for each topic. From these, the evaluation measures were calculated with Chris Buckley's trec_eval program. Additionally, the CLEF organizers translated the topics into many more languages, including English, and also provided a comparable English document collection, for use in the multilingual task. By grepping the English results out of the multilingual qrels, we were able to produce a comparable monolingual English test collection for diagnostic runs.

For some topics and languages, no documents were judged relevant. The precision scores are just averaged over the number of topics for which at least one document was judged relevant.

4.1   Submitted Runs

All submitted runs used both the Title and Description fields. Runs humDE01, humFR01, humIT01, humES01 and humNL01 used relevance method 'V2:3' and RELEVANCE_DLEN_IMP 500; these settings typically worked best on last year's collections. Runs humDE01x, humFR01x, humIT01x, humES01x, humNL01x used relevance method 'V2:4' and RELEVANCE_DLEN_IMP 750, which worked well on the TREC-9 Main Web Task last year [7]. After receiving the relevance assessments, preliminary experiments suggest that a combination of 'V2:3' and 750 would have been best for most languages this year, but it makes little difference.

In each of the 5 languages, SearchServer produced a run which scored in the top-3 in average precision, just counting the highest scoring Title+Description run from each group. In particular, the humDE01x run had the highest average precision score in the German task out of 12 groups. The precision scores of our submitted runs can be found in an appendix of this volume, or in the online workshop paper [6].

4.2   Impact of Stemming in 6 Languages

Table 3 shows runs which were done with a more recent SearchServer 5.0 build in August 2001. For each language, the runs vary in their VECTOR_GENERATOR setting. The first run set VECTOR_GENERATOR to the empty string, which disables stemming. The second run set VECTOR_GENERATOR to the recommended setting of Table 2, which enables stemming. For all of these runs, both the Title and Description were used, the relevance method was 'V2:3' and the RELEVANCE_DLEN_IMP setting was 750. Listed for each run are its average precision (AvgP), the precision after 5, 10 and 20 documents retrieved (P@5, P@10 and P@20 respectively), and the interpolated precision at 0% and 30% recall (Rec0 and Rec30 respectively). Additionally listed for the runs with stemming enabled is the number of topics on which the run scored higher, lower and equal (to 4 decimal places) in average precision to the corresponding run with stemming disabled. The languages investigated were German (DE), French (FR), Italian (IT), Spanish (ES), Dutch (NL) and English (EN).

Table 4 summarizes the percentage increases in the precision scores from stemming in each of the 6 languages. The rankings of the languages (in terms of stemming importance) are not the same for all measures. German and Dutch stand out as the top 2 beneficiaries in most measures. The percentage changes for French and Italian were generally larger than for Spanish, even though more topics were helped in Spanish. The results for English differ from what we found in the TREC-9 Main Web Task [7], where some scores, such as Precision@10, were a little lower with stemming enabled.

Table 3. Precision with Stemming Disabled and Enabled in 6 Languages

Run	AvgP	P@5	P@10	P@20	Rec0	Rec30	vs Stem Off
DE: stem off	0.3269	46.1%	43.7%	36.4%	0.7102	0.4038	
DE: stem on	0.4669	58.0%	52.4%	47.4%	0.8186	0.5699	42-6-1
FR: stem off	0.4114	46.9%	38.0%	33.0%	0.7301	0.5047	
FR: stem on	0.4855	52.2%	43.1%	36.2%	0.8121	0.5927	28-17-4
IT: stem off	0.3900	48.1%	43.0%	35.5%	0.7076	0.4729	
IT: stem on	0.4514	50.6%	48.5%	40.9%	0.7456	0.5553	28-16-3
ES: stem off	0.4848	63.3%	55.9%	47.1%	0.8117	0.6154	
ES: stem on	0.5429	70.6%	61.6%	51.9%	0.8842	0.6726	33-13-3
NL: stem off	0.3189	42.4%	36.8%	28.0%	0.6603	0.4197	
NL: stem on	0.4144	54.0%	45.6%	35.1%	0.7939	0.5313	37-10-3
EN: stem off	0.4732	48.9%	39.1%	29.7%	0.7765	0.5959	
EN: stem on	0.5317	52.8%	41.7%	31.7%	0.8213	0.7029	26-13-8

Table 4. Percentage Increase from Stemming

Language	AvgP	P@5	P@10	P@20	Rec0	Rec30	Range
German	+43%	+26%	+20%	+30%	+15%	+41%	15-43%
Dutch	+30%	+27%	+24%	+25%	+20%	+27%	20-30%
French	+18%	+11%	+13%	+10%	+11%	+17%	10-18%
Italian	+16%	+5%	+13%	+15%	+5%	+17%	5-17%
English	+12%	+8%	+7%	+7%	+6%	+18%	6-18%
Spanish	+12%	+12%	+10%	+10%	+9%	+9%	9-12%

Table 5. Significance Levels (Wilcoxon) of Impact from Stemming

Language	AvgP	P@5	P@10	P@20	Rec0	Rec30
German	0.0%	0.3%	0.5%	0.0%	1.9%	0.0%
Dutch	0.0%	0.1%	0.2%	0.0%	0.1%	0.0%
Spanish	0.2%	1.2%	1.1%	1.7%	8.3%	17.1%
English	0.6%	7.9%	11.5%	1.2%	44.5%	0.4%
French	0.7%	19.9%	4.6%	1.4%	3.5%	6.7%
Italian	5.4%	74.7%	18.3%	1.4%	37.5%	4.0%

The probabilities of these changes with stemming enabled happening by chance, making the assumptions associated with the two-sided Wilcoxon signed rank test [3], are given by the significance levels (also known as p-values) of Table 5. (We implemented an exact computation for the significance levels, estimators and confidence intervals (to the number of decimal places shown), including in the case of ties in the absolute values of the differences.) The table shows that many of the results are statistically significant at the 1% level, including the impact on average precision for 5 of the 6 languages (all except Italian), and the impact on all measures for Dutch. The impact on Precision@20 is statistically significant at the 5% level for all 6 languages.

Table 6. Estimators of Impact from Stemming

Language	AvgP	P@5	P@10	P@20	Rec0	Rec30
German	0.1091	0.1000	0.0500	0.0750	0.0022	0.1299
Dutch	0.0536	0.1000	0.0500	0.0500	0.0292	0.0476
Spanish	0.0360	0.1000	0.0500	0.0250	0.0000	0.0121
French	0.0342	0.0000	0.0500	0.0250	0.0024	0.0186
English	0.0217	0.0000	0.0000	0.0250	0.0000	0.0273
Italian	0.0197	0.0000	0.0000	0.0250	0.0070	0.0259

In Table 6 we show estimators of the impact of stemming on each measure. The estimator is the Walsh average [3] which, when subtracted from the scores of the stemming-enabled run, maximizes the significance level by the two-sided Wilcoxon signed rank test (for all of our experiments, there was just one such value). This estimator is usually the same as the Hodges-Lehmann Estimator [3] and is less sensitive to outliers than the average difference.

Table 7. Confidence Intervals for Impact of Stemming on Average Precision

Language	90% Confidence Int.	95% Confidence Int.	99% Confidence Int.
German	[0.0751, 0.1604]	[0.0703, 0.1752]	[0.0617, 0.2093]
Dutch	[0.0293, 0.0925]	[0.0263, 0.0990]	[0.0181, 0.1213]
Spanish	[0.0108, 0.0670]	[0.0089, 0.0748]	[0.0049, 0.0857]
French	[0.0078, 0.0640]	[0.0047, 0.0694]	[0.0000, 0.0872]
English	[0.0034, 0.0531]	[0.0018, 0.0611]	[0.0000, 0.0963]
Italian	[0.0024, 0.0430]	[−0.0001, 0.0504]	[−0.0062, 0.0699]

Finally, Table 7 shows 90%, 95% and 99% confidence intervals for the estimators for the average precision measure. The listed intervals are derived from the range of values for which, when subtracted from the scores of the stemming-enabled run, the significance level by the two-sided Wilcoxon signed rank test is at least 10%, 5% and 1% respectively. The listed boundary points might not need to be in the interval; we round the values so as to enlarge the interval when necessary to ensure the listed interval covers the minimal one. For example, we know that 0.0000 does not need to be in the 99% confidence interval for French because Table 5 lists a significance level of less than 1%, but because there are values less than 0.0001 which are in the interval, we list 0.0000 as the low point.

The low point of the 99% confidence interval for German gives strong evidence that there is at least a gain of 6 points of average precision from stemming, which is substantial. The high points for all languages are greater than 6 points, so we can't rule out a substantial impact from stemming in any language.

All points in the 95% confidence interval for German are greater than all points in the 95% confidence intervals for French, English and Italian, which is evidence that stemming is more beneficial to German than to French, English or Italian. Additionally, all points in the 90% confidence interval for German are greater than all points in the 90% confidence interval for Spanish. The intervals for Dutch, Spanish, French, English and Italian overlap, so we can't identify any significant difference in the importance of stemming for these 5 languages. We suspect a larger experiment (more than 50 topics) might at least identify Dutch as a clear second to German.

References

1. Cross-Language Evaluation Forum web site. http://www.clef-campaign.org/
2. Andrew Hodgson. Converting the Fulcrum Search Engine to Unicode. In Sixteenth International Unicode Conference, Amsterdam, The Netherlands, March 2000.
3. Myles Hollander and Douglas A. Wolfe. Nonparametric Statistical Methods. Second Edition, 1999. John Wiley & Sons.
4. S. E. Robertson, S. Walker, S. Jones, M. M. Hancock-Beaulieu, M. Gatford. (City University.) Okapi at TREC-3. In D. K. Harman, editor, Overview of the Third Text REtrieval Conference (TREC-3), 1995. NIST Special Publication 500-226. http://trec.nist.gov/pubs/trec3/t3_proceedings.html
5. Amit Singhal, John Choi, Donald Hindle, David Lewis and Fernando Pereira. AT&T at TREC-7. In E. M. Voorhees and D. K. Harman, editors, Proceedings of the Seventh Text REtrieval Conference (TREC-7), 1999. NIST Special Publication 500-242. http://trec.nist.gov/pubs/trec7/t7_proceedings.html
6. Stephen Tomlinson. Hummingbird's Fulcrum SearchServer at CLEF 2001. In Carol Peters, editor, Results of the CLEF 2001 Cross-Language System Evaluation Campaign: Working Notes for the CLEF 2001 Workshop. 3 September, Darmstadt, Germany. DELOS Network of Excellence on Digital Libraries Workshop Series. http://www.ercim.org/publication/ws-proceedings/CLEF2/index.html
7. Stephen Tomlinson and Tom Blackwell. Hummingbird's Fulcrum SearchServer at TREC-9. To appear in E. M. Voorhees and D. K. Harman, editors, Proceedings of the Ninth Text REtrieval Conference (TREC-9). NIST Special Publication 500-249. http://trec.nist.gov/pubs/trec9/t9_proceedings.html

Minimalistic Test Runs of the Eidetica Indexer

Teresita Frizzarin and Annius Groenink

Eidetica, Kruislaan 400, NL 1098 SM Amsterdam,
frizzarin@eidetica.com, avg@eidetica.com,
http://www.eidetica.com

Abstract. Participating in a text retrieval conference for the first time, Eidetica has run six minimalistic tests with its **t·repository** indexer, doing as little tuning as possible, in order to evaluate its "performance baseline". Since no tuning was done, we will only discuss the general properties of our indexing software and how it was run on the CLEF topic sets for the monolingual German and Dutch tasks.

1 Background

Eidetica is a service provider of search and text mining technology on the basis of a hosting model. We took part in the monolingual German and Dutch tracks of CLEF 2001, with the **t·repository** software – the core database and indexing software that drives Eidetica's hosting applications.

The **t·repository** software subjected to the test, has the following primary characteristics:

- Built for speed, reliability and stability
- Native data input format is flat-record XML
- The source XML is compiled to a generalized index: a mathematically motivated set of *string lexicons* and *matrices* between these lexicons, among which are both forward and backward term indexes.
- Record identifiers, data elements (authors, subjects, dates), terms, words and trigrams are all living in the same, unified, space. This provides for virtually unlimited text mining.
- On-the-fly context-free tagging: using simple UNIX shell pattern matching (for German/Dutch participle forms) and suffix co-occurrence rules (for singular/plural etc.), unknown words are automatically tagged and stemmed; only 5 different tags are used (noun, adword, verb, det, coor), and the tags are used only to aid term extraction.
- Use of dictionaries is very limited. Support for force/kill lists for search terms is used very sparingly.
- Compounding: words consisting of two parts that also exist as words, are split in their "internal representation". A compound form with and without a space or dash is considered to be identical (air craft = air-craft = aircraft).
- The indexer performs various types of term extraction (tagging-based, proper name recognition, and extraction from *full term only* - fields in the source data). Extracted terms are between 1 and 4 words (or parts-of-word in the case of compounds).

C.A. Peters et al. (Eds.): CLEF 2001, LNCS 2406, pp. 288–290, 2002.

- Because indexes take terms as entities, rather than single words, stop words and other irrelevant parts of text are automatically skipped.
- The *terms* by which documents are indexed, are living in a hierarchical space: parenthood, childhood, sibling, ancestors and descendant mappings are available as matrices after indexing. This allows for a form of flexible decompounding (e.g. do not decompound the topics, but do allow a term to match a narrower term in the document repository). Such partial decompounding was not used in CLEF 2001; instead, we performed literal matching of most specific forms (longest match).

2   Technique Description

The topics and text were first converted (with minimal changes) to fit the profile of a single database, where records happen to contain either the fields TI, LE, TE and CAP (article type), or the fields TITLE, DESC and NARR (topic type). Small CLEF-specific term kill lists were made with terms such as *"relevant documents"* and *"information"* that had not previously been any threat to Eidetica mining applications. Then, the standard Eidetica **t·repository** indexer was run without modifications. In other words, we have implemented *automatic runs*.

The indexer produces individual forward and backward indexes in the form of matrices between Document/Topic IDs and the terms appearing in the fields TI, LE, TE, CAP, TITLE, DESC and NARR. The vectors in these indexes are normalized, so that their sums are 1.

We then compute a linear combination of these indexes, where the DESC and TE fields are given a very high weight, and the remaining fields are blended in as "back-ups". The result is a matrix from document/topic IDs to terms. This matrix is transposed to a matrix from terms to document/topic IDs. Finally, we infer a Topic ID – Document ID matrix by composing the elementwise 4th power root of both matrices, producing a Topic-Document rank that is proportional to the sum of the square roots of individual term co-occurrences.

This ID – ID rank matrix is the basis for the Topic-ID – Article-ID lists that we submitted in various forms.

3   Submitted Runs

We have submitted the same three runs for both the Dutch monolingual task, and the German monolingual task. These runs are:

- **EidNL2001A**: use all topic fields (TITLE, DESC and NARR) and keep only results above a threshold score (0.80)
- **EidNL2001B**: use all topic fields, but produce the best 1000 results.
- **EidNL2001C**: use only the TITLE and DESC fields of the topics, and produce the best 1000 results.
- **EidDE2001A-C**: as their Dutch counterparts, but for German.

4 Conclusion

Participation in CLEF 2001 gave us a valuable indication where the **t·repository** is "standing" in the non-English retrieval landscape, and also which techniques native to **t·repository** are considered "standard" in TREC/CLEF context (query expansion), and which ones seem worthwhile to exploit and discuss in future CLEF workshops (hierarchical term relations and flexible decompounding). Eidetica aims to keep participating in next year's monolingual experiments, adjusting the "technique mix" to our experiences with these first test runs.

Across the Bridge: CLEF 2001 – Non-english Monolingual Retrieval. The French Task

Eugenia Matoyo and Tony Valsamidis

University of Greenwich,
Old Royal Naval College, Park Row, Greenwich, London SE10 9LS
me010@gre.ac.uk or A.Valsamidis@gre.ac.uk

Abstract. This paper presents work on document retrieval based on first time participation in the CLEF 2001 monolingual retrieval task using French. The experiment findings indicate that Okapi, the text retrieval system in use, can successfully be used for non-English text retrieval. A lot of internal pre-processing is required in the basic search system for conversion into Okapi access formats. Various shell scripts were written to achieve the conversion in a UNIX environment, failure of which would significantly have impeded the overall performance. Based on the experiment findings using Okapi - originally designed for English - it was clear that, although most European languages share conventional word boundaries and variant word morphemes formed by the addition of suffixes, there is significant difference between French and English retrieval depending on the adaptation of indexing and search strategies in use. No sophisticated method for higher recall and precision such as stemming techniques, phrase translation or de-compounding was employed for the experiment and our results were suggestively poor. Future participation would include more refined query translation tools.

1   Introduction

Participation in the CLEF 2001 monolingual task [2] for French served as a stepping stone toward the multilingual cross-language information retrieval. The background to the CLEF Campaigns as presented in the European Research Letter [4] triggered interest toward participation in this year's information retrieval task, which was our first attempt to participate in any of the CLEF tasks. The main task attempted was that of monolingual (non-English) Information Retrieval on French topics and documents as assigned by CLEF and retrieval was based on automatic query construction using Okapi. The main reason for choice of automatic query retrieval as opposed to manual query expansion was largely the time constraint. Automation implies that documents were automatically retrieved by the system without the intervention of the experimenter in interactive manual query expansion [9], which would have been time consuming and time was a limited resource given that the experiments had to be completed on time for the CLEF submission deadline. Due to the limitations on the time frame for completion of the experiments, we used the most basic, straightforward approach on Okapi, our standard retrieval system, without the application of great modification, stemming, decompounding or merging techniques. The additional tasks to the query processing involved use of a defined stoplist, followed by automated queries using previously used scripts for the processing.

C.A. Peters et al. (Eds.): CLEF 2001, LNCS 2406, pp. 291-299, 2002.
© Springer-Verlag Berlin Heidelberg 2002

2   Objectives

The primary aim of this experiment was three-fold:

- Crossing the Bridge: An attempt at participation in the CLEF tasks on Information Retrieval for better understanding of issues in cross-language information retrieval.
- To investigate whether Okapi, an experimental text retrieval system from City University of London [1], could successfully be used to provide a useful interface in the retrieval of French documents using indexing methods and stopwords.
- To investigate whether techniques applied for English text retrieval differ significantly from those used for French retrieval.

3   General System Description

The monolingual experiments for French documents were carried out using Okapi, a text retrieval system project based at City University, London, which is used solely for research purposes.   The Okapi software requires either a Solaris on Sun environment or Linux on Intel environment to run. It uses a probabilistic model [10] of information retrieval, which was first developed by Robertson [7]. This model performs in an iterative process, which uses the ranking of document listings based on indexing, term weighting function and word stemming rules for optimizing search queries.   The three major components of Okapi are:

- *Indexing Software,* which enables users to create and index Okapi type databases
- *The Basic Search System (BSS),* which is a set of low level commands to enable users to build their own interface.
- *Okapi Interactive Interface,* which is the graphical user interface, which calls the BSS command in a manner that hides the complexity from the user.

It is important to point out here that the Okapi system was originally designed for use with English. Although it has been used in similar text retrieval experiments for languages other than English including Chinese text collections [9], using it in the CLEF experiment for monolingual tasks was one of the few times that it has been used for French collections.   The section below describes the work that had to be done in the Okapi basic search system to allow for French monolingual retrieval.

4   Pre-processing Techniques

Prior to carrying out the formal runs, it was necessary to carry out various pre-processing tasks on the topics and the French collection using various shell scripts based on previous experiments in the Text Retrieval Conference (TREC)[6] series.

Database Integration: The two separate French collections, *Le_Monde.tar.gz* (Initial zipped file of 154 MB) and *sda_french* (Initial zipped file of 80 MB), were integrated into a single database, *le_m+sda_fr* upon which to carry out the query processing.

Conversion: A shell script (*convert_topic*) was written to reformat the 50 CLEF French topics by altering the title from *Fr-Title* to *Title* (because retrieval was required for the *Title* field) and changing the document numbers by removing the preceding *CO*. This reconstruction and manipulation of the topics and documents was necessary to convert the topics into Okapi access format as well as to enable the reuse of previous shell scripts, which had been used in similar TREC experiments. Various changes to the scripts were, however, required to customize them for the CLEF collection for French. Below is the script *Convert_Topic:*

```
# Script to convert CLEF French topics to TREC format

sed -e 's/FR-//g' \

-e 's/CO//'

#Substitute nothing for FR globally from the topic
titles to be plain <title>

# Substitute nothing for CO globally for the Document
numbers to be 'in plain numbers.
```

Stoplist: The *stoplist*, also referred to as *stopwords* or *stopterms*, is made up of common, generally used words in a language collection, which are considered irrelevant for the purpose of information retrieval because of their high frequency of occurrence. The stoplist comprised 248 terms and was derived from several sources to include common French terms[3], information compiled by Jaques Savoy of the University of Neuchatel for the CLEF web site [5] and Savoy's publication in the Journal of the American Society for Information Science [8]. All accented letters were removed from the stoplist because Okapi cannot handle accented characters.

A shell conversion script was required to convert the stoplist to Okapi-accessible formats because an *H* was required before each word, a comma [,] after each word and finally a colon [:] at the end of each line. An example of the conversion is from *avec* to *Havec,:* to comply with Okapi formats. This was achieved using an emacs editing utility in the UNIX environment to write a simple conversion script:

```
#For every line

#French stoplist

Replace string ^J with : H  # H to indicate stop term

Replace string ^J with : ,:  # to conform with Okapi
acceptable for stopterms
```

Stemming: There was no stemming applied at all for this experiment. Porter's stemming algorithm, which is configured to work for Muscat - an open source search engine - had been intended for use with Okapi but failed to run successfully. The Muscat stemmer depends on its own character coding, which Okapi could not recognize because it does not work with Unicode. A *front-end* shell script was written to adapt Okapi Basic Search System (BSS) to the stemmer but this also failed to work. Given more time, the script may have been successfully debugged and configured for Okapi but this was not accomplished due to time limitations. Since Porter's stemmer for English has successfully been used previously with Okapi in similar TREC experiments [9], it implies that Okapi could not properly handle the accented letters in the French language for the stemmer to work in this experiment. Thus stemming was omitted altogether and it may be worthwhile to note that this lack of stemming resulted in less accurate results in the final formal runs for the experiment.

Merging and indexing: We employed primitive database merging of the two French document collections into a single database for the query processing. Indexing of terms was accomplished in Okapi using an in-built Okapi indexing utility to index the integrated collection. The utility was called using two of Okapi's BSS (basic search system) programs *ix1* and *ixf* as shown below:

```
ix1 -delfinal le_m+sda_fr 1 | ixf le_m+sda_fr 1
```

The same programs were used to index the 50 CLEF topics for the combined collection:

```
ix1 -mem 50 -delfinal -doclens le_m+sda_fr 0 | ixf
le_m+sda_fr 0
```

Testing - Comparison with CLEF Input Checker: Throughout the experiments, it was important to ensure that the results would be in the required format for CLEF. The test runs were, therefore, validated against the CLEF input checker, CheckInput.pl. This was a Perl script, which compared the run results against the input checker for error identification in an effort to expose possible defects in the runs before submission of the formal runs. The input checker revealed that there were no serious errors in the run results, although a couple of topic sets yielded error on retrieval, possibly as a result of a segmentation bug in the Okapi BSS release.

5   The Formal Runs

The formal runs were automatic and query processing for the French topics and documents was done in three separate runs, each using the same French stoplist:

Run 1 - retrieval of documents by topic Title, Description and Narrative

Run 2 - retrieval by topic Title and Description only

Run 3 - retrieval by topic Title only

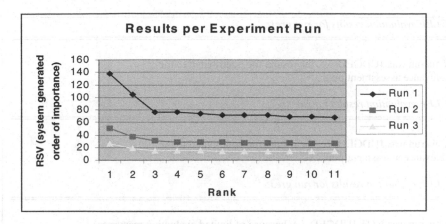

Fig. 1. Chart showing Results per Experiment Run for the same topic and ranked documents

The graph above indicates the order of importance as assigned by the system, and retrieval by Title, Description and Narrative received higher ranking.

Where:

Run 1 represents run gre1 for retrieval by Title, Description and Narrative

Run 2 represents run gre2 for retrieval by Title and Description

Run 3 represents run gre3 for retrieval by Title only

As expected and observed from Fig.1. above, all the three runs differed significantly from each other. Retrieval by *Title*, *Description* and *Narrative* gave the highest document relevance score of the three runs and retrieval by *Title* only of the same documents yielded the lowest document relevance score.

It may be significant to mention here that the general observed trends for the CLEF 2001 workshop revealed that the majority of the Information Retrieval experiments used mostly the *Title* and *Description* fields for the topics although some use of *Title*, *Description* and *Narrative* fields was employed.

6   Presentation and Analysis of Results

The formal runs were zipped using gZip in UNIX and were submitted by FTP to CLEF in ASCII as binary format and the results were sent out together with a README file describing the different runs. Our results for the experiment can be summarized as shown in Figure 2.

The formal results from CLEF for the submitted runs were as expected; Run *gre3*, which had the least priority was not judged. Similarly, in a graph of recall versus precision, run *gre3* scored the least precision values.

CLEF evaluation results for run gre1:
==

This run was JUDGED, i.e. the results file contributed to the
relevance assessment pool.

CLEF evaluation results for run gre2:
==

This run was JUDGED, i.e. the results file contributed to the
relevance assessment pool.

CLEF evaluation results for run gre3:
==

This run was NOT JUDGED, i.e. because of limited evaluation resources,
the result file did not directly contribute to the relevance assessment
pool. However, the run was subject to all other standard processing,
and is still scored as an official submission.

Fig. 2. Summary of Run Results

Although all of our experiment runs had a relatively poor performance against the comparison to the 'median' graph by topic from CLEF, which gave an indication of how well our results were according to other groups, run *gre1* had a considerably better performance than both runs *gre2* and *gre3*. Run *gre3* had the worst median performance of the three runs. The average precision (non - interpolated) for all relevant documents for run *gre1* was *0.3969* out of a scale of 1 and *0.3584* for run *gre2* and only *0.2806* for run *gre3*.

Our deduction from the runs is that document retrieval using the topic *Title*, *Description* and *Narrative* fields yields far better results than attempted document retrieval by omission of any of these fields.

7   Comparisons with Other Participants

The average precision of the top five participating groups in the monolingual task for French ranged between 0.392 and 0.502 for automatic runs where retrieval was by *Title* and *Description* topic fields. All of these groups were active CLEF participants and the best score was by the University of Neuchatel under Jaques Savoy. Savoy used Okapi for all of the monolingual experiments for automatic runs with the inclusion of stemming algorithms. He excluded letters with accents in the respective stopword lists and used an adaptation of indexing and other search strategies to perform equally well in all of the other monolingual tasks (Italian, German and Spanish). Our results would have had considerable improvement if we had made use of an effective stemming algorithm for use with Okapi as the University of Neuchatel had done.

8   Pictorial Summary of the Experiment

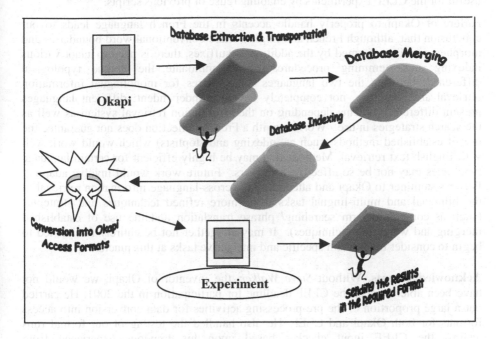

Fig. 3. Summary of the Experiment

9   Conclusions and Future Work

There is an adage that says, 'He who accepts not defeat is never a sportsman'; participation was more important than phenomenal results since this was the first time that the University of Greenwich had been represented in any of the CLEF workshops.   We did not really expect great results but it is our hope that future participation will yield considerably far better results, especially after the sharing experience of the CLEF 2001 Workshop.   Presentations by other participating groups, brain storming sessions in the open discussions as well as poster sessions in the workshop help participants to learn from each other and to be able to attempt new tasks, adapt/combine new strategies and techniques for future experiments. Previously participating groups almost always have better results than new comers do as a result of the workshop experience.   We employed the most basic of techniques and strategies in our experiment, such as database merging for the French documents, defining a suitable stoplist, working with an effective information retrieval system (Okapi) and use of full automation for query retrieval with no manual runs.   We did not include established methods such as word de-compounding, phrase translation or the employment of a suitable stemming algorithm based on morphological decomposition to work with Okapi. Work done on similar TREC experiments proved to be useful for the CLEF experiments by enabling reuse of previous scripts.

Failure of Okapi to properly handle accents in the French language leads to our conclusion that, although French and English share conventional word boundaries and morpheme variants formed by the addition of suffixes, there is need to adapt various indexing and stemming procedures to accommodate the unique typological differences between the two languages. Procedures for monolingual information retrieval are, therefore, not completely language independent; different languages present different problems depending on the information retrieval system as well as the search strategies in use. Working with a French collection does not guarantee the use of established methods (such as indexing and stoplists) which would work well with English text retrieval. Methods that may be highly efficient for certain language typologies may not be so effective for others. Future work would involve adapting Porter's stemmer to Okapi and attempting the cross-language information retrieval in the bilingual and multi-lingual tasks using more refined techniques and strategies (such as compound term searching/ phrase translation and the use of established merging and weighting techniques). It may altogether not be entirely far fetched to begin to consider the domain specific and interactive tasks at this juncture.

Acknowledgements. Without *Steve Walker*, the inventor of Okapi, we would not have been able to meet the CLEF deadline for participation in the 2001. He carried out a large proportion of the pre-processing activities for data conversion into access formats for both Okapi and CLEF. He also handled the testing of our formal runs against the CLEF input checker based upon his previous experience from participation in the TREC [6] series.

Special acknowledgement of help and collaboration also goes to *Surinder Singh Dio* of the UNIX help at the University of Greenwich. He set up the Okapi pack in the computing laboratory at the university and took great pains to set up the environment variable settings as required for the successful operation of the Okapi software.

References

1. Centre For Interactive Systems Research, City University: Introduction to Okapi Pack, 14 March 2000, available from: http://dotty.is.city.ac.uk/okapi-pack/okapi-pack.html (accessed 17 April 2001)
2. Cross Language Evaluation Forum, CLEF: CLEF Agenda for 2001, 14 March 2000, available from: http: www.clef-campaign.org (accessed May 2001)
3. Mueller, Erik T. 1998. Fluent French: Experiences of an English speaker. New York: Signiform. Available: http://www.signiform.com/french/ (accessed June 4, 2001)
4. Peters, C. & Braschler, M. (forthcoming). Cross-Language System Evaluation: the CLEF Campaigns. European Research Letter. In Journal of the American Society for Information Science and Technology, Vol 52(12) pp 1067-1072.
5. Savoy, J. 2001, Stopword List, available from : http://www.unine.ch/info/clef/ (accessed June 5, 2001)
6. Text Retrieval Conference, Test Collections, available from: http://trec.nist.gov/ (accessed May 2001)

7.   Centre for Interactive Systems Research, The Probabilistic Retrieval Model, available from: http://www.soi.city.ac.uk/research/cisr/okapi/prm.html (accessed May 2001)
8.   Savoy J. 1999. A stemming procedure and stopword list for general French corpora. Journal of the American Society for Information Science, 50(10), 944-952.
9.   M.Beaulieu, Experiments on Interfaces to Support Query Expansion (p8-19). S.E. Robertson, S. Walker and M. Beaulieu, Laboratory experiments with Okapi: participation in the TREC program (p20-34). S.E. Robertson and M. Beaulieu, Research and evaluation in information retrieval (p51-57). X. Huang and S.E. Robertson, Application of probabilistic methods to Chinese text retrieval (p74-79). Special issue of Journal of Documentation 53(1), (1997).
10. K. Sparck Jones, S. Walker and S.E. Robertson, A probabilistic model of information retrieval: development and status. See: http://citeseer.nj.nec.com/jones98probabilistic.html

Mpro-IR in CLEF 2001

Bärbel Ripplinger

IAI
Martin-Luther-Str. 14
D-66111 Saarbrücken

Abstract. The objective of this year's CLEF participation has been to evaluate an improved German morpho-syntactic component, focusing on the impact decomposition information has on performance.

The objective of IAI's CLEF participation in 2001 was to evaluate an improved German component. Only one official monolingual German run has been submitted. This year, the investigation focused on how improved linguistic processing affects the performance.

The cross-language information retrieval component, MPRO-IR (cf. [3]) exploits linguistic knowledge such as lexical unit (or base form), derivational root form, and, for German, information about decomposition produced by a morpho-syntactic analyser. This analyser, MPRO [2], has been improved by a far better tagging and lemmatisation component. Furthermore, the underlying German morpheme lexicon currently has 85.500 entries (morphemes, stems and word forms) compared to 42.000 entries used for last year's experiments. Our aim was to compare the behaviour of this component with respect to CLEF 2000, the contribution of decomposition information was of specific interest. In MPRO-IR, the decomposition information is applied in two different ways, once to find related concepts by evaluating the information provided by the decomposition feature, and, then, by using the decomposition information of compounds in the query to find syntactic variants. The first is used to retrieve documents which contain concepts related to the query term(s) in the form of compounds consisting of a search term as a constituent; the latter to find compounds expressed by nominal phrases.

1 Experimental Set-Up

The indexing of the German corpus has been carried out as described in [4]. Because last year the number of documents retrieved by MPRO-IR was low compared to other systems, the search algorithm was modified in this experiment: The restriction to one sentence as search window had been discarded. Furthermore, the condition that each meaning-bearing word (noun, verb, adjective) has to occur in a document to be relevant, has been weakened. For

C.A. Peters et al. (Eds.): CLEF 2001, LNCS 2406, pp. 300–302, 2002.

this experiment, all documents retrieved by a query are considered regardless whether all query terms occurred or not. For the ranking, the number of different terms occurring in a document is combined with the linguistic information type of each matching term (i.e. lexical unit, decompounding information or derivational root form) to calculate the final weight.

For the run only title and description of the topics are used as queries. No pre-processing, besides stopword removal (based on a closed class after the linguistic analysis), such as deleting fixed phrases like *finde alle relevanten Dokumente* (find all relevant documents), etc. was done. Each query was equally morpho-syntactically analysed, using the information extracted for meaning-bearing words such as lexical base form, derivational root, and decomposition to search in German documents.

2   Results

The overall result of our run shows a lower retrieval performance of MPRO-IR compared to other systems. In spite of a higher number of documents retrieved, the result is even worse than last year. The reasons are mani-fold: The new morpheme lexicon is still unstable in the sense that not all entries are examined with regard to allowed and forbidden decompounding information. (This information has to be encoded manually, and this process is still ongoing.) For instance, some important compounds are not split, as in query 61 *Ölkatastrophe* (oil catastrophe) or query 67 *Schiffkollisionen* (ship collisions). Another reason is certainly that corrupted lexicons were used for document and query analysis (unfortunately there was no time to redo the corpus analysis), resulting in incorrect or even not analysed terms. For instance, key words such as *Alpeninitiative* (initiative for the alps) in query 55 were not analysed. Because these key words were significant to find relevant documents, the results are not surprising. Furthermore, there is reason to suppose that the poorer results are mainly due to the modified search algorithm: MPRO-IR is not a probabilistic system but follows an exact match approach. With the search method as used in this experiment there was no longer control over the terms used to retrieve a document. Because only the number of different terms occurring in the document is considered, a document in which only the terms of a fixed phrase (i.e. document, relevant, find, etc.) occurs could be ranked higher than a document containing only one of the query's keywords. Using the linguistic information within a probabilistic system produces much better results as shown in [1] in this volume.

An investigation of the results per query in more detail shows more or less the same findings as last year: most hits could be retrieved by using precise lexical base forms, and a few on the basis of derivational information. Compositional information is valuable to detect syntactic variants of German compounds.

The better morpho-syntactic component results in less unknown words. However, a contribution with respect to a better decompounding could not be observed due to the errors in processing mentioned above.

Acknowledgements. Thanks to Peter Schäuble for allowing me to use EUROSPIDER resources to carry out this experiment.

References

1. Braschler, M., B. Ripplinger, P. Schäuble. Experiments with the Eurospider Retrieval System for CLEF 2001. In this volume.
2. Maas, D.: Multilinguale Textverarbeitung mit MPRO. In G. Lobin et al.(eds): Europäische Kommunikationskybernetik heute und morgen. KoPäd, München, 1999. http://www.iai.uni-sb.de/global/memos.html
3. Ripplinger, B.: Mpro-IR – A Cross-language Information Retrieval Component Enhanced by Linguistic Knowledge. Proceedings of the 6th RIAO 2000, Paris, 2000.
4. Ripplinger, B. The Use of NLP Techniques in CLIR. In Peters, C. (ed). Cross-Language Information Retrieval and Evaluation. Workshop of the CLEF 2000, Springer Verlag 2001.

Some Terms Are More Interchangeable than Others

Jakob Klok, Samuel Driessen, and Marvin Brunner

Océ Technologies
P.O. Box 101
NL-5900 MA Venlo
The Netherlands
{klok, sjdr, mbru}@oce.nl

Abstract. This paper describes the work done by the Information Retrieval Research Group at Océ Technologies B.V. for the Cross-Language Evaluation Forum (CLEF) 2001. We participated in the Dutch monolingual task and submitted three runs. In this paper we introduce a new model for relevance computation using two new query operators. It is our intention to apply this model to multilingual retrieval in the future.

1   Introduction

This is the first time the Information Retrieval Research Group at Océ Technologies B.V. participates in the CLEF evaluation campaign. We started in March 2001 with the implementation of a new method for relevance computation and were interested to see how it compares to other methods. In this paper we present our query model and accompanying ranking formulas. Only monolingual Dutch runs have been attempted so far, but the model has been created with multilingual IR in mind.

2   Heuristics

In our system the likelihood of relevance for a document with respect to a query is computed using term rareness, term frequency, document length, completeness, occurrence in important parts (topic & article), and occurrence of phrases / multiword terms. How these factors influence likelihood of relevance is formulated in seven heuristics. A document is more likely to be relevant if:
1. it contains rare terms from the query
2. it contains terms from the query many times (taking the length of the document into account)
3. it contains terms that originate from the topic title
4. it contains terms from the query in an important field (title or lead)
5. it contains phrases (consisting of more than one word) from the query
6. it contains terms that have a meaning similar to terms from the topic
7. it contains many (non-interchangeable) terms from the query

While heuristics 1 through 4 are common in Information Retrieval (cf. [1]), number 5, 6, and 7 need further explanation, which is given in the next three sections.

C. A. Peters et al. (Eds.): CLEF 2001, LNCS 2406, pp. 303-307, 2002.
© Springer-Verlag Berlin Heidelberg 2002

2.1   Phrases

Heuristic 5 says that documents containing phrases from the topic are more likely to be relevant. Phrases have a more specific meaning than the individual words that they are composed of. For instance, the words *Ierse, Republikeinse, Leger* (translation: Irish, Republic and Army) have meaning in themselves, but the combination *Ierse Republikeinse Leger* (translation: Irish Republic Army) has a narrower and more precise meaning. This example is obvious, but we also extracted phrase like *Japanse automobielindustrie* (translation: Japanese automotive industry), *Koreaanse president Kim Il Sung* (translation: Korean president Kim Il Sung), and *officiële devaluatie van de Chinese munt* (translation: official devaluation of the Chinese currency). We expect that including phrases like these in the query will improve the ranking.

The examples given above are all noun phrases. We choose to extract only noun phrases because they have the most obvious and specific meaning. In the future we might include other types of phrases like verb, preposition, adjective and determiner phrases.

A rule-based tagger/parser for Dutch was used to find and extract the noun phrases from the topics. This tagger/parser is called Amazon/Casus, mainly built by the Language and Speech department of the University of Nijmegen, The Netherlands. It tags and parses sentences syntactically and semantically. (For more information on Amazon/Casus refer to [2] and [3].) All Dutch determiners and pronouns that occur as the first word of the phrase were removed from the term phrase. We also made a short list of stop-phrases, which were removed as well.

We think that adding more phrases to the query should improve the ranking. Therefore we generated more phrases by extracting phrases that fall in between stop-words and added those to the queries as well.

2.2   Related Terms

Heuristic 6 implies that the retrieval system should add terms to the topic that are similar in meaning to the terms extracted from the topic. These added terms can, for instance, be the plural/singular form of a term. For example, synonyms from a dictionary could also be added. While the addition of similar terms should improve the performance of the system, there is a risk involved. Different terms rarely have the exact same meaning, so in some case adding terms does more harm than good. Suppose for instance that a topic contains the term "US". Adding the term "United States" would seem reasonable in that case, but not if "US" was used as a pronoun and just happened to be in uppercase. Other terms that could be added include morphological variants and split compounds.

2.3   Completeness and Interchangeable Terms

Heuristic 7 says that we expect a document to be more likely to be relevant when it contains a number of terms from the query. For instance if we have a query that contains the very different terms "babyvoeding" and "pesticide" (translation: "baby food" and "pesticide") then it is reasonable to expect that documents that contain both terms are more likely to be relevant than documents that contain only one of the terms. However, there are usually terms in the query that have a similar meaning (especially after adding terms as discussed in the previous section), in which case the occurrence of all these similar terms does not make the document more likely to be relevant than the occurrence of only one. For a query on "pesticide" and "pesticiden" (Dutch plural for pesticide), for instance, it does not really matter if a document contains both terms once or only one of them twice.

3   Queries

3.1   Query Definition

In the previous section we described two kinds of terms: words and phrases. The set of terms is defined as the union of those two:

Terms = Words ∪ Phrases

We also define two query operators, corresponding to the idea that some terms are interchangeable and others are not (cf. section 2.3). We will use the symbol 'I' as an operator for interchangeable terms and '&' for non-interchangeable terms. We will indicate these as 'interchange' and 'distinguish' respectively.

We define a query as follows:

- Q is a query, if Q ∈ Terms
- $Q_1 | .. | Q_n$ is a query, if $Q_1..Q_n$ are queries
- $Q_1 \& .. \& Q_n$ is a query, if $Q_1..Q_n$ are queries

Note that with the last two rules new queries can be constructed by combining (sub-) queries using our two operators (I and &). This means that not only terms can be distinguished or interchanged, but also sub-queries.

Actually we use weighted queries, so for each query there is a function w, that assigns a weight to each (sub-)query. In the light of the discussion in 2.2, added terms receive less weight than terms directly from the topic. Notice that interchangeability does not mean that the terms or queries are weighted equally.

3.2   Query Construction

The first step in constructing a query from a topic is extraction of terms from the topics. Words were extracted by splitting the texts at the white spaces. Phrases were extracted as explained in section 2.1. Below are some examples of the terms that were added and how they were fitted into the query:

morphological variants: *synagogen | synagoog | synagoge*
synonyms: *pesticide | bestrijdingsmiddel | verdelgingsmiddel*
compound splitting: *wereldkampioenschap | (wereld & kampioenschap)*
accent removal: *bosnië | bosnie*
article part: *in_title (pesticide) | in_lead (pesticide) |*
in_bodytext (pesticide)

Morphological variants and synonyms were taken from a semantic network [4]. Compounds were split using a simple algorithm that splits words in all possible ways and checks whether the parts are nouns using the before mentioned semantic network. Accents were removed using the Perl module Text::Unaccent.pm [5]. The parts of the article (title, context, and body) were indexed individually, so queries could be constructed that take this structure into account.

Weights for all added sub-queries are set to .5, while weights for sub-queries for terms from the topic are set to 1.

4   Relevance Computation

In this section we discuss the estimation of likelihood of relevance in our model. Since we work with a recursive definition of queries, it is logical to estimate likelihood of relevance for each of the sub-queries and combine those. The estimations for the sub-queries need to be comparable in the sense that they are on the same scale. We decided that likelihood of relevance estimations should fall between 0 and 1, where a value near 0 indicates a low estimated likelihood of relevance and near 1 high (1).

$$0 \le rel_j(Q) \le 1 \tag{1}$$

Recalling our definition of a query we see that some queries consists of just one term. We will use heuristics 1 and 2 for estimating likelihood of relevance for this type of query. First we define the normalized term frequency tf (2). In this formula $freq_{i,j}$ is the number of occurrences of term i in document j. The length of a document is defined as the total number of words in a document. The parameter p was set to 100 in our experiment.

$$tf_{i,j} = 1 - \left(\frac{length(d_j) - freq_{i,j}}{length(d_j)} \right)^p \tag{2}$$

The formula for the normalized document frequency is given in (3). In this formula n_i is the number of documents in the collection in which term i appears and N is the total number of documents in the collection. The parameter q was set to 300 in our experiment.

$$idf_i = \left(\frac{N - n_i + 1}{N} \right)^q \tag{3}$$

The relevance of a document j with respect to a query that consists only of term i is computed by multiplying the normalized term frequency and document frequency (4).

$$rel_{i,j} = tf_{i,j} \times idf_i \tag{4}$$

The likelihood of relevance with respect to queries that are constructed using the *interchange* operator '|' and the *distinguish* operator '&' can be computed with (5) and (6) respectively.

$$rel_j(Q_1 \mid Q_2 \mid .. \mid Q_k) = w_1 \times rel_j(Q_1) + (1 - w_1 \times rel_j(Q_1)) \times rel_j(Q_2 \mid .. \mid Q_k) \quad (5)$$

$$rel_j(Q_1 \& .. \& Q_k) = \frac{w_1 \times rel_j(Q_1) + .. + w_k \times rel_j(Q_k)}{k} \quad (6)$$

5   Results

We submitted three official runs. In all of these runs the title, description, and narrative parts of the topics were used. The best of these runs, named oce2, had a mean average precision of 0.24. After the workshop we modified the model in order to reduce the complexity. A run with this new model using title and description only results in a mean average precision of 0.20. A second unofficial run that added phrases to the queries had a mean average precision of 0.19. A third run included terms from the narrative - but not phrases - and resulted in 0.23 mean average precision. We have not yet tested by adding synonyms.

6   Conclusions and Future Work

As is shown in the previous section the scores were not very high for these runs. Considering that these were the first runs with a new model, this is not surprising. It is too soon to draw definitive conclusions from the few experiments done so far.

Tuning of parameters and experimenting with other query construction strategies could improve results. In the future we shall also attempt to do multilingual retrieval using this model.

References

1. Baeza-Yates, R. and Ribiero-Neto, B.: Modern Information Retrieval, ACM Press, 1999.
2. http://lands.let.kun.nl/projects/structuralist.en.html
3. http://lands.let.kun.nl/TSpublic/dreumel/amazon_casus.en.html
4. http://www.knowledge-concepts.com
5. http://www.cpan.org/modules/by-module/Catalog/LDACHARY/Text-Unaccent-1.01.readme

The CLEF 2001 Interactive Track

Douglas W. Oard[1] and Julio Gonzalo[2]

[1] Human Computer Interaction Laboratory
College of Information Studies and
Institute for Advanced Computer Studies
University of Maryland, College Park, MD 20742, USA
oard@glue.umd.edu.edu,
http://www.glue.umd.edu/~oard/

[2] Departamento de Lenguajes y Sistemas Informáticos
Universidad Nacional de Educación a Distancia
E.T.S.I Industriales, Ciudad Universitaria s/n, 28040 Madrid, SPAIN
julio@lsi.uned.es
http://sensei.lsi.uned.es/~julio/

Abstract. The problem of finding documents written in a language that the searcher cannot read is perhaps the most challenging application of cross-language information retrieval technology. In interactive applications, that task involves at least two steps: (1) the machine locates promising documents in a collection that is larger than the searcher could scan, and (2) the searcher recognizes documents relevant to their intended use from among those nominated by the machine. The goal of the 2001 Cross-Language Evaluation Forum's experimental interactive track was to explore the ability of present technology to support interactive relevance assessment. This paper describes the shared experiment design used at all three participating sites, summarizes preliminary results from the evaluation, and concludes with observations on lessons learned that can inform the design of subsequent evaluation campaigns.

1 Introduction

The problem of finding documents written in a language that the searcher cannot read is perhaps the most challenging application of Cross-Language Information Retrieval (CLIR) technology. In some cases (e.g., alerting the user to urgent new information), this might need to be a fully automatic process. In many applications, however, the effectiveness of fully automatic systems is limited by one or more of the following factors:

- The information need might initially be incompletely understood by the searcher.
- The information need might initially not be well articulated, either because the system's capabilities are underutilized or because the system's query language is insufficiently expressive.

C.A. Peters et al. (Eds.): CLEF 2001, LNCS 2406, pp. 308–319, 2002.
© Springer-Verlag Berlin Heidelberg 2002

- The ambiguity introduced by the use of natural (i.e., human) language within documents may cause the system to retrieve some documents that are not useful and/or to fail to retrieve some documents that are useful.

For this reason, automatic search technology is often embedded within interactive applications to achieve some degree of synergy between the machine's ability to rapidly cull through enormous collections using relatively simple techniques and a human searcher's ability to learn about their own information needs, to reformulate queries in ways that better express their needs and/or better match the system's capabilities, and to accurately recognize useful documents within a set of a limited size (perhaps 10-100 documents). The goal of the experimental interactive track at the 2001 Cross-Language Evaluation Forum (which we call iCLEF) is to begin the process of exploring these issues in the context of cross-language information retrieval.

The process by which searchers interact with information systems to find documents has been extensively studied (for an excellent overview, see [1]). Essentially, there are two key points at which the searcher and the system interact: query formulation and document selection. Query formulation is a complex cognitive process in which searchers apply three kinds of knowledge—what they think they want, what they think the information system can do, and what they think the document collection being searched contains—to develop a query. The query formulation process is typically iterative, with searchers learning about the collection and the system, and often about what it is that they really wanted to know, by posing queries and examining retrieval results. Ultimately we must study the query formulation process in a cross-language retrieval environment if we are to design systems that effectively support real information seeking behaviors. We were concerned, however, that the open-ended nature of the query formulation process might make it difficult to agree on a sharp focus for quantitative evaluation in the near term. We therefore chose to focus on cross-language document selection for the initial iCLEF evaluation.

Interactive document selection is essentially a manual detection problem—given the documents that are nominated by the system as being of possible interest, the searcher must recognize which documents are truly of interest. The main Cross-Language Evaluation Forum (CLEF) track evaluates the effectiveness of systems that develop a ranked list of documents that are possibly (and hopefully!) relevant to a query, so we took that as our starting point. The searcher's task thus becomes recognizing relevant documents in a language that they cannot read. Viewed from the perspective of system designers, the task is to present information (metadata, summaries, translations, etc.) that is sufficient to allow the user to make accurate relevance judgments.

Focusing on interactive CLIR is not actually such a radical departure for CLEF as it might first appear. The principal CLEF evaluation measure—mean average precision (MAP)—actually models the automatic component of an interactive search process [2]. MAP is defined as:

$$MAP = E_i[E_j[\frac{j}{r(i,j)}]]$$

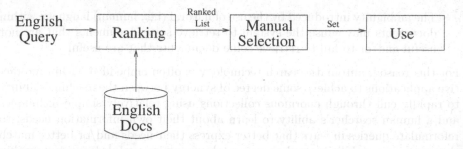

Fig. 1. A one-pass monolingual search process.

where $E_i[\;]$ is the sample expectation over a set of queries, $E_j[\;]$ is the sample expectation over the documents that are relevant to query i, and $r(i,j)$ is the rank of the jth relevant document for query i. One way to think of MAP is as a measure of effectiveness for the one-pass interactive retrieval process shown in Figure 1 in which:

1. The searcher creates a query in a manner similar to those over which the outer expectation is computed.
2. The system computes a ranked list in a way that seeks to place the topically relevant documents as close to the top of the list as is possible, given the available evidence (query terms, document terms, embedded knowledge of language characteristics such as stemming, ...).
3. The searcher starts at the top of the list and examines each document (and/or summaries of those documents) until they are satisfied.
4. The searcher becomes satisfied after finding some number of relevant documents, but we have no *a priori* knowledge of how many relevant documents it will take to satisfy the searcher.
5. The searcher's degree of satisfaction is related to the number of documents that they need to examine before finding the desired number of relevant documents.

Implicit in this process is the assumption that the user can recognize relevant documents when they see them. It is that question that we sought to explore at iCLEF.

The remainder of this paper is organized as follows. Section 2 presents the basic experiment design that all three sites adopted and describes the shared evaluation resources that were provided. Section 3 then summarizes the research questions that each site explored and briefly summarizes some of the preliminary insights gained through cross-site comparison. Finally, Section 4 provides a preliminary recapitulation of some of the lessons we have learned that could inform the design of subsequent evaluation campaigns.

2   Experiment Design

Our experiment design closely follows the framework established over several years at the interactive track of the Text Retrieval Conferences (TREC).

2.1   Data

Document collection. We decided to use data from the CLEF 2000 campaign for several reasons:

- Ranked lists from existing automatic CLIR systems provide a representative sample of the input that an interactive document selection stage must be designed to handle.
- The use of a common set of frozen ranked lists enhanced the potential for cross-site comparisons.
- Relevance judgments for most of the top-ranked documents found in this way were already available, which made it possible for us to set the deadline for the interactive track about one month after the main CLEF 2000 task deadline in order to facilitate participation by teams that wished to participate in both tasks.
- Rights to use the CLEF 2000 collection for research purposes have already been arranged for CLEF participants.

We used top-1000 results from John Hopkins University for English documents (found for CLEF 2000 using French queries) and from the University of Maryland for French documents (found after CLEF 2000 using English queries) as the basis for forming the ranked lists that would be used in the experiments. We chose to support more than one document language because alternatives were needed in order to satisfy our requirement that teams recruit only searchers that were not familiar with the document language. These top-1000 results were then used to produce top-50 English and top-50 French results for each topic by first removing any document for which a relevance judgment was unavailable and then selecting the top 50 remaining documents. This process made it possible to use runs that had not been included in the original CLEF 2000 judging pools without the added complexity of scoring documents for which no CLEF relevance judgments were available.

As a baseline Machine Translation (MT) system, we chose Systran professional 3.0 because it is representative of state-of-the-art systems for language pairs in which there is considerable interest. Another factor favoring selection of Systran is that its use by popular freely-available Web page translation services makes it a *de facto* baseline for this task. We chose to translate the French documents into English and the English documents into Spanish for the baseline translations since those language pairs met the needs of teams that we knew were planning to participate. Use of the baseline translations was not required, so in principle it would have been possible for teams that preferred other language pairs to participate as well. In practice, all participating teams did choose to use the baseline translations for at least one of their two conditions.

Topics. For our experiment design we needed two "broad" topics that asked about some general subject that we thought would have many aspects, and two "narrow" topics that asked about some specific event. We selected those topics from among the 40 CLEF 2000 topics in the following manner:

- Discard topics that do not fall clearly into either the "broad" or or the "narrow" category.
- Discard topics for which the relevance of a document could likely be judged simply by looking for a proper name (e.g. *Suicide of Pierre Beregovoy*).
- Favor topics that were relatively easy to judge for relevance based on:
  - a clear topic description, and
  - little need for specialized background knowledge.
- Favor topics with a greater number of known relevant documents in the top-50 for both languages.

Table 1. Selected topics

		Relevant Fraction	
Topic	Summary	English	French
11 (broad)	*New constitution for South Africa*	36/50	27/50
13 (broad)	*Conference on birth control*	16/50	11/50
17 (narrow)	*Bush fire near Sydney*	6/50	2/50
29 (narrow)	*Nobel Prize for Economics*	2/50	3/50

Our choice of topics according to these criteria turned out to be more limited than we had expected. Table 2.1 shows our choices and the density of relevant documents for each topic. One interesting outcome of our topic selection process is that it turned out that the narrow topics consistently had far fewer known relevant documents in the CLEF-2000 collection than the broad topics. Thus, for this collection, "narrow" roughly equates to "sparse" and "broad" roughly equates to "dense." In addition to the topics chosen for the experiment, we suggested the use of topic 33 (*Cancer genetics*, a broad topic) for training searchers at the outset of their session. The same standard resources (top-50 lists and baseline translations) were therefore provided for topic 33 as well.

2.2 Search Procedure

The task assigned to each participant in an experiment was to begin at the top of a ranked list that had been produced by a cross-language retrieval system (see above) and to determine for as many documents in the list as practical in the allowed time whether that document was "relevant," "somewhat relevant," or "not relevant" to a topic described by a written topic description. The written topic description included the text from the title, description, and narrative fields of the CLEF 2000 topic description. A maximum of 20 minutes was allowed for each topic, and participants were to be told that "more credit will be awarded for accurately assessing relevant documents than for the number of documents that are assessed, because in a real application you might need to pay for a high-quality translation [of] each selected document." The participants were also afforded the ability to indicate if they were unsure of their assessment for a document, and they could also choose to leave some documents unassessed.

The participants were asked to complete eight questionnaires at specific points during their session:

- Before the experiment, about computer/searching experience and attitudes, and their degree of knowledge of the document collection, and their foreign language skills. (1)
- After assessing the documents with respect to each topic. (4)
- After completing the use of each system. (2)
- After the experiment, about system comparisons and to provide feedback on the experiment design. (1)

These questionnaires closely followed the design of the questionnaires used in recent TREC interactive track evaluations. The questionnaires that we used, among with additional forms for recording the experimenter's observations during each search, can be found on the CLEF interactive track home page (which can be reached through http://www.clef-campaign.org). Each four-search session was designed to be completed in about three hours. This time included initial training, four 20-minute searches, all questionnaires, and two breaks (one following training, one between systems).

2.3 Presentation Order

We adopted a within-subject design in which each participant searched each topic with some system. Participants, topics and systems were distributed using a Latin square design in a manner similar to that used in the TREC interactive tracks. The presentation order for topics was varied systematically, with participants that saw the same topic-system combination seeing those topics in a different order. That design made it possible to control for fatigue and learning effects to some extent. An eight-participant presentation order matrix is shown in Table 2.3. The minimum number of participants was set at 4, in which case only the top half of the matrix would be used. Additional participants could be added in groups of 4, with the same matrix being reused as needed.

2.4 Evaluation

As our principal measure of effectiveness we selected an unbalanced version of van Rijsbergen's F measure that we called F_α:

Table 2. Presentation order for topics and association of topics with systems.

Participant	Block #1	Block #2
1	System 1: 11-17	System 2: 13-29
2	System 2: 11-17	System 1: 13-29
3	System 1: 17-11	System 2: 29-13
4	System 2: 17-11	System 1: 29-13
5	System 1: 11-17	System 2: 29-13
6	System 2: 11-17	System 1: 29-13
7	System 1: 17-11	System 2: 13-29
8	System 2: 17-11	System 1: 13-29

$$F_\alpha = \frac{1}{\alpha/P + (1-\alpha)/R}$$

where P is precision and R is recall [4]. Values of α above 0.5 emphasize precision, values below 0.5 emphasize recall. For this evaluation, $\alpha = 0.8$ was chosen, modeling the case in which missing some relevant documents would be less objectionable than finding too many documents that, after perhaps paying for professional translations, turn out not to be relevant. The CLEF relevance judgments are two-state (relevant or not relevant), so we treated all judgments other than "relevant" ("somewhat relevant," "not relevant," "not enough information") as not relevant when computing F_α. For contrast, we computed $F_{0.2}$ (which modeled a recall-biased searcher) in addition to $F_{0.8}$, and participating teams were encouraged to explore additional measures that might better model cross-language retrieval tasks in which they were interested.[1]

3   Results

We established an email reflector for teams that were interested in participating in the evaluation and other interested parties. Twenty people from 12 university, industry and government organizations joined that list. Three of those teams completed the experiment and submitted results: Universidad Nacional de Educación a Distancia (UNED) from Spain, the University of Maryland (UMD) from the USA, and the University of Sheffield (SHEF) from the United Kingdom. In this section we summarize the research questions explored by each team.

The **UNED** experiments used native Spanish speakers, Systran translations from English as a baseline, and "pseudo-translations" formed as lists of translated phrases as the contrastive condition. The hypotheses tested was that lists of translated phrases could permit faster judgments without significant loss in

---

[1] The more common subscript on F is β, which is defined such that $\alpha = 1/(\beta^2 + 1)$. $\alpha = 0.8$ corresponds to $\beta = 0.5$, which can be intuitively understood as valuing precision twice as much as recall. Similarly, $\alpha = 0.2$ corresponds to $\beta = 2.0$, which places a corresponding premium on recall.

precision. Eight monolingual Spanish-speaking searchers completed the task. In addition, a group of 8 searchers with a medium knowledge of English, and another 8-searcher group with a good knowledge of English, also completed the task.

The **University of Maryland** used four native English speakers to compare the utility of term-for-term gloss translations with results obtained using the baseline Systran translations. The hypothesis tested was that a combination of term-for-term gloss translation and query-term highlighting in the retrieved documents could provide a useful basis for relevance assessment.

The **University of Sheffield** used 8 native English-speaking searchers to compare monolingual and cross-language and document selection. The specific tasks included selecting French documents using Systran translations, and selecting documents from the (untranslated) English collection. Because both collections were used, the SHEF experiments offer a useful basis for comparison with both the UMD and UNED results.

Table 3 summarizes the results obtained for both languages. Figure 2 illustrates the French results using a recall-precision plot, and Figure 3 provides a similar depiction for English. For comparison, a naive searcher that marked every document as relevant would achieve a precision of 0.30 for English or 0.22 for French, with a recall of 1.0 in either case. This would have resulted in $F_{0.8} = 0.35$ for English and $F_{0.8} = 0.26$ for French.

Table 3. Overview of results.

English documents

System	P	R	$F_{0.8}$	$F_{0.2}$
SHEF-Monolingual	.59	.40	.45	.39
UNED-Phrases	.47	.34	.35	.32
UNED-MT	.48	.22	.28	.21

French documents

System	P	R	$F_{0.8}$	$F_{0.2}$
UMD-MT	.76	.58	.61	.57
SHEF-MT	.67	.46	.59	.48
UMD-Gloss	.51	.27	.29	.26

The papers submitted by each team describe system-specific results. By looking across the three systems we are also able to make the following observations:

- The fact that every system achieved better precision than could have been obtained through the naive selection of every document suggests that every technique that was tried has some merit.
- The usefulness of Systran translations for this task appears to be consistent across sites (for French-to-English, at SHEF and UMD), but not across languages (where both precision and recall with English-to-Spanish translations were well below that achieved with French-to-English translations).
- Monolingual assessment appears to be substantially better (in both precision and recall) than cross-language assessment using Systran, and cross-language assessment using Systran appears to be substantially better (in both precision and recall) than the term-for-term gloss translation technique that was tried at UMD.

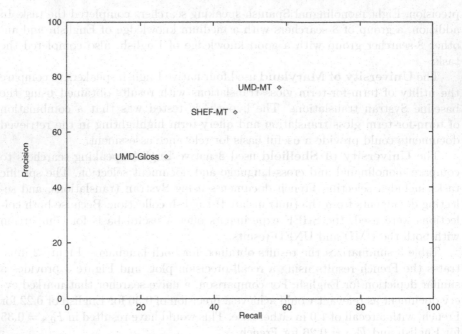

Fig. 2. Overview of French results.

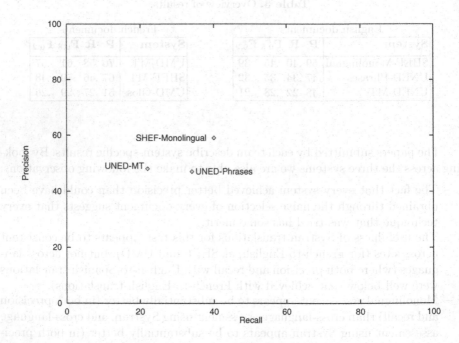

Fig. 3. Overview of English results.

- The display of translated phrases (UNED's pseudo-translations) appears to increase recall with no adverse affect on precision.
- There was a very substantial difference between CLEF relevance judgments (which would receive a F measure of 1.0 for any α) and monolingual assessment at iCLEF.

There are several possible explanations for this last point:

- Any pair of assessors will naturally disagree about some judgments, and assessors that that lack expertise in a topic typically exhibit less agreement than experts would.
- CLEF assessors must judge every document as *relevant/not relevant*, while our searchers could also choose *somewhat relevant, not enough information*, or leave the document unjudged.
- iCLEF searchers must make their judgments in a more sharply limited period.
- iCLEF searchers were given instructions that were intended to bias them in favor of precision. Pooled relevance assessment, by contract, places a premium on careful consideration of every document in the assessment pool.
- Assessors in a formal evaluation could discuss difficult judgments with other assessors, thereby reflecting some degree community consensus in those cases. The iCLEF searchers produce only personal opinions.
- CLEF assessors evaluate documents in an arbitrary order, while iCLEF searchers have additional information available (the order of the documents in the ranked list).

By characterizing the degree to which a time-constrained interactive searcher's judgment might differ from that exercised to establish ground truth for an information retrieval evaluation, we have gained an unexpected insight that might prove useful in the design of adaptive filtering and relevance feedback evaluations, even in a monolingual context.

4 Looking to the Future

With three participating teams in this first year and the limited number of particpants at each site, our conclusions must necessarily be preliminary. We have nonetheless learned a number of interesting things in these experiments. Our thinking on next steps is organized in two parts: what we might do to improve the evaluation of cross-language document selection, and how we might approach evaluation of some of the other tasks that are also important to interactive CLIR.

Some ideas that we are considering for future evaluations of document selection are:

- Consideration of measures other than F_α
- Establishing an agreed framework for statistical significance testing and then using that framework as a basis for establishing the minimum required number of participants in each experiment.

- Exploring experiment designs that could yield insight into the difference between monolingual and cross-language performance on the same document collection.
- Capturing separate values for confidence and relevance assessment, rather than treating "unsure" as an assessment value.
- Exploring tasks other than a simple yes/no decision (e.g., creating suitable ground truth for evaluating multi-valued relevance judgments, evaluating aspectual recall for topics that have a rich substructure, or designing a question answering task).
- Providing shared tools that can reduce barriers to participation in the evaluation campaign (e.g., user interface toolkits that include provisions for logging interactive relevance judgments).

There will be an iCLEF track in 2002, in which teams will have the opportunity to explore the effects of both interactive query translation and interactive document selection. The track design has not yet been finalized, but our intention is to measure the effect of interactive query translation as the difference in mean avearge precision obtained using automatic and interactive query translation techniques.

5   Conclusion

One of the most valuable products of iCLEF has been the emergence of a community of interest around the subject of interactive cross-language retrieval. One important part of this community of interest is a set of researchers that think of themselves as working on task-situated machine translation (where cross-language relevance assessment is the task). Task-based evaluation frameworks have recently been receiving greater attention from machine translation researchers (for example, see [3]). Addressing the CLIR challenge is naturally an interdisciplinary endeavor, and the potential for close links between CLIR and machine translation researchers should therefore be very much in our mutual interest.

Although only three sites participated in this first cooperative evaluation of interactive CLIR, we feel that we achieved our initial goals. We gained a better understanding of the issues that need to be addressed to conduct such evaluations, discovered other researchers with similar interests, and obtained some interesting results. We hope that our email reflector will help to nurture and grow that community as we discuss what we have learned and add people that will bring new perspectives. Next year's iCLEF should therefore benefit in many ways from what we have learned. But regardless of what happens next year, we believe that iCLEF has been an example of CLEF at its best—discovering interesting questions and providing the resources needed to begin to answer them.

Acknowledgments. The authors are grateful to Carol Peters (CNR-IEI Pisa) for her support and encouragement, Paul Over (NIST) and Bill Hersh (OHSU) for generously offering advice and resources based on their experience in the TREC interactive track, Paul McNamee (Johns Hopkins APL) for providing top-1000 automatic English results, Gina Levow (Maryland) for providing top-1000 automatic French results, Clara Cabezas (Maryland) for producing the final document lists used in the evaluation, Jianqiang Wang (Maryland) for providing the Systran translations, and Fernando López-Ostenero (UNED) for managing the iCLEF Web page and email reflector, developing the evaluation scripts, and helping with many other aspects of the evaluation.

References

1. Marti A. Hearst. User interfaces and visualization. In Ricardo Baeza-Yates and Berthier Ribeiro-Neto, editors, *Modern Information Retrieval*, chapter 10. Addison Wesley, New York, 1999. http://www.sims.berkeley.edu/~hearst/irbook/chapters/chap10.html.
2. Douglas W. Oard. Evaluating interactive cross-language information retrieval: Document selection. In Carol Peters, editor, *CLEF 2000 Proceedings, Lecture Notes in Computer Science 2069*, Springer 2001, 57-71.
3. Kathryn Taylor and John White. Predicting what MT is good for: User judgments and task performance. In David Farwell, Laurie Gerber, and Eduard Hovy, editors, *Third Conference of the Association for Machine Translation in the Americas*, pages 364–373. Springer, October 1998. Lecture Notes in Artificial Intelligence 1529.
4. C. J. van Rijsbergen. *Information Retrieval*. Butterworths, London, second edition, 1979.

Noun Phrase Translations for Cross-Language Document Selection

Fernando López-Ostenero, Julio Gonzalo, Anselmo Peñas, and Felisa Verdejo

Departamento de Lenguajes y Sistemas Informáticos
Universidad Nacional de Educación a Distancia
E.T.S.I Industriales, Ciudad Universitaria s/n, 28040 Madrid, SPAIN
{flopez,julio,anselmo,felisa}@lsi.uned.es
http://sensei.lsi.uned.es/NLP

Abstract. This paper presents results for the CLEF Interactive Cross-Language Document Selection task at the UNED. Two translation techniques were compared: the standard Systran translations provided by the CLEF organizers as a baseline, and a phrase-based pseudo-translation approach that uses a phrase alignment algorithm based on comparable corpora. The hypothesis being tested was that noun phrase translations could serve as summarized information for relevance judgment without compromising the precision of such judgments. In addition, we wanted to have an indirect measure of the quality of our phrase extraction process, that had been previously developed for an interactive CLIR application. The results of the experiment confirm that the hypothesis is reasonable: a set of 8 monolingual Spanish speakers judged English documents with the same precision for both systems, but achieved 52% more recall using phrasal translations than using full Systran translations.

1 Introduction

The goal of the CLEF 2001 interactive track (iCLEF) was to compare ways of informing a monolingual searcher about the content of documents written in foreign languages: a better system will allow for better relevance judgments and therefore better foreign-language document selection [2]. The baseline approach is using standard Machine Translation (MT) to produce translated versions of the documents.

Our intuition was that translations produced by MT are noisy and much harder to read and understand than hand-written documents. Perhaps a smaller amount of information, with the best translated phrases highlighted, could facilitate relevance judgment without a significant loss of precision.

To test such a hypothesis, we took advantage of a phrase extraction software previously developed within our research group for an interactive CLIR application [3]. This software is able to index noun phrases in large text collections in a variety of languages (including Spanish and English), providing a good starting material for a phrase-based summarized translation of the documents used in the iCLEF task. Then we performed the following steps:

C.A. Peters et al. (Eds.): CLEF 2001, LNCS 2406, pp. 320–331, 2002.

1. Extract phrasal information from the 200 documents (50 per iCLEF query) of the English CLEF 2000 collection.
2. Find a (large) Spanish corpus comparable with the iCLEF documents. This choice was easy, as the CLEF 2001 test set includes a comparable collection (EFE newswire 1994) of 250,000 Spanish documents (approximately 1Gb of text including SGML tags).
3. Extract phrasal information from the EFE 1994 collection.
4. Develop an alignment algorithm to obtain optimal Spanish translations for all phrases in the English documents.
5. Incorporate phrasal translations in a display strategy for the iCLEF document selection task.
6. Carry out the comparative evaluation between our system and Systran translations, following the iCLEF 2001 guidelines.

Besides testing our main hypothesis, we had three additional goals: first, scaling up the phrase extraction software to handle CLEF-size collections; second, enriching such software with a phrase-alignment algorithm that exploits comparable corpora; and third, obtaining an indirect measure (via document selection) of the quality of that software.

In Section 2, we describe our phrase-based approach to document translation. In Section 3, the experimental setup for the evaluation is explained. In Section 4, results are presented and discussed. Finally, in Section 5 we draw some conclusions.

2   Phrase-Based Pseudo-Translations

2.1   Phrase Extraction

We have used the phrase extraction software from the *UNED WTB Multilingual search engine* [3]. This software performs robust and efficient noun phrase extraction in several languages, and provides two kinds of indexes:

- an index that maps every (lemmatized) word to every noun phrase that contains a morphological variant of the word, and
- an index that maps every noun phrase to documents that contain that phrase.

Noun phrases are extracted using shallow NLP techniques:

1. Words are lemmatized using morphological analyzers. The Spanish processor uses MACO+ [1], and the English processor uses TreeTager [4].
2. Words are tagged for Part-Of-Speech (POS). No POS tagger, to our knowledge, is able to process gigabytes of text. Therefore, a fast approximation to tagging is performed: in the case of Spanish, a set of heuristics has been devised to ensure maximal recall in the phrase detection phase. For other languages, the most frequent POS is assigned to all occurrences of a word.

3. A shallow parsing process identifies noun phrases that satisfy the following (flexible) pattern:

$$[noun|adj][noun|adj|prep|det|conj]^*[noun|adj]$$

4. Finally, indexes for *lemma→phrases* and *phrase→documents* are created.

The collection of 200 English documents is very small and poses no problem for indexing. The EFE collection, however, consists of about 250,000 documents corresponding to about 1Gb of text. Before attempting this iCLEF experiment, the largest collection processed with our system contained 60,000 documents. In order to process the EFE collection with our (limited) hardware resources, it was necessary to re-program most of the system.

These are the approximate figures for the indexing process: 375,000 different words were detected, from which 250,000 were not recognized by the morphological analyzer, because they correspond to proper nouns, typos, foreign words, or words not covered by the dictionary.

Overall, 280,000 different lemmas (including unknown words) are considered, and 26,700,000 different candidate phrases are detected. From this set, we have retained the 3,600,000 phrases that appear more than once in the collection.

In the WTB search engine, such indexes are used to provide multilingual phrase-browsing capabilities in an interactive CLIR setting. In the present work, however, this data is used as statistical information to provide translations for English phrases in iCLEF documents.

2.2   Phrase Alignment

For each English phrase, we start translating all content words in the phrase using a bilingual dictionary. For instance:

```
phrase:       "abortion issue"
lemmas:       abortion, issue
translations: abortion -> aborto
              issue    -> asunto, tema, edición, número, emisión,
                         expedición, descendencia, publicar,
                         emitir, expedir, dar, promulgar
```

For each word in the translations set, we consider all Spanish phrases that contain that word. The set of all phrases forms the *pool of related Spanish phrases*.

Then we search all phrases that contain only (and exactly) one translation for every term of the original phrase. This subset of the Spanish related phrases forms the *set of candidate translations*. In the previous example, the system finds:

phrase	frequency
tema del aborto	16
asunto del aborto	12
asuntos como el aborto	5
asuntos del aborto	2
temas como el aborto	2
asunto aborto	2

abortion issue ⇒

If the subset is non-empty (as in the example above), the system selects the most frequent phrase as the best phrasal translation. Therefore *"tema del aborto"* is (correctly) chosen as translation for *"abortion issue"*. Note that all other candidate phrases also disambiguated *"issue"* correctly as *"tema, asunto"*. Other alignment examples include:

English	# candidates	selected	frequency
abortion issue	6	tema del aborto	16
birth control	3	control de los nacimientos	8
religious and cultural	10	culturales y religiosos	14
last year	52	año pasado	8837

The most appropriate translation for *"birth control"* would rather be *"control de la natalidad"* (with a frequency of 107), but the dictionary does not provide a link between *"birth"* and *"natalidad"*. The selected term *"control de los nacimientos"*, however, is unusual but understandable (in context) for a Spanish speaker.

If the set of candidate translations is empty, two steps are taken:

1. **Subphrase translation**: the system looks for maximal sub-phrases that can be aligned according to the previous step. These are used as partial translations.
2. **Word by word contextual translation**: The remaining words are translated using phrase statistics to take context into account: from all translation candidates for a word, we choose the candidate that is included in more phrases from the original pool of related Spanish phrases.

For instance:

```
phrase:  "day international conference on population and development"
lemmas:   day, international, conference, population, development
possible translations:
    day               -> día, jornada, época, tiempo
    international -> internacional
    conference        -> congreso, reunión
    population        -> población, habitantes
    development    -> desarrollo, avance, cambio, novedad, explotación,
                       urbanización, revelado
```

```
subphrase alignments:
    day international             -> jornadas internacionales
    day international conference -> jornada del congreso internacional
word by word translations:
    population                   -> población
    development                  -> desarrollo
final translation:
    "jornada del congreso internacional población desarrollo"
```

Note that, while the indexed phrase is not an optimal noun phrase (*"day"* should be removed) and the translation is not fully grammatical, the lexical selection is accurate, and the result is easily understandable for most purposes (including document selection).

2.3   Phrase-Based Document Translation

The pseudo-translation of the document is made using the information obtained in the alignment process. The basic process is:

1. Find all maximal (i.e., not included in bigger units) phrases in the document, and sort them by order of appearance in the document.
2. List the translations obtained for each original phrase according to the alignment phase, highligting:
   - Phrases that have an optimal alignment (boldface).
   - Phrases containing query terms (bright colour).

As an example, let us consider this sentence from one of iCLEF documents:

> ENGLISH SENTENCE
>
> the abortion issue dominated the nine-day International Conference on Population and Development.

A valid manual translation of the above sentence would be:

> MANUAL TRANSLATION
>
> el tema del aborto dominó las nueve jornadas del Congreso Internacional sobre Población y Desarrollo.

while Systran produces:

> SYSTRAN MT TRANSLATION
>
> la edición del aborto dominó el de nueve días Conferencia internacional sobre la población y el desarrollo.

Aside from grammatical correctness, Systran translation only makes one relevant mistake, interpreting *"issue"* as in *"journal issue"* and producing *"edición del aborto"*(meaningless) instead of *"tema del aborto"*.

Our phrase indexing process, on the other hand, identifies two maximal phrases:

abortion issue
day International Conference on Population and Development

which receive the translations showed in the previous section. The final display of our system is:

> PHRASAL PSEUDO-TRANSLATION
>
> **tema del aborto**
> **jornada del congreso internacional** población desarrollo

where boldface is used for optimal phrase alignments, which are supposed to be less noisy translations. If any of the phrases contain a (morphological variant of a) query term for a particular search, the phrase is further highlighted.

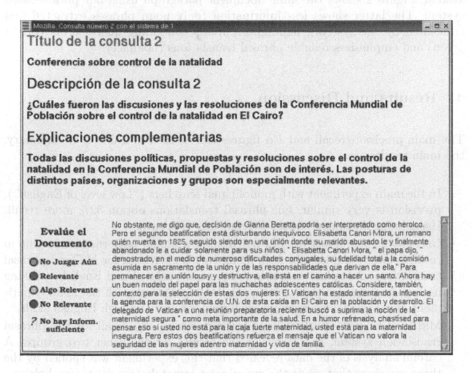

Fig. 1. Search interface: MT system

3   Experimental Setup

3.1   Experiments and Searchers

We conducted three experiments with different searcher profiles: for the main experiment, we recruited 8 volunteers with low or no proficiency at all in the English language. For purposes of comparison, we formed two additional 8-people groups with mid-level and high-level English skills.

3.2   Search Protocol and Interface Description

We followed closely the search protocol established in the iCLEF guidelines [2]. The time for each search, and the combination of topics and systems, were fully controlled by the system interface. Most of the searchers used the system locally, but five of them (UNED students) carried out the experiments via Internet from their study center (in the presence of the same supervisor).

Figure 1 shows an example of a document displayed using the Systran MT system. Figure 2 shows the same document paragraph using our phrase-based system. The latter shows less information (only noun phrases extracted and translated by the system), highlights phrases containing query terms (bright green) and emphasizes reliable phrasal translations (boldface).

4   Results and Discussion

The main precision/recall and $F\alpha$ figures can be seen in Table 4. In summary, the main results are:

- In the main experiment with monolingual searchers ("Low level of English"), precision is very similar, but phrasal translations obtain 52% more recall. Users judge documents faster without loss of accuracy.
- Users with good knowledge of English show a similar pattern, but the gain in recall is lower, and the absolute figures are higher both for MT and phrasal translations. As unknown words remain untranslated and English-speaking users may recognize them, these results are coherent with the main experiment. See Figure 3 for a comparison between low and high English skills.
- Mid-level English speakers have lower precision and recall for the phrasal translation system, contradicting the results for the other two groups. A careful analysis of the data revealed that this experiment was spoiled by the three searchers that made the experiment remotely (see discussion below).

A detailed discussion of each of the three experiments follows.

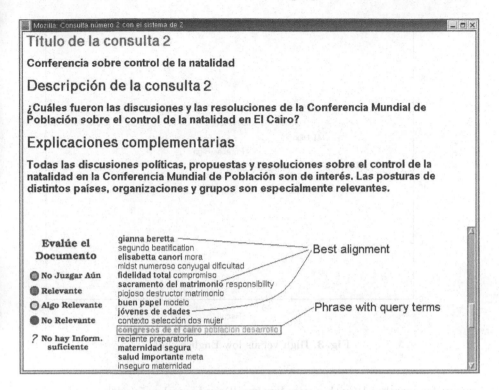

Fig. 2. Search interface: Phrases system

Table 1. Overview of results.

Main (Low level of English)

System	P	R	$F_{0.8}$	$F_{0.2}$
Systran MT	.48	.22	.28	.21
Phrases	.47(-2%)	.34(+52%)	.35(+25%)	.32(+52%)

Mid level of English

System	P	R	$F_{0.8}$	$F_{0.2}$
Systran MT	.62	.31	.41	.31
Phrases	.46(-25%)	.25(-19%)	.30(-26%)	.24(-22%)

High level of English

System	P	R	$F_{0.8}$	$F_{0.2}$
Systran MT	.58	.34	.42	.34
Phrases	.53(-12%)	.45(+32%)	.39(-7%)	.38(+11%)

4.1 Low Level of English Proficiency (Main Experiment)

The results of this experiment, detailed by searcher and topic, can be seen in
Table 2. Looking at the average figures per searcher, the results are consistent

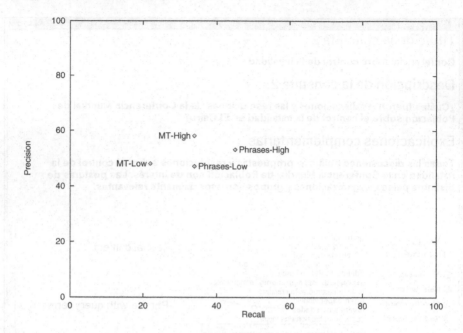

Fig. 3. High versus low English skills.

except for searcher 1 (with a very low recall) and searcher 5 (with very low recall and precision):

- Within this group, searcher 1 was the only one that carried out the experiment remotely, and problems with the net connection seriously affected recall for both systems and all topics. Unfortunately, this problem also affected three searchers in the mid-level English group and one in the high-level group.
- Examining the questionnaires filled in by Searcher 5, we concluded that he did not understand the task at all. He did not mark relevant documents in any of the questions, apparently judging the quality of the translations.

Only one of the eight searchers was familiar with MT systems, and most of them had little experience with search engines.

In the questionnaires, most searchers prefer the phrasal system, arguing that the information was more concise and thus decisions could be made faster. However, they felt that the phrases system demanded more interpretation from the user. The MT system was perceived as giving more detailed information, but too dense to reach easy judgments. All these impressions are coherent with the Precision/Recall figures obtained, and confirm our hypothesis about potential benefits of phrasal pseudo translations.

Table 2. Low Level of English (main experiment)

(Runs with the phrase system are in **boldface**, runs with MT in normal font)

Precision

User\Topic	T-1	T-2	T-3	T-4	Avg.
U-L-01	1	0	1	0	0.5
U-L-02	1	0.23	**0.66**	1	0.72
U-L-03	1	**0.34**	1	**0.25**	0.64
U-L-04	1	0.09	**0.33**	0	0.35
U-L-05	0	**0.2**	0	0	0.05
U-L-06	1	0	**0.57**	0.16	0.43
U-L-07	1	0	1	**0.33**	0.58
U-L-08	**0.95**	0.03	1	0.25	0.55
Avg.	0.86	0.11	0.69	0.24	0.47

Recall

User\Topic	T-1	T-2	T-3	T-4	Avg.
U-L-01	0.02	0	0.16	0	0.04
U-L-02	**0.19**	0.5	1	0.5	0.54
U-L-03	0.08	**0.93**	0.66	**0.5**	0.54
U-L-04	**0.11**	0.06	**0.5**	0	0.16
U-L-05	0	**0.18**	0	0	0.04
U-L-06	**0.13**	0	**0.66**	0.5	0.32
U-L-07	0.11	0	0.5	**0.5**	0.27
U-L-08	**0.55**	0.06	**0.33**	0.5	0.36
Avg.	0.14	0.21	0.47	0.31	0.28

$F_{0.2}$

User\Topic	T-1	T-2	T-3	T-4	Avg.
U-L-01	0.02	0	0.19	0	0.05
U-L-02	**0.22**	0.40	**0.90**	0.55	0.51
U-L-03	0.09	**0.69**	0.70	**0.41**	0.47
U-L-04	**0.13**	0.06	**0.45**	0	0.16
U-L-05	0	**0.18**	0	0	0.04
U-L-06	**0.15**	0	**0.63**	0.35	0.28
U-L-07	0.13	0	0.55	**0.45**	0.28
U-L-08	**0.60**	0.05	**0.38**	0.41	0.36
Avg.	0.16	0.17	0.47	0.27	0.26

$F_{0.8}$

User\Topic	T-1	T-2	T-3	T-4	Avg.
U-L-01	0.09	0	0.48	0	0.14
U-L-02	**0.53**	0.25	**0.70**	0.83	0.57
U-L-03	0.30	**0.38**	0.90	**0.27**	0.46
U-L-04	**0.38**	0.08	**0.35**	0	0.20
U-L-05	0	**0.19**	0	0	0.04
U-L-06	**0.42**	0	**0.58**	0.18	0.29
U-L-07	0.38	0	0.83	**0.35**	0.39
U-L-08	**0.82**	0.03	**0.71**	0.27	0.45
Avg.	0.36	0.11	0.56	0.23	0.31

4.2 Mid Level of English Proficiency

The results for this group (see Table 3) are apparently incompatible with the other two experiments. Taking a close look at the user averages, we detected that three users have extremely low recall figures, and these are precisely the users that performed the experiment remotely. Excluding them, the average recall would be similar for both systems. Of course the lesson learned from this spoiled experiment is that we have to be far more careful keeping the experiment conditions stable (and that we should not rely on Internet for this kind of experiment!).

4.3 High Level of English Proficiency

The detailed results for the group with good language skills can be seen in Table 4. Again, one searcher deviates from the rest with very low average recall, the only one that performed the experiment remotely (searcher 6). Aside from this, apparently better English skills lead to higher recall and precision rates. This is a reasonable result, as untranslated words can be understood, and translation errors can more easily be tracked back. Precision is 12% lower with the phrasal system, but recall is 32% higher. Overall, $F_{0.8}$ is higher for the MT system, and $F_{0.2}$ is higher for the phrasal system.

Table 3. Mid Level of English

(Runs with the phrase system are in **boldface**, runs with MT in normal font)

Precision

User\Topic	T-1	T-2	T-3	T-4	Avg.
U-M-01	1	0	1	0	0.5
U-M-02	1	0	1	0	0.5
U-M-03	1	**0.26**	1	**0.5**	0.69
U-M-04	1	0.31	0	0	0.32
U-M-05	1	**0.36**	1	**0.33**	0.67
U-M-06	**0.81**	0.30	**0.66**	0.33	0.52
U-M-07	1	0	1	0	0.5
U-M-08	**0.90**	0	**0.66**	1	0.64
Avg.	0.96	0.15	0.79	0.27	0.54

Recall

User\Topic	T-1	T-2	T-3	T-4	Avg.
U-M-01	0.11	0	0.66	0	0.19
U-M-02	**0.02**	0	**0.16**	0	0.04
U-M-03	0.13	**0.5**	0.5	**0.5**	0.40
U-M-04	**0.13**	0.31	0	0	0.11
U-M-05	0.11	**0.68**	0.66	**0.5**	0.48
U-M-06	**0.25**	0.87	**0.66**	0.5	0.57
U-M-07	0.08	0	0.16	0	0.06
U-M-08	**0.27**	0	**0.33**	1	0.4
Avg.	0.13	0.29	0.39	0.31	0.28

$F_{0.2}$

User\Topic	T-1	T-2	T-3	T-4	Avg.
U-M-01	0.13	0	0.70	0	0.20
U-M-02	**0.02**	0	**0.19**	0	0.05
U-M-03	0.15	**0.42**	0.55	**0.5**	0.40
U-M-04	**0.15**	0.31	0	0	0.11
U-M-05	0.13	**0.57**	0.70	**0.45**	0.46
U-M-06	**0.29**	0.63	**0.66**	0.45	0.50
U-M-07	0.09	0	0.19	0	0.07
U-M-08	**0.31**	0	**0.36**	1	0.41
Avg.	0.15	0.24	0.41	0.3	0.27

$F_{0.8}$

User\Topic	T-1	T-2	T-3	T-4	Avg.
U-M-01	0.38	0	0.90	0	0.32
U-M-02	**0.09**	0	**0.48**	0	0.14
U-M-03	0.42	**0.28**	0.83	**0.5**	0.50
U-M-04	**0.42**	0.31	0	0	0.18
U-M-05	0.38	**0.39**	0.90	**0.35**	0.50
U-M-06	**0.55**	0.34	**0.66**	0.35	0.47
U-M-07	0.30	0	0.48	0	0.19
U-M-08	**0.61**	0	**0.55**	1	0.54
Avg.	0.39	0.16	0.6	0.27	0.35

Besides having better English skills, searchers had more experience using graphical interfaces, search engines and Machine Translation programs. In agreement with the first group, they felt that the MT system gave too much information, and they also complained about the quality of the translations. However, overall they preferred the MT system to the phrasal one: translated phrases permitted faster judgments, but the searcher needed to add more subjective interpretation of the information presented. All these subjective impressions are in agreement with the final precision/recall figures.

5   Conclusions

Although the number of searchers does not allow for clear-cut conclusions, the results of the evaluation indicate that summarized translations, and in particular phrasal equivalents in the searcher's language, might be more appropriate for document selection than full-fledged MT. Our purpose is to reproduce a similar experiment with more users, and better-controlled experimental conditions, to have a better testing of our hypothesis in a near future.

As a side conclusion, we have proved that phrase detection and handling with shallow NLP techniques is feasible for large-scale IR collections. The major

Table 4. High Level of English

(Runs with the phrase system are in **boldface**, runs with MT in normal font)

Precision

User\Topic	T-1	T-2	T-3	T-4	Avg.
U-H-01	1	**0.27**	1	0	0.56
U-H-02	**0.91**	0.35	**0.8**	0.33	0.59
U-H-03	0.83	**0.17**	1	**0.66**	0.66
U-H-04	1	0	1	0.5	0.62
U-H-05	1	**0.34**	0.83	**0.25**	0.60
U-H-06	0	0.33	**0.66**	0	0.24
U-H-07	1	**0.33**	1	**0.13**	0.61
U-H-08	1	0.21	1	0	0.55
Avg.	0.84	0.25	0.91	0.23	0.55

Recall

User\Topic	T-1	T-2	T-3	T-4	Avg.
U-H-01	0.05	**0.37**	0.66	0	0.27
U-H-02	**0.30**	0.93	**0.66**	0.5	0.59
U-H-03	0.13	**0.18**	0.5	1	0.45
U-H-04	**0.02**	0	**0.83**	0.5	0.33
U-H-05	0.30	1	0.83	**0.5**	0.65
U-H-06	0	0.25	**0.33**	0	0.14
U-H-07	0.16	**0.62**	0.33	1	0.52
U-H-08	**0.08**	0.43	**0.33**	0	0.21
Avg.	0.13	0.47	0.55	0.43	0.39

$F_{0.2}$

User\Topic	T-1	T-2	T-3	T-4	Avg.
U-H-01	0.06	**0.34**	0.70	0	0.27
U-H-02	**0.34**	0.69	**0.68**	0.45	0.54
U-H-03	0.15	**0.17**	0.55	**0.90**	0.44
U-H-04	**0.02**	0	**0.85**	0.5	0.34
U-H-05	0.34	**0.72**	0.83	**0.41**	0.57
U-H-06	0	0.26	**0.36**	0	0.15
U-H-07	0.19	**0.52**	0.38	**0.42**	0.37
U-H-08	**0.09**	0.35	**0.38**	0	0.20
Avg.	0.14	0.38	0.59	0.33	0.36

$F_{0.8}$

User\Topic	T-1	T-2	T-3	T-4	Avg.
U-H-01	0.20	**0.28**	0.90	0	0.34
U-H-02	**0.64**	0.39	**0.76**	0.35	0.53
U-H-03	0.39	**0.17**	0.83	**0.70**	0.52
U-H-04	**0.09**	0	**0.96**	0.5	0.38
U-H-05	0.68	**0.39**	0.83	**0.27**	0.54
U-H-06	0	0.31	**0.55**	0	0.21
U-H-07	0.48	**0.36**	0.71	**0.15**	0.42
U-H-08	**0.30**	0.23	**0.71**	0	0.31
Avg.	0.34	0.26	0.78	0.24	0.40

bottleneck, Part-Of-Speech tagging, can be overcome with heuristic simplifications that do not compromise the usability of the results, at least in the present application.

Acknowledgments. This work has been funded by the Spanish *Comisión Interministerial de Ciencia y Tecnología*, project *Hermes* (TIC2000-0335-C03-01).

References

1. J. Carmona, S. Cervell, L. Màrquez, M. A. Martí, L. Padró, R. Placer, H. Rodríguez, M. Taulé, and J. Turmo. An environment for morphosyntactic processing of unrestricted spanish text. In *Proceedings of the First International Conference on Language Resources and Evaluation (LREC'98)*, 1998.
2. Douglas W. Oard and Julio Gonzalo. The CLEF 2001 interactive track. In Carol Peters, editor, *Proceedings of CLEF 2001*, Lecture Notes for Computer Science, Springer, forthcoming.
3. Anselmo Peñas, Julio Gonzalo, and Felisa Verdejo. Cross-language information access through phrase browsing. In *Applications of Natural Language to Information Systems*, Lecture Notes in Informatics, pages 121–130, 2001.
4. Helmut Schmid. Probabilistic part-of-speech tagging using decision trees. In *International Conference on New Methods in Language Processing*, 1994.

iCLEF at Sheffield

Mark Sanderson and Zoë Bathie

Department of Information Studies, University of Sheffield,
Western Bank, Sheffield, S10 2TN, UK
m.sanderson@shef.ac.uk

Abstract. Sheffield's contribution to the interactive cross language information retrieval track took the approach of comparing users' abilities to judge the relevance of machine translated French documents against ones written in the users' native language: English. Conducting such an experiment is challenging, and the issues surrounding the experimental design are discussed. Experimental results strongly suggest that users are just as capable of judging relevance of translated documents as they are for documents in their native language

1   Introduction

An important and relatively little studied aspect of Cross Language Information Retrieval research is user interaction with the CLIR system. Even the most fundamental aspects of retrieval, such as user ability to formulate effective queries or judge retrieved documents, have rarely been examined in a cross language context. As a consequence, the interactive Cross Language Evaluation Forum (iCLEF) was set up. Starting this year, the track studied one aspect of the interactive process: the user's ability to judge the relevance of retrieved foreign (i.e. target) language documents translated in some manner into the users' native (i.e. source) language. Using a test collection, user relevance judgements were compared to the judgements previously made by relevance assessors. The aim of the track was to compare different translation methods. However, at Sheffield, a different approach was taken: comparing user ability to judge the relevance of translated news articles against ability to judge articles written in the user's native language. The rest of this article describes the work at Sheffield: the experimental design is first described followed by a discussion of issues arising from this design: the results are then presented, and possible future work is outlined.

2   The Experiment

It might seem reasonable to assume that if a user is presented with a clearly written document that another has judged for relevance, the user will agree with the prior judgement. However, as is well known, relevance assessments are subjective depending on user interpretation of the query and document, which is based on prior

C.A. Peters et al. (Eds.): CLEF 2001, LNCS 2406, pp. 332–335, 2002.
© Springer-Verlag Berlin Heidelberg 2002

knowledge of the subject. Consequently, there can be a reasonable level of disagreement between judges. Voorhees (1988), amongst others, studied this issue.

The iCLEF experiments compare relevance judgements of users against those made previously by assessors, although in this case the assessors were reading the judged documents in their original language and the versions examined by the users were translations of some type. Although the aim of iCLEF was to assess the extent the translation had impaired users' ability to judge, any such measurement would also include disagreements between users and assessors on what constitutes relevance. Others conducting the iCLEF experiment choose to rely on past work on levels of disagreement to provide an indication of how important this factor is. Sheffield opted instead to attempt to separate out these factors by conducting a form of control experiment: comparing ability to judge relevance of translated documents against judgements made on native language documents. Specifically, users were presented with documents retrieved in response to iCLEF test collection queries: from either French newspaper articles (Le Monde) automatically translated using Systran software; or English language articles from the LA Times. Both newspaper collections covered the same time frame. Specifics about the queries used, collections searched and forms of relevance judgement made are outlined in the iCLEF overview paper elsewhere in the iCLEF section in this volume.

Designing an experiment to compare effectively user ability to judge relevance in native and translated documents is problematic. In the design chosen here any difference in relevance judgements across the two sets of documents can be attributed to factors other than the quality of English in the texts. Writing styles or assumptions of prior cultural knowledge may differ in Le Monde and the LA Times and such factors may affect user relevance judgement. In addition, the assessors (to whom user judgements are compared) are different for the two collections, as are the conditions under which they performed their assessment; again this might be an influencing factor. Even the retrieval system may have behaved differently on the two collections and this may influence the type of retrieved relevant documents presented to the user. Despite these issues, it was judged that continuing with the experiment as described was sensible as there appears to be no simple experimental design that can accurately measure user ability to judge relevance against translation quality that is not confounded by other factors[1]. Therefore, we take the position of assuming that the additional factors in this experiment do not contribute significantly to our experimental results.

Following the iCLEF design, eight subjects were presented with retrieved documents from four queries in two different situations: half of the queries retrieved on the French collection and the other half on the English collection. A latin square

---

[1] One could design an experiment where native English speakers judge the translated French documents and native French speakers judge the same (un-translated) French documents. However, the two groups of users are likely to have different cultural backgrounds, which may influence the results. Whether this difference would influence experimental results more or less than the design chosen here can only be determined through further experimentation. Note, there was a very pragmatic reason for not pursuing this design: finding a sufficient number of French speakers would have been hard to achieve.

design was used to ensure that query order and presentation of system did not confound the experiment. Users were given twenty minutes to judge the documents retrieved for each query. The subjects were Sheffield University students, who were native English speakers. They spent three hours in total on the experiment being paid £20 for their participation.

3   Results

Results from the initial data returned by iCLEF are shown in the table below. The effectiveness of users was determined using Van Rijsbergen's F measure [1], where user judgements were compared to those made previously by assessors. The variable a was set to values of 0.2 and 0.8 to bias F to indicate user preference for recall and precision respectively.

System	F (a=0.2)	F (a=0.8)
Le Monde	0.49	0.60
LA Times	0.40	0.46

As can be seen for both values of F users judge relevance better on the translated French documents than on the English originals, however use of a t-test indicated that the differences were not significant. We believe that despite the potential problems with the experimental design, we have shown with some degree of confidence that the users reading the retrieved machine translated documents are more than able to judge the relevance of the retrieved text.

As described in the overview iCLEF paper, users were asked to judge documents as relevant, not relevant, or somewhat relevant. The table above shows results of the user judgements focussing only on documents marked as relevant. The table below shows results re-calculated when documents marked as somewhat relevant are included. As can be seen, the difference in F values between Le Monde and LA Times is somewhat smaller particularly in the precision oriented F measure, indicating that users are more accurate in judging the relevance of marginally relevant native language documents than they are of translations.

System	F (a=0.2)	F (a=0.8)
Le Monde	0.65	0.59
LA Times	0.58	0.52

Finally, the degree of overlap between the sets of relevant documents (judged by the assessors) and the experimental subjects was measured. Overlap is defined as the intersection of the two sets divided by the union. In Voorhees's work [2] overlap between pairs of assessors was found to range between 0.42 and 0.49. Taking the user judgements of those judged both relevant and somewhat relevant, the overlap ranged between 0.39 and 0.47, a similar range.

4   Conclusions and Future Work

In this report, we have briefly described an experiment that compares user ability to judge relevance of documents written in different languages. The difficulty of designing such an experiment was discussed and the results of the experiment presented. The conclusion from the results was that for the documents tested here, French documents automatically translated into English using a good machine translation system are sufficiently readable to allow users to make accurate relevance judgements.

Extensions of this work would involve conducting further experiments to expand the number of users to try to find statistical significance in the data. In addition, exploring other experimental designs will also be a priority.

Acknowledgements. The second author conducted this work as part of her Master's course at Sheffield. Financial support for the work in this report was provided jointly by the MIND (IST-2000-26061, mind.cs.strath.ac.uk) and Clarity (IST-2000-25310, clarity.shef.ac.uk) projects.

References

1.   Van Rijsbergen, C.J. (1979): Information Retrieval (second edition), Butterworths, London
2.   Voorhees, E. (1998): Variations in Relevance Judgements and the Measurement of Retrieval Effectiveness, in Proceedings of the 21st Annual International ACM-SIGIR Conference on Research and Development in Information Retrieval: 315-323

iCLEF 2001 at Maryland: Comparing Term-for-Term Gloss and MT

Jianqiang Wang and Douglas W. Oard

Human Computer Interaction Laboratory
College of Information Studies and
Institute for Advanced Computer Studies
University of Maryland, College Park, MD 20742, USA
{oard,wangjq}@glue.umd.edu.edu,
http://www.glue.umd.edu/~oard/

Abstract. For the first interactive Cross-Language Evaluation Forum, the Maryland team focused on comparison of term-for-term gloss translation with full machine translation for the document selection task. The results show that (1) searchers are able to make relevance judgments with translations from either approach, and (2) the machine translation system achieved better effectiveness than the gloss translation strategy that we tried, although the difference is not statistically significant. It was noted that the "somewhat relevant" category was used differently by searchers presented with gloss translations than with machine translations, and some reasons for that difference are suggested. Finally, the results suggest that the F measure used in this evaluation is better suited for use with topics that have many known relevant documents than those with few.

1 Introduction

In the process of interactive cross-language information retrieval (CLIR), there are two points where interaction with the searcher is possible: query formulation and document selection. The focus of this paper is on the interactive document selection task. Ranked retrieval systems nominate promising documents for examination by the user by placing them higher in a ranked list. The searcher's task is then to examine those documents and select the ones that help to meet their information need. The query formulation process and the actual use of the documents selected by the user is outside the scope of the work reported in this paper. Focusing on one aspect of the problem in this way makes it possible to gain insight through the use of metrics that are appropriate for document selection, a well-studied problem in other contexts.

One important use for CLIR systems is to help searchers find information that is written in a language with which they are not familiar. In such an application, the query would be posed in a language for which the user has an adequate active (i.e., writing) vocabulary, and the document selection process would be performed in a language for which the searcher has at least an adequate passive

C.A. Peters et al. (Eds.): CLEF 2001, LNCS 2406, pp. 336–352, 2002.

(i.e., reading) vocabulary. Since we have assumed that the document(s) being sought are not expressed in such a language, some form of translation is required.

We view translation as a user interface design challenge, in which the goal is to provide the user with the information needed to perform some task—in this case document selection. There has been an extensive effort to develop so-called "Machine Translation" (MT) systems to produce (hopefully) fluent and accurate translation of every language that is presently studied at the Cross-Language Evaluation Forum (CLEF) into English. No such systems yet exist for most of the world's languages, however, and the cost of building a sophisticated MT system for every written language would indeed be staggering. This is an important challenge, since a substantial portion of the world's knowledge is presently recorded in English, and the vast majority of the world's people cannot even find that information. Supporting search by users that know only a lesser-developed language is only one of many capabilities that will be needed if we are to address what has been called the "digital divide" on a global scale. But it is one that we believe could be addressed with emerging broad-coverage language technologies. We therefore have chosen to use this first interactive CLEF (iCLEF) evaluation to begin to explore that question.

We have identified three factors that affect the utility of translation technology for the document selection task: accuracy, fluency, and focus. By "accuracy" we mean the degree to which a translation reflects the intent of the original author. Both lexical selection (word choice) and presentation order can affect accuracy.[1] By "fluency" we mean the degree to which a translation can be used quickly to achieve the intended purpose (in this case, document selection). Again, both lexical selection and presentation order can affect fluency.[2] By focus, we mean the degree to which the reader's attention can be focused on the portions of a translated document that best support the intended task–in this case the recognition of relevant documents from among those nominated by the system. Presentation of summaries and highlighting query terms in the retrieved documents are typical examples of focus. Our intuition suggests that accuracy is essential for the document selection task, but that there is a tradeoff between fluency and focus, with lower fluency being acceptable if effective focus mechanisms are provided. The iCLEF evaluation was well timed to allow us to begin to explore these questions.

For iCLEF, we chose to compare MT with a one-best term-by-term gloss translation technique that we had originally developed to demonstrate the degree of translation quality that could be achieved for resource-poor languages. We had already adapted this system to support controlled user studies for some exploratory work on interactive document selection in the CLIR track of the 2000 Text Retrieval Conference (TREC) [4], so only minor modifications were needed to conform to the iCLEF requirements. We obtained a number of interesting results, including:

---

[1] Consider the case of "Harry hit Tom" and "Tom hit Harry" to see why presentation order can be an accuracy issue.

[2] For example, "Tom hitting by Harry" is understandable, but disfluent.

- Searchers are able to make some useful relevance judgments with either type of translation
- MT achieved better effectiveness than gloss translation, although the difference was not statistically significant
- The "somewhat relevant" category was used differently by participants in our experiment depending on whether MT or gloss translations were being examined.
- The F_α effectiveness measure does not seem to be well suited for use with topics that have few relevant documents.

The remainder of the paper is organized as follows. Section 2 provides an overview of the iCLEF experiment design. Section 3 then describes the design and implementation of our system, details of the experiment procedure, and a description of the characteristics of the participants in our experiment. Section 4 presents the results, drawing on both quantitative and qualitative methods, and raises some experiment design issues. Finally, Section 5 concludes the paper.

2   Background

Over the past decade, research on CLIR has focused on development and evaluation of automatic approaches for ranking documents in a language different from that of the query. Present fully automatic techniques can do this fairly well, performing at perhaps 80% of what can be achieved by a monolingual information retrieval system under similar conditions when measured using mean average precision [3]. Ranking documents is only one step in a search process, however; some means of selecting documents from that list is needed. One possible strategy would be to build an automatic classifier that could make a sharp decision about whether each document is relevant or not. Such an approach would have problems, however, since users often don't express their information needs clearly. Indeed, they may not even *know* their information needs clearly at the outset of a search session. For this reason, ranked retrieval systems are often used interactively, with the user browsing the ranked list and selecting interesting documents. Research on interactive retrieval strongly suggests that people are quite good at this task, performing quite well even when using ranked lists produced by systems that are well below the current state-of-the-art [1]. It is an open question, however, whether a similar strategy would be effective if automatically produced translations of otherwise unreadable documents would be sufficient to obtain a similar effect in interactive CLIR applications. The goal of the iCLEF evaluation is to bring together a research community to explore that question [2].

The principal objective of the first iCLEF evaluation was to develop an experiment design that could yield insight into the effectiveness of alternative techniques for supporting cross-language document selection. Participating sites could choose from two tasks: Selection of French documents or selection of English documents. We chose to work on selection of French documents since knowledge of French among the pool of possible participants in our experiment was more limited than knowledge of English. The French test collection contained four search topics for use in the experiment, plus a fifth practice topic. For each topic, the following resources were provided:

- An English topic description, consisting of title, description, and narrative that served as a basis for the CLIR system's query,
- A ranked list of the top 50 documents produced automatically by a CLIR system using an English query,
- The original French version of each document, and
- An English translation of each document that was produced using Systran Professional 3.0.

The four topics included two "broad" topics that asked about a general subject (e.g. *Conference on Birth Control*) and two "narrow" topics that asked about some specific event (e.g., *Nobel Prize for Economics in 1994*). Relevance judgments for the top-50 documents for each topic were also known, but those judgments were used only to evaluate the results after the experiment was completed. As might be expected, it turned out that in every case there were more relevant documents in the top-50 for the broad topics than for the narrow ones.

The iCLEF experiment was designed in a manner similar to that used in the TREC Interactive Track, in which a Latin square design is used to block topic and searcher effects so that the system effect can be characterized. Table 2 shows the order in which topic-system combinations were presented to users. In this design, every searcher sees all four topics, two with one system and two with the other. The order in which topics and systems are presented is varied systematically in order to minimize the impact of fatigue and learning effect on the observability of the system effect. We realized at the outset that four participants was an undesirably small number given the large variability that has been observed in human performance of related tasks, but time and resource limitations precluded our use of a larger sample.

Table 1. iCLEF-2001 experiment design as run. Topics 11 and 13 are broad, Topic 17 and 29 are narrow.

Participant	Before break		After break	
umd01	MT	Topic 11, Topic 17	Gloss	Topic 13, Topic 29
umd02	Gloss	Topic 11, Topic 17	MT	Topic 13, Topic 29
umd03	MT	Topic 17, Topic 11	Gloss	Topic 29, Topic 13
umd04	Gloss	Topic 17, Topic 11	MT	Topic 29, Topic 13

The task to be performed at each participating site included:

- Design and implement two interactive document selection systems. Use of the Systran translations was optional, but we choose to use them as our MT system.

- Have participants make relevance judgments for each topic. Each participant was allowed 20 minutes for each topic (including reading the topic description, reading as many documents or document summaries as time allowed, and making relevance judgments). For each document, the participant was asked to select one of four possible judgments: "not relevant," "somewhat relevant," "relevant," or "unsure." A "not judged" response was also available.
- Ask each searcher to complete questionnaires regarding their background, each search, each system, and their subjective assessment of the two systems.
- Provide the participants judgments to the iCLEF coordinators in a standard format for scoring.
- Conduct data analysis using the scored results and other measurements that were recorded and retained locally.

An unbalanced version of van Rijsbergen's F measure was selected for use as the official effectiveness measure for the evaluation:

$$F_\alpha = \frac{1}{\alpha/P + (1 - \alpha)/R}$$

where P is precision and R is recall. Values of α could range between 0 and 1, with values above 0.5 emphasizing precision and values below 0.5 emphasizing recall [5]. For iCLEF, 0.8 was selected as the value for which the experiments were to be designed, modeling a situation in which finding documents accurately is more important than finding all the relevant documents. The participants were told that they should approach the task with that in mind. For the official results, judgments of "somewhat relevant," "unsure," and "not judged" were treated as "not relevant."

3   Maryland iCLEF Experiments

For the past few years, our team at Maryland has focused on low-cost techniques for extending CLIR capabilities to new languages. Our initial work was based on using existing bilingual term lists to perform dictionary-based CLIR, and it is that technique that we adapted to perform gloss translation for these experiments. The basic idea is to find source language (in this case, French) terms in the bilingual term list and then replace them with the corresponding target language term(s) (in this case, English). For resource-poor languages we could conceivably obtain bilingual term lists by scanning (or even rekeying) a printed bilingual dictionary or by training a statistical translation model on translation-equivalent text pairs that might be automatically farmed from the Web–for these experiments we used a bilingual term list that we had downloaded from the Web for CLEF 2000 [5]. This resource contained approximately 35,000 term pairs.

3.1   Gloss Translation

Bilingual term lists found on the Web often contain an eclectic combination of root and inflected forms. We therefore applied the same backoff translation strategy that we have previously used for automatic retrieval to extend the source-language (French) coverage of the term list. The first step was to remove all punctuation and convert every character to unaccented lower case in both the documents and the term list. This had the effect of minimizing problems due to character encoding. The translation process then proceeded in the normal reading order through the text, using greedy longest string matching to identify terms in the document that can be translated using the bilingual term list. If no multi-word or single word match is found, the French word in the document is stemmed and a match with the term list is attempted again. If that fails, the previous step is repeated using a second version of the bilingual term list in which all source language terms have been stemmed.[3] If the source-language term was still not found in the term list, it was copied unchanged into the translated document. We used the stemmer that we had developed for CLEF 2000 for this purpose. Bilingual term lists typically contain several possible translations for some terms. In past work, we have explored display strategies for presenting multiple alternatives, but for our iCLEF experiments we chose only a single translation for each term because we wanted to focus on a single factor (the translation strategy). As we have before, we chose the English translation that occurred most often in the Brown Corpus (a balanced corpus of English) when more than one possible translation was present in the term list.

3.2 Machine Translation

Maryland also performed full machine translation, contributing the results for use as the translations that were provided to all participating teams. Production of the English translations of the French documents was relatively straightforward. First, we used Systran Professional 3.0 to translate the French collection into English. We then corrected some SGML tags that were inadvertently translated or mangled in some way (e.g., white spaces was inserted within the tags) and corrected them using a simple Perl script. After the translated collection was released, we found some additional mangled SGML symbols in the document titles, so we deleted these symbols. Punctuation and untranslatable words are handled differently by Systran—punctuation and upper/lower case are retained and untranslatable words are displayed in upper case with accents retained.

3.3 User Interface

Because we wished to compare translation strategies, we sought to minimize the effect of presentation differences by using the same user interface with both types of translation. The user interface for our experiment was based on an existing system that we had developed for our TREC-9 CLIR track experiments [4]. The system uses a Web-based server-side architecture. Searchers interact with the system using a Web browser, and their relevance judgments are recorded by the

---

[3] Multi-word expressions in the source language are removed from the stemmed term list, so only single-word matches are possible in these last two steps.

server when a search is completed. A search starts when a searcher selects a topic and a translation option (MT or Gloss) and ends when the relevance judgments for that topic are finished. A search-ID is assigned to each search so that multiple searches can be tracked simultaneously, but participants in the study completed the task individually so this capability was not needed. The system included the following capabilities:

- Provide topic selection and translation option selection mechanisms.
- Display topic descriptions based on the searcher's selection. The topic is displayed separately prior to the ranked document list so that the searcher can read and understand it before making any relevance judgments, and it remains displayed at the top of the page once the ranked list is displayed as a ready reference.
- Display a ranked list providing summary information for the top 50 documents for the selected topic (see Figure 1). The summary information that we displayed for this experiment is simply the translation of its title, as specified by the appropriate SGML tag. Query terms (i.e., any term in the topic description) that appeared in a translated summary were detected using string matching and highlighted in red and rendered in italics. A set of five radio buttons under each title allowed relevance judgments to be selected, with "not judged" initially selected for all documents.
- Display the translation of the full text of a document in a separate window whenever that document is selected by a searcher. All translations are performed in advance and cached within the server, so no speed difference between translation types is apparent to the searcher. Again, query terms that appeared in a translated document were highlighted in red and rendered in italics.
- Record the amount of time spent on judging each document. This was implemented with a Javascript timer built in a CGI script. The timer was started when the title link was selected, and stopped when one of the relevance judgment radio buttons was selected. One can easily see this method fails to record the time correctly if the judgment was based solely on a displayed summary since in that case the title link would never be selected. It would be hard to do better without an eye tracker, since multiple summaries are displayed on the same page. On the other hand, since the summaries are very short (often only one line on the screen), the time required to render a judgment in such cases is likely to be quite small.
- Simultaneously record the relevance judgments for all documents when a search is completed. This design allows users to make a quick pass through the documents and then go back for a more detailed examination if they desire. The submit button is at the bottom of the ranked list page (not shown in the Figure 1).

3.4   Searcher Characteristics

We had originally intended to recruit graduate students in library science to participate in our experiment, since we expect that librarians could make ex-

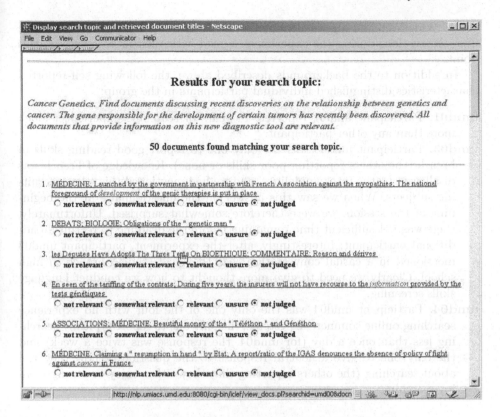

Fig. 1. Display of the ranked list of documents (MT).

tensive use of CLIR systems when conducting searches on behalf of people with
different language skills. The fact that the experiments were performed during
summer session limited the pool of potential participants, however, and the 3-
hour search session made participation less appealing even though we offered a
cash payment ($20) to each participant. As the deadline approached, we there-
fore became somewhat less selective. Of the four participants in our experiments,
two (umd01 and umd03) held a Masters degree in Library Science. Both of those
participants were doctoral students in the College of Information Studies, and
both have interests in information retrieval and human-computer interaction.
A third subject (umd02) has a Masters degree in Computer Science and some
familiarity with cross-language retrieval and is working as a user interface pro-
grammer. The fourth participant (umd04) has a Bachelors degree in religion,
is currently working as a financial controller, and professed no interest in the
technical details of what we were doing.

The ages of the four participants ranged between 28 and 35 at the time of the
experiment. None of the participants had been involved in previous interactive
retrieval experiments of this sort, but all had at least five years of online searching
experience. All four participants reported a great deal of experience searching the

World Wide Web and a great deal of experience of using a point-click interface. Our observations during the experiment agreed with their assessments on this point.

In addition to the backgrounds described above, the following self-reported characteristics distinguished individual participants in the group:

umd01. Participant umd01 reported 14 years of searching experience, much more than any other participant.

umd03. Participant umd03 was the only one to report good reading skills in French (the others reporting poor skills or none). Knowledge of French was disallowed by the track guidelines, and we had mentioned this when recruiting subjects. When we saw this answer on the questionnaire at the beginning of the session, we were therefore somewhat surprised. Unfortunately, there was not sufficient time remaining before the deadline to recruit an additional participant. Interestingly, after the experiment, participant umd03 mentioned in a casual conversation that they had studied French in high school. Clearly we need to give more thought to how we conduct language skills screening.

umd04. Participant umd04 was the only one of the four with no experience searching online commercial systems, the only one to report typically searching less than once a day (for umd04, the response was twice a week) and the only one to give a neutral response to the question of how they feel about searching (the others reporting that they either enjoy or strongly enjoy searching).

3.5   Experiment Procedure

The iCLEF experiment in Maryland started on June 27, 2001, and ended on July 9, 2001. We began with a small (two-user) pilot study, after which we made some changes to our system. We then conducted a half-hour peer review session with several graduate students who were working on computational linguistics. After a few further changes, we froze the configuration of the interface for the experiments reported in this paper.

The four search sessions were conducted individually by the first author of this paper. Upon arrival, a searcher was first given a 10-minute brief introduction to the goal of the study, the procedure of the experiment, the tasks he or she was expected to complete, and the time allocation for each step. Then a 5-minute pre-search questionnaire was completed. The major purpose of that questionnaire was to collect basic demographic information and information about the searcher's experience with searching, using point-click interface, and reading the document language. Following that was a 30-minute tutorial in which the two systems were introduced. The tutorial was conducted in a hands-on fashion—the searcher practiced using the systems while reading printed instructions line-by-line. The experimenter followed along with the searcher, pointing out, when necessary, specific details that might have been incompletely understood. We found that all the searchers learned how to use the systems in less than 30 minutes.

After this step, the searcher was asked to take a 10-minute break. Interestingly, no participant thought this break was necessary, and none took it. The first search then started.

For each search, the experimenter would tell the participant which topic and system to select, and then the experimenter would quietly observe the search process and take observation notes. Participants did occasionally ask questions of the experimenter, but we tried to minimize this tendency. Each search was followed by a 5-minute questionnaire regarding the searcher's familiarity with the topic, the ease of getting started with making relevance judgments for that topic, and their degree of confidence in the judgments that they had made. When two searches with the same system were completed, a questionnaire regarding the searcher's experience with that system was conducted. That was followed by a 10-minute break and then the process was repeated with the second system. After all the four searches were completed, an exit questionnaire was completed. That questionnaire sought the participant's subjective comparison of the two systems and provided an unstructured space for additional comments.

4   Results

The hypotheses that we wished to test was that MT and gloss translation can both support effective interactive cross-language document selection. Formally, we seek to reject two null hypotheses:

- The F_α measure achieved by gloss translation could be achieved by following a rule that does not involve looking at the translations at all.
- The F_α measure achieved using the MT system is the same as that which would be achieved using the gloss translation system.

In this section we first examine the results using the official measure ($F_{0.8}$), then look at two variants on the computation of F_α, and then conclude by suggesting some alternative metrics that could prove to be useful in future evaluations.

4.1   Official Results

Table 4.1 shows the official results on a per-search basis, and Table 4.1 shows the result of averaging the $F_{0.8}$ measures of the two participants that experienced each condition. Three of the four searchers did better with MT than gloss translation on broad topics, and all four searchers did better with MT on narrow topics. A two-tail paired t-test (p¡0.05), found no significant difference in either case, however, at $p < 0.05$). This is probably due to an insufficient number of degrees of freedom in our test (i.e., too few participants), since the trend seems quite clear. So although we cannot reject the second of our null hypothesis, the preponderance of the evidence suggests that MT is better for this task than our present implementation of gloss translation when scored using the official measure.

Table 2. $F_{0.8}$ by search, as run, strict relevance (official results).

Searcher	MT				GLOSS			
	Topic11	Topic13	Topic17	Topic29	Topic11	Topic13	Topic17	Topic29
umd01	0.62		1			0.28		0.78
umd02		0.34		0.78	0.13			0
umd03	0.13		1			0.10		0
umd04		0.13		0.90	0.27		0.83	

A couple of observations are easily made from Table 4.1. The values of $F_{0.8}$ for narrow topics are consistently higher than the values for broad topics. This suggests that searchers are typically able to make relevance judgments more accurately for narrow topics than for broad ones. Another interesting observation is that the values of $F_{0.8}$ for broad topics exhibit a strong central tendency by clustering fairly well around the mean, for narrow topics the values have a bimodal distribution with peaks near zero and one.

Table 3. Average $F_{0.8}$ by topic type and system, strict relevance (official results).

Topic	Broad		Narrow		Average	
Searcher	MT	GLOSS	MT	GLOSS	MT	GLOSS
umd01	0.62	0.28	1	0.78	0.81	0.53
umd02	0.34	0.13	0.78	0	0.56	0.07
umd03	0.13	0.10	1	0	0.52	0.05
umd04	0.13	0.27	0.9	0.83	0.52	0.55
Average	0.31	0.20	0.92	0.41	0.61	0.29

In order to test our first null hypothesis, we must construct some simple strategy that does not require looking at the documents. One way to do this is to simply select all 50 documents in the ranked list as relevant. That guarantees a recall of 1.0 (since we compute recall over the relevant documents in the top-50, not over all relevant documents known to CLEF). The precision is then the fraction of the entire list that happens to be relevant, which is much larger for broad topics than narrow ones. The average over all topics for $F_{0.8}$ when computed in this way is 0.26. All participants beat that value by at least a factor of two when using the MT system, and two of the four participants beat it by that much when using gloss translation. From this we tentatively conclude that both MT and gloss translation can be useful, but that there is substantial variation across the population of searchers with regard to their ability to use gloss translations for this purpose. The first part of this conclusion is tentative because we have not yet tried some other rules (e.g., always select the top 10 documents, or select different numbers of documents for broad and narrow topics) that might produce higher values for $F_{0.8}$.

4.2 Descriptive Data Analysis

No single measure can reflect every interesting aspect of the data, so we performed some descriptive data analysis to further explore our results. Figure 2 (a) shows the average number of documents to receive each type of relevance judgment by topic and system type. In that figure, we treat the official CLEF judgments as a third "system" for which only two types of judgment were provided. Clearly, many more documents were left unjudged for broad topics than for narrow ones. The highly skewed distribution of judgments on nonrelevant documents is particularly striking, suggesting that there is something about narrow topics that helps users to make more total judgments and to get the balance between relevant and not relevant judgments about right, regardless of the system type. One other observation that we could make is that for broad topics, our participants seemed to exhibit a greater proclivity to assess documents as relevant than as not relevant (based on the fraction of the official judgments that they achieved in each category). That may, however, be an artifact of the presence of a greater density of truly relevant documents near the top of any well constructed ranked list.

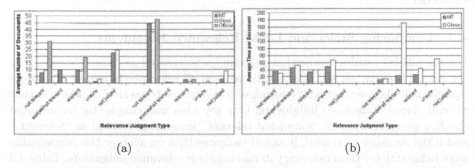

(a)   (b)

Fig. 2. (a) Average number of judgments (b) Average time per judgment, by judgment type. In each chart, broad topics are on the left and narrow topics are on the right.

Examining the time required to make relevance judgments provides another perspective on our results. As Figure 2 (b) shows, "unsure" and "somewhat relevant" judgments took longer on average than "relevant" judgments, and "not relevant" judgments could be performed the most quickly. This was true for both topic types, and it helps to explain why narrow topics (which have few relevant documents) had fewer "not judged" cases. The seemingly excessive time required to reach a judgment of "somewhat relevant" when using gloss translation results from a single data point, and therefore provides little basis for any sort of inference.

The total number of documents of each relevance judgment type (across both topic types) is: "not relevant:" 398, "somewhat relevant:" 57, "relevant:" 89, and "unsure:" 20. Comparing these numbers with the average amount of time per document of each relevance type in Figure 2 (b), we see a clear inverse relationship between the number of documents and time required to assign a document to that category. One possible explanation for this would be a within-topic learning effect, in which searchers learn to recognize documents in a category based on their recollection of documents that have been previously assigned to that category. Our observation of search behavior offers some evidence to support this speculation. We observed that some searchers often modified their relevance judgment, either right afterwards or later when they worked on a different document. In that second case, presumably their judgment of the relevance of the later document seemed to be related to the relevance of a previously judged document. We observed that other searchers rarely changed their relevance judgments, however, so it is not clear how pervasive this effect is.

It is interesting to note that the track guidelines did not provide any formal definition for the types of relevance judgments, presumably assuming that both experimenters and searchers would understand them based on the common meanings of the terms. In our study, we provided no further explanation of the judgment types to our participants, and no searcher expressed any confusion regarding this terminology. For this reason, we decided to explore whether the participants interpreted these terms consistently. That is the focus of the next subsection.

4.3 Comparing Strict and Loose Relevance Judgments

For the official results "somewhat relevant" was treated as "not relevant." For the sake of brevity, we will refer to that as "strict" relevance judgment. We could equally well choose to treat "somewhat relevant" as "relevant," a scenario that we call "loose" relevance judgments. Our key idea was simple: we recomputed the $F_{0.8}$ measure with all "somewhat relevant" judgments treated as "relevant," and if the measure increased, it would indicates that on average the participants were being stricter than necessary in making their relevance judgments. Table 4.3 shows the $F_{0.8}$ value by search with loose relevance judgments, and Table 4.3 compares the average $F_{0.8}$ value by systems and judgment type. Higher values are obtained from loose judgments in both cases, but the improvement is far larger for gloss translation than for MT.

Figure 3 depicts this difference for each of the 16 searches, with bars above the X axis indicating that loose judgments produce higher values and values below the axis indicating that strict judgments would have been better. Two trends are evident in this data. First, broad topics benefit more from loose judgments than narrow topics. Second, the improvement for gloss translation was more consistent than the improvement for MT. There were 40 judgments of "somewhat relevant" for MT, but only 17 for gloss translation, so more does not seem to be better in this case. It seems that the "somewhat relevant" judgments that people made with MT and and gloss translation were actually different in some fundamental

Table 4. $F_{0.8}$ by search, as run, loose relevance.

	MT				GLOSS			
Searcher	Topic11	Topic13	Topic17	Topic29	Topic11	Topic13	Topic17	Topic29
umd01	0.80		1			0.35		0.80
umd02		0.29		0.65	0.38		0	
umd03	0.74		1			0.17		0
umd04		0.20		0.67	0.68		1	

Table 5. Comparison of strict and loose relevance.

	Average $F_{0.8}$	
Relevance	MT	GLOSS
Strict	0.61	0.29
Loose	0.67	0.42
Relative improvement	10%	45%

way. One possibility is that our participants treated "somewhat relevant" as a variant of "unsure," perhaps assigning "somewhat relevant" when they had some inkling that a document might be relevant (i.e., they were not completely unsure).

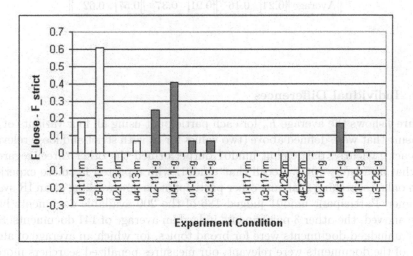

Fig. 3. Effect of loose (better above axis) and strict (better below axis) relevance on $F_{0.8}$. Left: broad topics, right: narrow topics. Each bar is labeled with searcher-topic-system (e.g., u1-t11-m means searcher umd01, Topic11, MT).

4.4   Recall-Oriented Measures

It is not possible to determine how a recall-oriented searcher would have behaved from our data because we gave the searchers instructions that we expected would cause them to be biased in favor of precision. Nonetheless, we can gain some insight into the behavior of recall-oriented measures by computing $F_{0.2}$ rather than $F_{0.8}$. Table 4.4 shows the average values for $F_{0.2}$ by topic and system type with strict judgments. Comparison with Table 4.1 shows that MT and gloss translation now achieve comparable results on broad topics, with one searcher doing better with gloss, a second doing better with MT, and the other two doing poorly with both. The results for narrow topics are more consistent, with MT beating gloss translation for every searcher with both precision-oriented and recall-oriented measures. This should not be too surprising, however, since there are so few relevant documents to be found in the case of narrow topics that recall may not be a discriminating factor.

Table 6. Average $F_{0.2}$ by topic type and system, strict relevance.

Topic	Broad		Narrow		Average	
Searcher	MT	GLOSS	MT	GLOSS	MT	GLOSS
umd01	0.33	0.43	1	0.93	0.67	0.68
umd02	0.52	0.03	0.93	0	0.73	0.01
umd03	0.03	0.09	1	0	0.52	0.05
umd04	0.09	0.08	0.70	0.55	0.40	0.31
Average	0.24	0.16	0.91	0.37	0.57	0.62

4.5   Individual Differences

Figure 4 shows the average F_α for each participant using all four variants of that measure that were defined above (two values for α, with strict and loose relevance for each). Clearly, participant umd01 outperformed the other three, regardless of what measure we use. Recall that umd01, who reported far more experience with online searching than any other participant, is now working as an IR system designer. Participant umd01 judged 186 of the 200 available documents in the time allowed, the other 3 participants judged an average of 141 documents. Since most unjudged documents were for broad topics, for which an average of almost 40% of the documents were relevant, our measures penalized searchers more for failing to finish their judgments for broad than for narrow topics.

Two other factors that had been of potential concern to us turned out not to make much of a difference. The first of these was that participant umd03 reported good reading skills in French. As Figure 4 shows, that participant actually achieved the lowest average values for three of the four measures (although

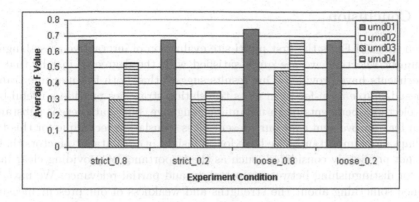

Fig. 4. Average F_α by searcher, α, and relevance type.

two or three other participants were close in every case), and Table 4.1 shows that this poor performance was consistent for both MT and gloss translation. The other factor we had concern about was that some of the subjects might actually know quite a bit about one of the topics. This actually did happen in one case, again with searcher umd03, for topic 29. As it turned out, the value of F_α for that search was zero for both values of α. See figure.

4.6 Subjective Evaluation

After each experiment, we solicited comments from our participants on the two systems and their degree of confidence in the relevance judgments that they had made. All searchers found the gloss translations were difficult to comprehend, and three of the four participants indicated that it was difficult or very difficult to judge the relevance of documents using gloss translations. All three of those participants felt that their judgment would have been even more accurate if they had been able to look at higher quality translations. The exception was participant umd01 who thought it was easy to judge relevance with gloss translations and had confidence in the judgments made with that system. All participants felt that it was easy to make relevance judgments with the MT system, and three of the four indicated that they liked the translation quality (umd02 didn't comment). Two felt that an even higher quality translation could still make relevance judgment much easier, while the other two thought it would only help a little bit.

In comparing the two systems, two participants felt that the difficulty of learning to use the two systems was comparable, while the other two felt that the MT system was easier to learn. Three of the four found the MT system easier to use while the remaining participant (umd01 again) found the gloss translation system easier to use. In amplifying on this, participant umd01 wrote that they believed that the gloss translation system seems easier to browse for "factual search questions."

5   Conclusion

Given that iCLEF is the first multi-site evaluation of interactive cross-language document selection, we are quite satisfied with the degree of insight that our experiments have provided. Our results suggest that both full machine translation and simple term-for-term gloss translation strategies provide a useful basis for selecting documents in an unfamiliar language, but that there is substantial room for improvement over our present gloss translation technique for this task. Perhaps more importantly, we have found insight in our data into factors that we had not previously considered, such as the importance of providing clear facilities for distinguishing between uncertainty and partial relevance. We have also learned something about the strengths and weakness of our present measures, with perhaps the most important point being that narrow topics pose a fundamentally different search task than broad topics. Perhaps we will ultimately find that it would be best to model those different tasks using different effectiveness measures. This first iCLEF has indeed pointed the way towards an interesting and important set of questions, but much remains to be done.

Acknowledgments. The authors would like to thank Clara Cabezas for assistance in setting up the systems used in the study, Gina Levow for help with gloss translation, Bob Allen for advice on statistical significance testing, our participants for their willingness to invest their time in this study, and members of the CLIP lab for performing peer review of our system. This work has been supported in part by DARPA cooperative agreement N660010028910.

References

1. William Hersh, Andrew Turpin, Susan Price, Benjamin Chan, Dale Kraemer, Lynetta Sacherek, and Daniel Olson. Do batch and user evaluations give the same results? In *Proceedings of the 23nd Annual International ACM SIGIR Conference on Research and Development in Information Retrieval*, pages 17–24, August 1998.
2. Douglas W. Oard. Evaluating interactive cross-language information retrieval: Document selection. In Carol Peters, editor, *Proceedings of the First Cross-Language Evaluation Forum*. 2001. http://www.glue.umd.edu/~oard/research.html.
3. Douglas W. Oard and Anne R. Diekema. Cross-language information retrieval. In *Annual Review of Information Science and Technology*, volume 33. American Society for Information Science, 1998.
4. Douglas W. Oard, Gina-Anne Levow, and Clara I. Cabezas. TREC-9 experiments at Maryland: Interactive CLIR. In *The Ninth Text Retrieval Conference (TREC-9)*, November 2000. http://trec.nist.gov.
5. Douglas W. Oard, Gina-Anne Levow, and Clara I. Cabezas. CLEF experiments at Maryland: Statistical stemming and backoff translation. In Carol Peters, editor, *Proceedings of the First Cross-Language Evaluation Forum*. 2001. http://www.glue.umd.edu/~oard/research.html.

Part II

Evaluation Issues and Results

The Philosophy of Information Retrieval Evaluation

Ellen M. Voorhees

National Institute of Standards and Technology, Gaithersburg MD 20899 USA
ellen.voorhees@nist.gov

Abstract. Evaluation conferences such as TREC, CLEF, and NTCIR are modern examples of the Cranfield evaluation paradigm. In Cranfield, researchers perform experiments on test collections to compare the relative effectiveness of different retrieval approaches. The test collections allow the researchers to control the effects of different system parameters, increasing the power and decreasing the cost of retrieval experiments as compared to user-based evaluations. This paper reviews the fundamental assumptions and appropriate uses of the Cranfield paradigm, especially as they apply in the context of the evaluation conferences.

1   Introduction

The evaluation of information retrieval (IR) systems is the process of assessing how well a system meets the information needs of its users. There are two broad classes of evaluation, system evaluation and user-based evaluation. User-based evaluation measures the user's satisfaction with the system, while system evaluation focuses on how well the system can rank documents. Since the goal is to determine how well a retrieval system meets the information needs of users, user-based evaluation would seem to be much preferable over system evaluation: it is a much more direct measure of the the overall goal. However, user-based evaluation is extremely expensive and difficult to do correctly. A properly designed user-based evaluation must use a sufficiently large, representative sample of actual users of the retrieval system (whose daily routine will be interrupted by the evaluation); each of the systems to be compared must be equally well developed and complete with an appropriate user interface; each subject must be equally well trained on all systems and care must be taken to control for the learning effect [18]. Such considerations lead IR researchers to use the less expensive system evaluation for some purposes.

System evaluation is, by design, an abstraction of the retrieval process that equates good performance with good document rankings. The abstraction allows experimenters to control some of the variables that affect retrieval performance thus increasing the power of comparative experiments. These laboratory tests are much less expensive than user-based evaluations while providing more diagnostic information regarding system behavior.

Laboratory testing of retrieval systems was first done in the Cranfield 2 experiment [3]. The experiment introduced a paradigm for system evaluation that

C.A. Peters et al. (Eds.): CLEF 2001, LNCS 2406, pp. 355–370, 2002.
© Springer-Verlag Berlin Heidelberg 2002

has been the dominant experimental IR model for four decades, and is the model used in evaluation efforts such as the Text REtrieval Conference (TREC), the Cross-Language Evaluation Forum (CLEF), and the NII-NACSIS Test Collection for IR Systems (NTCIR). This paper examines the assumptions inherent in the Cranfield paradigm, thereby prescribing when such system testing is appropriate. The first section reviews the history of the Cranfield tradition. Section 3 describes how test collections used in current evaluation conferences are built using pooling, and examines the effect of pooling on the quality of the test collection. Section 4 summarizes a series of experiments run on TREC collections that demonstrates that comparative evaluations are stable despite changes in the relevance judgments. The results of the experiments validate the utility of test collections as laboratory tools. The evaluation of cross-language retrieval systems presents special challenges that are considered in section 5. The paper concludes with some general reminders of the limits of laboratory tests.

2   The Cranfield Paradigm

The Cranfield experiments were an investigation into which of several alternative indexing languages was best [3]. A design goal for the Cranfield 2 experiment was to create "a laboratory type situation where, freed as far as possible from the contamination of operational variables, the performance of index languages could be considered in isolation" [4]. The experimental design called for the same set of documents and same set of information needs to be used for each language, and for the use of both precision and recall to evaluate the effectiveness of the search. (Recall is the proportion of relevant documents that are retrieved while precision is the proportion of retrieved documents that are relevant.) Relevance was based on topical similarity where the judgments were made by domain experts (i.e., aeronautics experts since the document collection was an aeronautics collection).

While the Cranfield 2 experiment had its detractors [16], many other researchers adopted the concept of retrieval test collections as a mechanism for comparing system performance [18,13,17]. A test collection consists of three distinct components: the documents, the statements of information need (called "topics" in this paper), and a set of relevance judgments. The relevance judgments are a list of which documents should be retrieved for each topic.

The Cranfield experiments made three major simplifying assumptions. The first assumption was that relevance can be approximated by topical similarity. This assumption has several implications: that all relevant documents are equally desirable, that the relevance of one document is independent of the relevance of any other document, and that the user information need is static. The second assumption was that a single set of judgments for a topic is representative of the user population. The final assumption was that the lists of relevant documents for each topic is complete (all relevant documents are known). The vast majority of test collection experiments since then have also assumed that relevance is a binary choice, though the original Cranfield experiments used a five-point relevance scale.

Of course, in general these assumptions are not true, which makes laboratory evaluation of retrieval systems a noisy process. Researchers have evolved a standard experimental design to decrease the noise, and this design has become an intrinsic part of the Cranfield paradigm. In the design, each retrieval strategy to be compared produces a ranked list of documents for each topic in a test collection, where the list is ordered by decreasing likelihood that the document should be retrieved for that topic. The effectiveness of a strategy for a single topic is computed as a function of the ranks of the relevant documents. The effectiveness of the strategy on the whole is then computed as the average score across the set of topics in the test collection.

This design contains three interrelated components—the number of topics used, the evaluation measures used, and the difference in scores required to consider one method better than the other—that can be manipulated to increase the reliability of experimental findings [2]. Since retrieval system effectiveness is known to vary widely across topics, the greater the number of topics used in an experiment the more confident the experimenter can be in its conclusions. TREC uses 25 topics as a minimum and 50 topics as the norm. A wide variety of different evaluation measures have been developed (see van Rijsbergen [22] for a summary), and some are inherently less stable than others. For example, measures based on very little data such as precision at one document retrieved (i.e., is the first retrieved document relevant?) are very noisy, and the mean average precision measure, which measures the area underneath the entire recall-precision curve, is much more stable. Requiring a larger difference between scores before considering the respective retrieval methods to be truly different increases reliability at the cost of not being able to discriminate between as many methods.

The remainder of this paper reviews a series of experiments that examine the reliability of test collections for comparing retrieval systems. The experiments show that the basic assumptions of the Cranfield paradigm need not be strictly true for test collections to be viable laboratory tools. The focus on comparative results is deliberate and important. A consequence of the abstraction used in the paradigm is that the absolute score of an evaluation measure for some retrieval run is not meaningful in isolation. The only valid use of such a score is to compare it to the score of a different retrieval run that used the exact same test collection. Note that this means that comparing the score a retrieval system obtained in TREC or CLEF one year to to the score the system obtained the following year is invalid since the test collection is different in the two years. It is also invalid to compare the score obtained over a subset of topics in a collection to the score obtained over the whole set of topics (or a different subset of topics).

3   Completeness of Relevance Judgments

A major departure from the original Cranfield 2 experiments and modern test collections such as the TREC collections is the relative emphasis given to collection size and the completeness of relevance judgments. In his account of the Cranfield experiments [4], Cleverdon remarks

Experience had shown that a large collection was not essential, but it was vital that there should be a complete set of relevance decisions for every question against every document, and, for this to be practical, the collection had to be limited in size.

However, further experience has shown that collection size (i.e., the number of documents in the collection) *does* matter. IR is challenging because of the large number of different ways the same concept can be expressed in natural language, and larger collections are generally more diverse. Unfortunately, even a moderately large collection cannot possibly have complete relevance judgments. Assuming a judgment rate of one document per 30 seconds, and judging round-the-clock with no breaks, it would still take more than nine months to judge one topic for a collection of 800,000 documents (the average size of a TREC collection). Instead, modern collections use a technique called pooling [15] to create a subset of the documents (the "pool") to judge for a topic. Each document in the pool for a topic is judged for relevance by the topic author, and documents not in the pool are assumed to be irrelevant to that topic.

Before describing the effects of incompleteness on a test collection, we will describe the process by which the collections are built in more detail. The building process will be described in terms of the TREC workshops here, but the process is similar for other evaluation conferences as well.

3.1   Building Large Test Collections

NIST provides a document set and a set of topics to the TREC participants. Each participant runs the topics against the documents using their retrieval system, and returns to NIST a ranked list of the top 1000 documents per topic. NIST forms pools from the participants' submissions, which are judged by the relevance assessors. Each submission is then evaluated using the resulting relevance judgments, and the evaluation results are returned to the participant.

The document set of a test collection should be a sample of the kinds of texts that will be encountered in the operational setting of interest. It is important that the document set reflect the diversity of subject matter, word choice, literary styles, document formats, etc. of the operational setting for the retrieval results to be representative of the performance in the real task. For example, if the operational setting is a medical library it makes little sense to use a collection of movie reviews as the document set. The TREC ad hoc collections contain mostly newspaper or newswire articles, though some government documents (the *Federal Register*, a small collection of patent applications) are also included in some of the collections to add variety. These collections contain about about 2 gigabytes of text (between 500,000 and 1,000,000 documents). The document sets used in various tracks have been smaller and larger depending on the needs of the track and the availability of data.

TREC distinguishes between a statement of information need (the topic) and the data structure that is actually given to a retrieval system (the query). The TREC test collections provide topics to allow a wide range of query construction methods to be tested and also to include a clear statement of what criteria make a document relevant. The format of a topic statement has evolved since the beginning of TREC, but it has been stable for the past several years. A topic statement generally consists of four sections: an identifier, a title, a description, and a narrative.

TREC topic statements are created by the same person who performs the relevance assessments for that topic. Usually, each assessor comes to NIST with ideas for topics based on his or her own interests, and searches the document collection using NIST's PRISE system to estimate the likely number of relevant documents per candidate topic. The NIST TREC team selects the final set of topics from among these candidate topics based on the estimated number of relevant documents and balancing the load across assessors. The TREC ad hoc collections contain 50 topics.

The relevance judgments are what turns a set of documents and topics into a test collection. TREC has almost always used binary relevance judgments—either a document is relevant to the topic or it is not. To define relevance for the assessors, the assessors are told to assume that they are writing a report on the subject of the topic statement. If they would use any information contained in the document in the report, then the (entire) document should be marked relevant, otherwise it should be marked irrelevant. The assessors are instructed to judge a document as relevant regardless of the number of other documents that contain the same information.

The judgment pools are created as follows. NIST selects the maximum number of runs that can be contributed to the pools by a single participating group; each group contributes this many runs to the pools unless they submitted fewer runs to NIST (in which case all their runs contribute to the pools). When participants submit their retrieval runs to NIST, they rank their runs in the order they prefer them to be judged. NIST merges the runs into the pools respecting this preferred ordering. For each selected run, the top X documents (usually, $X = 100$) per topic are added to the topics' pools. Since the retrieval results are ranked by decreasing similarity to the query, the top documents are the documents most likely to be relevant to the topic. Many documents are retrieved in the top X for more than one run, so the pools are generally much smaller the theoretical maximum of $X \times$ *the-number-of-selected-runs* documents (usually about 1/3 the maximum size). Each pool is sorted by document identifier so assessors cannot tell if a document was highly ranked by some system or how many systems (or which systems) retrieved the document.

3.2   Effects of Incompleteness

As mentioned above, pooling violates one of the original tenets of the Cranfield paradigm since it does not produce complete judgments. The concern is that evaluation scores for methods that did not contribute to the pools will be deflated relative to methods that did contribute because the non-contributors will have highly ranked unjudged documents that are assumed to be not relevant.

Figure 1 shows that there are relevant documents that are contributed to the pool by exactly one group (call these the unique relevant documents). The figure contains a histogram of the total number of unique relevant documents found by a group over the 50 test topics for four of the TREC ad hoc collections. The totals are subdivided into categories where "Automatic" designates documents that were retrieved only by completely automatic runs, "Manual" designates documents that were retrieved only by manual runs, "Mixture" designates documents that were retrieved by runs of different types, and "Others" designates documents that were retrieved by other tracks that contributed to the ad hoc pools. Each of the histograms in the figure uses the same scale. A dot underneath the x-axis indicates a group is plotted there, and all groups that retrieved at least one unique relevant document are plotted. For each year, the majority of unique documents was retrieved by manual runs. The distribution of unique relevant documents found was roughly the same over the four years.

Figure 1 suggests that the TREC collections contain relevant documents that have not been judged. If the particular group that contributed a unique relevant document had not participated in TREC that year, that document would not have been judged and would have been assumed to be not relevant. Presumably, there are other documents that did not make it into the pools that also would have been judged relevant. Indeed, a test of the TREC-2 and TREC-3 collections demonstrated the presence of unjudged relevant documents [8]. In this test, relevance assessors judged the documents in new pools formed from the second 100 documents in the ranked results submitted by participants. On average, the assessors found approximately one new relevant document per run (i.e., one relevant document that was not in the pool created from the top 100 documents of each ranking). The distribution of the new relevant documents was roughly uniform across runs, but was skewed across topics—topics that had many relevant documents initially also had many more new relevant documents.

Zobel found the same pattern of unjudged documents in his analysis of the effect of pooling [26]. He also demonstrated that the TREC collections could still be used to compare different retrieval methods since the collections were not biased against the unjudged runs. In this test, he evaluated each run that contributed to the pools using both the official set of relevant documents published for that collection and the set of relevant documents produced by removing the relevant documents uniquely retrieved by the run being evaluated. For the TREC-5 ad hoc collection, he found that using the unique relevant documents increased a run's 11 point average precision score by an average of 0.5 %. The maximum increase for any run was 3.5 %. The average increase for the TREC-3 ad hoc collection was somewhat higher at 2.2 %.

Most of the subsequent TREC collections have been examined using a similar test. In these tests, the entire set of uniquely retrieved relevant documents for a group across all of the runs that group submitted are removed from the relevance judgment set when evaluating a run from that group. This is a more stringent variation of the test used by Zobel in that it completely removes any effect of that group's participation. For the TREC-8 ad hoc collection, the mean

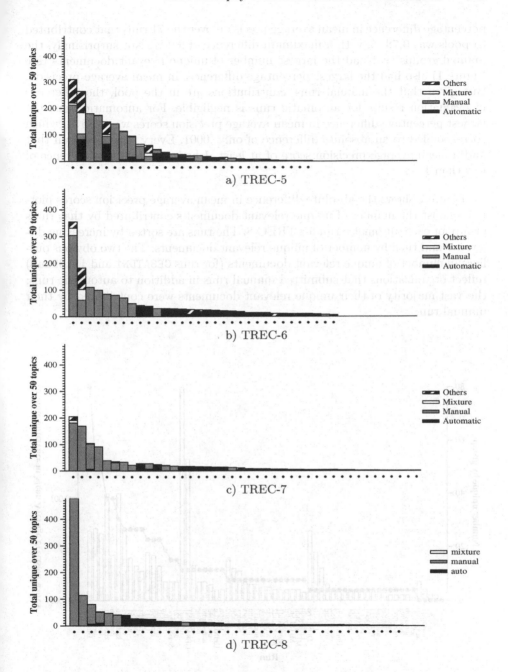

Fig. 1. Total number of unique relevant documents retrieved per TREC. Each total gives the percentages of the total that were retrieved by Automatic, Manual, Mixed, or Other runs. Groups are indicated by a dot beneath the x-axis. All groups that retrieved at least one unique relevant document are plotted.

percentage difference in mean average precision over the 71 runs that contributed to pools was 0.78 %, with a maximum difference of 9.9 %. Not surprisingly, the manual groups that had the largest number of unique relevant documents (see Figure 1) also had the largest percentage differences in mean average precision. But given that the manual runs' contributions are in the pool, the difference in evaluation results for automatic runs is negligible. For automatic runs, the largest percentage difference in mean average precision scores was 3.85 %, which corresponded to an absolute difference of only .0001. Every automatic run that had a mean average precision score of at least .1 had a percentage difference of less than 1 %.

Figure 2 shows the absolute difference in mean average precision scores plotted against the number of unique relevant documents contributed by that run's group for each automatic run for TREC-8. The runs are sorted by increasing difference and then by number of unique relevant documents. The two obvious outliers in number of unique relevant documents (for runs GE8ATDN1 and iit99au1) reflect organizations that submitted manual runs in addition to automatic runs; the vast majority of their unique relevant documents were contributed by their manual run.

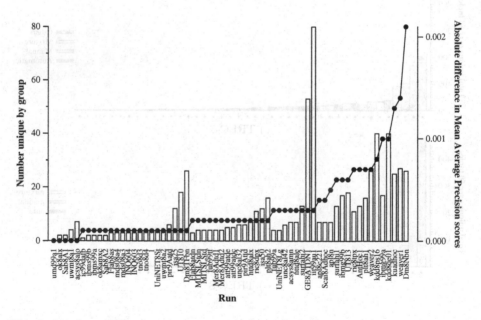

Fig. 2. Absolute difference in mean average precision scores when a run is evaluated using relevance pools with and without that group's unique relevant document for TREC-8 automatic, ad hoc runs. Also plotted is the number of unique relevant documents contributed to the pools by that group. Runs are ordered by increasing absolute difference and by increasing number of unique relevant documents.

While the lack of any appreciable difference in the scores of the automatic runs is not a guarantee that all relevant documents have been found, it is very strong evidence that the test collection is reliable for comparative evaluations of retrieval runs. Pool depth and diversity are important factors in building a test collection through pooling, but with adequate controls, the resulting test collection is not biased against runs that did not contribute to the pools. The quality of the pools is significantly enhanced by the presence of recall-oriented manual runs, an effect exploited by the organizers of the NTCIR workshops who perform their own manual runs to supplement the pools [11].

In the end, the concern regarding completeness is something of a red herring. Since test collections support only comparative evaluations, the important factor is whether the relevance judgments are unbiased. Having complete judgments ensures that there is no bias in the judgments; pooling with sufficiently diverse pools is a good approximation. The importance of an unbiased judgment set argues against the proposals for different pooling strategies that find more relevant documents in fewer total documents judged. Zobel suggests judging more documents for topics that have had many relevant documents found so far and fewer documents for topics with fewer relevant documents found so far [26]. However, assessors would know that documents added later in the pools came from lower in the systems' rankings and that may affect their judgments. Cormack et al. suggest judging more documents from runs that have returned more relevant documents recently and fewer documents from runs that have returned fewer relevant document recently [5]. But that would bias the pools toward systems that retrieve relevant documents early in their rankings. For test collections, a smaller, fair judgment set is always preferable to a larger biased set.

4   Differences in Relevance Judgments

Incompleteness is a relatively recent criticism of the Cranfield paradigm since the original test collections were complete. Inconsistency—the fact that different relevance assessors produce different relevance sets for the same topics—has been the main perceived problem with test collections since the initial Cranfield experiments [20,7,9]. The main gist of the critics' complaint is that relevance is inherently subjective. Relevance judgments are known to differ across judges and for the same judge at different times [14]. Critics question how valid conclusions can be drawn when the evaluation process is based on something as volatile as relevance.

To study the effect of different relevance judgments on the stability of comparative evaluation results, NIST obtained three independent sets of assessments for each of the 49 topics used in the TREC-4 evaluation (Topics 202–250). The TREC-4 relevance assessors were asked to judge additional topics once they had finished with the main TREC-4 assessing. Call the author of a topic its primary assessor. After the primary assessor was finished with a topic, a new document pool was created for it. This new pool consisted of all of the relevant documents as judged by the primary assessor up to a maximum of 200 relevant documents (a random sample of 200 relevant documents was used if there were more than 200 relevant documents) plus 200 randomly selected documents that the primary assessor judged not relevant. The new pool was sorted by document identifier and given to two additional assessors (the secondary assessors) who each independently judged the new pool for relevance. Because of the logistics involved, a topic was given to whatever secondary assessor was available at the time, so some individual assessors judged many more topics than others. However, each topic was judged by three individuals.

4.1   Assessor Agreement

The overlap of the relevant document sets can be used to quantify the level of agreement among different sets of relevance assessments [12]. Overlap is defined as the size of the intersection of the relevant document sets divided by the size of the union of the relevant document sets. Table 1 gives the mean overlap for each pair of assessors and the set of three assessors. Documents that the primary assessor judged relevant but that were not included in the secondary pool (because of the 200 document limit) were added as relevant documents to the secondary assessors' judgments for the analysis. The overlap is less than 50%, indicating that the assessors substantially disagreed on the judgments. Across all topics, 30% of the documents that the primary assessor marked relevant were judged nonrelevant by both secondary assessors.

Table 1. Mean overlap for each assessor pair and the set of three assessors.

Assessor Group	Overlap
Primary & A	.421
Primary & B	.494
A & B	.426
All three	.301

4.2   Effect of Inconsistency

To test how evaluation results change with these differences in assessments, we compare system rankings produced using different relevance judgments sets. A system ranking is a list of the systems under consideration sorted by the value each system obtained for some evaluation measure.

Each system is evaluated over a set of topics, and each topic has a different set of judgments produced by each assessor. Call the concatenation of one judgment set per topic a *qrels* (for query-relevance set). With three independent judgments for each of 49 topics, we can theoretically create 3^{49} different qrels by using different combinations of assessor's judgments for the topics, and evaluate the systems using each qrels. Note that each of these qrels might have been the qrels produced after the TREC conference if that set of assessors had been assigned those topics. To simplify the analysis that follows, we discarded Topic 214 since Secondary Assessor A judged no documents relevant for it. That leaves 48 topics and 3^{48} possible qrels.

Three of the 3^{48} possible qrels are special cases. The original qrels set consists of the primary assessments for each topic—this is the qrels released after TREC-4 except that it lacks Topic 214. The set of judgments produced by the Secondary A judge for each topic, and the set of judgments produced by the Secondary B judge for each topic constitute the Secondary A qrels and the Secondary B qrels respectively. We created a sample of size 100,000 of the remaining qrels by randomly selecting one of the primary or secondary assessors for each of the 48 topics and combining the selected judgments into a qrels. Adding the three distinguished qrels to the sample gives a total of 100,003 qrels that were used to evaluate retrieval systems. Finally, two additional qrels, the union and intersection qrels, were created from the relevance judgments. In the union qrels a document is considered to be relevant to a topic if any assessor judged it relevant to that topic; in the intersection qrels a document is considered to be relevant to a topic if all three assessors judged it relevant to that topic. Because two topics had no documents that all assessors agreed were relevant (219 and 232), the intersection qrels contains only 46 topics.

There were 33 category A ad hoc retrieval systems used in TREC-4. We evaluated each of these systems against each of the qrels in the sample of 100,003 qrels and computed the sample mean of the mean average precision for each system. The means are plotted in Figure 3 where the systems are sorted by decreasing mean. The error bars in Figure 3 indicate the minimum and the maximum mean average precision obtained for that system over the sample. Also plotted in the figure are the mean average precision scores computed using the original, union, and intersection qrels. These points demonstrate how the system ranking changes for an individual qrels versus the ranking by the mean: a system with a symbol higher than the corresponding symbol of a system to its left would be ranked differently in the individual qrels ranking. For example, the `pircs2` and `uwgcl1` systems (shown in position 2 and 3 in Figure 3) would switch positions when evaluated by the Original qrels.

The plot in Figure 3 demonstrates that the mean average precision score *does* change depending on the qrels used in the evaluation. The difference between the minimum and maximum mean average precision values is greater than .05 for most systems. However, the changes are very highly correlated across systems. That is, if a particular system gets a relatively high score with a particular qrels, then it is very likely that the other systems will also get a relatively high score with that qrels. The union qrels (the triangle in Figure 3) is close to the top of the range for each system, for example.

The correlation can be quantified by using a measure of association between the different system rankings. We used a correlation based on Kendall's tau [19] as the measure of association between two rankings. Kendall's tau computes the distance between two rankings as the minimum number of pairwise adjacent

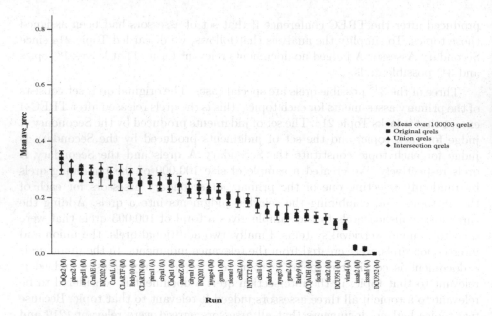

Fig. 3. Sample mean, min, and max of the mean average precision computed for each of 33 TREC-4 systems over a sample of 100,003 qrels. Also plotted are the mean average precision for the original, union, and intersection qrels. Systems are labeled as either manual (M) or automatic (A).

swaps to turn one ranking into the other. The distance is normalized by the number of items being ranked such that two identical rankings produce a correlation of 1.0, the correlation between a ranking and its perfect inverse is -1.0, and the expected correlation of two rankings chosen at random is 0.0.

We computed the mean of the Kendall correlations in the sample of 100,003 qrels in two ways. In the first case, we took the mean of the correlations between the ranking produced by the original qrels and the rankings produced by each of the other 100,002 qrels. In the second case, we took a random subsample of 1000 qrels and computed the mean correlation across all pairs in the subsample. The mean, minimum, and maximum Kendall correlations for the two methods are given in Table 2. The numbers in parentheses show the number of pairwise adjacent swaps a correlation represents given that there are 33 systems in the rankings. (Note that the way in which the qrels were constructed means that any two qrels are likely to contain the same judgments for 1/3 of the topics. Since the qrels are not independent of one another, the Kendall correlation is probably slightly higher than the correlation that would result from completely independent qrels.)

On average, it takes only 16 pairwise, adjacent swaps to turn one ranking into another ranking. The vast majority of the swaps that do take place are between systems whose mean average precisions are very close (a difference of less than .01).

Table 2. Kendall correlation of system rankings and corresponding number of pairwise adjacent swaps produced by different qrels. With 33 systems, there is a maximum of 528 possible pairwise adjacent swaps.

	Mean	Min	Max
with Original	.9380 (16)	.8712 (34)	.9962 (1)
in subsample	.9382 (16)	.8409 (42)	.9962 (1)

The plots of the union and intersection qrels evaluations in Figure 3 show that the evaluation using those qrels sets is not different from the evaluation using the other qrels sets. The intersection and union qrels differ from the other sets in that each topics' judgments are a combination of judges' opinions in the union and intersection qrels. The intersection qrels set represents a particularly stringent definition of relevance, and the union qrels a very weak definition of relevance. Nonetheless, in all but two cases (intersection qrels for systems pircs2 and uwgcl1), the mean average precision as computed by the union and intersection qrels falls within the range of values observed in the sample of 100,003 qrels. The corresponding rankings are also similar: the Kendall correlation between the original qrels ranking and the union qrels ranking is .9508, and between the original and intersection rankings is .9015.

This entire experiment was repeated several times using different evaluation measures, different topic sets, different systems, and different groups of assessors [23]. The correlation between system rankings was very high in each experiment, thus confirming that the comparative evaluation of ranked retrieval results is stable despite the idiosyncratic nature of relevance judgments.

5 Cross-Language Test Collections

The Cranfield paradigm is appropriate for cross-language retrieval experiments, though building a good cross-language test collection is more difficult than building a monolingual collection. In monolingual collections, the judgments for a topic are produced by one assessor. While this assessor's judgments may differ from another assessor's judgments, the judgment set represents an internally consistent sample of judgments. CLEF cross-language collections are produced using a separate set of assessors for each language represented in the document set. Thus multiple assessors judge a single topic across the entire collection. This necessitates close coordination among assessors so that "gray areas" can be judged consistently across languages.

Pooling is also much more difficult to coordinate for cross-language collections. As the results in section 3 demonstrate, the quality of the test collection depends on having diverse pools. Yet it is very difficult to get equally large, diverse pools for all languages contained within a multilingual collection. Both the number of runs submitted by participants and the documents retrieved within a run are usually skewed in favor of some languages at the expense of others. As a result, the pools for the minority languages are smaller and less diverse than the pools for the majority languages, which introduces an unknown bias into the judgments.

Another concern with the TREC cross-language collections is that the cross-language tasks have tended not to receive the recall-oriented manual runs that are beneficial for collection building. Analysis of the effect of incompleteness on the cross-language collections (as described in section 3) has sometimes showed mean differences in mean average precision scores computed with and without a group's unique relevant documents as large as 6–8 %, compared to mean percentage differences of less than 2 % for automatic runs for the monolingual TREC collections [24,25]. (The same analysis on the CLEF 2000 multilingual collection showed an average difference of less than 1 % [1].) The somewhat larger average differences do not invalidate the collections since comparative results are generally remain quite stable. However, experiments who find many unjudged documents in the top-ranked list of only one of a pair of runs to be contrasted should proceed with care.

6   Conclusion

Test collections are research tools that provide a means for researchers to explore the relative benefits of different retrieval strategies in a laboratory setting. As such they are abstractions of an operational retrieval environment. Test collections are useful because they allow researchers to control some of the variables that affect retrieval performance, increasing the power of comparative experiments while drastically decreasing the cost as compared to user-based evaluations.

This paper has summarized a set of experiments that demonstrate the validity of using test collections as laboratory tools. In response to the criticism that test collections use a static set of binary, topical relevance judgments to represent correct retrieval behavior, we showed that comparative retrieval results are stable despite changes in the relevance judgments. We also showed that an adequately controlled pooling process can produce an unbiased judgment set, which is all that is needed for comparative evaluation.

The final test of the Cranfield paradigm is whether the conclusions reached from the laboratory experiments transfer to operational settings. Hersh and his colleagues suggest that the results may not transfer since they were unable to verify the conclusions from a laboratory experiment in either of two user studies [10,21]. However, the first user study involved only 24 searchers and six topics, and the second user study involved 25 searchers and eight topics. The results of the user studies did not show that the conclusions from the laboratory test were wrong, simply that the user studies could not detect any differences. As such, the studies are a good illustration of the difficulties of performing user studies to evaluate retrieval systems. Any measure of the retrieval technology actually in use today demonstrates the results do transfer. Basic components of current web search engines and other commercial retrieval systems—including full text indexing, term weighting, and relevance feedback—were first developed on test collections.

Because the assumptions upon which the Cranfield paradigm is based are not strictly true, the evaluation of retrieval systems is a noisy process. The primary consequence of the noise is the fact that evaluation scores computed from a test collection are valid *only* in comparison to scores computed for other runs using the exact same collection. A second consequence of the noise is that there is an (unknown) amount of error when comparing two systems on the same collection. This error can be reduced by using many topics, by repeating the whole experiment (different sets of topics/judgments) multiple times, and by accepting two systems as different only if the delta between their respective scores is larger.

Acknowledgements. My thanks to Chris Buckley for many discussions regarding retrieval system evaluation, and for his comments on a draft of this paper.

References

1. Martin Braschler. CLEF 200 – Overview of results. In Carol Peters, editor, *Cross-Language Information Retrieval and Evaluation; Lecture Notes in Computer Science 2069*, pages 89–101. Springer, 2001.
2. Chris Buckley and Ellen M. Voorhees. Evaluating evaluation measure stability. In N. Belkin, P. Ingwersen, and M.K. Leong, editors, *Proceedings of the 23rd Annual International ACM SIGIR Conference on Research and Development in Information Retrieval*, pages 33–40, 2000.
3. C. W. Cleverdon. The Cranfield tests on index language devices. In *Aslib Proceedings*, volume 19, pages 173–192, 1967. (Reprinted in *Readings in Information Retrieval*, K. Sparck-Jones and P. Willett, editors, Morgan Kaufmann, 1997).
4. Cyril W. Cleverdon. The significance of the Cranfield tests on index languages. In *Proceedings of the Fourteenth Annual International ACM/SIGIR Conference on Research and Development in Information Retrieval*, pages 3–12, 1991.
5. Gordon V. Cormack, Christopher R. Palmer, and Charles L.A. Clarke. Efficient construction of large test collections. In Croft et al. [6], pages 282–289.
6. W. Bruce Croft, Alistair Moffat, C.J. van Rijsbergen, Ross Wilkinson, and Justin Zobel, editors. *Proceedings of the 21st Annual International ACM SIGIR Conference on Research and Development in Information Retrieval*, Melbourne, Australia, August 1998. ACM Press, New York.
7. C. A. Cuadra and R. V. Katter. Opening the black box of relevance. *Journal of Documentation*, 23(4):291–303, 1967.
8. Donna Harman. Overview of the fourth Text REtrieval Conference (TREC-4). In D. K. Harman, editor, *Proceedings of the Fourth Text REtrieval Conference (TREC-4)*, pages 1–23, October 1996. NIST Special Publication 500-236.
9. Stephen P. Harter. Variations in relevance assessments and the measurement of retrieval effectiveness. *Journal of the American Society for Information Science*, 47(1):37–49, 1996.

10. William Hersh, Andrew Turpin, Susan Price, Benjamin Chan, Dale Kraemer, Lynetta Sacherek, and Daniel Olson. Do batch and user evaluations give the same results? In N. Belkin, P. Ingwersen, and M.K. Leong, editors, *Proceedings of the 23rd Annual International ACM SIGIR Conference on Research and Development in Information Retrieval*, pages 17–24, 2000.

11. Noriko Kando, Kazuko Kuriyama, Toshihiko Nozue, Koji Eguchi, Hiroyuki Kato, and Souichiro Hidaka. Overview of IR tasks at the first NTCIR workshop. In *Proceedings of the First NTCIR Workshop on Research in Japanese Text Retrieval and Term Recognition*, pages 11–44, 1999.

12. M.E. Lesk and G. Salton. Relevance assessments and retrieval system evaluation. *Information Storage and Retrieval*, 4:343–359, 1969.

13. G. Salton, editor. *The SMART Retrieval System: Experiments in Automatic Document Processing*. Prentice-Hall, Inc. Englewood Cliffs, New Jersey, 1971.

14. Linda Schamber. Relevance and information behavior. *Annual Review of Information Science and Technology*, 29:3–48, 1994.

15. K. Sparck Jones and C. van Rijsbergen. Report on the need for and provision of an "ideal" information retrieval test collection. British Library Research and Development Report 5266, Computer Laboratory, University of Cambridge, 1975.

16. Karen Sparck Jones. The Cranfield tests. In Karen Sparck Jones, editor, *Information Retrieval Experiment*, chapter 13, pages 256–284. Butterworths, London, 1981.

17. Karen Sparck Jones. *Information Retrieval Experiment*. Butterworths, London, 1981.

18. Karen Sparck Jones and Peter Willett. Evaluation. In Karen Sparck Jones and Peter Willett, editors, *Readings in Information Retrieval*, chapter 4, pages 167–174. Morgan Kaufmann, 1997.

19. Alan Stuart. Kendall's tau. In Samuel Kotz and Norman L. Johnson, editors, *Encyclopedia of Statistical Sciences*, volume 4, pages 367–369. John Wiley & Sons, 1983.

20. M. Taube. A note on the pseudomathematics of relevance. *American Documentation*, 16(2):69–72, April 1965.

21. Andrew H. Turpin and William Hersh. Why batch and user evaluations do not give the same results. In *Proceedings of the 24th Annual International ACM SIGIR Conference on Research and Development in Information Retrieval*, pages 225–231, 2001.

22. C.J. van Rijsbergen. *Information Retrieval*, chapter 7. Butterworths, 2 edition, 1979.

23. Ellen M. Voorhees. Variations in relevance judgments and the measurement of retrieval effectiveness. *Information Processing and Management*, 36:697–716, 2000.

24. Ellen M. Voorhees and Donna Harman. Overview of the eighth Text REtrieval Conference (TREC-8). In E.M. Voorhees and D.K. Harman, editors, *Proceedings of the Eighth Text REtrieval Conference (TREC-8)*, pages 1–24, 2000. NIST Special Publication 500-246. Electronic version available at http://trec.nist.gov/pubs.html.

25. Ellen M. Voorhees and Donna Harman. Overview of TREC 2001. In *Proceedings of TREC 2001 (Draft)*, 2001. To appear.

26. Justin Zobel. How reliable are the results of large-scale information retrieval experiments? In Croft et al. [6], pages 307–314.

CLIR System Evaluation at the Second NTCIR Workshop

Noriko Kando

National Institute of Informatics (NII)
Tokyo 101-8430, Japan
kando@nii.ac.jp

Abstract. This paper introduces the *NTCIR Workshop*, a series of evaluation workshops, which are designed to enhance research in information retrieval and related text-processing techniques, such as summarization and extraction, by providing large-scale test collections and a forum for researchers. The paper gives a brief history of the Workshop, describes the tasks, participants, test collections and CLIR evaluation at the second workshop, and discusses the plans for the third workshop. In conclusion, some thoughts on future directions are suggested.

1 Introduction

The purposes of the *NTCIR[1] Workshop* [1] are as follows:

1. to encourage research in information retrieval (IR), and related text-processing technology, including term recognition and summarization, by providing large-scale reusable test collections and a common evaluation setting that allows cross-system comparisons;
2. to provide a forum for research groups interested in comparing results and exchanging ideas or opinions in an informal atmosphere;
3. to investigate methods for constructing test collections or data sets usable for experiments, and methods for laboratory-type testing of IR and related technology.

We call the whole process, from the data distribution to the final meeting, the "Workshop", since we have placed emphasis on interaction among participants, and on the experience gained as the participants learn from each other.

1.1 Brief History

The *First NTCIR Workshop* started with the distribution of the training data set on 1 November 1998, and ended with the meeting held in August 1999 in Tokyo, Japan [2]. It hosted three tasks; Ad Hoc IR, Cross-Lingual IR (CLIR), and Term Recognition using Japanese and English scientific abstracts. Thirty-one groups from six countries registered and twenty-eight groups submitted the results. The third day

---

[1] *NTCIR: NII-NACSIS* Test Collections for Information Retrieval and Text Processing

C.A. Peters et al. (Eds.): CLEF 2001, LNCS 2406, pp. 371–388, 2002.

of the meeting was organized as the *NTCIR/IREX Joint Workshop*. The *IREX Workshop* [3], another evaluation workshop of information retrieval and information extraction (named entities) using Japanese newspaper articles, was held immediately after *NTCIR*. *IREX* and *NTCIR* joined forces in April 2000 and have worked together since to organize the NTCIR Workshop. The new tasks of *Text Summarization* and *Question Answering* became feasible with this collaboration.

An international collaboration to organize Asian languages IR evaluation was proposed at the *4th International Workshop on Information Retrieval with Asian Languages (IRAL'99)*, which was held in November 1999, in Taipei, Taiwan R.O.C. In accordance with the proposal, the *Chinese Text Retrieval Tasks* have been organized by Hsin-Hsi Chen and Kuang-hua Chen, National Taiwan University, at the second workshop, and *Cross Language Retrieval* of Asian languages at the third workshop.

The first and second workshops were co-sponsored by the *National Institute of Informatics* (NII, formerly the National Center for Science Information Systems, NACSIS) and the *Japan Society for the Promotion of Sciences* (JSPS) as part of the "Research for the Future" Program (JSPS-RFTF 96P00602). After the first workshop, in April 2000, NACSIS reorganized and changed its name to NII. At the same time, the *Research Center for Information Resources* (RCIR), a permanent host of the NTCIR project was launched by NII. The third workshop will be sponsored by RCIR at NII.

The second workshop started with data delivery in June 2000 and ended with the meeting in March 2001. Since the second workshop [4], tasks have been proposed and organized by separate groups. This venture added a variety of tasks to the NTCIR Workshop and as a result attracted participants from various other groups.

In the next section we outline the second workshop. Section 3 describes the test collections used, and Section 4 reports the results. Section 5 introduces the tasks for the third workshop and discusses some ideas for future directions.

2 The Second NTCIR Workshop (2000/2001)

2.1 Tasks

Each participant conducted one or more of the following tasks at the workshop.

- *Chinese Text Retrieval Task (CHTR)*: including English-Chinese CLIR (ECIR; E - > C) and Chinese monolingual IR (CHIR tasks, C -> C) using the test collection *CIRB010*, containing newspaper articles from five newspapers in Taiwan R.O.C.
- *Japanese-English IR Task (JEIR)*: using the test collection of *NTCIR-1* and *-2*, including monolingual retrieval of Japanese and English (J -> J, E -> E), and CLIR of Japanese and English (J -> E, E -> J, J -> JE, E -> JE).
- *Text Summarization Task (TSC: Text Summarization Challenge):* text summarization of Japanese newspaper articles of various kinds. The *NTCIR-2 Summ* summarization test collection was used.

Each task was proposed and organized by a different research group in a relatively independent manner, while maintaining good contacts and discussion with the NTCIR Project organizing group. Evaluation issues, and what should be evaluated, were thoroughly discussed in a discussion group.

2.2 Participants

As shown in Table 1, 45 groups from eight countries registered for the *Second NTCIR Workshop* and 36 groups submitted results. Of the above, four groups submitted results to both CHTR and JEIR, three groups submitted results to both JEIR and TSC, and one group performed all three tasks. Table 2 shows the distribution of each type of participating group across the tasks. Below is a list of participating groups that submitted task results.

ATT Labs & Duke Univ. (US)
Communications Research Laboratory (Japan),
Fuji Xerox (Japan)
Fujitsu Laboratories (Japan)
Fujitsu R&D Center (China PRC)
Central Research Laboratory, Hitachi Co. (Japan)
Hong Kong Polytechnic (Hong Kong, China PRC)
Institute of Software, Chinese Academy of Sciences (China PRC)
Johns Hopkins Univ. (US)
JUSTSYSTEM Corp. (Japan)
Kanagawa Univ. (Japan)
KAIST/KORTERM (Korea)
Matsushita Electric Industrial (Japan)
National TsinHua Univ. (Taiwan, ROC)
NEC Media Research Laboratories (Japan)
National Institute of Informatics (Japan)
NTT-CS & NAIST (Japan)
OASIS, Aizu Univ. (Japan)
Osaka Kyoiku Univ. (Japan)
Queen College-City Univ. of New York (US)
Ricoh Co. (2) (Japan)
Surugadai Univ. (Japan)
Trans EZ Co. (Taiwan ROC)
Toyohashi Univ. of Technology (2) (Japan)
Univ. of California Berkeley (US)
Univ. of Cambridge/Toshiba/Microsoft (UK)
Univ. of Electro-Communications (2) (Japan)
Univ. of Library and Information Science (Japan)
Univ. of Maryland (US)
Univ. of Tokyo (2) (Japan),
Yokohama National Univ. (Japan)
Waseda Univ. (Japan).

Four of these groups participated in JEIR without any Japanese language expertise.

Table 1. Number of Participating Groups

Task	Subtask	Enrolled	Submitted (active)
CHTR	CHIR	14	10
	ECIR	13	7
	CHTR total	16	11
JEIR	J-J	22	17
	E-E	11	7
	monoLIR total	22	17
	J-E	16	12
	E-J	14	10
	J-JE	11	6
	E-JE	11	4
	J/E CLIR total	17	14
	JEIR total	31	25
TSC	A extrinsic		7
	B intrinsic		5
	TSC total	15	9
total		45	36

Table 2. Types of Active Participating Groups

	University	National Institution	Company
CHTR	7	2	2
JEIR	15	3	7
TSC	3	1	5
total	20	4	12

As shown in Figure 1, of the 18 active participants of the *Ad Hoc IR of Japanese and English* documents at the first workshop, 10 groups participated in the equivalent tasks at the second workshop, i.e., *JEIR monolingual IR* tasks, or added participating tasks; one changed the task to *JEIR CLIR*; one changed the task to *TSC*; and six did not participate.

Of 10 active *CLIR* participants at the first workshop, six continued to participate in the equivalent task, i.e., *JEIR-CLIR*; two groups changed tasks to *CHTR*; and two changed to *TSC*. Of nine active participating groups in the Term Recognition Task at the first workshop, six changed to *JEIR*, two changed to *TSC*, and two did not participate in the second workshop. Of the eight groups from the first workshop that did not participate in the second workshop, five are from Japanese universities, one is from a research institute/university in Australia, one is from a Japanese company, and one is from a university in the UK. Among the participants of *CHTR*, *JEIR*, and *TSC* at the second workshop, seven, twelve, and four groups, respectively, are new to the *NTCIR Workshop*.

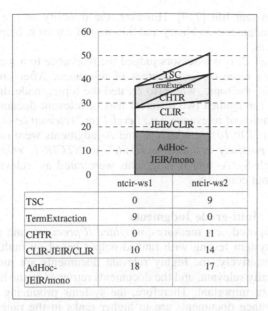

	ntcir-ws1	ntcir-ws2
TSC	0	9
TermExtraction	9	0
CHTR	0	11
CLIR-JEIR/CLIR	10	14
AdHoc-JEIR/mono	18	17

Fig. 1. Number of Active Participants for Each Task

2.3 CLIR Evaluation

The *second NTCIR Workshop* hosted two CLIR subtasks: one in the *Chinese Text Retrieval Tasks (CHTR)*, and the other in the *Japanese and English IR Tasks (JEIR)*. Both automatic and manual query constructions were allowed. In the case of automatic construction in the JEIR task, the participants had to submit at least one set of results of the searches using only <DESCRIPTION> fields of the topics as *the mandatory run*. The intention of this is to enhance cross-system comparison. For optional automatic runs and manual runs, any field, or fields, of the topics could be used. In addition, each participant had to complete a system description form describing the detailed features of the system.

The relevance judgments were undertaken by pooling methods. The same number of runs was selected from each participating group, and the same number of top ranked documents from each run for the topic was extracted and put into the document pool to be judged in order to retain "fairness" and "equal opportunity" for each participating group. In order to increase the exhaustiveness of the relevance judgments, additional manual searches were conducted for those topics with more relevant documents than a certain threshold (50 in *NTCIR-1*, and 100 in *NTCIR-2*). A detailed description of the pooling procedure has been reported in Kuriyama et al. [6].

Human analysts assessed the relevance of retrieved documents to each topic—three grades in NTCIR-1 and IREX-IR: relevant (A), partially relevant (B), irrelevant (C); and four grades in NTCIR-2 and CIRB010: highly relevant (S), A, B, and C. Some documents will be more relevant than others, either because they contain more relevant information, or because the information they contain is highly relevant. We believe that multi-grade relevance judgments are more natural, or closer to the judgments made in real life [7–9]. However, the majority of test collections have viewed relevance judgments as binary and this simplification is helpful for evaluators and system designers.

For *NTCIR-1* and *-2*, two assessors judged the relevance to a topic separately and assigned one of the three or four degrees of relevance. After cross-checking, the primary assessors of the topic, who also created the topic, made the final judgment. The *trec_eval* was run against two different lists of relevant documents produced by two different thresholds of relevance, i.e., *Level 1* (or "*relevant level file*" in *NTCIR*-1, *rigid relevance* in *CIRB010*), in which S- and A-judgments were rated as "relevant", and *Level 2* (or "*partially relevant level file*" in *NTCIR-1*, *relaxed relevance* in CIRB010), in which S-, A- and B-judgments were rated as "relevant", even though the *NTCIR-1* does not contain S.

2.3.1 Measure for Multi-grade Judgments

In addition, we proposed new measures, *weighted R precision* and *weighted average precision*, for IR system testing with ranked output based on multi-grade relevance judgments [10]. Intuitively, the highly relevant documents are more important for users than the partially relevant, and the documents retrieved in the higher ranks in the ranked list are more important. Therefore, the systems producing search results in which higher relevance documents are in higher ranks in the ranked list should be rated as better. Based on the review of existing IR system evaluation measures, it was decided that both of the proposed measures be a single number, and could be averaged over a number of topics.

Most IR systems and experiments have assumed that highly relevant items are useful to all users. However, some user-oriented studies have suggested that partially relevant items may be important for specific users and they should not be collapsed into relevant or irrelevant items, but should be analyzed separately [9]. More investigation is required.

3 Test Collections

Table 3 shows the IR test collections constructed through the *NTCIR* Workshops and with its partner *IREX*. In addition, *NTCIR-2Summ* and *NTCIR-2TAOSumm*, manually created summaries of various types of Japanese newspaper articles are available.

3.1 Documents

More than half of the documents in the *NTCIR-1 JE Collection* are English-Japanese paired. NTCIR-2 contains author abstracts of conference papers and extended summaries of grant reports. About one-third of the documents are Japanese- and English-paired, but the correspondence between English and Japanese is unknown during the workshop. Sample document records of *CIRB010* (Chinese), *NTCIR-2 J Collection* (Japanese) and *NTCIR-2 E Collection* (English) are shown in Figs. 2, 3 and 4 respectively. Documents are plain text with SGML-like tags.

Table 3. IR Test Collections

collection		rec#	documents size	genre	topic	rel judgment
CIRB010	C	132K	200MB	newspaper '98-99	C:50 E:50	4 grades
NTCIR-1	JE	340K	577MB	scientific abstract	J:83	3 grades
	J	333K	312MB		83	
	E	187K	218MB		J:60	
NTCIR-2	J	403K	600MB	scientific	49	4 grades
	E	135K	200MB	abstract	49	
IREX-IR	J	222K	221MB	newspaper '94-95	50	3 grades

```
<DOC>
<DOCNO>chinatimes_focus_0005660</DOCNO>
<LANG>CH</LANG>
<DATE>05071999</DATE>
<HEADLINE>解決高鐵融資 尋求第三管道</HEADLINE>
<TEXT>
<P>【記者羅兩莎台北報導】據負責台灣高速鐵路聯合貸款的主　銀行表示，高鐵
融資問題目前仍·在銀行團、交通部高鐵局以及台灣高鐵公司「三方合約」　容的
訂定。在銀行團和交通部一直未能就相關　見達成共識之下，三大主　銀行原則決
定，將尋求行政院經建會等第三管道與交通部協調，以儘早解決銀行團和交通部之
間對融資問題的　見。</P>
<P>高鐵案將向國　銀行融資二千八百多億元，這項聯貸案確定由交銀、台銀和中
國國際商業銀行共同主　。不過，由於高鐵是國　首宗ＢＯＴ案，潛在風險究竟有
多高，銀行無從評估。三大主　銀行與交通部和台灣高鐵公司訂定貸款合約時，重
點亦著重在風險控制以及債權確保。</P>
<P>據主　銀行主管表示，銀行當然希望債權確保不會有問題，譬如，在三方合約
中訂定，由政府出面保證萬一將來台灣高鐵公司蓋不下去時，政府可以出面買下，
負責把工程完成等。</P>
</TEXT>
</DOC>
```

Fig. 2. Sample Document (*CIRB010 Chinese document*)

```
<REC><ACCN>kaken-j-0924516300</ACCN>
<YEAR>1992</YEAR>
<SBJ1 TYPE="kanji">802: 情報学</SBJ1>
<PJNM
TYPE="kanji">文献の論理構造に基づく全文データベース検索システムの開発研
究</PJNM>
<ABST
TYPE="kanji"><ABST.P>本研究は、学術文献などの文書の全文を収容する全文デ
ータベースについて、それらの文書の論理構造に即した検索を可能とするシステ
ムを研究・開発しようとするものである。3年次にわたって下記の項目について
研究および開発を行なった。</ABST.P>
<ABST.P>1.全文データベースに対する検索要求の詳細分析を行ない、SGMLの文
書型定義に基づいて検索・表示要求を効率的に記述するための表記形式DQL(Doc
ument                                                              Query
Language)の詳細設計を行なった。SQLを拡張し、文書構造を扱うための記述を可
能にした。</ABST.P>
<ABST.P>2.文献の文書構造を図形的に表示し、要素をポインティングデバイス
で指定して検索条件・表示指示を行なうユーザ系のソフトウェアを設計し、ワー
クステーション上でグラフィカルユーザインタフェース(GUI)を用いて開発した
。</ABST.P>
<ABST.P>3.文書構造を各構成要素間の二項関係で関係データベース管理システ
ム上に表現し、DQLで記述された検索要求を処理するサーバ系のソフトウェアを
汎用大型計算機上に開発した。</ABST.P>
<ABST.P>4.サーバ系とユーザ系の接続方式を開発し、LANおよびISDNを介して
連動させて動作を確認した。</ABST.P>
<ABST.P>5.全体的な処理性能、使い心地、検索精度などについて評価を行ない
、実用に向けての課題と解決方式を検討した。</ABST.P>
<ABST.P>現在のシステムにはサーバ系の性能に改善の必要性が認められ、検討
の結果、二項関係に参照先のレコードIDを含めることが有効であることがわかっ
たので、今後これを実現することが課題となる。また、ユーザ系においては指定
した検索要求をよりわかりやすく表示する必要があることが明かとなり、考案し
たいくつかの方式について実験により検討することが課題となる。</ABST.P>
<ABST.P>以上の結果、本システムの設計概念、および実現方式の妥当性が確認
でき、課題への対処の方針も示すことができたことにより、実用化の可能性が示
された。</ABST.P></ABST>
<KYWD TYPE="kanji">全文データベース / 情報検索 / 文書構造 / SGML / GUI /
分散処理</KYWD></REC>
```

Fig. 3. Sample Document (*NTCIR-2, J Collection*)

```
<REC><ACCN>kaken-e-2469487463</ACCN>
<YEAR>1992</YEAR>
<SBE1 TYPE="alpha">802: *</SBE1>
<PJNE TYPE="alpha">Development of a Full Text Retrieval System based on Logical
Structure of Documents</PJNE>
<ABSE TYPE="alpha"><ABSE.P>The investigators have conducted research and
development of a system with which users can retrieve documents from a full text
database containing full documents such as academic papers. Results obtained were as
follows: </ABSE.P>
<ABSE.P>1. Based on detailed analysis of retrieval requests for full text databases, they
made detailed design of a formal notation DQL (Document Query Language) for
describing retrieval and display requests efficiently according to the document type
definition of SGML. </ABSE.P>
<ABSE.P>2. They designed a user system software which displays document structures
and let users select elements with pointing devices and specify retrieval conditions and
display instructions. The system w as developed on work-stations using graphical user
interface systems. </ABSE.P>
<ABSE.P>3. They developed a server system software on a main frame computer which
stores documents in a relational database management system by expressing the structure
as binomial relations among elements and processes retrieval requests described in DQL.
</ABSE.P>
<ABSE.P>4. They developed a communication method between sever and user systems
and confirmed the functionality by experiments using LAN and ISDN. </ABSE.P>
<ABSE.P>5. They evaluated the overall performance, usability, retrieval precision and so
on and considered on the problems and their solutions toward the practical
use.</ABSE.P>
<ABSE.P>Through evaluation, the necessity of performance improvement of the server
system was revealed. Further investigation has made it clear that including referenced
record identifiers within the binomial relation records is effective. It is the future issue to
implement this method. The necessity for the user system to represent specified retrieval
requests more understandably was also revealed. Several methods already proposed
should be studied by experiments.</ABSE.P>
<ABSE.P>As the result of the research, feasibility of the design concept and the
implementation method of this system was confirmed, the approach to the existing
problems was presented, and the reality of the full-fledged system was
shown.</ABSE.P></ABSE>
<KYWE TYPE="alpha">Full Text Database / Information Retrieval / Document
Structure / SGML / GUI / Distributed Processing</KYWE></REC>
```

Fig. 4. Sample Document (*NTCIR-2, E Collection*)

3.2 Topics

A sample topic record, which will be used in the CLIR task at the *NTCIR Workshop 3*, is shown in Fig. 5. Topics are defined as statements of "user's requests" rather than "queries", which are the strings actually submitted to the system, since we wish to allow both manual and automatic query construction from the topics. Of the 83 topics of *NTCIR-1*, 20 were translated into Korean and were used with the Korean *HANTEC Collection* [11].

```
<TOPIC>
<NUM>013</NUM>
<SLANG>CH</SLANG>
<TLANG>EN</TLANG>
<TITLE>NBA labor dispute</TITLE>
<DESC>To retrieve the labor dispute between the two parties of the US National
Basketball Association at the end of 1998 and the agreement that they reached. </DESC>
<NARR>The content of the related documents should include the causes of NBA labor
dispute, the relations between the players and the management, main controversial issues
of both sides, compromises after negotiation and content of the new agreement, etc. The
document will be regarded as irrelevant if it only touched upon the influences of closing
the court on each game of the season.</NARR>
<CONC>NBA (National Basketball Association), union, team, league, labor dispute,
league and union, negotiation, to sign an agreement, salary, lockout, Stern, Bird
Regulation.</CONC>
</TOPIC>
```

Fig. 5. A Sample Topic (CLIR at NTCIR WS 3)

The topics contain SGML-like tags. A topic in *NTCIR-1*, *NTCIR-2*, and *CIRB010* contains similar tag sets although tags are longer than above (ex. <DESCRIPTION>), and consists of the title of the topic, a description (question), a detailed narrative, and a list of concepts and field(s). The title is a very short description of the topic and can be used as a very short query that resembles those often submitted by users of Internet search engines. Each narrative may contain a detailed explanation of the topic, term definitions, background knowledge, the purpose of the search, criteria for judgment of relevance, etc.

3.3 Relevance Judgments (Right Answers)

The relevance judgments were conducted using multi-grades as stated in Section 2.3. In *NTCIR-1* and *-2*, relevance judgment files contained not only the relevance of each document in the pool, but also contained extracted phrases or passages showing the reason the analyst assessed the document as "relevant". These statements were used to confirm the judgments, and also in the hope of future use in experiments related to extracting answer passages.

3.4 Linguistic Analysis

NTCIR-1 contains a "*Tagged Corpus*". This contains detailed hand-tagged part-of-speech (POS) tags for 2,000 Japanese documents selected from *NTCIR-1*. Spelling errors are manually corrected. Because of the absence of explicit boundaries between words in Japanese sentences, we set three levels of lexical boundaries (i.e., word boundaries, and strong and weak morpheme boundaries). In *NTCIR-2*, the segmented data of the whole J (Japanese document) collection are provided. They are segmented into three levels of lexical boundaries using a commercially available morphological analyzer called *HAPPINESS* [12]. An analysis of the effect of segmentation is reported in Yoshioka et al. [13].

3.5 Robustness of the System Evaluation Using the Test Collections

The test collections *NTCIR-1* and *-2* have been tested with respect to (1) exhaustiveness of the document pool, and (2) inter-analyst consistency and its effect on system evaluation, to guarantee their use as a reliable tool for IR system testing:

The results have been reported and published on various occasions [13–16]. In terms of exhaustiveness, pooling the top 100 documents from each run worked well for topics with fewer than 100 relevant documents. For topics with more than 100 relevant documents, although the top 100 pooling covered only 51.9% of the total relevant documents, coverage was higher than 90% if combined with additional interactive searches. Therefore, we conducted additional interactive searches for topics with more than 50 relevant documents in the first workshop, and those with more than 100 relevant documents in the second workshop.

When the pool size was larger than 2500 for a specific topic, the number of documents collected from each submitted run was reduced to 90 or 80. This was done to keep the pool size practical and manageable for assessors and to keep consistency in the pool. Even though the numbers of documents collected in the pool were different for each topic, the number of documents collected from each run is exactly the same for a specific topic.

A strong correlation was found to exist between the system rankings produced using different relevance judgments and different pooling methods, regardless of the inconsistency of the relevance assessments among analysts and regardless of the different pooling methods used [6,13–15]. This served as an additional support to the analysis reported by Voorhees [17].

4 Evaluation Results of CLIR at NTCIR WS 2

4.1 English–Chinese CLIR (ECIR)

Ninety-eight runs for the Chinese monolingual task were submitted by 10 participating groups and 17 runs for the ECIR were submitted by seven groups. According to the task overview report [18], query expansion is a good method for increasing system performance. In general, the probabilistic model shows better performance. For the ECIR, the select-all approach seems to be better than other select-X approaches in dictionary look-up, if no further techniques are adopted. PIRCS used the MT approach and it out-performed other approaches. For the ECIR task, a word-based indexing approach is better.

4.2 CLIR of English and Japanese

There were 101 submitted runs for monolingual retrieval from 17 groups and 95 runs for CLIR from 14 groups. For J-E, E-J, J-JE, E-JE, 40 runs from 12, 30 runs from 10, 14 runs from six, and 11 runs from four groups, respectively, were submitted [19].

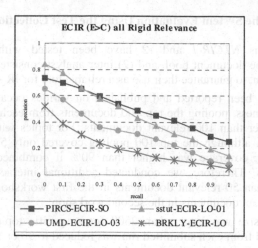

Fig. 6. Top ECIR Runs (All runs) Rigid Relevance

Most groups used query translation for CLIR but the LISIF group combined query and document translation; the top 1000 documents in the initial search were translated and further processed. Three groups used corpus-based approaches including LSI, segmented LSI, approximate dimension equalization, etc, but generally the performances were less effective compared with other approaches. Query expansion is generally effective and pseudo relevance feedback worked well. New approaches including flexible pseudo-relevance feedback and segmented LSI were proposed.

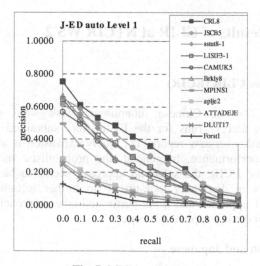

Fig. 7. J-E Runs (D) Level 1

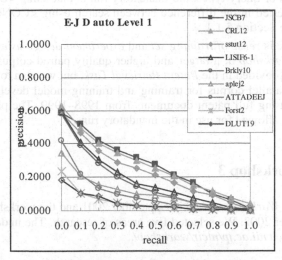

Fig. 8. E-J Runs (D) Level 1

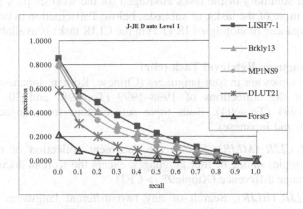

Fig. 9. J-JE Runs (D) Level 1

4.3 Issues for the Next CLIR Evaluation

In the round table discussion and at the program committee meeting, some issues were raised to conduct more appropriate and valid evaluation at the next workshop.

CHTR and *JEIR* at the *second workshop* were organized in rather an independent manner, but we aimed at following consistent, or at least compatible, procedures. However, regrettably, we found unintended incompatibility between *CHTR* and *JEIR*, including the categories of query types and pooling methods. The CLIR task at the *NTCIR Workshop 3* will be organized by the organizers of the *CHTR*, *JEIR*, and *HANTEC* groups. The organizers had face-to-face meetings and decided on detailed procedures for topic creation, topic format, document format, query types and mandatory runs. For query types, the mandatory run is that using <DESC> only, and we are also interested in the difference between search using <CONC>, or not using it. For details, see Section 5.1.1.

The other issue is *reuse of training set* and *experiment design using paired corpus*. At the *NTCIR Workshop 3*, a larger and higher quality paired corpus of English and Japanese will be provided in the *Patent Retrieval Task*, but we plan to allow the use of the 1995–1997 parallel corpus for training and training model development, and the test will be run using full patent documents from 1998–1999. The parallel corpus of 1998–1999 is not allowed for use in the mandatory runs.

5 NTCIR Workshop 3

The *third NTCIR Workshop* started in September 2001 and the workshop meeting will be held in October 2002. We selected five areas of research. The updated information is at *http://research.nii.ac.jp/ntcir/workshop/*.

5.1 Tasks

Below is a brief summary of the tasks envisaged for the workshop. A participant will conduct one or more of the tasks, or subtasks, below. Participation in only one subtask (for example Japanese monolingual IR (J-J) in the CLIR task) is available:

5.1.1 Cross-Language Retrieval Task (clir)
Documents and topics are in four languages (Chinese, Korean, Japanese and English). Fifty topics for the collections of 1998–1999 (Topic98) and 30 topics for the collection of 1994 (Topic94). Both topic sets contain four languages (Chinese, Korean, English and Japanese).

1. *Multilingual CLIR (MLIR)*: Search the document collection of more than one language by topics in one of four languages, except the Korean documents because of the time range difference (Xtopic98 -> CEJ).
2. *Bilingual CLIR (BLIR)*: Search of any two different languages as topics and documents, except the search of English documents (Xtopic98 -> C, Xtopic94 -> K, Xtopic98>J).
3. *Single Language IR (SLIR)*: Monolingual Search of Chinese, Korean, or Japanese. (Ctopic98 -> C, Ktopic94 -> K, Jtopic98 -> J).

DOCUMENT: newspapers articles published in Asia:

- Chinese: *CIRB010, United Daily News* (1998-1999)
- Korean: *Korea Economic Daily* (1994)
- Japanese: *Mainichi Newspaper* (1998–1999)
- English: *Taiwan News, China English News, Mainichi Daily News* (1998–1999).

5.1.2 Patent Retrieval Task (Patent)

1. Main Task
   - *Cross-language Cross-DB Retrieval*: retrieve patents in response to J/E/C newspaper articles associated with technology and commercial products. Thirty query articles with a short description of the search request.
   - *Monolingual Associative Retrieval*: retrieve patents associated with a Japanese patent as input. Thirty query patents with a short description of search requests.
2. Optional task: Any research reports are invited on patent processing using the above data, including, but not limited to: generating patent maps, paraphrasing claims, aligning claims and examples, summarization for patents, clustering patents.

DOCUMENT:
- Japanese patents: 1998–1999 (ca. 17GB, 700K docs)
- Japio patent abstracts: 1995–1999 (ca. 1750K docs)
- Patent Abstracts of Japan (English translations for Japio patent abstracts): 1995–1999 (ca. 1750K)
- Patolis test collection (34 topics and relevance assessment on the Patent 1998)
- Newspaper articles (Japanese/ English/ Traditional Chinese)

5.1.3 Question Answering Task (qac)

Task 1: System extracts five answers from the documents in some order. One hundred questions. The system is required to return support information for each answer to the questions. We assume the support information is a paragraph, a one hundred-character passage or a document that includes the answer.

Task 2: System extracts only one answer from the documents. One hundred questions. Support information is required.

Task 3: evaluation of a series of questions. The related questions are given for 30 of the questions of Task 2.

DOCUMENT: Japanese newspaper articles (Mainichi Newspaper 1998–1999).

5.1.4 Automatic Text Summarization Task (tsc2)

Task A (single-document summarization): Given the texts to be summarized and summarization lengths, the participants submit summaries for each text in plain text format.

Task B (multi-document summarization): Given a set of texts, the participants produce summaries of it in plain text format. The information, which was used to produce the document set, such as queries, as well as summarization lengths, is given to the participants.

DOCUMENT: Japanese newspaper articles (Mainichi Newspaper 1998–1999).

5.1.5 Web Retrieval Task

  A. Survey Retrieval (both recall and precision are evaluated)

    A1. Topic Retrieval

    A2. Similarity Retrieval

  B. Target Retrieval (precision-oriented)

  C. Optional Task

    C1.Search Results Classification

    C2. Speech-Driven Retrieval

    C3. Other

DOCUMENT: Web documents mainly collected from the jp domain (ca. 100GB and ca. 10GB). Available at the "*Open-Labo*" at NII.

5.2 Workshop Schedule

2001-09-30   Application Due

2001-10-01   Document release (newspaper)

2001-10/2002-01 Dry Run and Round-Table Discussion (varies with each task)

2001-12   Open Lab start

2001-12/2002-03 Formal Run (varies with each task)

2002-07-01   Evaluation Results Delivery

2002-08-20   Paper for Working Note Due

2002-10-08/10 NTCIR Workshop 3 Meeting

    Days 1–2: Closed session (task participants only)

    Day 3: Open session

2002-12-01   Paper for Final Proceedings Due

5.3 Features of the NTCIR Workshop 3 Tasks

For the next workshop, we plan some new ventures, including:

  1. multilingual CLIR (clir)

  2. search by document (patent, web)

  3. passage retrieval or submitting "evidential passages", passages to show the reason the documents are supposed to be relevant (patent, qac, web)

  4. optional task (patent, web)

  5. multi-grade relevance judgments (clir, patent, web)

  6. precision-oriented evaluation (qac, web).

  For (1), it is our first trial of the CLEF [20] model in Asia. For (3), we suppose that identifying the most relevant passage in the retrieved documents is required when retrieving longer documents such as Web documents or patents. The primary evaluation will be done document-based, but we will use the submitted passages as secondary information for further analysis.

  For patent and web tasks (4), we invite any research groups who are interested in the research using the document collection provided in the tasks for any research projects. These document collections are new to our research community and many interesting characteristics are included. We also expect that this venture will explore the new tasks possible for future workshops.

For (5), we have used multi-grade relevance judgments so far and have proposed new measures, Weighted Average Precision and Weighted R Precision, for this purpose. We will continue this line of investigation and will add "top relevant" for the Web task, as well as evaluation by *trec_eval*.

5.4 Future Directions

From the beginning of the NTCIR project, we have focused on two directions of investigation, i.e., (1) traditional laboratory-type text retrieval system testing, and (2) challenging issues. For the former, we have placed emphasis on retrieval with Japanese and other Asian languages and cross-lingual information retrieval (CLIR). Indexing texts written in Japanese or other East Asian languages, such as Chinese, is quite different from indexing texts in English, French or other European languages. CLIR is critical in the Internet environment, especially between languages with completely different origins and structure, such as English and Japanese [5]. The latter includes evaluation of technology to make information in the documents immediately usable and evaluation of retrieval of new document genres and more realistic evaluation.

One of the problems of CLIR is the availability of resources that can be used for translation. Enhancement of the processes of creating and sharing the resources is important. In the NTCIR workshops, some groups automatically constructed a bilingual lexicon from a quasi-paired document collection. Such paired documents can be easily found in non-English speaking countries and on the Web. Studying the algorithms to construct such resources and sharing them is one practical way to enrich the applicability of CLIR. International collaboration is needed to construct multilingual test collections and to organize the evaluation of CLIR systems, since creating topics and relevance judgments are language- and cultural-dependent, and must be performed by native speakers. Cross-lingual summarization and question answering are also being considered for future workshops.

References

1. NTCIR Project: http://research.nii.ac.jp/ntcir/
2. NTCIR Workshop 1: Proceedings of the First NTCIR Workshop on Research in Japanese Text Retrieval and Term Recognition, 30 Aug.–1 Sept., 1999, Tokyo, ISBN4-924600-77-6. http://research.nii.ac.jp/ntcir/workshop/OnlineProceedings/).
3. IREX URL:http://cs.nyu.edu/cs/projects/proteus/irex/
4. NTCIR Workshop 2: Proceedings of the Second NTCIR Workshop on Research in Chinese & Japanese Text Retrieval and Text Summarization, Tokyo, June 2000·March 2001 (ISBN4-924600-96-2)
5. Kando, N.: Cross-Linguistic Scholarly Information Transfer and Database Services in Japan. Annual Meeting of the ASIS, Washington DC. Nov. 1, 1997
6. Kuriyama, K., Yoshioka, M., Kando, N.: Effect of Cross-Lingual Pooling. In NTCIR Workshop 2: Proceedings of the Second NTCIR Workshop on Research in Chinese & Japanese Text Retrieval and Text Summarization, Tokyo, June 2000·March 2001 (ISBN : 4-924600-96-2)

7. Spink, A., Bateman, J. From highly relevant to not relevant: Examining different regions of relevance. Information Processing and Management, Vol.34, No.5, pp.599-622, 1998
8. Dunlop, M.D. Reflections on Mira, Journal of the American Society for Information Sciences, Vol.51, No.14, pp.1269-1274, 2000
9. Spink, A., Greisdorf, H. Regions and levels: Measuring and mapping users' relevance judgments. Journal of the American Society for Information Sciences, Vol.52, No.2, pp.161-173, 2001
10. Kando, N., Kuriyama, K., Yoshioka, M. Evaluation based on multi-grade relevance judgements. IPSJ SIG Notes, Vol.2001-FI-63, pp.105-112, July 2001.
11. Sung, H.M. "HANTEC Collection". Presented at the panel on IR Evaluation in the 4th IRAL, Hong Kong, 30 Sept.–3 Oct. 2000.
12. Yoshioka, M., Kuriyama, K., Kando, N.: Analysis on the Usage of Japanese Segmented Texts in the NTCIR Workshop 2. In NTCIR Workshop 2: Proceedings of the Second NTCIR Workshop on Research in Chinese & Japanese Text Retrieval and Text Summarization, Tokyo, June 2000·March 2001 (ISBN : 4-924600-96-2).
13. Kando, N, Nozue, T., Kuriyama, K., Oyama, K.: NTCIR-1: Its Policy and Practice, IPSJ SIG Notes, Vol.99, No.20, pp.33-40, 1999 [in Japanese].
14. Kuriyama, K., Nozue, T., Kando, N., Oyama, K.: Pooling for a Large Scale Test Collection: Analysis of the Search Results for the Pre-test of the NTCIR-1 Workshop, IPSJ SIG Notes, Vol.99-FI-54, pp.25-32 May, 1999 [in Japanese].
15. Kuriyama, K., Kando, K.: Construction of a Large Scale Test Collection: Analysis of the Training Topics of the NTCIR-1, IPSJ SIG Notes, Vol.99-FI-55, pp.41-48, July 1999 [in Japanese].
16. Kando, N., Eguchi, K., Kuriyama, K.: Construction of a Large Scale Test Collection: Analysis of the Test Topics of the NTCIR-1, In Proceedings of IPSJ Annual Meeting [in Japanese]. pp.3-107 -- 3-108, 30 Sept.–3 Oct. 1999.
17. Voorhees, E.M.: Variations in Relevance Judgments and the Measurement of Retrieval Effectiveness, In Proceedings of 21st Annual International ACM-SIGIR Conference on Research and Development in Information Retrieval. pp.315-323, Melbourne, Australia, August 1998.
18. Chen, K.H., Chen, H.H.: The Chinese Text Retrieval Tasks of NTCIR Workshop II. In NTCIR Workshop 2: Proceedings of the Second NTCIR Workshop on Research in Chinese & Japanese Text Retrieval and Text Summarization, Tokyo, June 2000·March 2001 (ISBN : 4-924600-96-2).
19. Kando, N., Kuriyama, K., Yoshioka, M.: Overview of Japanese and English Information Retrieval Tasks (JEIR) at the Second NTCIR Workshop. In NTCIR Workshop 2: Proceedings of the Second NTCIR Workshop on Research in Chinese & Japanese Text Retrieval and Text Summarization, Tokyo, June 2000-March 2001 (ISBN : 4-924600-96-2) .
20. CLEF: Cross-Language Evaluation Forum, http://www.iei.pi.cnr.it/DELOS/CLEF

Multilingual Topic Generation within the CLEF 2001 Experiments

Christa Womser-Hacker

University of Hildesheim, Information Science, Marienburger Platz 22,
31141 Hildesheim, Germany
womser@rz.uni-hildesheim.de
http://www.uni-hildesheim.de/~womser

Abstract. Topic generation is considered as one of the crucial elements in the information retrieval evaluation process. In the context of CLEF, the main focus lies on evaluating multilingual functions. With respect to topic generation this means that topics have to be created in various languages. Starting with TREC, the important parameters of topic generation are described.

1 Introduction

Since the beginning of information retrieval evaluation, topic generation is considered as one of the most important tasks. In the scope of discussions on well-formed and comparable collections, which came up in the early 90s, simple queries were increasingly replaced by "original user requests" or so-called topics.

This contribution addresses the topic generation process within CLEF with respect to the intercultural environment in particular.

2 Topic Generation in CLEF

Within CLEF, the topics are a very important component. Concerning the generation process, we could rely on valuable experiences made within TREC (cf. [1], [2]) where some effects of topic characteristics have been investigated and changed over time. In the beginning, topics were very elaborated and carefully formulated so that systems could start from a very good basis without applying query expansion techniques. Since this procedure seemed not to be very realistic, topics were later formulated in a less structured and much shorter way (cf. [3] p. 53).

C.A. Peters et al. (Eds.): CLEF 2001, LNCS 2406, pp. 389-393, 2002.
© Springer-Verlag Berlin Heidelberg 2002

2.1   Challenges of Generating Topics in a Multilingual Environment

Within the CLEF initiative, multilingual Information Retrieval is considered as the main task. In 2001, five core languages (English, French, German, Italian, and Spanish) formed the basis for documents and topics. Each language was to start with equal opportunities. Five language teams of the evaluation forum generated a certain number of topics in each of the core languages. Participants could choose which languages should be their starting points for performing retrieval.

2.2   Topic Generation Rules

Generally, the topics should meet the content of the documents which were drawn from different journals and newspapers of the year 1994. Events in politics, culture, sports, science etc. were addressed. A specific structure (see example below) was applied to the topics, which contain three textual fields: Title, Description and Narrative. The title should sketch in a very short way (maximum three words), the considered event, the description gives a more precise formulation in one sentence and the narrative states additional criteria for relevant or non-relevant documents.

The following example points out this structure:

```
<top lang="EN">
<num>1</num>
<EN-title>Shark Attacks</EN-title>
<EN-desc>Documents will report any information relating to shark attacks on humans.</EN-desc>
<EN-narr>Identify instances where a human was attacked by a shark, including where the attack took place and the circumstances surrounding the attack. Only documents concerning specific attacks are relevant; unconfirmed shark attacks or suspected bites are not relevant.>EN-narr></top>
```

Principally, there should be open topics and topics addressing specific facts. Roughly 20% should have answer documents containing pure fact information e.g. proper names. A heuristic rule stated that the topics should be related to either international, European or national issues. It was difficult to satisfy this rule because of the very different scope of the newspapers. Local events which took place in the South-West of France for example, were not discussed in US newspapers like the Los Angeles Times.

2.3   Topic Translation Process and Problems

Each language team generated a set of 15 potential topics which was more than would be used in the end. To make sure that related documents existed, pre-search processes were performed in the databases for all five languages. During a meeting in Pisa, all topic suggestions were discussed intensively with respect to their content and their formulation. A set of 50 topics was selected which were originally formulated in different languages. The groups elaborated the selected basic set and translated it from their original languages into English and the other core languages. The goal was to receive reliable formulations in the five languages. If there was no possibility to translate from an original language to a specific target language, translations were performed indirectly via the English master set. This process was performed in a very communicative and cooperative way to avoid any misunderstandings.

Translation processes aim at transferring an original text from one language to a second target language. As we know from translation science, the linguistic and cultural background are very important. A simple one-to-one translation is seldom possible. By translating the topics in a multilingual environment, different problems arise which should be met by the systems' functionalities. The most important of these challenges are dealing with proper names, abbreviations, compounds, idioms etc. Not only are domain specific terminology and culture specific knowledge involved, but also the recognition of the differences in English language usage in the UK and the USA, or the differences in German language usage in Germany and Switzerland.

2.4 Analysis of the English and German Topics

The 50 English and 50 German topics were analysed with respect to the systems' functionality.

Table 1. Analysis of English and German topics

	English	German
Stemming	345	471
Compound word	9	115
Proper name	73	62
Abbreviation	14	13
Negation	18	21
Idiom	2	2
Date	12	12
Noun phrase	98	42

Table 1 reflects the various language characteristics. In German, there were more linguistic problems concerning stemming and decomposition. On the other hand, the English topics contained more noun phrases than the German ones.

On average, English topics contained 11, and German topics 15 linguistic problems that had to be dealt with by the systems.

2.5   Cross-Checking of Topic Translations

The quality of the final topic set (i.e. 50 topics in English, French, German, Italian and Spanish) was checked by professional translators. The most important changes concerned stylistic, grammatical, and semantic factors, but corrections of spelling and formal mistakes were also proposed. All suggested alterations were discussed with the topic generators to ensure maintaining the intended meaning.

The following figure indicates the absolute values of changes to the topics:

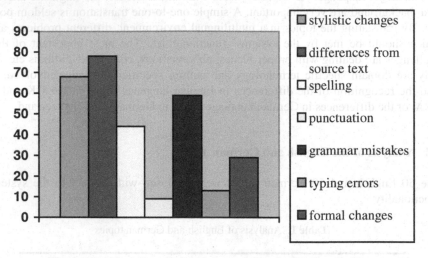

Fig. 1. Alterations in topic translations as a result of cross-checking

There were interesting examples which show that a simple word-by-word translation is not at all adequate. In many cases, additional explanations or the resolution of culture-specific abbreviations were necessary:

Table 2. Examples of translation problems

Original language	Target language
EN "CNG cars"	DE "mit Flüssiggas betriebene Autos"
NL „Muisarm"	FR „ordinateur: souris et tensions musculaires"
ES „Subasta de objetos de Lennon"	FR „Vente aux enchères de souvenirs de John Lennon"
DE „Schneider-Konkurs"	FR „Faillite de M. Schneider"

3   Conclusion

Topic generation is a crucial component of IR evaluation methodology. In CLEF, a lot of work has been done to ensure the high quality of the topic set. Further analyses are necessary to gain more experience in formalising appropriate topic characteristics and to find out what makes a topic difficult for IR systems.

References

1. Sparck Jones, K.: Reflections on TREC. Information Processing & Management 31 (1995) 291-314.
2. Harman, D.K.: The TREC Conferences. In: Kuhlen, R., Rittberger, M. (eds.): Hypertext – Information Retrieval – Multimedia. Proceedings HIM'95, 9-28, Konstanz (1995).
3. Sparck Jones, K.: Further Reflections on TREC. Information Processing & Management 36 (2000) 37-88.

CLEF Methodology and Metrics

Martin Braschler[1] and Carol Peters[2]

[1] Eurospider Information Technology AG
Schaffhauserstr. 18, 8006 Zürich, Switzerland
martin.braschler@eurospider.com

[2] IEI-CNR, Area di Ricerca, 56124 Pisa, Italy
carol@iei.pi.cnr.it

Abstract. We describe the organization of the CLEF 2001 evaluation campaign, outline the guidelines given to participants, and explain the techniques and measures used in CLEF campaigns for result calculation and analysis.

1 Introduction

Campaigns such as that organized by CLEF use a comparative evaluation approach. Comparative evaluation consists of deciding on a control task - which may correspond either to the function of a complete system or to that of a single component, of defining the protocol and metrics to be used, of identifying system or component developers interested in participating, and of organizing an evaluation campaign - which includes the acquisition and distribution of appropriate data for training and testing the systems.

A corpus-based, automatic scoring method is adopted, based on ideas first introduced in the Cranfield experiments [1] in the late 1960s. This methodology is widely used and accepted in the information retrieval community. Its properties have been thoroughly investigated and are well understood. This approach is also used by the popular series of TREC conferences [2], which are the "gold standard" for this form of evaluation campaigns. The implications of adopting the Cranfield paradigm are discussed in detail in [3].

In this paper, we describe the organization of the CLEF 2001 campaign. The aim is to give an exhaustive record of the technical setup of the CLEF 2001 campaign. In this way, we hope to provide readers, who have never participated in CLEF or similar evaluation campaigns, with the necessary background information in order to understand all the details of the experiments described in Part I of this volume and to be able to interpret the result pages in the Appendix.

The rest of the paper is organized as follows. In Section 2 we describe the tasks and the data collection provided for CLEF 2001 and briefly outline the instructions given to the participants, Section 3 describes the techniques and measures used for result calculation and analysis, and Section 4 explains how the results of the participating groups are presented. The Appendix presents the results for each track and task, run by run.

C.A. Peters et al. (Eds.): CLEF 2001, LNCS 2406, pp. 394-404, 2002.
© Springer-Verlag Berlin Heidelberg 2002

2   Agenda for CLEF 2001

CLEF campaigns are organized according to a predefined schedule, with a series of strict deadlines. The dates are determined in order to be compatible with those of the other two major Cross-Language Information Retrieval (CLIR) system evaluation activities: that organized by TREC and sponsored by the National Institute for Standards and Technology, which hosted English/French to Arabic retrieval in 2001 [4], and the NACSIS Test Collection for Information Retrieval (NTCIR) sponsored by the National Institute for Informatics of Tokyo, which offers cross-language system evaluation for Asian languages [5]. The three initiatives (US, Asian and European) aim at creating a network of complementary activities in the cross-language system evaluation area.

The main dates for 2001 were:

- First release of Call for Participation - November 2000
- Data Collection Release - 1 March 2001
- Topic Release - from 9 April 2001
- Receipt of runs from participants - 16 June 2001
- Release of relevance assessments and individual results - 25 July 2001
- Submission of paper for Working Notes - 6 August 2001
- Workshop - 3-4 September 2001

2.1   Tracks and Tasks

CLEF provides a series of evaluation tracks designed to test different aspects of information retrieval system development. The intention is to encourage systems to move from monolingual searching to the implementation of a full multilingual retrieval service. The design of these tracks has been modified over the years in order to meet the needs of the research community. Here below we describe the tracks and tasks offered by CLEF 2001.

Multilingual Information Retrieval. This is the main task in CLEF. It requires searching a multilingual collection of documents for relevant items, using a selected query language. Multilingual information retrieval is a complex task, testing the capability of a system to handle a number of different languages simultaneously and to merge the results, ordering them according to relevance. The multilingual collection for this track in CLEF 2001 contained English, German, French, Italian and Spanish documents. Using a selected topic (query) language, the goal was to retrieve documents for all languages in the collection, rather than just a given pair, listing the results in a merged, ranked list. Topics in twelve different languages were made available to participants in CLEF 2001.

Bilingual Information Retrieval. In this track, any query language can be used to search just one of the CLEF target document collections. Many newcomers to CLIR system evaluation prefer to begin with the simpler bilingual track before moving on to tackle the more complex issues involved in truly multilingual retrieval. CLEF 2001 offered 2 distinct bilingual tracks: the first consisted in querying a document collection of English texts in any of the other available topic languages. In order to assist participants who wanted to test their systems on a less familiar language, a second task provided the opportunity to query a Dutch document collection, again using any other topic language.

Monolingual (non-English) IR. Until recently, most IR system evaluation focused on English. However, many of the issues involved in IR are language dependent. CLEF provides the opportunity for monolingual system testing and tuning, and for building test suites in other European languages apart from English. In CLEF 2001, we provided the opportunity for monolingual system testing and tuning in Dutch, French, German, Italian and Spanish.

Domain-Specific Mono- and Cross-Language Information Retrieval. The rationale for this task is to study CLIR on other types of collections, serving a different kind of information need. The information that is provided by domain-specific scientific documents is far more targeted than news stories and contains much terminology. It is claimed that the users of this type of collection are typically interested in the completeness of results. This means that they are generally not satisfied with finding just some relevant documents in a collection that may contain much more. Developers of domain-specific cross-language retrieval systems need to be able to tune their systems to meet this requirement. See [6] for a discussion of this point. In CLEF 2001, this task was based on a data collection from a vertical domain (social sciences): the GIRT collection. Topics were made available in English, German and Russian.

For each of the tasks described above, the participating systems construct their queries (automatically or manually) from a common set of statements of information needs (known as topics) and search for relevant documents in the collections provided, listing the results in a ranked list.

Interactive CLIR. The aim of the tracks listed so far is to measure system performance mainly in terms of how good the document rankings are. However, this is not the only issue that interests the user. User satisfaction with an IR system is based on a number of factors, depending on the functionality of the particular system. For example, the way in which the results of a search are presented is of great importance in CLIR systems where it is common to have users retrieving documents in languages, which they do not understand. When users are unfamiliar with the target language, they need a presentation of the results, which will permit them to easily and accurately select documents of interest, discarding others. An interactive track that focused on this document selection problem was experimented with success in CLEF 2001 [7]

2.2   The Test Collections

The main CLEF test collection is formed of sets of documents in different European languages but with common features (same genre and time period, comparable content); a single set of topics rendered in a number of languages; relevance judgments determining the set of relevant documents for each topic. A separate test collection is being created for systems tuned for domain-specific tasks.

Document collection for CLEF 2001. This consisted of approximately 950,000 documents in six languages – Dutch, English, French, German, Italian and Spanish. It contains both newswires and national newspapers. Spanish and Dutch were introduced for the first time in CLEF 2001 for different reasons. Spanish was included because of its status as the fourth most widely spoken language in the world. Dutch was added not only to meet the demands of the considerable number of Dutch participants in CLEF but also because it provides a challenge for those who want to test the adaptability of their systems to a new, less well-known language.

The domain-specific collection was the GIRT database of about 80,000 German social science documents, which has controlled vocabularies for English-German and German-Russian.

Table 1 gives further details with respect to the source and dimensions of the 2001 multilingual document collection. It gives the overall size of each subcollection, number of documents contained, and three key figures indicating some typical characteristics of the individual documents: the median length in bytes, tokens and features. Tokens are "words", extracted by removing all formatting, tagging and punctuation, and the length in terms of features is defined as the number of distinct tokens occurring in a document.

Topics. The participating groups derive their queries in their preferred language from a set of topics created to simulate user information needs. Following the TREC philosophy, each topic consists of three parts: a brief title statement; a one-sentence description; a more complex narrative specifying the relevance assessment criteria.

The title contains the main keywords, the description is a "natural language" expression of the concept conveyed by the keywords, and the narrative adds additional syntax and semantics, stipulating the conditions for relevance assessment. Queries can be constructed from one or more fields. The motivation behind these structured topics is to provide query "input" for all kinds of IR systems, ranging from simple keyword-based procedures to more sophisticated systems supporting morphological analyses, parsing, query expansion and so on. In the cross-language context, the transfer component must also be considered, whether dictionary or corpus-based, a fully-fledged MT system or other. Different query structures may be more appropriate for testing one or the other methodology.

For CLEF 2001, 50 such topics were developed on the basis of the contents of the multilingual collection and topic sets were produced in all six document languages. Additional topic sets in Swedish, Russian, Japanese, Chinese and Thai were also prepared. The same topic set was used for the multilingual, bilingual and monolingual tasks. Participants could thus choose to formulate their queries in any one of at least nine European or three Asian languages. Separate topic sets were developed for the GIRT task in German, English and Russian for the GIRT task, The topic generation process and the issues involved is described in detail elsewhere in this volume [8].

Relevance Judgments. The number of documents in large test collections such as CLEF makes it impractical to judge every document for relevance. Instead, approximate recall figures are calculated by using pooling techniques. The results submitted by the participating groups are used to form a "pool" of documents for each

Table 1. Sources and dimensions of the CLEF 2001 document collection

Collection	Size (KB)	No. of Docs	Median Size of Docs. (Bytes)	Median Size of Docs. (Tokens)	Median Size of Docs . (Features)
Dutch: Algemeen Dagblad	247141	106483	1282	166	112
Dutch: NRC Handelsblad	306207	84121	2153	354	203
English: LA Times	435112	113005	2204	421	246
French: Le Monde	161423	44013	1994	361	213
French: SDA	88005	43178	1683	227	137
German: Frankfurter Rundschau	327652	139715	1598	225	161
German: Der Spiegel	64429	13979	1324	213	160
German: SDA	147494	71677	1672	186	131
Italian: La Stampa	198112	58051	1915	435	268
Italian: SDA	87592	50527	1454	187	129
Spanish: EFE	523497	215738	2172	290	171

SDA = Schweizerische Depeschenagentur (Swiss News Agency)
EFE = Agencia EFE S.A (Spanish News Agency)

topic and for each language by collecting the highly ranked documents from all the submissions. The pooling procedure is further discussed later in this paper.

2.3 Instructions to Participants

Guidelines were made available to CLEF 2001 participants shortly after the data release date. These Guidelines provide a definition of the system data structures and stipulate the conditions under which they can be used.

System Data Structures. The system data structures are defined to consist of the original documents, any new structures built automatically from the documents (such as inverted files, thesauri, conceptual networks, etc.), and any new structures built manually from the documents (such as thesauri, synonym lists, knowledge bases, rules, etc.). They may not be modified in response to the topics. For example, participants are not allowed to add topic words that are not already in the dictionaries used by their systems in order to extend coverage. The CLEF tasks are intended to represent the real-world problem of an ordinary user posing a question to a system. In the case of the cross-language tasks, the question is posed in one language and relevant documents must be retrieved whatever the language in which they have been written. If an ordinary user could not make the change to the system, the participating groups must not make it after receiving the topics.

There are several parts of the CLEF data collections that contain manually-assigned, controlled or uncontrolled index terms. These fields are delimited by SGML tags. Since the primary focus of CLEF is on retrieval of naturally occurring text over language boundaries, these manually-indexed terms must not be indiscriminately used as if they are a normal part of the text. If a group decides to use these terms, they should be part of a specific experiment that utilizes manual indexing terms, and these runs should be declared as manual runs. However, learning from (e.g. building translation sources from) such fields is permissible.

Constructing the Queries. There are many possible methods for converting the topics supplied into queries that a system can execute. We broadly defined two generic methods, "automatic" and "manual", based on whether manual intervention is used or not. When more than one set of results are submitted, the different sets may correspond to different query construction methods, or if desired, can be variants within the same method. The manual query construction method includes both runs in which the queries are constructed manually and then executed without looking at the results and runs in which the results are used to alter the queries using some manual operation. The distinction being made between runs in which there is no human involvement (automatic query construction) and runs in which there is some type of human involvement (manual query construction). It is clear that manual runs should be appropriately motivated in a CLIR context, e.g. a run where a proficient human simply translates the topic into the document language(s) is not what most people think of as cross-language retrieval.

Note that by including all types of human-involved runs in the manual query construction method we make it harder to do comparisons of work within this query construction method. Therefore groups are strongly encouraged to determine what constitutes a base run for their experiments and to do these runs (officially or unofficially) to allow useful interpretations of the results. Unofficial runs are those not submitted to CLEF but evaluated using the trec_eval package available from Cornell University [9].

Submission of Results. At CLEF 2001, we accepted a maximum of 4 runs per task for the multilingual, bilingual and GIRT tasks but participants were asked to specify run priority. We accepted a maximum of 5 monolingual experiments (there are 5 languages to choose from) but no more than 3 runs for any one of these languages and up to a maximum of 10 runs in total. This means that a group submitting monolingual experiments for all languages could not send more than two runs per language on average. In order to facilitate comparison between results, there was a mandatory run: Title + Description (per experiment, per topic language).

3 Result Calculation

3.1 Measures

The effectiveness of IR systems can be objectively evaluated by an analysis of a set of representative sample search results. To this end, test queries are used to retrieve the best matching documents. A human judge then decides the appropriateness of each of these documents for the given query ("relevance"). Ideally, such "relevance assessments" are available for every single document in the collection. Effectiveness measures are then calculated. Popular measures usually adopted for exercises of this type are Recall and Precision.

$$\text{Recall } \rho_r(q) := \frac{\left|D_r^{rel}(q)\right|}{\left|D^{rel}(q)\right|} \text{ and Precision } \pi_r(q) := \frac{\left|D_r^{rel}(q)\right|}{\left|D_r(q)\right|},$$

where $D_r(q) := \{d_1,...,d_r\}$ is the answer set to query q containing the first r documents. The choice of a specific value for r is necessary because recall and precision are set-based measures, and evaluate the quality of an unordered set of retrieved documents. Choosing a low value for r implies that the user is interested in few, high-precision documents, whereas a high value for r means that the user conducts an exhaustive search. $D^{rel}(q)$ is the set of all relevant documents, and $D_r^{rel}(q) := D^{rel}(q) \cap D_r(q)$ is the set of relevant documents contained in the answer set [10]. When precision and recall are determined for every possible size of the answer set, a plot of the corresponding values results in a sawtooth curve (see Table 2). In the next step, typically a replacement curve is defined by assigning for every recall value $\rho \in [0,1]$ a precision value as follows:

$$\Pi_q(\rho) := \max\{\pi_r(q) | \rho_r(q) \geq \rho\}$$

Using this "interpolation step", we obtain a monotonically decreasing curve where each recall value corresponds to a unique precision value (see Figure 1). This "ceiling operation" can be interpreted as looking only at the theoretically optimal answer sets for which recall and precision cannot be improved simultaneously by inspecting further documents.

When evaluating a system with a set of queries (typically 50 in CLEF), an averaging step is introduced that produces the final recall/precision curve:

$$\Pi(\rho) := \frac{1}{|Q|} \sum_{q \in Q} \Pi_q(\rho)$$

where $|Q|$ denotes the number of queries.

Often people prefer single value measures to a more complex performance indicator, such as a recall/precision curve. The advantage of such single value measures lies in easy comparison, their danger in too much abstraction: if relying exclusively on a single value, the ability to judge a system's effectiveness for different user preferences, such as exhaustive search or high-precision results, is lost.

The most popular single value measure for assessing the effectiveness of information retrieval systems is average precision. To calculate the average precision value, the precision after each relevant document found in the result list is determined as outlined above. The list of precision values that is obtained is then used to calculate an average. No interpolation is used to calculate the final average.

Table 2. Precision/recall figures for a sample query and its corresponding relevance assessments.

rank r	relevant to q.	$\rho_r(q)$	$\pi_r(q)$
1	+	0.20	1.00
2	-	0.20	0.50
3	-	0.20	0.33
4	+	0.40	0.50
5	-	0.40	0.40
6	-	0.40	0.33
7	+	0.60	0.43
8	+	0.80	0.50
9	-	0.80	0.44
10	+	1.00	0.50

3.2   Pooling

All evaluations in the CLEF campaigns are based on the use of relevance assessments, i.e. judgments made by human "assessors" with respect to the usefulness of a certain document to answer a user's information need. CLEF uses a set of topics as a sample of possible information needs that could be formulated by real users. Theoretically, for each of these topics, all documents in the test collection would have to be judged for relevance. Since this judging ("assessment") involves an assessor reading the complete document, this is a laborious process. With the size of today's test collections, which contain hundreds of thousands or even millions of documents (the CLEF multilingual track used around 750,000 documents for 2001), this becomes impractical.

Therefore, evaluation campaigns such as CLEF often use an alternative strategy, only assessing a fraction of the document collection for any given topic. This implies – for every query – eliminating all those documents from consideration that were not retrieved by any participant high up in their ranked list of results. The reasoning behind this strategy is discussed in detail in [11]. The remaining documents, which share the property of having been retrieved as a highly ranked document by at least one participant, form a "document pool" that is then judged for relevance. The number of result sets per participant that are used for pooling, and the establishing of the line between "highly ranked" and other documents (the so-called "pool depth") are dictated to a large extent by practical needs (i.e. available resources for assessment).

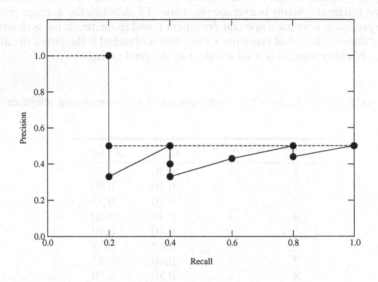

Fig. 1 Interpolation of recall/precision values

In the CLEF 2001 campaign, only selected results sets (slightly more than half of all results sets) were included in the pool. From these sets, the top 60 documents were used for pool formation. In [11] we discuss the implications of using a document pool vs. judging all documents in a collection

4   Results Presentation

4.1   Structure of Result Page

The Appendix contains one page for each result set submitted by a participating group. The page contains a set of tables and two graphs:
1.   The tables provide the following information:
     - Average precision figures for every individual query. This allows comparison of system performance for single queries, which is important since variation of performance across queries is often very high and can be significant.
     - Overall statistics, giving:
       - the total number of documents retrieved by the system
       - the total number of overall relevant documents in the collection, and
       - the total number of relevant documents actually found by the system

- interpolated precision averages at specific recall levels (see above)
- non-interpolated average precision over all queries (see above)
- precision numbers after inspecting a specific number of documents (see above)
- R-precision: precision after the last relevant document was retrieved.

2. The graphs consist of:

    • a recall/precision graph, providing a plot of the precision values for various recall levels. This is the standard statistic and is the one most commonly reported in the literature.

    • a comparison to median performance. For each query, the difference in average precision, when compared to the median performance for the given task, is plotted. This graph gives valuable insight into which type of queries is handled well by different systems.

The results page for a specific experiment can be most quickly located by using the table at the beginning of the appendix. This table is sorted by group, and gives the name of the track/task, run identifier, topic language, topic fields, run type (automatic/manual), and whether the run was used for pooling prior to producing the relevance assessment. The individual results pages are sorted by track/task, and further sorted by run identifier, as can be seen from the overview table.

Acknowledgments. Parts of this paper are based on material prepared by Donna Harman and Ellen Voorhees for the proceedings of the TREC conferences. We thank them for the permission to adapt their work to the CLEF context. Section 3.1. is based on a description contained in [10]. The authors would like to thank Peter Schäuble for his contribution.

References

1. Cleverdon, C. The Cranfield Tests on Index Language Devices. In K. Sparck-Jones and P. Willett (Eds.): Readings in Information Retrieval, pages 47-59. Morgan Kaufmann, 1997.
2. Harman, D. The TREC Conferences. In R. Kuhlen and M. Rittberger (Eds.): Hypertext - Information Retrieval - Multimedia: Synergieeffekte Elektronischer Informationssysteme, Proceedings of HIM '95, pages 9-28. Universitätsverlag Konstanz
3. Voorhees, E. The Philosophy of Information Retrieval Evaluation. This volume.
4. Gey, F.C. & Oard, D.W. The TREC-2001 Cross-Language Information Retrieval Track: Searching Arabic using English, French or Arabic Queries. NIST Special Publication 500-250: The Tenth Text REtrieval Conference (TREC 2001).
5. Kando, N., Aihara, K., Eguchi, K., Kato, H. (Eds.) Proceedings of the Second NTCIR Workshop Meeting on Evaluation of Chinese & Japanese Text Retrieval and Text Summarization, National Institute of Informatics (NII), ISBN 4-924600-89-X.
6. Gey, F.C. & Kluck, M. (2001). The Domain-Specific Task of CLEF – Specific Evaluation Strategies in Cross-Language Information Retrieval. In C. Peters (Ed.). Cross-Language Information Retrieval and Evaluation. Lecture Notes in Computer Science 2069, Springer Verlag, pp 48-56.4.
7. Oard, D.W. and Gonzalo, J. The CLEF 2001 Interactive Track. This volume.
8. Womser-Hacker, C. Multilingual Topic Generation within the CLEF 2001 Experiments. This volume.

9.   ftp://ftp.cs.cornell.edu/pub/smart/
10. Schäuble, P. Content-Based Information Retrieval from Large Text and Audio Databases. Section 1.6 Evaluation Issues, Pages 22-29, Kluwer Academic Publishers, 1997.
11. Braschler, M. CLEF 2001 - Overview of Results. This volume.

Appendix - Run Statistics

List of Run Characteristics

Institute	Country	Runtag	Track/Task	Top. lg.	Top. fld.	Type	Pool
APL/JHU	USA	aplbideen	Bi	DE	TD	Auto	
APL/JHU	USA	aplbiennl	Bi-NL	EN	TD	Auto	Y
APL/JHU	USA	aplbifren	Bi	FR	TD	Auto	
APL/JHU	USA	aplbijpen	Bi	JA	TD	Auto	
APL/JHU	USA	aplmodea	Mono	DE	TDN	Auto	Y
APL/JHU	USA	aplmodeb	Mono	DE	TD	Auto	Y
APL/JHU	USA	aplmoesa	Mono	ES	TDN	Auto	Y
APL/JHU	USA	aplmoesb	Mono	ES	TD	Auto	
APL/JHU	USA	aplmofra	Mono	FR	TDN	Auto	Y
APL/JHU	USA	aplmofrb	Mono	FR	TD	Auto	Y
APL/JHU	USA	aplmoita	Mono	IT	TDN	Auto	Y
APL/JHU	USA	aplmoitb	Mono	IT	TD	Auto	Y
APL/JHU	USA	aplmonla	Mono	NL	TDN	Auto	Y
APL/JHU	USA	aplmonlb	Mono	NL	TD	Auto	
APL/JHU	USA	aplmuena	Multi	EN	TD	Auto	Y
APL/JHU	USA	aplmuenb	Multi	EN	TDN	Auto	
APL/JHU	USA	aplmuenc	Multi	EN	TD	Auto	
APL/JHU	USA	aplmuend	Multi	EN	TD	Auto	
CMU	USA	CMUbll25e3tdn25	Bi	DE	TDN	Auto	Y
CMU	USA	CMUbnn15e2td15	Bi	DE	TD	Auto	
CMU	USA	CMUbnn25e2tdn15	Bi	DE	TDN	Auto	
CMU	USA	CMUmll15e200td	Mono	DE	TD	Auto	Y
CMU	USA	CMUmll15e300tdn	Mono	DE	TDN	Auto	Y
CMU	USA	CMUmll5e300td	Mono	DE	TD	Auto	
Eidetica	Netherlands	EidDE2001A	Mono	DE	TDN	Auto	Y
Eidetica	Netherlands	EidDE2001B	Mono	DE	TDN	Auto	
Eidetica	Netherlands	EidDE2001C	Mono	DE	TD	Auto	
Eidetica	Netherlands	EidNL2001A	Mono	NL	TDN	Auto	Y
Eidetica	Netherlands	EidNL2001B	Mono	NL	TDN	Auto	
Eidetica	Netherlands	EidNL2001C	Mono	NL	TD	Auto	
Eurospider	Switzerland	EIT01FFFN	Mono	FR	TDN	Auto	Y
Eurospider	Switzerland	EIT01FFLUN	Mono	FR	TDN	Auto	Y
Eurospider	Switzerland	EIT01GGLUD	Mono	DE	TD	Auto	
Eurospider	Switzerland	EIT01GGLUN	Mono	DE	TDN	Auto	
Eurospider	Switzerland	EIT01GGSN	Mono	DE	TDN	Auto	Y
Eurospider	Switzerland	EIT01M1N	Multi	DE	TDN	Auto	
Eurospider	Switzerland	EIT01M2N	Multi	DE	TDN	Auto	
Eurospider	Switzerland	EIT01M3D	Multi	DE	TD	Auto	
Eurospider	Switzerland	EIT01M3N	Multi	DE	TDN	Auto	Y
Greenwich U	UK	gre1	Mono	FR	TDN	Auto	Y
Greenwich U	UK	gre2	Mono	FR	TD	Auto	Y
Greenwich U	UK	gre3	Mono	FR	T	Auto	
HKUST	Hong Kong	hkust	Bi	FR	TD	Auto	Y
Hummingbird	Canada	humDE01	Mono	DE	TD	Auto	Y
Hummingbird	Canada	humDE01x	Mono	DE	TD	Auto	Y
Hummingbird	Canada	humES01	Mono	ES	TD	Auto	
Hummingbird	Canada	humES01x	Mono	ES	TD	Auto	Y
Hummingbird	Canada	humFR01	Mono	FR	TD	Auto	Y
Hummingbird	Canada	humFR01x	Mono	FR	TD	Auto	Y
Hummingbird	Canada	humIT01	Mono	IT	TD	Auto	Y

Hummingbird	Canada	humIT01x	Mono	IT	TD	Auto	Y
Hummingbird	Canada	humNL01	Mono	NL	TD	Auto	
Hummingbird	Canada	humNL01x	Mono	NL	TD	Auto	Y
IAI	Germany	iaidetd01	Mono	DE	TD	Auto	Y
IRIT	France	irit1bFr2En	Bi	FR	TD	Auto	
IRIT	France	irit2bFr2En	Bi	FR	TD	Auto	
IRIT	France	iritmonFR	Mono	FR	TD	Auto	Y
IRIT	France	iritmonGE	Mono	DE	TD	Auto	Y
IRIT	France	iritmonIT	Mono	IT	TD	Auto	Y
IRIT	France	iritmonSP	Mono	ES	TD	Auto	
IRIT	France	iritmuEn2A	Multi	EN	TD	Auto	Y
IRST	Italy	IRSTit1	Mono	IT	TDN	Auto	Y
IRST	Italy	IRSTit2	Mono	IT	TD	Auto	Y
IRST	Italy	IRSTit2en1	Bi	IT	TDN	Auto	
IRST	Italy	IRSTit2en2	Bi	IT	TD	Auto	
Kasetsart U	Thailand	thaiexp	Bi	TH	D	Auto	Y
Kasetsart U	Thailand	thaiexpa	Bi	TH	D	Auto	
Kasetsart U	Thailand	thaiseg	Bi	TH	D	Auto	
Kasetsart U	Thailand	thaithes	Bi	TH	D	Auto	
KCSL Inc.	Canada	kcslbilint	Bi	FR	T	Auto	
KCSL Inc.	Canada	kcslbilintd	Bi	FR	TD	Auto	Y
KCSL Inc.	Canada	kcslbilintdn	Bi	FR	TDN	Auto	
KCSL Inc.	Canada	kcslmonot	Mono	ES	T	Auto	Y
KCSL Inc.	Canada	kcslmonotd	Mono	ES	TD	Auto	Y
KCSL Inc.	Canada	kcslmonotdn	Mono	ES	TDN	Auto	
KCSL Inc.	Canada	kcslmultit	Multi	EN	T	Auto	
KCSL Inc.	Canada	kcslmultitd	Multi	EN	TD	Auto	Y
KCSL Inc.	Canada	kcslmultitdn	Multi	EN	TDN	Auto	
Medialab	Netherlands	medialab	Mono	NL	TDN	Auto	Y
Nara Inst. of Tech. NAIST	Japan	naraDOM	Bi	FR	TD	Manual	
Nara Inst. of Tech. NAIST	Japan	naraFEED	Bi	FR	TD	Manual	
Nara Inst. of Tech. NAIST	Japan	naraFR	Mono	FR	TD	Manual	Y
Nara Inst. of Tech. NAIST	Japan	naraORG	Bi	FR	TD	Manual	
Nara Inst. of Tech. NAIST	Japan	naraTR	Bi	FR	TD	Manual	Y
National Taiwan U	Taiwan	NTUa1wco	Bi	ZH	TD	Auto	
National Taiwan U	Taiwan	NTUaswtw	Bi	ZH	TD	Auto	
National Taiwan U	Taiwan	NTUco	Bi	ZH	TD	Auto	
National Taiwan U	Taiwan	NTUtpwn	Bi	ZH	TD	Auto	Y
OCE Technologies BV	Netherlands	oce1	Mono	NL	TDN	Auto	Y
OCE Technologies BV	Netherlands	oce2	Mono	NL	TDN	Auto	Y
OCE Technologies BV	Netherlands	oce3	Mono	NL	TDN	Auto	
SICS/Conexor	Sweden	sicsfed	Bi	FR	D	Auto	
SICS/Conexor	Sweden	sicsfen	Bi	FR	DN	Auto	
SICS/Conexor	Sweden	sicsfenf	Bi	FR	DN	Auto	
SICS/Conexor	Sweden	sicssen	Bi	SV	DN	Auto	Y
SINAI/U Jaen	Spain	sinaiewn	Bi	ES	T	Auto	Y
SINAI/U Jaen	Spain	sinaiewn2	Bi	ES	T	Auto	Y
SINAI/U Jaen	Spain	sinaiorg	Bi	ES	T	Auto	
Thomson L&R	USA	tlrdetd	Mono	DE	TD	Auto	Y
Thomson L&R	USA	tlrdetdn	Mono	DE	TDN	Auto	Y
Thomson L&R	USA	tlres2entdb	Bi	ES	TD	Auto	
Thomson L&R	USA	tlres2entdnb	Bi	ES	TDN	Auto	
Thomson L&R	USA	tlres2entdnw	Bi	ES	TDN	Auto	
Thomson L&R	USA	tlres2entdw	Bi	ES	TD	Auto	
Thomson L&R	USA	tlrestd	Mono	ES	TD	Auto	Y
Thomson L&R	USA	tlrestdnpc	Mono	ES	TDN	Auto	Y

Thomson L&R	USA	tlrestdpc	Mono	ES	TD	Auto	
Thomson L&R	USA	tlrfrtd	Mono	FR	TD	Auto	
Thomson L&R	USA	tlrfrtdn	Mono	FR	TDN	Auto	Y
Thomson L&R	USA	tlrfrtdnpc	Mono	FR	TDN	Auto	Y
Thomson L&R	USA	tlrittd	Mono	IT	TD	Auto	Y
Thomson L&R	USA	tlrnltd	Mono	NL	TD	Auto	Y
TNO	Netherlands	tnodd1	Mono	DE	TD	Auto	
TNO	Netherlands	tnodd3	Mono	DE	TD	Auto	Y
TNO	Netherlands	tnoen1	Bi-NL	EN	TD	Auto	Y
TNO	Netherlands	tnoex3	Multi	EN	TD	Auto	
TNO	Netherlands	tnoex4	Multi	EN	TD	Auto	
TNO	Netherlands	tnofe1	Bi	FR	TD	Auto	
TNO	Netherlands	tnofe2	Bi	FR	TD	Auto	
TNO	Netherlands	tnofe3	Bi	FR	TD	Auto	
TNO	Netherlands	tnoff1	Mono	FR	TD	Auto	Y
TNO	Netherlands	tnoff3	Mono	FR	TD	Auto	Y
TNO	Netherlands	tnoii3	Mono	IT	TD	Auto	Y
TNO	Netherlands	tnonn1	Mono	NL	TD	Auto	
TNO	Netherlands	tnonn1p	Mono	NL	TD	Auto	
TNO	Netherlands	tnonn3	Mono	NL	TD	Auto	Y
TNO	Netherlands	tnonx3	Multi	NL	TD	Auto	Y
TNO	Netherlands	tnoss1	Mono	ES	TD	Auto	
TNO	Netherlands	tnoss3	Mono	ES	TD	Auto	Y
U Alicante	Spain	ClefSPAutEl	Mono	ES	TD	Auto	
U Alicante	Spain	ClefSPAutM	Mono	ES	TDN	Auto	Y
U Alicante	Spain	ClefSPAutPR	Mono	ES	T	Auto	Y
U Alicante	Spain	ClefSPENAutEl	Bi	ES	TD	Auto	
U Alicante	Spain	ClefSPENAutEXP	Bi	ES	T	Auto	
U Alicante	Spain	ClefSPENAutM	Bi	ES	TDN	Auto	
U Alicante	Spain	ClefSPENAutPR	Bi	ES	T	Auto	
U Amsterdam	Netherlands	AmsDeM	Mono	DE	TD	Auto	Y
U Amsterdam	Netherlands	AmsDeNv	Mono	DE	TD	Auto	
U Amsterdam	Netherlands	AmsDeT	Mono	DE	T	Auto	Y
U Amsterdam	Netherlands	AmsItM	Mono	IT	TD	Auto	Y
U Amsterdam	Netherlands	AmsItNv	Mono	IT	TD	Auto	Y
U Amsterdam	Netherlands	AmsItT	Mono	IT	T	Auto	Y
U Amsterdam	Netherlands	AmsNlM	Mono	NL	TD	Auto	Y
U Amsterdam	Netherlands	AmsNlNv	Mono	NL	TD	Auto	
U Amsterdam	Netherlands	AmsNlT	Mono	NL	T	Auto	
U Exeter	UK	exece1	Bi	ZH	TD	Auto	
U Exeter	UK	exefe1	Bi	FR	TD	Auto	
U Exeter	UK	exege1	Bi	DE	TD	Auto	
U Exeter	UK	exeje1	Bi	JA	TD	Auto	Y
U Glasgow	UK	glaenl	Bi-NL	EN	TD	Auto	Y
U Montreal	Canada	RaliMidfF2E	Bi	FR	TDN	Auto	
U Montreal	Canada	RaliP01D2E	Bi	DE	TDN	Auto	
U Montreal	Canada	RaliP01F2E	Bi	FR	TDN	Auto	
U Montreal	Canada	RaliP01I2E	Bi	IT	TDN	Auto	Y
U Neuchatel	Switzerland	UniNEmoes	Mono	ES	TD	Auto	Y
U Neuchatel	Switzerland	UniNEmofr	Mono	FR	TD	Auto	Y
U Neuchatel	Switzerland	UniNEmofrM	Mono	FR	TDN	Manual	Y
U Neuchatel	Switzerland	UniNEmoge	Mono	DE	TD	Auto	Y
U Neuchatel	Switzerland	UniNEmoit	Mono	IT	TD	Auto	Y
U Neuchatel	Switzerland	UniNEmoitM	Mono	IT	TDN	Manual	Y
U Neuchatel	Switzerland	UniNEmu	Multi	EN	TD	Auto	
U Neuchatel	Switzerland	UniNEmuL	Multi	EN	TDN	Auto	

U Neuchatel	Switzerland	UniNEmum	Multi	EN	TD	Manual	Y
U Salamanca	Spain	usal01	Mono	ES	TDN	Auto	Y
U Salamanca	Spain	usal02	Mono	ES	TDN	Auto	
U Salamanca	Spain	usal03	Mono	ES	TDN	Auto	Y
U Tampere	Finland	TAYfinstr	Bi	FI	TD	Auto	Y
U Tampere	Finland	TAYgershort	Bi	DE	TD	Auto	
U Tampere	Finland	TAYgerstr	Bi	DE	TD	Auto	
U Tampere	Finland	TAYswestr	Bi	SV	TD	Auto	
U Twente	Netherlands	ut1	Mono	NL	TDN	Manual	Y
UC Berkeley 1	USA	BKBIGEM1	Bi	DE	TDN	Manual	
UC Berkeley 1	USA	BKBIREA1	Bi	RU	TDN	Auto	
UC Berkeley 1	USA	BKBIREM1	Bi	RU	TDN	Manual	Y
UC Berkeley 1	USA	BKGRGGA	GIRT	DE	TDN	Auto	Y
UC Berkeley 1	USA	BKGRRGA1	GIRT	RU	TDN	Auto	Y
UC Berkeley 1	USA	BKGRRGA2	GIRT	RU	TDN	Auto	Y
UC Berkeley 1	USA	BKGRRGA3	GIRT	RU	TD	Auto	Y
UC Berkeley 1	USA	BKMUEAA1	Multi	EN	TD	Auto	
UC Berkeley 1	USA	BKMUEAA2	Multi	EN	TDN	Auto	
UC Berkeley 1	USA	BKMUGAM1	Multi	DE	TDN	Manual	Y
UC Berkeley 1	USA	BKMURAA1	Multi	RU	TDN	Auto	Y
UC Berkeley 2	USA	BK2CEA1	Bi	ZH	TDN	Auto	
UC Berkeley 2	USA	BK2CEA2	Bi	ZH	TD	Auto	
UC Berkeley 2	USA	BK2GGA1	Mono	DE	TDN	Auto	Y
UC Berkeley 2	USA	BK2GGA2	Mono	DE	TD	Auto	
UC Berkeley 2	USA	BK2MUCAA1	Multi	ZH	TDN	Auto	Y
UC Berkeley 2	USA	BK2MUCAA2	Multi	ZH	TD	Auto	
UC Berkeley 2	USA	BK2MUEAA1	Multi	EN	TDN	Auto	
UC Berkeley 2	USA	BK2MUEAA2	Multi	EN	TD	Auto	
UC Berkeley 2	USA	BK2SSA1	Mono	ES	TDN	Auto	Y
UC Berkeley 2	USA	BK2SSA2	Mono	ES	TD	Auto	

Explanations:

Runtag	Experiment identifier. Matches the identifiers on the individual result pages.
Task	Multi = Multilingual, Bi = Bilingual to English, Bi-NL = Bilingual to Dutch
	Mono = Monolingual, GIRT = GIRT Special Subtask
Topic Language	DE = German, EN = English, ES = Spanish, FI = Finnish, FR = French,
	IT= Italian, JA = Japanese, NL = Dutch, RU = Russian, SV = Swedish,
	TH = Thai, ZH = Chinese
Topic Fields	Combination of T (Title), D (Description) and N (Narrative)
Type	Auto = automatic (no manual intervention), Manual = manual intervention
Pool	Y = run was used for formation of the pools judged by relevance assessors.

Run BK2MUCAA1, Multilingual, Chinese, Auto, title+desc+narr

Average precision (individual queries):		Overall statistics (for 50 queries):	

Average precision
(individual queries):

Query 41:	0.1004
Query 42:	0.2673
Query 43:	0.4580
Query 44:	0.1027
Query 45:	0.4113
Query 46:	0.0668
Query 47:	0.1901
Query 48:	0.1413
Query 49:	0.1298
Query 50:	0.2922
Query 51:	0.0091
Query 52:	0.0215
Query 53:	0.0219
Query 54:	0.0710
Query 55:	0.3652
Query 56:	0.0480
Query 57:	0.1778
Query 58:	0.5280
Query 59:	0.2412
Query 60:	0.2045
Query 61:	0.1668
Query 62:	0.3731
Query 63:	0.6989
Query 64:	0.0021
Query 65:	0.0874
Query 66:	0.0549
Query 67:	0.0304
Query 68:	0.0001
Query 69:	0.0011
Query 70:	0.3353
Query 71:	0.3008
Query 72:	0.1907
Query 73:	0.1133
Query 74:	0.2255
Query 75:	0.0106
Query 76:	0.2255
Query 77:	0.0542
Query 78:	0.0355
Query 79:	0.6267
Query 80:	0.4542
Query 81:	0.5588
Query 82:	0.3837
Query 83:	0.4170
Query 84:	0.2415
Query 85:	0.4750
Query 86:	0.1747
Query 87:	0.2310
Query 88:	0.6481
Query 89:	0.0209
Query 90:	0.0998

Overall statistics
(for 50 queries):

Total number of documents
over all queries

Retrieved:	50000
Relevant:	8138
Rel_ret:	4738

Interpolated Recall -
Precision Averages:

at 0.00	0.7604
at 0.10	0.4963
at 0.20	0.3658
at 0.30	0.2924
at 0.40	0.2462
at 0.50	0.2166
at 0.60	0.1584
at 0.70	0.1007
at 0.80	0.0602
at 0.90	0.0106
at 1.00	0.0010

Avg. prec. (non-interpolated)
for all rel. documents   0.2217

Precision:

At	5 docs:	0.5480
At	10 docs:	0.4940
At	15 docs:	0.4600
At	20 docs:	0.4280
At	30 docs:	0.3920
At	100 docs:	0.3070
At	200 docs:	0.2276
At	500 docs:	0.1467
At	1000 docs:	0.0948

R-Precision (prec. after R
(=num_rel) docs. retrieved):
Exact: 0.2731

Run BK2MUCAA1
Recall-Precision Values

Run BK2MUCAA1
Comparison to median by topic

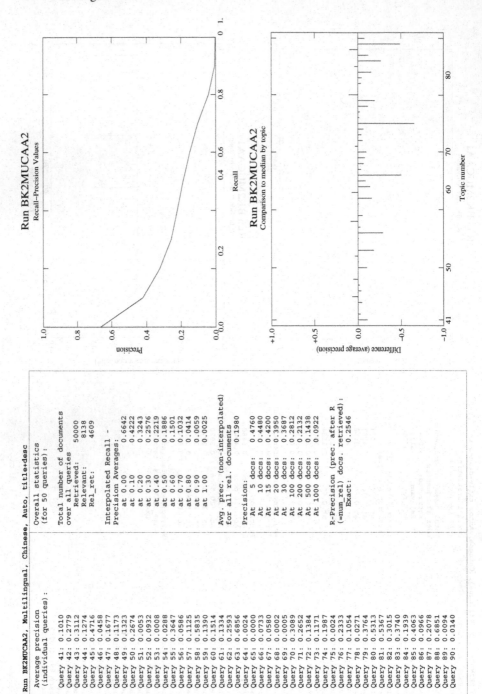

Run BK2MUCAA2
Recall-Precision Values

Precision

Recall

Run BK2MUCAA2
Comparison to median by topic

Difference (average precision)

Topic number

Run BK2MUCAA2, Multilingual, Chinese, Auto, title+desc

Average precision
(individual queries):

Query 41:	0.1010
Query 42:	0.2779
Query 43:	0.3112
Query 44:	0.1274
Query 45:	0.4716
Query 46:	0.0458
Query 47:	0.1677
Query 48:	0.1173
Query 49:	0.1323
Query 50:	0.2674
Query 51:	0.0053
Query 52:	0.0932
Query 53:	0.0008
Query 54:	0.0288
Query 55:	0.3647
Query 56:	0.0586
Query 57:	0.1125
Query 58:	0.5835
Query 59:	0.1390
Query 60:	0.1514
Query 61:	0.1334
Query 62:	0.2593
Query 63:	0.6856
Query 64:	0.0024
Query 65:	0.0000
Query 66:	0.0733
Query 67:	0.0580
Query 68:	0.0002
Query 69:	0.0005
Query 70:	0.3089
Query 71:	0.2652
Query 72:	0.1384
Query 73:	0.1171
Query 74:	0.1987
Query 75:	0.0024
Query 76:	0.2333
Query 77:	0.1054
Query 78:	0.0271
Query 79:	0.3764
Query 80:	0.5313
Query 81:	0.5367
Query 82:	0.3015
Query 83:	0.3740
Query 84:	0.1939
Query 85:	0.4063
Query 86:	0.0966
Query 87:	0.2078
Query 88:	0.6851
Query 89:	0.0094
Query 90:	0.0140

Overall statistics
(for 50 queries):

Total number of documents
over all queries
  Retrieved: 50000
  Relevant: 8138
  Rel_ret: 4609

Interpolated Recall -
Precision Averages:
  at 0.00   0.6642
  at 0.10   0.4222
  at 0.20   0.3243
  at 0.30   0.2576
  at 0.40   0.2219
  at 0.50   0.1886
  at 0.60   0.1501
  at 0.70   0.1032
  at 0.80   0.0414
  at 0.90   0.0059
  at 1.00   0.0025

Avg. prec. (non-interpolated)
for all rel. documents
                0.1980

Precision:
  At   5 docs: 0.4760
  At   10 docs: 0.4480
  At   15 docs: 0.4200
  At   20 docs: 0.3950
  At   30 docs: 0.3687
  At 100 docs: 0.2812
  At 200 docs: 0.2132
  At 500 docs: 0.1438
  At 1000 docs: 0.0922

R-Precision (prec. after R
(=num_rel) docs. retrieved):
  Exact: 0.2546

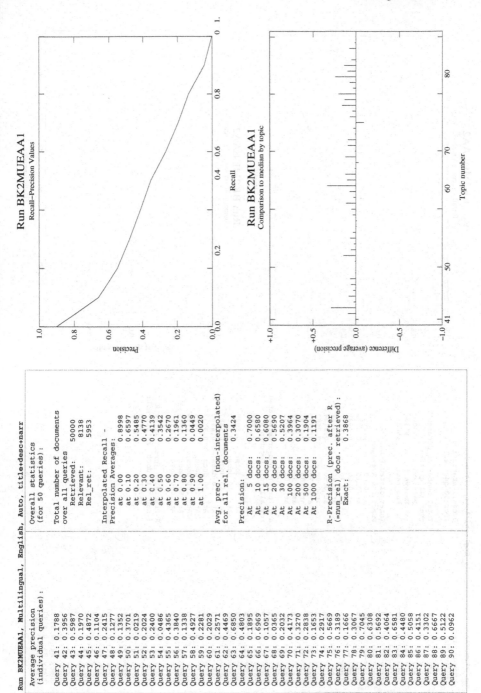

Run BK2MUEAA1
Recall–Precision Values

Recall

Precision

Run BK2MUEAA1
Comparison to median by topic

Topic number

Difference (average precision)

Run BK2MUEAA1, Multilingual, English, Auto, title+desc+narr

Average precision
(individual queries):

Query 41:	0.1788
Query 42:	0.3956
Query 43:	0.5987
Query 44:	0.1970
Query 45:	0.4872
Query 46:	0.1104
Query 47:	0.2415
Query 48:	0.1277
Query 49:	0.1352
Query 50:	0.3701
Query 51:	0.0219
Query 52:	0.2024
Query 53:	0.2400
Query 54:	0.0486
Query 55:	0.4365
Query 56:	0.3840
Query 57:	0.1338
Query 58:	0.4927
Query 59:	0.2281
Query 60:	0.2029
Query 61:	0.2571
Query 62:	0.4469
Query 63:	0.6850
Query 64:	0.4803
Query 65:	0.1895
Query 66:	0.6969
Query 67:	0.1057
Query 68:	0.0365
Query 69:	0.2032
Query 70:	0.4173
Query 71:	0.3270
Query 72:	0.2838
Query 73:	0.1653
Query 74:	0.2917
Query 75:	0.5669
Query 76:	0.3189
Query 77:	0.1666
Query 78:	0.3067
Query 79:	0.7045
Query 80:	0.6308
Query 81:	0.5692
Query 82:	0.4064
Query 83:	0.6581
Query 84:	0.4480
Query 85:	0.5058
Query 86:	0.4151
Query 87:	0.3302
Query 88:	0.6667
Query 89:	0.5122
Query 90:	0.0962

Overall statistics
(for 50 queries):

Total number of documents
over all queries:
Retrieved:	50000
Relevant:	8138
Rel_ret:	5953

Interpolated Recall –
Precision Averages:
at 0.00	0.8998
at 0.10	0.6597
at 0.20	0.5485
at 0.30	0.4770
at 0.40	0.4139
at 0.50	0.3542
at 0.60	0.2670
at 0.70	0.1961
at 0.80	0.1360
at 0.90	0.0449
at 1.00	0.0020

Avg. prec. (non-interpolated)
for all rel. documents
                0.3424

Precision:
At 5 docs:	0.7000
At 10 docs:	0.6580
At 15 docs:	0.6080
At 20 docs:	0.5690
At 30 docs:	0.5207
At 100 docs:	0.3964
At 200 docs:	0.3070
At 500 docs:	0.1904
At 1000 docs:	0.1191

R-Precision (prec. after R
(=num_rel) docs. retrieved):
Exact:	0.3868

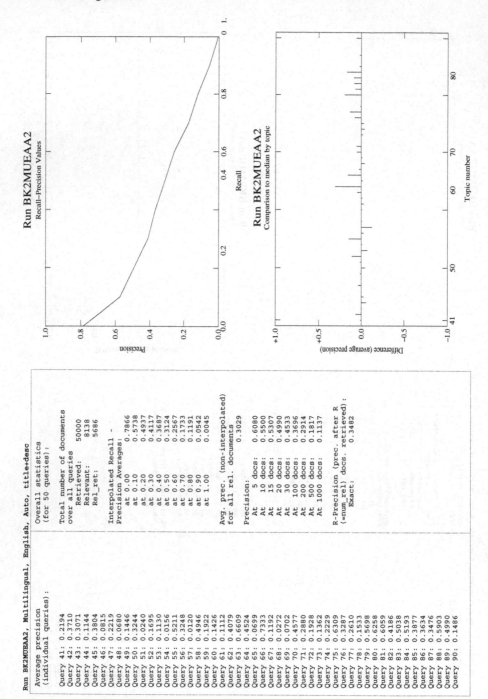

Run BK2MUEAA2
Recall-Precision Values

Run BK2MUEAA2
Comparison to median by topic

Run BK2MUEAA2, Multilingual, English, Auto, title+desc

Average precision
(individual queries):

Query 41:	0.2194	Query 64:	0.4524		
Query 42:	0.3710	Query 65:	0.0699		
Query 43:	0.3071	Query 66:	0.7333		
Query 44:	0.1144	Query 67:	0.1192		
Query 45:	0.3804	Query 68:	0.0272		
Query 46:	0.0815	Query 69:	0.0702		
Query 47:	0.2219	Query 70:	0.4577		
Query 48:	0.0680	Query 71:	0.2880		
Query 49:	0.1446	Query 72:	0.1928		
Query 50:	0.3244	Query 73:	0.1362		
Query 51:	0.0240	Query 74:	0.2229		
Query 52:	0.1695	Query 75:	0.6309		
Query 53:	0.1130	Query 76:	0.3287		
Query 54:	0.0156	Query 77:	0.2610		
Query 55:	0.5211	Query 78:	0.1533		
Query 56:	0.3248	Query 79:	0.5698		
Query 57:	0.0120	Query 80:	0.6258		
Query 58:	0.4946	Query 81:	0.6059		
Query 59:	0.1922	Query 82:	0.4186		
Query 60:	0.1426	Query 83:	0.5038		
Query 61:	0.1112	Query 84:	0.5193		
Query 62:	0.4079	Query 85:	0.3877		
Query 63:	0.6609	Query 86:	0.3634		
		Query 87:	0.3476		
		Query 88:	0.5903		
		Query 89:	0.4990		
		Query 90:	0.1486		

Overall statistics
(for 50 queries):

Total number of documents
over all queries
　　Retrieved:　　50000
　　Relevant:　　　8138
　　Rel_ret:　　　　5686

Interpolated Recall -
Precision Averages:
　　at 0.00　　0.7866
　　at 0.10　　0.5738
　　at 0.20　　0.4937
　　at 0.30　　0.4117
　　at 0.40　　0.3687
　　at 0.50　　0.3124
　　at 0.60　　0.2567
　　at 0.70　　0.1733
　　at 0.80　　0.1191
　　at 0.90　　0.0542
　　at 1.00　　0.0045

Avg. prec. (non-interpolated)
for all rel. documents
　　　　　　　0.3029

Precision:
　At　　5 docs:　　0.6080
　At　 10 docs:　　0.5500
　At　 15 docs:　　0.5307
　At　 20 docs:　　0.4990
　At　 30 docs:　　0.4533
　At　100 docs:　　0.3696
　At　200 docs:　　0.2914
　At　500 docs:　　0.1817
　At 1000 docs:　　0.1137

R-Precision (prec. after R
(=num_rel) docs. retrieved):
　　Exact:　　　　　0.3482

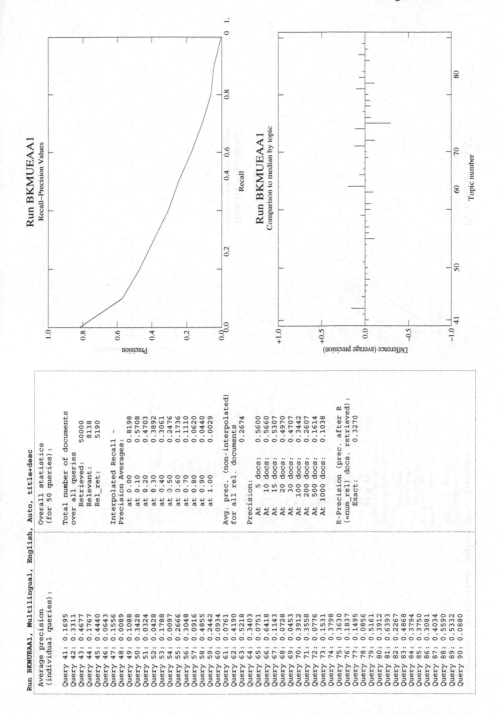

Run BKMUEAA1
Recall–Precision Values

Run BKMUEAA1
Comparison to median by topic

Run **BKMUEAA1**, Multilingual, English, Auto, title+desc

Average precision
(individual queries):

Query 41:	0.1695
Query 42:	0.3311
Query 43:	0.4677
Query 44:	0.1767
Query 45:	0.4440
Query 46:	0.0643
Query 47:	0.1556
Query 48:	0.0089
Query 49:	0.1088
Query 50:	0.3428
Query 51:	0.0324
Query 52:	0.0428
Query 53:	0.1788
Query 54:	0.0097
Query 55:	0.2666
Query 56:	0.3048
Query 57:	0.0916
Query 58:	0.4855
Query 59:	0.2442
Query 60:	0.0934
Query 61:	0.0761
Query 62:	0.4190
Query 63:	0.5218
Query 64:	0.3403
Query 65:	0.0751
Query 66:	0.6418
Query 67:	0.1143
Query 68:	0.0728
Query 69:	0.0453
Query 70:	0.3912
Query 71:	0.3558
Query 72:	0.0776
Query 73:	0.1531
Query 74:	0.3798
Query 75:	0.3630
Query 76:	0.1837
Query 77:	0.1495
Query 78:	0.0856
Query 79:	0.5161
Query 80:	0.3912
Query 81:	0.6393
Query 82:	0.2267
Query 83:	0.4868
Query 84:	0.3794
Query 85:	0.3750
Query 86:	0.3081
Query 87:	0.4034
Query 88:	0.5550
Query 89:	0.5332
Query 90:	0.0880

Overall statistics
(for 50 queries):

Total number of documents
over all queries
Retrieved:	50000
Relevant:	8138
Rel_ret:	5190

Interpolated Recall -
Precision Averages:
at 0.00	0.8198
at 0.10	0.5708
at 0.20	0.4703
at 0.30	0.3892
at 0.40	0.3061
at 0.50	0.2476
at 0.60	0.1736
at 0.70	0.1110
at 0.80	0.0620
at 0.90	0.0440
at 1.00	0.0029

Avg. prec. (non-interpolated)
for all rel. documents
                    0.2674

Precision:
At 5 docs:	0.5600
At 10 docs:	0.5660
At 15 docs:	0.5307
At 20 docs:	0.4970
At 30 docs:	0.4707
At 100 docs:	0.3442
At 200 docs:	0.2607
At 500 docs:	0.1614
At 1000 docs:	0.1038

R-Precision (prec. after R
(=num_rel) docs. retrieved):
        Exact: 0.3270

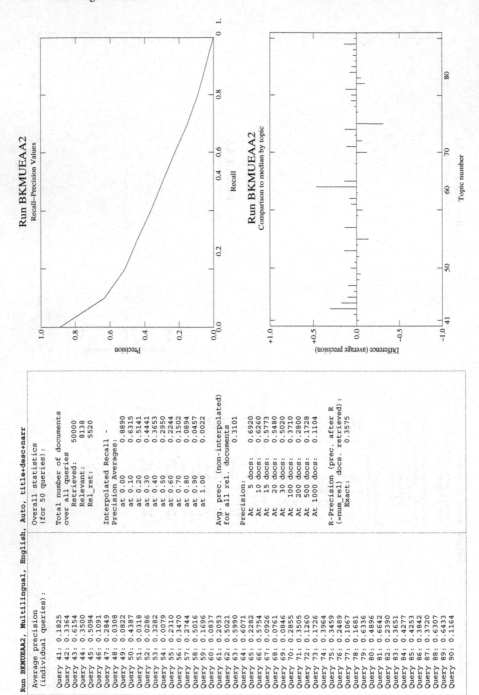

Run BKMUEAA2
Recall–Precision Values

Run BKMUEAA2
Comparison to median by topic

Run BKMUEAA2, Multilingual, English, Auto, title+desc+narr

Average precision
(individual queries):

Overall statistics
(for 50 queries):

Total number of documents
over all queries:
    Retrieved: 50000
    Relevant: 8138
    Rel_ret: 5520

Interpolated Recall -
Precision Averages:
    at 0.00   0.8890
    at 0.10   0.6315
    at 0.20   0.5141
    at 0.30   0.4441
    at 0.40   0.3653
    at 0.50   0.2950
    at 0.60   0.2244
    at 0.70   0.1502
    at 0.80   0.0894
    at 0.90   0.0457
    at 1.00   0.0022

Avg. prec. (non-interpolated)
for all rel. documents   0.3101

Precision:
    At   5 docs: 0.6920
    At   10 docs: 0.6260
    At   15 docs: 0.5773
    At   20 docs: 0.5480
    At   30 docs: 0.5020
    At 100 docs: 0.3710
    At 200 docs: 0.2800
    At 500 docs: 0.1728
    At 1000 docs: 0.1104

R-Precision (prec. after R
(=num_rel) docs. retrieved):
    Exact: 0.3575

Query 41:	0.1825
Query 42:	0.3364
Query 43:	0.6154
Query 44:	0.3500
Query 45:	0.5094
Query 46:	0.1091
Query 47:	0.2849
Query 48:	0.0308
Query 49:	0.0822
Query 50:	0.4387
Query 51:	0.0318
Query 52:	0.0286
Query 53:	0.3282
Query 54:	0.0079
Query 55:	0.2310
Query 56:	0.3470
Query 57:	0.2744
Query 58:	0.5016
Query 59:	0.1696
Query 60:	0.0837
Query 61:	0.2053
Query 62:	0.5021
Query 63:	0.5990
Query 64:	0.6071
Query 65:	0.2282
Query 66:	0.5754
Query 67:	0.0926
Query 68:	0.0761
Query 69:	0.0846
Query 70:	0.2855
Query 71:	0.3505
Query 72:	0.1260
Query 73:	0.1726
Query 74:	0.3964
Query 75:	0.3459
Query 76:	0.2489
Query 77:	0.1067
Query 78:	0.1681
Query 79:	0.6336
Query 80:	0.4896
Query 81:	0.6642
Query 82:	0.2390
Query 83:	0.3651
Query 84:	0.4277
Query 85:	0.4253
Query 86:	0.3842
Query 87:	0.3720
Query 88:	0.6307
Query 89:	0.6433
Query 90:	0.1164

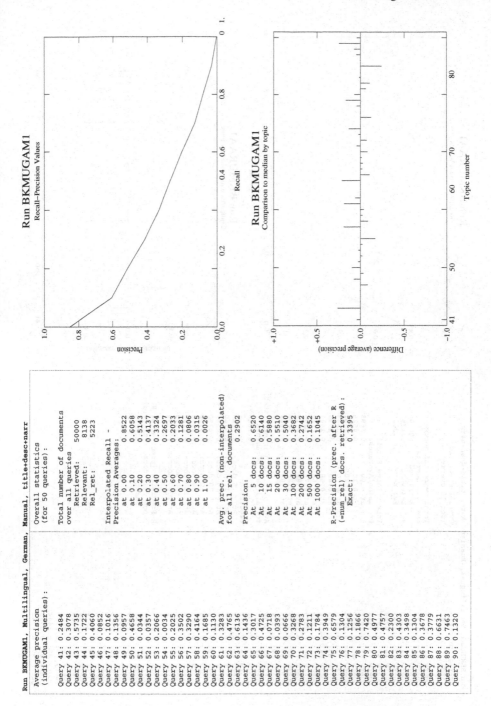

Run BKMUGAM1
Recall–Precision Values

Recall

Precision

Run BKMUGAM1
Comparison to median by topic

Difference (average precision)

Topic number

Run BKMUGAM1, Multilingual, German, Manual, title+desc+narr

Average precision
(individual queries):

Query 41:	0.2484
Query 42:	0.3078
Query 43:	0.5735
Query 44:	0.1722
Query 45:	0.4060
Query 46:	0.0852
Query 47:	0.1016
Query 48:	0.1356
Query 49:	0.0957
Query 50:	0.4658
Query 51:	0.0344
Query 52:	0.0357
Query 53:	0.2066
Query 54:	0.0034
Query 55:	0.2025
Query 56:	0.3502
Query 57:	0.3290
Query 58:	0.4164
Query 59:	0.1685
Query 60:	0.1130
Query 61:	0.3283
Query 62:	0.4765
Query 63:	0.6136
Query 64:	0.1436
Query 65:	0.3017
Query 66:	0.4725
Query 67:	0.0718
Query 68:	0.0393
Query 69:	0.0666
Query 70:	0.3268
Query 71:	0.2783
Query 72:	0.1211
Query 73:	0.1784
Query 74:	0.3949
Query 75:	0.6579
Query 76:	0.1304
Query 77:	0.1256
Query 78:	0.1866
Query 79:	0.7420
Query 80:	0.4977
Query 81:	0.4757
Query 82:	0.2300
Query 83:	0.4303
Query 84:	0.3498
Query 85:	0.1304
Query 86:	0.3678
Query 87:	0.3779
Query 88:	0.6631
Query 89:	0.7463
Query 90:	0.1320

Overall statistics
(for 50 queries):

Total number of documents
over all queries
Retrieved:	50000
Relevant:	8138
Rel_ret:	5223

Interpolated Recall -
Precision Averages:
at 0.00	0.8522
at 0.10	0.6058
at 0.20	0.5143
at 0.30	0.4137
at 0.40	0.3324
at 0.50	0.2697
at 0.60	0.2033
at 0.70	0.1281
at 0.80	0.0806
at 0.90	0.0315
at 1.00	0.0026

Avg. prec. (non-interpolated)
for all rel. documents
        0.2902

Precision:
At 5 docs:	0.6520
At 10 docs:	0.6140
At 15 docs:	0.5880
At 20 docs:	0.5510
At 30 docs:	0.5040
At 100 docs:	0.3682
At 200 docs:	0.2742
At 500 docs:	0.1652
At 1000 docs:	0.1045

R-Precision (prec. after R
(=num_rel) docs. retrieved):
        Exact: 0.3395

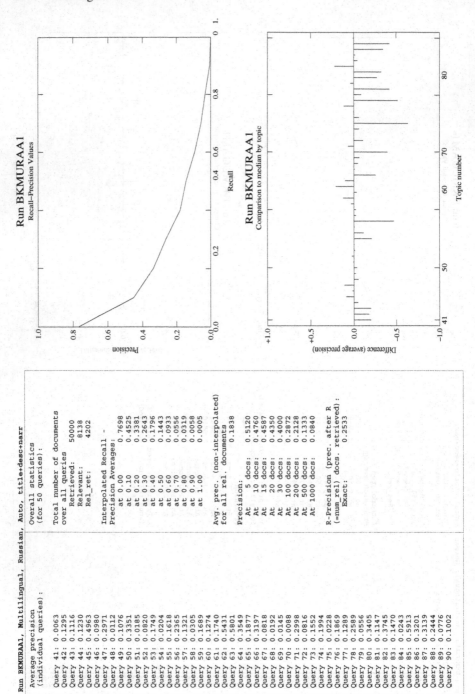

Run BKMURAA1
Recall-Precision Values

Run BKMURAA1
Comparison to median by topic

Run BKMURAA1, Multilingual, Russian, Auto, title+desc+narr

Average precision
(individual queries):

Query 41:	0.0063
Query 42:	0.1295
Query 43:	0.1116
Query 44:	0.1230
Query 45:	0.4963
Query 46:	0.0980
Query 47:	0.2971
Query 48:	0.0112
Query 49:	0.1076
Query 50:	0.3351
Query 51:	0.0185
Query 52:	0.0820
Query 53:	0.1749
Query 54:	0.0204
Query 55:	0.1618
Query 56:	0.2365
Query 57:	0.1321
Query 58:	0.0305
Query 59:	0.1689
Query 60:	0.1274
Query 61:	0.1740
Query 62:	0.5431
Query 63:	0.5801
Query 64:	0.3549
Query 65:	0.1877
Query 66:	0.3197
Query 67:	0.0818
Query 68:	0.0192
Query 69:	0.0145
Query 70:	0.0088
Query 71:	0.2998
Query 72:	0.0816
Query 73:	0.1552
Query 74:	0.1994
Query 75:	0.0228
Query 76:	0.1869
Query 77:	0.1289
Query 78:	0.2589
Query 79:	0.0556
Query 80:	0.3405
Query 81:	0.1147
Query 82:	0.3745
Query 83:	0.1470
Query 84:	0.0243
Query 85:	0.5913
Query 86:	0.3201
Query 87:	0.3139
Query 88:	0.2444
Query 89:	0.0776
Query 90:	0.1002

Overall statistics
(for 50 queries):

Total number of documents
over all queries
    Retrieved: 50000
    Relevant: 8138
    Rel_ret: 4202

Interpolated Recall -
Precision Averages:
    at 0.00   0.7698
    at 0.10   0.4525
    at 0.20   0.3381
    at 0.30   0.2643
    at 0.40   0.1796
    at 0.50   0.1443
    at 0.60   0.0933
    at 0.70   0.0556
    at 0.80   0.0319
    at 0.90   0.0058
    at 1.00   0.0005

Avg. prec. (non-interpolated)
for all rel. documents
                   0.1838

Precision:
    At   5 docs: 0.5120
    At   10 docs: 0.4760
    At   15 docs: 0.4587
    At   20 docs: 0.4350
    At   30 docs: 0.4000
    At 100 docs: 0.2872
    At 200 docs: 0.2128
    At 500 docs: 0.1333
    At 1000 docs: 0.0840

R-Precision (prec. after R
(=num_rel) docs. retrieved):
    Exact: 0.2533

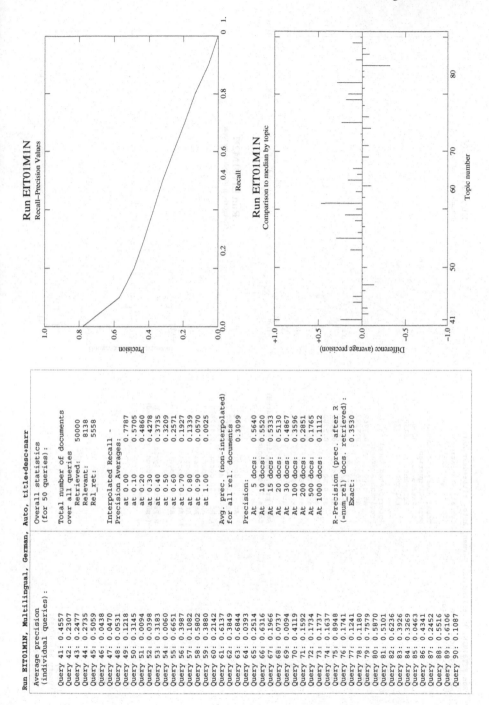

Run EIT01M1N
Recall–Precision Values

Precision

1.0

0.8

0.6

0.4

0.2

0.0

0.0   0.2   0.4   0.6   0.8   1.0

Recall

Run EIT01M1N
Comparison to median by topic

Difference (average precision)

+1.0

+0.5

0.0

−0.5

−1.0

41   50   60   70   80

Topic number

Run EIT01M1N, Multilingual, German, Auto, title+desc+narr

Average precision
(individual queries):

Query 41:	0.4557
Query 42:	0.2307
Query 43:	0.2477
Query 44:	0.2735
Query 45:	0.5059
Query 46:	0.0438
Query 47:	0.0470
Query 48:	0.0531
Query 49:	0.1218
Query 50:	0.3145
Query 51:	0.0094
Query 52:	0.0398
Query 53:	0.3183
Query 54:	0.0060
Query 55:	0.6651
Query 56:	0.3987
Query 57:	0.1082
Query 58:	0.5802
Query 59:	0.3880
Query 60:	0.2142
Query 61:	0.6137
Query 62:	0.3849
Query 63:	0.6844
Query 64:	0.0393
Query 65:	0.2514
Query 66:	0.6316
Query 67:	0.1966
Query 68:	0.0737
Query 69:	0.0094
Query 70:	0.4119
Query 71:	0.1592
Query 72:	0.1734
Query 73:	0.1737
Query 74:	0.1637
Query 75:	0.8948
Query 76:	0.1741
Query 77:	0.1241
Query 78:	0.1180
Query 79:	0.7579
Query 80:	0.5870
Query 81:	0.5101
Query 82:	0.6236
Query 83:	0.3926
Query 84:	0.3269
Query 85:	0.0463
Query 86:	0.4341
Query 87:	0.2452
Query 88:	0.5516
Query 89:	0.6106
Query 90:	0.1087

Overall statistics
(for 50 queries):

Total number of documents
over all queries
Retrieved:	50000
Relevant:	8138
Rel_ret:	5558

Interpolated Recall -
Precision Averages:
at 0.00	0.7787
at 0.10	0.5705
at 0.20	0.4860
at 0.30	0.4278
at 0.40	0.3735
at 0.50	0.3209
at 0.60	0.2571
at 0.70	0.1927
at 0.80	0.1339
at 0.90	0.0570
at 1.00	0.0025

Avg. prec. (non-interpolated)
for all rel. documents
                         0.3099

Precision:
At	5 docs:	0.5640
At	10 docs:	0.5520
At	15 docs:	0.5333
At	20 docs:	0.5130
At	30 docs:	0.4867
At	100 docs:	0.3596
At	200 docs:	0.2851
At	500 docs:	0.1765
At	1000 docs:	0.1112

R-Precision (prec. after R
(=num_rel) docs. retrieved):
Exact:	0.3530

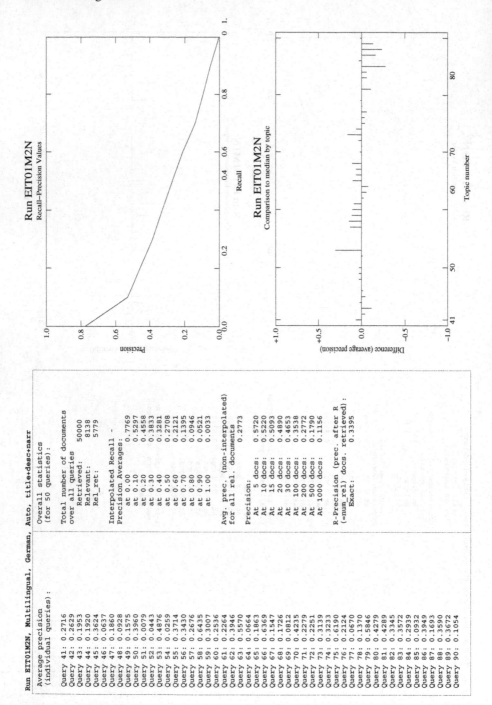

Run EIT01M2N, Multilingual, German, Auto, title+desc+narr

Average precision
(individual queries):

Query 41: 0.2716
Query 42: 0.2629
Query 43: 0.1953
Query 44: 0.1920
Query 45: 0.3624
Query 46: 0.0637
Query 47: 0.1860
Query 48: 0.0928
Query 49: 0.1575
Query 50: 0.3960
Query 51: 0.0079
Query 52: 0.0443
Query 53: 0.4876
Query 54: 0.0259
Query 55: 0.3714
Query 56: 0.3430
Query 57: 0.2676
Query 58: 0.6435
Query 59: 0.3007
Query 60: 0.2536
Query 61: 0.2264
Query 62: 0.3946
Query 63: 0.5570
Query 64: 0.0664
Query 65: 0.1863
Query 66: 0.6369
Query 67: 0.1547
Query 68: 0.1726
Query 69: 0.0812
Query 70: 0.4235
Query 71: 0.2279
Query 72: 0.2251
Query 73: 0.3139
Query 74: 0.3233
Query 75: 0.6190
Query 76: 0.2124
Query 77: 0.0670
Query 78: 0.1370
Query 79: 0.5846
Query 80: 0.4279
Query 81: 0.4289
Query 82: 0.3345
Query 83: 0.3572
Query 84: 0.2939
Query 85: 0.0932
Query 86: 0.3949
Query 87: 0.1693
Query 88: 0.3590
Query 89: 0.3672
Query 90: 0.1054

Overall statistics
(for 50 queries):

Total number of documents
over all queries
    Retrieved: 50000
    Relevant: 8138
    Rel_ret: 5779

Interpolated Recall -
Precision Averages:
    at 0.00   0.7769
    at 0.10   0.5297
    at 0.20   0.4558
    at 0.30   0.3833
    at 0.40   0.3281
    at 0.50   0.2708
    at 0.60   0.2121
    at 0.70   0.1395
    at 0.80   0.0946
    at 0.90   0.0521
    at 1.00   0.0033

Avg. prec. (non-interpolated)
for all rel. documents
                   0.2773

Precision:
    At   5 docs: 0.5720
    At   10 docs: 0.5220
    At   15 docs: 0.5093
    At   20 docs: 0.4890
    At   30 docs: 0.4653
    At 100 docs: 0.3538
    At 200 docs: 0.2772
    At 500 docs: 0.1790
    At 1000 docs: 0.1156

R-Precision (prec. after R
(=num_rel) docs. retrieved):
    Exact: 0.3395

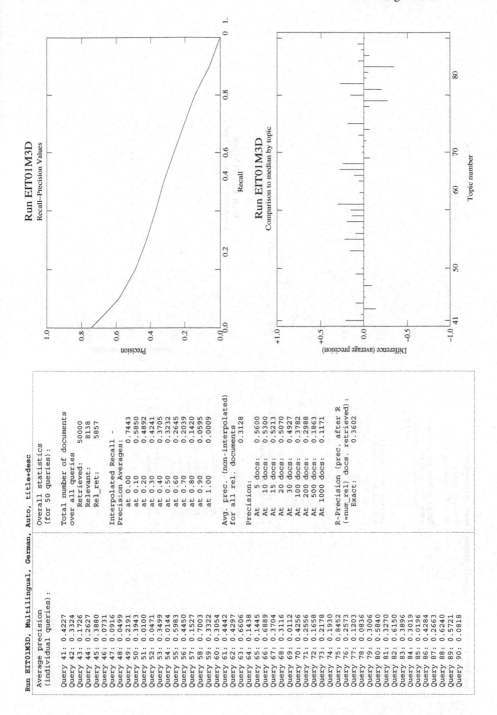

Run EIT01M3D
Recall–Precision Values

Run EIT01M3D
Comparison to median by topic

Run EIT01M3D, Multilingual, German, Auto, title+desc

Average precision
(individual queries):

Query 41:	0.4227
Query 42:	0.3324
Query 43:	0.1726
Query 44:	0.2627
Query 45:	0.3880
Query 46:	0.0731
Query 47:	0.0916
Query 48:	0.0499
Query 49:	0.2191
Query 50:	0.3943
Query 51:	0.0100
Query 52:	0.0471
Query 53:	0.3499
Query 54:	0.0144
Query 55:	0.5983
Query 56:	0.4450
Query 57:	0.1527
Query 58:	0.7003
Query 59:	0.3322
Query 60:	0.3054
Query 61:	0.4442
Query 62:	0.4297
Query 63:	0.6606
Query 64:	0.1438
Query 65:	0.1445
Query 66:	0.6889
Query 67:	0.3704
Query 68:	0.3116
Query 69:	0.0112
Query 70:	0.4256
Query 71:	0.2556
Query 72:	0.1658
Query 73:	0.2178
Query 74:	0.1930
Query 75:	0.8452
Query 76:	0.2573
Query 77:	0.1203
Query 78:	0.0836
Query 79:	0.3006
Query 80:	0.5840
Query 81:	0.3270
Query 82:	0.6150
Query 83:	0.3896
Query 84:	0.3019
Query 85:	0.0196
Query 86:	0.4284
Query 87:	0.2663
Query 88:	0.6240
Query 89:	0.5721
Query 90:	0.0818

Overall statistics
(for 50 queries):

Total number of documents
over all queries
Retrieved:	50000
Relevant:	8138
Rel_ret:	5857

Interpolated Recall -
Precision Averages:
at 0.00	0.7443
at 0.10	0.5850
at 0.20	0.4892
at 0.30	0.4241
at 0.40	0.3705
at 0.50	0.3232
at 0.60	0.2645
at 0.70	0.2039
at 0.80	0.1420
at 0.90	0.0595
at 1.00	0.0009

Avg. prec. (non-interpolated)
for all rel. documents
                          0.3128

Precision:
At 5 docs:	0.5600
At 10 docs:	0.5300
At 15 docs:	0.5213
At 20 docs:	0.5070
At 30 docs:	0.4927
At 100 docs:	0.3782
At 200 docs:	0.2988
At 500 docs:	0.1863
At 1000 docs:	0.1171

R-Precision (prec. after R
(=num_rel) docs. retrieved):
| Exact: | 0.3602 |

Run EIT01M3N
Recall-Precision Values

Run EIT01M3N
Comparison to median by topic

Run EIT01M3N, Multilingual, German, Auto, title+desc+narr

Average precision
(individual queries):

Query 41:	0.4473
Query 42:	0.3044
Query 43:	0.2545
Query 44:	0.2669
Query 45:	0.5004
Query 46:	0.0602
Query 47:	0.1378
Query 48:	0.0906
Query 49:	0.1553
Query 50:	0.3886
Query 51:	0.0103
Query 52:	0.0613
Query 53:	0.4429
Query 54:	0.0146
Query 55:	0.6289
Query 56:	0.4190
Query 57:	0.2038
Query 58:	0.6664
Query 59:	0.3854
Query 60:	0.2937
Query 61:	0.4923
Query 62:	0.4489
Query 63:	0.7040
Query 64:	0.0803
Query 65:	0.2750
Query 66:	0.6922
Query 67:	0.2186
Query 68:	0.1420
Query 69:	0.0391
Query 70:	0.4445
Query 71:	0.2378
Query 72:	0.2242
Query 73:	0.2796
Query 74:	0.2634
Query 75:	0.9020
Query 76:	0.2379
Query 77:	0.1084
Query 78:	0.1670
Query 79:	0.7641
Query 80:	0.5726
Query 81:	0.5156
Query 82:	0.5702
Query 83:	0.4080
Query 84:	0.3521
Query 85:	0.0720
Query 86:	0.4801
Query 87:	0.2836
Query 88:	0.6350
Query 89:	0.6177
Query 90:	0.1213

Overall statistics
(for 50 queries):

Total number of documents
over all queries

Retrieved:	50000
Relevant:	8138
Rel_ret:	6034

Interpolated Recall -
Precision Averages:

at 0.00	0.7570
at 0.10	0.6215
at 0.20	0.5390
at 0.30	0.4744
at 0.40	0.4159
at 0.50	0.3553
at 0.60	0.2859
at 0.70	0.2240
at 0.80	0.1457
at 0.90	0.0779
at 1.00	0.0018

Avg. prec. (non-interpolated)
for all rel. documents
          0.3416

Precision:

At	5 docs:	0.5720
At	10 docs:	0.5700
At	15 docs:	0.5587
At	20 docs:	0.5460
At	30 docs:	0.5220
At	100 docs:	0.3984
At	200 docs:	0.3119
At	500 docs:	0.1924
At	1000 docs:	0.1207

R-Precision (prec. after R
(=num_rel docs. retrieved):
          Exact: 0.3909

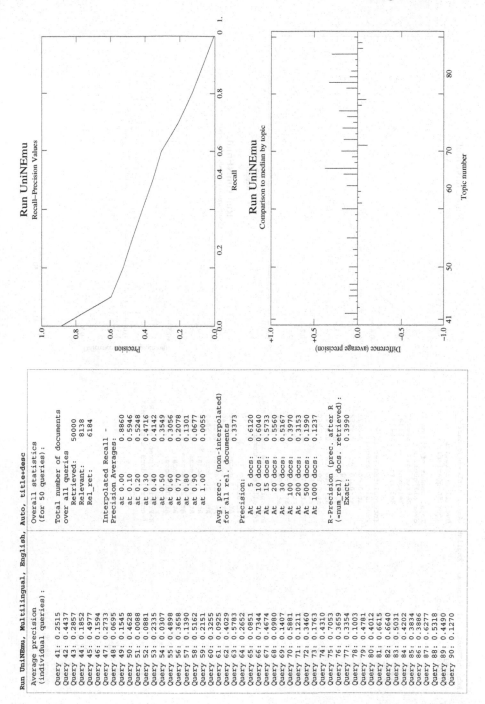

Run UniNEmu
Recall–Precision Values

Run UniNEmu
Comparison to median by topic

Run UniNEmu, Multilingual, English, Auto, title+desc

Average precision
(individual queries):

Query 41:	0.2515
Query 42:	0.4437
Query 43:	0.2857
Query 44:	0.1852
Query 45:	0.4977
Query 46:	0.1594
Query 47:	0.2733
Query 48:	0.0695
Query 49:	0.1545
Query 50:	0.4628
Query 51:	0.0088
Query 52:	0.0881
Query 53:	0.2335
Query 54:	0.0307
Query 55:	0.4898
Query 56:	0.3658
Query 57:	0.1390
Query 58:	0.5162
Query 59:	0.2151
Query 60:	0.3255
Query 61:	0.0925
Query 62:	0.4029
Query 63:	0.5783
Query 64:	0.2652
Query 65:	0.0851
Query 66:	0.7344
Query 67:	0.4674
Query 68:	0.0980
Query 69:	0.1407
Query 70:	0.5881
Query 71:	0.1211
Query 72:	0.3460
Query 73:	0.1763
Query 74:	0.4310
Query 75:	0.7053
Query 76:	0.3659
Query 77:	0.3354
Query 78:	0.1003
Query 79:	0.4781
Query 80:	0.4012
Query 81:	0.6615
Query 82:	0.6640
Query 83:	0.5031
Query 84:	0.4202
Query 85:	0.3834
Query 86:	0.3886
Query 87:	0.6277
Query 88:	0.5318
Query 89:	0.4490
Query 90:	0.1270

Overall statistics
(for 50 queries):

Total number of documents
over all queries
Retrieved:	50000
Relevant:	8138
Rel_ret:	6184

Interpolated Recall -
Precision Averages:
at 0.00	0.8860
at 0.10	0.5946
at 0.20	0.5248
at 0.30	0.4716
at 0.40	0.4142
at 0.50	0.3549
at 0.60	0.3056
at 0.70	0.2078
at 0.80	0.1301
at 0.90	0.0677
at 1.00	0.0055

Avg. prec. (non-interpolated)
for all rel. documents
                        0.3373

Precision:
At 5 docs:	0.6120
At 10 docs:	0.6040
At 15 docs:	0.5733
At 20 docs:	0.5560
At 30 docs:	0.5167
At 100 docs:	0.3970
At 200 docs:	0.3153
At 500 docs:	0.1990
At 1000 docs:	0.1237

R-Precision (prec. after R
(=num_rel) docs. retrieved):
Exact:	0.3990

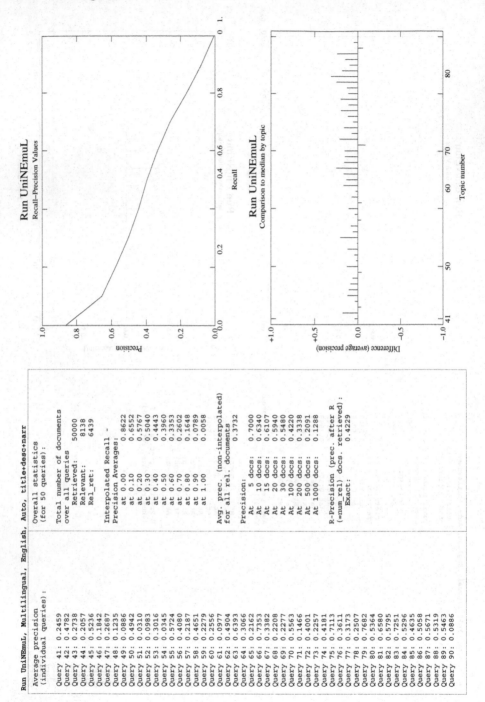

Run UniNEmuL
Recall–Precision Values

Precision

1.0
0.8
0.6
0.4
0.2
0.0

0.0   0.2   0.4   0.6   0.8   0. 1.

Recall

Run UniNEmuL
Comparison to median by topic

Difference (average precision)

+1.0
+0.5
0.0
-0.5
-1.0

41   50   60   70   80

Topic number

Run UniNEmuL, Multilingual, English, Auto, title+desc+narr

Average precision
(individual queries):

Query 41: 0.2459
Query 42: 0.4782
Query 43: 0.2738
Query 44: 0.2057
Query 45: 0.5236
Query 46: 0.1842
Query 47: 0.2687
Query 48: 0.1235
Query 49: 0.0886
Query 50: 0.4942
Query 51: 0.0310
Query 52: 0.0983
Query 53: 0.3016
Query 54: 0.0345
Query 55: 0.5724
Query 56: 0.4080
Query 57: 0.2187
Query 58: 0.4651
Query 59: 0.2279
Query 60: 0.2556
Query 61: 0.0977
Query 62: 0.4904
Query 63: 0.6393
Query 64: 0.3066
Query 65: 0.2162
Query 66: 0.7353
Query 67: 0.3382
Query 68: 0.2208
Query 69: 0.2277
Query 70: 0.5563
Query 71: 0.1466
Query 72: 0.4001
Query 73: 0.2257
Query 74: 0.4181
Query 75: 0.7113
Query 76: 0.3611
Query 77: 0.3173
Query 78: 0.2507
Query 79: 0.7682
Query 80: 0.5364
Query 81: 0.6580
Query 82: 0.5795
Query 83: 0.7251
Query 84: 0.5296
Query 85: 0.4635
Query 86: 0.5058
Query 87: 0.5671
Query 88: 0.5319
Query 89: 0.5463
Query 90: 0.0886

Overall statistics
(for 50 queries):

Total number of documents
over all queries
    Retrieved: 50000
    Relevant: 8138
    Rel_ret: 6439

Interpolated Recall -
Precision Averages:
    at 0.00   0.8622
    at 0.10   0.6552
    at 0.20   0.5767
    at 0.30   0.5040
    at 0.40   0.4443
    at 0.50   0.3960
    at 0.60   0.3353
    at 0.70   0.2602
    at 0.80   0.1648
    at 0.90   0.0789
    at 1.00   0.0058

Avg. prec. (non-interpolated)
for all rel. documents
                    0.3732

Precision:
    At   5 docs: 0.7000
    At   10 docs: 0.6340
    At   15 docs: 0.6107
    At   20 docs: 0.5940
    At   30 docs: 0.5480
    At 100 docs: 0.4220
    At 200 docs: 0.3338
    At 500 docs: 0.2091
    At 1000 docs: 0.1288

R-Precision (prec. after R
(=num_rel) docs. retrieved):
    Exact: 0.4229

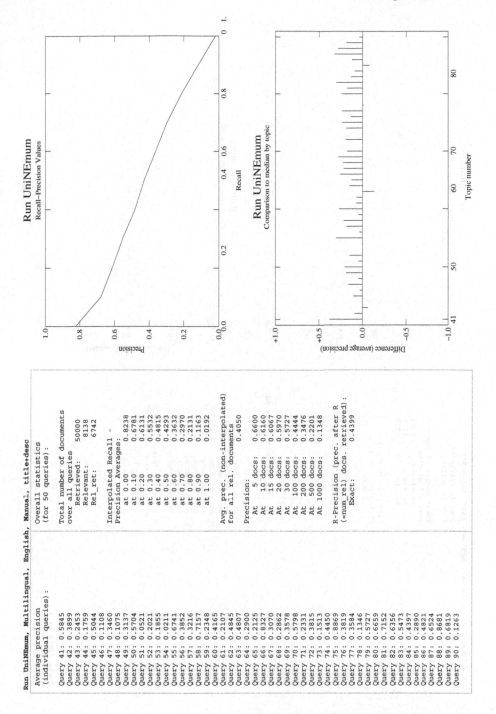

Run UniNEmum

Recall–Precision Values

Recall / Precision

Run UniNEmum

Comparison to median by topic

Difference (average precision) / Topic number

Run UniNEmum, Multilingual, English, Manual, title+desc

Average precision
(individual queries):

Query 41:	0.5845
Query 42:	0.3899
Query 43:	0.2453
Query 44:	0.1759
Query 45:	0.5044
Query 46:	0.1108
Query 47:	0.3460
Query 48:	0.1075
Query 49:	0.3137
Query 50:	0.5704
Query 51:	0.0521
Query 52:	0.2021
Query 53:	0.1855
Query 54:	0.0211
Query 55:	0.6741
Query 56:	0.3852
Query 57:	0.3216
Query 58:	0.7157
Query 59:	0.2348
Query 60:	0.4165
Query 61:	0.2107
Query 62:	0.4845
Query 63:	0.4807
Query 64:	0.2900
Query 65:	0.2125
Query 66:	0.8327
Query 67:	0.3070
Query 68:	0.2862
Query 69:	0.5798
Query 70:	0.5798
Query 71:	0.2331
Query 72:	0.3815
Query 73:	0.1513
Query 74:	0.4450
Query 75:	0.8869
Query 76:	0.3819
Query 77:	0.3584
Query 78:	0.1346
Query 79:	0.5727
Query 80:	0.6659
Query 81:	0.7152
Query 82:	0.6356
Query 83:	0.5473
Query 84:	0.4397
Query 85:	0.2890
Query 86:	0.4821
Query 87:	0.6524
Query 88:	0.8681
Query 89:	0.6819
Query 90:	0.1263

Overall statistics
(for 50 queries):

Total number of documents
over all queries
Retrieved:	50000
Relevant:	8138
Rel_ret:	6742

Interpolated Recall -
Precision Averages:
at 0.00	0.8238
at 0.10	0.6781
at 0.20	0.6131
at 0.30	0.5532
at 0.40	0.4815
at 0.50	0.4293
at 0.60	0.3632
at 0.70	0.2970
at 0.80	0.2131
at 0.90	0.1163
at 1.00	0.0192

Avg. prec. (non-interpolated)
for all rel. documents   0.4050

Precision:
At 5 docs:	0.6600
At 10 docs:	0.6160
At 15 docs:	0.6067
At 20 docs:	0.5970
At 30 docs:	0.5727
At 100 docs:	0.4444
At 200 docs:	0.3476
At 500 docs:	0.2201
At 1000 docs:	0.1348

R-Precision (prec. after R
(=num_rel) docs. retrieved):
Exact: 0.4399

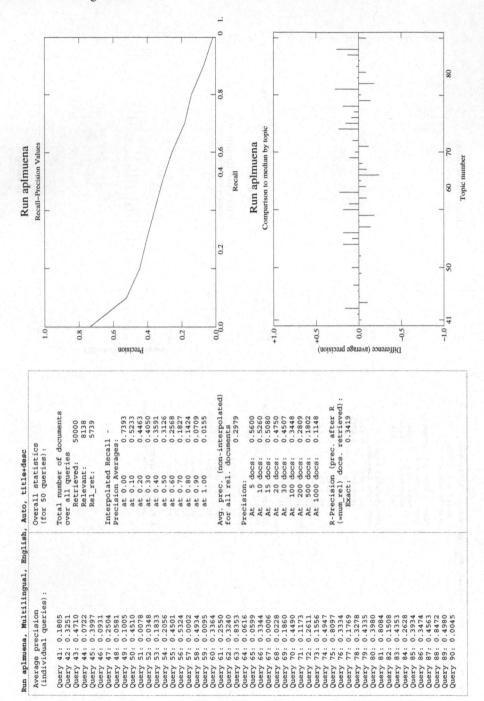

Run aplmuena
Recall–Precision Values

Run aplmuena
Comparison to median by topic

Run aplmuena, Multilingual, English, Auto, title+desc

Average precision
(individual queries):

Query 41:	0.1805
Query 42:	0.3251
Query 43:	0.4710
Query 44:	0.0722
Query 45:	0.3997
Query 46:	0.0931
Query 47:	0.2504
Query 48:	0.0581
Query 49:	0.1005
Query 50:	0.4510
Query 51:	0.0078
Query 52:	0.0348
Query 53:	0.1833
Query 54:	0.2056
Query 55:	0.4501
Query 56:	0.5324
Query 57:	0.0002
Query 58:	0.4934
Query 59:	0.0095
Query 60:	0.3364
Query 61:	0.2550
Query 62:	0.3240
Query 63:	0.8353
Query 64:	0.0616
Query 65:	0.0599
Query 66:	0.3344
Query 67:	0.0006
Query 68:	0.0228
Query 69:	0.1860
Query 70:	0.4490
Query 71:	0.1173
Query 72:	0.2611
Query 73:	0.1556
Query 74:	0.4947
Query 75:	0.8097
Query 76:	0.3334
Query 77:	0.1769
Query 78:	0.3278
Query 79:	0.4335
Query 80:	0.3980
Query 81:	0.8084
Query 82:	0.1508
Query 83:	0.4353
Query 84:	0.2628
Query 85:	0.3934
Query 86:	0.3474
Query 87:	0.4563
Query 88:	0.8472
Query 89:	0.4980
Query 90:	0.0045

Overall statistics
(for 50 queries):

Total number of documents
over all queries:
Retrieved:	50000
Relevant:	8138
Rel_ret:	5739

Interpolated Recall -
Precision Averages:
at 0.00	0.7393
at 0.10	0.5233
at 0.20	0.4463
at 0.30	0.4050
at 0.40	0.3591
at 0.50	0.3126
at 0.60	0.2568
at 0.70	0.1827
at 0.80	0.1424
at 0.90	0.0709
at 1.00	0.0155

Avg. prec. (non-interpolated)
for all rel. documents
0.2979

Precision:
At	5 docs:	0.5600
At	10 docs:	0.5260
At	15 docs:	0.5080
At	20 docs:	0.4750
At	30 docs:	0.4507
At	100 docs:	0.3448
At	200 docs:	0.2809
At	500 docs:	0.1802
At	1000 docs:	0.1148

R-Precision (prec. after R
(=num_rel) docs. retrieved):
Exact: 0.3419

Run aplmuenb

Recall–Precision Values

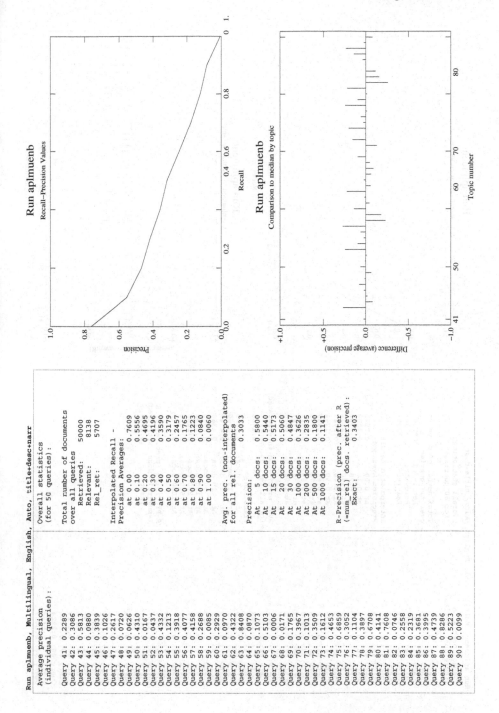

Run aplmuenb

Comparison to median by topic

Run aplmuenb, Multilingual, English, Auto, title+desc+narr

Average precision
(individual queries):

Query 41:	0.2289
Query 42:	0.3086
Query 43:	0.5813
Query 44:	0.0880
Query 45:	0.3839
Query 46:	0.1026
Query 47:	0.2617
Query 48:	0.0720
Query 49:	0.0626
Query 50:	0.4310
Query 51:	0.0167
Query 52:	0.0437
Query 53:	0.4332
Query 54:	0.1213
Query 55:	0.3918
Query 56:	0.4077
Query 57:	0.4158
Query 58:	0.2688
Query 59:	0.0085
Query 60:	0.2929
Query 61:	0.0970
Query 62:	0.4322
Query 63:	0.8408
Query 64:	0.0870
Query 65:	0.1073
Query 66:	0.5103
Query 67:	0.0006
Query 68:	0.0171
Query 69:	0.1765
Query 70:	0.3967
Query 71:	0.1013
Query 72:	0.3509
Query 73:	0.1612
Query 74:	0.4653
Query 75:	0.6859
Query 76:	0.3052
Query 77:	0.1104
Query 78:	0.3897
Query 79:	0.6708
Query 80:	0.4141
Query 81:	0.7608
Query 82:	0.0746
Query 83:	0.2558
Query 84:	0.2319
Query 85:	0.3681
Query 86:	0.3995
Query 87:	0.4739
Query 88:	0.8286
Query 89:	0.5223
Query 90:	0.0099

Overall statistics
(for 50 queries):

Total number of documents
over all queries:

Retrieved:	50000
Relevant:	8138
Rel_ret:	5707

Interpolated Recall -
Precision Averages:

at 0.00	0.7609
at 0.10	0.5556
at 0.20	0.4695
at 0.30	0.4196
at 0.40	0.3590
at 0.50	0.3179
at 0.60	0.2457
at 0.70	0.1765
at 0.80	0.1223
at 0.90	0.0840
at 1.00	0.0060

Avg. prec. (non-interpolated)
for all rel. documents
                    0.3033

Precision:

At	5 docs:	0.5800
At	10 docs:	0.5440
At	15 docs:	0.5173
At	20 docs:	0.5060
At	30 docs:	0.4847
At	100 docs:	0.3626
At	200 docs:	0.2835
At	500 docs:	0.1800
At	1000 docs:	0.1141

R-Precision (prec. after R
(=num_rel) docs. retrieved):
            Exact: 0.3403

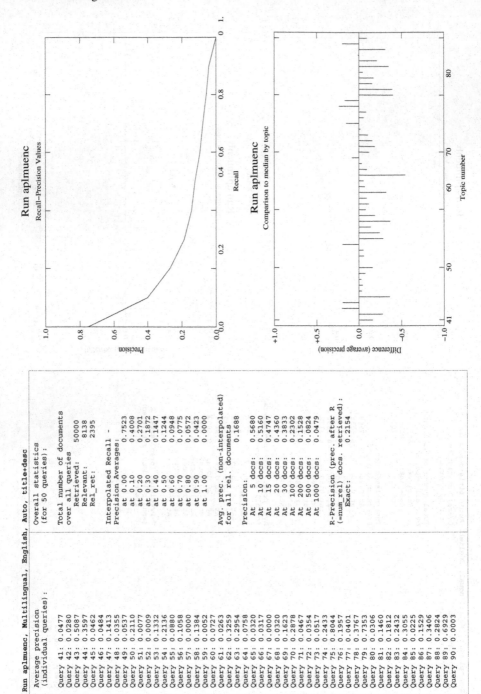

Run aplmuenc
Recall-Precision Values

Run aplmuenc
Comparison to median by topic

Run aplmuenc, Multilingual, English, Auto, title+desc

Average precision
(individual queries):

Query 41:	0.0477
Query 42:	0.0280
Query 43:	0.5087
Query 44:	0.3597
Query 45:	0.0462
Query 46:	0.0484
Query 47:	0.1413
Query 48:	0.0355
Query 49:	0.0537
Query 50:	0.2110
Query 51:	0.0077
Query 52:	0.0009
Query 53:	0.1332
Query 54:	0.2136
Query 55:	0.0880
Query 56:	0.1058
Query 57:	0.0000
Query 58:	0.1384
Query 59:	0.0052
Query 60:	0.0727
Query 61:	0.0263
Query 62:	0.3259
Query 63:	0.2954
Query 64:	0.0758
Query 65:	0.0320
Query 66:	0.0317
Query 67:	0.0000
Query 68:	0.0320
Query 69:	0.1623
Query 70:	0.2878
Query 71:	0.0467
Query 72:	0.0354
Query 73:	0.0517
Query 74:	0.2433
Query 75:	0.8044
Query 76:	0.1957
Query 77:	0.0401
Query 78:	0.3767
Query 79:	0.7353
Query 80:	0.0306
Query 81:	0.1460
Query 82:	0.1812
Query 83:	0.2432
Query 84:	0.3055
Query 85:	0.0225
Query 86:	0.1529
Query 87:	0.3406
Query 88:	0.2824
Query 89:	0.6929
Query 90:	0.0003

Overall statistics
(for 50 queries):

Total number of documents
over all queries
  Retrieved: 50000
  Relevant: 8138
  Rel_ret: 2395

Interpolated Recall -
Precision Averages:

at 0.00	0.7523
at 0.10	0.4008
at 0.20	0.2701
at 0.30	0.1872
at 0.40	0.1447
at 0.50	0.1244
at 0.60	0.0948
at 0.70	0.0775
at 0.80	0.0572
at 0.90	0.0423
at 1.00	0.0000

Avg. prec. (non-interpolated)
for all rel. documents
     0.1688

Precision:
At	5 docs:	0.5680
At	10 docs:	0.5160
At	15 docs:	0.4747
At	20 docs:	0.4360
At	30 docs:	0.3833
At	100 docs:	0.2302
At	200 docs:	0.1528
At	500 docs:	0.0824
At	1000 docs:	0.0479

R-Precision (prec. after R
(=num_rel) docs. retrieved):
    Exact: 0.2154

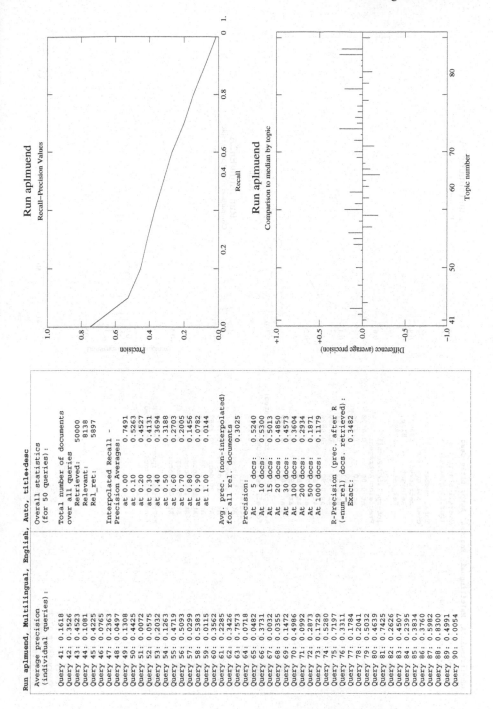

Run aplmuend

Recall–Precision Values

Recall

Precision

Run aplmuend

Comparison to median by topic

Topic number

Difference (average precision)

Run aplmuend, Multilingual, English, Auto, title+desc

Average precision
(individual queries):

Query 41:	0.1618
Query 42:	0.3526
Query 43:	0.4523
Query 44:	0.1081
Query 45:	0.4225
Query 46:	0.07765
Query 47:	0.2363
Query 48:	0.0497
Query 49:	0.1308
Query 50:	0.4425
Query 51:	0.0072
Query 52:	0.0575
Query 53:	0.2032
Query 54:	0.1263
Query 55:	0.4719
Query 56:	0.5093
Query 57:	0.0299
Query 58:	0.5383
Query 59:	0.0115
Query 60:	0.3562
Query 61:	0.2285
Query 62:	0.3426
Query 63:	0.7573
Query 64:	0.0718
Query 65:	0.0482
Query 66:	0.3731
Query 67:	0.0032
Query 68:	0.0355
Query 69:	0.1472
Query 70:	0.4986
Query 71:	0.0992
Query 72:	0.2873
Query 73:	0.1729
Query 74:	0.5280
Query 75:	0.7197
Query 76:	0.3311
Query 77:	0.1784
Query 78:	0.2041
Query 79:	0.5032
Query 80:	0.4639
Query 81:	0.7425
Query 82:	0.2626
Query 83:	0.4507
Query 84:	0.2395
Query 85:	0.3834
Query 86:	0.3760
Query 87:	0.5982
Query 88:	0.8300
Query 89:	0.4991
Query 90:	0.0054

Overall statistics
(for 50 queries):

Total number of documents
over all queries
Retrieved:	50000
Relevant:	8138
Rel_ret:	5897

Interpolated Recall -
Precision Averages:
at 0.00	0.7491
at 0.10	0.5263
at 0.20	0.4527
at 0.30	0.4131
at 0.40	0.3694
at 0.50	0.3188
at 0.60	0.2703
at 0.70	0.2005
at 0.80	0.1456
at 0.90	0.0782
at 1.00	0.0144

Avg. prec. (non-interpolated)
for all rel. documents
                0.3025

Precision:
At 5 docs:	0.5240
At 10 docs:	0.5300
At 15 docs:	0.5013
At 20 docs:	0.4850
At 30 docs:	0.4573
At 100 docs:	0.3604
At 200 docs:	0.2934
At 500 docs:	0.1871
At 1000 docs:	0.1179

R-Precision (prec. after R
(=num_rel) docs. retrieved) :
        Exact: 0.3482

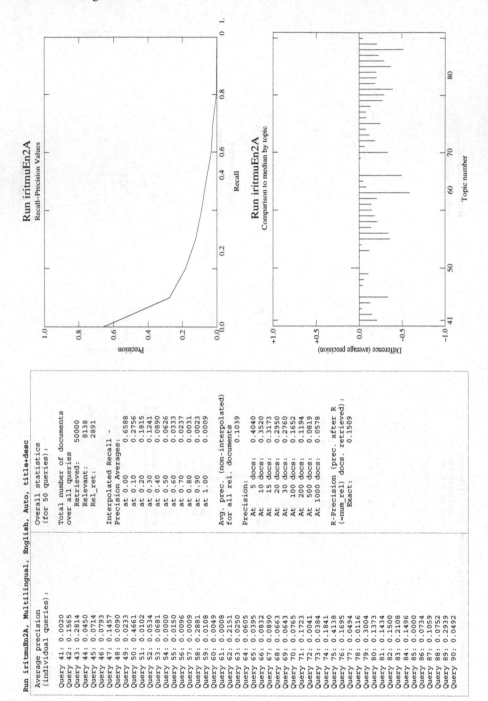

Run iritmuEn2A
Recall–Precision Values

Run iritmuEn2A
Comparison to median by topic

Run iritmuEn2A, Multilingual, English, Auto, title+desc

Average precision
(individual queries):

Query 41:	0.0020
Query 42:	0.1565
Query 43:	0.2814
Query 44:	0.0450
Query 45:	0.0714
Query 46:	0.0793
Query 47:	0.1457
Query 48:	0.0090
Query 49:	0.0233
Query 50:	0.4661
Query 51:	0.0102
Query 52:	0.0534
Query 53:	0.0681
Query 54:	0.0000
Query 55:	0.0150
Query 56:	0.0096
Query 57:	0.0009
Query 58:	0.2881
Query 59:	0.0108
Query 60:	0.0049
Query 61:	0.0008
Query 62:	0.2151
Query 63:	0.0250
Query 64:	0.0605
Query 65:	0.0395
Query 66:	0.0832
Query 67:	0.0890
Query 68:	0.0663
Query 69:	0.0643
Query 70:	0.0765
Query 71:	0.1723
Query 72:	0.0041
Query 73:	0.0384
Query 74:	0.1841
Query 75:	0.4138
Query 76:	0.1695
Query 77:	0.0494
Query 78:	0.0116
Query 79:	0.3004
Query 80:	0.1373
Query 81:	0.1434
Query 82:	0.1500
Query 83:	0.2108
Query 84:	0.1496
Query 85:	0.0000
Query 86:	0.0734
Query 87:	0.1059
Query 88:	0.0752
Query 89:	0.2939
Query 90:	0.0492

Overall statistics
(for 50 queries):

Total number of documents
over all queries:
Retrieved:	50000
Relevant:	8138
Rel_ret:	2891

Interpolated Recall -
Precision Averages:
at 0.00	0.6588
at 0.10	0.2756
at 0.20	0.1815
at 0.30	0.1241
at 0.40	0.0890
at 0.50	0.0626
at 0.60	0.0333
at 0.70	0.0237
at 0.80	0.0031
at 0.90	0.0023
at 1.00	0.0009

Avg. prec. (non-interpolated)
for all rel. documents
                     0.1039

Precision:
At 5 docs:	0.4040
At 10 docs:	0.3520
At 15 docs:	0.3173
At 20 docs:	0.2950
At 30 docs:	0.2760
At 100 docs:	0.1652
At 200 docs:	0.1194
At 500 docs:	0.0819
At 1000 docs:	0.0578

R-Precision (prec. after R
(=num_rel) docs. retrieved):
| Exact: | 0.1509 |

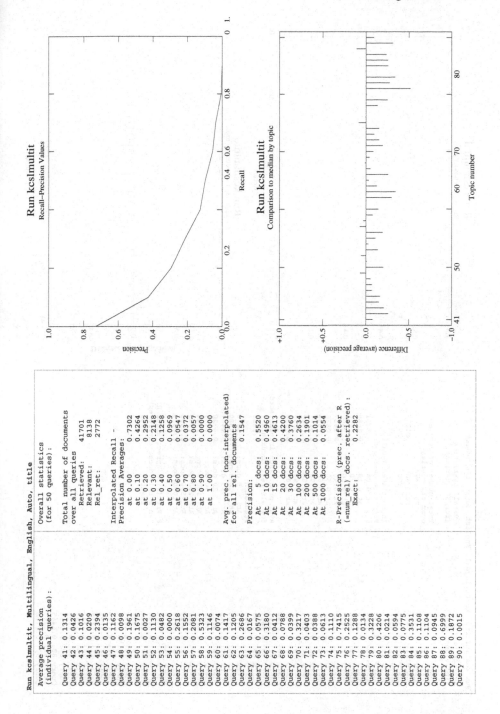

Run kcslmultit

Recall-Precision Values

Precision

1.0
0.8
0.6
0.4
0.2
0.0

0.0   0.2   0.4   0.6   0.8   0. 1.

Recall

Run kcslmultit

Comparison to median by topic

Difference (average precision)

+1.0
+0.5
0.0
-0.5
-1.0

41   50   60   70   80

Topic number

Run kcslmultit, Multilingual, English, Auto, title

Average precision
(individual queries):

Query	41:	0.1314
Query	42:	0.0426
Query	43:	0.1016
Query	44:	0.0209
Query	45:	0.2394
Query	46:	0.0135
Query	47:	0.1162
Query	48:	0.0098
Query	49:	0.1961
Query	50:	0.1675
Query	51:	0.0027
Query	52:	0.1130
Query	53:	0.0482
Query	54:	0.0000
Query	55:	0.2618
Query	56:	0.1552
Query	57:	0.2081
Query	58:	0.5323
Query	59:	0.1146
Query	60:	0.0074
Query	61:	0.1417
Query	62:	0.1205
Query	63:	0.2686
Query	64:	0.0167
Query	65:	0.0575
Query	66:	0.3180
Query	67:	0.0412
Query	68:	0.0788
Query	69:	0.0399
Query	70:	0.3217
Query	71:	0.0403
Query	72:	0.0388
Query	73:	0.0613
Query	74:	0.1110
Query	75:	0.7415
Query	76:	0.2525
Query	77:	0.1288
Query	78:	0.0134
Query	79:	0.3228
Query	80:	0.4206
Query	81:	0.0214
Query	82:	0.0594
Query	83:	0.0775
Query	84:	0.3531
Query	85:	0.1108
Query	86:	0.1104
Query	87:	0.0945
Query	88:	0.6999
Query	89:	0.1872
Query	90:	0.0015

Overall statistics
(for 50 queries):

Total number of documents
over all queries
Retrieved: 41701
Relevant: 8138
Rel_ret: 2772

Interpolated Recall -
Precision Averages:

at 0.00	0.7302
at 0.10	0.4264
at 0.20	0.2952
at 0.30	0.2148
at 0.40	0.1258
at 0.50	0.0969
at 0.60	0.0547
at 0.70	0.0372
at 0.80	0.0057
at 0.90	0.0000
at 1.00	0.0000

Avg. prec. (non-interpolated)
for all rel. documents
                 0.1547

Precision:

At 5 docs:	0.5520
At 10 docs:	0.4960
At 15 docs:	0.4613
At 20 docs:	0.4200
At 30 docs:	0.3760
At 100 docs:	0.2634
At 200 docs:	0.1901
At 500 docs:	0.1014
At 1000 docs:	0.0554

R-Precision (prec. after R
(=num_rel) docs. retrieved):
     Exact: 0.2282

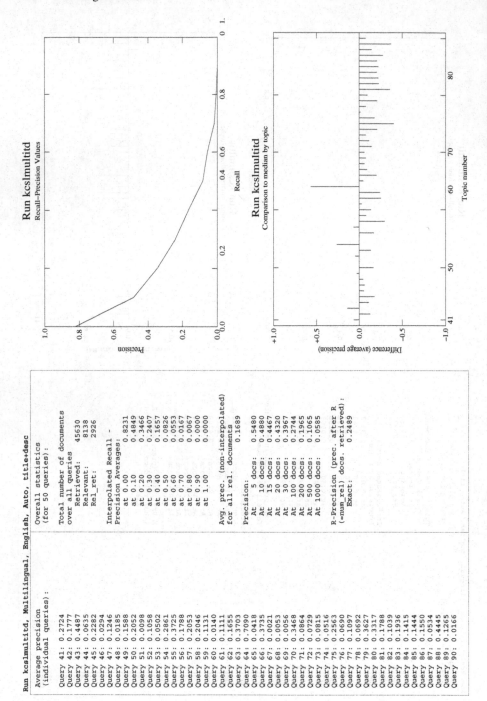

Run kcslmultitd
Recall-Precision Values

Run kcslmultitd
Comparison to median by topic

Run kcslmultitd, Multilingual, English, Auto, title+desc

Average precision
(individual queries):

Query 41:	0.2724
Query 42:	0.1777
Query 43:	0.4487
Query 44:	0.0635
Query 45:	0.2282
Query 46:	0.0294
Query 47:	0.1246
Query 48:	0.0185
Query 49:	0.1588
Query 50:	0.2052
Query 51:	0.0098
Query 52:	0.1058
Query 53:	0.0502
Query 54:	0.2861
Query 55:	0.3725
Query 56:	0.1788
Query 57:	0.2053
Query 58:	0.2046
Query 59:	0.1131
Query 60:	0.0140
Query 61:	0.1111
Query 62:	0.1655
Query 63:	0.3703
Query 64:	0.7090
Query 65:	0.0418
Query 66:	0.3735
Query 67:	0.0021
Query 68:	0.0053
Query 69:	0.0056
Query 70:	0.3468
Query 71:	0.0864
Query 72:	0.0729
Query 73:	0.0815
Query 74:	0.0516
Query 75:	0.2563
Query 76:	0.0690
Query 77:	0.1097
Query 78:	0.0692
Query 79:	0.3627
Query 80:	0.3317
Query 81:	0.1788
Query 82:	0.1039
Query 83:	0.1936
Query 84:	0.1415
Query 85:	0.1444
Query 86:	0.1550
Query 87:	0.0534
Query 88:	0.4445
Query 89:	0.1265
Query 90:	0.0166

Overall statistics
(for 50 queries):

Total number of documents
over all queries
  Retrieved: 45630
  Relevant: 8138
  Rel_ret: 2926

Interpolated Recall -
Precision Averages:
at 0.00	0.8231
at 0.10	0.4849
at 0.20	0.3466
at 0.30	0.2407
at 0.40	0.1657
at 0.50	0.0826
at 0.60	0.0553
at 0.70	0.0167
at 0.80	0.0067
at 0.90	0.0000
at 1.00	0.0000

Avg. prec. (non-interpolated)
for all rel. documents
           0.1689

Precision:
At 5 docs:	0.5480
At 10 docs:	0.4880
At 15 docs:	0.4467
At 20 docs:	0.4320
At 30 docs:	0.3967
At 100 docs:	0.2744
At 200 docs:	0.1965
At 500 docs:	0.1065
At 1000 docs:	0.0585

R-Precision (prec. after R
(=num_rel) docs. retrieved):
  Exact: 0.2489

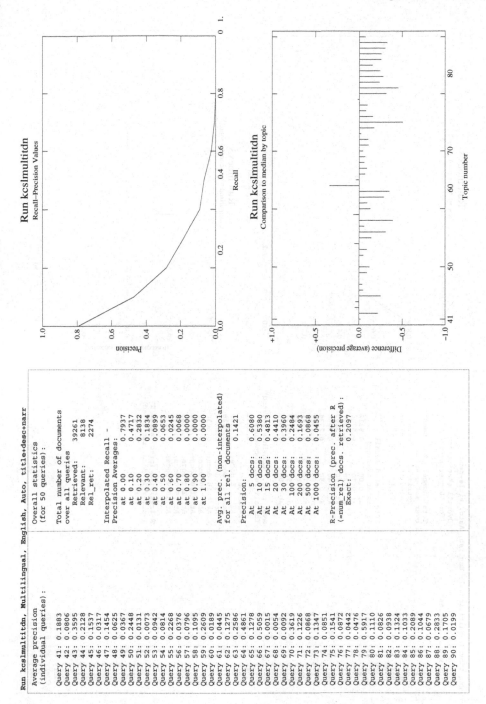

Run kcslmultitdn, Multilingual, English, Auto, title+desc+narr

Average precision
(individual queries):

Query 41:	0.1883
Query 42:	0.0806
Query 43:	0.3595
Query 44:	0.2128
Query 45:	0.1537
Query 46:	0.0317
Query 47:	0.1454
Query 48:	0.0625
Query 49:	0.0367
Query 50:	0.2448
Query 51:	0.0131
Query 52:	0.0073
Query 53:	0.0942
Query 54:	0.0814
Query 55:	0.2268
Query 56:	0.0376
Query 57:	0.0796
Query 58:	0.1095
Query 59:	0.2609
Query 60:	0.0189
Query 61:	0.0445
Query 62:	0.1275
Query 63:	0.2586
Query 64:	0.4861
Query 65:	0.1278
Query 66:	0.5059
Query 67:	0.0015
Query 68:	0.0054
Query 69:	0.0092
Query 70:	0.3619
Query 71:	0.1226
Query 72:	0.0868
Query 73:	0.1347
Query 74:	0.0851
Query 75:	0.1541
Query 76:	0.0872
Query 77:	0.0442
Query 78:	0.0476
Query 79:	0.5917
Query 80:	0.1110
Query 81:	0.0826
Query 82:	0.0938
Query 83:	0.1324
Query 84:	0.1033
Query 85:	0.2089
Query 86:	0.1044
Query 87:	0.0679
Query 88:	0.2833
Query 89:	0.1705
Query 90:	0.0199

Overall statistics
(for 50 queries):

Total number of documents
over all queries
  Retrieved: 39261
  Relevant: 8138
  Rel_ret: 2274

Interpolated Recall -
Precision Averages:
  at 0.00   0.7937
  at 0.10   0.4717
  at 0.20   0.2832
  at 0.30   0.1834
  at 0.40   0.0899
  at 0.50   0.0653
  at 0.60   0.0245
  at 0.70   0.0068
  at 0.80   0.0000
  at 0.90   0.0000
  at 1.00   0.0000
Avg. prec. (non-interpolated)
for all rel. documents
               0.1421

Precision:
  At   5 docs: 0.6080
  At   10 docs: 0.5380
  At   15 docs: 0.4813
  At   20 docs: 0.4410
  At   30 docs: 0.3960
  At 100 docs: 0.2484
  At 200 docs: 0.1693
  At 500 docs: 0.0868
  At 1000 docs: 0.0455

R-Precision (prec. after R
(=num_rel) docs. retrieved):
  Exact: 0.2097

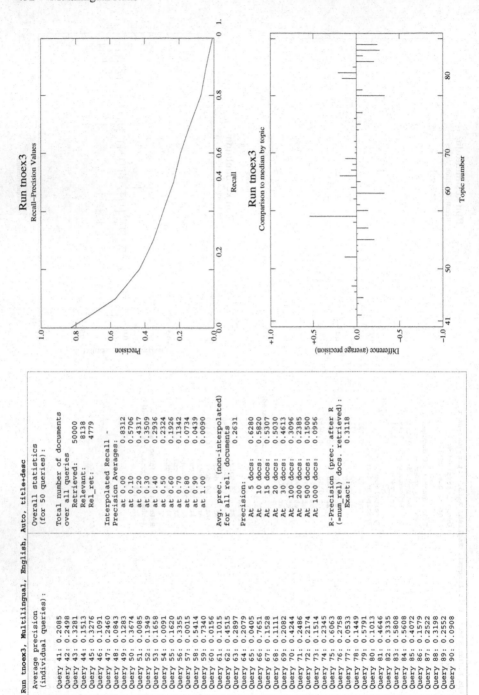

Run tnoex3, Multilingual, English, Auto, title-desc

Average precision
(individual queries):

Query 41:	0.2085
Query 42:	0.2498
Query 43:	0.3281
Query 44:	0.1513
Query 45:	0.3276
Query 46:	0.1091
Query 47:	0.2460
Query 48:	0.0843
Query 49:	0.1283
Query 50:	0.3674
Query 51:	0.0085
Query 52:	0.1949
Query 53:	0.1658
Query 54:	0.0091
Query 55:	0.1620
Query 56:	0.3355
Query 57:	0.0015
Query 58:	0.5414
Query 59:	0.7340
Query 60:	0.0156
Query 61:	0.1015
Query 62:	0.4515
Query 63:	0.2897
Query 64:	0.2079
Query 65:	0.0405
Query 66:	0.7651
Query 67:	0.1528
Query 68:	0.1111
Query 69:	0.2082
Query 70:	0.4244
Query 71:	0.2486
Query 72:	0.2174
Query 73:	0.1514
Query 74:	0.2345
Query 75:	0.6063
Query 76:	0.2758
Query 77:	0.0533
Query 78:	0.1449
Query 79:	0.5791
Query 80:	0.1013
Query 81:	0.4646
Query 82:	0.3335
Query 83:	0.5808
Query 84:	0.5608
Query 85:	0.4072
Query 86:	0.1579
Query 87:	0.2522
Query 88:	0.3198
Query 89:	0.2552
Query 90:	0.0908

Overall statistics
(for 50 queries):

Total number of documents
over all queries:
  Retrieved: 50000
  Relevant: 8138
  Rel_ret: 4779

Interpolated Recall -
Precision Averages:
  at 0.00   0.8312
  at 0.10   0.5706
  at 0.20   0.4317
  at 0.30   0.3509
  at 0.40   0.2936
  at 0.50   0.2324
  at 0.60   0.1926
  at 0.70   0.1342
  at 0.80   0.0734
  at 0.90   0.0439
  at 1.00   0.0090

Avg. prec. (non-interpolated)
for all rel. documents
                0.2631

Precision:
  At   5 docs: 0.6280
  At   10 docs: 0.5820
  At   15 docs: 0.5307
  At   20 docs: 0.5030
  At   30 docs: 0.4613
  At 100 docs: 0.3096
  At 200 docs: 0.2385
  At 500 docs: 0.1500
  At 1000 docs: 0.0956

R-Precision (prec. after R
(=num_rel) docs. retrieved):
    Exact: 0.3118

Run tnoex3
Recall-Precision Values

Run tnoex3
Comparison to median by topic

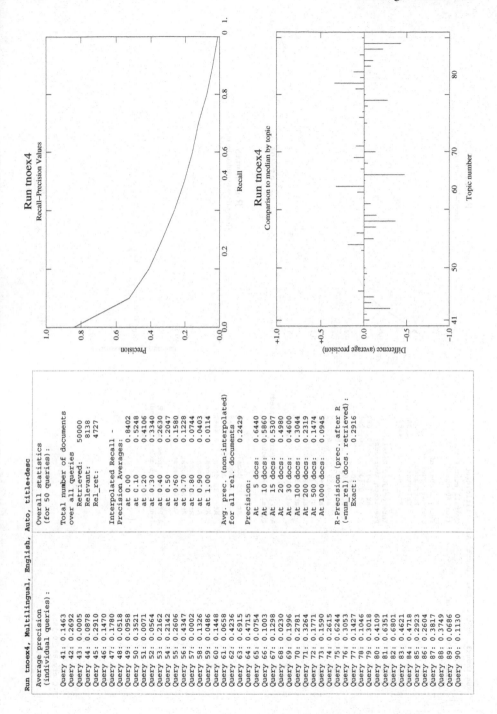

Run tnoex4
Recall–Precision Values

Run tnoex4
Comparison to median by topic

Run tnoex4, Multilingual, English, Auto, title+desc

Average precision
(individual queries):

Query 41:	0.1463
Query 42:	0.2692
Query 43:	0.0005
Query 44:	0.0878
Query 45:	0.2910
Query 46:	0.1470
Query 47:	0.1780
Query 48:	0.0518
Query 49:	0.0958
Query 50:	0.3521
Query 51:	0.0071
Query 52:	0.0564
Query 53:	0.2162
Query 54:	0.2142
Query 55:	0.2606
Query 56:	0.4347
Query 57:	0.0002
Query 58:	0.1326
Query 59:	0.0486
Query 60:	0.1448
Query 61:	0.0658
Query 62:	0.4236
Query 63:	0.6915
Query 64:	0.4715
Query 65:	0.0754
Query 66:	0.1003
Query 67:	0.1298
Query 68:	0.0230
Query 69:	0.1996
Query 70:	0.2781
Query 71:	0.3264
Query 72:	0.1771
Query 73:	0.1590
Query 74:	0.2615
Query 75:	0.6244
Query 76:	0.3053
Query 77:	0.1427
Query 78:	0.1046
Query 79:	0.3018
Query 80:	0.4109
Query 81:	0.6351
Query 82:	0.6801
Query 83:	0.4621
Query 84:	0.4718
Query 85:	0.2923
Query 86:	0.2604
Query 87:	0.3817
Query 88:	0.3749
Query 89:	0.0686
Query 90:	0.1130

Overall statistics
(for 50 queries):

Total number of documents
over all queries
Retrieved: 50000
Relevant: 8138
Rel_ret: 4727

Interpolated Recall -
Precision Averages:
at 0.00	0.8402
at 0.10	0.5248
at 0.20	0.4106
at 0.30	0.3340
at 0.40	0.2630
at 0.50	0.2047
at 0.60	0.1580
at 0.70	0.1228
at 0.80	0.0744
at 0.90	0.0403
at 1.00	0.0114

Avg. prec. (non-interpolated)
for all rel. documents
                    0.2429

Precision:
At 5 docs:	0.6440
At 10 docs:	0.5860
At 15 docs:	0.5307
At 20 docs:	0.4980
At 30 docs:	0.4600
At 100 docs:	0.3044
At 200 docs:	0.2319
At 500 docs:	0.1474
At 1000 docs:	0.0945

R-Precision (prec. after R
(=num_rel) docs. retrieved):
Exact: 0.2916

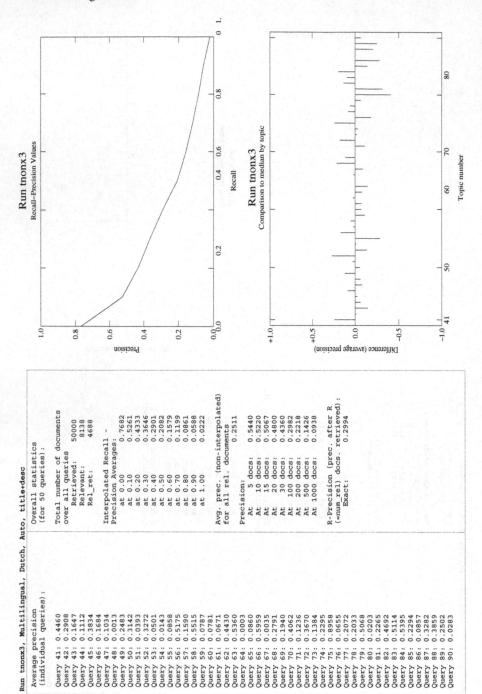

Run tnonx3
Recall–Precision Values

Precision

Recall

Run tnonx3
Comparison to median by topic

Difference (average precision)

Topic number

Run tnonx3, Multilingual, Dutch, Auto, title+desc

Average precision
(individual queries):

Query 41: 0.4460
Query 42: 0.2908
Query 43: 0.1647
Query 44: 0.1112
Query 45: 0.3834
Query 46: 0.1684
Query 47: 0.1034
Query 48: 0.0013
Query 49: 0.2483
Query 50: 0.3142
Query 51: 0.0393
Query 52: 0.3272
Query 53: 0.0501
Query 54: 0.0143
Query 55: 0.0858
Query 56: 0.5175
Query 57: 0.1590
Query 58: 0.5515
Query 59: 0.0787
Query 60: 0.0781
Query 61: 0.0671
Query 62: 0.4430
Query 63: 0.5360
Query 64: 0.0003
Query 65: 0.0860
Query 66: 0.5959
Query 67: 0.0035
Query 68: 0.2791
Query 69: 0.1940
Query 70: 0.4062
Query 71: 0.1236
Query 72: 0.3670
Query 73: 0.1384
Query 74: 0.2295
Query 75: 0.8958
Query 76: 0.0655
Query 77: 0.2072
Query 78: 0.2033
Query 79: 0.5068
Query 80: 0.0203
Query 81: 0.2265
Query 82: 0.4692
Query 83: 0.5114
Query 84: 0.5395
Query 85: 0.2294
Query 86: 0.0857
Query 87: 0.3282
Query 88: 0.3859
Query 89: 0.2502
Query 90: 0.0283

Overall statistics
(for 50 queries):

Total number of documents
over all queries
    Retrieved: 50000
    Relevant: 8138
    Rel_ret: 4688

Interpolated Recall -
Precision Averages:
    at 0.00   0.7682
    at 0.10   0.5261
    at 0.20   0.4333
    at 0.30   0.3646
    at 0.40   0.2901
    at 0.50   0.2082
    at 0.60   0.1579
    at 0.70   0.1199
    at 0.80   0.0861
    at 0.90   0.0588
    at 1.00   0.0222

Avg. prec. (non-interpolated)
for all rel. documents
                   0.2511

Precision:
    At   5 docs: 0.5440
    At 10 docs: 0.5220
    At 15 docs: 0.5067
    At 20 docs: 0.4800
    At 30 docs: 0.4360
    At 100 docs: 0.2982
    At 200 docs: 0.2218
    At 500 docs: 0.1426
    At 1000 docs: 0.0938

R-Precision (prec. after R
(=num_rel) docs. retrieved):
    Exact: 0.2994

Run BK2CEA1, Bilingual to English, Chinese, Auto, title+desc+narr

Average precision
(individual queries):

Query 41:	0.0433
Query 42:	0.3493
Query 43:	0.7986
Query 44:	0.5667
Query 45:	0.5716
Query 46:	0.3542
Query 47:	0.9144
Query 48:	0.3261
Query 49:	0.3234
Query 50:	0.8106
Query 51:	0.0388
Query 52:	0.0607
Query 53:	0.0375
Query 55:	0.4370
Query 56:	0.0008
Query 58:	0.2888
Query 59:	0.0159
Query 61:	0.3788
Query 62:	1.0000
Query 63:	1.0000
Query 64:	0.0192
Query 65:	0.0369
Query 66:	0.6640
Query 67:	0.0029
Query 68:	0.0110
Query 69:	0.0027
Query 70:	0.5544
Query 71:	0.3772
Query 72:	0.1744
Query 73:	1.0000
Query 74:	0.3269
Query 75:	0.5000
Query 76:	0.3990
Query 77:	0.0806
Query 78:	0.0127
Query 79:	1.0000
Query 80:	0.4473
Query 81:	1.0000
Query 82:	0.4715
Query 83:	0.2180
Query 84:	0.3832
Query 85:	0.5551
Query 86:	0.3805
Query 87:	0.6579
Query 88:	1.0000
Query 89:	0.4685
Query 90:	0.3145

Overall statistics
(for 47 queries):

Total number of documents
over all queries

Retrieved:	47000
Relevant:	856
Rel_ret:	755

Interpolated Recall -
Precision Averages:

at 0.00	0.7107
at 0.10	0.6666
at 0.20	0.5926
at 0.30	0.5157
at 0.40	0.4567
at 0.50	0.4066
at 0.60	0.3385
at 0.70	0.2992
at 0.80	0.2698
at 0.90	0.2407
at 1.00	0.1914

Avg. prec. (non-interpolated)
for all rel. documents
0.4122

Precision:

At	5 docs:	0.4128
At	10 docs:	0.3447
At	15 docs:	0.2936
At	20 docs:	0.2660
At	30 docs:	0.2227
At	100 docs:	0.1113
At	200 docs:	0.0677
At	500 docs:	0.0307
At	1000 docs:	0.0161

R-Precision (prec. after R
(=num_rel) docs. retrieved):
Exact: 0.3889

Run BK2CEA1
Recall-Precision Values

Run BK2CEA1
Comparison to median by topic

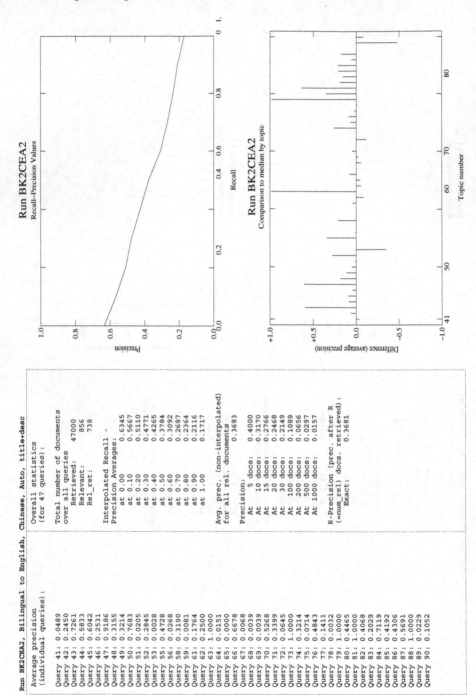

Run BK2CEA2
Recall-Precision Values

Run BK2CEA2
Comparison to median by topic

Run BK2CEA2, Bilingual to English, Chinese, Auto, title+desc

Average precision
(individual queries):

Query 41:	0.0489
Query 42:	0.2450
Query 43:	0.7261
Query 44:	0.5833
Query 45:	0.6042
Query 46:	0.2531
Query 47:	0.9186
Query 48:	0.3155
Query 49:	0.3214
Query 50:	0.7683
Query 51:	0.0205
Query 52:	0.2845
Query 53:	0.0028
Query 55:	0.4728
Query 56:	0.0268
Query 58:	0.3190
Query 59:	0.0081
Query 61:	0.1764
Query 62:	0.2500
Query 63:	1.0000
Query 64:	0.0151
Query 65:	0.0000
Query 66:	0.6678
Query 67:	0.0068
Query 68:	0.0039
Query 69:	0.0039
Query 70:	0.5268
Query 71:	0.3399
Query 72:	0.0645
Query 73:	1.0000
Query 74:	0.3214
Query 75:	0.0714
Query 76:	0.4843
Query 77:	0.1411
Query 78:	0.0032
Query 79:	1.0000
Query 80:	0.4465
Query 81:	1.0000
Query 82:	0.4068
Query 83:	0.2029
Query 84:	0.7119
Query 85:	0.4192
Query 86:	0.4306
Query 87:	0.5691
Query 88:	1.0000
Query 89:	0.0229
Query 90:	0.1052

Overall statistics
(for 47 queries):

Total number of documents
over all queries   47000
    Retrieved: 856
    Relevant: 738
    Rel_ret:

Interpolated Recall -
Precision Averages:
    at 0.00   0.6345
    at 0.10   0.5667
    at 0.20   0.5110
    at 0.30   0.4771
    at 0.40   0.4265
    at 0.50   0.3784
    at 0.60   0.3092
    at 0.70   0.2687
    at 0.80   0.2364
    at 0.90   0.2116
    at 1.00   0.1717

Avg. prec. (non-interpolated)
for all rel. documents
                 0.3683

Precision:
    At   5 docs: 0.4000
    At   10 docs: 0.3170
    At   15 docs: 0.2766
    At   20 docs: 0.2468
    At   30 docs: 0.2149
    At   100 docs: 0.1089
    At   200 docs: 0.0656
    At   500 docs: 0.0297
    At 1000 docs: 0.0157

R-Precision (prec. after R
(=num_rel) docs. retrieved):
    Exact: 0.3681

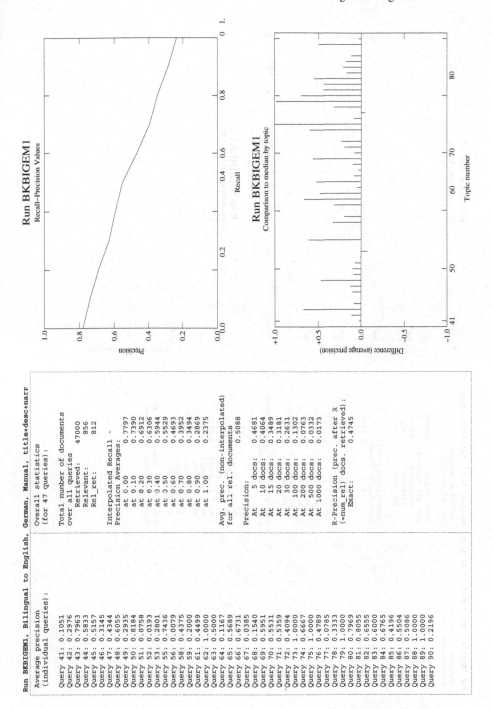

Run BKBIGEM1
Recall–Precision Values

Precision

Recall

Run BKBIGEM1
Comparison to median by topic

Difference (average precision)

Topic number

Run BKBIGEM1, Bilingual to English, German, Manual, title+desc+narr

Average precision
(individual queries):

Query 41:	0.1051
Query 42:	0.2976
Query 43:	0.7963
Query 44:	0.5833
Query 45:	0.5157
Query 46:	0.3145
Query 47:	0.4344
Query 48:	0.6055
Query 49:	0.2935
Query 50:	0.8184
Query 51:	0.0758
Query 52:	0.0193
Query 53:	0.2801
Query 55:	0.7436
Query 56:	0.0079
Query 58:	0.4375
Query 59:	0.2000
Query 61:	0.4499
Query 62:	1.0000
Query 63:	0.5000
Query 64:	0.1167
Query 65:	0.5689
Query 66:	0.6731
Query 67:	0.0385
Query 68:	0.1540
Query 69:	0.5951
Query 70:	0.5531
Query 71:	0.5359
Query 72:	0.4094
Query 73:	1.0000
Query 74:	0.6667
Query 75:	1.0000
Query 76:	0.4789
Query 77:	0.0785
Query 78:	0.3333
Query 79:	1.0000
Query 80:	0.7969
Query 81:	0.8055
Query 82:	0.6555
Query 83:	0.6000
Query 84:	0.6765
Query 85:	0.4196
Query 86:	0.5504
Query 87:	0.5086
Query 88:	1.0000
Query 89:	1.0000
Query 90:	0.2196

Overall statistics
(for 47 queries):

Total number of documents
over all queries
    Retrieved: 47000
    Relevant: 856
    Rel_ret: 812

Interpolated Recall –
Precision Averages:
    at 0.00   0.7797
    at 0.10   0.7390
    at 0.20   0.6912
    at 0.30   0.6306
    at 0.40   0.5944
    at 0.50   0.5529
    at 0.60   0.4693
    at 0.70   0.3952
    at 0.80   0.3494
    at 0.90   0.2869
    at 1.00   0.2375

Avg. prec. (non-interpolated)
for all rel. documents
                    0.5088

Precision:
    At   5 docs: 0.4681
    At   10 docs: 0.4064
    At   15 docs: 0.3489
    At   20 docs: 0.3181
    At   30 docs: 0.2631
    At 100 docs: 0.1302
    At 200 docs: 0.0763
    At 500 docs: 0.0332
    At 1000 docs: 0.0173

R-Precision (prec. after R
(=num_rel) docs. retrieved):
    Exact: 0.4745

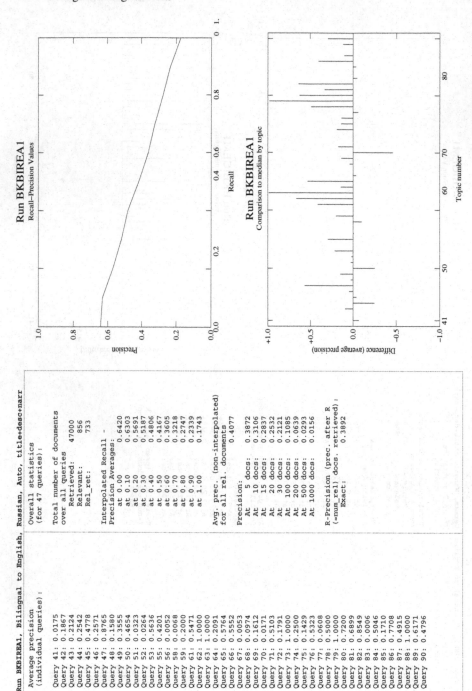

Run BKBIREA1
Recall-Precision Values

Run BKBIREA1
Comparison to median by topic

Run BKBIREA1, Bilingual to English, Russian, Auto, title+desc+narr

Average precision
(individual queries):

Query 41:	0.0175
Query 42:	0.1867
Query 43:	0.2124
Query 44:	0.2542
Query 45:	0.4778
Query 46:	0.2571
Query 47:	0.8765
Query 48:	0.1580
Query 49:	0.3555
Query 50:	0.4654
Query 51:	0.0323
Query 52:	0.0264
Query 53:	0.5636
Query 55:	0.4201
Query 56:	0.0052
Query 58:	0.0068
Query 59:	0.2000
Query 61:	0.5471
Query 62:	1.0000
Query 63:	1.0000
Query 64:	0.2091
Query 65:	0.5764
Query 66:	0.5552
Query 67:	0.0053
Query 68:	0.0974
Query 69:	0.1612
Query 70:	0.0171
Query 71:	0.5103
Query 72:	0.1791
Query 73:	1.0000
Query 74:	0.2500
Query 75:	0.1429
Query 76:	0.5323
Query 77:	0.0608
Query 78:	0.5000
Query 79:	1.0000
Query 80:	0.7200
Query 81:	0.6899
Query 82:	0.8549
Query 83:	0.0006
Query 84:	0.5046
Query 85:	0.1710
Query 86:	0.7708
Query 87:	0.4915
Query 88:	1.0000
Query 89:	0.6171
Query 90:	0.4796

Overall statistics
(for 47 queries):

Total number of documents
over all queries:
  Retrieved: 47000
  Relevant: 856
  Rel_ret: 733

Interpolated Recall -
Precision Averages:
  at 0.00   0.6420
  at 0.10   0.6303
  at 0.20   0.5691
  at 0.30   0.5187
  at 0.40   0.4806
  at 0.50   0.4167
  at 0.60   0.3605
  at 0.70   0.3218
  at 0.80   0.2747
  at 0.90   0.2339
  at 1.00   0.1743

Avg. prec. (non-interpolated)
for all rel. documents
                    0.4077

Precision:
  At   5 docs: 0.3872
  At   10 docs: 0.3106
  At   15 docs: 0.2837
  At   20 docs: 0.2532
  At   30 docs: 0.2121
  At 100 docs: 0.1085
  At 200 docs: 0.0639
  At 500 docs: 0.0293
  At 1000 docs: 0.0156

R-Precision (prec. after R
(=num_rel) docs. retrieved):
  Exact: 0.3892

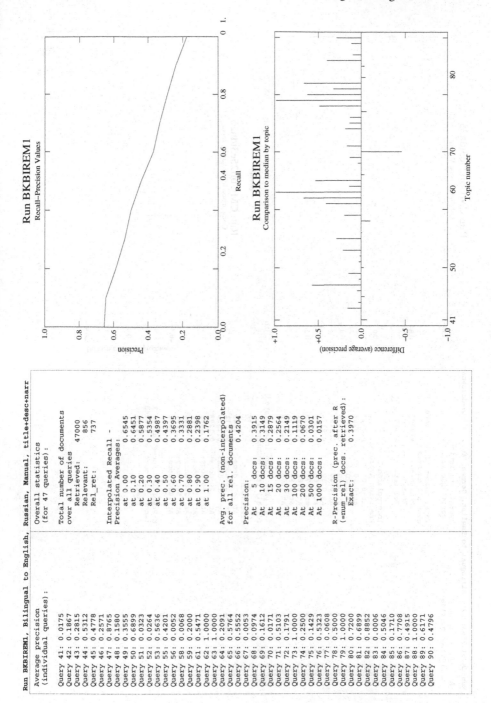

Run **BKBIREM1**
Recall–Precision Values

Run **BKBIREM1**
Comparison to median by topic

Run **BKBIREM1**, Bilingual to English, Russian, Manual, title+desc+narr

Average precision
(individual queries):

Query 41:	0.0175
Query 42:	0.1867
Query 43:	0.2815
Query 44:	0.5312
Query 45:	0.4778
Query 46:	0.2571
Query 47:	0.8765
Query 48:	0.1580
Query 49:	0.3555
Query 50:	0.6899
Query 51:	0.0323
Query 52:	0.0264
Query 53:	0.5636
Query 55:	0.4201
Query 56:	0.0052
Query 58:	0.0068
Query 59:	0.2000
Query 61:	0.5471
Query 62:	1.0000
Query 63:	1.0000
Query 64:	0.2091
Query 65:	0.5764
Query 66:	0.5552
Query 67:	0.0053
Query 68:	0.0974
Query 69:	0.1612
Query 70:	0.0171
Query 71:	0.5103
Query 72:	0.1791
Query 73:	1.0000
Query 74:	0.2500
Query 75:	0.1429
Query 76:	0.5323
Query 77:	0.0608
Query 78:	0.5000
Query 79:	1.0000
Query 80:	0.7200
Query 81:	0.6899
Query 82:	0.8852
Query 83:	0.0006
Query 84:	0.5046
Query 85:	0.1710
Query 86:	0.7708
Query 87:	0.4915
Query 88:	1.0000
Query 89:	0.6171
Query 90:	0.4796

Overall statistics
(for 47 queries):

Total number of documents
over all queries
Retrieved:	47000
Relevant:	856
Rel_ret:	737

Interpolated Recall -
Precision Averages:
at 0.00	0.6545
at 0.10	0.6451
at 0.20	0.5877
at 0.30	0.5354
at 0.40	0.4987
at 0.50	0.4397
at 0.60	0.3695
at 0.70	0.3331
at 0.80	0.2881
at 0.90	0.2398
at 1.00	0.1762

Avg. prec. (non-interpolated)
for all rel. documents
0.4204

Precision:
At	5 docs:	0.3915
At	10 docs:	0.3149
At	15 docs:	0.2879
At	20 docs:	0.2564
At	30 docs:	0.2149
At	100 docs:	0.1119
At	200 docs:	0.0670
At	500 docs:	0.0301
At 1000 docs:		0.0157

R-Precision (prec. after R
(=num rel) docs. retrieved):
Exact:	0.3970

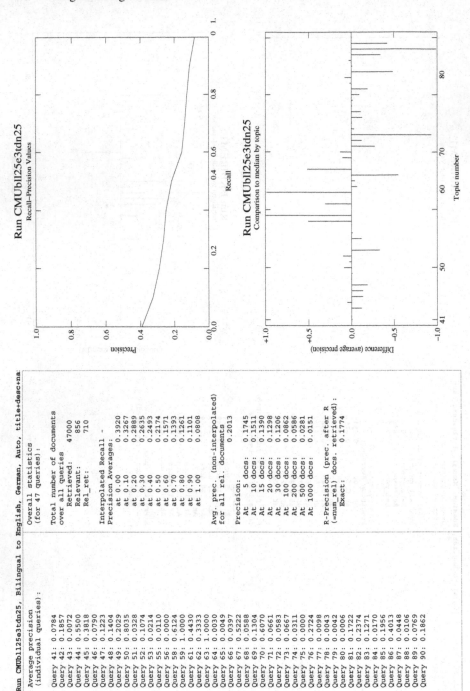

Run CMUbll25e3tdn25
Recall-Precision Values

Run CMUbll25e3tdn25
Comparison to median by topic

Run CMUbll25e3tdn25, Bilingual to English, German, Auto, title+desc+na:

Average precision
(individual queries):

Query 41:	0.0784
Query 42:	0.1857
Query 43:	0.0072
Query 44:	0.5500
Query 45:	0.3818
Query 46:	0.0790
Query 47:	0.1223
Query 48:	0.1404
Query 49:	0.2029
Query 50:	0.8035
Query 51:	0.0328
Query 52:	0.1074
Query 53:	0.0214
Query 55:	0.0110
Query 56:	0.0000
Query 58:	0.6124
Query 59:	1.0000
Query 61:	0.4430
Query 62:	0.3333
Query 63:	1.0000
Query 64:	0.0030
Query 65:	0.0049
Query 66:	0.0397
Query 67:	0.5222
Query 68:	0.0588
Query 69:	0.1304
Query 70:	0.6070
Query 71:	0.0661
Query 72:	0.0583
Query 73:	0.0667
Query 74:	0.0311
Query 75:	0.0000
Query 76:	0.2724
Query 77:	0.0098
Query 78:	0.0043
Query 79:	0.0042
Query 80:	0.0006
Query 81:	0.1722
Query 82:	0.2374
Query 83:	0.1271
Query 84:	0.0170
Query 85:	0.1956
Query 86:	0.4013
Query 87:	0.0448
Query 88:	0.0106
Query 89:	0.0769
Query 90:	0.1862

Overall statistics
(for 47 queries):

Total number of documents
over all queries):
Retrieved:	47000
Relevant:	856
Rel_ret:	710

Interpolated Recall -
Precision Averages:
at 0.00	0.3920
at 0.10	0.3267
at 0.20	0.2889
at 0.30	0.2635
at 0.40	0.2493
at 0.50	0.2174
at 0.60	0.1571
at 0.70	0.1393
at 0.80	0.1261
at 0.90	0.1101
at 1.00	0.0808

Avg. prec. (non-interpolated)
for all rel. documents
    0.2013

Precision:
At 5 docs:	0.1745
At 10 docs:	0.1511
At 15 docs:	0.1390
At 20 docs:	0.1298
At 30 docs:	0.1206
At 100 docs:	0.0862
At 200 docs:	0.0586
At 500 docs:	0.0281
At 1000 docs:	0.0151

R-Precision (prec. after R
(=num_rel) docs. retrieved) :
    Exact: 0.1774

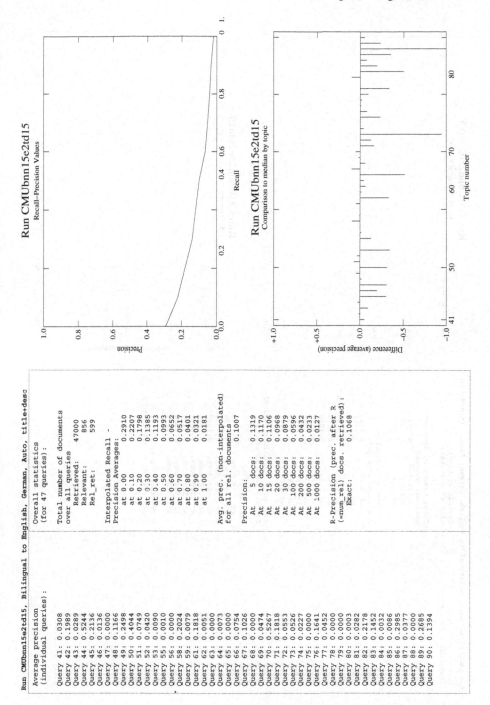

Run CMUbnn15e2td15
Recall–Precision Values

Run CMUbnn15e2td15
Comparison to median by topic

Run CMUbnn15e2td15, Bilingual to English, German, Auto, title+desc

Average precision
(individual queries):

Query 41:	0.0308
Query 42:	0.1989
Query 43:	0.0289
Query 44:	0.5244
Query 45:	0.2136
Query 46:	0.0136
Query 47:	0.0000
Query 48:	0.1166
Query 49:	0.2498
Query 50:	0.4044
Query 51:	0.0749
Query 52:	0.0420
Query 53:	0.0090
Query 55:	0.0010
Query 56:	0.0000
Query 58:	0.2024
Query 59:	0.0079
Query 61:	0.1818
Query 62:	0.0051
Query 63:	0.0000
Query 64:	0.0073
Query 65:	0.0000
Query 66:	0.0754
Query 67:	0.1026
Query 68:	0.0000
Query 69:	0.0474
Query 70:	0.5267
Query 71:	0.1818
Query 72:	0.0553
Query 73:	0.0526
Query 74:	0.0227
Query 75:	0.0000
Query 76:	0.1641
Query 77:	0.0452
Query 78:	0.0000
Query 79:	0.0000
Query 80:	0.0003
Query 81:	0.0282
Query 82:	0.2178
Query 83:	0.1452
Query 84:	0.0032
Query 85:	0.0086
Query 86:	0.2985
Query 87:	0.0377
Query 88:	0.0000
Query 89:	0.2685
Query 90:	0.1394

Overall statistics
(for 47 queries):

Total number of documents
over all queries:

Retrieved:	47000
Relevant:	856
Rel_ret:	599

Interpolated Recall -
Precision Averages:

at 0.00	0.2910
at 0.10	0.2207
at 0.20	0.1798
at 0.30	0.1385
at 0.40	0.1193
at 0.50	0.0993
at 0.60	0.0652
at 0.70	0.0517
at 0.80	0.0401
at 0.90	0.0321
at 1.00	0.0181

Avg. prec. (non-interpolated)
for all rel. documents
                              0.1007

Precision:

At	5 docs:	0.1319
At	10 docs:	0.1170
At	15 docs:	0.1106
At	20 docs:	0.0968
At	30 docs:	0.0879
At	100 docs:	0.0596
At	200 docs:	0.0432
At	500 docs:	0.0233
At	1000 docs:	0.0127

R-Precision (prec. after R
(=num_rel) docs. retrieved):
            Exact: 0.1068

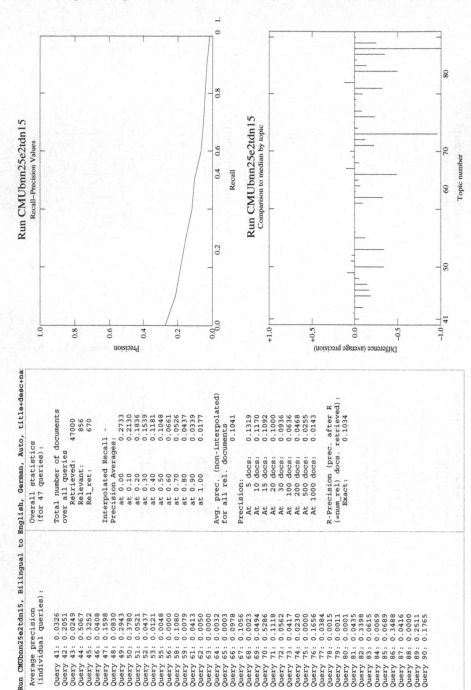

Run CMUbnn25e2tdn15   Recall-Precision Values

Run CMUbnn25e2tdn15   Comparison to median by topic

Run CMUbnn25e2tdn15, Bilingual to English, German, Auto, title+desc+na:

Average precision
(individual queries):

Query 41:	0.0326
Query 42:	0.2051
Query 43:	0.0249
Query 44:	0.5067
Query 45:	0.3252
Query 46:	0.0408
Query 47:	0.1598
Query 48:	0.0830
Query 49:	0.2943
Query 50:	0.3780
Query 51:	0.0521
Query 52:	0.0437
Query 53:	0.0121
Query 55:	0.0048
Query 56:	0.0000
Query 58:	0.1080
Query 59:	0.0079
Query 61:	0.0413
Query 62:	0.0050
Query 63:	0.0000
Query 64:	0.0032
Query 65:	0.0003
Query 66:	0.0978
Query 67:	0.1056
Query 68:	0.0023
Query 69:	0.0494
Query 70:	0.5286
Query 71:	0.1118
Query 72:	0.0562
Query 73:	0.0417
Query 74:	0.0230
Query 75:	0.0000
Query 76:	0.1656
Query 77:	0.0384
Query 78:	0.0015
Query 79:	0.0011
Query 80:	0.0001
Query 81:	0.0435
Query 82:	0.3398
Query 83:	0.0615
Query 84:	0.0069
Query 85:	0.0689
Query 86:	0.3488
Query 87:	0.0416
Query 88:	0.0000
Query 89:	0.2511
Query 90:	0.1765

Overall statistics
(for 47 queries):

Total number of documents
over all queries
Retrieved:	47000
Relevant:	856
Rel_ret:	670

Interpolated Recall -
Precision Averages:
at 0.00	0.2733
at 0.10	0.2130
at 0.20	0.1836
at 0.30	0.1539
at 0.40	0.1181
at 0.50	0.1048
at 0.60	0.0661
at 0.70	0.0526
at 0.80	0.0437
at 0.90	0.0339
at 1.00	0.0177

Avg. prec. (non-interpolated)
for all rel. documents
        0.1041

Precision:
At	5 docs:	0.1319
At	10 docs:	0.1170
At	15 docs:	0.1092
At	20 docs:	0.1000
At	30 docs:	0.0936
At	100 docs:	0.0636
At	200 docs:	0.0468
At	500 docs:	0.0255
At	1000 docs:	0.0143

R-Precision (prec. after R
(=num_rel) docs. retrieved):
        Exact: 0.1034

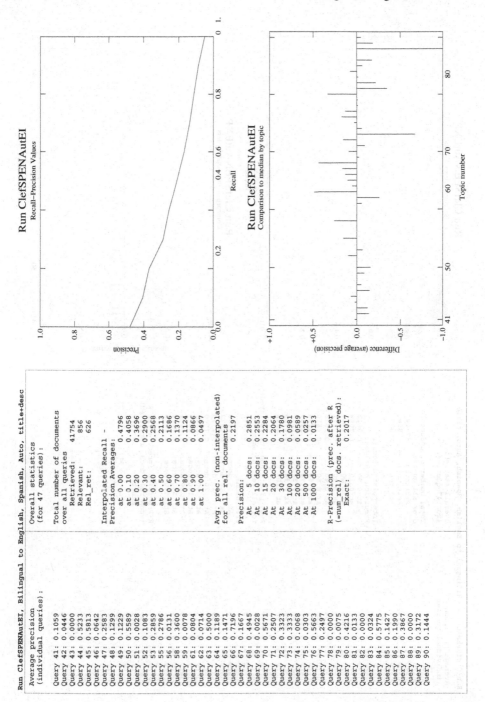

Run ClefSPENAutEI, Bilingual to English, Spanish, Auto, title+desc

Average precision
(individual queries):

Query 41:	0.1059
Query 42:	0.0446
Query 43:	0.0000
Query 44:	0.5233
Query 45:	0.5813
Query 46:	0.0642
Query 47:	0.2583
Query 48:	0.1299
Query 49:	0.1229
Query 50:	0.5589
Query 51:	0.0028
Query 52:	0.1083
Query 53:	0.2859
Query 55:	0.2786
Query 56:	0.0131
Query 58:	0.3600
Query 59:	0.0078
Query 61:	0.0804
Query 62:	0.0714
Query 63:	0.5000
Query 64:	0.1189
Query 65:	0.1471
Query 66:	0.7196
Query 67:	0.1667
Query 68:	0.4945
Query 69:	0.0028
Query 70:	0.5671
Query 71:	0.2507
Query 72:	0.3323
Query 73:	0.3333
Query 74:	0.0068
Query 75:	0.0303
Query 76:	0.5663
Query 77:	0.2497
Query 78:	0.0000
Query 79:	0.0075
Query 80:	0.4216
Query 81:	0.0133
Query 82:	0.0000
Query 83:	0.0324
Query 84:	0.5775
Query 85:	0.1427
Query 86:	0.1990
Query 87:	0.3867
Query 88:	0.0000
Query 89:	0.3172
Query 90:	0.1444

Overall statistics
(for 47 queries):

Total number of documents
over all queries
    Retrieved: 41754
    Relevant: 856
    Rel_ret: 626

Interpolated Recall -
Precision Averages:
    at 0.00   0.4796
    at 0.10   0.4058
    at 0.20   0.3696
    at 0.30   0.2900
    at 0.40   0.2568
    at 0.50   0.2113
    at 0.60   0.1686
    at 0.70   0.1370
    at 0.80   0.1124
    at 0.90   0.0866
    at 1.00   0.0497

Avg. prec. (non-interpolated)
for all rel. documents
                   0.2197

Precision:
    At   5 docs: 0.2851
    At   10 docs: 0.2553
    At   15 docs: 0.2284
    At   20 docs: 0.2064
    At   30 docs: 0.1780
    At 100 docs: 0.0981
    At 200 docs: 0.0589
    At 500 docs: 0.0257
    At 1000 docs: 0.0133

R-Precision (prec. after R
(=num rel) docs. retrieved):
    Exact: 0.2017

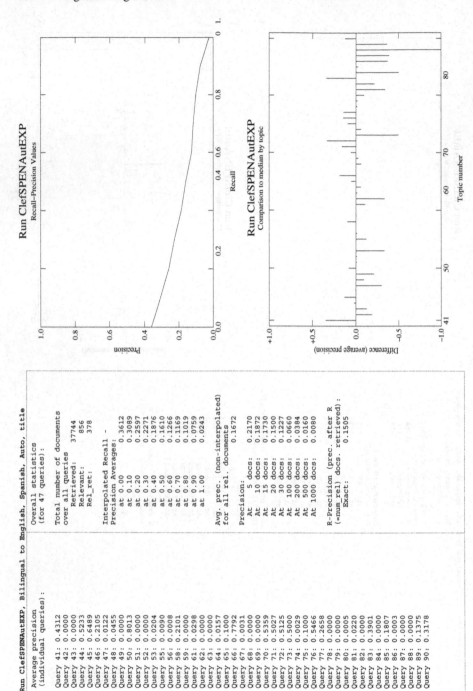

Run ClefSPENAutEXP
Recall-Precision Values

Run ClefSPENAutEXP
Comparison to median by topic

Run ClefSPENAutEXP, Bilingual to English, Spanish, Auto, title

Average precision
(individual queries):

Query 41:	0.4312
Query 42:	0.0000
Query 43:	0.0000
Query 44:	0.5233
Query 45:	0.6489
Query 46:	0.2105
Query 47:	0.0122
Query 48:	0.0455
Query 49:	0.0000
Query 50:	0.8013
Query 51:	0.0000
Query 52:	0.0000
Query 53:	0.0204
Query 55:	0.0090
Query 56:	0.0008
Query 58:	0.2101
Query 59:	0.0000
Query 61:	0.0298
Query 62:	0.0000
Query 63:	0.0000
Query 64:	0.0157
Query 65:	0.1000
Query 66:	0.7792
Query 67:	0.0031
Query 68:	0.0000
Query 69:	0.0000
Query 70:	0.5359
Query 71:	0.5027
Query 72:	0.5125
Query 73:	0.5000
Query 74:	0.0029
Query 75:	0.1000
Query 76:	0.5466
Query 77:	0.2658
Query 78:	0.0000
Query 79:	0.0000
Query 80:	0.0005
Query 81:	0.0220
Query 82:	0.0000
Query 83:	0.3901
Query 84:	0.0000
Query 85:	0.1807
Query 86:	0.0003
Query 87:	0.0000
Query 88:	0.0000
Query 89:	0.1375
Query 90:	0.3178

Overall statistics
(for 47 queries):

Total number of documents
over all queries:
Retrieved: 37744
Relevant: 856
Rel_ret: 378

Interpolated Recall -
Precision Averages:
at 0.00   0.3612
at 0.10   0.3089
at 0.20   0.2597
at 0.30   0.2271
at 0.40   0.1876
at 0.50   0.1610
at 0.60   0.1266
at 0.70   0.1169
at 0.80   0.1019
at 0.90   0.0759
at 1.00   0.0243

Avg. prec. (non-interpolated)
for all rel. documents
             0.1672

Precision:
At   5 docs: 0.2170
At   10 docs: 0.1872
At   15 docs: 0.1730
At   20 docs: 0.1500
At   30 docs: 0.1227
At 100 docs: 0.0660
At 200 docs: 0.0384
At 500 docs: 0.0160
At 1000 docs: 0.0080

R-Precision (prec. after R
(=num_rel) docs. retrieved):
    Exact: 0.1505

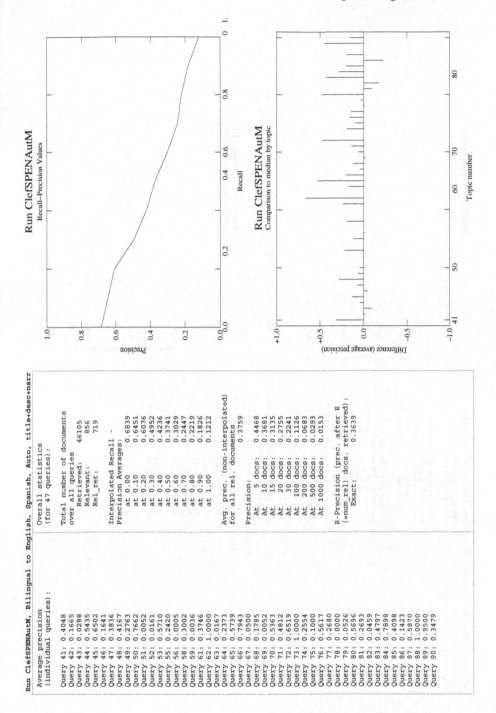

Run ClefSPENAutM
Recall–Precision Values

Precision

Recall

Run ClefSPENAutM
Comparison to median by topic

Difference (average precision)

Topic number

Run ClefSPENAutM, Bilingual to English, Spanish, Auto, title+desc+narr

Average precision
(individual queries):

Query 41:	0.4048
Query 42:	0.1665
Query 43:	0.0288
Query 44:	0.5435
Query 45:	0.6502
Query 46:	0.1641
Query 47:	0.3836
Query 48:	0.4167
Query 49:	0.2763
Query 50:	0.7662
Query 51:	0.0052
Query 52:	0.0161
Query 53:	0.5710
Query 55:	0.2420
Query 56:	0.0005
Query 58:	0.3002
Query 59:	0.0036
Query 61:	0.3746
Query 62:	1.0000
Query 63:	0.0167
Query 64:	0.2373
Query 65:	0.5739
Query 66:	0.7943
Query 67:	0.0500
Query 68:	0.1785
Query 69:	0.0052
Query 70:	0.5363
Query 71:	0.4812
Query 72:	0.6519
Query 73:	1.0000
Query 74:	0.2554
Query 75:	0.1000
Query 76:	0.5617
Query 77:	0.2680
Query 78:	0.0000
Query 79:	0.0526
Query 80:	0.5696
Query 81:	0.2693
Query 82:	0.0459
Query 83:	0.4797
Query 84:	0.7898
Query 85:	0.4098
Query 86:	0.1423
Query 87:	0.5870
Query 88:	1.0000
Query 89:	0.9500
Query 90:	0.3479

Overall statistics
(for 47 queries):

Total number of documents
over all queries
    Retrieved: 46105
    Relevant: 856
    Rel_ret: 719

Interpolated Recall -
Precision Averages:
    at 0.00   0.6839
    at 0.10   0.6451
    at 0.20   0.6076
    at 0.30   0.4952
    at 0.40   0.4236
    at 0.50   0.3741
    at 0.60   0.3029
    at 0.70   0.2447
    at 0.80   0.2219
    at 0.90   0.1826
    at 1.00   0.1212

Avg. prec. (non-interpolated)
for all rel. documents
                    0.3759

Precision:
    At   5 docs: 0.4468
    At   10 docs: 0.3681
    At   15 docs: 0.3135
    At   20 docs: 0.2755
    At   30 docs: 0.2241
    At 100 docs: 0.1126
    At 200 docs: 0.0683
    At 500 docs: 0.0293
    At 1000 docs: 0.0153

R-Precision (prec. after R
(=num rel) docs. retrieved):
    Exact: 0.3639

Run ClefSPENAutPR
Recall–Precision Values

Run ClefSPENAutPR
Comparison to median by topic

Run ClefSPENAutPR, Bilingual to English, Spanish, Auto, title

Average precision
(individual queries):

Query 41:	0.3771
Query 42:	0.0505
Query 43:	0.0000
Query 44:	0.5476
Query 45:	0.6566
Query 46:	0.3095
Query 47:	0.2483
Query 48:	0.2001
Query 49:	0.1829
Query 50:	0.7175
Query 51:	0.0085
Query 52:	0.0190
Query 53:	0.5604
Query 55:	0.1520
Query 56:	0.0007
Query 58:	0.2870
Query 59:	0.0043
Query 61:	0.0497
Query 62:	0.0667
Query 63:	0.0204
Query 64:	0.4245
Query 65:	0.2565
Query 66:	0.7761
Query 67:	0.0294
Query 68:	0.5041
Query 69:	0.0051
Query 70:	0.5314
Query 71:	0.4629
Query 72:	0.4142
Query 73:	0.5000
Query 74:	0.0093
Query 75:	0.0213
Query 76:	0.5836
Query 77:	0.2374
Query 78:	0.0000
Query 79:	0.0017
Query 80:	0.4872
Query 81:	0.0935
Query 82:	0.0000
Query 83:	0.4369
Query 84:	0.6917
Query 85:	0.2743
Query 86:	0.2961
Query 87:	0.6989
Query 88:	0.0000
Query 89:	0.1617
Query 90:	0.4532

Overall statistics
(for 47 queries):

Total number of documents
over all queries:
Retrieved:	41754
Relevant:	856
Rel_ret:	624

Interpolated Recall –
Precision Averages:
at 0.00	0.5585
at 0.10	0.5366
at 0.20	0.4715
at 0.30	0.3796
at 0.40	0.3011
at 0.50	0.2708
at 0.60	0.2036
at 0.70	0.1639
at 0.80	0.1374
at 0.90	0.0936
at 1.00	0.0448

Avg. prec. (non-interpolated)
for all rel. documents   0.2725

Precision:
At 5 docs:	0.3872
At 10 docs:	0.3340
At 15 docs:	0.2837
At 20 docs:	0.2511
At 30 docs:	0.2170
At 100 docs:	0.1034
At 200 docs:	0.0616
At 500 docs:	0.0258
At 1000 docs:	0.0133

R-Precision (prec. after R
(=num_rel) docs. retrieved):
| Exact: | 0.2573 |

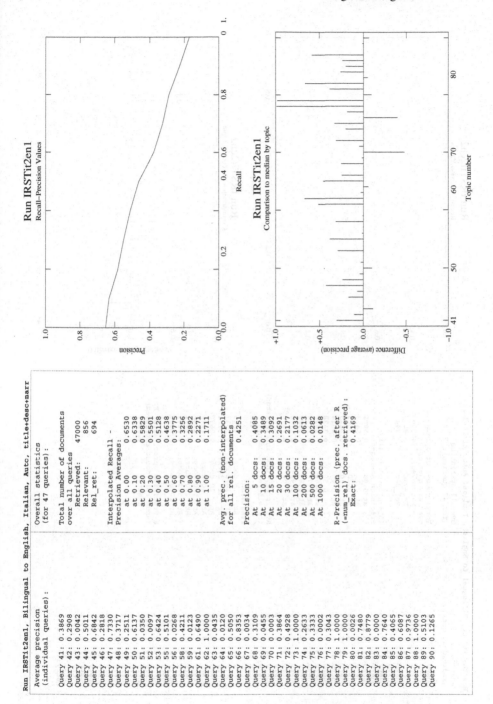

Run IRSTit2en1
Recall–Precision Values

Run IRSTit2en1
Comparison to median by topic

Run IRSTit2en1, Bilingual to English, Italian, Auto, title+desc+narr

Average precision
(individual queries):

Query 41:	0.3869		
Query 42:	0.2908		
Query 43:	0.0042		
Query 44:	0.5011		
Query 45:	0.6842		
Query 46:	0.2818		
Query 47:	0.7330		
Query 48:	0.3717		
Query 49:	0.2511		
Query 50:	0.6137		
Query 51:	0.0350		
Query 52:	0.0097		
Query 53:	0.6424		
Query 55:	0.5101		
Query 56:	0.0268		
Query 58:	0.4211		
Query 59:	0.0123		
Query 61:	0.6490		
Query 62:	1.0000		
Query 63:	0.0435		
Query 64:	0.0120		
Query 65:	0.5050		
Query 66:	0.8353		
Query 67:	0.0034		
Query 68:	0.3109		
Query 69:	0.0455		
Query 70:	0.0003		
Query 71:	0.3864		
Query 72:	0.4928		
Query 73:	1.0000		
Query 74:	0.2633		
Query 75:	0.3333		
Query 76:	0.0002		
Query 77:	0.3043		
Query 78:	1.0000		
Query 79:	1.0000		
Query 80:	0.0026		
Query 81:	0.7480		
Query 82:	0.8779		
Query 83:	0.0000		
Query 84:	0.7640		
Query 85:	0.4065		
Query 86:	0.6087		
Query 87:	0.9736		
Query 88:	1.0000		
Query 89:	0.5103		
Query 90:	0.1265		

Overall statistics
(for 47 queries):

Total number of documents
over all queries
  Retrieved: 47000
  Relevant: 856
  Rel_ret: 694

Interpolated Recall -
Precision Averages:
  at 0.00   0.6530
  at 0.10   0.6338
  at 0.20   0.5829
  at 0.30   0.5501
  at 0.40   0.5128
  at 0.50   0.4638
  at 0.60   0.3775
  at 0.70   0.3256
  at 0.80   0.2892
  at 0.90   0.2271
  at 1.00   0.1711

Avg. prec. (non-interpolated)
for all rel. documents
                0.4251

Precision:
  At   5 docs: 0.4085
  At   10 docs: 0.3489
  At   15 docs: 0.3092
  At   20 docs: 0.2691
  At   30 docs: 0.2177
  At 100 docs: 0.1032
  At 200 docs: 0.0613
  At 500 docs: 0.0282
  At 1000 docs: 0.0148

R-Precision (prec. after R
(=num_rel) docs. retrieved):
       Exact: 0.4169

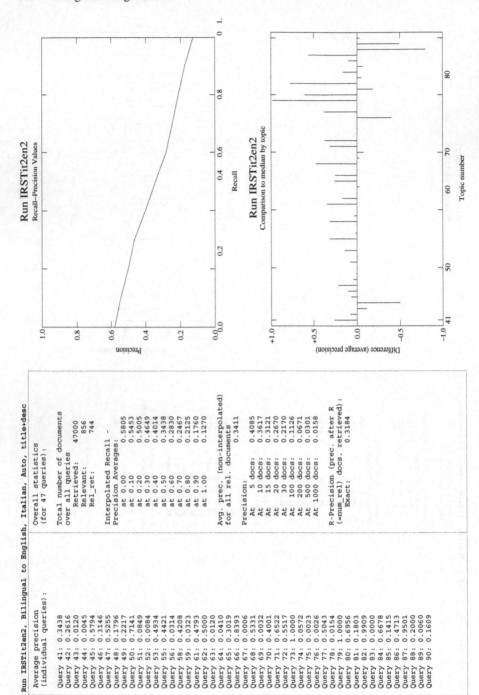

Run IRSTit2en2
Recall–Precision Values

Run IRSTit2en2
Comparison to median by topic

Run IRSTit2en2, Bilingual to English, Italian, Auto, title+desc

Average precision (individual queries):		Overall statistics (for 47 queries):	
Query 41: 0.3438		Total number of documents over all queries:	
Query 42: 0.2616		Retrieved:	47000
Query 43: 0.0120		Relevant:	856
Query 44: 0.0045		Rel_ret:	744
Query 45: 0.5794			
Query 46: 0.3146		Interpolated Recall -	
Query 47: 0.5255		Precision Averages:	
Query 48: 0.1796		at 0.00	0.5805
Query 49: 0.2217		at 0.10	0.5453
Query 50: 0.7141		at 0.20	0.5005
Query 51: 0.0849		at 0.30	0.4649
Query 52: 0.0084		at 0.40	0.4014
Query 53: 0.4934		at 0.50	0.3438
Query 55: 0.4421		at 0.60	0.2830
Query 56: 0.0314		at 0.70	0.2467
Query 58: 0.4208		at 0.80	0.2125
Query 59: 0.0323		at 0.90	0.1760
Query 61: 0.4793		at 1.00	0.1270
Query 62: 0.5000			
Query 63: 0.0120		Avg. prec. (non-interpolated)	
Query 64: 0.0410		for all rel. documents	0.3411
Query 65: 0.3019			
Query 66: 0.8393		Precision:	
Query 67: 0.0006		At 5 docs:	0.4085
Query 68: 0.5331		At 10 docs:	0.3617
Query 69: 0.0032		At 15 docs:	0.3121
Query 70: 0.4001		At 20 docs:	0.2670
Query 71: 0.6522		At 30 docs:	0.2170
Query 72: 0.5517		At 100 docs:	0.1126
Query 73: 1.0000		At 200 docs:	0.0671
Query 74: 0.0572		At 500 docs:	0.0301
Query 75: 0.0023		At 1000 docs:	0.0158
Query 76: 0.0026			
Query 77: 0.5043		R-Precision (prec. after R	
Query 78: 0.0154		(=num_rel) docs. retrieved):	
Query 79: 1.0000		Exact:	0.3184
Query 80: 0.6956			
Query 81: 0.1803			
Query 82: 0.9909			
Query 83: 0.0000			
Query 84: 0.6678			
Query 85: 0.1415			
Query 86: 0.4713			
Query 87: 0.9501			
Query 88: 0.2000			
Query 89: 0.0060			
Query 90: 0.1609			

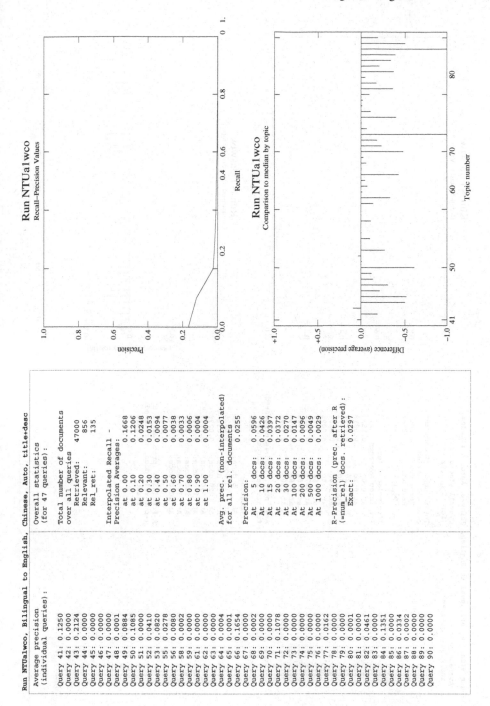

Run NTUa1wco
Recall–Precision Values

Run NTUa1wco
Comparison to median by topic

Run NTUa1wco, Bilingual to English, Chinese, Auto, title+desc

Average precision
(individual queries):

Query 41:	0.1250
Query 42:	0.0000
Query 43:	0.2124
Query 44:	0.0000
Query 45:	0.0000
Query 46:	0.0000
Query 47:	0.0000
Query 48:	0.0001
Query 49:	0.0884
Query 50:	0.1085
Query 51:	0.0000
Query 52:	0.0410
Query 53:	0.0820
Query 55:	0.0278
Query 56:	0.0080
Query 58:	0.0002
Query 59:	0.0000
Query 61:	0.0000
Query 62:	0.0000
Query 63:	0.0000
Query 64:	0.0004
Query 65:	0.0001
Query 66:	0.1654
Query 67:	0.0000
Query 68:	0.0002
Query 69:	0.0000
Query 70:	0.0000
Query 71:	0.1078
Query 72:	0.0000
Query 73:	0.0000
Query 74:	0.0000
Query 75:	0.0000
Query 76:	0.0000
Query 77:	0.0162
Query 78:	0.0000
Query 79:	0.0000
Query 80:	0.0001
Query 81:	0.0000
Query 82:	0.0461
Query 83:	0.0000
Query 84:	0.1351
Query 85:	0.0000
Query 86:	0.0334
Query 87:	0.0002
Query 88:	0.0000
Query 89:	0.0000
Query 90:	0.0000

Overall statistics
(for 47 queries):

Total number of documents
over all queries
    Retrieved: 47000
    Relevant: 856
    Rel_ret: 135

Interpolated Recall -
Precision Averages:
    at 0.00   0.1668
    at 0.10   0.1206
    at 0.20   0.0248
    at 0.30   0.0153
    at 0.40   0.0094
    at 0.50   0.0077
    at 0.60   0.0038
    at 0.70   0.0033
    at 0.80   0.0006
    at 0.90   0.0004
    at 1.00   0.0004

Avg. prec. (non-interpolated)
for all rel. documents
            0.0255

Precision:
    At   5 docs: 0.0596
    At   10 docs: 0.0426
    At   15 docs: 0.0397
    At   20 docs: 0.0372
    At   30 docs: 0.0270
    At 100 docs: 0.0147
    At 200 docs: 0.0096
    At 500 docs: 0.0049
    At 1000 docs: 0.0029

R-Precision (prec. after R
(=num rel) docs. retrieved):
    Exact: 0.0297

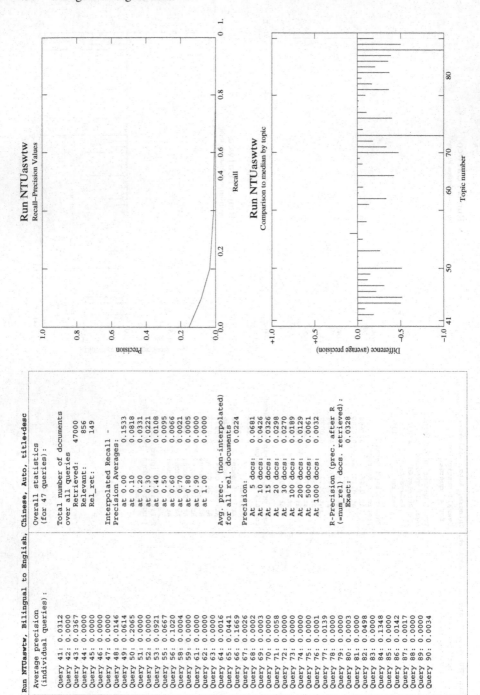

Run NTUaswtw
Recall–Precision Values

Run NTUaswtw
Comparison to median by topic

Run NTUaswtw, Bilingual to English, Chinese, Auto, title+desc

Average precision
(individual queries):

Query 41:	0.0312
Query 42:	0.0000
Query 43:	0.0367
Query 44:	0.0000
Query 45:	0.0000
Query 46:	0.0000
Query 47:	0.0000
Query 48:	0.0146
Query 49:	0.0614
Query 50:	0.2065
Query 51:	0.0000
Query 52:	0.0000
Query 53:	0.0921
Query 55:	0.0667
Query 56:	0.1020
Query 58:	0.0004
Query 59:	0.0000
Query 61:	0.0000
Query 62:	0.0000
Query 63:	0.0000
Query 64:	0.0016
Query 65:	0.0441
Query 66:	0.1669
Query 67:	0.0026
Query 68:	0.0002
Query 69:	0.0003
Query 70:	0.0000
Query 71:	0.0058
Query 72:	0.0000
Query 73:	0.0000
Query 74:	0.0000
Query 75:	0.0000
Query 76:	0.0001
Query 77:	0.0139
Query 78:	0.0000
Query 79:	0.0000
Query 80:	0.0003
Query 81:	0.0000
Query 82:	0.0498
Query 83:	0.0000
Query 84:	0.1348
Query 85:	0.0000
Query 86:	0.0142
Query 87:	0.0017
Query 88:	0.0000
Query 89:	0.0000
Query 90:	0.0034

Overall statistics
(for 47 queries):

Total number of documents
over all queries:
Retrieved: 47000
Relevant: 856
Rel_ret: 149

Interpolated Recall -
Precision Averages:

at 0.00	0.1533
at 0.10	0.0818
at 0.20	0.0331
at 0.30	0.0221
at 0.40	0.0108
at 0.50	0.0095
at 0.60	0.0066
at 0.70	0.0021
at 0.80	0.0005
at 0.90	0.0000
at 1.00	0.0000

Avg. prec. (non-interpolated)
for all rel. documents
                 0.0224

Precision:
At 5 docs:	0.0681
At 10 docs:	0.0426
At 15 docs:	0.0326
At 20 docs:	0.0298
At 30 docs:	0.0270
At 100 docs:	0.0189
At 200 docs:	0.0129
At 500 docs:	0.0061
At 1000 docs:	0.0032

R-Precision (prec. after R
(=num_rel) docs. retrieved):
Exact: 0.0328

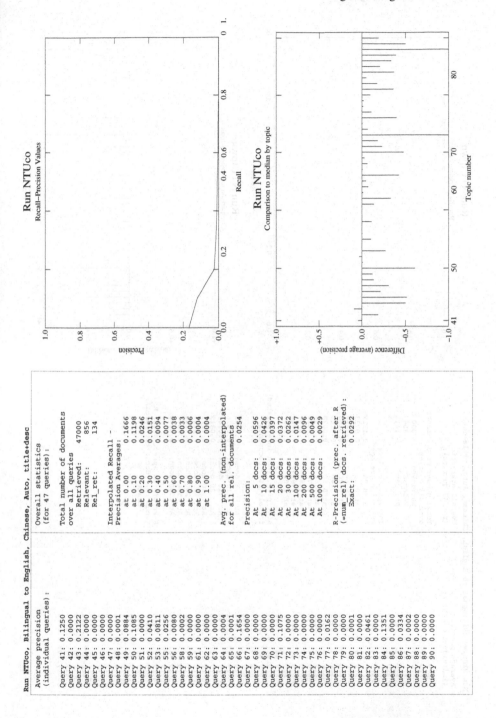

Run NTUco, Bilingual to English, Chinese, Auto, title+desc

Average precision
(individual queries):

Query 41:	0.1250
Query 42:	0.0000
Query 43:	0.2122
Query 44:	0.0000
Query 45:	0.0000
Query 46:	0.0000
Query 47:	0.0000
Query 48:	0.0001
Query 49:	0.0884
Query 50:	0.1085
Query 51:	0.0000
Query 52:	0.0410
Query 53:	0.0811
Query 55:	0.0256
Query 56:	0.0080
Query 58:	0.0002
Query 59:	0.0001
Query 61:	0.0000
Query 62:	0.0000
Query 63:	0.0000
Query 64:	0.0004
Query 65:	0.0001
Query 66:	0.1654
Query 67:	0.0000
Query 68:	0.0000
Query 69:	0.0000
Query 70:	0.0000
Query 71:	0.1075
Query 72:	0.0000
Query 73:	0.0000
Query 74:	0.0000
Query 75:	0.0000
Query 76:	0.0000
Query 77:	0.0162
Query 78:	0.0000
Query 79:	0.0000
Query 80:	0.0001
Query 81:	0.0000
Query 82:	0.0461
Query 83:	0.0000
Query 84:	0.1351
Query 85:	0.0000
Query 86:	0.0334
Query 87:	0.0002
Query 88:	0.0000
Query 89:	0.0000
Query 90:	0.0000

Overall statistics
(for 47 queries):

Total number of documents
over all queries
Retrieved: 47000
Relevant: 856
Rel_ret: 134

Interpolated Recall -
Precision Averages:
at 0.00   0.1666
at 0.10   0.1198
at 0.20   0.0246
at 0.30   0.0151
at 0.40   0.0094
at 0.50   0.0077
at 0.60   0.0038
at 0.70   0.0033
at 0.80   0.0006
at 0.90   0.0004
at 1.00   0.0004

Avg. prec. (non-interpolated)
for all rel. documents
                0.0254

Precision:
At   5 docs: 0.0596
At   10 docs: 0.0426
At   15 docs: 0.0397
At   20 docs: 0.0372
At   30 docs: 0.0262
At 100 docs: 0.0147
At 200 docs: 0.0096
At 500 docs: 0.0049
At 1000 docs: 0.0029

R-Precision (prec. after R
(=num_rel) docs. retrieved):
     Exact: 0.0292

Run NTUco
Recall-Precision Values

Run NTUco
Comparison to median by topic

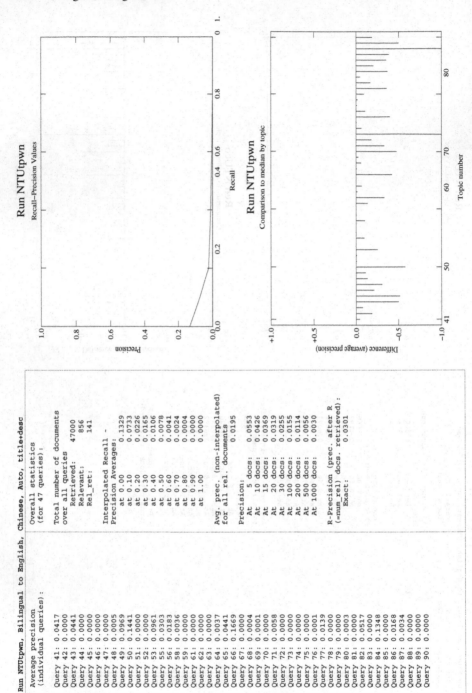

Run NTUtpwn
Recall-Precision Values

Run NTUtpwn
Comparison to median by topic

Run NTUtpwn, Bilingual to English, Chinese, Auto, title+desc

Average precision
(individual queries):

Query 41: 0.0417
Query 42: 0.0000
Query 43: 0.0441
Query 44: 0.0000
Query 45: 0.0000
Query 46: 0.0000
Query 47: 0.0000
Query 48: 0.0005
Query 49: 0.0969
Query 50: 0.1441
Query 51: 0.0000
Query 52: 0.0000
Query 53: 0.0961
Query 55: 0.0303
Query 56: 0.0183
Query 58: 0.0036
Query 59: 0.0000
Query 61: 0.0000
Query 62: 0.0000
Query 63: 0.0000
Query 64: 0.0037
Query 65: 0.0441
Query 66: 0.1669
Query 67: 0.0000
Query 68: 0.0004
Query 69: 0.0001
Query 70: 0.0000
Query 71: 0.0058
Query 72: 0.0000
Query 73: 0.0000
Query 74: 0.0000
Query 75: 0.0000
Query 76: 0.0001
Query 77: 0.0139
Query 78: 0.0000
Query 79: 0.0000
Query 80: 0.0003
Query 81: 0.0000
Query 82: 0.0517
Query 83: 0.0000
Query 84: 0.1348
Query 85: 0.0000
Query 86: 0.0168
Query 87: 0.0034
Query 88: 0.0000
Query 89: 0.0000
Query 90: 0.0000

Overall statistics
(for 47 queries):

Total number of documents
over all queries:
Retrieved: 47000
Relevant: 856
Rel_ret: 141

Interpolated Recall -
Precision Averages:
    at 0.00   0.1329
    at 0.10   0.0733
    at 0.20   0.0226
    at 0.30   0.0165
    at 0.40   0.0106
    at 0.50   0.0078
    at 0.60   0.0041
    at 0.70   0.0024
    at 0.80   0.0004
    at 0.90   0.0000
    at 1.00   0.0000

Avg. prec. (non-interpolated)
for all rel. documents
                0.0195

Precision:
    At   5 docs: 0.0553
    At   10 docs: 0.0426
    At   15 docs: 0.0369
    At   20 docs: 0.0319
    At   30 docs: 0.0255
    At 100 docs: 0.0155
    At 200 docs: 0.0114
    At 500 docs: 0.0056
    At 1000 docs: 0.0030

R-Precision (prec. after R
(=num_rel) docs. retrieved):
    Exact: 0.0301

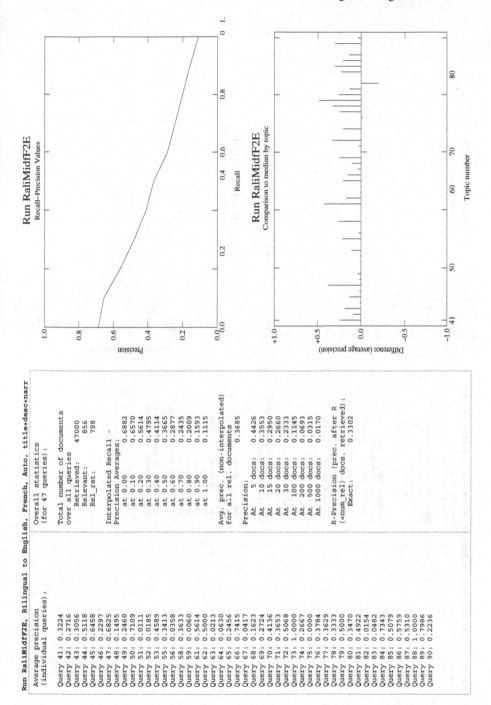

Run RaliMidfF2E, Bilingual to English, French, Auto, title+desc+narr

Average precision
(individual queries):

Query 41:	0.3224
Query 42:	0.2716
Query 43:	0.3056
Query 44:	0.5118
Query 45:	0.6458
Query 46:	0.2297
Query 47:	0.6825
Query 48:	0.1495
Query 49:	0.2460
Query 50:	0.7109
Query 51:	0.0111
Query 52:	0.0185
Query 53:	0.4589
Query 55:	0.3413
Query 56:	0.0358
Query 58:	0.3633
Query 59:	0.0060
Query 61:	0.5614
Query 62:	0.5000
Query 63:	0.0213
Query 64:	0.0630
Query 65:	0.2456
Query 66:	0.7415
Query 67:	0.0417
Query 68:	0.1623
Query 69:	0.2724
Query 70:	0.4136
Query 71:	0.3653
Query 72:	0.5068
Query 73:	1.0000
Query 74:	0.2667
Query 75:	0.0000
Query 76:	0.3784
Query 77:	0.3629
Query 78:	0.3333
Query 79:	0.5000
Query 80:	0.3470
Query 81:	0.4922
Query 82:	0.0154
Query 83:	0.0482
Query 84:	0.7343
Query 85:	0.5079
Query 86:	0.5759
Query 87:	0.5310
Query 88:	1.0000
Query 89:	0.7986
Query 90:	0.2236

Overall statistics
(for 47 queries):

Total number of documents
over all queries

Retrieved:	47000
Relevant:	856
Rel_ret:	798

Interpolated Recall -
Precision Averages:

at 0.00	0.6882
at 0.10	0.6570
at 0.20	0.5614
at 0.30	0.4795
at 0.40	0.4114
at 0.50	0.3665
at 0.60	0.2877
at 0.70	0.2435
at 0.80	0.2009
at 0.90	0.1593
at 1.00	0.1115

Avg. prec. (non-interpolated)
for all rel. documents
        0.3685

Precision:

At	5 docs:	0.4426
At	10 docs:	0.3553
At	15 docs:	0.2950
At	20 docs:	0.2660
At	30 docs:	0.2333
At	100 docs:	0.1145
At	200 docs:	0.0693
At	500 docs:	0.0315
At	1000 docs:	0.0170

R-Precision (prec. after R
(=num_rel) docs. retrieved):
        Exact: 0.3302

Run RaliMidfF2E
Recall-Precision Values

Run RaliMidfF2E
Comparison to median by topic

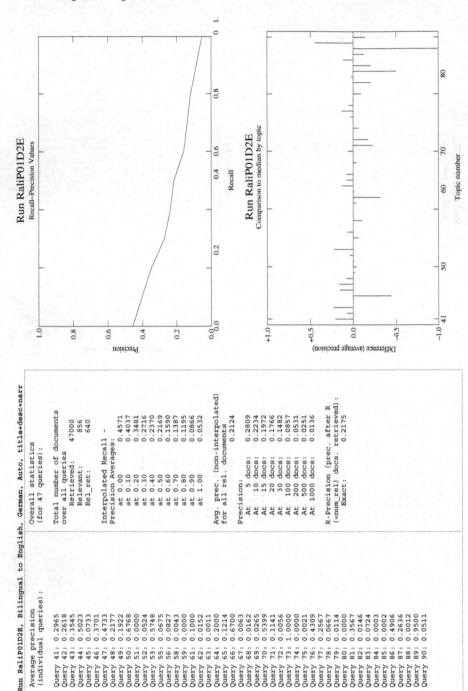

Run RaliP01D2E
Recall-Precision Values

Run RaliP01D2E
Comparison to median by topic

Run RaliP01D2E, Bilingual to English, German, Auto, title+desc+narr

Average precision
(individual queries):

Query 41:	0.2965
Query 42:	0.2618
Query 43:	0.3545
Query 44:	0.5023
Query 45:	0.0733
Query 46:	0.3701
Query 47:	0.4733
Query 48:	0.2177
Query 49:	0.1922
Query 50:	0.6768
Query 51:	0.0000
Query 52:	0.0524
Query 53:	0.5748
Query 55:	0.0675
Query 56:	0.0827
Query 58:	0.0043
Query 59:	0.0000
Query 61:	0.1000
Query 62:	0.0152
Query 63:	0.0011
Query 64:	0.2000
Query 65:	0.1214
Query 66:	0.6700
Query 67:	0.0063
Query 68:	0.0162
Query 69:	0.0265
Query 70:	0.5399
Query 71:	0.1141
Query 72:	0.0056
Query 73:	1.0000
Query 74:	0.0000
Query 75:	0.0021
Query 76:	0.4309
Query 77:	0.2567
Query 78:	0.0667
Query 79:	0.0114
Query 80:	0.0000
Query 81:	0.3567
Query 82:	0.0146
Query 83:	0.0724
Query 84:	0.0003
Query 85:	0.0002
Query 86:	0.4906
Query 87:	0.2636
Query 88:	0.0012
Query 89:	0.9500
Query 90:	0.0511

Overall statistics
(for 47 queries):

Total number of documents
over all queries:
    Retrieved: 47000
    Relevant: 856
    Rel_ret: 640

Interpolated Recall -
Precision Averages:
    at 0.00   0.4571
    at 0.10   0.4037
    at 0.20   0.3481
    at 0.30   0.2716
    at 0.40   0.2370
    at 0.50   0.2169
    at 0.60   0.1590
    at 0.70   0.1387
    at 0.80   0.1195
    at 0.90   0.0866
    at 1.00   0.0532

Avg. prec. (non-interpolated)
for all rel. documents
            0.2124

Precision:
    At   5 docs: 0.2809
    At   10 docs: 0.2234
    At   15 docs: 0.1972
    At   20 docs: 0.1766
    At   30 docs: 0.1482
    At 100 docs: 0.0857
    At 200 docs: 0.0531
    At 500 docs: 0.0251
    At 1000 docs: 0.0136

R-Precision (prec. after R
(=num_rel) docs. retrieved):
    Exact: 0.2175

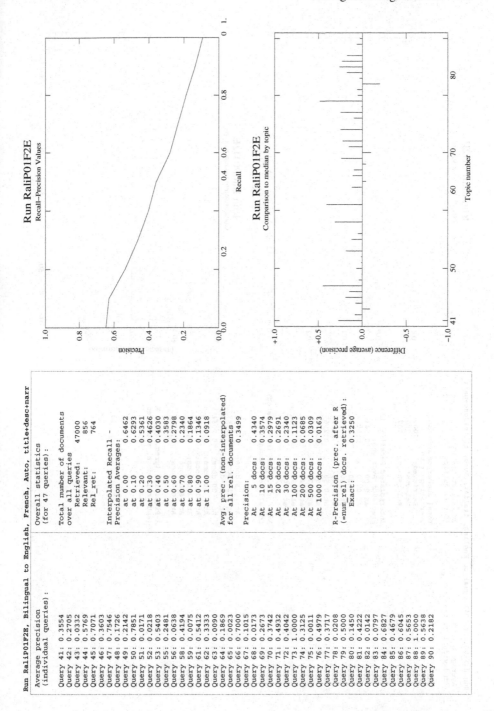

Run RaliP01F2E
Recall–Precision Values

Run RaliP01F2E
Comparison to median by topic

Run RaliP01F2B, Bilingual to English, French, Auto, title+desc+narr

Average precision
(individual queries):

Query 41:	0.3554
Query 42:	0.2705
Query 43:	0.0332
Query 44:	0.5769
Query 45:	0.7071
Query 46:	0.3603
Query 47:	0.7546
Query 48:	0.1726
Query 49:	0.2142
Query 50:	0.7851
Query 51:	0.0171
Query 52:	0.0218
Query 53:	0.5403
Query 55:	0.2481
Query 56:	0.0638
Query 58:	0.4194
Query 59:	0.0075
Query 61:	0.5412
Query 62:	0.3333
Query 63:	0.0090
Query 64:	0.1869
Query 65:	0.0023
Query 66:	0.7000
Query 67:	0.1015
Query 68:	0.0173
Query 69:	0.2673
Query 70:	0.3742
Query 71:	0.4932
Query 72:	0.4042
Query 73:	1.0000
Query 74:	0.3125
Query 75:	0.0011
Query 76:	0.4979
Query 77:	0.3717
Query 78:	0.0208
Query 79:	0.5000
Query 80:	0.1450
Query 81:	0.4222
Query 82:	0.0142
Query 83:	0.0797
Query 84:	0.6827
Query 85:	0.4679
Query 86:	0.6045
Query 87:	0.5653
Query 88:	1.0000
Query 89:	0.5638
Query 90:	0.2182

Overall statistics
(for 47 queries):

Total number of documents
over all queries
    Retrieved: 47000
    Relevant: 856
    Rel_ret: 764

Interpolated Recall -
Precision Averages:
    at 0.00   0.6462
    at 0.10   0.6293
    at 0.20   0.5361
    at 0.30   0.4626
    at 0.40   0.4030
    at 0.50   0.3583
    at 0.60   0.2798
    at 0.70   0.2340
    at 0.80   0.1864
    at 0.90   0.1346
    at 1.00   0.0918

Avg. prec. (non-interpolated)
for all rel. documents
                   0.3499

Precision:
    At   5 docs: 0.4340
    At   10 docs: 0.3574
    At   15 docs: 0.2979
    At   20 docs: 0.2691
    At   30 docs: 0.2340
    At 100 docs: 0.1123
    At 200 docs: 0.0685
    At 500 docs: 0.0309
    At 1000 docs: 0.0163

R-Precision (prec. after R
(=num_rel) docs. retrieved):
    Exact: 0.3250

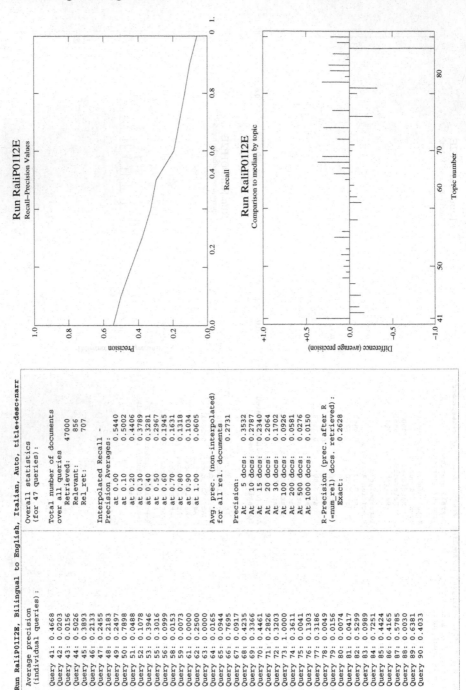

Run RaliP0lI2E
Recall–Precision Values

Run RaliP0lI2E
Comparison to median by topic

Run RaliP0lI2E, Bilingual to English, Italian, Auto, title+desc+narr

Average precision
(individual queries) :

Query 41:	0.4668
Query 42:	0.0203
Query 43:	0.0156
Query 44:	0.5026
Query 45:	0.3893
Query 46:	0.2133
Query 47:	0.2455
Query 48:	0.2183
Query 49:	0.2497
Query 50:	0.7898
Query 51:	0.0488
Query 52:	0.1078
Query 53:	0.3946
Query 55:	0.3016
Query 56:	0.0999
Query 58:	0.0153
Query 59:	0.0073
Query 61:	0.0000
Query 62:	0.2500
Query 63:	0.0000
Query 64:	0.0165
Query 65:	0.0944
Query 66:	0.7695
Query 67:	0.0917
Query 68:	0.4235
Query 69:	0.3366
Query 70:	0.4461
Query 71:	0.2826
Query 72:	0.3203
Query 73:	1.0000
Query 74:	0.3611
Query 75:	0.0041
Query 76:	0.1303
Query 77:	0.3186
Query 78:	0.0049
Query 79:	0.0156
Query 80:	0.0074
Query 81:	0.0417
Query 82:	0.5299
Query 83:	0.0989
Query 84:	0.7251
Query 85:	0.4424
Query 86:	0.4165
Query 87:	0.5785
Query 88:	0.0030
Query 89:	0.6381
Query 90:	0.4033

Overall statistics
(for 47 queries) :

Total number of documents
over all queries :
    Retrieved: 47000
    Relevant: 856
    Rel_ret: 707

Interpolated Recall -
Precision Averages:
    at 0.00   0.5440
    at 0.10   0.5002
    at 0.20   0.4406
    at 0.30   0.3789
    at 0.40   0.3281
    at 0.50   0.2967
    at 0.60   0.1945
    at 0.70   0.1631
    at 0.80   0.1318
    at 0.90   0.1034
    at 1.00   0.0605

Avg. prec. (non-interpolated)
for all rel. documents
                   0.2731

Precision:
    At   5 docs: 0.3532
    At   10 docs: 0.2787
    At   15 docs: 0.2340
    At   20 docs: 0.2064
    At   30 docs: 0.1702
    At 100 docs: 0.0926
    At 200 docs: 0.0581
    At 500 docs: 0.0276
    At 1000 docs: 0.0150

R-Precision (prec. after R
(=num_rel) docs. retrieved) :
    Exact: 0.2628

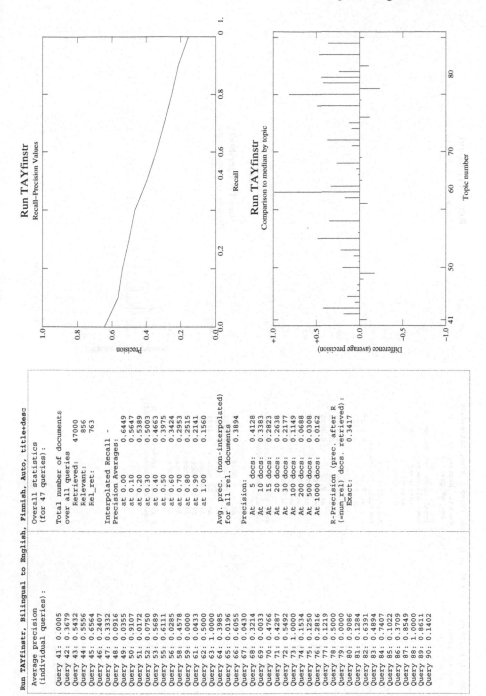

Run **TAYfinstr**, Bilingual to English, Finnish, Auto, title+desc

Average precision
(individual queries):

Query 41:	0.0005
Query 42:	0.3679
Query 43:	0.5432
Query 44:	0.5556
Query 45:	0.5564
Query 46:	0.2407
Query 47:	0.3332
Query 48:	0.0916
Query 49:	0.0355
Query 50:	0.9107
Query 51:	0.0172
Query 52:	0.0750
Query 53:	0.5689
Query 55:	0.6111
Query 56:	0.0285
Query 58:	0.4578
Query 59:	0.0000
Query 61:	0.0433
Query 62:	0.5000
Query 63:	1.0000
Query 64:	0.3985
Query 65:	0.0196
Query 66:	0.6055
Query 67:	0.0430
Query 68:	0.3214
Query 69:	0.0033
Query 70:	0.4766
Query 71:	0.4287
Query 72:	0.5492
Query 73:	1.0000
Query 74:	0.1534
Query 75:	0.1250
Query 76:	0.2816
Query 77:	0.1219
Query 78:	0.5000
Query 79:	0.0000
Query 80:	0.9086
Query 81:	0.1284
Query 82:	0.6391
Query 83:	0.4894
Query 84:	0.7407
Query 85:	0.1022
Query 86:	0.3709
Query 87:	0.8549
Query 88:	1.0000
Query 89:	0.8611
Query 90:	0.1402

Overall statistics
(for 47 queries):

Total number of documents
over all queries
   Retrieved: 47000
   Relevant: 856
   Rel_ret: 763

Interpolated Recall -
Precision Averages:
at 0.00	0.6449
at 0.10	0.5647
at 0.20	0.5389
at 0.30	0.5003
at 0.40	0.4663
at 0.50	0.3975
at 0.60	0.3424
at 0.70	0.2953
at 0.80	0.2515
at 0.90	0.2141
at 1.00	0.1560

Avg. prec. (non-interpolated)
for all rel. documents
                0.3894

Precision:
At 5 docs:	0.4128
At 10 docs:	0.3383
At 15 docs:	0.2823
At 20 docs:	0.2638
At 30 docs:	0.2177
At 100 docs:	0.1149
At 200 docs:	0.0688
At 500 docs:	0.0308
At 1000 docs:	0.0162

R-Precision (prec. after R
(=num rel) docs. retrieved):
    Exact: 0.3417

Run **TAYfinstr**
Recall–Precision Values

Run **TAYfinstr**
Comparison to median by topic

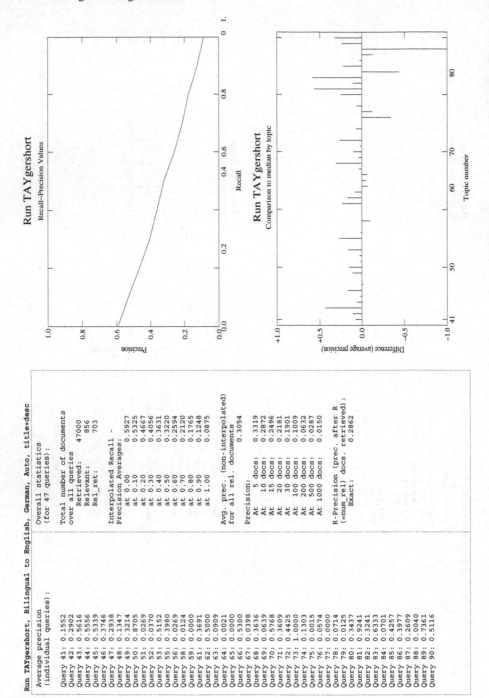

Run TAYgershort
Recall-Precision Values

Run TAYgershort
Comparison to median by topic

Run TAYgershort, Bilingual to English, German, Auto, title+desc

Average precision
(individual queries):

Query 41:	0.1552
Query 42:	0.2902
Query 43:	0.5616
Query 44:	0.5556
Query 45:	0.5339
Query 46:	0.3746
Query 47:	0.2938
Query 48:	0.1347
Query 49:	0.3214
Query 50:	0.8705
Query 51:	0.0269
Query 52:	0.0370
Query 53:	0.5152
Query 55:	0.3980
Query 56:	0.0269
Query 58:	0.0124
Query 59:	0.0000
Query 61:	0.3691
Query 62:	0.5000
Query 63:	0.0909
Query 64:	0.0021
Query 65:	0.0000
Query 66:	0.5300
Query 67:	0.0398
Query 68:	0.3636
Query 69:	0.0639
Query 70:	0.5768
Query 71:	0.3609
Query 72:	0.4425
Query 73:	1.0000
Query 74:	0.13303
Query 75:	0.0015
Query 76:	0.0574
Query 77:	0.0000
Query 78:	0.0714
Query 79:	0.0125
Query 80:	0.3437
Query 81:	0.9241
Query 82:	0.3241
Query 83:	0.6333
Query 84:	0.0701
Query 85:	0.4257
Query 86:	0.3977
Query 87:	0.2609
Query 88:	0.0040
Query 89:	0.7361
Query 90:	0.5116

Overall statistics
(for 47 queries):

Total number of documents
over all queries:
Retrieved: 47000
Relevant: 856
Rel_ret: 703

Interpolated Recall -
Precision Averages:

at 0.00	0.5927
at 0.10	0.5325
at 0.20	0.4667
at 0.30	0.4056
at 0.40	0.3631
at 0.50	0.3220
at 0.60	0.2594
at 0.70	0.2120
at 0.80	0.1765
at 0.90	0.1248
at 1.00	0.0875

Avg. prec. (non-interpolated)
for all rel. documents
                    0.3054

Precision:

At	5 docs:	0.3319
At	10 docs:	0.2872
At	15 docs:	0.2496
At	20 docs:	0.2181
At	30 docs:	0.1901
At	100 docs:	0.1009
At	200 docs:	0.0632
At	500 docs:	0.0287
At	1000 docs:	0.0150

R-Precision (prec. after R
(=num_rel) docs. retrieved):
Exact: 0.2862

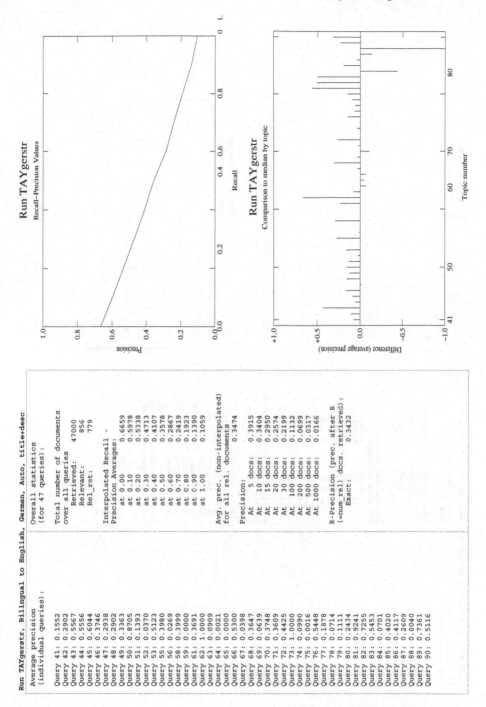

Run TAYgerstr
Recall–Precision Values

Run TAYgerstr
Comparison to median by topic

Run TAYgerstr, Bilingual to English, German, Auto, title+desc

Average precision
(individual queries):

Overall statistics
(for 47 queries):

Total number of documents
over all queries
    Retrieved: 47000
    Relevant: 856
    Rel_ret: 779

Interpolated Recall –
Precision Averages:
    at 0.00   0.6659
    at 0.10   0.5978
    at 0.20   0.5338
    at 0.30   0.4713
    at 0.40   0.4107
    at 0.50   0.3578
    at 0.60   0.2867
    at 0.70   0.2419
    at 0.80   0.1923
    at 0.90   0.1390
    at 1.00   0.1059

Avg. prec. (non-interpolated)
for all rel. documents
                   0.3474

Precision:
    At   5 docs: 0.3915
    At   10 docs: 0.3404
    At   15 docs: 0.2950
    At   20 docs: 0.2574
    At   30 docs: 0.2199
    At 100 docs: 0.1132
    At 200 docs: 0.0699
    At 500 docs: 0.0317
    At 1000 docs: 0.0166

R-Precision (prec. after R
(=num_rel) docs. retrieved):
    Exact: 0.3432

Query 41:	0.1552
Query 42:	0.2902
Query 43:	0.5567
Query 44:	0.5556
Query 45:	0.6044
Query 46:	0.3746
Query 47:	0.2938
Query 48:	0.2902
Query 49:	0.3363
Query 50:	0.8705
Query 51:	0.1393
Query 52:	0.0370
Query 53:	0.5123
Query 55:	0.3980
Query 56:	0.0269
Query 58:	0.3999
Query 59:	0.0000
Query 61:	0.3691
Query 62:	1.0000
Query 63:	0.0909
Query 64:	0.0021
Query 65:	0.0000
Query 66:	0.5300
Query 67:	0.0398
Query 68:	0.3647
Query 69:	0.0639
Query 70:	0.3748
Query 71:	0.3609
Query 72:	0.4425
Query 73:	1.0000
Query 74:	0.0990
Query 75:	0.0016
Query 76:	0.5448
Query 77:	0.1878
Query 78:	0.0714
Query 79:	0.1111
Query 80:	0.2434
Query 81:	0.9241
Query 82:	0.7255
Query 83:	0.5453
Query 84:	0.0701
Query 85:	0.4020
Query 86:	0.4117
Query 87:	0.2609
Query 88:	0.0040
Query 89:	0.7361
Query 90:	0.5116

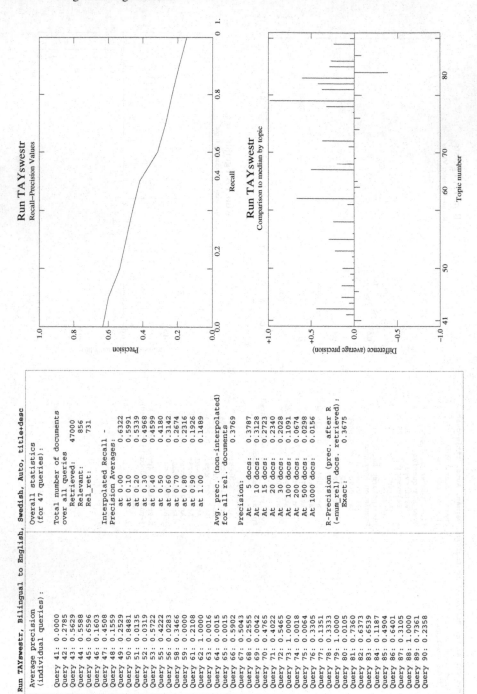

Run TAYswestr
Recall–Precision Values

Run TAYswestr
Comparison to median by topic

Run TAYswestr, Bilingual to English, Swedish, Auto, title+desc

Average precision
(individual queries):

Query 41:	0.0000
Query 42:	0.2785
Query 43:	0.5629
Query 44:	0.5588
Query 45:	0.6596
Query 46:	0.1603
Query 47:	0.4508
Query 48:	0.1559
Query 49:	0.2529
Query 50:	0.8481
Query 51:	0.0135
Query 52:	0.0319
Query 53:	0.5722
Query 55:	0.4222
Query 56:	0.0283
Query 58:	0.3466
Query 59:	0.0000
Query 61:	0.2108
Query 62:	1.0000
Query 63:	0.0016
Query 64:	0.0015
Query 65:	0.0015
Query 66:	0.5902
Query 67:	0.5043
Query 68:	0.2555
Query 69:	0.0042
Query 70:	0.4765
Query 71:	0.4022
Query 72:	0.5465
Query 73:	1.0000
Query 74:	0.0018
Query 75:	0.0064
Query 76:	0.3305
Query 77:	0.1351
Query 78:	0.3333
Query 79:	1.0000
Query 80:	0.0105
Query 81:	0.7360
Query 82:	0.6373
Query 83:	0.6539
Query 84:	0.1187
Query 85:	0.4904
Query 86:	0.6401
Query 87:	0.3105
Query 88:	1.0000
Query 89:	0.7361
Query 90:	0.2358

Overall statistics
(for 47 queries):

Total number of documents
over all queries:
  Retrieved: 47000
  Relevant: 856
  Rel_ret: 731

Interpolated Recall –
Precision Averages:
  at 0.00   0.6322
  at 0.10   0.5991
  at 0.20   0.5339
  at 0.30   0.4968
  at 0.40   0.4599
  at 0.50   0.4180
  at 0.60   0.3142
  at 0.70   0.2674
  at 0.80   0.2316
  at 0.90   0.1926
  at 1.00   0.1489

Avg. prec. (non-interpolated)
for all rel. documents
                0.3769

Precision:
  At   5 docs: 0.3787
  At   10 docs: 0.3128
  At   15 docs: 0.2723
  At   20 docs: 0.2340
  At   30 docs: 0.2028
  At 100 docs: 0.1091
  At 200 docs: 0.0674
  At 500 docs: 0.0298
  At 1000 docs: 0.0156

R-Precision (prec. after R
(=num_rel) docs. retrieved):
  Exact: 0.3675

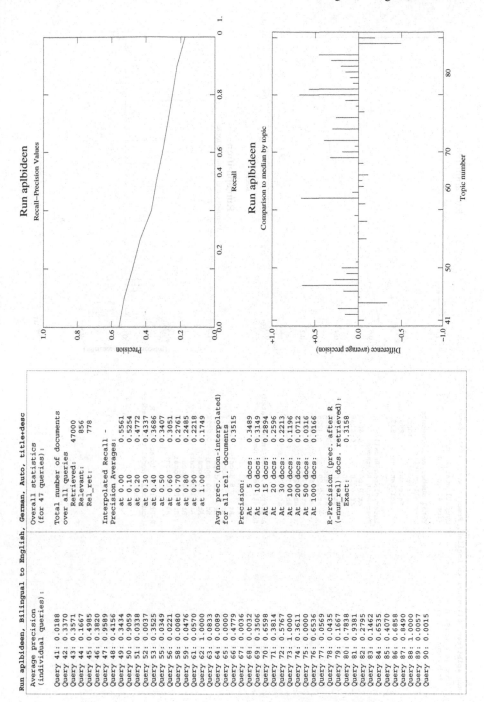

Run aplbideen, Bilingual to English, German, Auto, title+desc

Average precision
(individual queries):

Query 41: 0.0188
Query 42: 0.3370
Query 43: 0.3571
Query 44: 0.1667
Query 45: 0.4985
Query 46: 0.3820
Query 47: 0.9589
Query 48: 0.4156
Query 49: 0.3434
Query 50: 0.9059
Query 51: 0.0338
Query 52: 0.0037
Query 53: 0.3525
Query 55: 0.0349
Query 56: 0.0221
Query 58: 0.0080
Query 59: 0.0476
Query 61: 0.0570
Query 62: 1.0000
Query 63: 0.0833
Query 64: 0.0089
Query 65: 0.0000
Query 66: 0.4779
Query 67: 0.0036
Query 68: 0.0032
Query 69: 0.3506
Query 70: 0.6598
Query 71: 0.3814
Query 72: 0.5767
Query 73: 1.0000
Query 74: 0.3611
Query 75: 0.0000
Query 76: 0.6536
Query 77: 0.0569
Query 78: 0.0435
Query 79: 0.1667
Query 80: 0.7838
Query 81: 0.9381
Query 82: 0.2795
Query 83: 0.1462
Query 84: 0.6535
Query 85: 0.4070
Query 86: 0.6858
Query 87: 0.8490
Query 88: 1.0000
Query 89: 0.0057
Query 90: 0.0015

Overall statistics
(for 47 queries)

Total number of documents
over all queries
   Retrieved: 47000
   Relevant: 856
   Rel_ret: 778

Interpolated Recall -
Precision Averages:
   at 0.00   0.5561
   at 0.10   0.5254
   at 0.20   0.4772
   at 0.30   0.4337
   at 0.40   0.3686
   at 0.50   0.3407
   at 0.60   0.3051
   at 0.70   0.2761
   at 0.80   0.2485
   at 0.90   0.2218
   at 1.00   0.1749
Avg. prec. (non-interpolated)
for all rel. documents
                  0.3515

Precision:
   At   5 docs: 0.3489
   At   10 docs: 0.3149
   At   15 docs: 0.2894
   At   20 docs: 0.2596
   At   30 docs: 0.2213
   At 100 docs: 0.1196
   At 200 docs: 0.0712
   At 500 docs: 0.0316
   At 1000 docs: 0.0166

R-Precision (prec. after R
(=num_rel) docs. retrieved):
   Exact: 0.3158

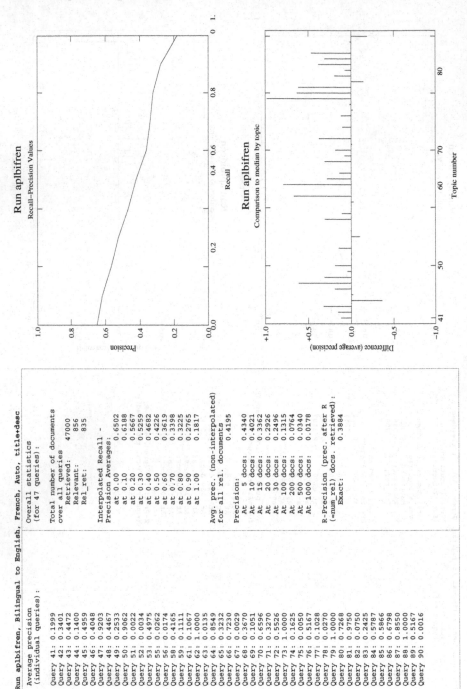

Run aplbifren

Recall–Precision Values

Precision

Recall

Run aplbifren

Comparison to median by topic

Difference (average precision)

Topic number

Run aplbifren, Bilingual to English, French, Auto, title+desc

Average precision
(individual queries):

Query 41:	0.1999
Query 42:	0.3401
Query 43:	0.4472
Query 44:	0.1400
Query 45:	0.4959
Query 46:	0.4048
Query 47:	0.9203
Query 48:	0.4467
Query 49:	0.2533
Query 50:	0.9062
Query 51:	0.0022
Query 52:	0.0034
Query 53:	0.4975
Query 55:	0.0262
Query 56:	0.0174
Query 58:	0.4165
Query 59:	0.1111
Query 61:	0.1067
Query 62:	1.0000
Query 63:	0.0135
Query 64:	0.8549
Query 65:	0.3232
Query 66:	0.7230
Query 67:	0.0029
Query 68:	0.3670
Query 69:	0.1051
Query 70:	0.6596
Query 71:	0.3270
Query 72:	0.5526
Query 73:	1.0000
Query 74:	0.1625
Query 75:	0.0050
Query 76:	0.5167
Query 77:	0.1028
Query 78:	0.0270
Query 79:	1.0000
Query 80:	0.7268
Query 81:	0.9750
Query 82:	0.0750
Query 83:	0.2425
Query 84:	0.5787
Query 85:	0.5866
Query 86:	0.6798
Query 87:	0.8550
Query 88:	1.0000
Query 89:	0.5167
Query 90:	0.0016

Overall statistics
(for 47 queries):

Total number of documents
over all queries:

Retrieved:	47000
Relevant:	856
Rel_ret:	835

Interpolated Recall –
Precision Averages:

at 0.00	0.6502
at 0.10	0.6188
at 0.20	0.5667
at 0.30	0.5259
at 0.40	0.4682
at 0.50	0.4226
at 0.60	0.3619
at 0.70	0.3398
at 0.80	0.3225
at 0.90	0.2765
at 1.00	0.1817

Avg. prec. (non-interpolated)
for all rel. documents
0.4195

Precision:

At 5 docs:	0.4340
At 10 docs:	0.4021
At 15 docs:	0.3362
At 20 docs:	0.2926
At 30 docs:	0.2496
At 100 docs:	0.1315
At 200 docs:	0.0764
At 500 docs:	0.0340
At 1000 docs:	0.0178

R-Precision (prec. after R
(=num_rel) docs. retrieved):
Exact: 0.3884

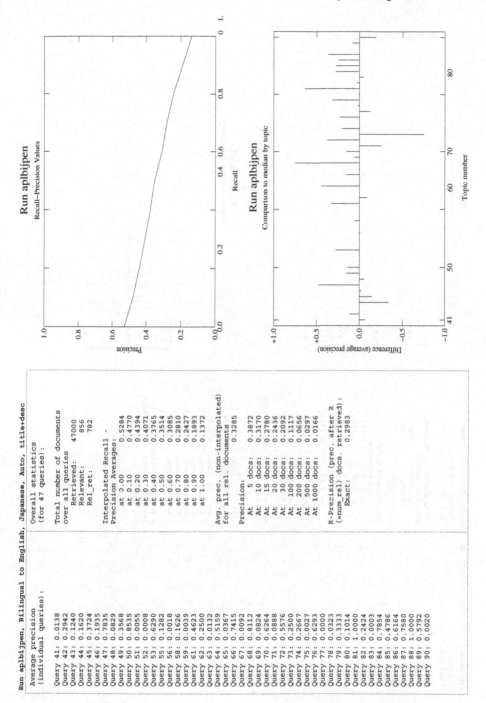

Run aplbijpen
Recall–Precision Values

Run aplbijpen
Comparison to median by topic

Run aplbijpen, Bilingual to English, Japanese, Auto, title+desc

Average precision
(individual queries):

Query 41:	0.0138		
Query 42:	0.2942		
Query 43:	0.1240		
Query 44:	0.1620		
Query 45:	0.3724		
Query 46:	0.1935		
Query 47:	0.7835		
Query 48:	0.0829		
Query 49:	0.3568		
Query 50:	0.8535		
Query 51:	0.0055		
Query 52:	0.0008		
Query 53:	0.6290		
Query 55:	0.1282		
Query 56:	0.0018		
Query 58:	0.1626		
Query 59:	0.0039		
Query 61:	0.4623		
Query 62:	0.2500		
Query 63:	0.0132		
Query 64:	0.5159		
Query 65:	0.0367		
Query 66:	0.7415		
Query 67:	0.0092		
Query 68:	0.8112		
Query 69:	0.0824		
Query 70:	0.6264		
Query 71:	0.0888		
Query 72:	0.5576		
Query 73:	0.2500		
Query 74:	0.2667		
Query 75:	0.0027		
Query 76:	0.6293		
Query 77:	0.0000		
Query 78:	0.0323		
Query 79:	0.3333		
Query 80:	0.1014		
Query 81:	1.0000		
Query 82:	0.2424		
Query 83:	0.0003		
Query 84:	0.7854		
Query 85:	0.4786		
Query 86:	0.6164		
Query 87:	0.7580		
Query 88:	1.0000		
Query 89:	0.5792		
Query 90:	0.0020		

Overall statistics
(for 47 queries):

Total number of documents over all queries
Retrieved: 47000
Relevant: 856
Rel_ret: 782

Interpolated Recall -
Precision Averages:
    at 0.00   0.5284
    at 0.10   0.4770
    at 0.20   0.4394
    at 0.30   0.4071
    at 0.40   0.3765
    at 0.50   0.3514
    at 0.60   0.3085
    at 0.70   0.2810
    at 0.80   0.2427
    at 0.90   0.1893
    at 1.00   0.1372
Avg. prec. (non-interpolated)
for all rel. documents
                   0.3285

Precision:
   At   5 docs: 0.3872
   At   10 docs: 0.3170
   At   15 docs: 0.2780
   At   20 docs: 0.2436
   At   30 docs: 0.2092
   At 100 docs: 0.1117
   At 200 docs: 0.0656
   At 500 docs: 0.0297
   At 1000 docs: 0.0166
R-Precision (prec. after R
(=num_rel) docs. retrieved):
     Exact: 0.2983

Run execel
Recall–Precision Values

Run execel
Comparison to median by topic

Run execel, Bilingual to English, Chinese, Auto, title+desc

Average precision
(individual queries):

Query 41:	0.2596
Query 42:	0.0390
Query 43:	0.3980
Query 44:	0.0190
Query 45:	0.6893
Query 46:	0.3293
Query 47:	0.9415
Query 48:	0.0036
Query 49:	0.4805
Query 50:	0.8854
Query 51:	0.0317
Query 52:	0.0262
Query 53:	0.5977
Query 55:	0.3739
Query 56:	0.0023
Query 58:	0.4028
Query 59:	0.1250
Query 61:	0.4069
Query 62:	0.3333
Query 63:	0.0164
Query 64:	0.1199
Query 65:	0.0099
Query 66:	0.7222
Query 67:	0.3667
Query 68:	0.0002
Query 69:	0.0022
Query 70:	0.5138
Query 71:	0.4474
Query 72:	0.2332
Query 73:	1.0000
Query 74:	1.0000
Query 75:	0.2000
Query 76:	0.6408
Query 77:	0.1164
Query 78:	0.5000
Query 79:	0.0022
Query 80:	0.0396
Query 81:	1.0000
Query 82:	0.7142
Query 83:	0.0064
Query 84:	0.5835
Query 85:	0.0032
Query 86:	0.2019
Query 87:	0.6438
Query 88:	1.0000
Query 89:	0.0080
Query 90:	0.0094

Overall statistics
(for 47 queries):

Total number of documents
over all queries:

Retrieved:	46001
Relevant:	856
Rel_ret:	687

Interpolated Recall -
Precision Averages:

at 0.00	0.5417
at 0.10	0.5269
at 0.20	0.4584
at 0.30	0.4297
at 0.40	0.3599
at 0.50	0.2994
at 0.60	0.2742
at 0.70	0.2484
at 0.80	0.2309
at 0.90	0.2081
at 1.00	0.1590

Avg. prec. (non-interpolated)
for all rel. documents   0.3286

Precision:

At	5 docs:	0.3489
At	10 docs:	0.2894
At	15 docs:	0.2525
At	20 docs:	0.2191
At	30 docs:	0.1872
At	100 docs:	0.0977
At	200 docs:	0.0583
At	500 docs:	0.0267
At	1000 docs:	0.0146

R-Precision (prec. after R
(=num_rel) docs. retrieved):

Exact:	0.2890

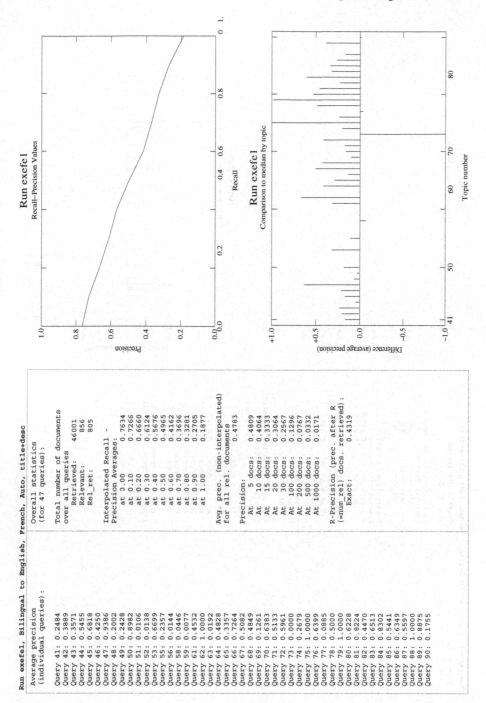

Run exefe1
Recall-Precision Values

Run exefe1
Comparison to median by topic

Run exefe1, Bilingual to English, French, Auto, title+desc

Average precision
(individual queries):

Query 41:	0.2484
Query 42:	0.3889
Query 43:	0.3571
Query 44:	0.5455
Query 45:	0.6818
Query 46:	0.4250
Query 47:	0.9386
Query 48:	0.2002
Query 49:	0.2428
Query 50:	0.8982
Query 51:	0.0106
Query 52:	0.0138
Query 53:	0.6699
Query 55:	0.2357
Query 56:	0.0144
Query 58:	0.0446
Query 59:	0.0077
Query 61:	0.4532
Query 62:	1.0000
Query 63:	0.0192
Query 64:	0.4828
Query 65:	0.3357
Query 66:	0.7264
Query 67:	0.5082
Query 68:	0.4849
Query 69:	0.1261
Query 70:	0.6383
Query 71:	0.5133
Query 72:	0.5961
Query 73:	0.0000
Query 74:	0.2679
Query 75:	1.0000
Query 76:	0.6399
Query 77:	0.0885
Query 78:	0.5000
Query 79:	1.0000
Query 80:	0.6228
Query 81:	0.8224
Query 82:	0.4470
Query 83:	0.6513
Query 84:	0.8302
Query 85:	0.5441
Query 86:	0.6349
Query 87:	0.5597
Query 88:	1.0000
Query 89:	0.8875
Query 90:	0.1755

Overall statistics
(for 47 queries):

Total number of documents
over all queries

Retrieved:	46001
Relevant:	856
Rel_ret:	805

Interpolated Recall -
Precision Averages:

at 0.00	0.7634
at 0.10	0.7266
at 0.20	0.6660
at 0.30	0.6124
at 0.40	0.5676
at 0.50	0.4965
at 0.60	0.4162
at 0.70	0.3696
at 0.80	0.3281
at 0.90	0.2705
at 1.00	0.1877

Avg. prec. (non-interpolated)
for all rel. documents
                  0.4783

Precision:

At 5 docs:	0.4809
At 10 docs:	0.4064
At 15 docs:	0.3333
At 20 docs:	0.3064
At 30 docs:	0.2567
At 100 docs:	0.1296
At 200 docs:	0.0767
At 500 docs:	0.0332
At 1000 docs:	0.0171

R-Precision (prec. after R
(=num_rel) docs. retrieved):
        Exact: 0.4319

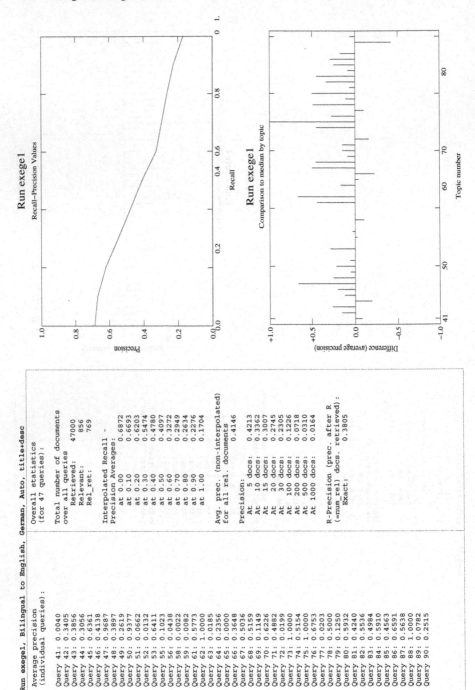

Run exege1
Recall–Precision Values

Run exege1
Comparison to median by topic

Run exege1, Bilingual to English, German, Auto, title+desc

Average precision
(individual queries):

Query 41:	0.0040
Query 42:	0.3405
Query 43:	0.3886
Query 44:	0.3056
Query 45:	0.6361
Query 46:	0.4138
Query 47:	0.9687
Query 48:	0.3897
Query 49:	0.2619
Query 50:	0.9377
Query 51:	0.0662
Query 52:	0.0132
Query 53:	0.6411
Query 55:	0.1023
Query 56:	0.0438
Query 58:	0.0022
Query 59:	0.0082
Query 61:	0.5773
Query 62:	1.0000
Query 63:	0.0185
Query 64:	0.2356
Query 65:	0.0000
Query 66:	0.3648
Query 67:	0.5036
Query 68:	0.5159
Query 69:	0.1149
Query 70:	0.6226
Query 71:	0.4882
Query 72:	0.0199
Query 73:	1.0000
Query 74:	0.5154
Query 75:	1.0000
Query 76:	0.6753
Query 77:	0.0203
Query 78:	0.5000
Query 79:	0.1250
Query 80:	0.5932
Query 81:	0.4240
Query 82:	0.5536
Query 83:	0.4984
Query 84:	0.5910
Query 85:	0.4563
Query 86:	0.6591
Query 87:	0.5638
Query 88:	1.0000
Query 89:	0.0782
Query 90:	0.2515

Overall statistics
(for 47 queries):

Total number of documents
over all queries:
Retrieved: 47000
Relevant: 856
Rel_ret: 769

Interpolated Recall –
Precision Averages:

at 0.00	0.6872
at 0.10	0.6693
at 0.20	0.6203
at 0.30	0.5474
at 0.40	0.4780
at 0.50	0.4097
at 0.60	0.3272
at 0.70	0.2949
at 0.80	0.2634
at 0.90	0.2276
at 1.00	0.1704

Avg. prec. (non-interpolated)
for all rel. documents
                    0.4146

Precision:

At 5 docs:	0.4213
At 10 docs:	0.3362
At 15 docs:	0.3007
At 20 docs:	0.2745
At 30 docs:	0.2305
At 100 docs:	0.1226
At 200 docs:	0.0718
At 500 docs:	0.0310
At 1000 docs:	0.0164

R-Precision (prec. after R
(=num_rel) docs. retrieved):
    Exact: 0.3805

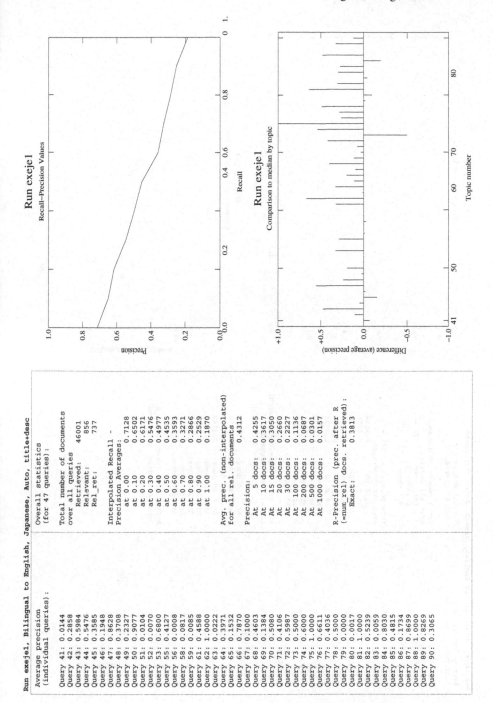

Run exeje1

Recall–Precision Values

Run exeje1

Comparison to median by topic

Run exeje1, Bilingual to English, Japanese, Auto, title+desc

Average precision
(individual queries):

Query 41:	0.0144
Query 42:	0.2858
Query 43:	0.5984
Query 44:	0.5476
Query 45:	0.3585
Query 46:	0.1948
Query 47:	0.8628
Query 48:	0.3708
Query 49:	0.2327
Query 50:	0.9077
Query 51:	0.0104
Query 52:	0.0070
Query 53:	0.6800
Query 55:	0.4127
Query 56:	0.0008
Query 58:	0.0817
Query 59:	0.0085
Query 61:	0.4588
Query 62:	1.0000
Query 63:	0.0222
Query 64:	0.3971
Query 65:	0.1532
Query 66:	0.7870
Query 67:	0.1000
Query 68:	0.4603
Query 69:	0.1384
Query 70:	0.5080
Query 71:	0.4106
Query 72:	0.5987
Query 73:	0.5000
Query 74:	0.6000
Query 75:	1.0000
Query 76:	0.6611
Query 77:	0.4036
Query 78:	0.5000
Query 79:	0.0000
Query 80:	0.0017
Query 81:	1.0000
Query 82:	0.5239
Query 83:	0.0059
Query 84:	0.8030
Query 85:	0.4815
Query 86:	0.1734
Query 87:	0.8699
Query 88:	1.0000
Query 89:	0.8269
Query 90:	0.3065

Overall statistics
(for 47 queries):

Total number of documents
over all queries
Retrieved:	46001
Relevant:	856
Rel_ret:	737

Interpolated Recall -
Precision Averages:
at 0.00	0.7128
at 0.10	0.6502
at 0.20	0.6171
at 0.30	0.5476
at 0.40	0.4977
at 0.50	0.4535
at 0.60	0.3593
at 0.70	0.3271
at 0.80	0.2866
at 0.90	0.2529
at 1.00	0.1870

Avg. prec. (non-interpolated)
for all rel. documents
                    0.4312

Precision:
At 5 docs:	0.4255
At 10 docs:	0.3617
At 15 docs:	0.3050
At 20 docs:	0.2660
At 30 docs:	0.2227
At 100 docs:	0.1136
At 200 docs:	0.0687
At 500 docs:	0.0301
At 1000 docs:	0.0157

R-Precision (prec. after R
(=num_rel) docs. retrieved) :
    Exact: 0.3813

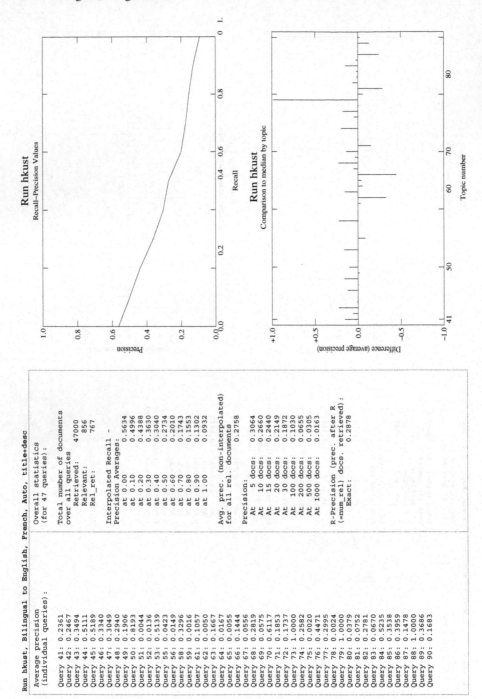

Run hkust
Recall-Precision Values

Run hkust
Comparison to median by topic

Run hkust, Bilingual to English, French, Auto, title+desc

Average precision
(individual queries):

Query 41:	0.2361
Query 42:	0.2467
Query 43:	0.3494
Query 44:	0.5111
Query 45:	0.5189
Query 46:	0.3340
Query 47:	0.3049
Query 48:	0.2940
Query 49:	0.1906
Query 50:	0.8193
Query 51:	0.0044
Query 52:	0.0136
Query 53:	0.5139
Query 55:	0.0423
Query 56:	0.0149
Query 58:	0.3296
Query 59:	0.0016
Query 61:	0.1057
Query 62:	0.0050
Query 63:	0.1667
Query 64:	0.0167
Query 65:	0.0055
Query 66:	0.1444
Query 67:	0.0556
Query 68:	0.2819
Query 69:	0.0575
Query 70:	0.6117
Query 71:	0.1853
Query 72:	0.1737
Query 73:	1.0000
Query 74:	0.2582
Query 75:	0.0020
Query 76:	0.4471
Query 77:	0.2995
Query 78:	0.0024
Query 79:	1.0000
Query 80:	0.0379
Query 81:	0.0752
Query 82:	0.2781
Query 83:	0.0670
Query 84:	0.5235
Query 85:	0.3538
Query 86:	0.3959
Query 87:	0.1478
Query 88:	1.0000
Query 89:	0.3686
Query 90:	0.1683

Overall statistics
(for 47 queries):

Total number of documents
over all queries
    Retrieved: 47000
    Relevant: 856
    Rel_ret: 767

Interpolated Recall -
Precision Averages:
    at 0.00   0.5634
    at 0.10   0.4996
    at 0.20   0.4388
    at 0.30   0.3630
    at 0.40   0.3040
    at 0.50   0.2734
    at 0.60   0.2010
    at 0.70   0.1743
    at 0.80   0.1553
    at 0.90   0.1302
    at 1.00   0.0932
Avg. prec. (non-interpolated)
for all rel. documents
                   0.2758

Precision:
    At   5 docs: 0.3064
    At   10 docs: 0.2660
    At   15 docs: 0.2440
    At   20 docs: 0.2149
    At   30 docs: 0.1872
    At 100 docs: 0.1030
    At 200 docs: 0.0655
    At 500 docs: 0.0305
    At 1000 docs: 0.0163

R-Precision (prec. after R
(=num_rel) docs. retrieved):
    Exact: 0.2878

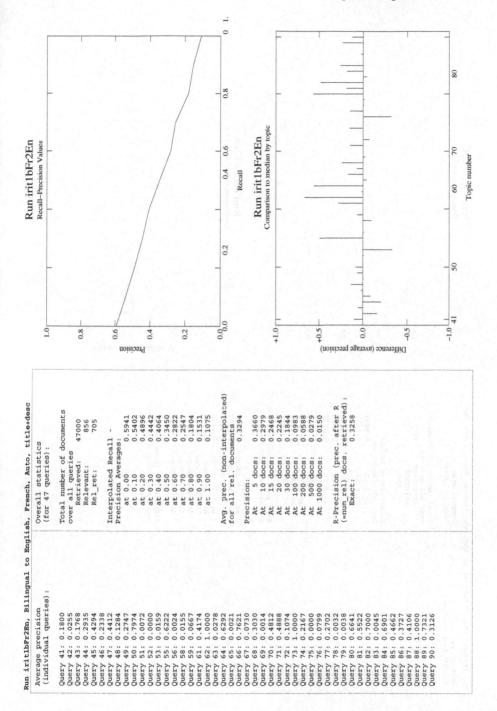

Run irit1bFr2En
Recall–Precision Values

Run irit1bFr2En
Comparison to median by topic

Run irit1bFr2En, Bilingual to English, French, Auto, title+desc

Average precision
(individual queries):

Query 41:	0.1800	Query 64:	0.6292		
Query 42:	0.0255	Query 65:	0.0021		
Query 43:	0.1768	Query 66:	0.7621		
Query 44:	0.2935	Query 67:	0.0730		
Query 45:	0.4294	Query 68:	0.3030		
Query 46:	0.2338	Query 69:	0.0014		
Query 47:	0.4412	Query 70:	0.4812		
Query 48:	0.1284	Query 71:	0.4888		
Query 49:	0.2747	Query 72:	0.1074		
Query 50:	0.7974	Query 73:	1.0000		
Query 51:	0.0072	Query 74:	0.2167		
Query 52:	0.0000	Query 75:	0.0000		
Query 53:	0.0159	Query 76:	0.0799		
Query 55:	0.6222	Query 77:	0.2702		
Query 56:	0.0024	Query 78:	0.0032		
Query 58:	0.0155	Query 79:	0.0038		
Query 59:	0.0667	Query 80:	0.6641		
Query 61:	0.4174	Query 81:	0.5522		
Query 62:	1.0000	Query 82:	0.7000		
Query 63:	0.0278	Query 83:	0.0045		
		Query 84:	0.6901		
		Query 85:	0.4662		
		Query 86:	0.3727		
		Query 87:	0.4106		
		Query 88:	1.0000		
		Query 89:	0.7321		
		Query 90:	0.3126		

Overall statistics
(for 47 queries):

Total number of documents
over all queries
        Retrieved: 47000
        Relevant: 856
        Rel_ret: 705

Interpolated Recall -
Precision Averages:
        at 0.00   0.5941
        at 0.10   0.5402
        at 0.20   0.4896
        at 0.30   0.4442
        at 0.40   0.4064
        at 0.50   0.3450
        at 0.60   0.2822
        at 0.70   0.2547
        at 0.80   0.1804
        at 0.90   0.1531
        at 1.00   0.1075

Avg. prec. (non-interpolated)
for all rel. documents
                    0.3294

Precision:
        At   5 docs: 0.3660
        At   10 docs: 0.2979
        At   15 docs: 0.2468
        At   20 docs: 0.2245
        At   30 docs: 0.1844
        At 100 docs: 0.0983
        At 200 docs: 0.0588
        At 500 docs: 0.0279
        At 1000 docs: 0.0150

R-Precision (prec. after R
(=num_rel) docs. retrieved):
        Exact: 0.3258

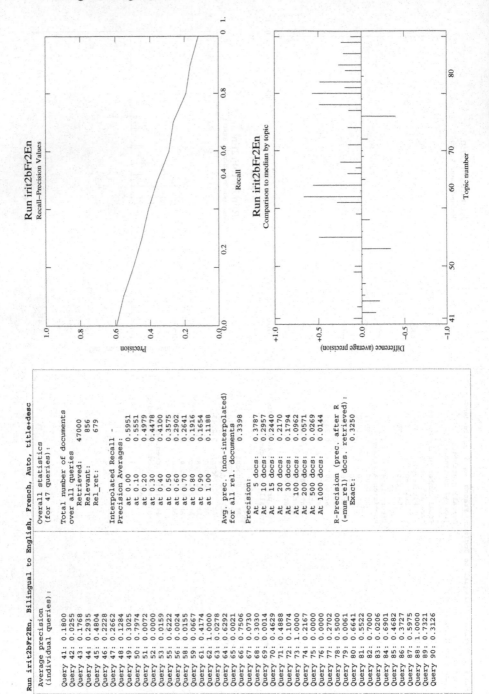

Run irit2bFr2En
Recall–Precision Values

Run irit2bFr2En
Comparison to median by topic

Run irit2bFr2En, Bilingual to English, French, Auto, title+desc

Average precision
(individual queries):

Query 41:	0.1800		
Query 42:	0.0255		
Query 43:	0.1768		
Query 44:	0.2935		
Query 45:	0.4804		
Query 46:	0.2228		
Query 47:	0.2662		
Query 48:	0.1284		
Query 49:	0.3025		
Query 50:	0.7974		
Query 51:	0.0072		
Query 52:	0.0000		
Query 53:	0.0159		
Query 55:	0.6222		
Query 56:	0.0024		
Query 58:	0.0155		
Query 59:	0.0667		
Query 61:	0.4174		
Query 62:	1.0000		
Query 63:	0.0278		
Query 64:	0.6292		
Query 65:	0.0021		
Query 66:	0.7506		
Query 67:	0.0730		
Query 68:	0.3030		
Query 69:	0.0014		
Query 70:	0.4629		
Query 71:	0.4888		
Query 72:	0.1074		
Query 73:	1.0000		
Query 74:	0.2167		
Query 75:	0.0000		
Query 76:	0.0000		
Query 77:	0.2702		
Query 78:	0.5000		
Query 79:	0.0061		
Query 80:	0.6641		
Query 81:	0.5522		
Query 82:	0.7000		
Query 83:	0.0206		
Query 84:	0.6901		
Query 85:	0.4682		
Query 86:	0.3727		
Query 87:	0.5975		
Query 88:	1.0000		
Query 89:	0.7321		
Query 90:	0.3126		

Overall statistics
(for 47 queries):

Total number of documents
over all queries:
    Retrieved: 47000
    Relevant: 856
    Rel_ret: 679

Interpolated Recall -
Precision Averages:
    at 0.00   0.5951
    at 0.10   0.5551
    at 0.20   0.4979
    at 0.30   0.4478
    at 0.40   0.4100
    at 0.50   0.3575
    at 0.60   0.2902
    at 0.70   0.2641
    at 0.80   0.1916
    at 0.90   0.1654
    at 1.00   0.1188

Avg. prec. (non-interpolated)
for all rel. documents
                0.3398

Precision:
    At   5 docs: 0.3787
    At   10 docs: 0.2957
    At   15 docs: 0.2440
    At   20 docs: 0.2170
    At   30 docs: 0.1794
    At 100 docs: 0.0962
    At 200 docs: 0.0571
    At 500 docs: 0.0269
    At 1000 docs: 0.0144

R-Precision (prec. after R
(=num_rel) docs. retrieved):
    Exact: 0.3250

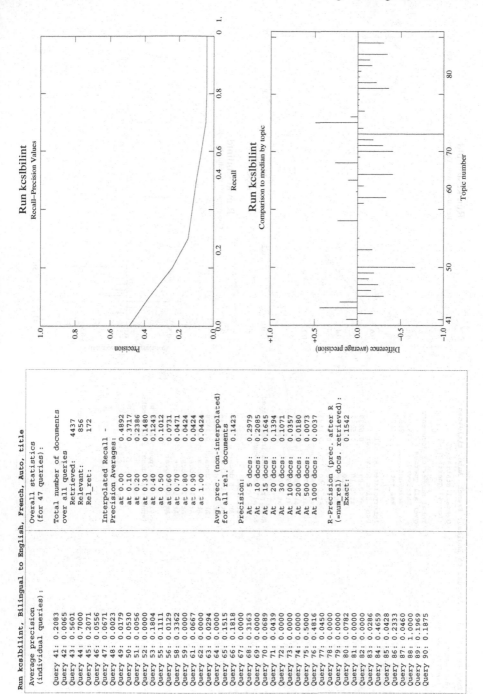

Run kcslbilint, Bilingual to English, French, Auto, title

Average precision
(individual queries):

Query 41:	0.2083
Query 42:	0.0065
Query 43:	0.5601
Query 44:	0.7000
Query 45:	0.2071
Query 46:	0.0556
Query 47:	0.0671
Query 48:	0.0023
Query 49:	0.0179
Query 50:	0.0530
Query 51:	0.0056
Query 52:	0.0000
Query 53:	0.1804
Query 55:	0.1111
Query 56:	0.0129
Query 58:	0.3362
Query 59:	0.0000
Query 61:	0.0667
Query 62:	0.0000
Query 63:	0.0294
Query 64:	0.0000
Query 65:	0.1515
Query 66:	0.1818
Query 67:	0.0000
Query 69:	0.3163
Query 70:	0.0689
Query 71:	0.0439
Query 72:	0.0000
Query 73:	0.0000
Query 74:	0.0000
Query 75:	0.5000
Query 76:	0.4816
Query 77:	0.0450
Query 78:	0.0000
Query 79:	0.0000
Query 80:	0.0782
Query 81:	0.0000
Query 82:	0.0000
Query 83:	0.0286
Query 84:	0.4659
Query 85:	0.0428
Query 86:	0.2333
Query 87:	0.0460
Query 88:	1.0000
Query 89:	0.1969
Query 90:	0.1875

Overall statistics
(for 47 queries):

Total number of documents
over all queries
Retrieved:	4437
Relevant:	856
Rel_ret:	172

Interpolated Recall -
Precision Averages:
at 0.00	0.4892
at 0.10	0.3717
at 0.20	0.2386
at 0.30	0.1480
at 0.40	0.1243
at 0.50	0.1012
at 0.60	0.0731
at 0.70	0.0471
at 0.80	0.0424
at 0.90	0.0424
at 1.00	0.0424

Avg. prec. (non-interpolated)
for all rel. documents
           0.1423

Precision:
At	5 docs:	0.2979
At	10 docs:	0.2085
At	15 docs:	0.1645
At	20 docs:	0.1394
At	30 docs:	0.1071
At	100 docs:	0.0357
At	200 docs:	0.0180
At	500 docs:	0.0073
At	1000 docs:	0.0037

R-Precision (prec. after R
(=num_rel) docs. retrieved) :
           Exact: 0.1542

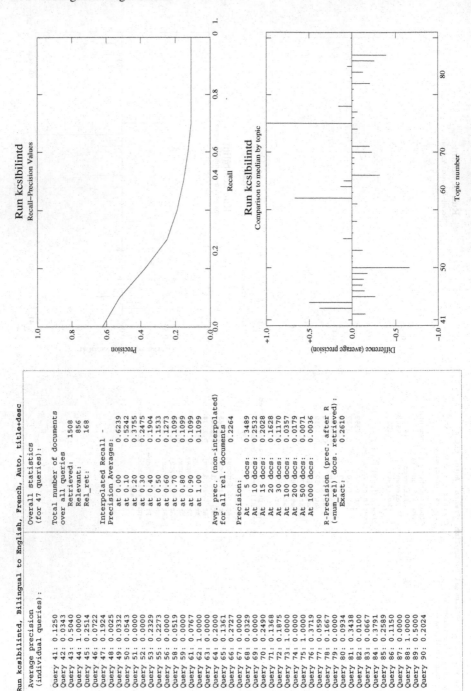

Run kcslbilintd, Bilingual to English, French, Auto, title+desc

Average precision
(individual queries):

Query 41:	0.1250
Query 42:	0.0343
Query 43:	0.5040
Query 44:	1.0000
Query 45:	0.2514
Query 46:	0.0722
Query 47:	0.1924
Query 48:	0.0025
Query 49:	0.0332
Query 50:	0.0543
Query 51:	0.0000
Query 52:	0.0000
Query 53:	0.2329
Query 55:	0.2273
Query 56:	0.0000
Query 58:	0.0519
Query 59:	0.0000
Query 61:	0.0767
Query 62:	1.0000
Query 63:	0.0000
Query 64:	0.2000
Query 65:	0.1361
Query 66:	0.2727
Query 67:	0.0000
Query 68:	0.0329
Query 69:	0.0000
Query 70:	0.2490
Query 71:	0.1368
Query 72:	0.1875
Query 73:	1.0000
Query 74:	0.0000
Query 75:	1.0000
Query 76:	0.3719
Query 77:	0.0590
Query 78:	0.1667
Query 79:	0.0000
Query 80:	0.0934
Query 81:	0.3438
Query 82:	0.0100
Query 83:	0.0667
Query 84:	0.3791
Query 85:	0.2589
Query 86:	0.1150
Query 87:	0.0000
Query 88:	1.0000
Query 89:	0.5000
Query 90:	0.2024

Overall statistics
(for 47 queries):

Total number of documents
over all queries:
Retrieved: 1508
Relevant: 856
Rel_ret: 168

Interpolated Recall -
Precision Averages:
at 0.00   0.6239
at 0.10   0.5242
at 0.20   0.3755
at 0.30   0.2475
at 0.40   0.1904
at 0.50   0.1533
at 0.60   0.1273
at 0.70   0.1099
at 0.80   0.1099
at 0.90   0.1099
at 1.00   0.1099

Avg. prec. (non-interpolated)
for all rel. documents
           0.2264

Precision:
At   5 docs: 0.3489
At   10 docs: 0.2532
At   15 docs: 0.2028
At   20 docs: 0.1628
At   30 docs: 0.1170
At 100 docs: 0.0357
At 200 docs: 0.0179
At 500 docs: 0.0071
At 1000 docs: 0.0036

R-Precision (prec. after R
(=num_rel) docs. retrieved):
    Exact: 0.2610

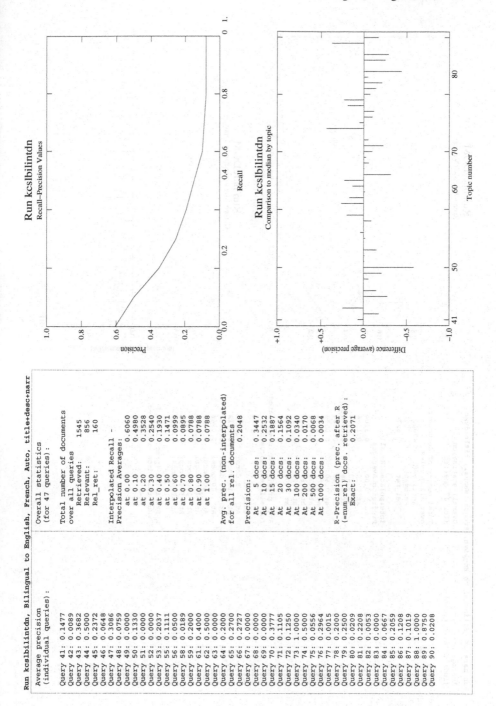

Run kcslbilintdn
Recall–Precision Values

Run kcslbilintdn
Comparison to median by topic

Run kcslbilintdn, Bilingual to English, French, Auto, title+desc+narr

Average precision
(individual queries):

Query 41:	0.1477
Query 42:	0.0089
Query 43:	0.3682
Query 44:	0.5000
Query 45:	0.2372
Query 46:	0.0648
Query 47:	0.3086
Query 48:	0.0759
Query 49:	0.0000
Query 50:	0.1330
Query 51:	0.0000
Query 52:	0.0000
Query 53:	0.2037
Query 55:	0.1111
Query 56:	0.0500
Query 58:	0.0189
Query 59:	0.2000
Query 61:	0.4000
Query 62:	0.5000
Query 63:	0.0000
Query 64:	0.2000
Query 65:	0.2700
Query 66:	0.2727
Query 67:	0.0000
Query 68:	0.0000
Query 69:	0.0000
Query 70:	0.3777
Query 71:	0.1105
Query 72:	0.1250
Query 73:	1.0000
Query 74:	0.5000
Query 75:	0.0556
Query 76:	0.2964
Query 77:	0.0015
Query 78:	0.2000
Query 79:	0.2500
Query 80:	0.0209
Query 81:	0.2208
Query 82:	0.0053
Query 83:	0.0000
Query 84:	0.0667
Query 85:	0.2059
Query 86:	0.1208
Query 87:	0.1019
Query 88:	1.0000
Query 89:	0.8750
Query 90:	0.0208

Overall statistics
(for 47 queries):

Total number of documents
over all queries
    Retrieved: 1545
    Relevant: 856
    Rel_ret: 160

Interpolated Recall -
Precision Averages:
    at 0.00   0.6060
    at 0.10   0.4980
    at 0.20   0.3528
    at 0.30   0.2540
    at 0.40   0.1930
    at 0.50   0.1471
    at 0.60   0.0999
    at 0.70   0.0895
    at 0.80   0.0788
    at 0.90   0.0788
    at 1.00   0.0788

Avg. prec. (non-interpolated)
for all rel. documents
                      0.2048

Precision:
    At   5 docs: 0.3447
    At   10 docs: 0.2532
    At   15 docs: 0.1887
    At   20 docs: 0.1564
    At   30 docs: 0.1092
    At 100 docs: 0.0340
    At 200 docs: 0.0170
    At 500 docs: 0.0068
    At 1000 docs: 0.0034

R-Precision (prec. after R
(=num_rel) docs. retrieved):
    Exact: 0.2071

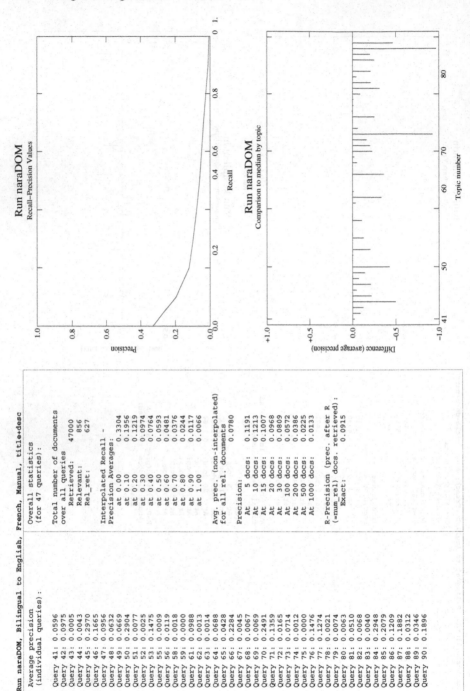

Run naraDOM, Bilingual to English, French, Manual, title+desc

Average precision
(individual queries):

Query 41:	0.0596
Query 42:	0.0975
Query 43:	0.0005
Query 44:	0.0043
Query 45:	0.2970
Query 46:	0.1665
Query 47:	0.0956
Query 48:	0.0632
Query 49:	0.0669
Query 50:	0.2904
Query 51:	0.0077
Query 52:	0.0025
Query 53:	0.1475
Query 55:	0.0009
Query 56:	0.0119
Query 58:	0.0018
Query 59:	0.0000
Query 61:	0.0988
Query 62:	0.0013
Query 63:	0.0014
Query 64:	0.0688
Query 65:	0.0428
Query 66:	0.2284
Query 67:	0.0045
Query 68:	0.0067
Query 69:	0.0069
Query 70:	0.2491
Query 71:	0.1359
Query 72:	0.0165
Query 73:	0.0714
Query 74:	0.0012
Query 75:	0.0000
Query 76:	0.1476
Query 77:	0.1274
Query 78:	0.0021
Query 79:	0.0074
Query 80:	0.0063
Query 81:	0.0510
Query 82:	0.0068
Query 83:	0.0040
Query 84:	0.2948
Query 85:	0.2079
Query 86:	0.1209
Query 87:	0.1882
Query 88:	0.0312
Query 89:	0.0346
Query 90:	0.1896

Overall statistics
(for 47 queries):

Total number of documents
over all queries
  Retrieved: 47000
  Relevant: 856
  Rel_ret: 627

Interpolated Recall -
Precision Averages:
  at 0.00   0.3304
  at 0.10   0.1956
  at 0.20   0.1219
  at 0.30   0.0974
  at 0.40   0.0764
  at 0.50   0.0593
  at 0.60   0.0481
  at 0.70   0.0376
  at 0.80   0.0244
  at 0.90   0.0117
  at 1.00   0.0066

Avg. prec. (non-interpolated)
for all rel. documents
            0.0780

Precision:
  At   5 docs: 0.1191
  At 10 docs: 0.1213
  At 15 docs: 0.1007
  At 20 docs: 0.0968
  At 30 docs: 0.0809
  At 100 docs: 0.0572
  At 200 docs: 0.0386
  At 500 docs: 0.0225
  At 1000 docs: 0.0133

R-Precision (prec. after R
(=num_rel) docs. retrieved):
  Exact: 0.0915

Run naraDOM
Recall-Precision Values

Run naraDOM
Comparison to median by topic

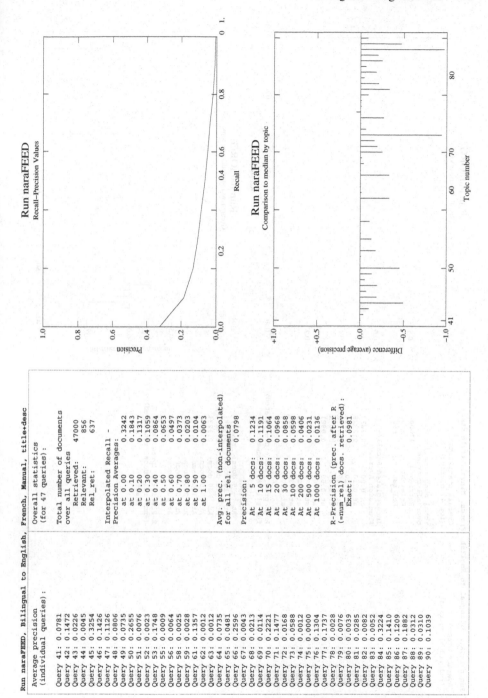

Run naraFEED, Bilingual to English, French, Manual, title+desc

Average precision
(individual queries):

Query 41:	0.0781
Query 42:	0.1472
Query 43:	0.0226
Query 44:	0.0045
Query 45:	0.3254
Query 46:	0.1426
Query 47:	0.1126
Query 48:	0.0806
Query 49:	0.0735
Query 50:	0.2655
Query 51:	0.0076
Query 52:	0.0023
Query 53:	0.1748
Query 55:	0.0009
Query 56:	0.0064
Query 58:	0.0025
Query 59:	0.0028
Query 61:	0.1357
Query 62:	0.0012
Query 63:	0.0012
Query 64:	0.0735
Query 65:	0.0481
Query 66:	0.2596
Query 67:	0.0043
Query 68:	0.0213
Query 69:	0.0114
Query 70:	0.2221
Query 71:	0.1477
Query 72:	0.0168
Query 73:	0.0588
Query 74:	0.0012
Query 75:	0.0000
Query 76:	0.1304
Query 77:	0.1737
Query 78:	0.0028
Query 79:	0.0076
Query 80:	0.0039
Query 81:	0.0285
Query 82:	0.0082
Query 83:	0.0052
Query 84:	0.3224
Query 85:	0.1410
Query 86:	0.1209
Query 87:	0.1882
Query 88:	0.0312
Query 89:	0.0310
Query 90:	0.1039

Overall statistics
(for 47 queries):

Total number of documents
over all queries
   Retrieved: 47000
   Relevant: 856
   Rel_ret: 637

Interpolated Recall -
Precision Averages:
   at 0.00   0.3242
   at 0.10   0.1843
   at 0.20   0.1317
   at 0.30   0.1059
   at 0.40   0.0864
   at 0.50   0.0653
   at 0.60   0.0497
   at 0.70   0.0373
   at 0.80   0.0203
   at 0.90   0.0104
   at 1.00   0.0063

Avg. prec. (non-interpolated)
for all rel. documents
           0.0798

Precision:
  At   5 docs: 0.1234
  At 10 docs: 0.1191
  At 15 docs: 0.1064
  At 20 docs: 0.0968
  At 30 docs: 0.0858
  At 100 docs: 0.0598
  At 200 docs: 0.0406
  At 500 docs: 0.0231
  At 1000 docs: 0.0136

R-Precision (prec. after R
(=num rel) docs. retrieved):
   Exact: 0.0981

Run naraFEED
Recall–Precision Values

Run naraFEED
Comparison to median by topic

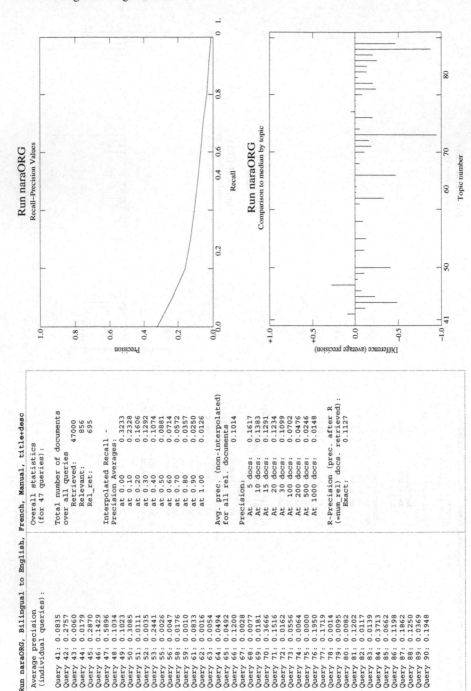

Run naraORG
Recall-Precision Values

Run naraORG
Comparison to median by topic

Run naraORG, Bilingual to English, French, Manual, title+desc

Average precision
(individual queries):

Query 41:	0.0835
Query 42:	0.2757
Query 43:	0.0060
Query 44:	0.0179
Query 45:	0.2870
Query 46:	0.1429
Query 47:	0.5896
Query 48:	0.1034
Query 49:	0.1023
Query 50:	0.3085
Query 51:	0.0111
Query 52:	0.0035
Query 53:	0.2441
Query 55:	0.0026
Query 56:	0.0047
Query 58:	0.0176
Query 59:	0.0010
Query 61:	0.0833
Query 62:	0.0016
Query 63:	0.0054
Query 64:	0.0494
Query 65:	0.0492
Query 66:	0.1200
Query 67:	0.0028
Query 68:	0.0077
Query 69:	0.0181
Query 70:	0.3666
Query 71:	0.1516
Query 72:	0.0162
Query 73:	0.0556
Query 74:	0.0064
Query 75:	0.0000
Query 76:	0.1950
Query 77:	0.1719
Query 78:	0.0014
Query 79:	0.0095
Query 80:	0.0082
Query 81:	0.1202
Query 82:	0.0117
Query 83:	0.0139
Query 84:	0.3713
Query 85:	0.0662
Query 86:	0.1198
Query 87:	0.1862
Query 88:	0.1250
Query 89:	0.0369
Query 90:	0.1948

Overall statistics
(for 47 queries):

Total number of documents
over all queries:
Retrieved: 47000
Relevant: 856
Rel_ret: 695

Interpolated Recall -
Precision Averages:
at 0.00	0.3233
at 0.10	0.2328
at 0.20	0.1606
at 0.30	0.1292
at 0.40	0.1074
at 0.50	0.0881
at 0.60	0.0714
at 0.70	0.0572
at 0.80	0.0357
at 0.90	0.0250
at 1.00	0.0126

Avg. prec. (non-interpolated)
for all rel. documents
                   0.1014

Precision:
At 5 docs:	0.1617
At 10 docs:	0.1383
At 15 docs:	0.1291
At 20 docs:	0.1234
At 30 docs:	0.1099
At 100 docs:	0.0702
At 200 docs:	0.0476
At 500 docs:	0.0246
At 1000 docs:	0.0148

R-Precision (prec. after R
(=num_rel) docs. retrieved):
Exact: 0.1127

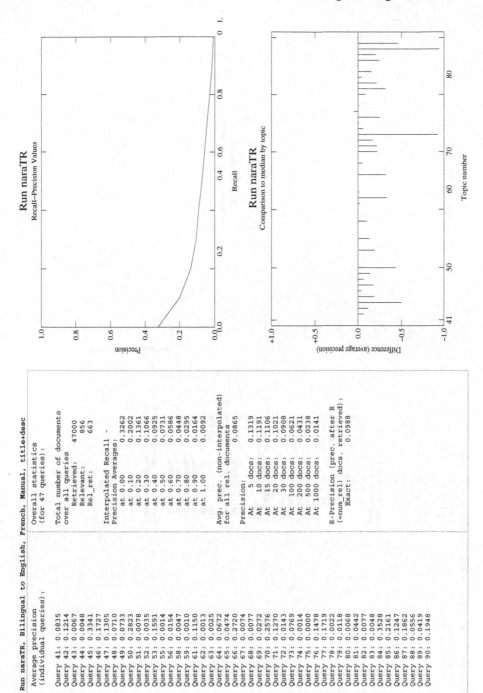

Run naraTR
Recall–Precision Values

Run naraTR
Comparison to median by topic

Run naraTR, Bilingual to English, French, Manual, title+desc

Average precision
(individual queries):

Query 41:	0.0835
Query 42:	0.1214
Query 43:	0.0067
Query 44:	0.0048
Query 45:	0.3341
Query 46:	0.1727
Query 47:	0.1305
Query 48:	0.0710
Query 49:	0.0733
Query 50:	0.2823
Query 51:	0.0078
Query 52:	0.0035
Query 53:	0.1591
Query 55:	0.0014
Query 56:	0.0154
Query 58:	0.0047
Query 59:	0.0010
Query 61:	0.1150
Query 62:	0.0013
Query 63:	0.0025
Query 64:	0.0672
Query 65:	0.0474
Query 66:	0.2720
Query 67:	0.0074
Query 68:	0.0077
Query 69:	0.0272
Query 70:	0.2576
Query 71:	0.1270
Query 72:	0.0143
Query 73:	0.0769
Query 74:	0.0014
Query 75:	0.0000
Query 76:	0.1478
Query 77:	0.1719
Query 78:	0.0022
Query 79:	0.0118
Query 80:	0.0068
Query 81:	0.0442
Query 82:	0.0077
Query 83:	0.0048
Query 84:	0.3528
Query 85:	0.2161
Query 86:	0.1247
Query 87:	0.1862
Query 88:	0.0556
Query 89:	0.0419
Query 90:	0.1948

Overall statistics
(for 47 queries):

Total number of documents
over all queries:

Retrieved:	47000
Relevant:	856
Rel_ret:	663

Interpolated Recall -
Precision Averages:

at 0.00	0.3262
at 0.10	0.2002
at 0.20	0.1361
at 0.30	0.1066
at 0.40	0.0925
at 0.50	0.0731
at 0.60	0.0586
at 0.70	0.0448
at 0.80	0.0295
at 0.90	0.0164
at 1.00	0.0092

Avg. prec. (non-interpolated)
for all rel. documents
    0.0865

Precision:

At 5 docs:	0.1319
At 10 docs:	0.1191
At 15 docs:	0.1106
At 20 docs:	0.1021
At 30 docs:	0.0908
At 100 docs:	0.0621
At 200 docs:	0.0431
At 500 docs:	0.0238
At 1000 docs:	0.0141

R-Precision (prec. after R
(=num_rel) docs. retrieved):
    Exact: 0.0988

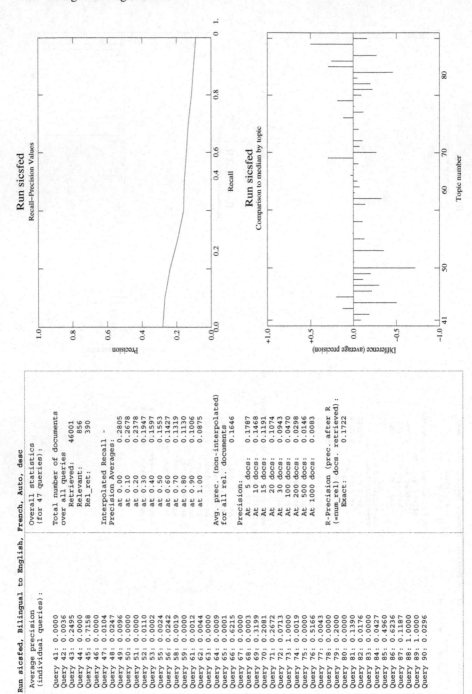

Run sicsfed, Bilingual to English, French, Auto, desc

Average precision
(individual queries):

Query 41:	0.0000
Query 42:	0.0036
Query 43:	0.2495
Query 44:	0.0000
Query 45:	0.7158
Query 46:	0.0000
Query 47:	0.0104
Query 48:	0.0247
Query 49:	0.0096
Query 50:	0.0000
Query 51:	0.0000
Query 52:	0.0110
Query 53:	0.0002
Query 55:	0.0024
Query 56:	0.0242
Query 58:	0.0019
Query 59:	0.0000
Query 61:	0.0012
Query 62:	0.0044
Query 63:	0.0000
Query 64:	0.0009
Query 65:	0.0001
Query 66:	0.6215
Query 67:	0.0000
Query 68:	0.0003
Query 69:	0.3199
Query 70:	0.2081
Query 71:	0.2672
Query 72:	0.0713
Query 73:	1.0000
Query 74:	0.0019
Query 75:	0.0000
Query 76:	0.5166
Query 77:	0.0043
Query 78:	0.0000
Query 79:	0.2000
Query 80:	0.0000
Query 81:	0.1390
Query 82:	0.0176
Query 83:	0.0000
Query 84:	0.0427
Query 85:	0.4960
Query 86:	0.6236
Query 87:	0.1187
Query 88:	1.0000
Query 89:	1.0000
Query 90:	0.0296

Overall statistics
(for 47 queries):

Total number of documents
over all queries:
Retrieved: 46001
Relevant: 856
Rel_ret: 390

Interpolated Recall -
Precision Averages:

at 0.00	0.2805
at 0.10	0.2678
at 0.20	0.2378
at 0.30	0.1947
at 0.40	0.1597
at 0.50	0.1553
at 0.60	0.1427
at 0.70	0.1319
at 0.80	0.1130
at 0.90	0.1006
at 1.00	0.0875

Avg. prec. (non-interpolated)
for all rel. documents
              0.1646

Precision:

At	5 docs:	0.1787
At	10 docs:	0.1468
At	15 docs:	0.1191
At	20 docs:	0.1074
At	30 docs:	0.0943
At	100 docs:	0.0470
At	200 docs:	0.0298
At	500 docs:	0.0146
At	1000 docs:	0.0083

R-Precision (prec. after R
(=num_rel) docs. retrieved):
    Exact: 0.1722

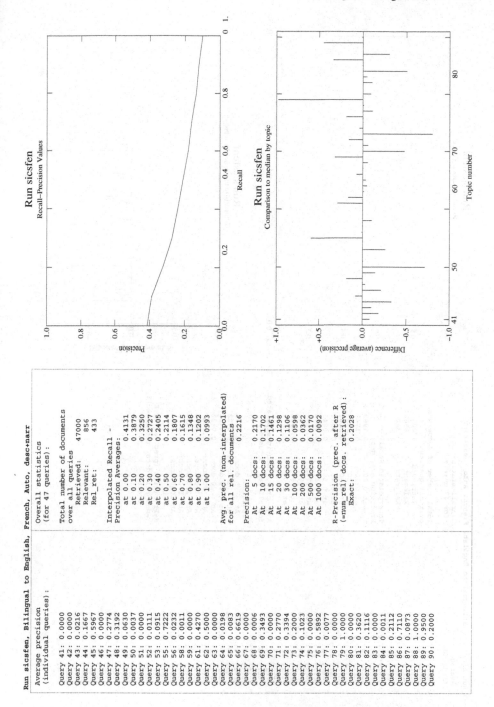

Run sicsfen
Recall–Precision Values

Run sicsfen
Comparison to median by topic

Run sicsfen, Bilingual to English, French, Auto, desc+narr

Average precision
(individual queries):

Query 41:	0.0000
Query 42:	0.0000
Query 43:	0.0216
Query 44:	0.1667
Query 45:	0.5967
Query 46:	0.0000
Query 47:	0.2774
Query 48:	0.3192
Query 49:	0.0630
Query 50:	0.0037
Query 51:	0.0000
Query 52:	0.0111
Query 53:	0.0915
Query 55:	0.7222
Query 56:	0.0232
Query 58:	0.0011
Query 59:	0.0000
Query 61:	0.4270
Query 62:	0.5000
Query 63:	0.0000
Query 64:	0.0198
Query 65:	0.0083
Query 66:	0.6619
Query 67:	0.0000
Query 68:	0.0006
Query 69:	0.3493
Query 70:	0.0000
Query 71:	0.2770
Query 72:	0.3394
Query 73:	0.2000
Query 74:	0.1023
Query 75:	0.0000
Query 76:	0.5892
Query 77:	0.0077
Query 78:	0.0000
Query 79:	1.0000
Query 80:	0.0000
Query 81:	0.3620
Query 82:	0.1116
Query 83:	0.0000
Query 84:	0.0011
Query 85:	0.2112
Query 86:	0.7110
Query 87:	0.0873
Query 88:	1.0000
Query 89:	0.9500
Query 90:	0.2000

Overall statistics
(for 47 queries):

Total number of documents
over all queries
Retrieved: 47000
Relevant: 856
Rel_ret: 433

Interpolated Recall -
Precision Averages:
at 0.00   0.4131
at 0.10   0.3879
at 0.20   0.3250
at 0.30   0.2727
at 0.40   0.2405
at 0.50   0.2114
at 0.60   0.1807
at 0.70   0.1615
at 0.80   0.1348
at 0.90   0.1202
at 1.00   0.0993

Avg. prec. (non-interpolated)
for all rel. documents   0.2216

Precision:
At   5 docs: 0.2170
At   10 docs: 0.1702
At   15 docs: 0.1461
At   20 docs: 0.1298
At   30 docs: 0.1106
At 100 docs: 0.0598
At 200 docs: 0.0362
At 500 docs: 0.0170
At 1000 docs: 0.0092

R-Precision (prec. after R
(=num_rel) docs. retrieved):
Exact: 0.2028

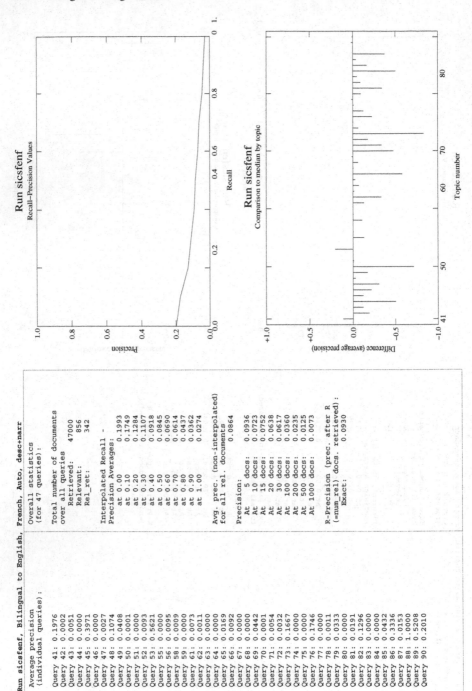

Run sicsfenf
Recall–Precision Values

Run sicsfenf
Comparison to median by topic

Run sicsfenf. Bilingual to English, French, Auto, desc+narr

Average precision
(individual queries):

Query 41:	0.1976
Query 42:	0.0002
Query 43:	0.0051
Query 44:	0.0000
Query 45:	0.3971
Query 46:	0.0000
Query 47:	0.0027
Query 48:	0.1074
Query 49:	0.0408
Query 50:	0.0001
Query 51:	0.0000
Query 52:	0.0093
Query 53:	0.5621
Query 55:	0.0000
Query 56:	0.0095
Query 58:	0.0009
Query 59:	0.0000
Query 61:	0.0073
Query 62:	0.0011
Query 63:	0.0000
Query 64:	0.0000
Query 65:	0.0169
Query 66:	0.0092
Query 67:	0.0000
Query 68:	0.0000
Query 69:	0.0442
Query 70:	0.0001
Query 71:	0.0054
Query 72:	0.0032
Query 73:	0.1667
Query 74:	0.0000
Query 75:	0.0000
Query 76:	0.1746
Query 77:	0.0000
Query 78:	0.0011
Query 79:	0.0333
Query 80:	0.0000
Query 81:	0.01191
Query 82:	0.1296
Query 83:	0.0000
Query 84:	0.0000
Query 85:	0.0432
Query 86:	0.3336
Query 87:	0.0153
Query 88:	1.0000
Query 89:	0.5208
Query 90:	0.2010

Overall statistics
(for 47 queries):

Total number of documents
over all queries:

Retrieved:	47000
Relevant:	856
Rel_ret:	342

Interpolated Recall -
Precision Averages:

at 0.00	0.1993
at 0.10	0.1749
at 0.20	0.1284
at 0.30	0.1107
at 0.40	0.0918
at 0.50	0.0845
at 0.60	0.0690
at 0.70	0.0614
at 0.80	0.0437
at 0.90	0.0362
at 1.00	0.0274

Avg. prec. (non-interpolated)
for all rel. documents
0.0864

Precision:

At 5 docs:	0.0936
At 10 docs:	0.0723
At 15 docs:	0.0752
At 20 docs:	0.0638
At 30 docs:	0.0617
At 100 docs:	0.0360
At 200 docs:	0.0235
At 500 docs:	0.0125
At 1000 docs:	0.0073

R-Precision (prec. after R
(=num_rel) docs. retrieved):
Exact: 0.0930

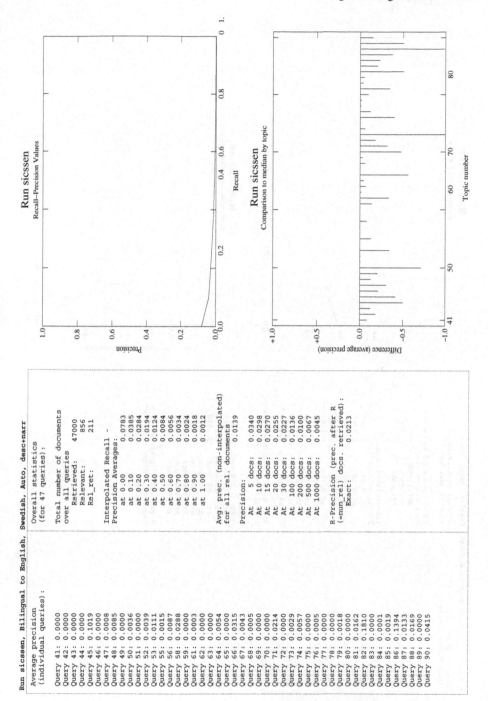

Run sicssen
Recall–Precision Values

Run sicssen
Comparison to median by topic

Run sicssen, Bilingual to English, Swedish, Auto, desc+narr

Average precision
(individual queries):

Query 41:	0.0000
Query 42:	0.0000
Query 43:	0.0000
Query 44:	0.0000
Query 45:	0.1019
Query 46:	0.0000
Query 47:	0.0008
Query 48:	0.0085
Query 49:	0.0000
Query 50:	0.0036
Query 51:	0.0000
Query 52:	0.0039
Query 53:	0.0111
Query 55:	0.0015
Query 56:	0.0087
Query 58:	0.0288
Query 59:	0.0000
Query 61:	0.0003
Query 62:	0.0000
Query 63:	0.0000
Query 64:	0.0054
Query 65:	0.0000
Query 66:	0.0315
Query 67:	0.0043
Query 68:	0.0005
Query 69:	0.0000
Query 70:	0.0000
Query 71:	0.0214
Query 72:	0.0000
Query 73:	0.0029
Query 74:	0.0057
Query 75:	0.0000
Query 76:	0.0005
Query 77:	0.0000
Query 78:	0.0000
Query 79:	0.0018
Query 80:	0.0000
Query 81:	0.0162
Query 82:	0.1810
Query 83:	0.0000
Query 84:	0.0001
Query 85:	0.0019
Query 86:	0.1394
Query 87:	0.0133
Query 88:	0.0169
Query 89:	0.0000
Query 90:	0.0415

Overall statistics
(for 47 queries):

Total number of documents
over all queries
Retrieved:	47000
Relevant:	856
Rel_ret:	211

Interpolated Recall -
Precision Averages:
at 0.00	0.0783
at 0.10	0.0385
at 0.20	0.0284
at 0.30	0.0194
at 0.40	0.0124
at 0.50	0.0084
at 0.60	0.0056
at 0.70	0.0034
at 0.80	0.0024
at 0.90	0.0018
at 1.00	0.0012

Avg. prec. (non-interpolated)
for all rel. documents
                     0.0139

Precision:
At 5 docs:	0.0340
At 10 docs:	0.0298
At 15 docs:	0.0270
At 20 docs:	0.0255
At 30 docs:	0.0227
At 100 docs:	0.0136
At 200 docs:	0.0100
At 500 docs:	0.0067
At 1000 docs:	0.0045

R-Precision (prec. after R
(=num rel) docs. retrieved):
| Exact: | 0.0213 |

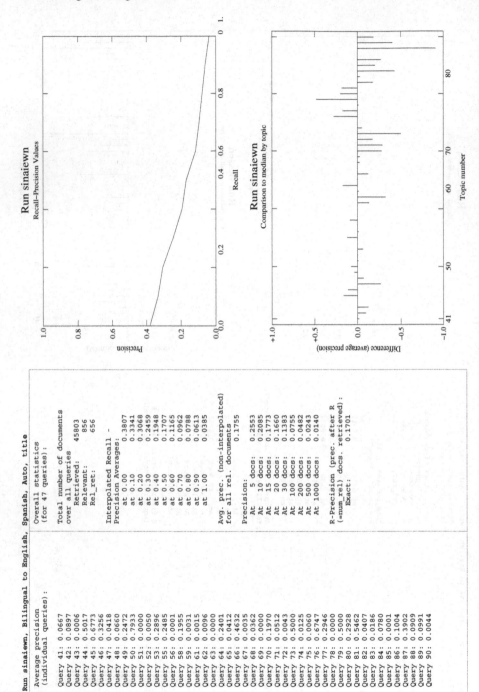

Run sinaiewn
Recall–Precision Values

Run sinaiewn
Comparison to median by topic

Run sinaiewn, Bilingual to English, Spanish, Auto, title

Average precision
(individual queries):

Query 41:	0.0667
Query 42:	0.0897
Query 43:	0.0006
Query 44:	0.5017
Query 45:	0.6773
Query 46:	0.3256
Query 47:	0.0418
Query 48:	0.0660
Query 49:	0.2472
Query 50:	0.7933
Query 51:	0.0000
Query 52:	0.0050
Query 53:	0.2896
Query 55:	0.2485
Query 56:	0.0001
Query 58:	0.1955
Query 59:	0.0031
Query 61:	0.0015
Query 62:	0.0096
Query 63:	0.0000
Query 64:	0.2401
Query 65:	0.0412
Query 66:	0.4632
Query 67:	0.0035
Query 68:	0.0362
Query 69:	0.0000
Query 70:	0.1970
Query 71:	0.0512
Query 72:	0.0043
Query 73:	0.5000
Query 74:	0.0125
Query 75:	0.0060
Query 76:	0.6747
Query 77:	0.2946
Query 78:	0.0000
Query 79:	0.5000
Query 80:	0.2928
Query 81:	0.5462
Query 82:	0.0407
Query 83:	0.0186
Query 84:	0.0780
Query 85:	0.0001
Query 86:	0.1004
Query 87:	0.3902
Query 88:	0.0909
Query 89:	0.0991
Query 90:	0.0044

Overall statistics
(for 47 queries):

Total number of documents
over all queries:
  Retrieved: 45803
  Relevant: 856
  Rel_ret: 656

Interpolated Recall –
Precision Averages:
  at 0.00   0.3807
  at 0.10   0.3341
  at 0.20   0.3068
  at 0.30   0.2459
  at 0.40   0.1948
  at 0.50   0.1707
  at 0.60   0.1165
  at 0.70   0.0962
  at 0.80   0.0788
  at 0.90   0.0613
  at 1.00   0.0385

Avg. prec. (non-interpolated)
for all rel. documents
                   0.1755

Precision:
  At   5 docs: 0.2553
  At   10 docs: 0.2085
  At   15 docs: 0.1773
  At   20 docs: 0.1660
  At   30 docs: 0.1383
  At 100 docs: 0.0755
  At 200 docs: 0.0482
  At 500 docs: 0.0243
  At 1000 docs: 0.0140

R-Precision (prec. after R
(=num_rel) docs. retrieved):
  Exact: 0.1701

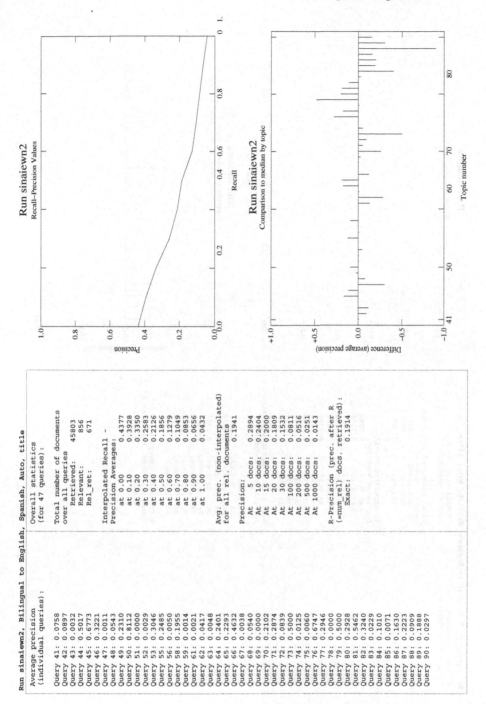

Run sinaiewn2, Bilingual to English, Spanish, Auto, title

Average precision
(individual queries):

Query 41:	0.0758
Query 42:	0.0897
Query 43:	0.0032
Query 44:	0.5017
Query 45:	0.6773
Query 46:	0.3221
Query 47:	0.0011
Query 48:	0.0543
Query 49:	0.2310
Query 50:	0.8112
Query 51:	0.0000
Query 52:	0.0029
Query 53:	0.3046
Query 55:	0.2485
Query 56:	0.0050
Query 58:	0.1955
Query 59:	0.0014
Query 61:	0.0021
Query 63:	0.0048
Query 64:	0.2401
Query 65:	0.2293
Query 66:	0.4632
Query 67:	0.0038
Query 68:	0.0540
Query 69:	0.0000
Query 70:	0.2102
Query 71:	0.2874
Query 72:	0.0839
Query 73:	0.5000
Query 74:	0.0125
Query 75:	0.0060
Query 76:	0.6747
Query 77:	0.2946
Query 78:	0.0000
Query 79:	0.5000
Query 80:	0.2928
Query 81:	0.5462
Query 82:	0.3240
Query 83:	0.0229
Query 84:	0.1010
Query 85:	0.0071
Query 86:	0.1630
Query 87:	0.2223
Query 88:	0.0909
Query 89:	0.1888
Query 90:	0.0297

Overall statistics
(for 47 queries):

Total number of documents
over all queries
   Retrieved: 45803
   Relevant: 856
   Rel_ret: 671

Interpolated Recall -
Precision Averages:
   at 0.00   0.4377
   at 0.10   0.3928
   at 0.20   0.3350
   at 0.30   0.2583
   at 0.40   0.2126
   at 0.50   0.1856
   at 0.60   0.1279
   at 0.70   0.1049
   at 0.80   0.0853
   at 0.90   0.0656
   at 1.00   0.0432

Avg. prec. (non-interpolated)
for all rel. documents
          0.1941

Precision:
 At   5 docs: 0.2894
 At 10 docs: 0.2404
 At 15 docs: 0.2000
 At 20 docs: 0.1809
 At 30 docs: 0.1532
 At 100 docs: 0.0811
 At 200 docs: 0.0516
 At 500 docs: 0.0251
 At 1000 docs: 0.0143

R-Precision (prec. after R
(=num_rel) docs. retrieved):
   Exact: 0.1914

Run sinaiewn2
Recall–Precision Values

Precision / Recall

Run sinaiewn2
Comparison to median by topic

Difference (average precision) / Topic number

Run sinaiorg
Recall–Precision Values

Run sinaiorg
Comparison to median by topic

Run sinaiorg, Bilingual to English, Spanish, Auto, title

Average precision
(individual queries):

Query 41:	0.3517		Query 67:	0.5625	
Query 42:	0.3736		Query 68:	0.6294	
Query 43:	0.2780		Query 69:	0.1363	
Query 44:	0.5145		Query 70:	0.5327	
Query 45:	0.7011		Query 71:	0.5033	
Query 46:	0.3606		Query 72:	0.2337	
Query 47:	0.9716		Query 73:	1.0000	
Query 48:	0.1650		Query 74:	0.5141	
Query 49:	0.2545		Query 75:	0.1429	
Query 50:	0.8440		Query 76:	0.6472	
Query 51:	0.0259		Query 77:	0.2518	
Query 52:	0.0194		Query 78:	0.0109	
Query 53:	0.5555		Query 79:	1.0000	
Query 55:	0.1467		Query 80:	0.2928	
Query 56:	0.0415		Query 81:	0.8203	
Query 58:	0.3505		Query 82:	0.5998	
Query 59:	0.0278		Query 83:	0.1659	
Query 61:	0.3872		Query 84:	0.7259	
Query 62:	0.5000		Query 85:	0.2768	
Query 63:	0.0588		Query 86:	0.2451	
Query 64:	0.2128		Query 87:	0.4867	
Query 65:	0.2467		Query 88:	1.0000	
Query 66:	0.7320		Query 89:	0.4539	
			Query 90:	0.4253	

Overall statistics
(for 47 queries):

Total number of documents
over all queries:

Retrieved:	45340
Relevant:	856
Rel_ret:	783

Interpolated Recall -
Precision Averages:

at 0.00	0.7583
at 0.10	0.7278
at 0.20	0.6476
at 0.30	0.5632
at 0.40	0.4904
at 0.50	0.4389
at 0.60	0.3315
at 0.70	0.2825
at 0.80	0.2343
at 0.90	0.1925
at 1.00	0.1317

Avg. prec. (non-interpolated)
for all rel. documents

0.4208

Precision:

At 5 docs:	0.4638
At 10 docs:	0.3872
At 15 docs:	0.3135
At 20 docs:	0.2851
At 30 docs:	0.2383
At 100 docs:	0.1215
At 200 docs:	0.0705
At 500 docs:	0.0318
At 1000 docs:	0.0167

R-Precision (prec. after R
(=num_rel) docs. retrieved):

Exact: 0.4009

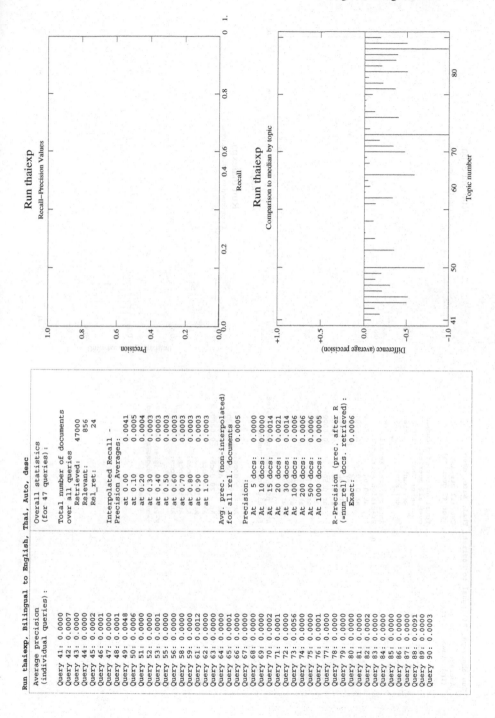

Run thaiexp
Recall–Precision Values

Run thaiexp
Comparison to median by topic

Run thaiexp, Bilingual to English, Thai, Auto, desc

Average precision
(individual queries):

Overall statistics
(for 47 queries):

Total number of documents
over all queries
    Retrieved: 47000
    Relevant: 856
    Rel_ret: 24

Interpolated Recall -
Precision Averages:
    at 0.00   0.0041
    at 0.10   0.0005
    at 0.20   0.0004
    at 0.30   0.0003
    at 0.40   0.0003
    at 0.50   0.0003
    at 0.60   0.0003
    at 0.70   0.0003
    at 0.80   0.0003
    at 0.90   0.0003
    at 1.00   0.0003

Avg. prec. (non-interpolated)
for all rel. documents
                    0.0005

Precision:
    At   5 docs: 0.0000
    At   10 docs: 0.0000
    At   15 docs: 0.0014
    At   20 docs: 0.0021
    At   30 docs: 0.0014
    At 100 docs: 0.0006
    At 200 docs: 0.0006
    At 500 docs: 0.0006
    At 1000 docs: 0.0005

R-Precision (prec. after R
(=num_rel) docs. retrieved):
    Exact: 0.0006

Query 41: 0.0000
Query 42: 0.0007
Query 43: 0.0000
Query 44: 0.0000
Query 45: 0.0002
Query 46: 0.0001
Query 47: 0.0000
Query 48: 0.0001
Query 49: 0.0048
Query 50: 0.0006
Query 51: 0.0000
Query 52: 0.0000
Query 53: 0.0001
Query 55: 0.0000
Query 56: 0.0000
Query 58: 0.0000
Query 59: 0.0000
Query 61: 0.0012
Query 62: 0.0000
Query 63: 0.0000
Query 64: 0.0000
Query 65: 0.0001
Query 66: 0.0000
Query 67: 0.0000
Query 68: 0.0000
Query 69: 0.0000
Query 70: 0.0002
Query 71: 0.0001
Query 72: 0.0000
Query 73: 0.0056
Query 74: 0.0000
Query 75: 0.0000
Query 76: 0.0001
Query 77: 0.0000
Query 78: 0.0000
Query 79: 0.0000
Query 80: 0.0000
Query 81: 0.0000
Query 82: 0.0002
Query 83: 0.0000
Query 84: 0.0000
Query 85: 0.0000
Query 86: 0.0000
Query 87: 0.0000
Query 88: 0.0091
Query 89: 0.0000
Query 90: 0.0003

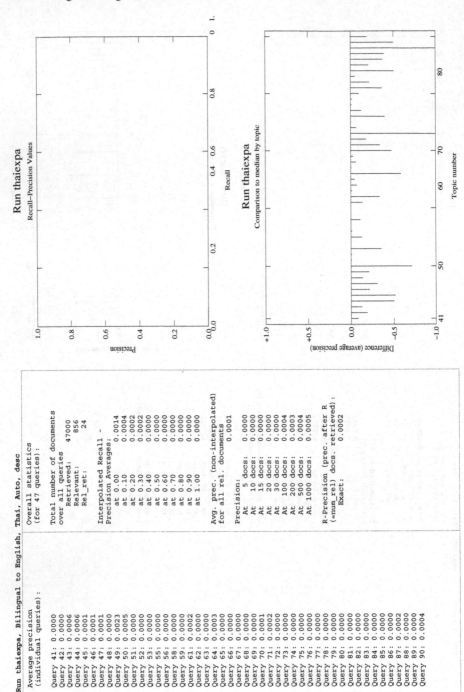

Run thaiexpa
Recall–Precision Values

Run thaiexpa
Comparison to median by topic

Run thaiexpa, Bilingual to English, Thai, Auto, desc

Average precision
(individual queries):

Query 41:	0.0000
Query 42:	0.0000
Query 43:	0.0006
Query 44:	0.0006
Query 45:	0.0001
Query 46:	0.0001
Query 47:	0.0001
Query 48:	0.0000
Query 49:	0.0023
Query 50:	0.0005
Query 51:	0.0000
Query 52:	0.0000
Query 53:	0.0000
Query 55:	0.0000
Query 56:	0.0000
Query 58:	0.0000
Query 59:	0.0000
Query 61:	0.0002
Query 62:	0.0000
Query 63:	0.0000
Query 64:	0.0003
Query 65:	0.0000
Query 66:	0.0000
Query 67:	0.0000
Query 68:	0.0000
Query 69:	0.0000
Query 70:	0.0001
Query 71:	0.0002
Query 72:	0.0000
Query 73:	0.0000
Query 74:	0.0000
Query 75:	0.0000
Query 76:	0.0000
Query 77:	0.0000
Query 78:	0.0000
Query 79:	0.0000
Query 80:	0.0000
Query 81:	0.0000
Query 82:	0.0000
Query 83:	0.0000
Query 84:	0.0000
Query 85:	0.0000
Query 86:	0.0000
Query 87:	0.0002
Query 88:	0.0000
Query 89:	0.0000
Query 90:	0.0004

Overall statistics
(for 47 queries):

Total number of documents
over all queries
    Retrieved: 47000
    Relevant: 856
    Rel_ret: 24

Interpolated Recall -
Precision Averages:
    at 0.00   0.0014
    at 0.10   0.0004
    at 0.20   0.0002
    at 0.30   0.0002
    at 0.40   0.0000
    at 0.50   0.0000
    at 0.60   0.0000
    at 0.70   0.0000
    at 0.80   0.0000
    at 0.90   0.0000
    at 1.00   0.0000

Avg. prec. (non-interpolated)
for all rel. documents
                 0.0001

Precision:
    At   5 docs: 0.0000
    At   10 docs: 0.0000
    At   15 docs: 0.0000
    At   20 docs: 0.0000
    At   30 docs: 0.0000
    At   100 docs: 0.0004
    At   200 docs: 0.0003
    At   500 docs: 0.0004
    At 1000 docs: 0.0005

R-Precision (prec. after R
(=num_rel) docs. retrieved):
    Exact: 0.0002

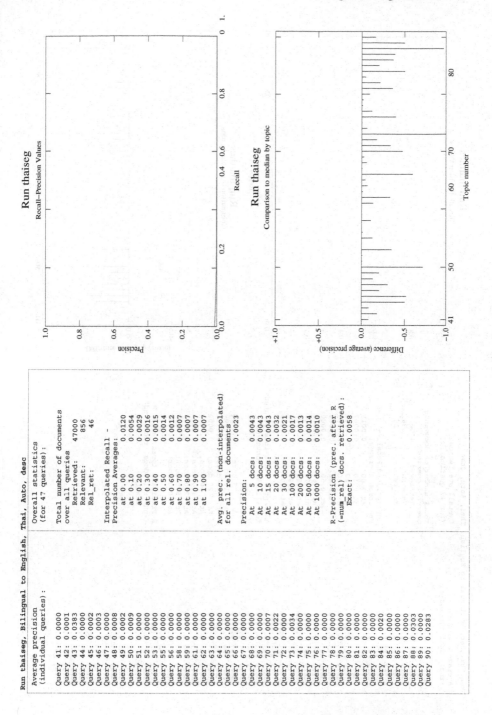

Run thaiseg
Recall-Precision Values

Run thaiseg
Comparison to median by topic

Run thaiseg, Bilingual to English, Thai, Auto, desc

Average precision
(individual queries):

Query 41:	0.0000
Query 42:	0.0001
Query 43:	0.0383
Query 44:	0.0000
Query 45:	0.0002
Query 46:	0.0003
Query 47:	0.0000
Query 48:	0.0008
Query 49:	0.0002
Query 50:	0.0009
Query 51:	0.0000
Query 52:	0.0000
Query 53:	0.0000
Query 55:	0.0000
Query 56:	0.0000
Query 58:	0.0000
Query 59:	0.0000
Query 61:	0.0000
Query 62:	0.0000
Query 63:	0.0000
Query 64:	0.0000
Query 65:	0.0000
Query 66:	0.0000
Query 67:	0.0000
Query 68:	0.0000
Query 69:	0.0000
Query 70:	0.0007
Query 71:	0.0022
Query 72:	0.0000
Query 73:	0.0034
Query 74:	0.0000
Query 75:	0.0000
Query 76:	0.0000
Query 77:	0.0000
Query 78:	0.0000
Query 79:	0.0000
Query 80:	0.0000
Query 81:	0.0000
Query 82:	0.0000
Query 83:	0.0020
Query 84:	0.0000
Query 85:	0.0000
Query 86:	0.0000
Query 87:	0.0000
Query 88:	0.0303
Query 89:	0.0000
Query 90:	0.0283

Overall statistics
(for 47 queries):

Total number of documents
over all queries
Retrieved:	47000
Relevant:	856
Rel_ret:	46

Interpolated Recall -
Precision Averages:
at 0.00	0.0120
at 0.10	0.0054
at 0.20	0.0029
at 0.30	0.0016
at 0.40	0.0015
at 0.50	0.0014
at 0.60	0.0012
at 0.70	0.0007
at 0.80	0.0007
at 0.90	0.0007
at 1.00	0.0007

Avg. prec. (non-interpolated)
for all rel. documents
                0.0023

Precision:
At	5 docs:	0.0043
At	10 docs:	0.0043
At	15 docs:	0.0043
At	20 docs:	0.0032
At	30 docs:	0.0021
At	100 docs:	0.0017
At	200 docs:	0.0013
At	500 docs:	0.0014
At	1000 docs:	0.0010

R-Precision (prec. after R
(=num rel) docs. retrieved):
           Exact: 0.0058

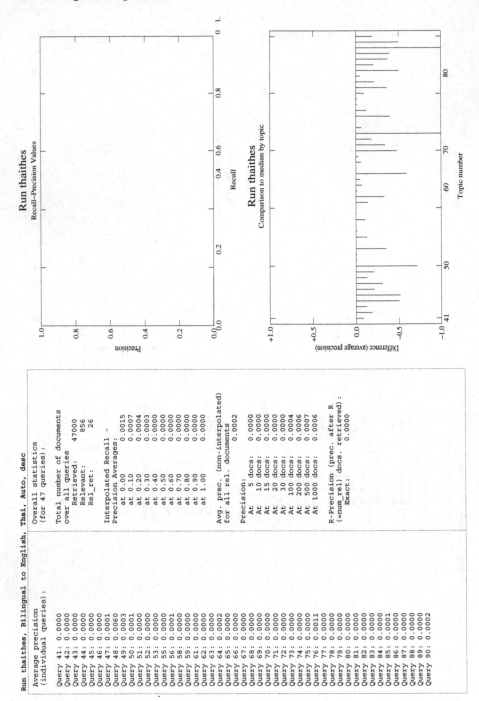

Run thaithes
Recall–Precision Values

Run thaithes
Comparison to median by topic

Run thaithes, Bilingual to English, Thai, Auto, desc

Average precision
(individual queries):

Query 41:	0.0000
Query 42:	0.0000
Query 43:	0.0000
Query 44:	0.0000
Query 45:	0.0000
Query 46:	0.0000
Query 47:	0.0001
Query 48:	0.0060
Query 49:	0.0003
Query 50:	0.0001
Query 51:	0.0000
Query 52:	0.0000
Query 53:	0.0000
Query 55:	0.0000
Query 56:	0.0001
Query 58:	0.0000
Query 59:	0.0000
Query 61:	0.0000
Query 62:	0.0000
Query 63:	0.0000
Query 64:	0.0002
Query 65:	0.0000
Query 66:	0.0000
Query 67:	0.0000
Query 68:	0.0000
Query 69:	0.0000
Query 70:	0.0000
Query 71:	0.0000
Query 72:	0.0000
Query 73:	0.0000
Query 74:	0.0000
Query 75:	0.0000
Query 76:	0.0011
Query 77:	0.0000
Query 78:	0.0000
Query 79:	0.0000
Query 80:	0.0000
Query 81:	0.0000
Query 82:	0.0000
Query 83:	0.0000
Query 84:	0.0000
Query 85:	0.0001
Query 86:	0.0000
Query 87:	0.0000
Query 88:	0.0000
Query 89:	0.0000
Query 90:	0.0002

Overall statistics
(for 47 queries):

Total number of documents
over all queries:
    Retrieved: 47000
    Relevant: 856
    Rel_ret: 26

Interpolated Recall -
Precision Averages:
    at 0.00   0.0015
    at 0.10   0.0007
    at 0.20   0.0004
    at 0.30   0.0003
    at 0.40   0.0000
    at 0.50   0.0000
    at 0.60   0.0000
    at 0.70   0.0000
    at 0.80   0.0000
    at 0.90   0.0000
    at 1.00   0.0000

Avg. prec. (non-interpolated)
for all rel. documents
                 0.0002

Precision:
    At   5 docs: 0.0000
    At   10 docs: 0.0000
    At   15 docs: 0.0000
    At   20 docs: 0.0000
    At   30 docs: 0.0000
    At 100 docs: 0.0004
    At 200 docs: 0.0006
    At 500 docs: 0.0007
    At 1000 docs: 0.0006

R-Precision (prec. after R
(=num_rel) docs. retrieved):
    Exact: 0.0000

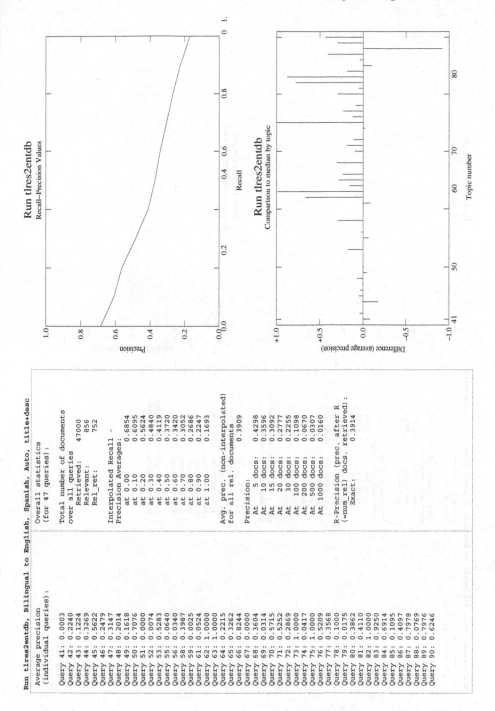

Run tlres2entdb, Bilingual to English, Spanish, Auto, title+desc

Average precision
(individual queries):

Query 41:	0.0003
Query 42:	0.2240
Query 43:	0.1224
Query 44:	0.3269
Query 45:	0.5622
Query 46:	0.2479
Query 47:	0.3147
Query 48:	0.2014
Query 49:	0.1618
Query 50:	0.7076
Query 51:	0.0000
Query 52:	0.0074
Query 53:	0.5283
Query 55:	0.0640
Query 56:	0.0340
Query 58:	0.3987
Query 59:	0.0025
Query 61:	0.0524
Query 62:	1.0000
Query 63:	1.0000
Query 64:	0.2215
Query 65:	0.3262
Query 66:	0.8244
Query 67:	0.0000
Query 68:	0.3604
Query 69:	0.0314
Query 70:	0.5715
Query 71:	0.5252
Query 72:	0.2869
Query 73:	1.0000
Query 74:	0.0417
Query 75:	1.0000
Query 76:	0.5209
Query 77:	0.3568
Query 78:	0.1000
Query 79:	0.0175
Query 80:	0.3862
Query 81:	0.4110
Query 82:	1.0000
Query 83:	0.9250
Query 84:	0.6914
Query 85:	0.1095
Query 86:	0.4097
Query 87:	0.7978
Query 88:	0.0769
Query 89:	0.7976
Query 90:	0.6246

Overall statistics
(for 47 queries):

Total number of documents over all queries
Retrieved: 47000
Relevant: 856
Rel_ret: 752

Interpolated Recall -
Precision Averages:

at 0.00:	0.6854
at 0.10:	0.6095
at 0.20:	0.5624
at 0.30:	0.4840
at 0.40:	0.4119
at 0.50:	0.3720
at 0.60:	0.3420
at 0.70:	0.3052
at 0.80:	0.2686
at 0.90:	0.2247
at 1.00:	0.1693

Avg. prec. (non-interpolated)
for all rel. documents
0.3909

Precision:

At 5 docs:	0.4298
At 10 docs:	0.3596
At 15 docs:	0.3092
At 20 docs:	0.2777
At 30 docs:	0.2255
At 100 docs:	0.1098
At 200 docs:	0.0670
At 500 docs:	0.0307
At 1000 docs:	0.0160

R-Precision (prec. after R
(=num_rel) docs. retrieved):
Exact: 0.3914

Run tlres2entdb
Recall-Precision Values

Run tlres2entdb
Comparison to median by topic

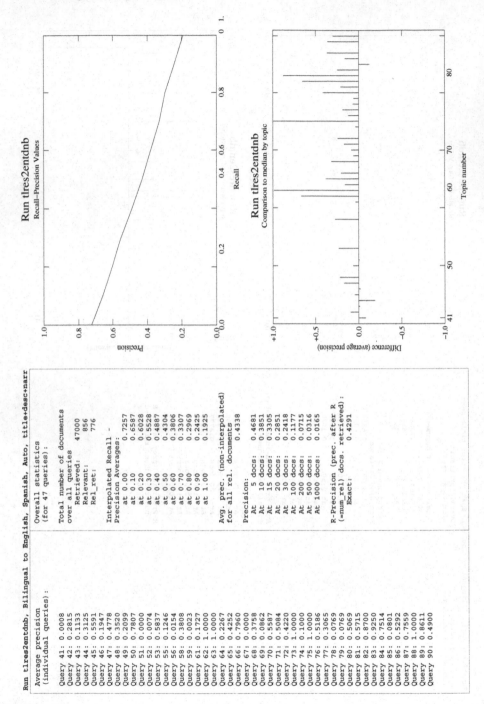

Run tlres2entdnb
Recall-Precision Values

Run tlres2entdnb
Comparison to median by topic

Run tlres2entdnb, Bilingual to English, Spanish, Auto, title+desc+narr

Average precision
(individual queries):

Query 41:	0.0008
Query 42:	0.2815
Query 43:	0.1133
Query 44:	0.3125
Query 45:	0.5591
Query 46:	0.1947
Query 47:	0.4778
Query 48:	0.3520
Query 49:	0.2099
Query 50:	0.7807
Query 51:	0.0000
Query 52:	0.0074
Query 53:	0.5837
Query 55:	0.1246
Query 56:	0.0154
Query 58:	0.3808
Query 59:	0.0023
Query 61:	0.1727
Query 62:	1.0000
Query 63:	1.0000
Query 64:	0.2267
Query 65:	0.4252
Query 66:	0.7960
Query 67:	0.0000
Query 68:	0.3758
Query 69:	0.0862
Query 70:	0.5587
Query 71:	0.5084
Query 72:	0.4220
Query 73:	1.0000
Query 74:	0.1000
Query 75:	1.0000
Query 76:	0.5186
Query 77:	0.3065
Query 78:	0.0769
Query 79:	0.0769
Query 80:	0.5069
Query 81:	0.5715
Query 82:	0.8700
Query 83:	0.9250
Query 84:	0.7514
Query 85:	0.0801
Query 86:	0.5292
Query 87:	0.7559
Query 88:	1.0000
Query 89:	0.8611
Query 90:	0.4900

Overall statistics
(for 47 queries):

Total number of documents
over all queries

Retrieved:	47000
Relevant:	856
Rel_ret:	776

Interpolated Recall -
Precision Averages:

at 0.00	0.7257
at 0.10	0.6587
at 0.20	0.6028
at 0.30	0.5528
at 0.40	0.4887
at 0.50	0.4304
at 0.60	0.3806
at 0.70	0.3307
at 0.80	0.2969
at 0.90	0.2425
at 1.00	0.1925

Avg. prec. (non-interpolated)
for all rel. documents
0.4338

Precision:

At 5 docs:	0.4681
At 10 docs:	0.3851
At 15 docs:	0.3305
At 20 docs:	0.2851
At 30 docs:	0.2418
At 100 docs:	0.1177
At 200 docs:	0.0715
At 500 docs:	0.0316
At 1000 docs:	0.0165

R-Precision (prec. after R
(=num_rel) docs. retrieved):
Exact: 0.4291

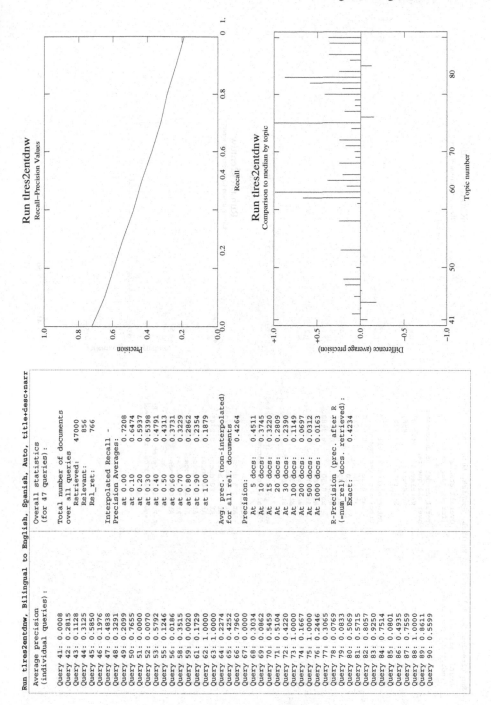

Run tlres2entdnw, Bilingual to English, Spanish, Auto, title+desc+narr

Average precision
(individual queries):

Query 41:	0.0008
Query 42:	0.2815
Query 43:	0.1128
Query 44:	0.3125
Query 45:	0.5850
Query 46:	0.1976
Query 47:	0.4838
Query 48:	0.3291
Query 49:	0.2099
Query 50:	0.7655
Query 51:	0.0000
Query 52:	0.0070
Query 53:	0.5792
Query 55:	0.1246
Query 56:	0.0186
Query 58:	0.3515
Query 59:	0.0020
Query 61:	0.1729
Query 62:	1.0000
Query 63:	1.0000
Query 64:	0.2274
Query 65:	0.4252
Query 66:	0.7960
Query 67:	0.0000
Query 68:	0.3034
Query 69:	0.0862
Query 70:	0.5459
Query 71:	0.5104
Query 72:	0.4220
Query 73:	1.0000
Query 74:	0.1667
Query 75:	1.0000
Query 76:	0.2446
Query 77:	0.3065
Query 78:	0.0769
Query 79:	0.0833
Query 80:	0.5069
Query 81:	0.5715
Query 82:	0.8057
Query 83:	0.9250
Query 84:	0.7514
Query 85:	0.0801
Query 86:	0.4935
Query 87:	0.7559
Query 88:	1.0000
Query 89:	0.8611
Query 90:	0.5599

Overall statistics
(for 47 queries):

Total number of documents
over all queries
Retrieved:	47000
Relevant:	856
Rel_ret:	766

Interpolated Recall -
Precision Averages:
at 0.00	0.7208
at 0.10	0.6474
at 0.20	0.5937
at 0.30	0.5398
at 0.40	0.4791
at 0.50	0.4313
at 0.60	0.3731
at 0.70	0.3229
at 0.80	0.2862
at 0.90	0.2354
at 1.00	0.1879

Avg. prec. (non-interpolated)
for all rel. documents
                        0.4264

Precision:
At 5 docs:	0.4511
At 10 docs:	0.3745
At 15 docs:	0.3220
At 20 docs:	0.2809
At 30 docs:	0.2390
At 100 docs:	0.1149
At 200 docs:	0.0697
At 500 docs:	0.0312
At 1000 docs:	0.0163

R-Precision (prec. after R
(=num rel) docs. retrieved):
| Exact: | 0.4234 |

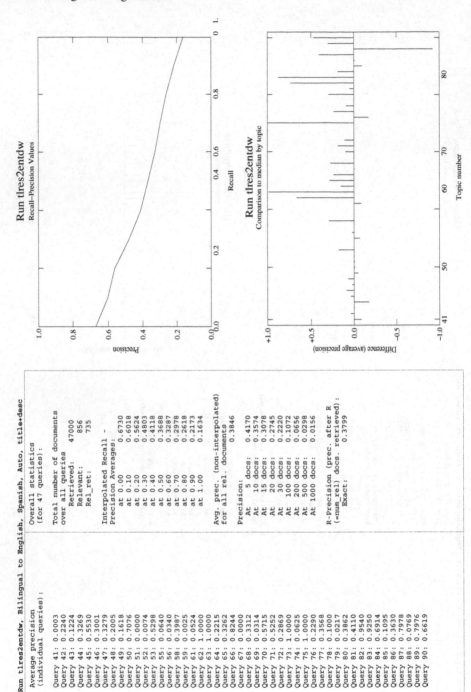

Run tlres2entdw
Recall-Precision Values

Run tlres2entdw
Comparison to median by topic

Run tlres2entdw, Bilingual to English, Spanish, Auto, title+desc

Average precision
(individual queries):

Query 41:	0.0003		
Query 42:	0.2240		
Query 43:	0.1224		
Query 44:	0.3269		
Query 45:	0.5530		
Query 46:	0.3001		
Query 47:	0.3279		
Query 48:	0.2005		
Query 49:	0.1618		
Query 50:	0.7076		
Query 51:	0.0000		
Query 52:	0.0074		
Query 53:	0.5298		
Query 55:	0.0640		
Query 56:	0.0340		
Query 58:	0.3987		
Query 59:	0.0025		
Query 61:	0.0524		
Query 62:	1.0000		
Query 63:	1.0000		
Query 64:	0.2215		
Query 65:	0.3262		
Query 66:	0.8244		
Query 67:	0.0000		
Query 68:	0.3312		
Query 69:	0.0314		
Query 70:	0.5715		
Query 71:	0.5252		
Query 72:	0.2869		
Query 73:	1.0000		
Query 74:	0.0625		
Query 75:	1.0000		
Query 76:	0.2290		
Query 77:	0.3568		
Query 78:	0.1000		
Query 79:	0.0217		
Query 80:	0.3862		
Query 81:	0.4110		
Query 82:	0.9540		
Query 83:	0.9250		
Query 84:	0.6914		
Query 85:	0.1095		
Query 86:	0.3630		
Query 87:	0.7978		
Query 88:	0.0769		
Query 89:	0.7976		
Query 90:	0.6619		

Overall statistics
(for 47 queries):

Total number of documents
over all queries

Retrieved:	47000
Relevant:	856
Rel_ret:	735

Interpolated Recall -
Precision Averages:

at 0.00	0.6730
at 0.10	0.6018
at 0.20	0.5624
at 0.30	0.4803
at 0.40	0.4118
at 0.50	0.3688
at 0.60	0.3287
at 0.70	0.2978
at 0.80	0.2618
at 0.90	0.2173
at 1.00	0.1634

Avg. prec. (non-interpolated)
for all rel. documents
                    0.3846

Precision:

At	5 docs:	0.4170
At	10 docs:	0.3574
At	15 docs:	0.3078
At	20 docs:	0.2745
At	30 docs:	0.2220
At	100 docs:	0.1072
At	200 docs:	0.0656
At	500 docs:	0.0298
At	1000 docs:	0.0156

R-Precision (prec. after R
(=num_rel) docs. retrieved):
                    Exact: 0.3799

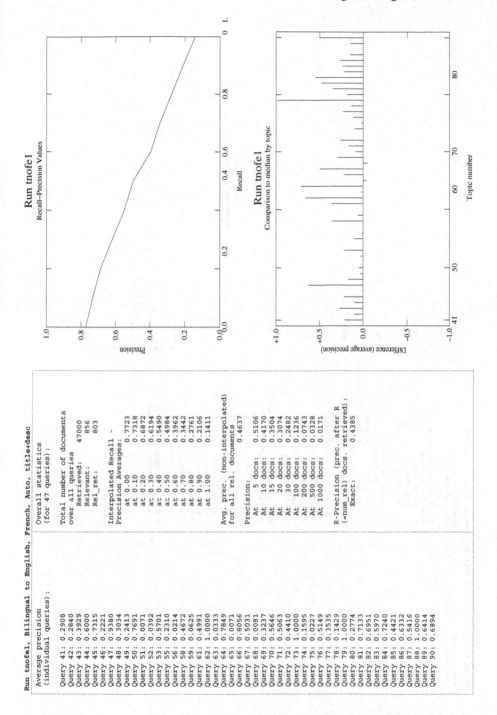

Run tnofe1, Bilingual to English, French, Auto, title+desc

Average precision
(individual queries):

Query 41:	0.2908
Query 42:	0.2840
Query 43:	0.3929
Query 44:	0.6000
Query 45:	0.7315
Query 46:	0.2221
Query 47:	0.9380
Query 48:	0.3034
Query 49:	0.2413
Query 50:	0.7691
Query 51:	0.0071
Query 52:	0.0392
Query 53:	0.5701
Query 55:	0.2310
Query 56:	0.0214
Query 58:	0.4672
Query 59:	0.0625
Query 61:	0.4991
Query 62:	1.0000
Query 63:	0.0333
Query 64:	0.7849
Query 65:	0.0071
Query 66:	0.8056
Query 67:	0.5031
Query 68:	0.0081
Query 69:	0.3237
Query 70:	0.5646
Query 71:	0.5063
Query 72:	0.4410
Query 73:	1.0000
Query 74:	0.1595
Query 75:	0.0227
Query 76:	0.5149
Query 77:	0.3535
Query 78:	0.1429
Query 79:	1.0000
Query 80:	0.2774
Query 81:	0.7133
Query 82:	0.6951
Query 83:	0.5970
Query 84:	0.7240
Query 85:	0.4421
Query 86:	0.6332
Query 87:	0.5416
Query 88:	1.0000
Query 89:	0.6414
Query 90:	0.6894

Overall statistics
(for 47 queries):

Total number of documents
over all queries
    Retrieved: 47000
    Relevant: 856
    Rel_ret: 803

Interpolated Recall -
Precision Averages:
    at 0.00   0.7723
    at 0.10   0.7318
    at 0.20   0.6872
    at 0.30   0.6194
    at 0.40   0.5490
    at 0.50   0.4984
    at 0.60   0.3962
    at 0.70   0.3442
    at 0.80   0.2761
    at 0.90   0.2106
    at 1.00   0.1411
Avg. prec. (non-interpolated)
for all rel. documents
                   0.4637

Precision:
    At   5 docs: 0.5106
    At   10 docs: 0.4170
    At   15 docs: 0.3504
    At   20 docs: 0.3074
    At   30 docs: 0.2482
    At 100 docs: 0.1236
    At 200 docs: 0.0743
    At 500 docs: 0.0328
    At 1000 docs: 0.0171

R-Precision (prec. after R
(=num rel) docs. retrieved):
        Exact: 0.4385

Run tnofe1
Recall-Precision Values

Run tnofe1
Comparison to median by topic

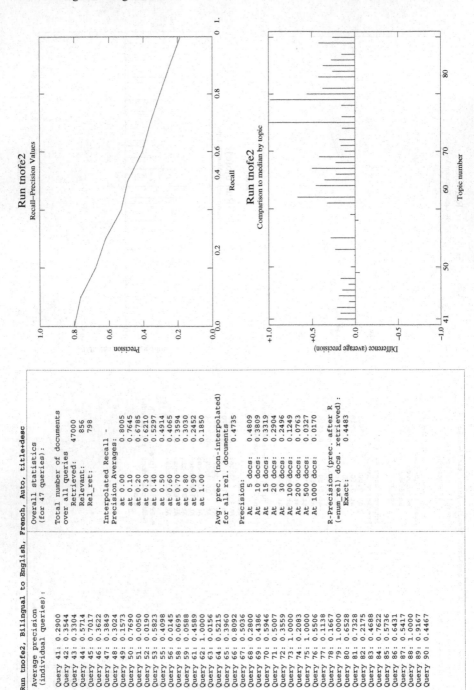

Run tnofe2
Recall–Precision Values

Run tnofe2
Comparison to median by topic

Run tnofe2, Bilingual to English, French, Auto, title+desc

Average precision
(individual queries):

Query 41:	0.2900
Query 42:	0.3544
Query 43:	0.3304
Query 44:	0.5714
Query 45:	0.7017
Query 46:	0.3622
Query 47:	0.3849
Query 48:	0.3024
Query 49:	0.1573
Query 50:	0.7690
Query 51:	0.0050
Query 52:	0.0190
Query 53:	0.5823
Query 55:	0.4098
Query 56:	0.0145
Query 58:	0.0695
Query 59:	0.0588
Query 61:	0.4589
Query 62:	1.0000
Query 63:	0.0156
Query 64:	0.5215
Query 65:	0.3960
Query 66:	0.8092
Query 67:	0.5036
Query 68:	0.2800
Query 69:	0.4386
Query 70:	0.5946
Query 71:	0.5007
Query 72:	0.3559
Query 73:	1.0000
Query 74:	0.2083
Query 75:	1.0000
Query 76:	0.5506
Query 77:	0.1138
Query 78:	0.1667
Query 79:	1.0000
Query 80:	0.6528
Query 81:	0.7328
Query 82:	0.2175
Query 83:	0.4688
Query 84:	0.7622
Query 85:	0.5736
Query 86:	0.6431
Query 87:	0.5417
Query 88:	1.0000
Query 89:	0.9167
Query 90:	0.4467

Overall statistics
(for 47 queries):

Total number of documents
over all queries:
Retrieved: 47000
Relevant: 856
Rel_ret: 798

Interpolated Recall -
Precision Averages:

at 0.00	0.8005
at 0.10	0.7645
at 0.20	0.6785
at 0.30	0.6210
at 0.40	0.5297
at 0.50	0.4914
at 0.60	0.4065
at 0.70	0.3594
at 0.80	0.3030
at 0.90	0.2452
at 1.00	0.1850

Avg. prec. (non-interpolated)
for all rel. documents
                0.4735

Precision:

At 5 docs:	0.4809
At 10 docs:	0.3809
At 15 docs:	0.3319
At 20 docs:	0.2904
At 30 docs:	0.2496
At 100 docs:	0.1249
At 200 docs:	0.0763
At 500 docs:	0.0327
At 1000 docs:	0.0170

R-Precision (prec. after R
(=num_rel) docs. retrieved):
        Exact: 0.4483

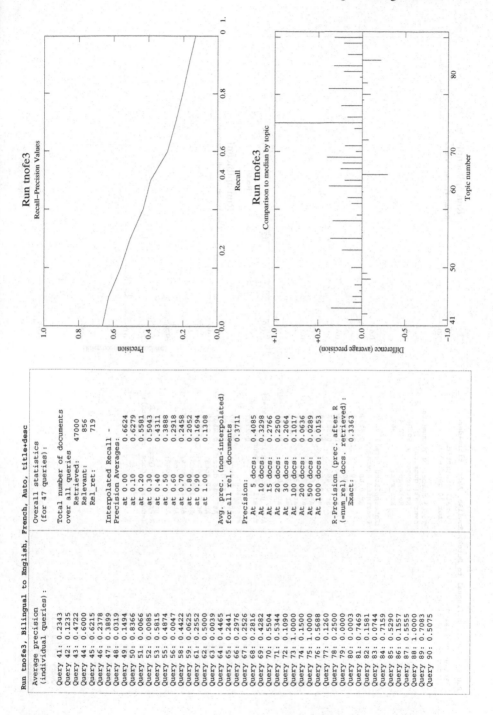

Run tnofe3
Recall–Precision Values

Precision

1.0

0.8

0.6

0.4

0.2

0.0

0.0   0.2   0.4   0.6   0.8   1. 0

Recall

Run tnofe3
Comparison to median by topic

Difference (average precision)

+1.0

+0.5

0.0

−0.5

−1.0

41   50   60   70   80

Topic number

Run tnofe3, Bilingual to English, French, Auto, title+desc

Average precision
(individual queries):

Query 41:	0.2343
Query 42:	0.1235
Query 43:	0.4722
Query 44:	0.6000
Query 45:	0.6215
Query 46:	0.2378
Query 47:	0.3899
Query 48:	0.0319
Query 49:	0.1494
Query 50:	0.8366
Query 51:	0.0066
Query 52:	0.0085
Query 53:	0.5815
Query 55:	0.4874
Query 56:	0.0047
Query 58:	0.4422
Query 59:	0.0625
Query 61:	0.2552
Query 62:	0.5000
Query 63:	0.0039
Query 64:	0.4465
Query 65:	0.2441
Query 66:	0.2976
Query 67:	0.2526
Query 68:	0.2816
Query 69:	0.4282
Query 70:	0.5504
Query 71:	0.5344
Query 72:	0.1090
Query 73:	1.0000
Query 74:	0.1500
Query 75:	1.0000
Query 76:	0.5688
Query 77:	0.1260
Query 78:	0.2500
Query 79:	0.0000
Query 80:	0.0003
Query 81:	0.7469
Query 82:	0.1581
Query 83:	0.0744
Query 84:	0.7159
Query 85:	0.5290
Query 86:	0.1557
Query 87:	0.5555
Query 88:	1.0000
Query 89:	0.7083
Query 90:	0.5075

Overall statistics
(for 47 queries):

Total number of documents
over all queries
Retrieved:	47000
Relevant:	856
Rel_ret:	719

Interpolated Recall -
Precision Averages:
at 0.00	0.6624
at 0.10	0.6279
at 0.20	0.5581
at 0.30	0.5043
at 0.40	0.4311
at 0.50	0.3888
at 0.60	0.2918
at 0.70	0.2458
at 0.80	0.2052
at 0.90	0.1694
at 1.00	0.1308

Avg. prec. (non-interpolated)
for all rel. documents
0.3711

Precision:
At	5 docs:	0.4085
At	10 docs:	0.3298
At	15 docs:	0.2766
At	20 docs:	0.2500
At	30 docs:	0.2064
At	100 docs:	0.1017
At	200 docs:	0.0636
At	500 docs:	0.0289
At	1000 docs:	0.0153

R-Precision (prec. after R
(=num_rel) docs. retrieved):
Exact:	0.3363

Run aplbiennl

Recall-Precision Values

Run aplbiennl

Comparison to median by topic

Run aplbiennl, Bilingual to Dutch, English, Auto, title+desc

Average precision
(individual queries):

Query 41:	0.0034
Query 42:	0.2415
Query 43:	0.0774
Query 44:	0.1876
Query 45:	0.4850
Query 46:	0.1030
Query 47:	0.0125
Query 48:	0.1335
Query 49:	0.1355
Query 50:	0.3261
Query 51:	0.0015
Query 52:	0.0561
Query 53:	0.0168
Query 54:	0.0011
Query 55:	0.7106
Query 56:	0.0732
Query 57:	0.6247
Query 58:	0.4972
Query 59:	0.6584
Query 60:	0.0001
Query 61:	0.0574
Query 62:	0.5600
Query 63:	0.5484
Query 64:	0.8284
Query 65:	0.0402
Query 66:	0.6784
Query 67:	0.0325
Query 68:	0.4148
Query 69:	0.0000
Query 70:	0.2451
Query 71:	0.0075
Query 72:	0.3577
Query 73:	0.3700
Query 74:	0.4229
Query 75:	0.5000
Query 76:	0.2837
Query 77:	0.0120
Query 78:	0.2345
Query 79:	0.1019
Query 80:	0.6336
Query 81:	0.5854
Query 82:	0.0413
Query 83:	0.1256
Query 84:	0.3850
Query 85:	0.0769
Query 86:	0.0004
Query 87:	0.4115
Query 88:	0.3702
Query 89:	0.8518
Query 90:	0.0117

Overall statistics
(for 50 queries):

Total number of documents
over all queries
Retrieved:	50000
Relevant:	1224
Rel_ret:	963

Interpolated Recall -
Precision Averages:

at 0.00	0.5399
at 0.10	0.4516
at 0.20	0.3993
at 0.30	0.3361
at 0.40	0.3137
at 0.50	0.2860
at 0.60	0.2336
at 0.70	0.2151
at 0.80	0.1855
at 0.90	0.1331
at 1.00	0.0851

Avg. prec. (non-interpolated)
for all rel. documents
                    0.2707

Precision:
At 5 docs:	0.3280
At 10 docs:	0.2600
At 15 docs:	0.2507
At 20 docs:	0.2260
At 30 docs:	0.2067
At 100 docs:	0.1198
At 200 docs:	0.0768
At 500 docs:	0.0352
At 1000 docs:	0.0193

R-Precision (prec. after R
(=num_rel) docs. retrieved):
        Exact: 0.2493

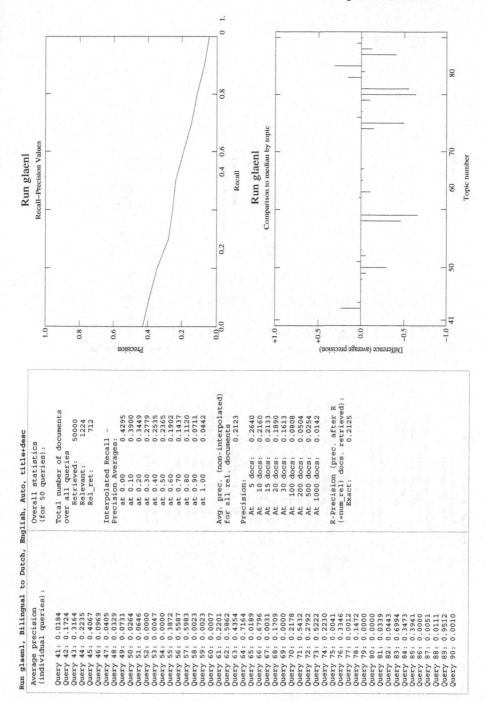

Run glaenl
Recall–Precision Values

Run glaenl
Comparison to median by topic

Run glaenl, Bilingual to Dutch, English, Auto, title+desc

Average precision
(individual queries):

Query 41:	0.0184
Query 42:	0.1724
Query 43:	0.3164
Query 44:	0.2235
Query 45:	0.4067
Query 46:	0.0969
Query 47:	0.0405
Query 48:	0.0329
Query 49:	0.0731
Query 50:	0.0264
Query 51:	0.0646
Query 52:	0.0000
Query 53:	0.0047
Query 54:	0.0000
Query 55:	0.3872
Query 56:	0.5587
Query 57:	0.5983
Query 58:	0.0023
Query 59:	0.0023
Query 60:	0.0007
Query 61:	0.2201
Query 62:	0.5862
Query 63:	0.4354
Query 64:	0.7164
Query 65:	0.0189
Query 66:	0.6796
Query 67:	0.0031
Query 68:	0.1709
Query 69:	0.0000
Query 70:	0.2178
Query 71:	0.5432
Query 72:	0.2792
Query 73:	0.5222
Query 74:	0.2230
Query 75:	0.0041
Query 76:	0.3346
Query 77:	0.0012
Query 78:	0.1472
Query 79:	0.0000
Query 80:	0.0339
Query 81:	0.0443
Query 82:	0.6994
Query 83:	0.3473
Query 84:	0.3941
Query 85:	0.0000
Query 86:	0.0051
Query 87:	0.0111
Query 88:	0.9512
Query 89:	0.0010
Query 90:	0.0010

Overall statistics
(for 50 queries):

Total number of documents
over all queries
Retrieved:	50000
Relevant:	1224
Rel_ret:	712

Interpolated Recall -
Precision Averages:
at 0.00	0.4295
at 0.10	0.3900
at 0.20	0.3449
at 0.30	0.2779
at 0.40	0.2535
at 0.50	0.2365
at 0.60	0.1902
at 0.70	0.1437
at 0.80	0.1120
at 0.90	0.0711
at 1.00	0.0442

Avg. prec. (non-interpolated)
for all rel. documents
0.2123

Precision:
At	5 docs:	0.2640
At	10 docs:	0.2160
At	15 docs:	0.2133
At	20 docs:	0.1890
At	30 docs:	0.1613
At	100 docs:	0.0808
At	200 docs:	0.0504
At	500 docs:	0.0254
At	1000 docs:	0.0142

R-Precision (prec. after R
(=num_rel) docs. retrieved) :
Exact:	0.2125

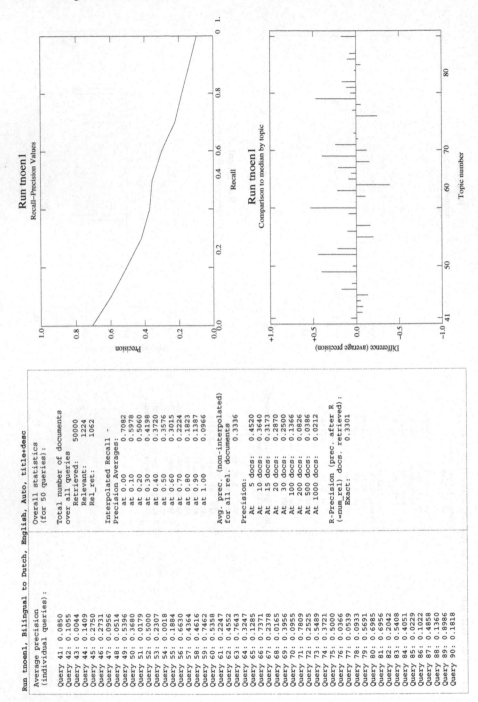

Run tnoen1, Bilingual to Dutch, English, Auto, title+desc

Average precision
(individual queries):

Query 41:	0.0850
Query 42:	0.1055
Query 43:	0.0044
Query 44:	0.1409
Query 45:	0.2750
Query 46:	0.2731
Query 47:	0.0956
Query 48:	0.0514
Query 49:	0.5396
Query 50:	0.3680
Query 51:	0.0179
Query 52:	0.5000
Query 53:	0.2307
Query 54:	0.0018
Query 55:	0.1884
Query 56:	0.6630
Query 57:	0.4364
Query 58:	0.4616
Query 59:	0.7462
Query 60:	0.5358
Query 61:	0.2247
Query 62:	0.4552
Query 63:	0.7643
Query 64:	0.3247
Query 65:	0.1285
Query 66:	0.7371
Query 67:	0.2378
Query 68:	0.0165
Query 69:	0.3956
Query 70:	0.0955
Query 71:	0.7809
Query 72:	0.2525
Query 73:	0.5489
Query 74:	0.3721
Query 75:	0.5000
Query 76:	0.0366
Query 77:	0.0539
Query 78:	0.0933
Query 79:	0.5691
Query 80:	0.6985
Query 81:	0.6956
Query 82:	0.2042
Query 83:	0.5408
Query 84:	0.4051
Query 85:	0.0229
Query 86:	0.1022
Query 87:	0.4858
Query 88:	0.1360
Query 89:	0.8986
Query 90:	0.1818

Overall statistics
(for 50 queries):

Total number of documents
over all queries:
Retrieved: 50000
Relevant: 1224
Rel_ret: 1062

Interpolated Recall -
Precision Averages:
at 0.00   0.7082
at 0.10   0.5978
at 0.20   0.5060
at 0.30   0.4198
at 0.40   0.3720
at 0.50   0.3576
at 0.60   0.3015
at 0.70   0.2224
at 0.80   0.1823
at 0.90   0.1387
at 1.00   0.0966

Avg. prec. (non-interpolated)
for all rel. documents
                   0.3336

Precision:
At   5 docs: 0.4520
At   10 docs: 0.3640
At   15 docs: 0.3173
At   20 docs: 0.2870
At   30 docs: 0.2500
At 100 docs: 0.1366
At 200 docs: 0.0826
At 500 docs: 0.0386
At 1000 docs: 0.0212

R-Precision (prec. after R
(=num_rel) docs. retrieved):
     Exact: 0.3301

Run AmsNIM
Recall–Precision Values

Run AmsNIM
Comparison to median by topic

Run AmsNIM, Monolingual, Dutch, Auto, title+desc

Average precision
(individual queries):

Query 41:	0.2934
Query 42:	0.2466
Query 43:	0.0434
Query 44:	0.1926
Query 45:	0.3406
Query 46:	0.2018
Query 47:	0.2456
Query 48:	0.1055
Query 49:	0.0048
Query 50:	0.4676
Query 51:	0.0312
Query 52:	0.5000
Query 53:	0.0191
Query 54:	0.0473
Query 55:	0.0871
Query 56:	0.4819
Query 57:	0.4443
Query 58:	0.4584
Query 59:	0.5842
Query 60:	0.0684
Query 61:	0.7313
Query 62:	0.5186
Query 63:	0.7207
Query 64:	0.0026
Query 65:	0.0002
Query 66:	0.5875
Query 67:	0.3598
Query 68:	0.0002
Query 69:	0.0364
Query 70:	0.2029
Query 71:	0.4583
Query 72:	0.0580
Query 73:	0.4512
Query 74:	0.4491
Query 75:	1.0000
Query 76:	0.0024
Query 77:	0.1242
Query 78:	0.1009
Query 79:	0.6473
Query 80:	0.1045
Query 81:	0.0912
Query 82:	0.0076
Query 83:	0.0658
Query 84:	0.3920
Query 85:	0.2940
Query 86:	0.5548
Query 87:	0.4148
Query 88:	0.0187
Query 89:	0.9056
Query 90:	0.0005

Overall statistics
(for 50 queries):

Total number of documents
over all queries
Retrieved: 50000
Relevant: 1224
Rel_ret: 963

Interpolated Recall -
Precision Averages:
at 0.00   0.5513
at 0.10   0.4718
at 0.20   0.4318
at 0.30   0.3899
at 0.40   0.3536
at 0.50   0.3266
at 0.60   0.2327
at 0.70   0.1896
at 0.80   0.1595
at 0.90   0.1107
at 1.00   0.0597

Avg. prec. (non-interpolated)
for all rel. documents
          0.2833

Precision:
At   5 docs: 0.3440
At   10 docs: 0.3080
At   15 docs: 0.2667
At   20 docs: 0.2500
At   30 docs: 0.2173
At 100 docs: 0.1194
At 200 docs: 0.0767
At 500 docs: 0.0367
At 1000 docs: 0.0193

R-Precision (prec. after R
(=num_rel) docs. retrieved):
Exact: 0.2864

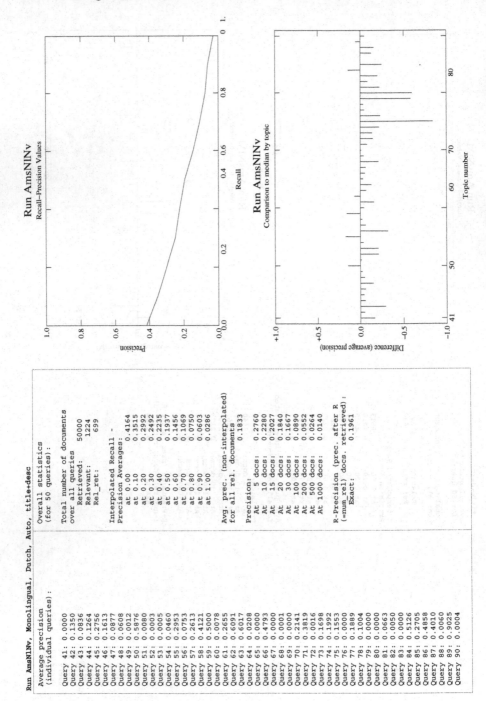

Run AmsNlNv

Recall–Precision Values

Run AmsNlNv

Comparison to median by topic

Run AmsNlNv, Monolingual, Dutch, Auto, title+desc

Average precision
(individual queries):

Query 41:	0.0000
Query 42:	0.1350
Query 43:	0.0836
Query 44:	0.1264
Query 45:	0.2756
Query 46:	0.1613
Query 47:	0.0877
Query 48:	0.0608
Query 49:	0.0012
Query 50:	0.5876
Query 51:	0.0080
Query 52:	0.0003
Query 53:	0.0005
Query 54:	0.0460
Query 55:	0.2953
Query 56:	0.0753
Query 57:	0.2613
Query 58:	0.4121
Query 59:	0.5000
Query 60:	0.0078
Query 61:	0.2655
Query 62:	0.6091
Query 63:	0.6017
Query 64:	0.0208
Query 65:	0.0000
Query 66:	0.4793
Query 67:	0.0000
Query 68:	0.0001
Query 69:	0.0000
Query 70:	0.2141
Query 71:	0.3819
Query 72:	0.0016
Query 73:	0.1698
Query 74:	0.1992
Query 75:	0.1553
Query 76:	0.0000
Query 77:	0.1889
Query 78:	0.1004
Query 79:	0.0000
Query 80:	0.0000
Query 81:	0.0663
Query 82:	0.0050
Query 83:	0.0000
Query 84:	0.5126
Query 85:	0.2705
Query 86:	0.4858
Query 87:	0.4010
Query 88:	0.0060
Query 89:	0.9025
Query 90:	0.0004

Overall statistics
(for 50 queries):

Total number of documents
over all queries
   Retrieved: 50000
   Relevant: 1224
   Rel_ret: 699

Interpolated Recall -
Precision Averages:
   at 0.00   0.4164
   at 0.10   0.3515
   at 0.20   0.2992
   at 0.30   0.2492
   at 0.40   0.2235
   at 0.50   0.1937
   at 0.60   0.1456
   at 0.70   0.1069
   at 0.80   0.0750
   at 0.90   0.0603
   at 1.00   0.0286

Avg. prec. (non-interpolated)
for all rel. documents
            0.1833

Precision:
  At   5 docs: 0.2760
  At   10 docs: 0.2280
  At   15 docs: 0.2027
  At   20 docs: 0.1840
  At   30 docs: 0.1667
  At 100 docs: 0.0890
  At 200 docs: 0.0552
  At 500 docs: 0.0264
  At 1000 docs: 0.0140

R-Precision (prec. after R
(=num_rel) docs. retrieved):
   Exact: 0.1961

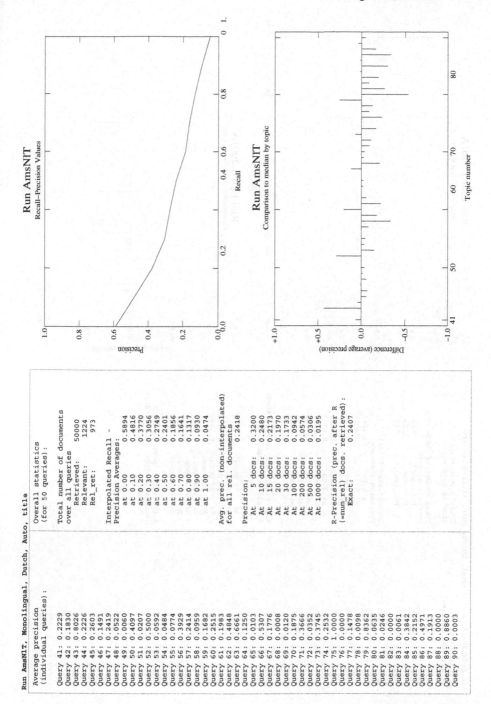

Run AmsNIT, Monolingual, Dutch, Auto, title

Average precision
(individual queries):

Query 41:	0.2229
Query 42:	0.1830
Query 43:	0.8026
Query 44:	0.2226
Query 45:	0.2603
Query 46:	0.1491
Query 47:	0.2419
Query 48:	0.0522
Query 49:	0.0060
Query 50:	0.4097
Query 51:	0.0207
Query 52:	0.5000
Query 53:	0.0592
Query 54:	0.0484
Query 55:	0.0774
Query 56:	0.3929
Query 57:	0.2414
Query 58:	0.0959
Query 59:	0.1682
Query 60:	0.2515
Query 61:	0.1983
Query 62:	0.4848
Query 63:	0.6661
Query 64:	0.1250
Query 65:	0.0103
Query 66:	0.5307
Query 67:	0.1776
Query 68:	0.0008
Query 69:	0.0120
Query 70:	0.1875
Query 71:	0.3666
Query 72:	0.0352
Query 73:	0.3745
Query 74:	0.2532
Query 75:	1.0000
Query 76:	0.0000
Query 77:	0.1478
Query 78:	0.0098
Query 79:	0.8362
Query 80:	0.0635
Query 81:	0.0246
Query 82:	0.0000
Query 83:	0.0061
Query 84:	0.3842
Query 85:	0.2152
Query 86:	0.4971
Query 87:	0.1913
Query 88:	0.0000
Query 89:	0.8860
Query 90:	0.0003

Overall statistics
(for 50 queries):

Total number of documents
over all queries
Retrieved: 50000
Relevant: 1224
Rel_ret: 973

Interpolated Recall -
Precision Averages:
at 0.00   0.5894
at 0.10   0.4816
at 0.20   0.3770
at 0.30   0.3056
at 0.40   0.2749
at 0.50   0.2401
at 0.60   0.1856
at 0.70   0.1641
at 0.80   0.1317
at 0.90   0.0930
at 1.00   0.0474

Avg. prec. (non-interpolated)
for all rel. documents
                 0.2418

Precision:
At   5 docs: 0.3200
At   10 docs: 0.2480
At   15 docs: 0.2173
At   20 docs: 0.1970
At   30 docs: 0.1733
At 100 docs: 0.0942
At 200 docs: 0.0574
At 500 docs: 0.0306
At 1000 docs: 0.0195

R-Precision (prec. after R
(=num rel) docs. retrieved):
    Exact: 0.2407

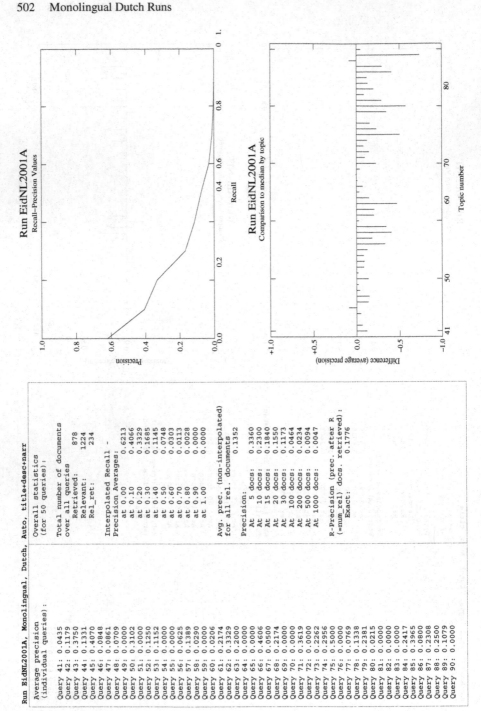

Run EidNL2001A
Recall–Precision Values

Run EidNL2001A
Comparison to median by topic

Run EidNL2001A, Monolingual, Dutch, Auto, title+desc+narr

Average precision
(individual queries):

Query 41:	0.0435
Query 42:	0.1179
Query 43:	0.3750
Query 44:	0.1331
Query 45:	0.4070
Query 46:	0.0848
Query 47:	0.0861
Query 48:	0.0709
Query 49:	0.0000
Query 50:	0.3102
Query 51:	0.0000
Query 52:	0.1250
Query 53:	0.1152
Query 54:	0.0000
Query 55:	0.0000
Query 56:	0.0625
Query 57:	0.1389
Query 58:	0.0290
Query 59:	0.0000
Query 60:	0.0206
Query 61:	0.2174
Query 62:	0.3329
Query 63:	0.2000
Query 64:	0.0000
Query 65:	0.0000
Query 66:	0.4606
Query 67:	0.0500
Query 68:	0.2174
Query 69:	0.0000
Query 70:	0.0000
Query 71:	0.3619
Query 72:	0.0000
Query 73:	0.2262
Query 74:	0.2956
Query 75:	0.5000
Query 76:	0.0000
Query 77:	0.0769
Query 78:	0.1338
Query 79:	0.2381
Query 80:	0.0215
Query 81:	0.0000
Query 82:	0.0000
Query 83:	0.0000
Query 84:	0.2417
Query 85:	0.3965
Query 86:	0.0800
Query 87:	0.2308
Query 88:	0.2500
Query 89:	0.1079
Query 90:	0.0000

Overall statistics
(for 50 queries):

Total number of documents
over all queries:
    Retrieved: 878
    Relevant: 1224
    Rel_ret: 234

Interpolated Recall -
Precision Averages:
    at 0.00   0.6213
    at 0.10   0.4066
    at 0.20   0.3329
    at 0.30   0.1685
    at 0.40   0.1145
    at 0.50   0.0748
    at 0.60   0.0303
    at 0.70   0.0113
    at 0.80   0.0028
    at 0.90   0.0000
    at 1.00   0.0000

Avg. prec. (non-interpolated)
for all rel. documents
                    0.1352

Precision:
    At   5 docs: 0.3360
    At   10 docs: 0.2300
    At   15 docs: 0.1840
    At   20 docs: 0.1550
    At   30 docs: 0.1173
    At 100 docs: 0.0464
    At 200 docs: 0.0234
    At 500 docs: 0.0094
    At 1000 docs: 0.0047

R-Precision (prec. after R
(=num_rel) docs. retrieved):
    Exact: 0.1776

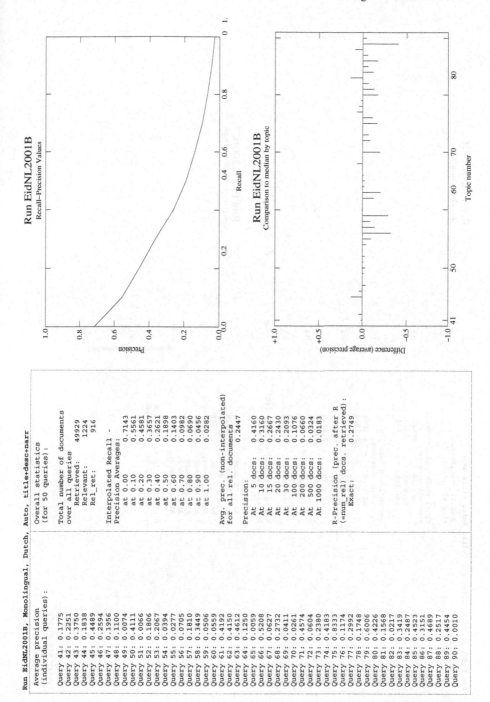

Run EidNL2001B, Monolingual, Dutch, Auto, title+desc+narr

Average precision
(individual queries):

Query 41:	0.1775
Query 42:	0.2251
Query 43:	0.3750
Query 44:	0.1838
Query 45:	0.4489
Query 46:	0.2594
Query 47:	0.1956
Query 48:	0.1100
Query 49:	0.0074
Query 50:	0.4111
Query 51:	0.0066
Query 52:	0.1806
Query 53:	0.2067
Query 54:	0.0394
Query 55:	0.0277
Query 56:	0.0705
Query 57:	0.1810
Query 58:	0.3449
Query 59:	0.0506
Query 60:	0.0559
Query 61:	0.4192
Query 62:	0.4150
Query 63:	0.4612
Query 64:	0.1250
Query 65:	0.0059
Query 66:	0.5208
Query 67:	0.0627
Query 68:	0.2732
Query 69:	0.0411
Query 70:	0.0261
Query 71:	0.4574
Query 72:	0.0604
Query 73:	0.2380
Query 74:	0.4183
Query 75:	0.8333
Query 76:	0.1174
Query 77:	0.2992
Query 78:	0.1748
Query 79:	0.6006
Query 80:	0.4226
Query 81:	0.1568
Query 82:	0.0217
Query 83:	0.3419
Query 84:	0.2487
Query 85:	0.4523
Query 86:	0.3151
Query 87:	0.4689
Query 88:	0.2517
Query 89:	0.4454
Query 90:	0.0010

Overall statistics
(for 50 queries):

Total number of documents
over all queries
Retrieved:	49929
Relevant:	1224
Rel_ret:	916

Interpolated Recall -
Precision Averages:
at 0.00	0.7143
at 0.10	0.5561
at 0.20	0.4581
at 0.30	0.3557
at 0.40	0.2621
at 0.50	0.1898
at 0.60	0.1403
at 0.70	0.0982
at 0.80	0.0690
at 0.90	0.0456
at 1.00	0.0282

Avg. prec. (non-interpolated)
for all rel. documents
                         0.2447

Precision:
At 5 docs:	0.4160
At 10 docs:	0.3160
At 15 docs:	0.2667
At 20 docs:	0.2430
At 30 docs:	0.2093
At 100 docs:	0.1076
At 200 docs:	0.0660
At 500 docs:	0.0324
At 1000 docs:	0.0183

R-Precision (prec. after R
(=num rel) docs. retrieved):
| Exact: | 0.2749 |

Run EidNL2001B
Recall-Precision Values

Run EidNL2001B
Comparison to median by topic

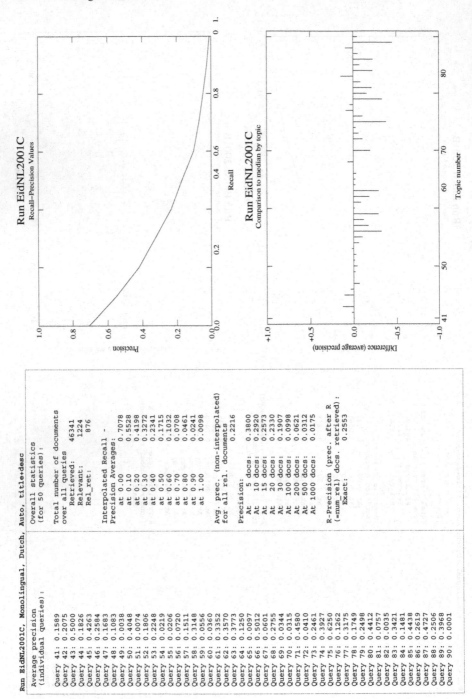

Run EidNL2001C
Recall–Precision Values

Run EidNL2001C
Comparison to median by topic

Run EidNL2001C, Monolingual, Dutch, Auto, title+desc

Average precision
(individual queries):

Query 41:	0.1589
Query 42:	0.2075
Query 43:	0.5000
Query 44:	0.1826
Query 45:	0.4263
Query 46:	0.2584
Query 47:	0.1683
Query 48:	0.1083
Query 49:	0.0038
Query 50:	0.4048
Query 51:	0.0074
Query 52:	0.1806
Query 53:	0.2248
Query 54:	0.0219
Query 55:	0.0206
Query 56:	0.0720
Query 57:	0.1511
Query 58:	0.3148
Query 59:	0.0556
Query 60:	0.0360
Query 61:	0.3352
Query 62:	0.3570
Query 63:	0.3773
Query 64:	0.1250
Query 65:	0.0097
Query 66:	0.5012
Query 67:	0.0601
Query 68:	0.2755
Query 69:	0.0344
Query 70:	0.0315
Query 71:	0.4580
Query 72:	0.0410
Query 73:	0.2461
Query 74:	0.3927
Query 75:	0.6250
Query 76:	0.1262
Query 77:	0.3175
Query 78:	0.1749
Query 79:	0.2498
Query 80:	0.4412
Query 81:	0.0757
Query 82:	0.0035
Query 83:	0.3421
Query 84:	0.1481
Query 85:	0.4438
Query 86:	0.2619
Query 87:	0.4727
Query 88:	0.2506
Query 89:	0.3968
Query 90:	0.0001

Overall statistics
(for 50 queries):

Total number of documents
over all queries
  Retrieved: 46341
  Relevant: 1224
  Rel_ret: 876

Interpolated Recall -
Precision Averages:
  at 0.00   0.7078
  at 0.10   0.5528
  at 0.20   0.4198
  at 0.30   0.3272
  at 0.40   0.2341
  at 0.50   0.1715
  at 0.60   0.1032
  at 0.70   0.0708
  at 0.80   0.0461
  at 0.90   0.0241
  at 1.00   0.0098

Avg. prec. (non-interpolated)
for all rel. documents
     0.2216

Precision:
  At   5 docs: 0.3800
  At 10 docs: 0.2920
  At 15 docs: 0.2573
  At 20 docs: 0.2330
  At 30 docs: 0.1907
  At 100 docs: 0.0998
  At 200 docs: 0.0621
  At 500 docs: 0.0312
  At 1000 docs: 0.0175

R-Precision (prec. after R
(=num_rel) docs. retrieved):
    Exact: 0.2553

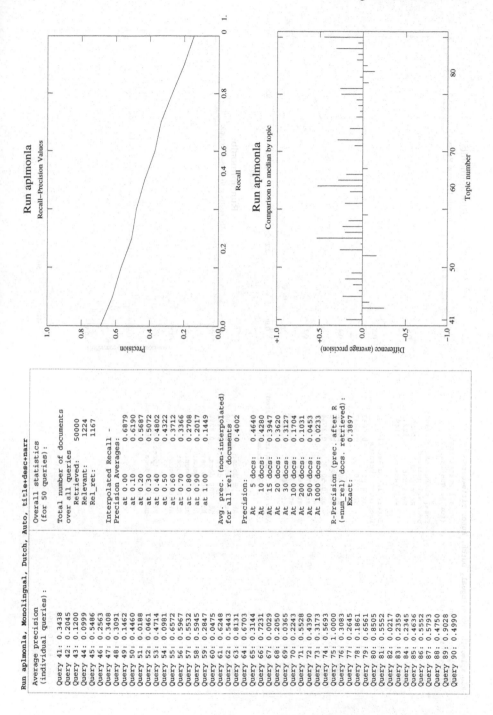

Run aplmon1a
Recall–Precision Values

Run aplmon1a
Comparison to median by topic

Run aplmon1a, Monolingual, Dutch, Auto, title+desc+narr

Average precision
(individual queries):

Query 41:	0.3438
Query 42:	0.2045
Query 43:	0.1200
Query 44:	0.0999
Query 45:	0.5486
Query 46:	0.2563
Query 47:	0.3408
Query 48:	0.3091
Query 49:	0.1462
Query 50:	0.4460
Query 51:	0.0188
Query 52:	0.0461
Query 53:	0.4714
Query 54:	0.0981
Query 55:	0.6572
Query 56:	0.5967
Query 57:	0.5532
Query 58:	0.5945
Query 59:	0.2847
Query 60:	0.0475
Query 61:	0.6248
Query 62:	0.5443
Query 63:	0.8131
Query 64:	0.6703
Query 65:	0.3144
Query 66:	0.7231
Query 67:	0.0029
Query 68:	0.2050
Query 69:	0.0365
Query 70:	0.2243
Query 71:	0.5528
Query 72:	0.4390
Query 73:	0.3173
Query 74:	0.5693
Query 75:	1.0000
Query 76:	0.3083
Query 77:	0.2645
Query 78:	0.1861
Query 79:	0.6561
Query 80:	0.8505
Query 81:	0.5552
Query 82:	0.0217
Query 83:	0.2359
Query 84:	0.2345
Query 85:	0.4636
Query 86:	0.5552
Query 87:	0.5793
Query 88:	0.4750
Query 89:	0.9028
Query 90:	0.4990

Overall statistics
(for 50 queries):

Total number of documents
over all queries
    Retrieved: 50000
    Relevant: 1224
    Rel_ret: 1167

Interpolated Recall -
Precision Averages:
    at 0.00   0.6879
    at 0.10   0.6190
    at 0.20   0.5687
    at 0.30   0.5072
    at 0.40   0.4802
    at 0.50   0.4322
    at 0.60   0.3712
    at 0.70   0.3366
    at 0.80   0.2708
    at 0.90   0.2017
    at 1.00   0.1449

Avg. prec. (non-interpolated)
for all rel. documents
                   0.4002

Precision:
    At   5 docs: 0.4640
    At   10 docs: 0.4280
    At   15 docs: 0.3947
    At   20 docs: 0.3620
    At   30 docs: 0.3127
    At 100 docs: 0.1704
    At 200 docs: 0.1031
    At 500 docs: 0.0453
    At 1000 docs: 0.0233

R-Precision (prec. after R
(=num rel) docs. retrieved):
    Exact: 0.3897

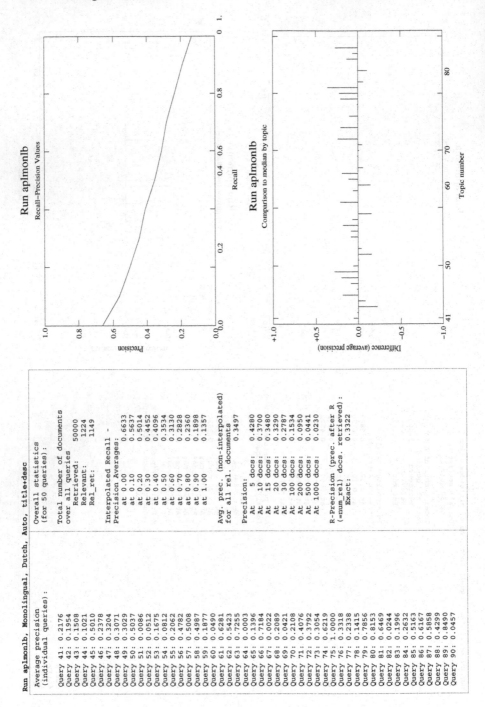

Run aplmonlb

Recall–Precision Values

Recall

Precision

Run aplmonlb

Comparison to median by topic

Topic number

Difference (average precision)

Run aplmonlb, Monolingual, Dutch, Auto, title+desc

Average precision
(individual queries):

Query 41:	0.2176
Query 42:	0.1954
Query 43:	0.1508
Query 44:	0.1021
Query 45:	0.5010
Query 46:	0.2378
Query 47:	0.3204
Query 48:	0.3071
Query 49:	0.3029
Query 50:	0.5037
Query 51:	0.0086
Query 52:	0.0512
Query 53:	0.1675
Query 54:	0.0812
Query 55:	0.2062
Query 56:	0.4782
Query 57:	0.5008
Query 58:	0.4987
Query 59:	0.1877
Query 60:	0.0490
Query 61:	0.6281
Query 62:	0.5423
Query 63:	0.7255
Query 64:	0.0003
Query 65:	0.1396
Query 66:	0.7184
Query 67:	0.0022
Query 68:	0.2089
Query 69:	0.0421
Query 70:	0.2108
Query 71:	0.4076
Query 72:	0.3792
Query 73:	0.3054
Query 74:	0.6219
Query 75:	1.0000
Query 76:	0.3318
Query 77:	0.2338
Query 78:	0.1415
Query 79:	0.7856
Query 80:	0.8153
Query 81:	0.6469
Query 82:	0.0244
Query 83:	0.1996
Query 84:	0.2632
Query 85:	0.5163
Query 86:	0.6167
Query 87:	0.5858
Query 88:	0.4299
Query 89:	0.8490
Query 90:	0.0457

Overall statistics
(for 50 queries):

Total number of documents
over all queries:
Retrieved: 50000
Relevant: 1224
Rel_ret: 1149

Interpolated Recall -
Precision Averages:
at 0.00   0.6633
at 0.10   0.5637
at 0.20   0.5014
at 0.30   0.4452
at 0.40   0.4096
at 0.50   0.3534
at 0.60   0.3130
at 0.70   0.2828
at 0.80   0.2360
at 0.90   0.1898
at 1.00   0.1357

Avg. prec. (non-interpolated)
for all rel. documents   0.3497

Precision:
At   5 docs: 0.4280
At   10 docs: 0.3700
At   15 docs: 0.3480
At   20 docs: 0.3290
At   30 docs: 0.2787
At 100 docs: 0.1534
At 200 docs: 0.0950
At 500 docs: 0.0441
At 1000 docs: 0.0230

R-Precision (prec. after R
(=num_rel) docs. retrieved):
Exact: 0.3322

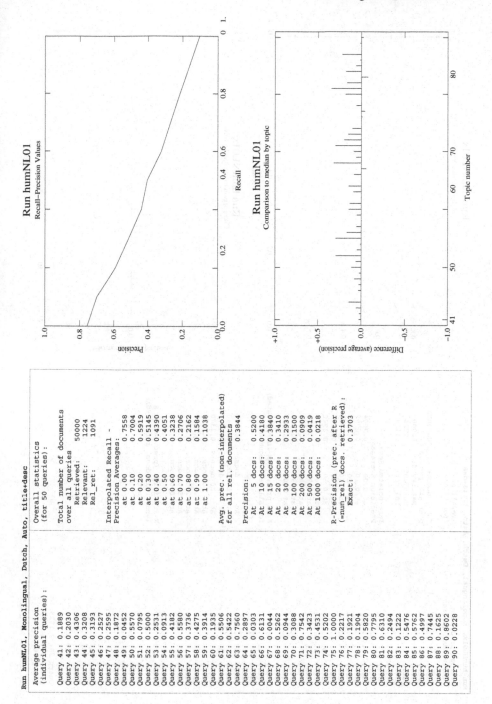

Run humNL01
Recall–Precision Values

Run humNL01
Comparison to median by topic

Run humNL01, Monolingual, Dutch, Auto, title+desc

Average precision
(individual queries):

Query 41:	0.1889
Query 42:	0.2030
Query 43:	0.4306
Query 44:	0.3208
Query 45:	0.3193
Query 46:	0.2527
Query 47:	0.2595
Query 48:	0.1872
Query 49:	0.0452
Query 50:	0.5570
Query 51:	0.0795
Query 52:	0.5000
Query 53:	0.2531
Query 54:	0.0913
Query 55:	0.4182
Query 56:	0.5580
Query 57:	0.3736
Query 58:	0.4275
Query 59:	0.3914
Query 60:	0.1935
Query 61:	0.5506
Query 62:	0.5422
Query 63:	0.7560
Query 64:	0.2897
Query 65:	0.0303
Query 66:	0.6131
Query 67:	0.0044
Query 68:	0.5262
Query 69:	0.0944
Query 70:	0.3088
Query 71:	0.7542
Query 72:	0.3423
Query 73:	0.4531
Query 74:	0.5202
Query 75:	1.0000
Query 76:	0.2217
Query 77:	0.1921
Query 78:	0.1904
Query 79:	0.5820
Query 80:	0.7795
Query 81:	0.6310
Query 82:	0.2494
Query 83:	0.1222
Query 84:	0.5476
Query 85:	0.5762
Query 86:	0.4997
Query 87:	0.7445
Query 88:	0.1625
Query 89:	0.8602
Query 90:	0.0228

Overall statistics
(for 50 queries):

Total number of documents
over all queries
    Retrieved: 50000
    Relevant: 1224
    Rel_ret: 1091

Interpolated Recall -
Precision Averages:
    at 0.00   0.7558
    at 0.10   0.7004
    at 0.20   0.5919
    at 0.30   0.5145
    at 0.40   0.4390
    at 0.50   0.4051
    at 0.60   0.3238
    at 0.70   0.2706
    at 0.80   0.2162
    at 0.90   0.1584
    at 1.00   0.1038

Avg. prec. (non-interpolated)
for all rel. documents
                     0.3844

Precision:
    At   5 docs: 0.5200
    At   10 docs: 0.4180
    At   15 docs: 0.3840
    At   20 docs: 0.3410
    At   30 docs: 0.2933
    At 100 docs: 0.1500
    At 200 docs: 0.0909
    At 500 docs: 0.0419
    At 1000 docs: 0.0218

R-Precision (prec. after R
(=num rel) docs. retrieved):
    Exact: 0.3703

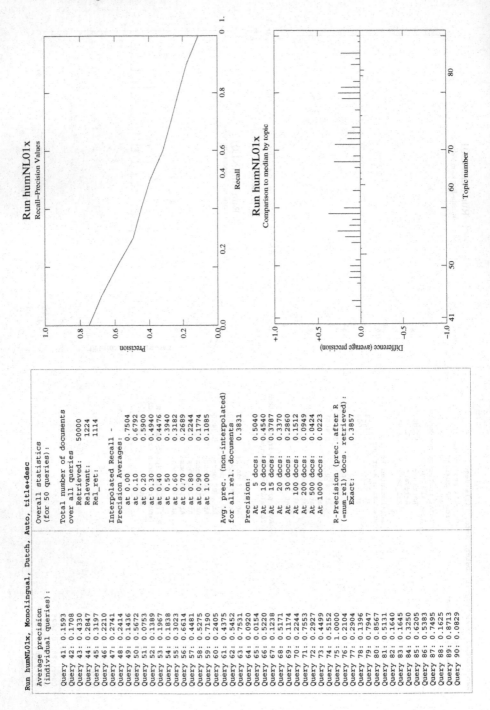

Run humNL01x
Recall–Precision Values

Run humNL01x
Comparison to median by topic

Run humNL01x, Monolingual, Dutch, Auto, title+desc

Average precision
(individual queries):

Query 41:	0.1593
Query 42:	0.1708
Query 43:	0.4330
Query 44:	0.2847
Query 45:	0.3197
Query 46:	0.2210
Query 47:	0.2741
Query 48:	0.2414
Query 49:	0.1436
Query 50:	0.5672
Query 51:	0.0753
Query 52:	0.1389
Query 53:	0.1967
Query 54:	0.1838
Query 55:	0.3023
Query 56:	0.6614
Query 57:	0.4481
Query 58:	0.5275
Query 59:	0.7190
Query 60:	0.2405
Query 61:	0.4375
Query 62:	0.5452
Query 63:	0.7531
Query 64:	0.0920
Query 65:	0.0154
Query 66:	0.5220
Query 67:	0.1238
Query 68:	0.5171
Query 69:	0.1174
Query 70:	0.2244
Query 71:	0.7553
Query 72:	0.2927
Query 73:	0.4499
Query 74:	0.5152
Query 75:	1.0000
Query 76:	0.2104
Query 77:	0.2904
Query 78:	0.1396
Query 79:	0.7947
Query 80:	0.8567
Query 81:	0.5131
Query 82:	0.1640
Query 83:	0.1645
Query 84:	0.3250
Query 85:	0.6205
Query 86:	0.5383
Query 87:	0.7495
Query 88:	0.1625
Query 89:	0.8713
Query 90:	0.0829

Overall statistics
(for 50 queries):

Total number of documents
over all queries
Retrieved: 50000
Relevant: 1224
Rel_ret: 1114

Interpolated Recall -
Precision Averages:
at 0.00   0.7504
at 0.10   0.6792
at 0.20   0.5900
at 0.30   0.4940
at 0.40   0.4476
at 0.50   0.3940
at 0.60   0.3182
at 0.70   0.2689
at 0.80   0.2244
at 0.90   0.1774
at 1.00   0.1085

Avg. prec. (non-interpolated)
for all rel. documents
          0.3831

Precision:
At   5 docs: 0.5040
At   10 docs: 0.4540
At   15 docs: 0.3787
At   20 docs: 0.3370
At   30 docs: 0.2860
At 100 docs: 0.1512
At 200 docs: 0.0949
At 500 docs: 0.0424
At 1000 docs: 0.0223

R-Precision (prec. after R
(=num_rel) docs. retrieved):
Exact: 0.3857

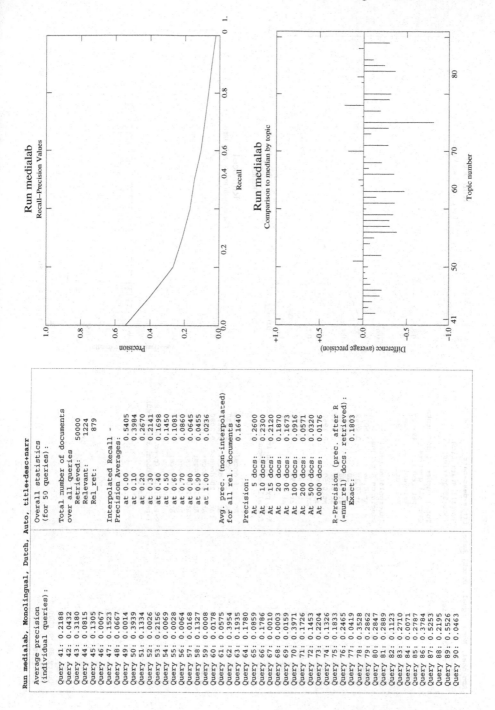

Run medialab
Recall–Precision Values

Run medialab
Comparison to median by topic

Run medialab, Monolingual, Dutch, Auto, title+desc+narr

Average precision
(individual queries):

Query 41:	0.2188
Query 42:	0.0432
Query 43:	0.3180
Query 44:	0.0815
Query 45:	0.1305
Query 46:	0.0067
Query 47:	0.1523
Query 48:	0.0667
Query 49:	0.0014
Query 50:	0.3939
Query 51:	0.1334
Query 52:	0.0026
Query 53:	0.2156
Query 54:	0.0069
Query 55:	0.0028
Query 56:	0.0064
Query 57:	0.0168
Query 58:	0.1327
Query 59:	0.0008
Query 60:	0.0178
Query 61:	0.0575
Query 62:	0.3954
Query 63:	0.1935
Query 64:	0.1780
Query 65:	0.0859
Query 66:	0.1786
Query 67:	0.0010
Query 68:	0.0003
Query 69:	0.0159
Query 70:	0.3971
Query 71:	0.1726
Query 72:	0.1453
Query 73:	0.2204
Query 74:	0.1326
Query 75:	0.1833
Query 76:	0.2465
Query 77:	0.0419
Query 78:	0.3528
Query 79:	0.2862
Query 80:	0.2847
Query 81:	0.2889
Query 82:	0.1123
Query 83:	0.2710
Query 84:	0.0071
Query 85:	0.2787
Query 86:	0.3784
Query 87:	0.5253
Query 88:	0.2195
Query 89:	0.5526
Query 90:	0.0463

Overall statistics
(for 50 queries):

Total number of documents
over all queries:
Retrieved: 50000
Relevant: 1224
Rel_ret: 879

Interpolated Recall -
Precision Averages:

at 0.00	0.5405
at 0.10	0.3984
at 0.20	0.2670
at 0.30	0.2141
at 0.40	0.1698
at 0.50	0.1450
at 0.60	0.1081
at 0.70	0.0860
at 0.80	0.0645
at 0.90	0.0455
at 1.00	0.0236

Avg. prec. (non-interpolated)
for all rel. documents
                    0.1640

Precision:

At 5 docs:	0.2600
At 10 docs:	0.2300
At 15 docs:	0.2120
At 20 docs:	0.1870
At 30 docs:	0.1673
At 100 docs:	0.0916
At 200 docs:	0.0571
At 500 docs:	0.0320
At 1000 docs:	0.0176

R-Precision (prec. after R
(=num rel) docs. retrieved):
    Exact: 0.1803

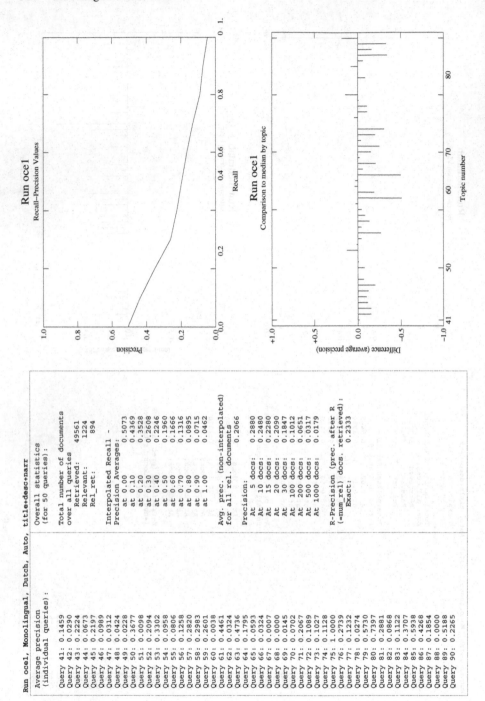

Run ocel, Monolingual, Dutch, Auto, title+desc+narr

Average precision
(individual queries):

Query 41:	0.1459
Query 42:	0.0290
Query 43:	0.2224
Query 44:	0.0673
Query 45:	0.2197
Query 46:	0.0989
Query 47:	0.0312
Query 48:	0.0424
Query 49:	0.0228
Query 50:	0.3677
Query 51:	0.0098
Query 52:	0.2094
Query 53:	0.3302
Query 54:	0.0958
Query 55:	0.0806
Query 56:	0.1258
Query 57:	0.2820
Query 58:	0.2983
Query 59:	0.2601
Query 60:	0.0038
Query 61:	0.4461
Query 62:	0.0324
Query 63:	0.4736
Query 64:	0.1795
Query 65:	0.0593
Query 66:	0.0324
Query 67:	0.0007
Query 68:	0.0000
Query 69:	0.0145
Query 70:	0.0702
Query 71:	0.2067
Query 72:	0.1089
Query 73:	0.1027
Query 74:	0.1128
Query 75:	1.0000
Query 76:	0.2739
Query 77:	0.1232
Query 78:	0.0274
Query 79:	0.5730
Query 80:	0.7397
Query 81:	0.2881
Query 82:	0.0868
Query 83:	0.1122
Query 84:	0.3707
Query 85:	0.5938
Query 86:	0.4268
Query 87:	0.1854
Query 88:	0.0000
Query 89:	0.5188
Query 90:	0.2265

Overall statistics
(for 50 queries):

Total number of documents
over all queries:
    Retrieved: 49561
    Relevant: 1224
    Rel_ret: 894

Interpolated Recall -
Precision Averages:
    at 0.00   0.5073
    at 0.10   0.4369
    at 0.20   0.3528
    at 0.30   0.2608
    at 0.40   0.2246
    at 0.50   0.1960
    at 0.60   0.1666
    at 0.70   0.1316
    at 0.80   0.0895
    at 0.90   0.0715
    at 1.00   0.0462

Avg. prec. (non-interpolated)
for all rel. documents
                   0.2066

Precision:
    At   5 docs: 0.2880
    At   10 docs: 0.2480
    At   15 docs: 0.2280
    At   20 docs: 0.2090
    At   30 docs: 0.1847
    At 100 docs: 0.1012
    At 200 docs: 0.0651
    At 500 docs: 0.0317
    At 1000 docs: 0.0179

R-Precision (prec. after R
(=num_rel) docs. retrieved):
    Exact: 0.2333

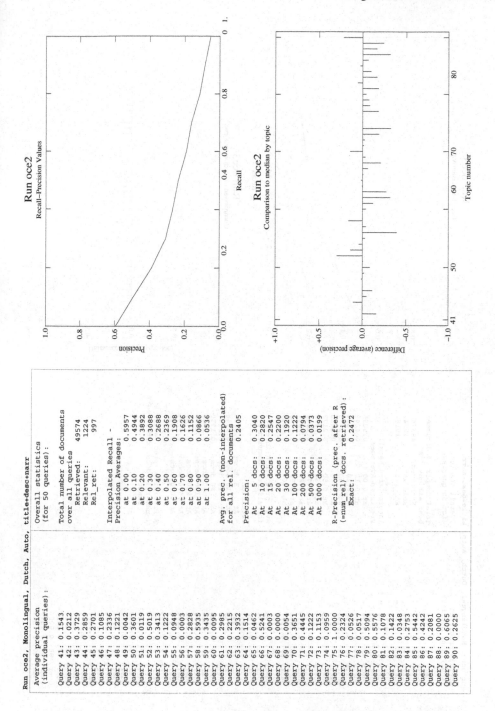

Run oce2
Recall-Precision Values

Run oce2
Comparison to median by topic

Run oce2, Monolingual, Dutch, Auto, title+desc+narr

Average precision
(individual queries):

Query 41:	0.1543
Query 42:	0.0212
Query 43:	0.3729
Query 44:	0.2859
Query 45:	0.2701
Query 46:	0.1085
Query 47:	0.2336
Query 48:	0.1221
Query 49:	0.0042
Query 50:	0.3601
Query 51:	0.0119
Query 52:	0.5019
Query 53:	0.3413
Query 54:	0.1222
Query 55:	0.0948
Query 56:	0.0003
Query 57:	0.2828
Query 58:	0.5935
Query 59:	0.3435
Query 60:	0.0095
Query 61:	0.2985
Query 62:	0.2215
Query 63:	0.3932
Query 64:	0.1514
Query 65:	0.0462
Query 66:	0.5241
Query 67:	0.0003
Query 68:	0.0000
Query 69:	0.0054
Query 70:	0.3651
Query 71:	0.4445
Query 72:	0.1222
Query 73:	0.1153
Query 74:	0.0959
Query 75:	1.0000
Query 76:	0.2324
Query 77:	0.0526
Query 78:	0.0517
Query 79:	0.5094
Query 80:	0.5576
Query 81:	0.1078
Query 82:	0.1422
Query 83:	0.0348
Query 84:	0.2753
Query 85:	0.5442
Query 86:	0.4242
Query 87:	0.2081
Query 88:	0.0000
Query 89:	0.6065
Query 90:	0.2625

Overall statistics
(for 50 queries):

Total number of documents
over all queries
    Retrieved: 49574
    Relevant: 1224
    Rel_ret: 997

Interpolated Recall -
Precision Averages:
    at 0.00   0.5957
    at 0.10   0.4944
    at 0.20   0.3892
    at 0.30   0.3088
    at 0.40   0.2688
    at 0.50   0.2369
    at 0.60   0.1908
    at 0.70   0.1626
    at 0.80   0.1152
    at 0.90   0.0886
    at 1.00   0.0536

Avg. prec. (non-interpolated)
for all rel. documents
                    0.2405

Precision:
    At   5 docs: 0.3040
    At   10 docs: 0.2820
    At   15 docs: 0.2547
    At   20 docs: 0.2200
    At   30 docs: 0.1920
    At 100 docs: 0.1222
    At 200 docs: 0.0794
    At 500 docs: 0.0373
    At 1000 docs: 0.0199

R-Precision (prec. after R
(=num rel) docs. retrieved):
    Exact: 0.2472

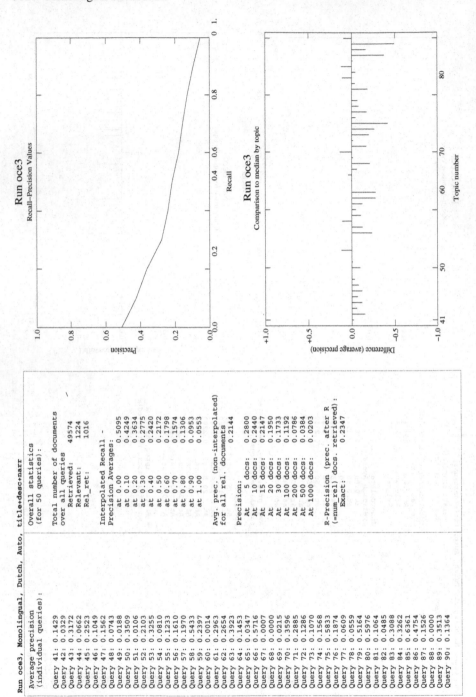

Run oce3 — Recall–Precision Values

Run oce3 — Comparison to median by topic

Run oce3, Monolingual, Dutch, Auto, title+desc+narr

Average precision (individual queries):

Query 41:	0.1429	Query 66:	0.5716
Query 42:	0.0329	Query 67:	0.0007
Query 43:	0.3172	Query 68:	0.0000
Query 44:	0.0662	Query 69:	0.0215
Query 45:	0.2523	Query 70:	0.3596
Query 46:	0.1049	Query 71:	0.2885
Query 47:	0.1562	Query 72:	0.1286
Query 48:	0.0743	Query 73:	0.1070
Query 49:	0.0188	Query 74:	0.1568
Query 50:	0.3509	Query 75:	0.5833
Query 51:	0.0106	Query 76:	0.1874
Query 52:	0.2103	Query 77:	0.0609
Query 53:	0.3255	Query 78:	0.0559
Query 54:	0.0810	Query 79:	0.5164
Query 55:	0.1233	Query 80:	0.5976
Query 56:	0.1610	Query 81:	0.1064
Query 57:	0.1970	Query 82:	0.0485
Query 58:	0.5433	Query 83:	0.3088
Query 59:	0.2397	Query 84:	0.3262
Query 60:	0.0014	Query 85:	0.6361
Query 61:	0.2963	Query 86:	0.4754
Query 62:	0.2654	Query 87:	0.1526
Query 63:	0.3923	Query 88:	0.0000
Query 64:	0.1453	Query 89:	0.3513
Query 65:	0.0347	Query 90:	0.1364

Overall statistics (for 50 queries):

Total number of documents over all queries

Retrieved: 49574
Relevant: 1224
Rel_ret: 1016

Interpolated Recall - Precision Averages:

at 0.00	0.5095
at 0.10	0.4249
at 0.20	0.3634
at 0.30	0.2775
at 0.40	0.2420
at 0.50	0.2172
at 0.60	0.1798
at 0.70	0.1574
at 0.80	0.1306
at 0.90	0.0953
at 1.00	0.0553

Avg. prec. (non-interpolated) for all rel. documents
0.2144

Precision:

At 5 docs:	0.2800
At 10 docs:	0.2440
At 15 docs:	0.2147
At 20 docs:	0.1950
At 30 docs:	0.1733
At 100 docs:	0.1192
At 200 docs:	0.0786
At 500 docs:	0.0384
At 1000 docs:	0.0203

R-Precision (prec. after R (=num_rel) docs. retrieved):
Exact: 0.2347

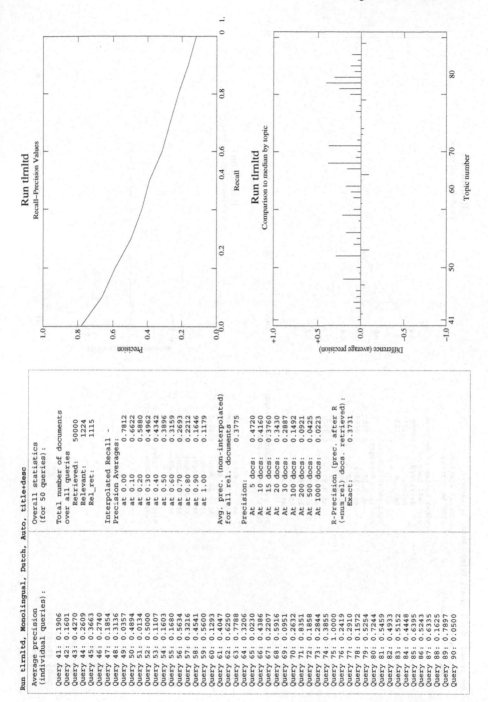

Run tlrnltd
Recall-Precision Values

Run tlrnltd
Comparison to median by topic

Run tlrnltd, Monolingual, Dutch, Auto, title+desc

Average precision (individual queries):			Overall statistics (for 50 queries):	
Query 41:	0.1906			
Query 42:	0.1601		Total number of documents	
Query 43:	0.4270		over all queries	
Query 44:	0.2609		Retrieved:	50000
Query 45:	0.3663		Relevant:	1224
Query 46:	0.2740		Rel_ret:	1115
Query 47:	0.1854			
Query 48:	0.3136		Interpolated Recall -	
Query 49:	0.0357		Precision Averages:	
Query 50:	0.4894		at 0.00	0.7812
Query 51:	0.0134		at 0.10	0.6622
Query 52:	0.5000		at 0.20	0.5880
Query 53:	0.1107		at 0.30	0.4962
Query 54:	0.1603		at 0.40	0.4342
Query 55:	0.1680		at 0.50	0.3896
Query 56:	0.5634		at 0.60	0.3159
Query 57:	0.3216		at 0.70	0.2693
Query 58:	0.4541		at 0.80	0.2212
Query 59:	0.5600		at 0.90	0.1646
Query 60:	0.1293		at 1.00	0.1179
Query 61:	0.4047			
Query 62:	0.6250		Avg. prec. (non-interpolated)	
Query 63:	0.7788		for all rel. documents	0.3775
Query 64:	0.3206			
Query 65:	0.0230		Precision:	
Query 66:	0.4386		At 5 docs:	0.4720
Query 67:	0.2207		At 10 docs:	0.4160
Query 68:	0.5916		At 15 docs:	0.3760
Query 69:	0.0951		At 20 docs:	0.3430
Query 70:	0.2632		At 30 docs:	0.2887
Query 71:	0.8351		At 100 docs:	0.1492
Query 72:	0.1858		At 200 docs:	0.0921
Query 73:	0.2844		At 500 docs:	0.0425
Query 74:	0.3855		At 1000 docs:	0.0223
Query 75:	1.0000			
Query 76:	0.2419		R-Precision (prec. after R	
Query 77:	0.2910		(=num_rel) docs. retrieved):	
Query 78:	0.1572		Exact:	0.3731
Query 79:	0.5254			
Query 80:	0.7244			
Query 81:	0.5459			
Query 82:	0.4933			
Query 83:	0.5152			
Query 84:	0.4448			
Query 85:	0.6395			
Query 86:	0.5243			
Query 87:	0.6335			
Query 88:	0.1625			
Query 89:	0.7897			
Query 90:	0.0500			

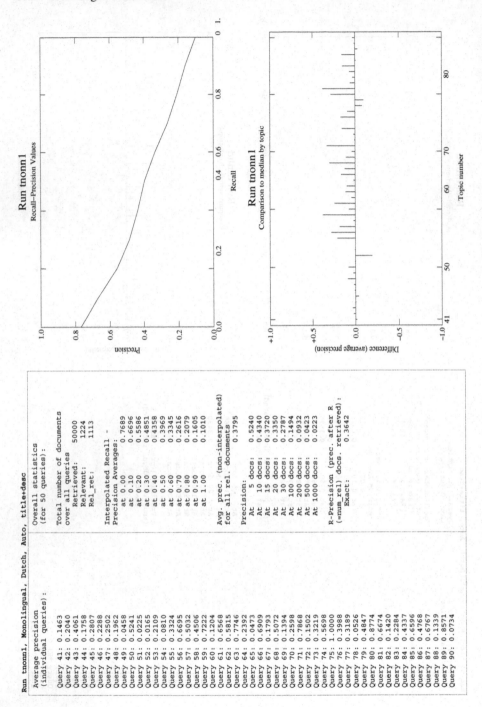

Run tnonn1
Recall–Precision Values

Run tnonn1
Comparison to median by topic

Run tnonn1, Monolingual, Dutch, Auto, title+desc

Average precision
(individual queries):

Query 41:	0.1463				
Query 42:	0.2040				
Query 43:	0.4061				
Query 44:	0.1758				
Query 45:	0.2807				
Query 46:	0.2288				
Query 47:	0.2502				
Query 48:	0.1962				
Query 49:	0.0458				
Query 50:	0.5241				
Query 51:	0.0225				
Query 52:	0.0165				
Query 53:	0.2109				
Query 54:	0.0810				
Query 55:	0.3324				
Query 56:	0.6695				
Query 57:	0.5032				
Query 58:	0.4506				
Query 59:	0.7222				
Query 60:	0.1204				
Query 61:	0.6568				
Query 62:	0.5815				
Query 63:	0.7746				
Query 64:	0.2392				
Query 65:	0.0473				
Query 66:	0.6909				
Query 67:	0.1793				
Query 68:	0.5072				
Query 69:	0.1394				
Query 70:	0.2598				
Query 71:	0.7868				
Query 72:	0.1502				
Query 73:	0.3219				
Query 74:	0.5698				
Query 75:	1.0000				
Query 76:	0.3988				
Query 77:	0.3189				
Query 78:	0.0526				
Query 79:	0.4847				
Query 80:	0.8774				
Query 81:	0.6674				
Query 82:	0.1420				
Query 83:	0.2284				
Query 84:	0.4337				
Query 85:	0.6596				
Query 86:	0.4768				
Query 87:	0.6767				
Query 88:	0.1339				
Query 89:	0.8571				
Query 90:	0.0734				

Overall statistics
(for 50 queries):

Total number of documents
over all queries:
  Retrieved: 50000
  Relevant: 1224
  Rel_ret: 1113

Interpolated Recall -
Precision Averages:
  at 0.00   0.7689
  at 0.10   0.6696
  at 0.20   0.5586
  at 0.30   0.4851
  at 0.40   0.4358
  at 0.50   0.3969
  at 0.60   0.3345
  at 0.70   0.2616
  at 0.80   0.2079
  at 0.90   0.1605
  at 1.00   0.1010

Avg. prec. (non-interpolated)
for all rel. documents
                 0.3795

Precision:
  At   5 docs: 0.5240
  At   10 docs: 0.4340
  At   15 docs: 0.3720
  At   20 docs: 0.3350
  At   30 docs: 0.2787
  At 100 docs: 0.1494
  At 200 docs: 0.0932
  At 500 docs: 0.0423
  At 1000 docs: 0.0223

R-Precision (prec. after R
(=num_rel) docs. retrieved):
  Exact: 0.3642

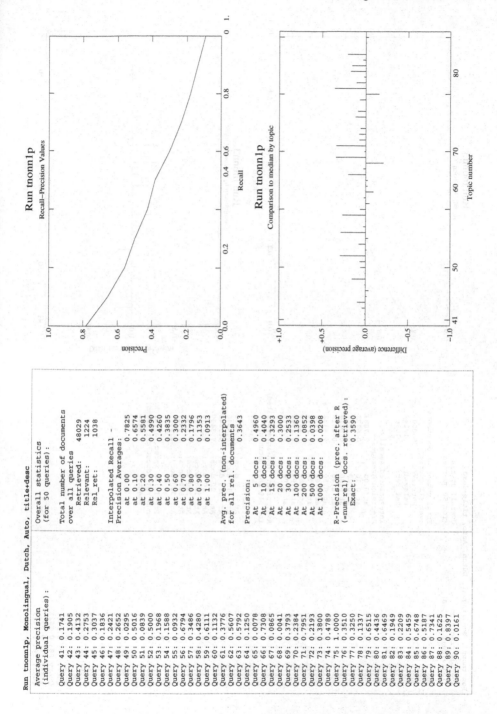

Run tnonn1p

Recall-Precision Values

Run tnonn1p

Comparison to median by topic

Run tnonn1p, Monolingual, Dutch, Auto, title+desc

Average precision
(individual queries):

Query 41:	0.1741
Query 42:	0.1905
Query 43:	0.4132
Query 44:	0.2753
Query 45:	0.3037
Query 46:	0.1836
Query 47:	0.2421
Query 48:	0.2652
Query 49:	0.0295
Query 50:	0.5016
Query 51:	0.0839
Query 52:	0.5000
Query 53:	0.1968
Query 54:	0.1588
Query 55:	0.0932
Query 56:	0.6794
Query 57:	0.3486
Query 58:	0.4280
Query 59:	0.6111
Query 60:	0.1132
Query 61:	0.3776
Query 62:	0.5607
Query 63:	0.5792
Query 64:	0.1250
Query 65:	0.0078
Query 66:	0.7308
Query 67:	0.0865
Query 68:	0.0041
Query 69:	0.3793
Query 70:	0.2384
Query 71:	0.7951
Query 72:	0.2193
Query 73:	0.3800
Query 74:	0.4789
Query 75:	1.0000
Query 76:	0.3510
Query 77:	0.3250
Query 78:	0.1337
Query 79:	0.6515
Query 80:	0.4436
Query 81:	0.6469
Query 82:	0.1949
Query 83:	0.2209
Query 84:	0.5459
Query 85:	0.6748
Query 86:	0.5187
Query 87:	0.7341
Query 88:	0.1625
Query 89:	0.8397
Query 90:	0.0161

Overall statistics
(for 50 queries):

Total number of documents
over all queries

Retrieved:	48029
Relevant:	1224
Rel_ret:	1038

Interpolated Recall -
Precision Averages:

at 0.00	0.7825
at 0.10	0.6574
at 0.20	0.5581
at 0.30	0.4990
at 0.40	0.4260
at 0.50	0.3835
at 0.60	0.3000
at 0.70	0.2332
at 0.80	0.1796
at 0.90	0.1353
at 1.00	0.0913

Avg. prec. (non-interpolated)
for all rel. documents
                     0.3643

Precision:

At 5 docs:	0.4960
At 10 docs:	0.4040
At 15 docs:	0.3293
At 20 docs:	0.3000
At 30 docs:	0.2533
At 100 docs:	0.1360
At 200 docs:	0.0852
At 500 docs:	0.0398
At 1000 docs:	0.0208

R-Precision (prec. after R
(=num_rel) docs. retrieved):
      Exact: 0.3590

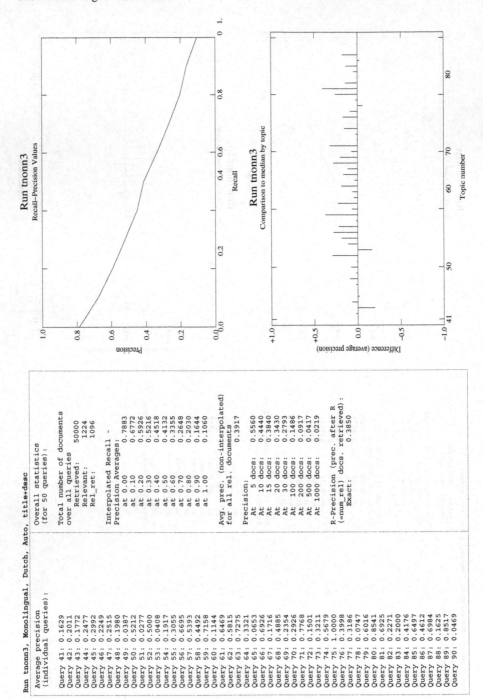

Run tnonn3

Recall-Precision Values

Recall

Precision

Run tnonn3

Comparison to median by topic

Topic number

Difference (average precision)

Run tnonn3, Monolingual, Dutch, Auto, title+desc

Average precision
(individual queries):

Query 41:	0.1629
Query 42:	0.2011
Query 43:	0.1772
Query 44:	0.2477
Query 45:	0.2992
Query 46:	0.2249
Query 47:	0.2515
Query 48:	0.1980
Query 49:	0.0387
Query 50:	0.5212
Query 51:	0.0277
Query 52:	0.5000
Query 53:	0.0408
Query 54:	0.1917
Query 55:	0.3055
Query 56:	0.6695
Query 57:	0.53393
Query 58:	0.4492
Query 59:	0.7158
Query 60:	0.1144
Query 61:	0.6469
Query 62:	0.5815
Query 63:	0.7275
Query 64:	0.3321
Query 65:	0.0653
Query 66:	0.6926
Query 67:	0.1716
Query 68:	0.4885
Query 69:	0.2354
Query 70:	0.2926
Query 71:	0.7768
Query 72:	0.1501
Query 73:	0.3211
Query 74:	0.5679
Query 75:	1.0000
Query 76:	0.3998
Query 77:	0.3186
Query 78:	0.0747
Query 79:	0.6016
Query 80:	0.8541
Query 81:	0.6925
Query 82:	0.2271
Query 83:	0.2000
Query 84:	0.4176
Query 85:	0.6497
Query 86:	0.4612
Query 87:	0.6984
Query 88:	0.1625
Query 89:	0.8517
Query 90:	0.0469

Overall statistics
(for 50 queries):

Total number of documents
over all queries
Retrieved:	50000
Relevant:	1224
Rel_ret:	1096

Interpolated Recall -
Precision Averages:
at 0.00	0.7883
at 0.10	0.6772
at 0.20	0.5926
at 0.30	0.5216
at 0.40	0.4518
at 0.50	0.4132
at 0.60	0.3355
at 0.70	0.2648
at 0.80	0.2030
at 0.90	0.1644
at 1.00	0.1060

Avg. prec. (non-interpolated)
for all rel. documents
                    0.3917

Precision:
At 5 docs:	0.5560
At 10 docs:	0.4440
At 15 docs:	0.3840
At 20 docs:	0.3430
At 30 docs:	0.2793
At 100 docs:	0.1486
At 200 docs:	0.0917
At 500 docs:	0.0417
At 1000 docs:	0.0219

R-Precision (prec. after R
(=num_rel) docs. retrieved):
| Exact: | 0.3850 |

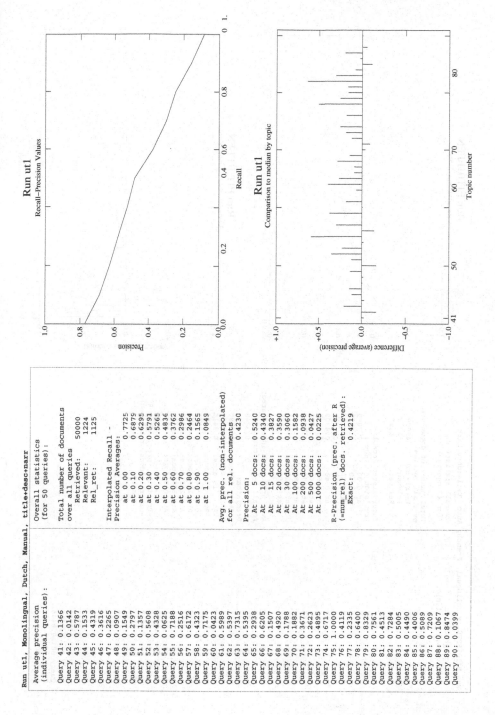

Run ut1
Recall–Precision Values

Run ut1
Comparison to median by topic

Run ut1, Monolingual, Dutch, Manual, title+desc+narr

Average precision
(individual queries):

Query 41:	0.1366
Query 42:	0.0142
Query 43:	0.5787
Query 44:	0.1533
Query 45:	0.4319
Query 46:	0.3616
Query 47:	0.2265
Query 48:	0.0907
Query 49:	0.1549
Query 50:	0.2797
Query 51:	0.1357
Query 52:	0.5608
Query 53:	0.4328
Query 54:	0.0625
Query 55:	0.7188
Query 56:	0.2516
Query 57:	0.6172
Query 58:	0.4323
Query 59:	0.7175
Query 60:	0.0423
Query 61:	0.5989
Query 62:	0.5397
Query 63:	0.7315
Query 64:	0.5395
Query 65:	0.2938
Query 66:	0.6205
Query 67:	0.1507
Query 68:	0.4920
Query 69:	0.1788
Query 70:	0.1882
Query 71:	0.3671
Query 72:	0.2623
Query 73:	0.4895
Query 74:	0.6717
Query 75:	1.0000
Query 76:	0.4119
Query 77:	0.2335
Query 78:	0.6400
Query 79:	0.8329
Query 80:	0.7561
Query 81:	0.4513
Query 82:	0.7284
Query 83:	0.5005
Query 84:	0.4490
Query 85:	0.4006
Query 86:	0.5089
Query 87:	0.7209
Query 88:	0.1067
Query 89:	0.8474
Query 90:	0.0399

Overall statistics
(for 50 queries):

Total number of documents
over all queries
Retrieved:	50000
Relevant:	1224
Rel_ret:	1125

Interpolated Recall –
Precision Averages:
at 0.00	0.7725
at 0.10	0.6879
at 0.20	0.6295
at 0.30	0.5791
at 0.40	0.5265
at 0.50	0.4836
at 0.60	0.3762
at 0.70	0.2986
at 0.80	0.2464
at 0.90	0.1565
at 1.00	0.0849

Avg. prec. (non-interpolated)
for all rel. documents
0.4230

Precision:
At 5 docs:	0.5240
At 10 docs:	0.4340
At 15 docs:	0.3827
At 20 docs:	0.3590
At 30 docs:	0.3060
At 100 docs:	0.1582
At 200 docs:	0.0938
At 500 docs:	0.0427
At 1000 docs:	0.0225

R-Precision (prec. after R
(=num rel) docs. retrieved):
Exact: 0.4219

Run EIT01FFFN

Recall-Precision Values

Run EIT01FFFN

Comparison to median by topic

Run EIT01FFFN, Monolingual, French, Auto, title+desc+narr

Average precision (individual queries):		Overall statistics (for 49 queries):	

Query 41:	0.1909
Query 42:	0.0930
Query 43:	0.5000
Query 44:	0.7323
Query 45:	0.5518
Query 46:	0.0144
Query 47:	0.3297
Query 48:	0.0367
Query 49:	0.3125
Query 50:	0.3782
Query 51:	0.0393
Query 52:	0.0109
Query 53:	0.0033
Query 54:	0.6294
Query 55:	0.4477
Query 56:	0.6306
Query 57:	0.5176
Query 58:	0.7147
Query 59:	0.5783
Query 60:	0.3781
Query 61:	0.1277
Query 62:	0.6907
Query 63:	0.5471
Query 65:	0.0381
Query 66:	0.8241
Query 67:	0.3098
Query 68:	0.5279
Query 69:	0.2139
Query 70:	0.7228
Query 71:	0.0436
Query 72:	0.2316
Query 73:	0.1184
Query 74:	0.3141
Query 75:	1.0000
Query 76:	0.4192
Query 77:	0.2267
Query 78:	0.2238
Query 79:	0.7098
Query 80:	0.1270
Query 81:	0.4677
Query 82:	0.0554
Query 83:	1.0000
Query 84:	0.5000
Query 85:	0.2305
Query 86:	0.2850
Query 87:	0.2316
Query 88:	0.8445
Query 89:	0.6800
Query 90:	0.0537

Total number of documents
over all queries:
Retrieved: 49000
Relevant: 1212
Rel_ret: 1127

Interpolated Recall -
Precision Averages:
  at 0.00   0.7079
  at 0.10   0.6032
  at 0.20   0.5252
  at 0.30   0.4642
  at 0.40   0.4309
  at 0.50   0.4036
  at 0.60   0.3718
  at 0.70   0.2860
  at 0.80   0.2480
  at 0.90   0.1839
  at 1.00   0.1329

Avg. prec. (non-interpolated)
for all rel. documents
      0.3848

Precision:
  At   5 docs: 0.4490
  At   10 docs: 0.3796
  At   15 docs: 0.3415
  At   20 docs: 0.3153
  At   30 docs: 0.2707
  At 100 docs: 0.1561
  At 200 docs: 0.0959
  At 500 docs: 0.0438
  At 1000 docs: 0.0230

R-Precision (prec. after R
(=num_rel) docs. retrieved):
      Exact: 0.3641

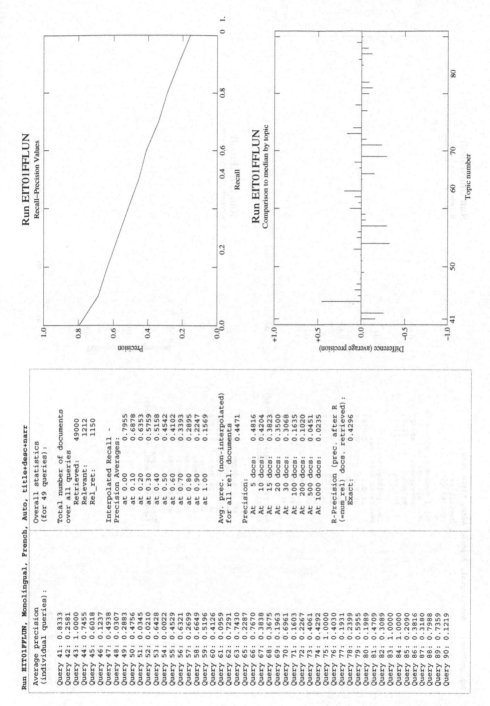

Run EIT01FFLUN
Recall–Precision Values

Run EIT01FFLUN
Comparison to median by topic

Run EIT01FFLUN, Monolingual, French, Auto, title+desc+narr

Average precision
(individual queries):

Query 41:	0.8333	
Query 42:	0.2581	
Query 43:	1.0000	
Query 44:	0.7455	
Query 45:	0.6018	
Query 46:	0.1237	
Query 47:	0.4938	
Query 48:	0.0307	
Query 49:	0.2883	
Query 50:	0.4756	
Query 51:	0.0345	
Query 52:	0.0210	
Query 53:	0.6428	
Query 54:	0.0022	
Query 55:	0.4529	
Query 56:	0.6321	
Query 57:	0.2699	
Query 58:	0.6649	
Query 59:	0.5196	
Query 60:	0.4126	
Query 61:	0.0959	
Query 62:	0.7291	
Query 63:	0.7430	
Query 65:	0.2287	
Query 66:	0.7670	
Query 67:	0.3838	
Query 68:	0.3675	
Query 69:	0.1963	
Query 70:	0.6961	
Query 71:	0.1603	
Query 72:	0.2267	
Query 73:	0.4061	
Query 74:	0.4292	
Query 75:	1.0000	
Query 76:	0.4030	
Query 77:	0.1931	
Query 78:	0.2399	
Query 79:	0.5955	
Query 80:	0.1989	
Query 81:	0.4709	
Query 82:	0.3089	
Query 83:	1.0000	
Query 84:	1.0000	
Query 85:	0.2090	
Query 86:	0.3816	
Query 87:	0.3180	
Query 88:	0.7988	
Query 89:	0.7359	
Query 90:	0.1219	

Overall statistics
(for 49 queries):

Total number of documents
over all queries
    Retrieved: 49000
    Relevant: 1212
    Rel_ret: 1150

Interpolated Recall -
Precision Averages:
    at 0.00   0.7955
    at 0.10   0.6878
    at 0.20   0.6353
    at 0.30   0.5759
    at 0.40   0.5158
    at 0.50   0.4542
    at 0.60   0.4102
    at 0.70   0.3393
    at 0.80   0.2895
    at 0.90   0.2247
    at 1.00   0.1569
Avg. prec. (non-interpolated)
for all rel. documents
            0.4471

Precision:
  At   5 docs: 0.4816
  At 10 docs: 0.4204
  At 15 docs: 0.3823
  At 20 docs: 0.3500
  At 30 docs: 0.3068
  At 100 docs: 0.1635
  At 200 docs: 0.1020
  At 500 docs: 0.0451
  At 1000 docs: 0.0235

R-Precision (prec. after R
(=num rel) docs. retrieved):
    Exact: 0.4296

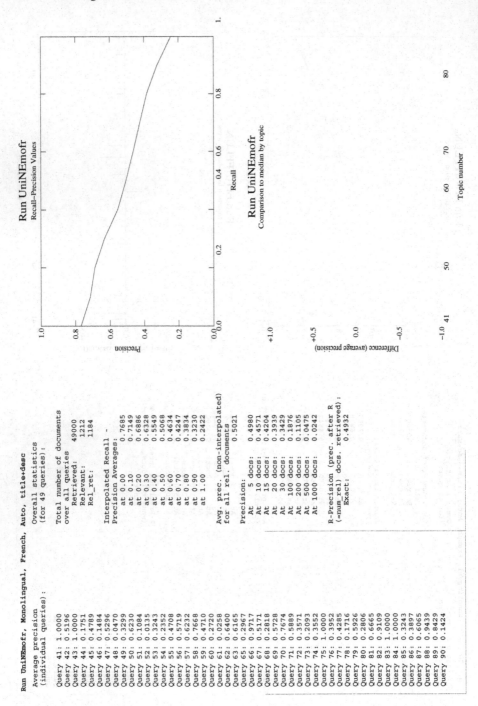

Run UniNEmofr
Recall-Precision Values

Run UniNEmofr
Comparison to median by topic

Run UniNEmofr, Monolingual, French, Auto, title+desc

Average precision
(individual queries):

Query 41:	1.0000
Query 42:	0.5196
Query 43:	1.0000
Query 44:	0.1751
Query 45:	0.4789
Query 46:	0.1484
Query 47:	0.5296
Query 48:	0.0470
Query 49:	0.3299
Query 50:	0.6230
Query 51:	0.1084
Query 52:	0.0135
Query 53:	0.3243
Query 54:	0.2352
Query 55:	0.4708
Query 56:	0.5719
Query 57:	0.6232
Query 58:	0.7668
Query 59:	0.4710
Query 60:	0.2720
Query 61:	0.0258
Query 62:	0.6400
Query 63:	0.6165
Query 65:	0.2967
Query 66:	0.9717
Query 67:	0.5171
Query 68:	0.2818
Query 69:	0.5728
Query 70:	0.7674
Query 71:	0.5889
Query 72:	0.3571
Query 73:	0.2093
Query 74:	0.3552
Query 75:	1.0000
Query 76:	0.3952
Query 77:	0.4285
Query 78:	0.1716
Query 79:	0.5926
Query 80:	0.2806
Query 81:	0.6665
Query 82:	0.9109
Query 83:	1.0000
Query 84:	1.0000
Query 85:	0.3243
Query 86:	0.3897
Query 87:	0.6065
Query 88:	0.9439
Query 89:	0.8429
Query 90:	0.1424

Overall statistics
(for 49 queries):

Total number of documents
over all queries
   Retrieved: 49000
   Relevant: 1212
   Rel_ret: 1184

Interpolated Recall -
Precision Averages:
   at 0.00   0.7685
   at 0.10   0.7149
   at 0.20   0.6886
   at 0.30   0.6328
   at 0.40   0.5549
   at 0.50   0.5068
   at 0.60   0.4634
   at 0.70   0.4247
   at 0.80   0.3834
   at 0.90   0.3230
   at 1.00   0.2422

Avg. prec. (non-interpolated)
for all rel. documents
         0.5021

Precision:
  At   5 docs: 0.4980
  At 10 docs: 0.4571
  At 15 docs: 0.4204
  At 20 docs: 0.3939
  At 30 docs: 0.3429
  At 100 docs: 0.1876
  At 200 docs: 0.1105
  At 500 docs: 0.0475
  At 1000 docs: 0.0242

R-Precision (prec. after R
(=num_rel) docs. retrieved):
   Exact: 0.4932

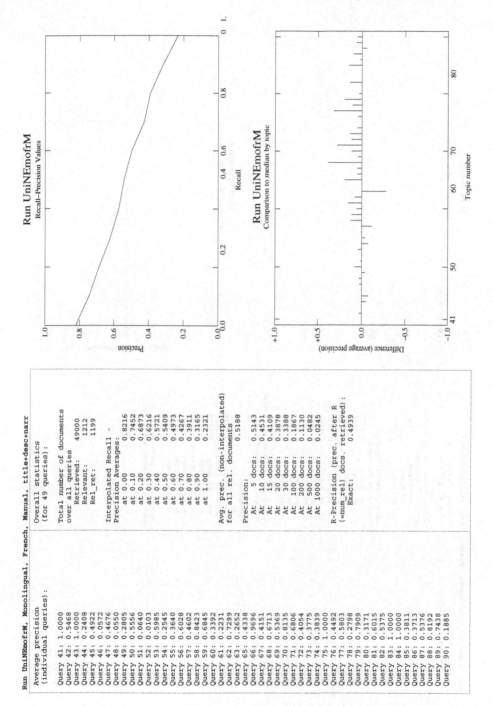

Run UniNEmofrM
Recall–Precision Values

Run UniNEmofrM
Comparison to median by topic

Run **UniNEmofrM**, Monolingual, French, Manual, title+desc+narr

Average precision
(individual queries):

Query 41:	1.0000
Query 42:	0.5468
Query 43:	1.0000
Query 44:	0.2408
Query 45:	0.4922
Query 46:	0.0572
Query 47:	0.4676
Query 48:	0.0550
Query 49:	0.2805
Query 50:	0.5556
Query 51:	0.0640
Query 52:	0.0103
Query 53:	0.5985
Query 54:	0.2545
Query 55:	0.3640
Query 56:	0.6028
Query 57:	0.4602
Query 58:	0.8423
Query 59:	0.6845
Query 60:	0.3392
Query 61:	0.2231
Query 62:	0.7299
Query 63:	0.2652
Query 65:	0.4338
Query 66:	0.9696
Query 67:	0.4151
Query 68:	0.6713
Query 69:	0.5369
Query 70:	0.8135
Query 71:	0.6806
Query 72:	0.4054
Query 73:	0.3775
Query 74:	0.3839
Query 75:	1.0000
Query 76:	0.4492
Query 77:	0.5803
Query 78:	0.2798
Query 79:	0.7909
Query 80:	0.3171
Query 81:	0.6015
Query 82:	0.5375
Query 83:	1.0000
Query 84:	1.0000
Query 85:	0.3811
Query 86:	0.3713
Query 87:	0.5376
Query 88:	0.8192
Query 89:	0.7438
Query 90:	0.1885

Overall statistics
(for 49 queries):

Total number of documents
over all queries
   Retrieved: 49000
   Relevant: 1212
   Rel_ret: 1199

Interpolated Recall -
Precision Averages:
   at 0.00   0.8216
   at 0.10   0.7452
   at 0.20   0.6873
   at 0.30   0.6216
   at 0.40   0.5721
   at 0.50   0.5409
   at 0.60   0.4973
   at 0.70   0.4267
   at 0.80   0.3911
   at 0.90   0.3165
   at 1.00   0.2321
Avg. prec. (non-interpolated)
for all rel. documents   0.5188

Precision:
  At   5 docs: 0.5143
  At 10 docs: 0.4531
  At 15 docs: 0.4109
  At 20 docs: 0.3878
  At 30 docs: 0.3388
  At 100 docs: 0.1867
  At 200 docs: 0.1130
  At 500 docs: 0.0482
  At 1000 docs: 0.0245

R-Precision (prec. after R
(=num_rel) docs. retrieved):
   Exact: 0.4939

Run aplmofra

Recall–Precision Values

Run aplmofra

Comparison to median by topic

Run aplmofra, Monolingual, French, Auto, title+desc+narr

Average precision
(individual queries):

Query 41:	0.7500
Query 42:	0.6027
Query 43:	1.0000
Query 44:	0.1529
Query 45:	0.7371
Query 46:	0.0137
Query 47:	0.5840
Query 48:	0.0212
Query 49:	0.2857
Query 50:	0.6113
Query 51:	0.0451
Query 52:	0.0064
Query 53:	0.5955
Query 54:	0.2485
Query 55:	0.3626
Query 56:	0.4446
Query 57:	0.5324
Query 58:	0.8719
Query 59:	0.1991
Query 60:	0.2766
Query 61:	0.1744
Query 62:	0.5846
Query 63:	0.8666
Query 65:	0.2764
Query 66:	0.8614
Query 67:	0.0467
Query 68:	0.1636
Query 69:	0.5043
Query 70:	0.8468
Query 71:	0.0467
Query 72:	0.1898
Query 73:	0.2377
Query 74:	0.4150
Query 75:	0.3333
Query 76:	0.3823
Query 77:	0.2162
Query 78:	0.5033
Query 79:	0.6516
Query 80:	0.3536
Query 81:	0.6490
Query 82:	0.6260
Query 83:	0.1603
Query 84:	0.0278
Query 85:	0.2385
Query 86:	0.3947
Query 87:	0.6535
Query 88:	0.9703
Query 89:	0.7758
Query 90:	0.1358

Overall statistics
(for 49 queries):

Total number of documents
over all queries:
Retrieved: 49000
Relevant: 1212
Rel_ret: 1202

Interpolated Recall -
Precision Averages:

at 0.00	0.6979
at 0.10	0.6008
at 0.20	0.5498
at 0.30	0.5243
at 0.40	0.4997
at 0.50	0.4484
at 0.60	0.3964
at 0.70	0.3516
at 0.80	0.3248
at 0.90	0.2587
at 1.00	0.1710

Avg. prec. (non-interpolated)
for all rel. documents   0.4210

Precision:

At	5 docs:	0.4449
At	10 docs:	0.4020
At	15 docs:	0.3810
At	20 docs:	0.3459
At	30 docs:	0.3224
At	100 docs:	0.1851
At	200 docs:	0.1103
At	500 docs:	0.0476
At	1000 docs:	0.0245

R-Precision (prec. after R
(=num_rel) docs. retrieved) :
   Exact: 0.3837

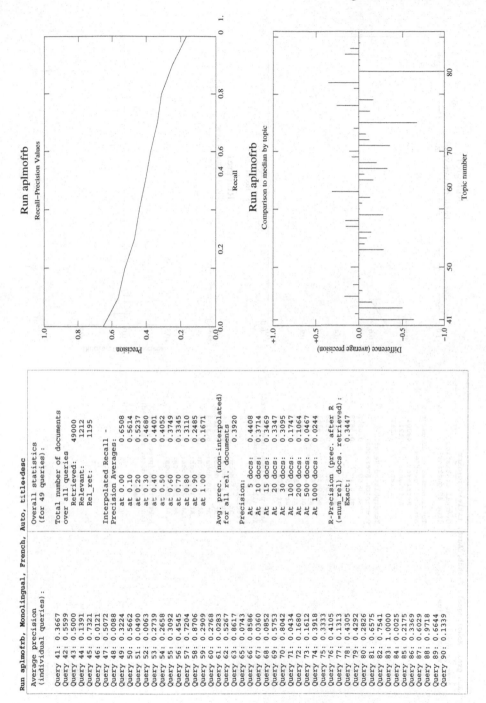

Run aplmofrb
Recall-Precision Values

Run aplmofrb
Comparison to median by topic

Run aplmofrb, Monolingual, French, Auto, title+desc

Average precision
(individual queries):

Query 41:	0.3667
Query 42:	0.5599
Query 43:	0.5000
Query 44:	0.1391
Query 45:	0.7321
Query 46:	0.0121
Query 47:	0.5072
Query 48:	0.0088
Query 49:	0.3224
Query 50:	0.5662
Query 51:	0.0490
Query 52:	0.0063
Query 53:	0.2739
Query 54:	0.2658
Query 55:	0.3092
Query 56:	0.4545
Query 57:	0.7204
Query 58:	0.8706
Query 59:	0.2909
Query 60:	0.2768
Query 61:	0.0283
Query 62:	0.5267
Query 63:	0.8617
Query 65:	0.0743
Query 66:	0.8586
Query 67:	0.0360
Query 68:	0.0852
Query 69:	0.5753
Query 70:	0.8042
Query 71:	0.0434
Query 72:	0.1680
Query 73:	0.1612
Query 74:	0.3918
Query 75:	0.3333
Query 76:	0.4105
Query 77:	0.1313
Query 78:	0.4305
Query 79:	0.4292
Query 80:	0.2826
Query 81:	0.6575
Query 82:	0.7541
Query 83:	1.0000
Query 84:	0.0025
Query 85:	0.2175
Query 86:	0.3369
Query 87:	0.6029
Query 88:	0.9718
Query 89:	0.6644
Query 90:	0.1339

Overall statistics
(for 49 queries):

Total number of documents
over all queries
Retrieved:	49000
Relevant:	1212
Rel_ret:	1195

Interpolated Recall -
Precision Averages:
at 0.00	0.6508
at 0.10	0.5614
at 0.20	0.5237
at 0.30	0.4680
at 0.40	0.4401
at 0.50	0.4052
at 0.60	0.3749
at 0.70	0.3345
at 0.80	0.3110
at 0.90	0.2485
at 1.00	0.1671

Avg. prec. (non-interpolated)
for all rel. documents
                0.3920

Precision:
At 5 docs:	0.4408
At 10 docs:	0.3714
At 15 docs:	0.3469
At 20 docs:	0.3347
At 30 docs:	0.3095
At 100 docs:	0.1747
At 200 docs:	0.1064
At 500 docs:	0.0467
At 1000 docs:	0.0244

R-Precision (prec. after R
(=num_rel) docs. retrieved):
        Exact: 0.3447

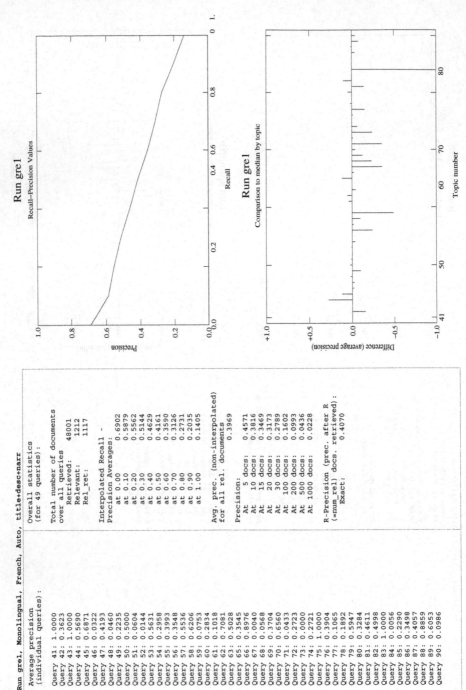

Run gre1

Recall–Precision Values

Recall

Run gre1

Comparison to median by topic

Topic number

Run gre1, Monolingual, French, Auto, title+desc+narr

Average precision (individual queries):		Overall statistics (for 49 queries):	
Query 41:	1.0000	Total number of documents over all queries:	
Query 42:	0.3623	Retrieved:	48001
Query 43:	1.0000	Relevant:	1212
Query 44:	0.5590	Rel_ret:	1117
Query 45:	0.6871		
Query 46:	0.0322	Interpolated Recall -	
Query 47:	0.4193	Precision Averages:	
Query 48:	0.0460	at 0.00	0.6902
Query 49:	0.2235	at 0.10	0.5879
Query 50:	0.5000	at 0.20	0.5562
Query 51:	0.0604	at 0.30	0.5144
Query 52:	0.0144	at 0.40	0.4629
Query 53:	0.5631	at 0.50	0.4161
Query 54:	0.2958	at 0.60	0.3590
Query 55:	0.3993	at 0.70	0.3126
Query 56:	0.3548	at 0.80	0.2731
Query 57:	0.5536	at 0.90	0.2035
Query 58:	0.6206	at 1.00	0.1405
Query 59:	0.0753		
Query 60:	0.2834	Avg. prec. (non-interpolated)	
Query 61:	0.1018	for all rel. documents	0.3969
Query 62:	0.7081		
Query 63:	0.5028	Precision:	
Query 65:	0.3545	At 5 docs:	0.4571
Query 66:	0.8976	At 10 docs:	0.3816
Query 67:	0.0040	At 15 docs:	0.3469
Query 68:	0.0568	At 20 docs:	0.3173
Query 69:	0.3704	At 30 docs:	0.2789
Query 70:	0.6560	At 100 docs:	0.1602
Query 71:	0.0433	At 200 docs:	0.0993
Query 72:	0.2723	At 500 docs:	0.0436
Query 73:	0.0000	At 1000 docs:	0.0228
Query 74:	0.2721		
Query 75:	1.0000	R-Precision (prec. after R	
Query 76:	0.3904	(=num_rel) docs. retrieved):	
Query 77:	0.1065	Exact:	0.4070
Query 78:	0.1892		
Query 79:	0.5947		
Query 80:	0.3284		
Query 81:	0.4611		
Query 82:	0.4998		
Query 83:	1.0000		
Query 84:	0.0056		
Query 85:	0.2290		
Query 86:	0.3498		
Query 87:	0.4057		
Query 88:	0.8859		
Query 89:	0.6053		
Query 90:	0.0986		

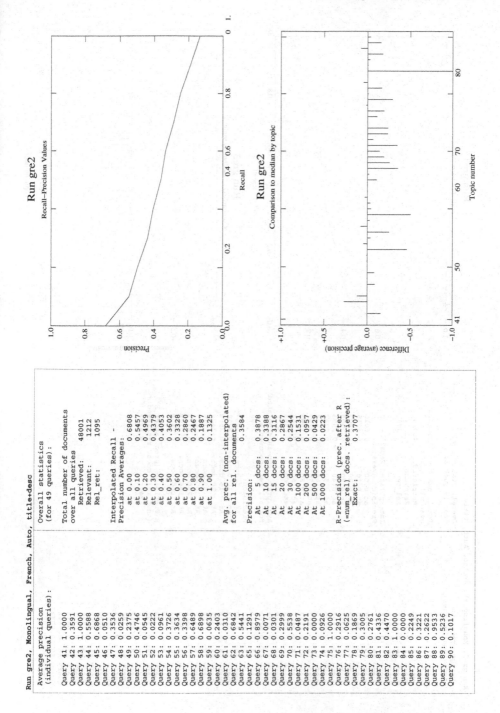

Run gre2, Monolingual, French, Auto, title+desc

Average precision
(individual queries):

Query 41:	1.0000
Query 42:	0.3591
Query 43:	1.0000
Query 44:	0.5588
Query 45:	0.6868
Query 46:	0.0510
Query 47:	0.3536
Query 48:	0.0259
Query 49:	0.2375
Query 50:	0.4746
Query 51:	0.0545
Query 52:	0.0222
Query 53:	0.0961
Query 54:	0.3726
Query 55:	0.3634
Query 56:	0.3398
Query 57:	0.6489
Query 58:	0.6998
Query 59:	0.0635
Query 60:	0.2403
Query 61:	0.0310
Query 62:	0.6842
Query 63:	0.5441
Query 65:	0.1291
Query 66:	0.8979
Query 67:	0.0071
Query 68:	0.0301
Query 69:	0.2999
Query 70:	0.5538
Query 71:	0.0487
Query 72:	0.2191
Query 73:	0.0000
Query 74:	0.0926
Query 75:	1.0000
Query 76:	0.2916
Query 77:	0.0625
Query 78:	0.1869
Query 79:	0.3005
Query 80:	0.2761
Query 81:	0.4336
Query 82:	0.4470
Query 83:	1.0000
Query 84:	0.0000
Query 85:	0.2249
Query 86:	0.3221
Query 87:	0.2622
Query 88:	0.9533
Query 89:	0.5236
Query 90:	0.1017

Overall statistics
(for 49 queries):

Total number of documents
over all queries:
Retrieved:	48001
Relevant:	1212
Rel_ret:	1095

Interpolated Recall -
Precision Averages:
at 0.00	0.6808
at 0.10	0.5457
at 0.20	0.4969
at 0.30	0.4379
at 0.40	0.4053
at 0.50	0.3602
at 0.60	0.3328
at 0.70	0.2860
at 0.80	0.2467
at 0.90	0.1887
at 1.00	0.1325

Avg. prec. (non-interpolated)
for all rel. documents
0.3584

Precision:
At	5 docs:	0.3878
At	10 docs:	0.3388
At	15 docs:	0.3116
At	20 docs:	0.2867
At	30 docs:	0.2544
At	100 docs:	0.1531
At	200 docs:	0.0957
At	500 docs:	0.0429
At	1000 docs:	0.0223

R-Precision (prec. after R
(=num_rel) docs. retrieved):
Exact:	0.3707

Run gre2
Recall-Precision Values

Run gre2
Comparison to median by topic

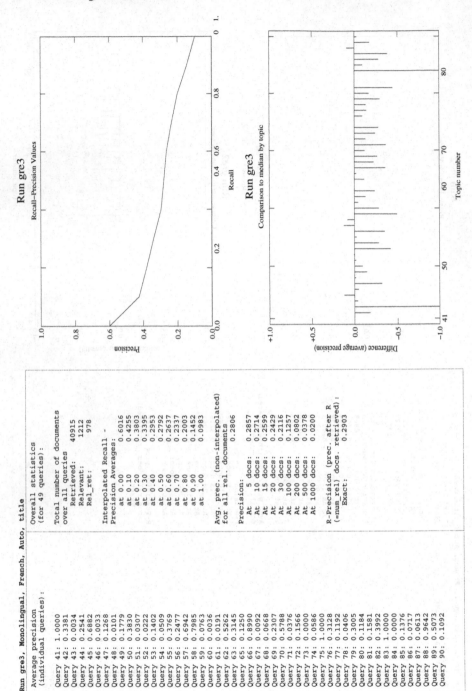

Run gre3

Recall-Precision Values

Run gre3

Comparison to median by topic

Run gre3, Monolingual, French, Auto, title

Average precision
(individual queries):

Query 41:	1.0000
Query 42:	0.3381
Query 43:	0.0034
Query 44:	0.2541
Query 45:	0.6882
Query 46:	0.0033
Query 47:	0.1268
Query 48:	0.0101
Query 49:	0.1779
Query 50:	0.3830
Query 51:	0.0307
Query 52:	0.0222
Query 53:	0.1402
Query 54:	0.0509
Query 55:	0.3769
Query 56:	0.2477
Query 57:	0.6942
Query 58:	0.7985
Query 59:	0.0763
Query 60:	0.0036
Query 61:	0.0191
Query 62:	0.5262
Query 63:	0.3145
Query 65:	0.1250
Query 66:	0.8990
Query 67:	0.0092
Query 68:	0.0668
Query 69:	0.2307
Query 70:	0.5788
Query 71:	0.0376
Query 72:	0.1566
Query 73:	0.0000
Query 74:	0.0586
Query 75:	1.0000
Query 76:	0.3128
Query 77:	0.1192
Query 78:	0.0406
Query 79:	0.3005
Query 80:	0.1184
Query 81:	0.1581
Query 82:	0.3992
Query 83:	1.0000
Query 84:	0.0000
Query 85:	0.1376
Query 86:	0.0717
Query 87:	0.0613
Query 88:	0.9642
Query 89:	0.5073
Query 90:	0.1092

Overall statistics
(for 49 queries):

Total number of documents
over all queries
  Retrieved: 40915
  Relevant: 1212
  Rel_ret: 978

Interpolated Recall -
Precision Averages:
  at 0.00   0.6016
  at 0.10   0.4255
  at 0.20   0.3803
  at 0.30   0.3395
  at 0.40   0.2953
  at 0.50   0.2792
  at 0.60   0.2637
  at 0.70   0.2337
  at 0.80   0.2003
  at 0.90   0.1452
  at 1.00   0.0983

Avg. prec. (non-interpolated)
for all rel. documents
               0.2806

Precision:
  At   5 docs: 0.2857
  At   10 docs: 0.2714
  At   15 docs: 0.2599
  At   20 docs: 0.2429
  At   30 docs: 0.2116
  At 100 docs: 0.1257
  At 200 docs: 0.0802
  At 500 docs: 0.0378
  At 1000 docs: 0.0200

R-Precision (prec. after R
(=num_rel) docs. retrieved):
  Exact: 0.2903

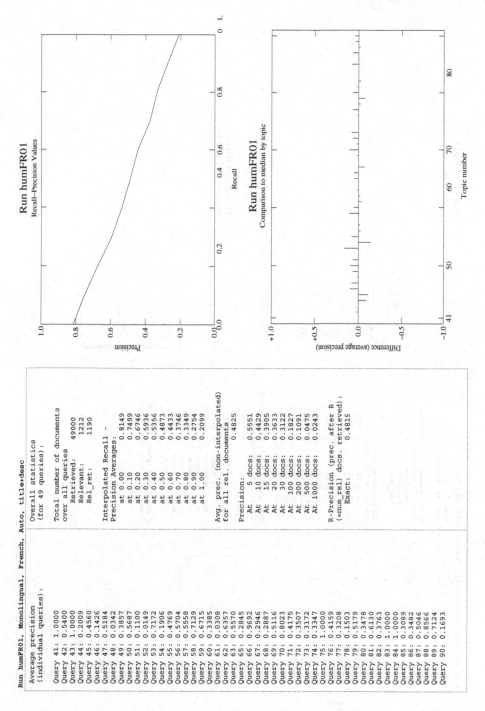

Run humFR01
Recall–Precision Values

Precision

Recall

Run humFR01
Comparison to median by topic

Difference (average precision)

Topic number

Run humFR01, Monolingual, French, Auto, title-desc

Average precision
(individual queries):

Overall statistics
(for 49 queries):

Total number of documents
over all queries
          Retrieved: 49000
          Relevant: 1212
          Rel_ret: 1190

Interpolated Recall -
Precision Averages:
          at 0.00   0.8149
          at 0.10   0.7499
          at 0.20   0.6746
          at 0.30   0.5936
          at 0.40   0.5356
          at 0.50   0.4873
          at 0.60   0.4433
          at 0.70   0.3746
          at 0.80   0.3349
          at 0.90   0.2754
          at 1.00   0.2099

Avg. prec. (non-interpolated)
for all rel. documents
                     0.4825

Precision:
     At   5 docs: 0.5551
     At   10 docs: 0.4429
     At   15 docs: 0.3905
     At   20 docs: 0.3633
     At   30 docs: 0.3122
     At 100 docs: 0.1827
     At 200 docs: 0.1091
     At 500 docs: 0.0475
     At 1000 docs: 0.0243

R-Precision (prec. after R
(=num_rel) docs. retrieved):
     Exact: 0.4815

Query 41: 1.0000
Query 42: 0.5400
Query 43: 1.0000
Query 44: 0.2009
Query 45: 0.4560
Query 46: 0.1426
Query 47: 0.5184
Query 48: 0.0342
Query 49: 0.3857
Query 50: 0.5687
Query 51: 0.1100
Query 52: 0.0149
Query 53: 0.7172
Query 54: 0.1906
Query 55: 0.4769
Query 56: 0.5704
Query 57: 0.5558
Query 58: 0.7129
Query 59: 0.6715
Query 60: 0.3385
Query 61: 0.0308
Query 62: 0.6357
Query 63: 0.5570
Query 65: 0.2845
Query 66: 0.9692
Query 67: 0.2946
Query 68: 0.2887
Query 69: 0.5116
Query 70: 0.8023
Query 71: 0.4175
Query 72: 0.3507
Query 73: 0.3172
Query 74: 0.3347
Query 75: 1.0000
Query 76: 0.4159
Query 77: 0.3208
Query 78: 0.1503
Query 79: 0.5179
Query 80: 0.3478
Query 81: 0.6130
Query 82: 0.3763
Query 83: 1.0000
Query 84: 1.0000
Query 85: 0.3089
Query 86: 0.3482
Query 87: 0.5046
Query 88: 0.8566
Query 89: 0.7124
Query 90: 0.1693

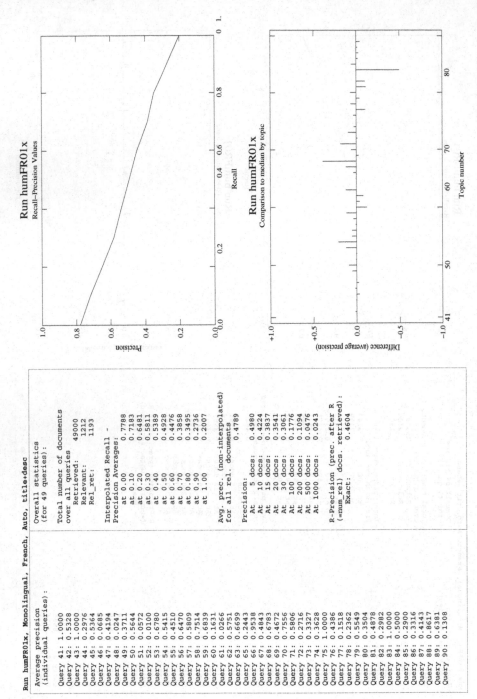

Run humFR01x
Recall–Precision Values

Run humFR01x
Comparison to median by topic

Run humFR01x, Monolingual, French, Auto, title+desc

Average precision
(individual queries):

Query 41:	1.0000	
Query 42:	0.5328	
Query 43:	1.0000	
Query 44:	0.2976	
Query 45:	0.5364	
Query 46:	0.0685	
Query 47:	0.4194	
Query 48:	0.0247	
Query 49:	0.3711	
Query 50:	0.5644	
Query 51:	0.0572	
Query 52:	0.0100	
Query 53:	0.6780	
Query 54:	0.5415	
Query 55:	0.4510	
Query 56:	0.6470	
Query 57:	0.5809	
Query 58:	0.7514	
Query 59:	0.6839	
Query 60:	0.1631	
Query 61:	0.0266	
Query 62:	0.5751	
Query 63:	0.6699	
Query 65:	0.2443	
Query 66:	0.9538	
Query 67:	0.4843	
Query 68:	0.6783	
Query 69:	0.4672	
Query 70:	0.7556	
Query 71:	0.5806	
Query 72:	0.2716	
Query 73:	0.3327	
Query 74:	0.3628	
Query 75:	1.0000	
Query 76:	0.4386	
Query 77:	0.1518	
Query 78:	0.2362	
Query 79:	0.5549	
Query 80:	0.3504	
Query 81:	0.4878	
Query 82:	0.2982	
Query 83:	1.0000	
Query 84:	0.5000	
Query 85:	0.2900	
Query 86:	0.3316	
Query 87:	0.4143	
Query 88:	0.8617	
Query 89:	0.6381	
Query 90:	0.1308	

Overall statistics
(for 49 queries):

Total number of documents
over all queries:
Retrieved: 49000
Relevant: 1212
Rel_ret: 1193

Interpolated Recall -
Precision Averages:
  at 0.00   0.7788
  at 0.10   0.7183
  at 0.20   0.6481
  at 0.30   0.5811
  at 0.40   0.5389
  at 0.50   0.4928
  at 0.60   0.4476
  at 0.70   0.3858
  at 0.80   0.3495
  at 0.90   0.2736
  at 1.00   0.2007

Avg. prec. (non-interpolated)
for all rel. documents
                   0.4789

Precision:
  At   5 docs: 0.4980
  At   10 docs: 0.4224
  At   15 docs: 0.3837
  At   20 docs: 0.3541
  At   30 docs: 0.3061
  At 100 docs: 0.1776
  At 200 docs: 0.1094
  At 500 docs: 0.0476
  At 1000 docs: 0.0243

R-Precision (prec. after R
(=num rel) docs. retrieved):
  Exact: 0.4604

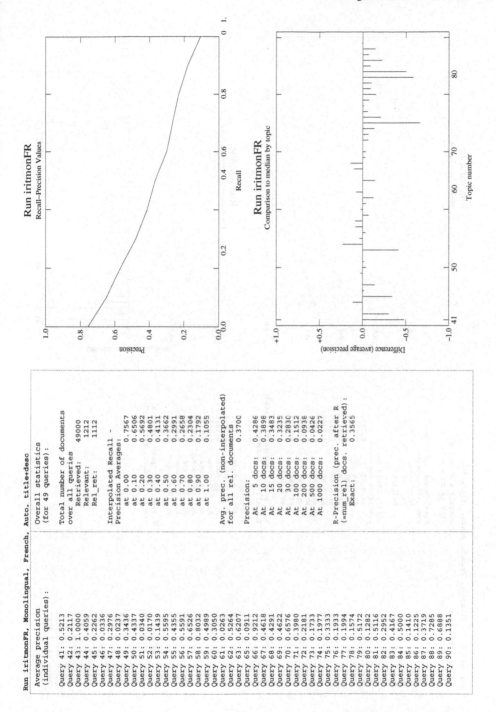

Run iritmonFR
Recall–Precision Values

Run iritmonFR
Comparison to median by topic

Run iritmonFR, Monolingual, French, Auto, title+desc

Average precision
(individual queries):

Query 41:	0.5213
Query 42:	0.2117
Query 43:	1.0000
Query 44:	0.4059
Query 45:	0.2262
Query 46:	0.0336
Query 47:	0.2976
Query 48:	0.0237
Query 49:	0.3436
Query 50:	0.4337
Query 51:	0.0340
Query 52:	0.0170
Query 53:	0.1439
Query 54:	0.5595
Query 55:	0.4355
Query 56:	0.5591
Query 57:	0.6526
Query 58:	0.8032
Query 59:	0.4989
Query 60:	0.3050
Query 61:	0.0263
Query 62:	0.5264
Query 63:	0.6207
Query 65:	0.0911
Query 66:	0.9212
Query 67:	0.4618
Query 68:	0.4291
Query 69:	0.4622
Query 70:	0.5576
Query 71:	0.3980
Query 72:	0.2181
Query 73:	0.1733
Query 74:	0.1977
Query 75:	0.3333
Query 76:	0.1933
Query 77:	0.1994
Query 78:	0.1574
Query 79:	0.5172
Query 80:	0.1282
Query 81:	0.5116
Query 82:	0.2952
Query 83:	0.4167
Query 84:	0.5000
Query 85:	0.1410
Query 86:	0.1225
Query 87:	0.3719
Query 88:	0.7285
Query 89:	0.6888
Query 90:	0.1351

Overall statistics
(for 49 queries):

Total number of documents
over all queries:

Retrieved:	49000
Relevant:	1212
Rel_ret:	1112

Interpolated Recall –
Precision Averages:

at 0.00	0.7567
at 0.10	0.6506
at 0.20	0.5692
at 0.30	0.4801
at 0.40	0.4131
at 0.50	0.3662
at 0.60	0.2991
at 0.70	0.2658
at 0.80	0.2304
at 0.90	0.1792
at 1.00	0.1055

Avg. prec. (non-interpolated)
for all rel. documents
                    0.3700

Precision:

At 5 docs:	0.4286
At 10 docs:	0.3898
At 15 docs:	0.3483
At 20 docs:	0.3235
At 30 docs:	0.2830
At 100 docs:	0.1512
At 200 docs:	0.0938
At 500 docs:	0.0426
At 1000 docs:	0.0227

R-Precision (prec. after R
(=num_rel) docs. retrieved):
Exact: 0.3565

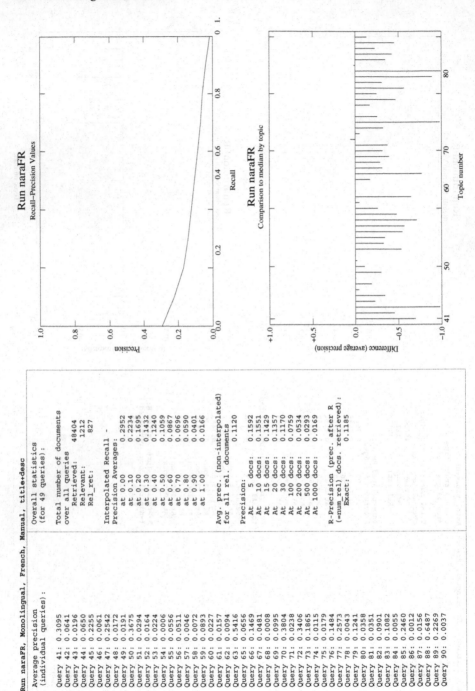

Run naraFR
Recall–Precision Values

Run naraFR
Comparison to median by topic

Run naraFR, Monolingual, French, Manual, title+desc

Average precision
(individual queries):

Query 41:	0.3095
Query 42:	0.0641
Query 43:	0.0196
Query 44:	0.0650
Query 45:	0.2255
Query 46:	0.0061
Query 47:	0.2542
Query 48:	0.0172
Query 49:	0.0191
Query 50:	0.3675
Query 51:	0.0294
Query 52:	0.0164
Query 53:	0.0224
Query 54:	0.0006
Query 55:	0.0556
Query 56:	0.0511
Query 57:	0.0046
Query 58:	0.0072
Query 59:	0.0893
Query 60:	0.0227
Query 61:	0.0157
Query 62:	0.0094
Query 63:	0.5416
Query 65:	0.0656
Query 66:	0.1469
Query 67:	0.0481
Query 68:	0.0008
Query 69:	0.0995
Query 70:	0.3804
Query 71:	0.0238
Query 72:	0.3406
Query 73:	0.1865
Query 74:	0.0115
Query 75:	0.0179
Query 76:	0.1484
Query 77:	0.2573
Query 78:	0.0043
Query 79:	0.1241
Query 80:	0.0358
Query 81:	0.0351
Query 82:	0.0901
Query 83:	0.1082
Query 84:	0.0055
Query 85:	0.2460
Query 86:	0.0012
Query 87:	0.0156
Query 88:	0.6487
Query 89:	0.2269
Query 90:	0.0037

Overall statistics
(for 49 queries):

Total number of documents
over all queries:
Retrieved: 48404
Relevant: 1212
Rel_ret: 827

Interpolated Recall -
Precision Averages:

at 0.00	0.2952
at 0.10	0.2234
at 0.20	0.1695
at 0.30	0.1432
at 0.40	0.1240
at 0.50	0.1059
at 0.60	0.0867
at 0.70	0.0696
at 0.80	0.0590
at 0.90	0.0401
at 1.00	0.0166

Avg. prec. (non-interpolated)
for all rel. documents
                          0.1120

Precision:

At 5 docs:	0.1592
At 10 docs:	0.1551
At 15 docs:	0.1429
At 20 docs:	0.1357
At 30 docs:	0.1170
At 100 docs:	0.0759
At 200 docs:	0.0534
At 500 docs:	0.0293
At 1000 docs:	0.0169

R-Precision (prec. after R
(=num_rel) docs. retrieved):
          Exact: 0.1185

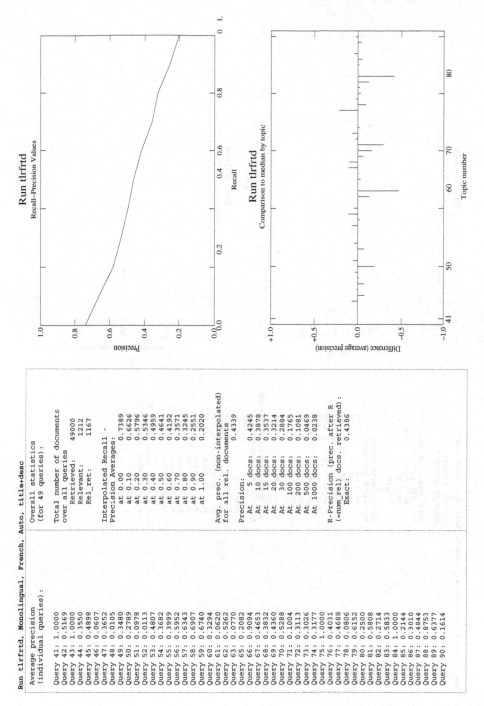

Run tlrfrtd
Recall–Precision Values

Precision

Recall

Run tlrfrtd
Comparison to median by topic

Difference (average precision)

Topic number

Run tlrfrtd, Monolingual, French, Auto, title+desc

Average precision
(individual queries):

Query 41:	1.0000
Query 42:	0.5169
Query 43:	1.0000
Query 44:	0.3350
Query 45:	0.4898
Query 46:	0.0607
Query 47:	0.3652
Query 48:	0.0105
Query 49:	0.3480
Query 50:	0.2789
Query 51:	0.0978
Query 52:	0.0113
Query 53:	0.4807
Query 54:	0.3682
Query 55:	0.3999
Query 56:	0.5952
Query 57:	0.6343
Query 58:	0.6907
Query 59:	0.6740
Query 60:	0.3294
Query 61:	0.0620
Query 62:	0.5262
Query 63:	0.0770
Query 65:	0.2082
Query 66:	0.9094
Query 67:	0.4653
Query 68:	0.3832
Query 69:	0.4360
Query 70:	0.5288
Query 71:	0.1004
Query 72:	0.3113
Query 73:	0.3026
Query 74:	0.3177
Query 75:	1.0000
Query 76:	0.4031
Query 77:	0.4688
Query 78:	0.0806
Query 79:	0.6152
Query 80:	0.2500
Query 81:	0.5808
Query 82:	0.2714
Query 83:	0.5833
Query 84:	1.0000
Query 85:	0.2144
Query 86:	0.3010
Query 87:	0.4844
Query 88:	0.8753
Query 89:	0.6377
Query 90:	0.1614

Overall statistics
(for 49 queries):

Total number of documents
over all queries
    Retrieved: 49000
    Relevant: 1212
    Rel_ret: 1167

Interpolated Recall -
Precision Averages:
    at 0.00   0.7389
    at 0.10   0.6626
    at 0.20   0.5796
    at 0.30   0.5346
    at 0.40   0.4959
    at 0.50   0.4641
    at 0.60   0.4192
    at 0.70   0.3571
    at 0.80   0.3245
    at 0.90   0.2551
    at 1.00   0.2020

Avg. prec. (non-interpolated)
for all rel. documents
                 0.4339

Precision:
    At   5 docs: 0.4245
    At   10 docs: 0.3878
    At   15 docs: 0.3537
    At   20 docs: 0.3214
    At   30 docs: 0.2884
    At 100 docs: 0.1765
    At 200 docs: 0.1081
    At 500 docs: 0.0469
    At 1000 docs: 0.0238

R-Precision (prec. after R
(=num_rel) docs. retrieved):
    Exact: 0.4336

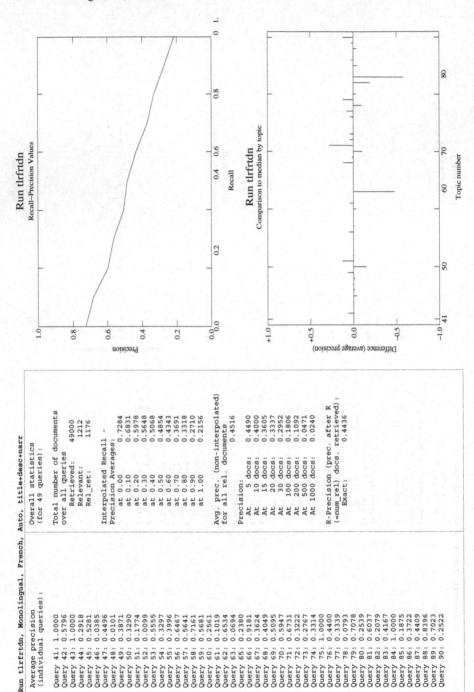

Run tlrfrtdn
Recall–Precision Values

Run tlrfrtdn
Comparison to median by topic

Run tlrfrtdn, Monolingual, French, Auto, title+desc-narr

Average precision
(individual queries):

Query 41:	1.0000
Query 42:	0.5796
Query 43:	1.0000
Query 44:	0.2918
Query 45:	0.5281
Query 46:	0.0385
Query 47:	0.4496
Query 48:	0.0101
Query 49:	0.3871
Query 50:	0.3290
Query 51:	0.1774
Query 52:	0.0099
Query 53:	0.5555
Query 54:	0.3297
Query 55:	0.3996
Query 56:	0.6467
Query 57:	0.5641
Query 58:	0.7161
Query 59:	0.5681
Query 60:	0.2561
Query 61:	0.1019
Query 62:	0.6534
Query 63:	0.0694
Query 65:	0.2380
Query 66:	0.9181
Query 67:	0.3624
Query 68:	0.4049
Query 69:	0.5095
Query 70:	0.5947
Query 71:	0.6731
Query 72:	0.3222
Query 73:	0.2767
Query 74:	0.3314
Query 75:	1.0000
Query 76:	0.4400
Query 77:	0.3339
Query 78:	0.0793
Query 79:	0.7078
Query 80:	0.2539
Query 81:	0.6037
Query 82:	0.2079
Query 83:	0.4167
Query 84:	1.0000
Query 85:	0.1875
Query 86:	0.3722
Query 87:	0.4409
Query 88:	0.8396
Query 89:	0.7023
Query 90:	0.2522

Overall statistics
(for 49 queries):

Total number of documents
over all queries
Retrieved:	49000
Relevant:	1212
Rel_ret:	1176

Interpolated Recall -
Precision Averages:
at 0.00	0.7284
at 0.10	0.6831
at 0.20	0.5978
at 0.30	0.5648
at 0.40	0.5068
at 0.50	0.4854
at 0.60	0.4343
at 0.70	0.3691
at 0.80	0.3318
at 0.90	0.2710
at 1.00	0.2156

Avg. prec. (non-interpolated)
for all rel. documents
0.4516

Precision:
At 5 docs:	0.4490
At 10 docs:	0.4000
At 15 docs:	0.3605
At 20 docs:	0.3337
At 30 docs:	0.2952
At 100 docs:	0.1806
At 200 docs:	0.1092
At 500 docs:	0.0471
At 1000 docs:	0.0240

R-Precision (prec. after R
(=num_rel) docs. retrieved):
Exact: 0.4436

Run tlrfrtdnpc

Recall–Precision Values

Run tlrfrtdnpc

Comparison to median by topic

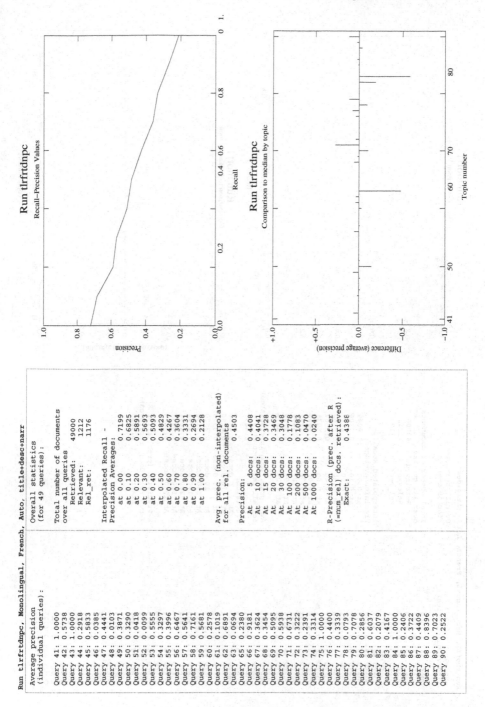

Run tlrfrtdnpc, Monolingual, French, Auto, title+desc+narr

Average precision
(individual queries):

Query 41:	1.0000
Query 42:	0.5738
Query 43:	1.0000
Query 44:	0.2918
Query 45:	0.5833
Query 46:	0.0385
Query 47:	0.4441
Query 48:	0.0103
Query 49:	0.3871
Query 50:	0.3290
Query 51:	0.0418
Query 52:	0.0099
Query 53:	0.5555
Query 54:	0.3297
Query 55:	0.3996
Query 56:	0.6467
Query 57:	0.5641
Query 58:	0.7161
Query 59:	0.5681
Query 60:	0.2578
Query 61:	0.1019
Query 62:	0.6891
Query 63:	0.0694
Query 65:	0.2380
Query 66:	0.9181
Query 67:	0.3624
Query 68:	0.3454
Query 69:	0.5095
Query 70:	0.5938
Query 71:	0.6731
Query 72:	0.3222
Query 73:	0.2391
Query 74:	0.3314
Query 75:	1.0000
Query 76:	0.4400
Query 77:	0.3339
Query 78:	0.0793
Query 79:	0.7078
Query 80:	0.2856
Query 81:	0.6037
Query 82:	0.2079
Query 83:	0.4167
Query 84:	1.0000
Query 85:	0.2406
Query 86:	0.3722
Query 87:	0.4409
Query 88:	0.8396
Query 89:	0.7023
Query 90:	0.2522

Overall statistics
(for 49 queries):

Total number of documents
over all queries
    Retrieved: 49000
    Relevant: 1212
    Rel_ret: 1176

Interpolated Recall -
Precision Averages:
    at 0.00   0.7199
    at 0.10   0.6825
    at 0.20   0.5891
    at 0.30   0.5693
    at 0.40   0.5093
    at 0.50   0.4829
    at 0.60   0.4267
    at 0.70   0.3604
    at 0.80   0.3331
    at 0.90   0.2694
    at 1.00   0.2128

Avg. prec. (non-interpolated)
for all rel. documents
               0.4503

Precision:
    At   5 docs: 0.4408
    At   10 docs: 0.4041
    At   15 docs: 0.3728
    At   20 docs: 0.3469
    At   30 docs: 0.3048
    At 100 docs: 0.1778
    At 200 docs: 0.1083
    At 500 docs: 0.0470
    At 1000 docs: 0.0240

R-Precision (prec. after R
(=num rel) docs. retrieved):
    Exact: 0.4388

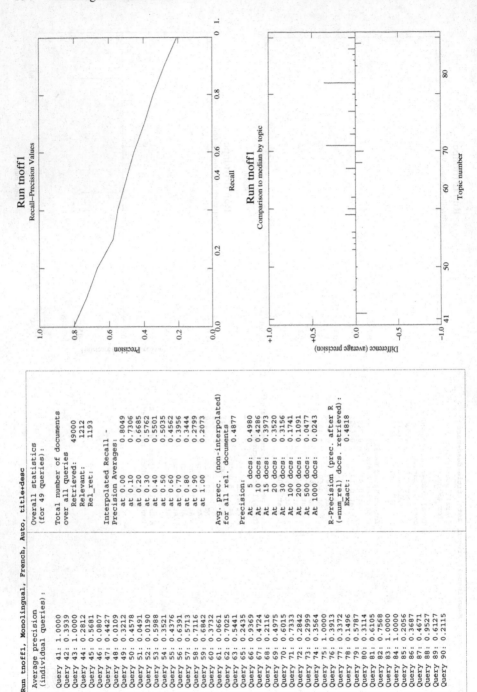

Run tnoff1
Recall–Precision Values

Run tnoff1
Comparison to median by topic

Run tnoff1, Monolingual, French, Auto, title+desc

Average precision
(individual queries):

Query 41:	1.0000	Query 65:	0.2435
Query 42:	0.3939	Query 66:	0.9369
Query 43:	1.0000	Query 67:	0.4724
Query 44:	0.2812	Query 68:	0.2116
Query 45:	0.5681	Query 69:	0.4975
Query 46:	0.0807	Query 70:	0.6015
Query 47:	0.4427	Query 71:	0.7333
Query 48:	0.0109	Query 72:	0.2842
Query 49:	0.3212	Query 73:	0.2999
Query 50:	0.4578	Query 74:	0.3564
Query 51:	0.0491	Query 75:	1.0000
Query 52:	0.0190	Query 76:	0.3913
Query 53:	0.5988	Query 77:	0.3372
Query 54:	0.3521	Query 78:	0.1496
Query 55:	0.4376	Query 79:	0.5787
Query 56:	0.6391	Query 80:	0.3114
Query 57:	0.5713	Query 81:	0.6105
Query 58:	0.7116	Query 82:	0.7568
Query 59:	0.6842	Query 83:	1.0000
Query 60:	0.3732	Query 84:	1.0000
Query 61:	0.0661	Query 85:	0.2056
Query 62:	0.7025	Query 86:	0.3687
Query 63:	0.5441	Query 87:	0.4671
		Query 88:	0.9527
		Query 89:	0.6127
		Query 90:	0.2115

Overall statistics
(for 49 queries):

Total number of documents
over all queries
Retrieved: 49000
Relevant: 1212
Rel_ret: 1193

Interpolated Recall -
Precision Averages:

at	0.00	0.8049
at	0.10	0.7306
at	0.20	0.6685
at	0.30	0.5762
at	0.40	0.5501
at	0.50	0.5035
at	0.60	0.4562
at	0.70	0.3956
at	0.80	0.3444
at	0.90	0.2799
at	1.00	0.2073

Avg. prec. (non-interpolated)
for all rel. documents
                    0.4877

Precision:

At	5 docs:	0.4980
At	10 docs:	0.4286
At	15 docs:	0.3973
At	20 docs:	0.3520
At	30 docs:	0.3156
At	100 docs:	0.1741
At	200 docs:	0.1091
At	500 docs:	0.0477
At	1000 docs:	0.0243

R-Precision (prec. after R
(=num_rel) docs. retrieved):
    Exact: 0.4818

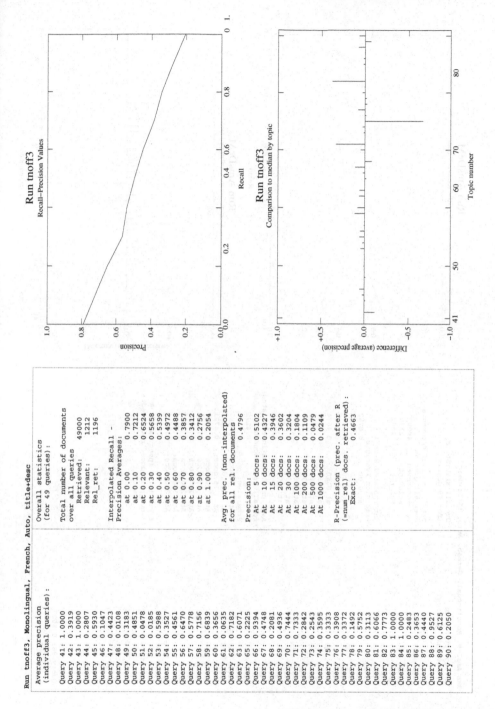

Run tnoff3, Monolingual, French, Auto, title+desc

Average precision
(individual queries):

Query 41:	1.0000
Query 42:	0.3919
Query 43:	1.0000
Query 44:	0.2807
Query 45:	0.5930
Query 46:	0.1047
Query 47:	0.4423
Query 48:	0.0108
Query 49:	0.3183
Query 50:	0.4851
Query 51:	0.0478
Query 52:	0.0185
Query 53:	0.5988
Query 54:	0.3527
Query 55:	0.4561
Query 56:	0.6470
Query 57:	0.5778
Query 58:	0.7156
Query 59:	0.6839
Query 60:	0.3656
Query 61:	0.0635
Query 62:	0.7182
Query 63:	0.6071
Query 65:	0.2225
Query 66:	0.9394
Query 67:	0.4748
Query 68:	0.2081
Query 69:	0.4936
Query 70:	0.7444
Query 71:	0.7333
Query 72:	0.2842
Query 73:	0.2543
Query 74:	0.3595
Query 75:	0.3333
Query 76:	0.3908
Query 77:	0.3372
Query 78:	0.1492
Query 79:	0.5752
Query 80:	0.3113
Query 81:	0.6066
Query 82:	0.7773
Query 83:	1.0000
Query 84:	1.0000
Query 85:	0.2483
Query 86:	0.3653
Query 87:	0.4440
Query 88:	0.9527
Query 89:	0.6125
Query 90:	0.2050

Overall statistics
(for 49 queries):

Total number of documents
over all queries:
Retrieved:	49000
Relevant:	1212
Rel_ret:	1196

Interpolated Recall -
Precision Averages:
at 0.00	0.7900
at 0.10	0.7212
at 0.20	0.6524
at 0.30	0.5658
at 0.40	0.5399
at 0.50	0.4972
at 0.60	0.4488
at 0.70	0.3857
at 0.80	0.3412
at 0.90	0.2756
at 1.00	0.2054

Avg. prec. (non-interpolated)
for all rel. documents
                       0.4796

Precision:
At 5 docs:	0.5102
At 10 docs:	0.4327
At 15 docs:	0.3946
At 20 docs:	0.3602
At 30 docs:	0.3204
At 100 docs:	0.1804
At 200 docs:	0.1109
At 500 docs:	0.0479
At 1000 docs:	0.0244

R-Precision (prec. after R
(=num_rel) docs. retrieved):
         Exact: 0.4663

Run tnoff3
Recall-Precision Values

Run tnoff3
Comparison to median by topic

Monolingual French...

Run AmsDeM
Recall–Precision Values

Run AmsDeM
Comparison to median by topic

Run AmsDeM, Monolingual, German, Auto, title+desc

Average precision
(individual queries):

Overall statistics
(for 49 queries):

Total number of documents	
over all queries	
Retrieved:	49000
Relevant:	2130
Rel_ret:	2007

Interpolated Recall -
Precision Averages:

at	0.00	0.6762
at	0.10	0.6192
at	0.20	0.5495
at	0.30	0.5023
at	0.40	0.4674
at	0.50	0.4307
at	0.60	0.3985
at	0.70	0.3629
at	0.80	0.3155
at	0.90	0.2501
at	1.00	0.1203

Avg. prec. (non-interpolated)
for all rel. documents   0.4172

Precision:

At	5 docs:	0.5102
At	10 docs:	0.5102
At	15 docs:	0.4721
At	20 docs:	0.4582
At	30 docs:	0.4102
At	100 docs:	0.2504
At	200 docs:	0.1669
At	500 docs:	0.0793
At	1000 docs:	0.0410

R-Precision (prec. after R
(=num_rel) docs. retrieved):
Exact: 0.3922

Query 41:	0.8707
Query 42:	0.6938
Query 43:	0.0014
Query 45:	0.7276
Query 46:	0.0447
Query 47:	0.2280
Query 48:	0.1174
Query 49:	0.3378
Query 50:	0.6802
Query 51:	0.0508
Query 52:	0.0438
Query 53:	0.2600
Query 54:	0.0019
Query 55:	0.8259
Query 56:	0.3623
Query 57:	0.9860
Query 58:	0.8094
Query 59:	0.2223
Query 60:	0.5422
Query 61:	0.0432
Query 62:	0.7421
Query 63:	0.8496
Query 64:	0.0096
Query 65:	0.1717
Query 66:	0.7971
Query 67:	0.6959
Query 68:	0.3652
Query 69:	0.0215
Query 70:	0.3392
Query 71:	0.1651
Query 72:	0.0600
Query 73:	0.3532
Query 74:	0.4751
Query 75:	0.9694
Query 76:	0.2632
Query 77:	0.0782
Query 78:	0.4333
Query 79:	0.4400
Query 80:	0.8804
Query 81:	0.7179
Query 82:	0.8737
Query 83:	0.0767
Query 84:	0.0304
Query 85:	0.1584
Query 86:	0.5120
Query 87:	0.6271
Query 88:	0.8567
Query 89:	0.5893
Query 90:	0.0418

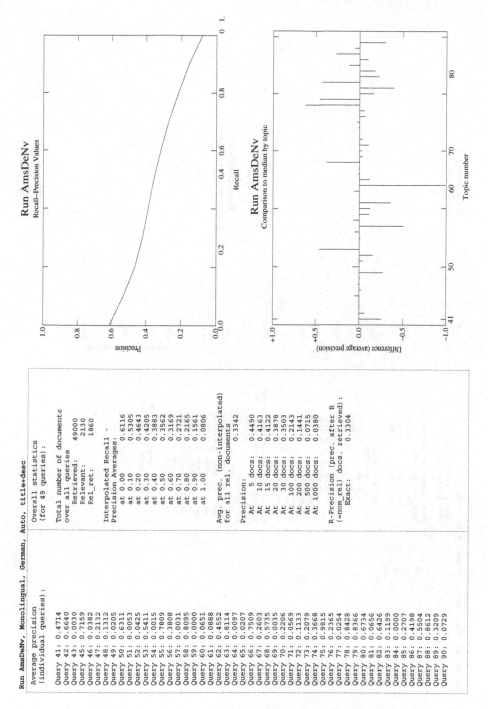

Run AmsDeNv

Recall–Precision Values

Run AmsDeNv

Comparison to median by topic

Run AmsDeNv, Monolingual, German, Auto, title+desc

Average precision
(individual queries):

Query 41:	0.4714
Query 42:	0.6640
Query 43:	0.0030
Query 45:	0.7159
Query 46:	0.0382
Query 47:	0.2132
Query 48:	0.1312
Query 49:	0.0205
Query 50:	0.6311
Query 51:	0.0053
Query 52:	0.0425
Query 53:	0.5411
Query 54:	0.0015
Query 55:	0.7809
Query 56:	0.3808
Query 57:	0.0031
Query 58:	0.8095
Query 59:	0.0000
Query 60:	0.0651
Query 61:	0.0888
Query 62:	0.4552
Query 63:	0.8114
Query 64:	0.0097
Query 65:	0.0207
Query 66:	0.7509
Query 67:	0.2603
Query 68:	0.5735
Query 69:	0.0035
Query 70:	0.2206
Query 71:	0.0569
Query 72:	0.1133
Query 73:	0.2079
Query 74:	0.3668
Query 75:	0.9815
Query 76:	0.2365
Query 77:	0.0254
Query 78:	0.8828
Query 79:	0.8366
Query 80:	0.6734
Query 81:	0.0656
Query 82:	0.6426
Query 83:	0.1199
Query 84:	0.0000
Query 85:	0.2707
Query 86:	0.4198
Query 87:	0.5504
Query 88:	0.8612
Query 89:	0.3209
Query 90:	0.0729

Overall statistics
(for 49 queries):

Total number of documents
over all queries
    Retrieved: 49000
    Relevant: 2130
    Rel_ret: 1860

Interpolated Recall -
Precision Averages:
    at 0.00   0.6116
    at 0.10   0.5305
    at 0.20   0.4643
    at 0.30   0.4205
    at 0.40   0.3883
    at 0.50   0.3562
    at 0.60   0.3169
    at 0.70   0.2721
    at 0.80   0.2165
    at 0.90   0.1561
    at 1.00   0.0806

Avg. prec. (non-interpolated)
for all rel. documents
                 0.3342

Precision:
    At   5 docs: 0.4490
    At 10 docs: 0.4163
    At 15 docs: 0.4122
    At 20 docs: 0.3878
    At 30 docs: 0.3503
    At 100 docs: 0.2143
    At 200 docs: 0.1441
    At 500 docs: 0.0715
    At 1000 docs: 0.0380

R-Precision (prec. after R
(=num_rel) docs. retrieved):
    Exact: 0.3304

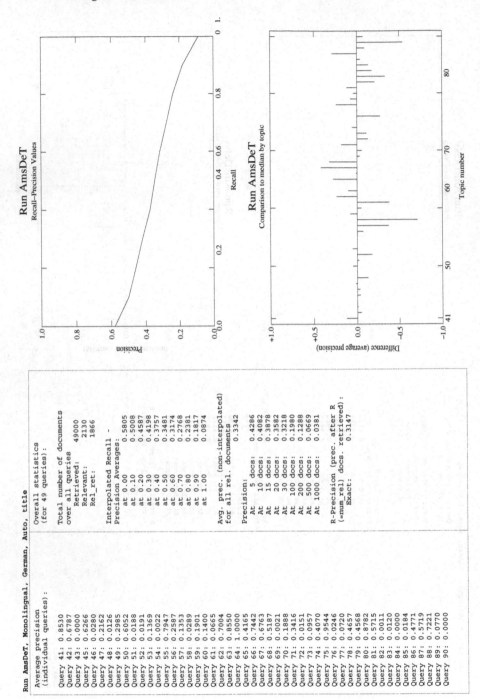

Run AmsDeT
Recall–Precision Values

Run AmsDeT
Comparison to median by topic

Run AmsDeT, Monolingual, German, Auto, title

Average precision
(individual queries):

Query 41:	0.8530
Query 42:	0.6787
Query 43:	0.0000
Query 45:	0.6266
Query 46:	0.0280
Query 47:	0.2162
Query 48:	0.0126
Query 49:	0.2985
Query 50:	0.6052
Query 51:	0.0188
Query 52:	0.0191
Query 53:	0.1369
Query 54:	0.0022
Query 55:	0.7947
Query 56:	0.2587
Query 57:	0.1353
Query 58:	0.0289
Query 59:	0.1901
Query 60:	0.1400
Query 61:	0.0665
Query 62:	0.7004
Query 63:	0.8550
Query 64:	1.0000
Query 65:	0.4165
Query 66:	0.7442
Query 67:	0.6763
Query 68:	0.5187
Query 69:	0.0021
Query 70:	0.1888
Query 71:	0.3416
Query 72:	0.0151
Query 73:	0.0957
Query 74:	0.4070
Query 75:	0.9544
Query 76:	0.0246
Query 77:	0.0720
Query 78:	0.4657
Query 79:	0.4568
Query 80:	0.8782
Query 81:	0.5715
Query 82:	0.0011
Query 83:	0.0120
Query 84:	0.0000
Query 85:	0.0184
Query 86:	0.4771
Query 87:	0.5719
Query 88:	0.7221
Query 89:	0.0770
Query 90:	0.0000

Overall statistics
(for 49 queries):

Total number of documents
over all queries:

Retrieved:	49000
Relevant:	2130
Rel_ret:	1866

Interpolated Recall -
Precision Averages:

at 0.00	0.5805
at 0.10	0.5008
at 0.20	0.4587
at 0.30	0.4198
at 0.40	0.3757
at 0.50	0.3481
at 0.60	0.3174
at 0.70	0.2768
at 0.80	0.2381
at 0.90	0.1817
at 1.00	0.0874

Avg. prec. (non-interpolated)
for all rel. documents
                    0.3342

Precision:
At 5 docs:	0.4286
At 10 docs:	0.4082
At 15 docs:	0.3878
At 20 docs:	0.3582
At 30 docs:	0.3218
At 100 docs:	0.1980
At 200 docs:	0.1288
At 500 docs:	0.0669
At 1000 docs:	0.0381

R-Precision (prec. after R
(=num_rel) docs. retrieved):
| Exact: | 0.3147 |

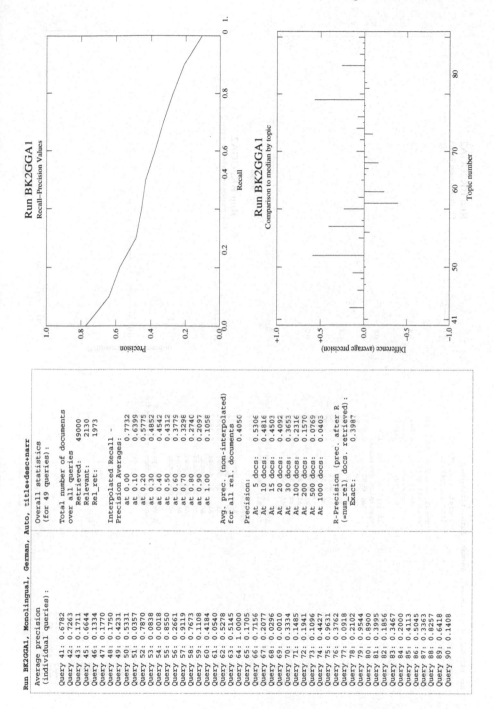

Run BK2GGA1, Monolingual, German, Auto, title+desc+narr

Average precision
(individual queries):

Query 41:	0.6782
Query 42:	0.7263
Query 43:	0.1711
Query 45:	0.6644
Query 46:	0.1334
Query 47:	0.1770
Query 48:	0.1750
Query 49:	0.4231
Query 50:	0.5331
Query 51:	0.0357
Query 52:	0.7870
Query 53:	0.0838
Query 54:	0.0018
Query 55:	0.8550
Query 56:	0.2661
Query 57:	0.9119
Query 58:	0.7673
Query 59:	0.1108
Query 60:	0.4184
Query 61:	0.0540
Query 62:	0.5278
Query 63:	0.5145
Query 64:	1.0000
Query 65:	0.1705
Query 66:	0.7156
Query 67:	0.2077
Query 68:	0.0296
Query 69:	0.0010
Query 70:	0.3334
Query 71:	0.1485
Query 72:	0.1941
Query 73:	0.1096
Query 74:	0.4427
Query 75:	0.9631
Query 76:	0.3762
Query 77:	0.0918
Query 78:	0.2102
Query 79:	0.9544
Query 80:	0.8900
Query 81:	0.3995
Query 82:	0.1856
Query 83:	0.3467
Query 84:	0.2000
Query 85:	0.4113
Query 86:	0.5045
Query 87:	0.3363
Query 88:	0.8257
Query 89:	0.6418
Query 90:	0.1408

Overall statistics
(for 49 queries):

Total number of documents
over all queries:
Retrieved: 49000
Relevant: 2130
Rel_ret: 1973

Interpolated Recall -
Precision Averages:
at 0.00	0.7732
at 0.10	0.6399
at 0.20	0.5775
at 0.30	0.4852
at 0.40	0.4542
at 0.50	0.4312
at 0.60	0.3779
at 0.70	0.3298
at 0.80	0.2740
at 0.90	0.2097
at 1.00	0.1058

Avg. prec. (non-interpolated)
for all rel. documents   0.4050

Precision:
At 5 docs:	0.5306
At 10 docs:	0.4816
At 15 docs:	0.4503
At 20 docs:	0.4092
At 30 docs:	0.3653
At 100 docs:	0.2316
At 200 docs:	0.1570
At 500 docs:	0.0769
At 1000 docs:	0.0403

R-Precision (prec. after R
(=num_rel) docs. retrieved):
Exact: 0.3987

Run BK2GGA1
Recall-Precision Values

Run BK2GGA1
Comparison to median by topic

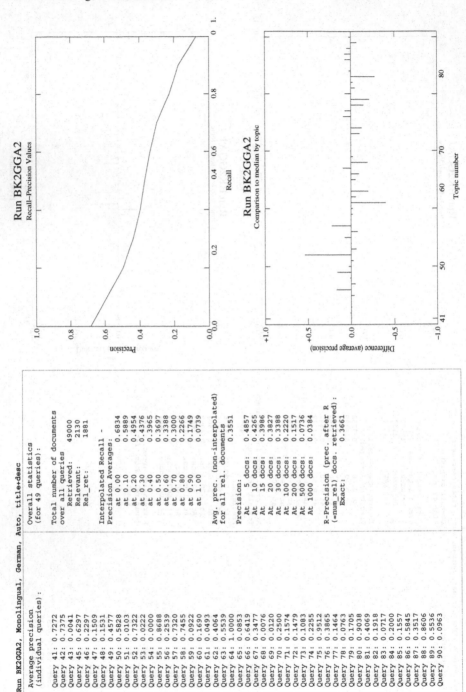

Run BK2GGA2
Recall–Precision Values

Run BK2GGA2
Comparison to median by topic

Run BK2GGA2, Monolingual, German, Auto, title+desc

Average precision
(individual queries):

Query 41:	0.7272
Query 42:	0.7375
Query 43:	0.0041
Query 45:	0.6297
Query 46:	0.2297
Query 47:	0.1509
Query 48:	0.1531
Query 49:	0.4577
Query 50:	0.5828
Query 51:	0.0103
Query 52:	0.7322
Query 53:	0.0222
Query 54:	0.0000
Query 55:	0.8688
Query 56:	0.2539
Query 57:	0.7320
Query 58:	0.7455
Query 59:	0.0922
Query 60:	0.1690
Query 61:	0.0493
Query 62:	0.4064
Query 63:	0.5539
Query 64:	1.0000
Query 65:	0.0853
Query 66:	0.6419
Query 67:	0.3477
Query 68:	0.0076
Query 69:	0.0120
Query 70:	0.2500
Query 71:	0.1574
Query 72:	0.1479
Query 73:	0.1083
Query 74:	0.2255
Query 75:	0.9512
Query 76:	0.3865
Query 77:	0.1464
Query 78:	0.0763
Query 79:	0.1705
Query 80:	0.9038
Query 81:	0.4069
Query 82:	0.1918
Query 83:	0.0717
Query 84:	0.2000
Query 85:	0.1557
Query 86:	0.5845
Query 87:	0.3517
Query 88:	0.8606
Query 89:	0.5536
Query 90:	0.0963

Overall statistics
(for 49 queries):

Total number of documents
over all queries:
    Retrieved: 49000
    Relevant: 2130
    Rel_ret: 1881

Interpolated Recall –
Precision Averages:
    at 0.00   0.6834
    at 0.10   0.5889
    at 0.20   0.4954
    at 0.30   0.4376
    at 0.40   0.3965
    at 0.50   0.3697
    at 0.60   0.3388
    at 0.70   0.3000
    at 0.80   0.2266
    at 0.90   0.1749
    at 1.00   0.0739

Avg. prec. (non-interpolated)
for all rel. documents
                   0.3551

Precision:
    At   5 docs: 0.4857
    At   10 docs: 0.4265
    At   15 docs: 0.3986
    At   20 docs: 0.3827
    At   30 docs: 0.3388
    At 100 docs: 0.2220
    At 200 docs: 0.1517
    At 500 docs: 0.0736
    At 1000 docs: 0.0384

R-Precision (prec. after R
(=num_rel) docs. retrieved):
    Exact: 0.3661

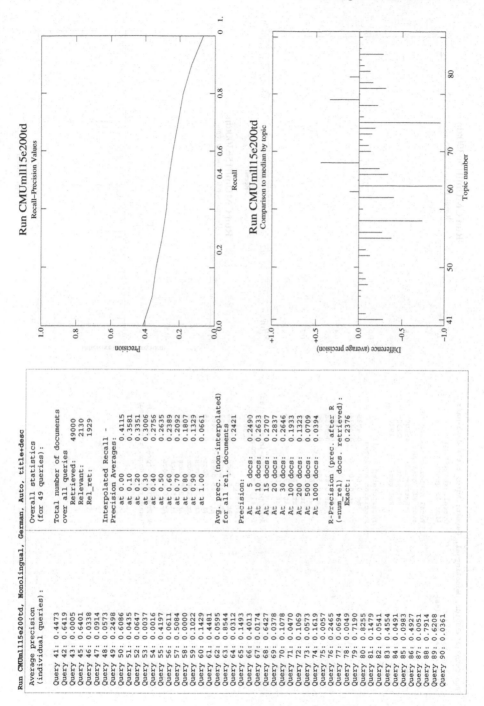

Run CMUmll15e200td

Recall-Precision Values

Precision

Recall

Run CMUmll15e200td

Comparison to median by topic

Difference (average precision)

Topic number

Run CMUmll15e200td, Monolingual, German, Auto, title+desc

Average precision
(individual queries):

Query 41:	0.4473
Query 42:	0.6419
Query 43:	0.0005
Query 45:	0.6401
Query 46:	0.0338
Query 47:	0.0914
Query 48:	0.0573
Query 49:	0.2498
Query 50:	0.6086
Query 51:	0.0435
Query 52:	0.0647
Query 53:	0.0037
Query 54:	0.0016
Query 55:	0.4197
Query 56:	0.0611
Query 57:	0.5084
Query 58:	0.0000
Query 59:	0.1022
Query 60:	0.1429
Query 61:	0.4481
Query 62:	0.0595
Query 63:	0.8544
Query 64:	0.0312
Query 65:	0.1493
Query 66:	0.4013
Query 67:	0.0174
Query 68:	0.6427
Query 69:	0.0378
Query 70:	0.1078
Query 71:	0.0470
Query 72:	0.1069
Query 73:	0.0573
Query 74:	0.1619
Query 75:	0.0057
Query 76:	0.2465
Query 77:	0.0694
Query 78:	0.0049
Query 79:	0.7190
Query 80:	0.8255
Query 81:	0.1479
Query 82:	0.0541
Query 83:	0.4554
Query 84:	0.0491
Query 85:	0.0983
Query 86:	0.4927
Query 87:	0.0051
Query 88:	0.7914
Query 89:	0.6208
Query 90:	0.0361

Overall statistics
(for 49 queries):

Total number of documents
over all queries
  Retrieved: 49000
  Relevant: 2130
  Rel_ret: 1929

Interpolated Recall -
Precision Averages:
  at 0.00   0.4115
  at 0.10   0.3581
  at 0.20   0.3351
  at 0.30   0.3006
  at 0.40   0.2756
  at 0.50   0.2635
  at 0.60   0.2389
  at 0.70   0.2092
  at 0.80   0.1807
  at 0.90   0.1329
  at 1.00   0.0661

Avg. prec. (non-interpolated)
for all rel. documents   0.2421

Precision:
  At   5 docs: 0.2490
  At   10 docs: 0.2633
  At   15 docs: 0.2707
  At   20 docs: 0.2837
  At   30 docs: 0.2646
  At 100 docs: 0.1933
  At 200 docs: 0.1323
  At 500 docs: 0.0709
  At 1000 docs: 0.0394

R-Precision (prec. after R
(=num_rel) docs. retrieved):
  Exact: 0.2376

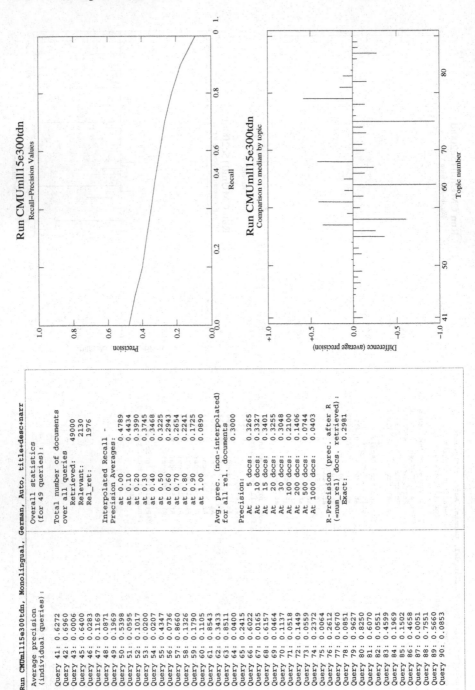

Run CMUmll15e300tdn
Recall–Precision Values

Run CMUmll15e300tdn
Comparison to median by topic

Run CMUmll15e300tdn, Monolingual, German, Auto, title+desc+narr

Average precision
(individual queries):

Query 41:	0.6272
Query 42:	0.6960
Query 43:	0.0006
Query 45:	0.6400
Query 46:	0.0283
Query 47:	0.1169
Query 48:	0.0871
Query 49:	0.1969
Query 50:	0.5398
Query 51:	0.0595
Query 52:	0.1017
Query 53:	0.0200
Query 54:	0.0207
Query 55:	0.4347
Query 56:	0.0736
Query 57:	0.8660
Query 58:	0.1326
Query 59:	0.1790
Query 60:	0.1105
Query 61:	0.8543
Query 62:	0.3433
Query 63:	0.8511
Query 64:	0.0400
Query 65:	0.2415
Query 66:	0.6022
Query 67:	0.0165
Query 68:	0.6157
Query 69:	0.0464
Query 70:	0.1137
Query 71:	0.0518
Query 72:	0.1449
Query 73:	0.0559
Query 74:	0.2372
Query 75:	0.0064
Query 76:	0.2612
Query 77:	0.0670
Query 78:	0.0851
Query 79:	0.9627
Query 80:	0.8250
Query 81:	0.6070
Query 82:	0.0551
Query 83:	0.4599
Query 84:	0.1969
Query 85:	0.1502
Query 86:	0.4658
Query 87:	0.0051
Query 88:	0.7551
Query 89:	0.5660
Query 90:	0.0853

Overall statistics
(for 49 queries):

Total number of documents
over all queries:
Retrieved:	49000
Relevant:	2130
Rel_ret:	1976

Interpolated Recall -
Precision Averages:
at 0.00	0.4789
at 0.10	0.4434
at 0.20	0.3990
at 0.30	0.3745
at 0.40	0.3468
at 0.50	0.3225
at 0.60	0.2943
at 0.70	0.2654
at 0.80	0.2241
at 0.90	0.1725
at 1.00	0.0890

Avg. prec. (non-interpolated)
for all rel. documents
0.3000

Precision:
At 5 docs:	0.3265
At 10 docs:	0.3327
At 15 docs:	0.3401
At 20 docs:	0.3255
At 30 docs:	0.3048
At 100 docs:	0.2100
At 200 docs:	0.1406
At 500 docs:	0.0744
At 1000 docs:	0.0403

R-Precision (prec. after R
(=num_rel) docs. retrieved):
| Exact: | 0.2981 |

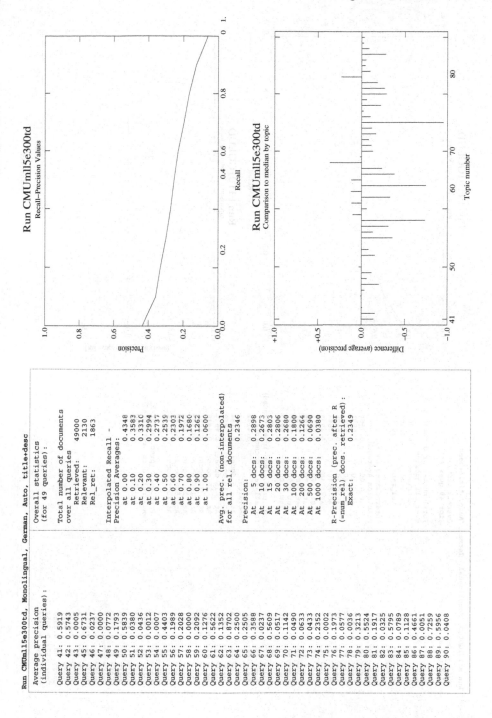

Run CMUml15e300td
Recall–Precision Values

Run CMUml15e300td
Comparison to median by topic

Run CMUml15e300td, Monolingual, German, Auto, title+desc

Average precision
(individual queries):

Query 41:	0.5919
Query 42:	0.5743
Query 43:	0.0005
Query 45:	0.6731
Query 46:	0.0237
Query 47:	0.0000
Query 48:	0.0772
Query 49:	0.1793
Query 50:	0.5839
Query 51:	0.0380
Query 52:	0.0436
Query 53:	0.0012
Query 54:	0.0007
Query 55:	0.4403
Query 56:	0.1989
Query 57:	0.2028
Query 58:	0.0000
Query 59:	0.2092
Query 60:	0.1276
Query 61:	0.5622
Query 62:	0.1352
Query 63:	0.8702
Query 64:	0.2500
Query 65:	0.2505
Query 66:	0.3588
Query 67:	0.0237
Query 68:	0.5609
Query 69:	0.0517
Query 70:	0.1142
Query 71:	0.0490
Query 72:	0.0633
Query 73:	0.0433
Query 74:	0.2352
Query 75:	0.0002
Query 76:	0.1973
Query 77:	0.0577
Query 78:	0.0036
Query 79:	0.3213
Query 80:	0.5524
Query 81:	0.1917
Query 82:	0.0325
Query 83:	0.5795
Query 84:	0.0789
Query 85:	0.1128
Query 86:	0.4661
Query 87:	0.0051
Query 88:	0.7259
Query 89:	0.5956
Query 90:	0.0408

Overall statistics
(for 49 queries):

Total number of documents
over all queries
    Retrieved: 49000
    Relevant: 2130
    Rel_ret: 1863

Interpolated Recall -
Precision Averages:
    at 0.00   0.4348
    at 0.10   0.3583
    at 0.20   0.3310
    at 0.30   0.2994
    at 0.40   0.2737
    at 0.50   0.2539
    at 0.60   0.2303
    at 0.70   0.1972
    at 0.80   0.1680
    at 0.90   0.1262
    at 1.00   0.0600

Avg. prec. (non-interpolated)
for all rel. documents
                   0.2346

Precision:
    At   5 docs: 0.2898
    At   10 docs: 0.2673
    At   15 docs: 0.2803
    At   20 docs: 0.2806
    At   30 docs: 0.2680
    At 100 docs: 0.1800
    At 200 docs: 0.1264
    At 500 docs: 0.0690
    At 1000 docs: 0.0380

R-Precision (prec. after R
(=num_rel) docs. retrieved):
    Exact: 0.2349

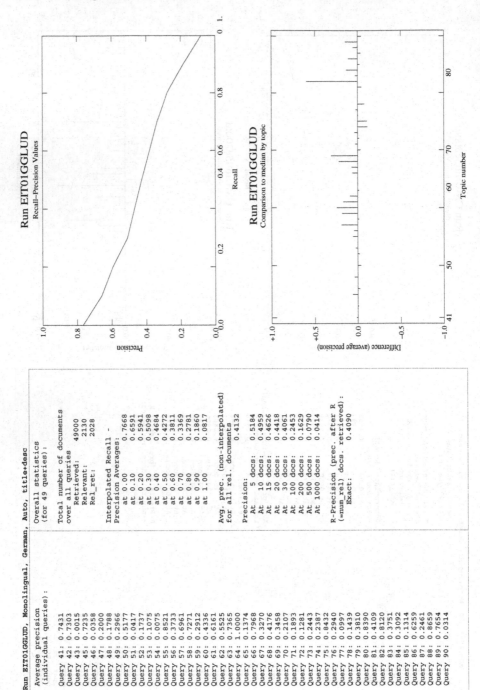

Run **EIT01GGLUD**, Monolingual, German, Auto, title+desc

Average precision
(individual queries):

Query 41:	0.7431
Query 42:	0.7303
Query 43:	0.0015
Query 45:	0.7235
Query 46:	0.0358
Query 47:	0.2000
Query 48:	0.1788
Query 49:	0.2966
Query 50:	0.5177
Query 51:	0.0417
Query 52:	0.1737
Query 53:	0.1075
Query 54:	0.0075
Query 55:	0.8521
Query 56:	0.3733
Query 57:	0.6961
Query 58:	0.7271
Query 59:	0.2912
Query 60:	0.4336
Query 61:	0.6161
Query 62:	0.5525
Query 63:	0.7365
Query 64:	1.0000
Query 65:	0.1374
Query 66:	0.7968
Query 67:	0.3270
Query 68:	0.4176
Query 69:	0.3458
Query 70:	0.2107
Query 71:	0.1893
Query 72:	0.1281
Query 73:	0.2443
Query 74:	0.2387
Query 75:	0.8432
Query 76:	0.2940
Query 77:	0.0997
Query 78:	0.1439
Query 79:	0.3810
Query 80:	0.8390
Query 81:	0.4109
Query 82:	0.8120
Query 83:	0.3751
Query 84:	0.3092
Query 85:	0.1314
Query 86:	0.6259
Query 87:	0.2461
Query 88:	0.8659
Query 89:	0.7654
Query 90:	0.0314

Overall statistics
(for 49 queries):

Total number of documents
over all queries:
Retrieved:	49000
Relevant:	2130
Rel_ret:	2028

Interpolated Recall -
Precision Averages:
at 0.00	0.7668
at 0.10	0.6591
at 0.20	0.5941
at 0.30	0.5098
at 0.40	0.4684
at 0.50	0.4272
at 0.60	0.3811
at 0.70	0.3369
at 0.80	0.2781
at 0.90	0.1860
at 1.00	0.0817

Avg. prec. (non-interpolated)
for all rel. documents
0.4132

Precision:
At 5 docs:	0.5184
At 10 docs:	0.4959
At 15 docs:	0.4626
At 20 docs:	0.4418
At 30 docs:	0.4061
At 100 docs:	0.2453
At 200 docs:	0.1629
At 500 docs:	0.0790
At 1000 docs:	0.0414

R-Precision (prec. after R
(=num_rel) docs. retrieved):
| Exact: | 0.4090 |

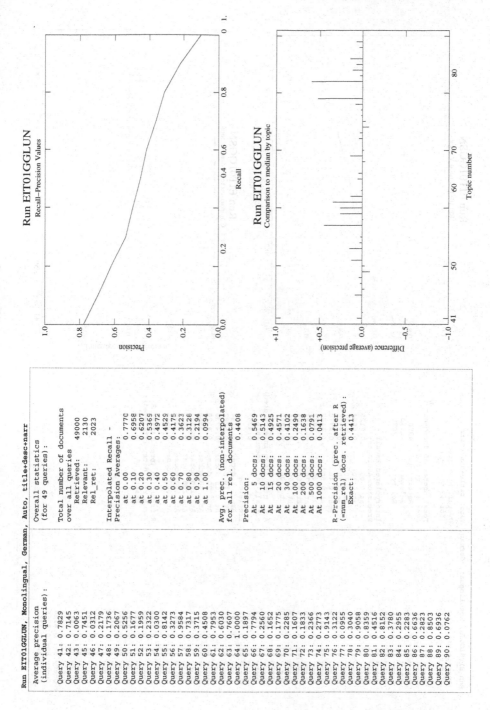

Run EIT01GGLUN
Recall-Precision Values

Run EIT01GGLUN
Comparison to median by topic

Run EIT01GGLUN, Monolingual, German, Auto, title+desc+narr

Average precision
(individual queries):

Overall statistics
(for 49 queries):

Total number of documents
over all queries:
Retrieved: 49000
Relevant: 2130
Rel_ret: 2023

Query 41:	0.7829
Query 42:	0.7145
Query 43:	0.0063
Query 45:	0.7451
Query 46:	0.0312
Query 47:	0.2179
Query 48:	0.1736
Query 49:	0.2067
Query 50:	0.5256
Query 51:	0.1677
Query 52:	0.1959
Query 53:	0.2322
Query 54:	-0.0300
Query 55:	0.8142
Query 56:	0.3273
Query 57:	0.9584
Query 58:	0.7317
Query 59:	0.3715
Query 60:	0.4508
Query 61:	0.7953
Query 62:	0.6030
Query 63:	0.7607
Query 64:	1.0000
Query 65:	0.1897
Query 66:	0.7794
Query 67:	0.2560
Query 68:	0.1652
Query 69:	0.1775
Query 70:	0.2285
Query 71:	0.1607
Query 72:	0.1833
Query 73:	0.2366
Query 74:	0.2773
Query 75:	0.9143
Query 76:	0.3122
Query 77:	0.0955
Query 78:	0.3040
Query 79:	0.9058
Query 80:	0.8359
Query 81:	0.4516
Query 82:	0.8152
Query 83:	0.3780
Query 84:	0.2955
Query 85:	0.2283
Query 86:	0.6636
Query 87:	0.2823
Query 88:	0.8503
Query 89:	0.6936
Query 90:	0.0762

Interpolated Recall -
Precision Averages:
at 0.00	0.7770
at 0.10	0.6958
at 0.20	0.6207
at 0.30	0.5369
at 0.40	0.4972
at 0.50	0.4529
at 0.60	0.4175
at 0.70	0.3623
at 0.80	0.3128
at 0.90	0.2194
at 1.00	0.0994

Avg. prec. (non-interpolated)
for all rel. documents   0.4408

Precision:
At 5 docs:	0.5469
At 10 docs:	0.5143
At 15 docs:	0.4925
At 20 docs:	0.4571
At 30 docs:	0.4102
At 100 docs:	0.2490
At 200 docs:	0.1638
At 500 docs:	0.0791
At 1000 docs:	0.0413

R-Precision (prec. after R
(=num_rel) docs. retrieved):
Exact: 0.4413

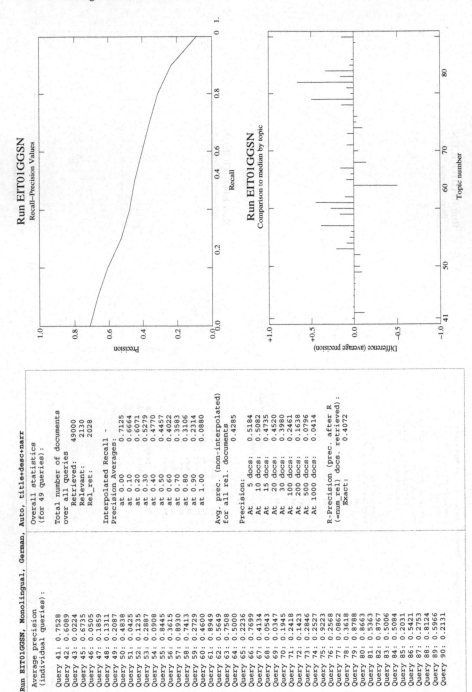

Run EIT01GGSN
Recall-Precision Values

Run EIT01GGSN
Comparison to median by topic

Run EIT01GGSN, Monolingual, German, Auto, title+desc+narr

Average precision
(individual queries):

Query 41:	0.7528	Query 66:	0.7699
Query 42:	0.6089	Query 67:	0.4134
Query 43:	0.0224	Query 68:	0.0543
Query 45:	0.6735	Query 69:	0.0347
Query 46:	0.0505	Query 70:	0.1945
Query 47:	0.1859	Query 71:	0.2418
Query 48:	0.1311	Query 72:	0.1423
Query 49:	0.2087	Query 73:	0.2846
Query 50:	0.4838	Query 74:	0.2527
Query 51:	0.0425	Query 75:	0.9223
Query 52:	0.1235	Query 76:	0.2568
Query 53:	0.2887	Query 77:	0.0862
Query 55:	0.0908	Query 78:	0.3618
Query 56:	0.8445	Query 79:	0.8788
Query 56:	0.3615	Query 80:	0.8663
Query 57:	0.8930	Query 81:	0.5363
Query 58:	0.7413	Query 82:	0.8767
Query 59:	0.2729	Query 83:	0.5006
Query 60:	0.4600	Query 84:	0.5084
Query 61:	0.8949	Query 85:	0.2031
Query 62:	0.5649	Query 86:	0.5421
Query 63:	0.7508	Query 87:	0.2753
Query 64:	0.5000	Query 88:	0.8124
Query 65:	0.2236	Query 89:	0.5966
		Query 90:	0.2131

Overall statistics
(for 49 queries):

Total number of documents
over all queries:
Retrieved: 49000
Relevant: 2130
Rel_ret: 2028

Interpolated Recall -
Precision Averages:
at 0.00   0.7125
at 0.10   0.6664
at 0.20   0.6071
at 0.30   0.5279
at 0.40   0.4770
at 0.50   0.4457
at 0.60   0.4022
at 0.70   0.3583
at 0.80   0.3106
at 0.90   0.2314
at 1.00   0.0880

Avg. prec. (non-interpolated)
for all rel. documents
                 0.4285

Precision:
At   5 docs: 0.5184
At   10 docs: 0.5082
At   15 docs: 0.4735
At   20 docs: 0.4520
At   30 docs: 0.3980
At 100 docs: 0.2461
At 200 docs: 0.1638
At 500 docs: 0.0796
At 1000 docs: 0.0414

R-Precision (prec. after R
(=num rel) docs. retrieved):
Exact: 0.4072

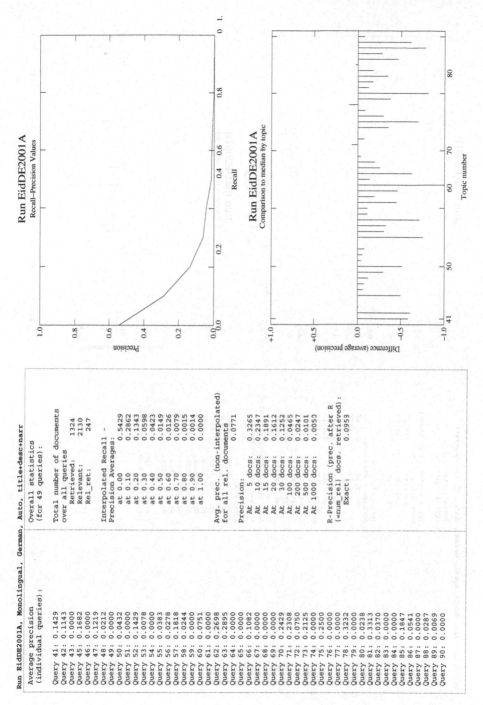

Run EidDE2001A
Recall-Precision Values

Run EidDE2001A
Comparison to median by topic

Run EidDE2001A, Monolingual, German, Auto, title+desc+narr

Average precision
(individual queries):

Query 41:	0.1429
Query 42:	0.1143
Query 43:	0.0000
Query 45:	0.1682
Query 46:	0.0000
Query 47:	0.1219
Query 48:	0.0212
Query 49:	0.0000
Query 50:	0.0432
Query 51:	0.0000
Query 52:	0.1429
Query 53:	0.0078
Query 54:	0.0000
Query 55:	0.0383
Query 56:	0.0278
Query 57:	0.1818
Query 58:	0.0244
Query 59:	0.0000
Query 60:	0.0751
Query 61:	0.0000
Query 62:	0.2698
Query 63:	0.2895
Query 64:	0.0000
Query 65:	0.0000
Query 66:	0.1082
Query 67:	0.0000
Query 68:	0.0000
Query 69:	0.0000
Query 70:	0.2429
Query 71:	0.2308
Query 72:	0.0750
Query 73:	0.2125
Query 74:	0.0000
Query 75:	0.2500
Query 76:	0.0000
Query 77:	0.0000
Query 78:	0.3232
Query 79:	0.0000
Query 80:	0.0238
Query 81:	0.3313
Query 82:	0.0370
Query 83:	0.0000
Query 84:	0.0000
Query 85:	0.1847
Query 86:	0.0541
Query 87:	0.0000
Query 88:	0.0287
Query 89:	0.0069
Query 90:	0.0000

Overall statistics
(for 49 queries):

Total number of documents
over all queries
    Retrieved: 1324
    Relevant: 2130
    Rel_ret: 247

Interpolated Recall -
Precision Averages:
    at 0.00   0.5429
    at 0.10   0.2862
    at 0.20   0.1343
    at 0.30   0.0598
    at 0.40   0.0423
    at 0.50   0.0149
    at 0.60   0.0126
    at 0.70   0.0079
    at 0.80   0.0015
    at 0.90   0.0014
    at 1.00   0.0000
Avg. prec. (non-interpolated)
for all rel. documents
    0.0771

Precision:
  At   5 docs: 0.3265
  At   10 docs: 0.2347
  At   15 docs: 0.1891
  At   20 docs: 0.1612
  At   30 docs: 0.1252
  At 100 docs: 0.0465
  At 200 docs: 0.0247
  At 500 docs: 0.0101
  At 1000 docs: 0.0050

R-Precision (prec. after R
(=num_rel) docs. retrieved):
    Exact: 0.0953

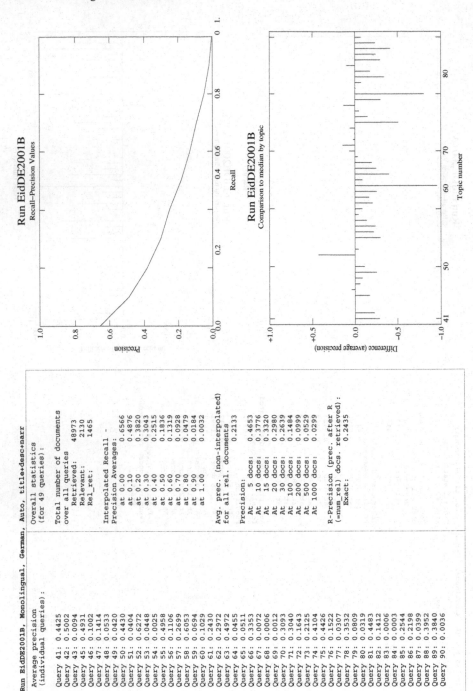

Run EidDE2001B, Monolingual, German, Auto, title+desc+narr

Average precision
(individual queries):

Query 41:	0.4425
Query 42:	0.5002
Query 43:	0.0094
Query 45:	0.4931
Query 46:	0.1002
Query 47:	0.1414
Query 48:	0.0533
Query 49:	0.0420
Query 50:	0.4430
Query 51:	0.0404
Query 52:	0.6272
Query 53:	0.0448
Query 54:	0.0025
Query 55:	0.4958
Query 56:	0.1106
Query 57:	0.2699
Query 58:	0.6053
Query 59:	0.0694
Query 60:	0.1029
Query 61:	0.2430
Query 62:	0.2972
Query 63:	0.4972
Query 64:	0.0455
Query 65:	0.0511
Query 66:	0.3353
Query 67:	0.0072
Query 68:	0.0006
Query 69:	0.0012
Query 70:	0.3093
Query 71:	0.3040
Query 72:	0.1643
Query 73:	0.2125
Query 74:	0.4104
Query 75:	0.4426
Query 76:	0.1522
Query 77:	0.0307
Query 78:	0.3532
Query 79:	0.0809
Query 80:	0.0319
Query 81:	0.4483
Query 82:	0.1412
Query 83:	0.0006
Query 84:	0.0003
Query 85:	0.2544
Query 86:	0.2198
Query 87:	0.0399
Query 88:	0.3952
Query 89:	0.3840
Query 90:	0.0036

Overall statistics
(for 49 queries):

Total number of documents
over all queries:

Retrieved:	48973
Relevant:	2130
Rel_ret:	1465

Interpolated Recall -
Precision Averages:

at 0.00	0.6566
at 0.10	0.4876
at 0.20	0.3820
at 0.30	0.3043
at 0.40	0.2515
at 0.50	0.1836
at 0.60	0.1319
at 0.70	0.0928
at 0.80	0.0479
at 0.90	0.0184
at 1.00	0.0032

Avg. prec. (non-interpolated)
for all rel. documents   0.2133

Precision:

At	5 docs:	0.4553
At	10 docs:	0.3776
At	15 docs:	0.3320
At	20 docs:	0.2980
At	30 docs:	0.2639
At	100 docs:	0.1484
At	200 docs:	0.0999
At	500 docs:	0.0529
At	1000 docs:	0.0299

R-Precision (prec. after R
(=num_rel) docs. retrieved):

Exact:	0.2435

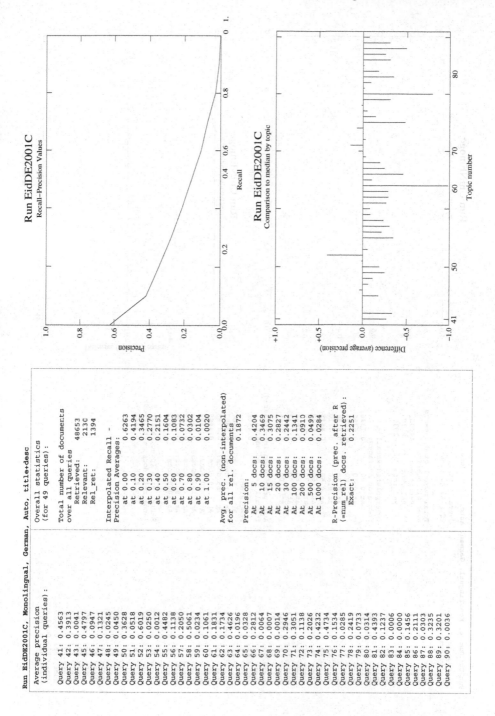

Run EidDE2001C
Recall-Precision Values

Run EidDE2001C
Comparison to median by topic

Run EidDE2001C, Monolingual, German, Auto, title+desc

Average precision
(individual queries):

Query 41:	0.4563
Query 42:	0.3913
Query 43:	0.0041
Query 45:	0.4797
Query 46:	0.0947
Query 47:	0.1321
Query 48:	0.0245
Query 49:	0.0450
Query 50:	0.3628
Query 51:	0.0518
Query 52:	0.6019
Query 53:	0.0250
Query 54:	0.0012
Query 55:	0.4482
Query 56:	0.1138
Query 57:	0.2050
Query 58:	0.5061
Query 59:	0.0234
Query 60:	0.1061
Query 61:	0.1831
Query 62:	0.1734
Query 63:	0.4626
Query 64:	0.0196
Query 65:	0.0328
Query 66:	0.2812
Query 67:	0.0064
Query 68:	0.0007
Query 69:	0.0014
Query 70:	0.2946
Query 71:	0.3051
Query 72:	0.1138
Query 73:	0.2026
Query 74:	0.4232
Query 75:	0.4734
Query 76:	0.1534
Query 77:	0.0285
Query 78:	0.2419
Query 79:	0.0733
Query 80:	0.0314
Query 81:	0.4393
Query 82:	0.1237
Query 83:	0.0006
Query 84:	0.0000
Query 85:	0.1456
Query 86:	0.2111
Query 87:	0.0303
Query 88:	0.3235
Query 89:	0.3201
Query 90:	0.0036

Overall statistics
(for 49 queries):

Total number of documents
over all queries:
Retrieved: 48653
Relevant: 2130
Rel_ret: 1394

Interpolated Recall -
Precision Averages:
at 0.00   0.6263
at 0.10   0.4194
at 0.20   0.3465
at 0.30   0.2770
at 0.40   0.2151
at 0.50   0.1604
at 0.60   0.1083
at 0.70   0.0732
at 0.80   0.0302
at 0.90   0.0104
at 1.00   0.0020

Avg. prec. (non-interpolated)
for all rel. documents
0.1872

Precision:
At   5 docs: 0.4204
At   10 docs: 0.3469
At   15 docs: 0.3075
At   20 docs: 0.2827
At   30 docs: 0.2442
At 100 docs: 0.1341
At 200 docs: 0.0910
At 500 docs: 0.0499
At 1000 docs: 0.0284

R-Precision (prec. after R
(=num_rel) docs. retrieved):
Exact: 0.2251

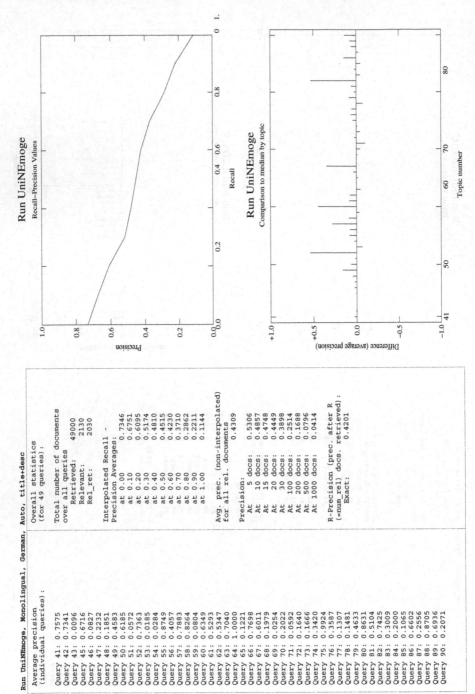

Run UniNEmoge
Recall-Precision Values

Precision / Recall

Run UniNEmoge
Comparison to median by topic

Difference (average precision) / Topic number

Run UniNEmoge, Monolingual, German, Auto, title+desc

Average precision
(individual queries):

Query 41:	0.7575
Query 42:	0.7341
Query 43:	0.0096
Query 45:	0.6716
Query 46:	0.0827
Query 47:	0.2232
Query 48:	0.1851
Query 49:	0.4583
Query 50:	0.6185
Query 51:	0.0572
Query 52:	0.7363
Query 53:	0.0185
Query 54:	0.0284
Query 55:	0.8749
Query 56:	0.4057
Query 57:	0.7883
Query 58:	0.8264
Query 59:	0.0804
Query 60:	0.6349
Query 61:	0.5293
Query 62:	0.5347
Query 63:	0.7040
Query 64:	1.0000
Query 65:	0.1221
Query 66:	0.7698
Query 67:	0.6011
Query 68:	0.1979
Query 69:	0.0254
Query 70:	0.2022
Query 71:	0.0592
Query 72:	0.1640
Query 73:	0.1666
Query 74:	0.3420
Query 75:	0.9924
Query 76:	0.3587
Query 77:	0.1307
Query 78:	0.1481
Query 79:	0.4633
Query 80:	0.8631
Query 81:	0.5104
Query 82:	0.7425
Query 83:	0.3009
Query 84:	0.2000
Query 85:	0.1065
Query 86:	0.6602
Query 87:	0.2556
Query 88:	0.8705
Query 89:	0.6936
Query 90:	0.2071

Overall statistics
(for 49 queries):

Total number of documents
over all queries:
Retrieved:	49000
Relevant:	2130
Rel_ret:	2030

Interpolated Recall -
Precision Averages:
at 0.00	0.7346
at 0.10	0.6751
at 0.20	0.6095
at 0.30	0.5174
at 0.40	0.4810
at 0.50	0.4515
at 0.60	0.4230
at 0.70	0.3710
at 0.80	0.2862
at 0.90	0.2211
at 1.00	0.1144

Avg. prec. (non-interpolated)
for all rel. documents
          0.4309

Precision:
At	5 docs:	0.5306
At	10 docs:	0.4857
At	15 docs:	0.4748
At	20 docs:	0.4449
At	30 docs:	0.3898
At	100 docs:	0.2514
At	200 docs:	0.1688
At	500 docs:	0.0796
At	1000 docs:	0.0414

R-Precision (prec. after R
(=num_rel) docs. retrieved):
      Exact: 0.4201

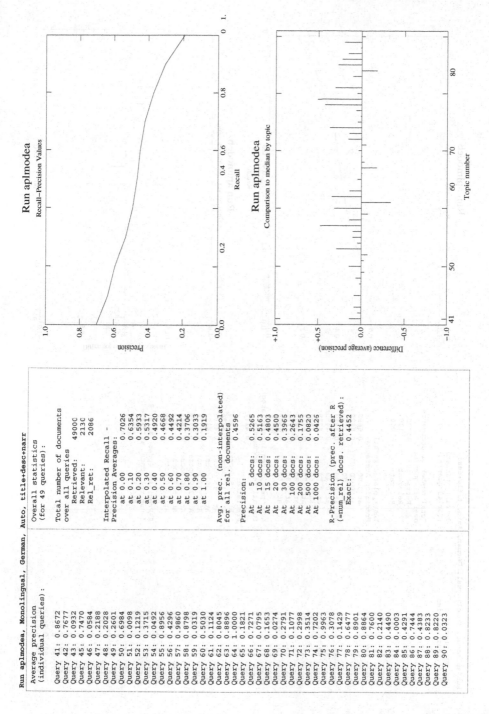

Run aplmodea
Recall–Precision Values

Run aplmodea
Comparison to median by topic

Run aplmodea, Monolingual, German, Auto, title+desc+narr

Average precision
(individual queries):

Query 41:	0.8672		Query 66:	0.7271	
Query 42:	0.7677		Query 67:	0.0795	
Query 43:	0.0932		Query 68:	0.1653	
Query 45:	0.7470		Query 69:	0.0274	
Query 46:	0.0584		Query 70:	0.2791	
Query 47:	0.2188		Query 71:	0.1077	
Query 48:	0.2028		Query 72:	0.2998	
Query 49:	0.2601		Query 73:	0.3514	
Query 50:	0.6984		Query 74:	0.7202	
Query 51:	0.0098		Query 75:	0.9963	
Query 52:	0.1219		Query 76:	0.3078	
Query 53:	0.3715		Query 77:	0.1429	
Query 54:	0.0492		Query 78:	0.6477	
Query 55:	0.8956		Query 79:	0.8901	
Query 56:	0.4296		Query 80:	0.8864	
Query 57:	0.9860		Query 81:	0.7600	
Query 58:	0.8798		Query 82:	0.2140	
Query 59:	0.0319		Query 83:	0.4490	
Query 60:	0.5030		Query 84:	0.0003	
Query 61:	0.1124		Query 85:	0.4291	
Query 62:	0.8045		Query 86:	0.7444	
Query 63:	0.8896		Query 87:	0.4383	
Query 64:	1.0000		Query 88:	0.8233	
Query 65:	0.1821		Query 89:	0.8220	
			Query 90:	0.0323	

Overall statistics
(for 49 queries):

Total number of documents
over all queries
   Retrieved: 49000
   Relevant: 2130
   Rel_ret: 2086

Interpolated Recall -
Precision Averages:
   at 0.00   0.7026
   at 0.10   0.6354
   at 0.20   0.5933
   at 0.30   0.5317
   at 0.40   0.4920
   at 0.50   0.4668
   at 0.60   0.4492
   at 0.70   0.4214
   at 0.80   0.3706
   at 0.90   0.3033
   at 1.00   0.1919

Avg. prec. (non-interpolated)
for all rel. documents
            0.4596

Precision:
  At   5 docs: 0.5265
  At   10 docs: 0.5163
  At   15 docs: 0.4803
  At   20 docs: 0.4500
  At   30 docs: 0.3965
  At 100 docs: 0.2643
  At 200 docs: 0.1755
  At 500 docs: 0.0820
  At 1000 docs: 0.0425

R-Precision (prec. after R
(=num_rel) docs. retrieved):
   Exact: 0.4452

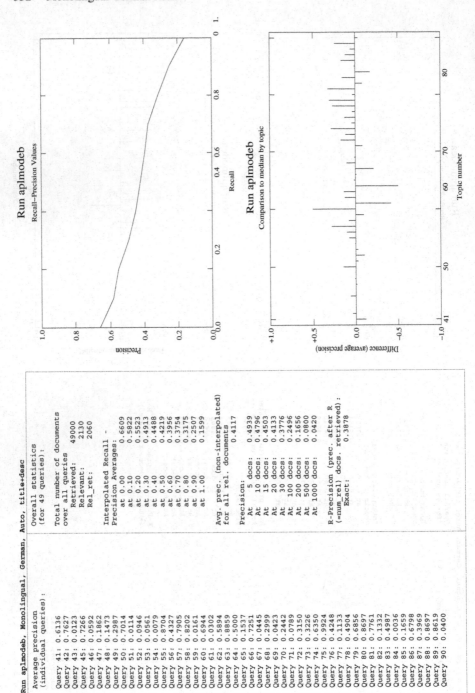

Run aplmodeb

Recall-Precision Values

Run aplmodeb

Comparison to median by topic

Run aplmodeb, Monolingual, German, Auto, title+desc

Average precision
(individual queries):

Query 41:	0.6136	
Query 42:	0.7627	
Query 43:	0.0123	
Query 45:	0.7266	
Query 46:	0.0592	
Query 47:	0.1862	
Query 48:	0.1473	
Query 49:	0.2987	
Query 50:	0.7014	
Query 51:	0.0114	
Query 52:	0.0946	
Query 53:	0.0561	
Query 54:	0.0079	
Query 55:	0.8704	
Query 56:	0.4327	
Query 57:	0.7905	
Query 58:	0.8202	
Query 59:	0.0161	
Query 60:	0.6944	
Query 61:	0.0302	
Query 62:	0.5894	
Query 63:	0.8859	
Query 64:	0.5000	
Query 65:	0.1537	
Query 66:	0.7251	
Query 67:	0.0445	
Query 68:	0.2999	
Query 69:	0.0423	
Query 70:	0.2442	
Query 71:	0.0789	
Query 72:	0.3150	
Query 73:	0.3226	
Query 74:	0.6350	
Query 75:	0.9924	
Query 76:	0.4248	
Query 77:	0.1133	
Query 78:	0.4904	
Query 79:	0.6856	
Query 80:	0.8697	
Query 81:	0.7761	
Query 82:	0.1332	
Query 83:	0.4987	
Query 84:	0.0036	
Query 85:	0.1659	
Query 86:	0.6798	
Query 87:	0.3969	
Query 88:	0.8697	
Query 89:	0.8619	
Query 90:	0.0400	

Overall statistics
(for 49 queries):

Total number of documents
over all queries:
Retrieved: 49000
Relevant: 2130
Rel_ret: 2060

Interpolated Recall -
Precision Averages:

at 0.00	0.6609
at 0.10	0.5822
at 0.20	0.5523
at 0.30	0.4913
at 0.40	0.4488
at 0.50	0.4219
at 0.60	0.3956
at 0.70	0.3754
at 0.80	0.3175
at 0.90	0.2507
at 1.00	0.1599

Avg. prec. (non-interpolated)
for all rel. documents
                 0.4117

Precision:
At 5 docs:	0.4939
At 10 docs:	0.4796
At 15 docs:	0.4503
At 20 docs:	0.4133
At 30 docs:	0.3776
At 100 docs:	0.2496
At 200 docs:	0.1656
At 500 docs:	0.0800
At 1000 docs:	0.0420

R-Precision (prec. after R
(=num_rel) docs. retrieved):
        Exact: 0.3878

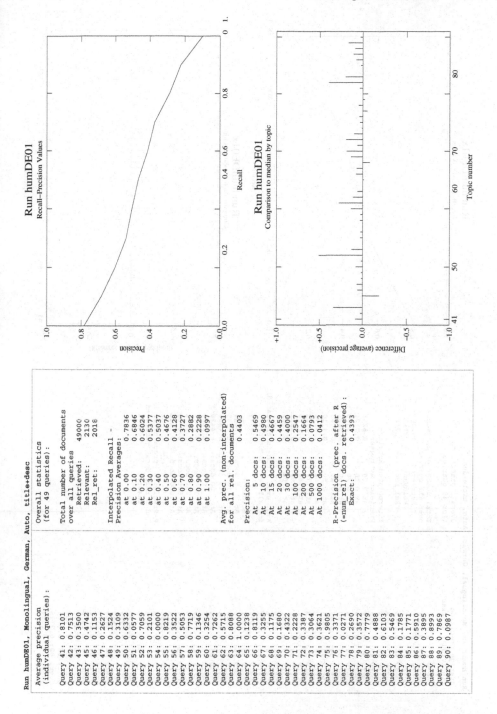

Run humDE01
Recall-Precision Values

Run humDE01
Comparison to median by topic

Run humDE01, Monolingual, German, Auto, title+desc

Average precision
(individual queries):

Query 41:	0.8101
Query 42:	0.7513
Query 43:	0.3500
Query 45:	0.4742
Query 46:	0.1153
Query 47:	0.2627
Query 48:	0.1524
Query 49:	0.3109
Query 50:	0.6332
Query 51:	0.0577
Query 52:	0.7059
Query 53:	0.2101
Query 54:	0.0000
Query 55:	0.8219
Query 56:	0.3522
Query 57:	0.5053
Query 58:	0.7719
Query 59:	0.1346
Query 60:	0.3254
Query 61:	0.7262
Query 62:	0.5715
Query 63:	0.8088
Query 64:	1.0000
Query 65:	0.1238
Query 66:	0.8119
Query 67:	0.3255
Query 68:	0.1175
Query 69:	0.1680
Query 70:	0.4322
Query 71:	0.2228
Query 72:	0.3387
Query 73:	0.3064
Query 74:	0.3621
Query 75:	0.9805
Query 76:	0.3371
Query 77:	0.0271
Query 78:	0.2690
Query 79:	0.3572
Query 80:	0.7779
Query 81:	0.4888
Query 82:	0.6103
Query 83:	0.5469
Query 84:	0.1785
Query 85:	0.1771
Query 86:	0.5910
Query 87:	0.3895
Query 88:	0.8993
Query 89:	0.7869
Query 90:	0.0987

Overall statistics
(for 49 queries):

Total number of documents
over all queries:
Retrieved:	49000
Relevant:	2130
Rel_ret:	2018

Interpolated Recall -
Precision Averages:
at 0.00	0.7836
at 0.10	0.6846
at 0.20	0.6024
at 0.30	0.5377
at 0.40	0.5037
at 0.50	0.4676
at 0.60	0.4128
at 0.70	0.3727
at 0.80	0.2882
at 0.90	0.2228
at 1.00	0.0997

Avg. prec. (non-interpolated)
for all rel. documents
0.4403

Precision:
At 5 docs:	0.5469
At 10 docs:	0.4980
At 15 docs:	0.4667
At 20 docs:	0.4459
At 30 docs:	0.4000
At 100 docs:	0.2547
At 200 docs:	0.1664
At 500 docs:	0.0793
At 1000 docs:	0.0412

R-Precision (prec. after R
(=num_rel) docs. retrieved):
| Exact: | 0.4393 |

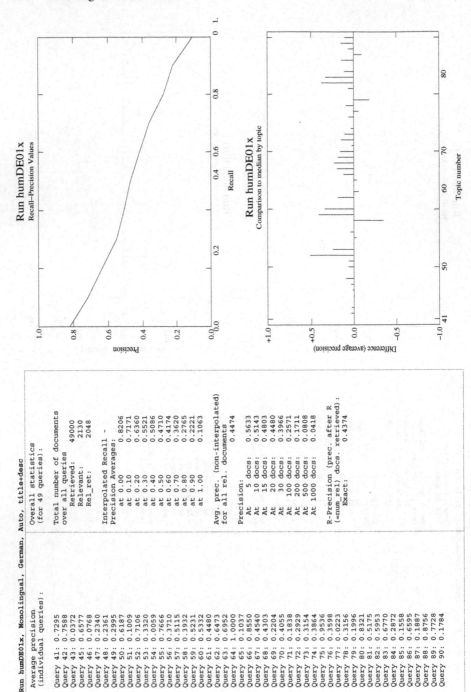

Run humDE01x

Recall-Precision Values

Run humDE01x

Comparison to median by topic

Run humDE01x, Monolingual, German, Auto, title+desc

Average precision
(individual queries):

Query 41:	0.7295
Query 42:	0.7588
Query 43:	0.0372
Query 45:	0.6577
Query 46:	0.0768
Query 47:	0.2340
Query 48:	0.2361
Query 49:	0.2995
Query 50:	0.6187
Query 51:	0.1009
Query 52:	0.7106
Query 53:	0.3320
Query 54:	0.0059
Query 55:	0.7666
Query 56:	0.3710
Query 57:	0.5115
Query 58:	0.3932
Query 59:	0.5231
Query 60:	0.5332
Query 61:	0.4480
Query 62:	0.6473
Query 63:	0.6952
Query 64:	1.0000
Query 65:	0.1037
Query 66:	0.8550
Query 67:	0.4540
Query 68:	0.4303
Query 69:	0.2204
Query 70:	0.4055
Query 71:	0.1838
Query 72:	0.2929
Query 73:	0.3154
Query 74:	0.3864
Query 75:	0.9536
Query 76:	0.3598
Query 77:	0.0223
Query 78:	0.3156
Query 79:	0.1996
Query 80:	0.8321
Query 81:	0.5175
Query 82:	0.5953
Query 83:	0.6770
Query 84:	0.2872
Query 85:	0.1558
Query 86:	0.6595
Query 87:	0.1887
Query 88:	0.8756
Query 89:	0.7728
Query 90:	0.1784

Overall statistics
(for 49 queries):

Total number of documents
over all queries

Retrieved:	49000
Relevant:	2130
Rel_ret:	2048

Interpolated Recall -
Precision Averages:

at 0.00	0.8206
at 0.10	0.7171
at 0.20	0.6360
at 0.30	0.5521
at 0.40	0.5086
at 0.50	0.4710
at 0.60	0.4174
at 0.70	0.3620
at 0.80	0.2765
at 0.90	0.2221
at 1.00	0.1063

Avg. prec. (non-interpolated)
for all rel. documents
                        0.4474

Precision:

At	5 docs:	0.5633
At	10 docs:	0.5143
At	15 docs:	0.4803
At	20 docs:	0.4480
At	30 docs:	0.3966
At	100 docs:	0.2571
At	200 docs:	0.1711
At	500 docs:	0.0808
At	1000 docs:	0.0418

R-Precision (prec. after R
(=num rel) docs. retrieved):
        Exact: 0.4374

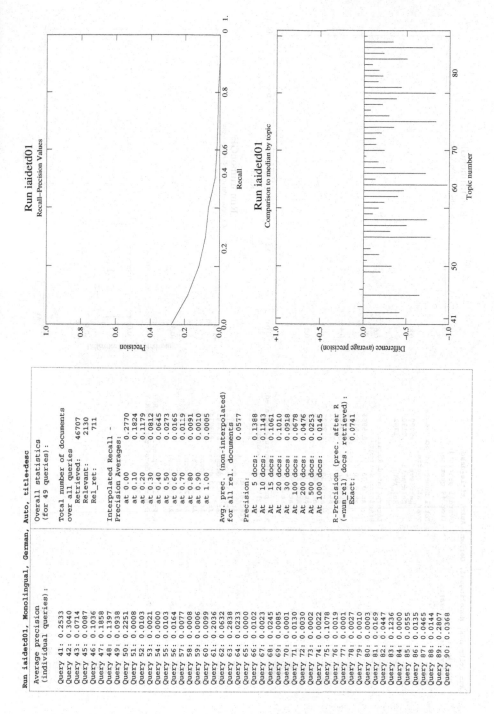

Run iaidetd01

Recall–Precision Values

Recall

Precision

Run iaidetd01

Comparison to median by topic

Topic number

Difference (average precision)

Run iaidetd01, Monolingual, German, Auto, title+desc

Average precision
(individual queries):

Overall statistics
(for 49 queries):

Total number of documents
over all queries:
    Retrieved: 46707
    Relevant: 2130
    Rel_ret: 711

Interpolated Recall -
Precision Averages:
    at 0.00   0.2770
    at 0.10   0.1824
    at 0.20   0.1179
    at 0.30   0.0812
    at 0.40   0.0645
    at 0.50   0.0273
    at 0.60   0.0165
    at 0.70   0.0119
    at 0.80   0.0091
    at 0.90   0.0010
    at 1.00   0.0005

Avg. prec. (non-interpolated)
for all rel. documents
                   0.0577

Precision:
    At   5 docs: 0.1388
    At 10 docs: 0.1143
    At 15 docs: 0.1061
    At 20 docs: 0.1010
    At 30 docs: 0.0918
    At 100 docs: 0.0678
    At 200 docs: 0.0476
    At 500 docs: 0.0253
    At 1000 docs: 0.0145

R-Precision (prec. after R
(=num_rel) docs. retrieved):
    Exact: 0.0741

Query 41: 0.2533
Query 42: 0.3040
Query 43: 0.0714
Query 45: 0.0087
Query 46: 0.1036
Query 47: 0.1858
Query 48: 0.1397
Query 49: 0.0938
Query 50: 0.2251
Query 51: 0.0008
Query 52: 0.0103
Query 53: 0.0021
Query 54: 0.0000
Query 55: 0.0103
Query 56: 0.0164
Query 57: 0.0077
Query 58: 0.0008
Query 59: 0.0006
Query 60: 0.0099
Query 61: 0.2036
Query 62: 0.0632
Query 63: 0.2838
Query 64: 0.0233
Query 65: 0.0000
Query 66: 0.0102
Query 67: 0.0023
Query 68: 0.0245
Query 69: 0.0085
Query 70: 0.0001
Query 71: 0.0130
Query 72: 0.0030
Query 73: 0.0002
Query 74: 0.0022
Query 75: 0.1078
Query 76: 0.0019
Query 77: 0.0001
Query 78: 0.0027
Query 79: 0.0010
Query 80: 0.0003
Query 81: 0.0169
Query 82: 0.0447
Query 83: 0.1236
Query 84: 0.0000
Query 85: 0.0555
Query 86: 0.0135
Query 87: 0.0465
Query 88: 0.0144
Query 89: 0.2807
Query 90: 0.0368

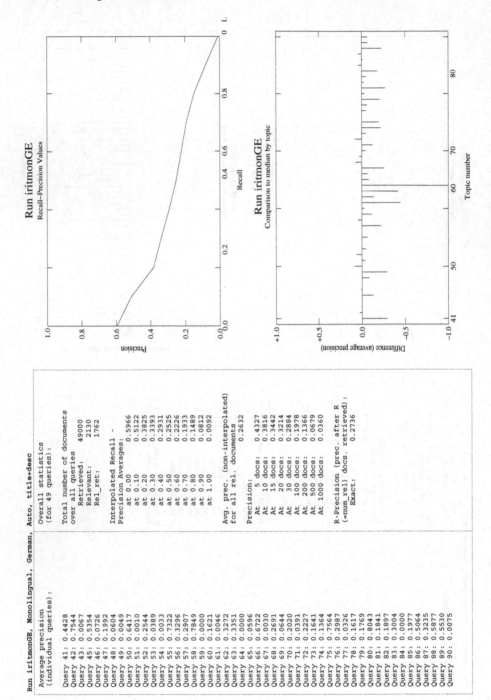

Run iritmonGE
Recall-Precision Values

Run iritmonGE
Comparison to median by topic

Run iritmonGE, Monolingual, German, Auto, title+desc

Average precision
(individual queries):

Query 41:	0.4428
Query 42:	0.7544
Query 43:	0.0067
Query 45:	0.5354
Query 46:	0.0726
Query 47:	0.1992
Query 48:	0.0604
Query 49:	0.0049
Query 50:	0.6417
Query 51:	0.0010
Query 52:	0.2544
Query 53:	0.0389
Query 54:	0.0033
Query 55:	0.7322
Query 56:	0.3296
Query 57:	0.2907
Query 58:	0.7849
Query 59:	0.0000
Query 60:	0.1621
Query 61:	0.0046
Query 62:	0.3272
Query 63:	0.3351
Query 64:	0.0000
Query 65:	0.0596
Query 66:	0.6722
Query 67:	0.0030
Query 68:	0.2691
Query 69:	0.0644
Query 70:	0.2020
Query 71:	0.0391
Query 72:	0.2227
Query 73:	0.1641
Query 74:	0.1364
Query 75:	0.7564
Query 76:	0.2987
Query 77:	0.0326
Query 78:	0.1617
Query 79:	0.1769
Query 80:	0.8043
Query 81:	0.1841
Query 82:	0.1897
Query 83:	0.3004
Query 84:	0.0000
Query 85:	0.1977
Query 86:	0.5064
Query 87:	0.3235
Query 88:	0.5877
Query 89:	0.5530
Query 90:	0.0075

Overall statistics
(for 49 queries):

Total number of documents
over all queries:
  Retrieved: 49000
  Relevant: 2130
  Rel_ret: 1762

Interpolated Recall -
Precision Averages:
  at 0.00   0.5966
  at 0.10   0.5122
  at 0.20   0.3825
  at 0.30   0.3393
  at 0.40   0.2931
  at 0.50   0.2525
  at 0.60   0.2226
  at 0.70   0.1933
  at 0.80   0.1489
  at 0.90   0.0812
  at 1.00   0.0092

Avg. prec. (non-interpolated)
for all rel. documents
                    0.2632

Precision:
  At   5 docs: 0.4327
  At   10 docs: 0.3816
  At   15 docs: 0.3442
  At   20 docs: 0.3214
  At   30 docs: 0.2884
  At 100 docs: 0.1978
  At 200 docs: 0.1366
  At 500 docs: 0.0679
  At 1000 docs: 0.0360

R-Precision (prec. after R
(=num_rel) docs. retrieved):
  Exact: 0.2736

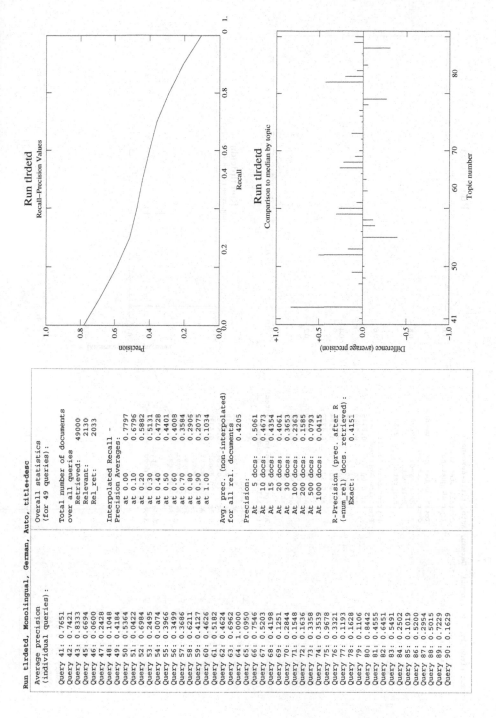

Run tlrdetd
Recall–Precision Values

Run tlrdetd
Comparison to median by topic

Run tlrdetd, Monolingual, German, Auto, title+desc

Average precision (individual queries):		Overall statistics (for 49 queries):
Query 41: 0.7651		Total number of documents over all queries:
Query 42: 0.7421		Retrieved: 49000
Query 43: 0.8333		Relevant: 2130
Query 45: 0.6694		Rel_ret: 2033
Query 46: 0.0600		
Query 47: 0.2428		Interpolated Recall –
Query 48: 0.1048		Precision Averages:
Query 49: 0.4184		at 0.00 0.7797
Query 50: 0.5364		at 0.10 0.6796
Query 51: 0.0422		at 0.20 0.5882
Query 52: 0.6984		at 0.30 0.5131
Query 53: 0.2495		at 0.40 0.4728
Query 54: 0.0074		at 0.50 0.4401
Query 55: 0.3966		at 0.60 0.4008
Query 56: 0.3499		at 0.70 0.3584
Query 57: 0.3686		at 0.80 0.2905
Query 58: 0.6211		at 0.90 0.2075
Query 59: 0.4127		at 1.00 0.1034
Query 60: 0.4626		
Query 61: 0.5182		Avg. prec. (non-interpolated)
Query 62: 0.4624		for all rel. documents
Query 63: 0.6962		0.4205
Query 64: 1.0000		
Query 65: 0.0950		Precision:
Query 66: 0.7546		At 5 docs: 0.5061
Query 67: 0.5203		At 10 docs: 0.4673
Query 68: 0.4198		At 15 docs: 0.4354
Query 69: 0.1251		At 20 docs: 0.4061
Query 70: 0.2844		At 30 docs: 0.3653
Query 71: 0.1548		At 100 docs: 0.2363
Query 72: 0.1636		At 200 docs: 0.1585
Query 73: 0.3358		At 500 docs: 0.0793
Query 74: 0.3539		At 1000 docs: 0.0415
Query 75: 0.9678		
Query 76: 0.3321		R-Precision (prec. after R
Query 77: 0.1193		(=num_rel) docs. retrieved):
Query 78: 0.1628		Exact: 0.4151
Query 79: 0.1106		
Query 80: 0.8442		
Query 81: 0.4555		
Query 82: 0.6451		
Query 83: 0.5491		
Query 84: 0.2502		
Query 85: 0.1019		
Query 86: 0.5200		
Query 87: 0.2954		
Query 88: 0.5015		
Query 89: 0.7229		
Query 90: 0.1629		

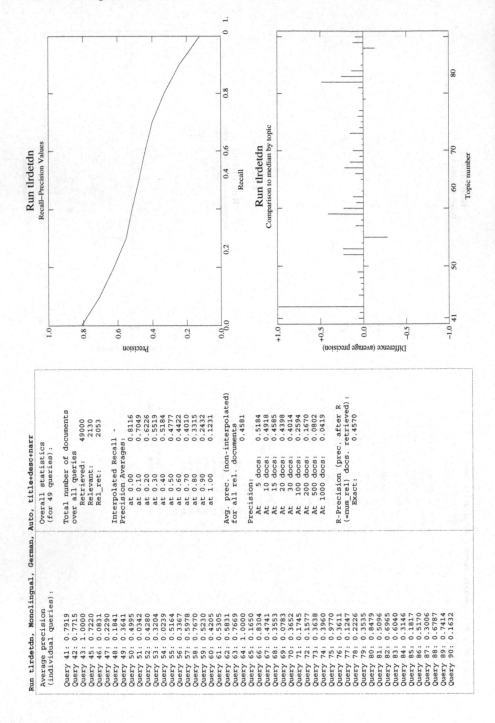

Run tlrdetdn
Recall–Precision Values

Precision

Recall

Run tlrdetdn
Comparison to median by topic

Difference (average precision)

Topic number

Run tlrdetdn, Monolingual, German, Auto, title+desc+narr

Average precision
(individual queries):

Query 41:	0.7919
Query 42:	0.7715
Query 43:	1.0000
Query 45:	0.7220
Query 46:	0.0831
Query 47:	0.2290
Query 48:	0.1841
Query 49:	0.3641
Query 50:	0.4995
Query 51:	0.0342
Query 52:	0.4280
Query 53:	0.3204
Query 54:	0.0239
Query 55:	0.5164
Query 56:	0.3367
Query 57:	0.5978
Query 58:	0.7670
Query 59:	0.5230
Query 60:	0.4205
Query 61:	0.5305
Query 62:	0.5831
Query 63:	0.7669
Query 64:	1.0000
Query 65:	0.1650
Query 66:	0.8304
Query 67:	0.4741
Query 68:	0.3553
Query 69:	0.0783
Query 70:	0.3652
Query 71:	0.1745
Query 72:	0.1577
Query 73:	0.3638
Query 74:	0.3960
Query 75:	0.9770
Query 76:	0.3611
Query 77:	0.1247
Query 78:	0.2226
Query 79:	0.3535
Query 80:	0.8479
Query 81:	0.5096
Query 82:	0.6965
Query 83:	0.6040
Query 84:	0.3146
Query 85:	0.1817
Query 86:	0.5170
Query 87:	0.3006
Query 88:	0.6787
Query 89:	0.7414
Query 90:	0.1632

Overall statistics
(for 49 queries):

Total number of documents
over all queries
   Retrieved: 49000
   Relevant: 2130
   Rel_ret: 2053

Interpolated Recall -
Precision Averages:
   at 0.00   0.8116
   at 0.10   0.7049
   at 0.20   0.6226
   at 0.30   0.5519
   at 0.40   0.5184
   at 0.50   0.4777
   at 0.60   0.4422
   at 0.70   0.4010
   at 0.80   0.3315
   at 0.90   0.2432
   at 1.00   0.1231

Avg. prec. (non-interpolated)
for all rel. documents
          0.4581

Precision:
  At   5 docs: 0.5184
  At 10 docs: 0.4918
  At 15 docs: 0.4585
  At 20 docs: 0.4398
  At 30 docs: 0.4014
  At 100 docs: 0.2594
  At 200 docs: 0.1670
  At 500 docs: 0.0802
  At 1000 docs: 0.0419

R-Precision (prec. after R
(=num rel) docs. retrieved):
   Exact: 0.4570

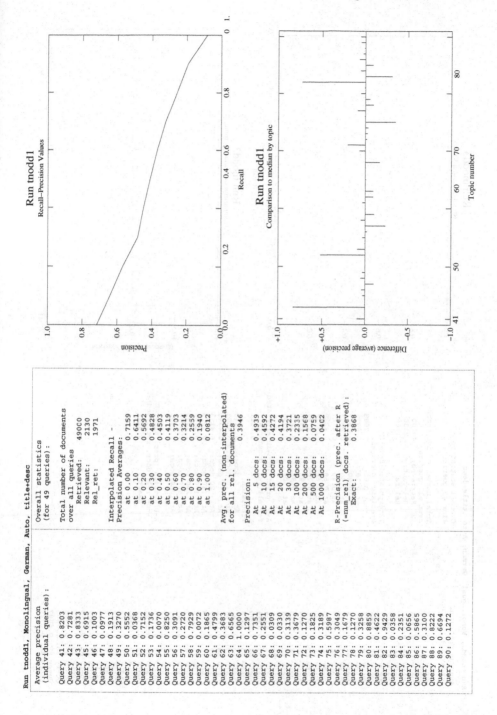

Run tnodd1, Monolingual, German, Auto, title+desc

Average precision
(individual queries):

Query 41:	0.8203
Query 42:	0.7281
Query 43:	0.8333
Query 45:	0.6915
Query 46:	0.1003
Query 47:	0.0977
Query 48:	0.1913
Query 49:	0.3270
Query 50:	0.5552
Query 51:	0.0368
Query 52:	0.7152
Query 53:	0.1736
Query 54:	0.0070
Query 55:	0.8250
Query 56:	0.3091
Query 57:	0.2720
Query 58:	0.7929
Query 59:	0.0072
Query 61:	0.1865
Query 62:	0.4799
Query 63:	0.3683
Query 64:	1.0000
Query 65:	0.6565
Query 66:	0.1297
Query 67:	0.7351
Query 68:	0.2551
Query 69:	0.0309
Query 70:	0.0330
Query 71:	0.3139
Query 72:	0.3679
Query 73:	0.1270
Query 74:	0.1825
Query 75:	0.3189
Query 76:	0.5987
Query 77:	0.3049
Query 78:	0.1679
Query 79:	0.1270
Query 80:	0.3258
Query 81:	0.8859
Query 82:	0.4622
Query 83:	0.9429
Query 84:	0.0358
Query 85:	0.2351
Query 86:	0.0656
Query 87:	0.5865
Query 88:	0.3100
Query 89:	0.8222
Query 90:	0.6694
	0.1272

Overall statistics
(for 49 queries):

Total number of documents
over all queries
Retrieved:	49000
Relevant:	2130
Rel_ret:	1971

Interpolated Recall -
Precision Averages:
at 0.00	0.7159
at 0.10	0.6411
at 0.20	0.5692
at 0.30	0.4828
at 0.40	0.4503
at 0.50	0.4119
at 0.60	0.3703
at 0.70	0.3214
at 0.80	0.2559
at 0.90	0.1940
at 1.00	0.0812

Avg. prec. (non-interpolated)
for all rel. documents
0.3946

Precision:
At 5 docs:	0.4939
At 10 docs:	0.4592
At 15 docs:	0.4272
At 20 docs:	0.4194
At 30 docs:	0.3721
At 100 docs:	0.2335
At 200 docs:	0.1568
At 500 docs:	0.0759
At 1000 docs:	0.0402

R-Precision (prec. after R
(=num_rel) docs. retrieved):
Exact: 0.3868

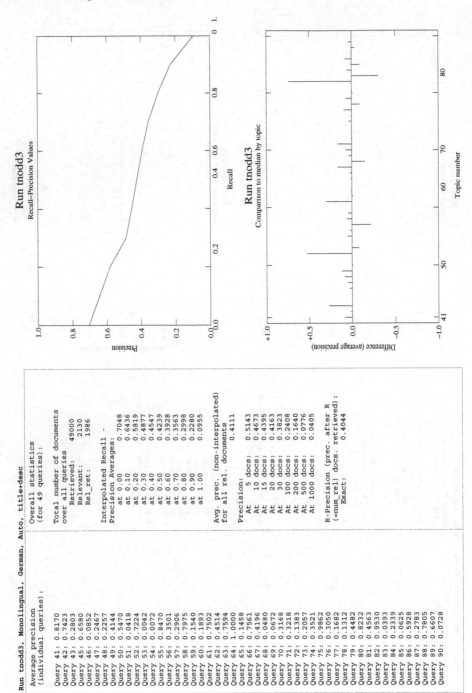

Run tnodd3
Recall–Precision Values

Recall

Precision

Run tnodd3
Comparison to median by topic

Difference (average precision)

Topic number

Run tnodd3, Monolingual, German, Auto, title+desc

Average precision
(individual queries):

Query 41:	0.8170
Query 42:	0.7423
Query 43:	0.2803
Query 45:	0.6580
Query 46:	0.0852
Query 47:	0.2467
Query 48:	0.2257
Query 49:	0.4144
Query 50:	0.5470
Query 51:	0.0418
Query 52:	0.7224
Query 53:	0.0042
Query 54:	0.0072
Query 55:	0.8470
Query 56:	0.3501
Query 57:	0.2906
Query 58:	0.7975
Query 59:	0.1540
Query 60:	0.1893
Query 61:	0.7502
Query 62:	0.4514
Query 63:	0.7594
Query 64:	1.0000
Query 65:	0.1458
Query 66:	0.7561
Query 67:	0.4196
Query 68:	0.0480
Query 69:	0.0672
Query 70:	0.3168
Query 71:	0.3218
Query 72:	0.1383
Query 73:	0.2057
Query 74:	0.3521
Query 75:	0.9862
Query 76:	0.3050
Query 77:	0.1682
Query 78:	0.1312
Query 79:	0.4482
Query 80:	0.8232
Query 81:	0.4563
Query 82:	0.9530
Query 83:	0.0393
Query 84:	0.2339
Query 85:	0.0625
Query 86:	0.5928
Query 87:	0.2783
Query 88:	0.7805
Query 89:	0.6607
Query 90:	0.0728

Overall statistics
(for 49 queries):

Total number of documents
over all queries:
Retrieved: 49000
Relevant: 2130
Rel_ret: 1986

Interpolated Recall –
Precision Averages:

at 0.00	0.7048
at 0.10	0.6436
at 0.20	0.5819
at 0.30	0.4877
at 0.40	0.4547
at 0.50	0.4239
at 0.60	0.3928
at 0.70	0.3563
at 0.80	0.2998
at 0.90	0.2280
at 1.00	0.0955

Avg. prec. (non-interpolated)
for all rel. documents
                 0.4111

Precision:
At	5 docs:	0.5143
At	10 docs:	0.4673
At	15 docs:	0.4395
At	20 docs:	0.4163
At	30 docs:	0.3823
At	100 docs:	0.2408
At	200 docs:	0.1640
At	500 docs:	0.0776
At	1000 docs:	0.0405

R-Precision (prec. after R
(=num_rel) docs. retrieved):
    Exact: 0.4044

Run AmsItM

Recall–Precision Values

Run AmsItM

Comparison to median by topic

Run AmsItM, Monolingual, Italian, Auto, title+desc

Average precision
(individual queries):

Query 41:	0.9240
Query 42:	0.4102
Query 44:	0.0507
Query 45:	0.2558
Query 46:	0.3152
Query 47:	0.2070
Query 48:	0.1244
Query 49:	0.3175
Query 50:	0.7999
Query 51:	0.0801
Query 53:	0.4517
Query 54:	0.0258
Query 55:	0.6991
Query 56:	0.5609
Query 57:	0.2435
Query 58:	0.6384
Query 59:	0.1614
Query 60:	0.8454
Query 61:	0.5769
Query 62:	0.5779
Query 63:	0.8291
Query 65:	0.3247
Query 66:	0.6687
Query 67:	0.4663
Query 68:	0.8301
Query 69:	0.1270
Query 70:	0.2275
Query 71:	0.0394
Query 72:	0.4645
Query 73:	0.1222
Query 74:	0.3939
Query 75:	1.0000
Query 76:	0.2626
Query 77:	0.0734
Query 78:	0.1666
Query 79:	0.6434
Query 80:	0.7894
Query 81:	0.4723
Query 82:	0.6401
Query 83:	0.5873
Query 84:	0.2042
Query 85:	0.5999
Query 86:	0.3395
Query 87:	0.6044
Query 88:	0.9125
Query 89:	0.9660
Query 90:	0.0590

Overall statistics
(for 47 queries):

Total number of documents
over all queries
```
Retrieved:   47000
Relevant:     1246
Rel_ret:      1199
```

Interpolated Recall -
Precision Averages:
```
at 0.00   0.7713
at 0.10   0.6978
at 0.20   0.6119
at 0.30   0.5562
at 0.40   0.5012
at 0.50   0.4624
at 0.60   0.4131
at 0.70   0.3648
at 0.80   0.3083
at 0.90   0.2493
at 1.00   0.1755
```

Avg. prec. (non-interpolated)
for all rel. documents
```
          0.4485
```

Precision:
```
At    5 docs:   0.5660
At   10 docs:   0.5170
At   15 docs:   0.4638
At   20 docs:   0.4330
At   30 docs:   0.3695
At  100 docs:   0.1970
At  200 docs:   0.1147
At  500 docs:   0.0502
At 1000 docs:   0.0255
```

R-Precision (prec. after R
(=num_rel) docs. retrieved):
```
Exact:   0.4211
```

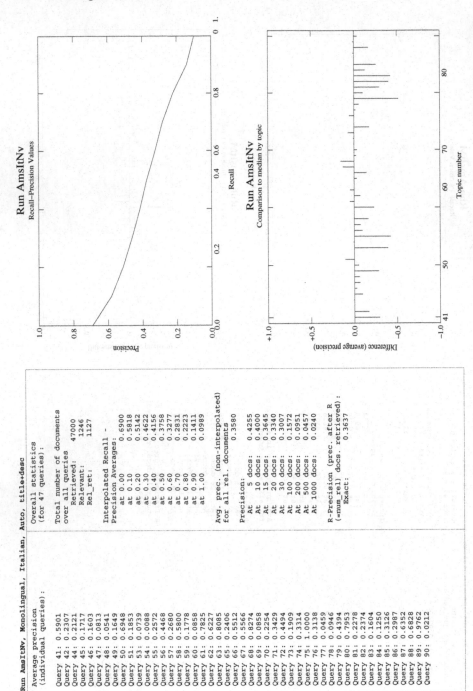

Run AmsItNv
Recall-Precision Values

Run AmsItNv
Comparison to median by topic

Run AmsItNv, Monolingual, Italian, Auto, title+desc

Average precision
(individual queries):

Query 41: 0.5901
Query 42: 0.2307
Query 44: 0.2121
Query 45: 0.1717
Query 46: 0.1603
Query 47: 0.0813
Query 48: 0.0541
Query 49: 0.1649
Query 50: 0.6948
Query 51: 0.1853
Query 53: 0.0739
Query 54: 0.0088
Query 55: 0.2572
Query 56: 0.4468
Query 57: 0.2680
Query 58: 0.5800
Query 59: 0.1778
Query 60: 0.0858
Query 61: 0.7825
Query 62: 0.6227
Query 63: 0.8085
Query 65: 0.2406
Query 66: 0.5512
Query 67: 0.5566
Query 68: 0.8274
Query 69: 0.0858
Query 70: 0.2254
Query 71: 0.3429
Query 72: 0.4494
Query 73: 0.1909
Query 74: 0.3314
Query 75: 1.0000
Query 76: 0.3138
Query 77: 0.0459
Query 78: 0.0946
Query 79: 0.4394
Query 80: 0.7953
Query 81: 0.2278
Query 82: 0.2374
Query 83: 0.1604
Query 84: 0.1250
Query 85: 0.3126
Query 86: 0.2987
Query 87: 0.6352
Query 88: 0.6828
Query 89: 0.9762
Query 90: 0.0212

Overall statistics
(for 47 queries):

Total number of documents
over all queries:
Retrieved: 47000
Relevant: 1246
Rel_ret: 1127

Interpolated Recall -
Precision Averages:
  at 0.00:   0.6900
  at 0.10:   0.5818
  at 0.20:   0.5142
  at 0.30:   0.4622
  at 0.40:   0.4156
  at 0.50:   0.3758
  at 0.60:   0.3277
  at 0.70:   0.2831
  at 0.80:   0.2223
  at 0.90:   0.1411
  at 1.00:   0.0989

Avg. prec. (non-interpolated)
for all rel. documents
            0.3580

Precision:
  At   5 docs: 0.4255
  At   10 docs: 0.4000
  At   15 docs: 0.3645
  At   20 docs: 0.3340
  At   30 docs: 0.3007
  At 100 docs: 0.1572
  At 200 docs: 0.0951
  At 500 docs: 0.0457
  At 1000 docs: 0.0240

R-Precision (prec. after R
(=num_rel) docs. retrieved):
  Exact: 0.3637

Run AmsItT
Recall-Precision Values

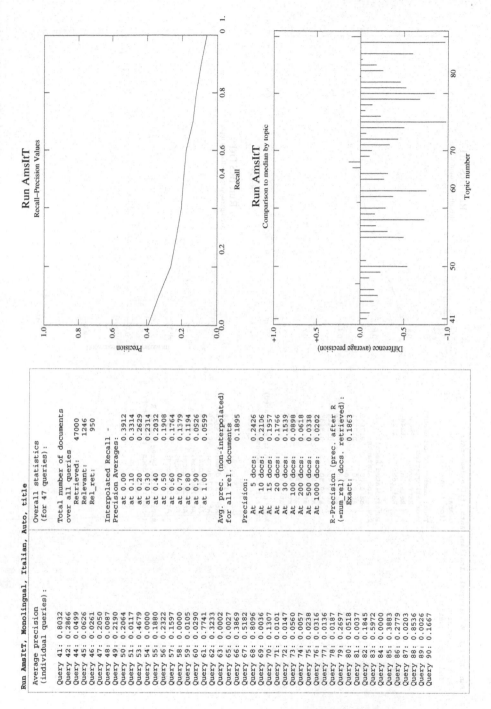

Run AmsItT
Comparison to median by topic

Run AmsItT, Monolingual, Italian, Auto, title

Average precision
(individual queries):

Query 41:	0.8032
Query 42:	0.2866
Query 44:	0.0499
Query 45:	0.0626
Query 46:	0.0261
Query 47:	0.2050
Query 48:	0.0087
Query 49:	0.2190
Query 50:	0.2064
Query 51:	0.0117
Query 53:	0.4679
Query 54:	0.0000
Query 55:	0.1880
Query 56:	0.2322
Query 57:	0.1597
Query 58:	0.0000
Query 59:	0.0105
Query 60:	0.0290
Query 61:	0.7741
Query 62:	0.3233
Query 63:	0.0002
Query 65:	0.0027
Query 66:	0.3869
Query 67:	0.5182
Query 68:	0.8096
Query 69:	0.0036
Query 70:	0.1307
Query 71:	0.0101
Query 72:	0.0147
Query 73:	0.0560
Query 74:	0.0057
Query 75:	0.0238
Query 76:	0.0316
Query 77:	0.0136
Query 78:	0.0187
Query 79:	0.2697
Query 80:	0.0518
Query 81:	0.0037
Query 82:	0.1845
Query 83:	0.5972
Query 84:	0.0000
Query 85:	0.3883
Query 86:	0.2779
Query 87:	0.0203
Query 88:	0.8536
Query 89:	0.0026
Query 90:	0.1667

Overall statistics
(for 47 queries):

Total number of documents
over all queries:
Retrieved:	47000
Relevant:	1246
Rel_ret:	950

Interpolated Recall -
Precision Averages:
at 0.00	0.3912
at 0.10	0.3314
at 0.20	0.2629
at 0.30	0.2314
at 0.40	0.2032
at 0.50	0.1908
at 0.60	0.1764
at 0.70	0.1379
at 0.80	0.1194
at 0.90	0.0926
at 1.00	0.0599

Avg. prec. (non-interpolated)
for all rel. documents
0.1895

Precision:
At 5 docs:	0.2426
At 10 docs:	0.2106
At 15 docs:	0.1957
At 20 docs:	0.1766
At 30 docs:	0.1539
At 100 docs:	0.0898
At 200 docs:	0.0618
At 500 docs:	0.0338
At 1000 docs:	0.0202

R-Precision (prec. after R
(=num_rel) docs. retrieved):
Exact: 0.1863

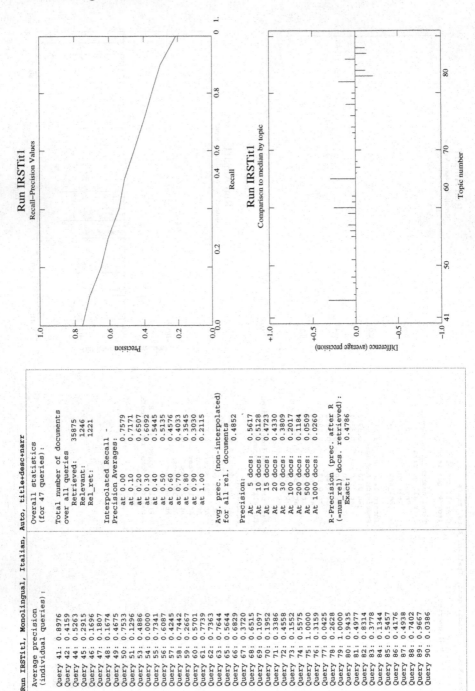

Run IRSTit1
Recall–Precision Values

Run IRSTit1
Comparison to median by topic

Run IRSTit1, Monolingual, Italian, Auto, title+desc+narr

Average precision
(individual queries):

Query 41:	0.8976
Query 42:	0.4159
Query 44:	0.5263
Query 45:	0.2915
Query 46:	0.1696
Query 47:	0.1807
Query 48:	0.1674
Query 49:	0.4675
Query 50:	0.7533
Query 51:	0.1296
Query 53:	0.4886
Query 54:	0.0000
Query 55:	0.7341
Query 56:	0.6087
Query 57:	0.4245
Query 58:	0.7442
Query 59:	0.2667
Query 60:	0.5701
Query 61:	0.7739
Query 62:	0.7363
Query 63:	0.7644
Query 65:	0.5644
Query 66:	0.6829
Query 67:	0.3720
Query 68:	0.6515
Query 69:	0.1097
Query 70:	0.1952
Query 71:	0.3386
Query 72:	0.4558
Query 73:	0.1552
Query 74:	0.5575
Query 75:	1.0000
Query 76:	0.3159
Query 77:	0.0425
Query 78:	0.2628
Query 79:	1.0000
Query 80:	0.9435
Query 81:	0.4977
Query 82:	0.8314
Query 83:	0.3778
Query 84:	0.1344
Query 85:	0.5457
Query 86:	0.4176
Query 87:	0.4938
Query 88:	0.7402
Query 89:	0.9667
Query 90:	0.0386

Overall statistics
(for 47 queries):

Total number of documents
over all queries
Retrieved: 35875
Relevant: 1246
Rel_ret: 1221

Interpolated Recall -
Precision Averages:
   at 0.00   0.7579
   at 0.10   0.7171
   at 0.20   0.6507
   at 0.30   0.6092
   at 0.40   0.5445
   at 0.50   0.5135
   at 0.60   0.4576
   at 0.70   0.4033
   at 0.80   0.3545
   at 0.90   0.3030
   at 1.00   0.2115

Avg. prec. (non-interpolated)
for all rel. documents
              0.4852

Precision:
   At   5 docs: 0.5617
   At   10 docs: 0.5128
   At   15 docs: 0.4723
   At   20 docs: 0.4330
   At   30 docs: 0.3809
   At 100 docs: 0.2017
   At 200 docs: 0.1184
   At 500 docs: 0.0509
   At 1000 docs: 0.0260

R-Precision (prec. after R
(=num_rel) docs. retrieved):
   Exact: 0.4786

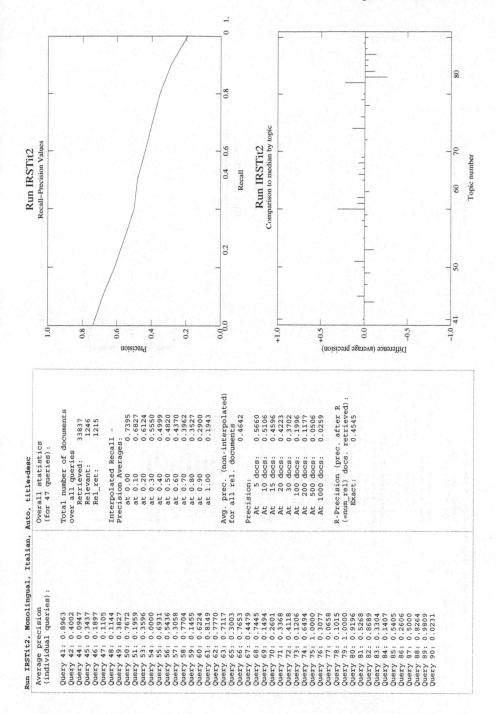

Run IRSTit2, Monolingual, Italian, Auto, title+desc

Average precision
(individual queries):

Query 41:	0.8963
Query 42:	0.4002
Query 44:	0.0947
Query 45:	0.3437
Query 46:	0.1897
Query 47:	0.1105
Query 48:	0.1144
Query 49:	0.3827
Query 50:	0.7672
Query 51:	0.1959
Query 53:	0.3596
Query 54:	0.0000
Query 55:	0.6931
Query 56:	0.5436
Query 57:	0.3058
Query 58:	0.7704
Query 59:	0.1455
Query 60:	0.6224
Query 61:	0.8149
Query 62:	0.7770
Query 63:	0.7117
Query 65:	0.3003
Query 66:	0.7653
Query 67:	0.4479
Query 68:	0.7445
Query 69:	0.1494
Query 70:	0.2601
Query 71:	0.3368
Query 72:	0.4118
Query 73:	0.1206
Query 74:	0.6494
Query 75:	1.0000
Query 76:	0.3077
Query 77:	0.0658
Query 78:	0.1015
Query 79:	1.0000
Query 80:	0.9196
Query 81:	0.5268
Query 82:	0.8689
Query 83:	0.3304
Query 84:	0.1407
Query 85:	0.5405
Query 86:	0.2606
Query 87:	0.5000
Query 88:	0.8264
Query 89:	0.9809
Query 90:	0.0231

Overall statistics
(for 47 queries):

Total number of documents
over all queries:

Retrieved:	33837
Relevant:	1246
Rel_ret:	1215

Interpolated Recall -
Precision Averages:

at 0.00	0.7395
at 0.10	0.6827
at 0.20	0.6124
at 0.30	0.5550
at 0.40	0.4999
at 0.50	0.4820
at 0.60	0.4370
at 0.70	0.3962
at 0.80	0.3527
at 0.90	0.2900
at 1.00	0.1943

Avg. prec. (non-interpolated)
for all rel. documents
                    0.4642

Precision:

At 5 docs:	0.5660
At 10 docs:	0.5106
At 15 docs:	0.4596
At 20 docs:	0.4223
At 30 docs:	0.3702
At 100 docs:	0.1996
At 200 docs:	0.1177
At 500 docs:	0.0506
At 1000 docs:	0.0259

R-Precision (prec. after R
(=num_rel) docs. retrieved):
    Exact: 0.4545

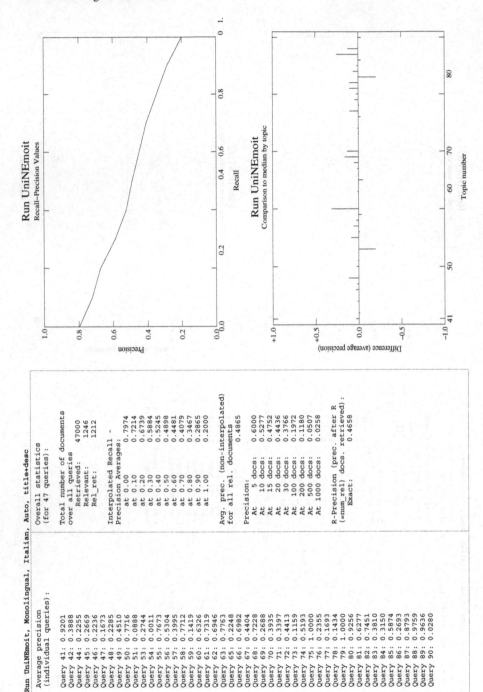

Run UniNEmoit
Recall–Precision Values

Run UniNEmoit
Comparison to median by topic

Run UniNEmoit, Monolingual, Italian, Auto, title+desc

Average precision
(individual queries):

Query 41:	0.9201
Query 42:	0.3888
Query 44:	0.2255
Query 45:	0.2669
Query 46:	0.2236
Query 47:	0.1673
Query 48:	0.2285
Query 49:	0.4510
Query 50:	0.7716
Query 51:	0.0888
Query 53:	0.2744
Query 54:	0.0011
Query 55:	0.7673
Query 56:	0.5304
Query 57:	0.3995
Query 58:	0.7712
Query 59:	0.1419
Query 60:	0.6326
Query 61:	0.7319
Query 62:	0.6946
Query 63:	0.7763
Query 65:	0.2248
Query 66:	0.6982
Query 67:	0.4404
Query 68:	0.7228
Query 69:	0.2688
Query 70:	0.3935
Query 71:	0.3397
Query 72:	0.4413
Query 73:	0.1159
Query 74:	0.5193
Query 75:	1.0000
Query 76:	0.2355
Query 77:	0.1693
Query 78:	0.1434
Query 79:	1.0000
Query 80:	0.9256
Query 81:	0.6277
Query 82:	0.7451
Query 83:	0.3810
Query 84:	0.3150
Query 85:	0.5874
Query 86:	0.2693
Query 87:	0.8793
Query 88:	0.9759
Query 89:	0.9636
Query 90:	0.0280

Overall statistics
(for 47 queries):

Total number of documents
over all queries
Retrieved:	47000
Relevant:	1246
Rel_ret:	1212

Interpolated Recall -
Precision Averages:
at 0.00	0.7974
at 0.10	0.7214
at 0.20	0.6739
at 0.30	0.5884
at 0.40	0.5245
at 0.50	0.4898
at 0.60	0.4481
at 0.70	0.4079
at 0.80	0.3467
at 0.90	0.2865
at 1.00	0.2000

Avg. prec. (non-interpolated)
for all rel. documents
0.4865

Precision:
At	5 docs:	0.6000
At	10 docs:	0.5277
At	15 docs:	0.4752
At	20 docs:	0.4436
At	30 docs:	0.3766
At	100 docs:	0.1972
At	200 docs:	0.1180
At	500 docs:	0.0507
At	1000 docs:	0.0258

R-Precision (prec. after R
(=num_rel) docs. retrieved):
Exact: 0.4658

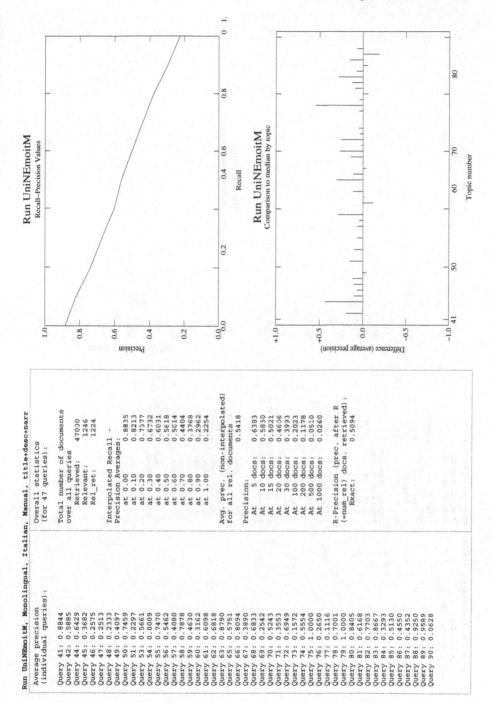

Run UniNEmoitM
Recall–Precision Values

Run UniNEmoitM
Comparison to median by topic

Run UniNEmoitM, Monolingual, Italian, Manual, title+desc+narr

Average precision
(individual queries):

		Overall statistics
		(for 47 queries):

Query 41:	0.8844
Query 42:	0.5885
Query 44:	0.6429
Query 45:	0.3682
Query 46:	0.2575
Query 47:	0.2513
Query 48:	0.2333
Query 49:	0.4097
Query 50:	0.7459
Query 51:	0.2297
Query 53:	0.5661
Query 54:	0.0009
Query 55:	0.7470
Query 56:	0.5462
Query 57:	0.4080
Query 58:	0.7878
Query 59:	0.4630
Query 60:	0.3162
Query 61:	0.6098
Query 62:	0.6618
Query 63:	0.8790
Query 65:	0.5751
Query 66:	0.8094
Query 67:	0.3890
Query 68:	0.6833
Query 69:	0.2542
Query 70:	0.5243
Query 71:	0.3553
Query 72:	0.6949
Query 73:	0.1572
Query 74:	0.5554
Query 75:	1.0000
Query 76:	0.2650
Query 77:	0.1116
Query 78:	0.7001
Query 79:	1.0000
Query 80:	0.8405
Query 81:	0.5168
Query 82:	0.7703
Query 83:	0.8667
Query 84:	0.3293
Query 85:	0.5130
Query 86:	0.4550
Query 87:	0.4352
Query 88:	0.9250
Query 89:	0.9589
Query 90:	0.0628

Total number of documents
over all queries
Retrieved:	47030
Relevant:	1246
Rel_ret:	1224

Interpolated Recall -
Precision Averages:
at 0.00	0.8835
at 0.10	0.8213
at 0.20	0.7377
at 0.30	0.6732
at 0.40	0.6031
at 0.50	0.5618
at 0.60	0.5014
at 0.70	0.4404
at 0.80	0.3768
at 0.90	0.2962
at 1.00	0.2254

Avg. prec. (non-interpolated)
for all rel. documents
0.5418

Precision:
At	5 docs:	0.6383
At	10 docs:	0.5830
At	15 docs:	0.5021
At	20 docs:	0.4606
At	30 docs:	0.3993
At	100 docs:	0.2023
At	200 docs:	0.1178
At	500 docs:	0.0510
At	1000 docs:	0.0260

R-Precision (prec. after R
(=num_rel) docs. retrieved):
Exact: 0.5094

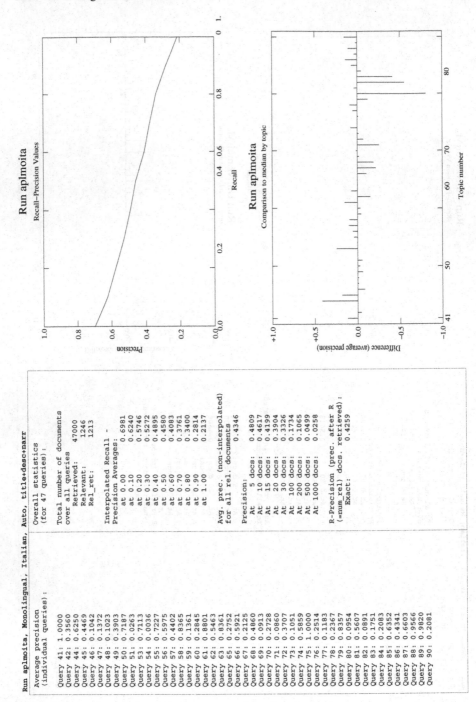

Run aplmoita

Recall–Precision Values

Run aplmoita

Comparison to median by topic

Run aplmoita, Monolingual, Italian, Auto, title+desc+narr

Average precision
(individual queries):

Query 41:	1.0000	Query 67:	0.2125
Query 42:	0.3560	Query 68:	0.4860
Query 44:	0.6250	Query 69:	0.0913
Query 45:	0.4469	Query 70:	0.2728
Query 46:	0.1042	Query 71:	0.0860
Query 47:	0.1372	Query 72:	0.3707
Query 48:	0.1023	Query 73:	0.1051
Query 49:	0.3903	Query 74:	0.5859
Query 50:	0.7187	Query 75:	1.0000
Query 51:	0.0263	Query 76:	0.2514
Query 53:	0.7113	Query 77:	0.1183
Query 54:	0.0036	Query 78:	0.2367
Query 55:	0.7227	Query 79:	0.8357
Query 56:	0.5975	Query 80:	0.0954
Query 57:	0.4402	Query 81:	0.5607
Query 58:	0.8365	Query 82:	0.0891
Query 59:	0.1361	Query 83:	0.1751
Query 60:	0.2845	Query 84:	0.2083
Query 61:	0.8801	Query 85:	0.6352
Query 62:	0.5463	Query 86:	0.4341
Query 63:	0.8361	Query 87:	0.6603
Query 65:	0.2752	Query 88:	0.9566
Query 66:	0.5921	Query 89:	0.9820
		Query 90:	0.2081

Overall statistics
(for 47 queries):

Total number of documents
over all queries:
  Retrieved: 47000
  Relevant: 1246
  Rel_ret: 1213

Interpolated Recall -
Precision Averages:
  at 0.00   0.6981
  at 0.10   0.6240
  at 0.20   0.5746
  at 0.30   0.5272
  at 0.40   0.4895
  at 0.50   0.4580
  at 0.60   0.4083
  at 0.70   0.3761
  at 0.80   0.3400
  at 0.90   0.2814
  at 1.00   0.2137
Avg. prec. (non-interpolated)
for all rel. documents
              0.4346

Precision:
  At   5 docs: 0.4809
  At 10 docs: 0.4617
  At 15 docs: 0.4199
  At 20 docs: 0.3904
  At 30 docs: 0.3326
  At 100 docs: 0.1734
  At 200 docs: 0.1065
  At 500 docs: 0.0499
  At 1000 docs: 0.0258

R-Precision (prec. after R
(=num_rel) docs. retrieved):
  Exact: 0.4259

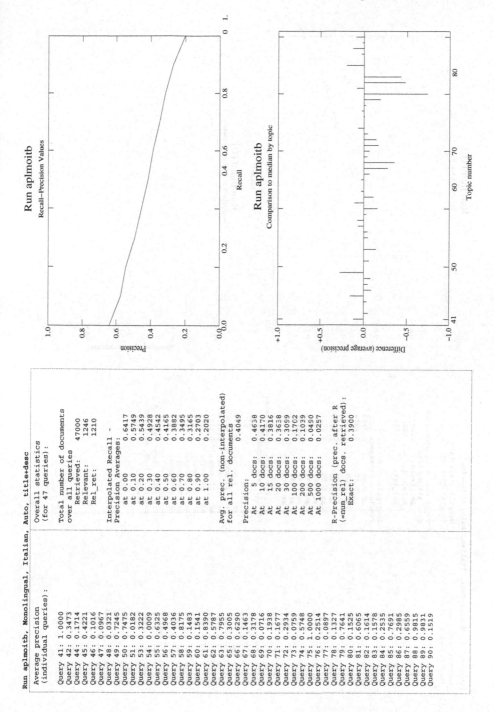

Run aplmoitb, Monolingual, Italian, Auto, title+desc

Average precision
(individual queries):

Query 41:	1.0000
Query 42:	0.3473
Query 44:	0.1714
Query 45:	0.4221
Query 46:	0.1016
Query 47:	0.0967
Query 48:	0.0321
Query 49:	0.7245
Query 50:	0.7475
Query 51:	0.0182
Query 53:	0.3222
Query 54:	0.0009
Query 55:	0.6325
Query 56:	0.4968
Query 57:	0.4036
Query 58:	0.8175
Query 59:	0.1483
Query 60:	0.1541
Query 61:	0.8390
Query 62:	0.5787
Query 63:	0.7955
Query 65:	0.3005
Query 66:	0.6290
Query 67:	0.1463
Query 68:	0.3178
Query 69:	0.0716
Query 70:	0.1938
Query 71:	0.1677
Query 72:	0.2934
Query 73:	0.0759
Query 74:	0.5748
Query 75:	1.0000
Query 76:	0.2514
Query 77:	0.0897
Query 78:	0.1327
Query 79:	0.7641
Query 80:	0.1525
Query 81:	0.6065
Query 82:	0.1614
Query 83:	0.1578
Query 84:	0.2535
Query 85:	0.7691
Query 86:	0.2985
Query 87:	0.6559
Query 88:	0.9815
Query 89:	0.9831
Query 90:	0.1519

Overall statistics
(for 47 queries):

Total number of documents
over all queries:
  Retrieved: 47000
  Relevant: 1246
  Rel_ret: 1210

Interpolated Recall -
Precision Averages:
  at 0.00   0.6417
  at 0.10   0.5749
  at 0.20   0.5439
  at 0.30   0.4928
  at 0.40   0.4542
  at 0.50   0.4165
  at 0.60   0.3882
  at 0.70   0.3495
  at 0.80   0.3165
  at 0.90   0.2703
  at 1.00   0.2020

Avg. prec. (non-interpolated)
for all rel. documents
              0.4049

Precision:
  At   5 docs: 0.4638
  At   10 docs: 0.4170
  At   15 docs: 0.3816
  At   20 docs: 0.3638
  At   30 docs: 0.3099
  At 100 docs: 0.1702
  At 200 docs: 0.1039
  At 500 docs: 0.0490
  At 1000 docs: 0.0257

R-Precision (prec. after R
(=num_rel) docs. retrieved):
  Exact: 0.3900

Run aplmoitb
Recall-Precision Values

Run aplmoitb
Comparison to median by topic

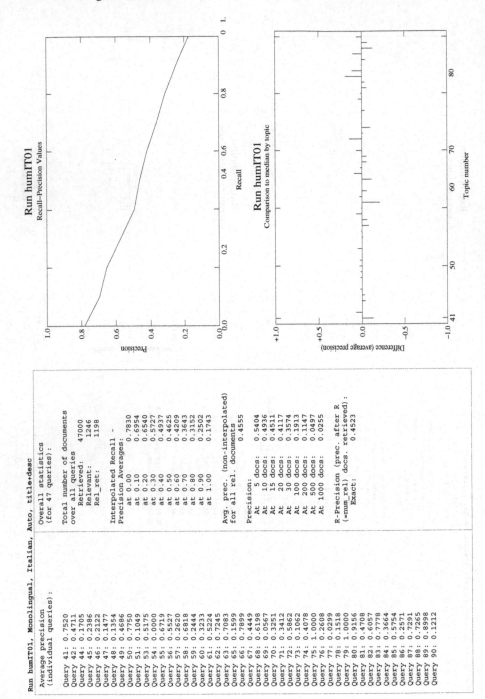

Run humITO1

Recall–Precision Values

Run humITO1

Comparison to median by topic

Run humITO1, Monolingual, Italian, Auto, title+desc

Average precision
(individual queries):

Query 41:	0.7520
Query 42:	0.4711
Query 44:	0.1705
Query 45:	0.2386
Query 46:	0.2122
Query 47:	0.1477
Query 48:	0.1354
Query 49:	0.4686
Query 50:	0.7750
Query 51:	0.1049
Query 53:	0.5175
Query 54:	0.0000
Query 55:	0.6719
Query 56:	0.5527
Query 57:	0.2620
Query 58:	0.6818
Query 59:	0.2444
Query 60:	0.3233
Query 61:	0.5224
Query 62:	0.7245
Query 63:	0.7083
Query 65:	0.1599
Query 66:	0.7899
Query 67:	0.4449
Query 68:	0.6198
Query 69:	0.05067
Query 70:	0.3251
Query 71:	0.3412
Query 72:	0.5862
Query 73:	0.1062
Query 74:	0.4078
Query 75:	1.0000
Query 76:	0.2608
Query 77:	0.0299
Query 78:	0.1518
Query 79:	1.0000
Query 80:	0.9156
Query 81:	0.4708
Query 82:	0.6057
Query 83:	0.7778
Query 84:	0.3664
Query 85:	0.5754
Query 86:	0.2571
Query 87:	0.7291
Query 88:	0.7265
Query 89:	0.8998
Query 90:	0.1212

Overall statistics
(for 47 queries):

Total number of documents
over all queries:
Retrieved:　47000
Relevant:　1246
Rel_ret:　1198

Interpolated Recall　-
Precision Averages:

at 0.00	0.7830
at 0.10	0.6954
at 0.20	0.6540
at 0.30	0.5727
at 0.40	0.4937
at 0.50	0.4625
at 0.60	0.4209
at 0.70	0.3643
at 0.80	0.3152
at 0.90	0.2502
at 1.00	0.1743

Avg. prec. (non-interpolated)
for all rel. documents
0.4555

Precision:

At	5 docs:	0.5404
At	10 docs:	0.4936
At	15 docs:	0.4511
At	20 docs:	0.4117
At	30 docs:	0.3574
At	100 docs:	0.1913
At	200 docs:	0.1147
At	500 docs:	0.0497
At	1000 docs:	0.0255

R-Precision (prec. after R
(=num_rel) docs. retrieved):
Exact:　0.4523

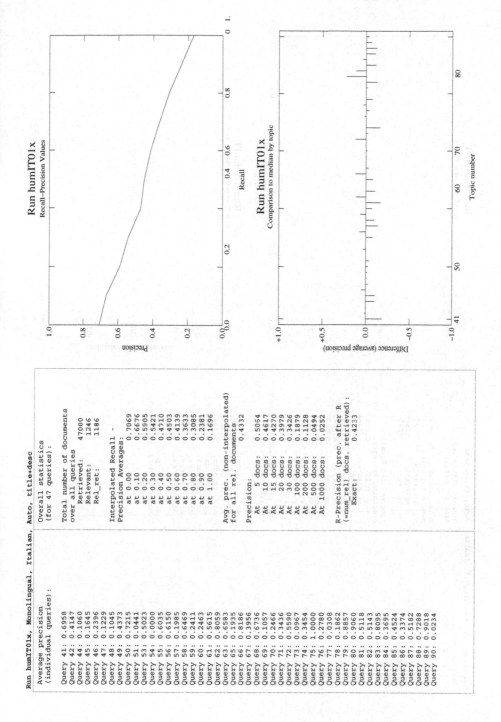

Run humIT01x
Recall-Precision Values

Precision

1.0
0.8
0.6
0.4
0.2
0.0
0.0   0.2   0.4   0.6   0.8   1.0
Recall

Run humIT01x
Comparison to median by topic

Difference (average precision)

+1.0
+0.5
0.0
-0.5
-1.0
41   50   60   70   80
Topic number

Run humIT01x, Monolingual, Italian, Auto, title+desc

Average precision
(individual queries):

Query 41: 0.6958
Query 42: 0.4147
Query 44: 0.1060
Query 45: 0.1645
Query 46: 0.2396
Query 47: 0.1229
Query 48: 0.1045
Query 49: 0.4373
Query 50: 0.7215
Query 51: 0.0441
Query 53: 0.5023
Query 54: 0.0000
Query 55: 0.6035
Query 56: 0.6150
Query 57: 0.1985
Query 58: 0.6469
Query 59: 0.2411
Query 60: 0.2463
Query 61: 0.5615
Query 62: 0.8059
Query 63: 0.6583
Query 65: 0.1935
Query 66: 0.8186
Query 67: 0.3956
Query 68: 0.6736
Query 69: 0.1057
Query 70: 0.2466
Query 71: 0.3436
Query 72: 0.5590
Query 73: 0.0967
Query 74: 0.3454
Query 75: 1.0000
Query 76: 0.2780
Query 77: 0.0308
Query 78: 0.1862
Query 79: 0.8857
Query 80: 0.9060
Query 81: 0.5118
Query 82: 0.5143
Query 83: 0.8095
Query 84: 0.3695
Query 85: 0.4524
Query 86: 0.3374
Query 87: 0.5182
Query 88: 0.7288
Query 89: 0.9018
Query 90: 0.0234

Overall statistics
(for 47 queries):

Total number of documents
over all queries
    Retrieved: 47000
    Relevant: 1246
    Rel_ret: 1186

Interpolated Recall -
Precision Averages:
    at 0.00   0.7069
    at 0.10   0.6676
    at 0.20   0.5905
    at 0.30   0.5421
    at 0.40   0.4710
    at 0.50   0.4503
    at 0.60   0.4139
    at 0.70   0.3633
    at 0.80   0.3085
    at 0.90   0.2381
    at 1.00   0.1696

Avg. prec. (non-interpolated)
for all rel. documents
                0.4332

Precision:
    At   5 docs: 0.5054
    At   10 docs: 0.4617
    At   15 docs: 0.4270
    At   20 docs: 0.3979
    At   30 docs: 0.3426
    At   100 docs: 0.1879
    At   200 docs: 0.1128
    At   500 docs: 0.0494
    At 1000 docs: 0.0252

R-Precision (prec. after R
(=num_rel) docs. retrieved):
    Exact: 0.4233

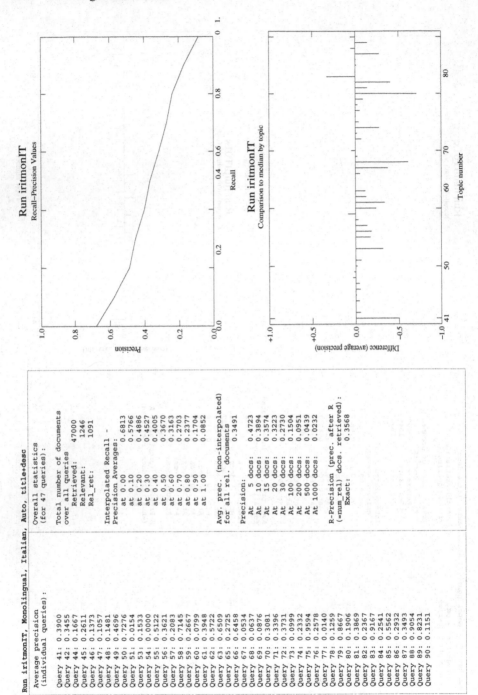

Run iritmonIT
Recall-Precision Values

Run iritmonIT
Comparison to median by topic

Run iritmonIT, Monolingual, Italian, Auto, title-desc

Average precision
(individual queries):

Query 41:	0.3900
Query 42:	0.3455
Query 44:	0.1667
Query 45:	0.2611
Query 46:	0.1373
Query 47:	0.1057
Query 48:	0.1481
Query 49:	0.4696
Query 50:	0.7276
Query 51:	0.0154
Query 53:	0.1533
Query 54:	0.0000
Query 55:	0.5122
Query 56:	0.3621
Query 57:	0.2083
Query 58:	0.7145
Query 59:	0.2667
Query 60:	0.0799
Query 61:	0.3948
Query 62:	0.5722
Query 63:	0.6509
Query 65:	0.2725
Query 66:	0.6458
Query 67:	0.0534
Query 68:	0.0637
Query 69:	0.0876
Query 70:	0.3081
Query 71:	0.3396
Query 72:	0.3731
Query 73:	0.0999
Query 74:	0.2332
Query 75:	0.5594
Query 76:	0.2578
Query 77:	0.0140
Query 78:	0.1259
Query 79:	0.8667
Query 80:	0.1906
Query 81:	0.3869
Query 82:	0.2367
Query 83:	0.9167
Query 84:	0.2541
Query 85:	0.5562
Query 86:	0.2932
Query 87:	0.3493
Query 88:	0.9054
Query 89:	0.8231
Query 90:	0.1151

Overall statistics
(for 47 queries):

Total number of documents
over all queries:
Retrieved:	47000
Relevant:	1246
Rel_ret:	1091

Interpolated Recall -
Precision Averages:
at 0.00	0.6813
at 0.10	0.5766
at 0.20	0.4886
at 0.30	0.4527
at 0.40	0.4005
at 0.50	0.3670
at 0.60	0.3163
at 0.70	0.2703
at 0.80	0.2377
at 0.90	0.1704
at 1.00	0.0852

Avg. prec. (non-interpolated)
for all rel. documents
0.3491

Precision:
At	5 docs:	0.4723
At	10 docs:	0.3894
At	15 docs:	0.3574
At	20 docs:	0.3223
At	30 docs:	0.2730
At	100 docs:	0.1504
At	200 docs:	0.0951
At	500 docs:	0.0439
At	1000 docs:	0.0232

R-Precision (prec. after R
(=num_rel) docs. retrieved):
Exact: 0.3568

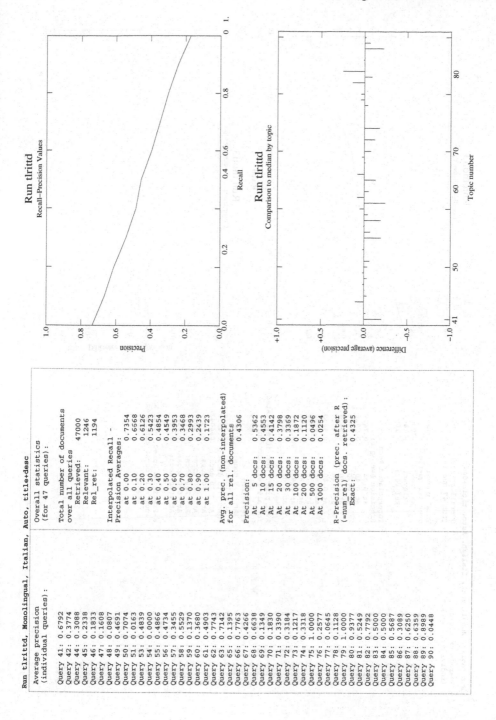

Run tlrittd, Monolingual, Italian, Auto, title+desc

Average precision
(individual queries):

Query 41:	0.6792
Query 42:	0.3774
Query 44:	0.3088
Query 45:	0.2338
Query 46:	0.1833
Query 47:	0.1608
Query 48:	0.0807
Query 49:	0.4691
Query 50:	0.7074
Query 51:	0.0163
Query 53:	0.4839
Query 54:	0.0000
Query 55:	0.4866
Query 56:	0.4734
Query 57:	0.3455
Query 58:	0.5529
Query 59:	0.1370
Query 60:	0.3680
Query 61:	0.4903
Query 62:	0.7743
Query 63:	0.7142
Query 65:	0.1395
Query 66:	0.7763
Query 67:	0.4266
Query 68:	0.6638
Query 69:	0.1349
Query 70:	0.1830
Query 71:	0.3390
Query 72:	0.3184
Query 73:	0.1217
Query 74:	0.3318
Query 75:	1.0000
Query 76:	0.2577
Query 77:	0.0645
Query 78:	0.1128
Query 79:	1.0000
Query 80:	0.9377
Query 81:	0.5249
Query 82:	0.7792
Query 83:	0.5000
Query 84:	0.5000
Query 85:	0.5687
Query 86:	0.3089
Query 87:	0.6250
Query 88:	0.6359
Query 89:	0.8989
Query 90:	0.0448

Overall statistics
(for 47 queries):

Total number of documents
over all queries
    Retrieved: 47000
    Relevant: 1246
    Rel_ret: 1194

Interpolated Recall -
Precision Averages:
   at 0.00   0.7354
   at 0.10   0.6668
   at 0.20   0.6126
   at 0.30   0.5423
   at 0.40   0.4854
   at 0.50   0.4549
   at 0.60   0.3953
   at 0.70   0.3468
   at 0.80   0.2993
   at 0.90   0.2439
   at 1.00   0.1723

Avg. prec. (non-interpolated)
for all rel. documents
              0.4306

Precision:
  At   5 docs: 0.5362
  At 10 docs: 0.4553
  At 15 docs: 0.4142
  At 20 docs: 0.3798
  At 30 docs: 0.3369
  At 100 docs: 0.1872
  At 200 docs: 0.1120
  At 500 docs: 0.0496
  At 1000 docs: 0.0254

R-Precision (prec. after R
(=num_rel) docs. retrieved):
    Exact: 0.4325

Run tlrittd
Recall-Precision Values

Precision

Recall

Run tlrittd
Comparison to median by topic

Difference (average precision)

Topic number

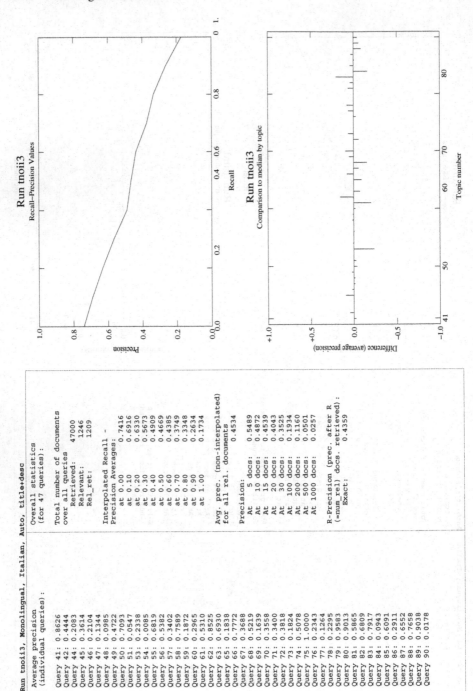

Run tnoii3

Recall–Precision Values

Run tnoii3

Comparison to median by topic

Run tnoii3, Monolingual, Italian, Auto, title+desc

Average precision
(individual queries):

Query 41:	0.8626	Query 67:	0.3688
Query 42:	0.4444	Query 68:	0.5219
Query 44:	0.2083	Query 69:	0.1639
Query 45:	0.3614	Query 70:	0.3558
Query 46:	0.2104	Query 71:	0.3400
Query 47:	0.1344	Query 72:	0.3818
Query 48:	0.0985	Query 73:	0.1824
Query 49:	0.4722	Query 74:	0.5078
Query 50:	0.7093	Query 75:	1.0000
Query 51:	0.0547	Query 76:	0.2343
Query 53:	0.2338	Query 77:	0.1264
Query 54:	0.0085	Query 78:	0.2295
Query 55:	0.6819	Query 79:	0.9583
Query 56:	0.5382	Query 80:	0.9013
Query 57:	0.3402	Query 81:	0.5865
Query 58:	0.7589	Query 82:	0.6809
Query 59:	0.1872	Query 83:	0.7917
Query 60:	0.2965	Query 84:	0.0943
Query 61:	0.5310	Query 85:	0.6091
Query 62:	0.8525	Query 86:	0.2911
Query 63:	0.6930	Query 87:	0.6552
Query 65:	0.1838	Query 88:	0.7658
Query 66:	0.7772	Query 89:	0.9038
		Query 90:	0.0178

Overall statistics
(for 47 queries):

Total number of documents
over all queries
  Retrieved: 47000
  Relevant: 1246
  Rel_ret: 1209

Interpolated Recall –
Precision Averages:
  at 0.00   0.7416
  at 0.10   0.6916
  at 0.20   0.6330
  at 0.30   0.5673
  at 0.40   0.4909
  at 0.50   0.4669
  at 0.60   0.4385
  at 0.70   0.3749
  at 0.80   0.3348
  at 0.90   0.2634
  at 1.00   0.1734
Avg. prec. (non-interpolated)
for all rel. documents
           0.4534

Precision:
  At   5 docs: 0.5489
  At 10 docs: 0.4872
  At 15 docs: 0.4539
  At 20 docs: 0.4043
  At 30 docs: 0.3525
  At 100 docs: 0.1934
  At 200 docs: 0.1160
  At 500 docs: 0.0501
  At 1000 docs: 0.0257

R-Precision (prec. after R
(=num rel) docs. retrieved):
    Exact: 0.4359

Run BK2SSA1, Monolingual, Spanish, Auto, title+desc-narr

Average precision
(individual queries):

Query 41:	0.1510
Query 42:	0.7162
Query 43:	0.6581
Query 44:	0.4943
Query 45:	0.6823
Query 46:	0.0820
Query 47:	0.4081
Query 48:	0.3116
Query 49:	0.1496
Query 50:	0.6687
Query 51:	0.1086
Query 52:	0.3159
Query 53:	0.3890
Query 54:	0.0244
Query 55:	0.3658
Query 56:	0.4760
Query 57:	0.1819
Query 58:	0.8754
Query 59:	0.9094
Query 60:	0.4358
Query 62:	0.3768
Query 63:	0.8560
Query 64:	1.0000
Query 65:	0.4568
Query 66:	0.9377
Query 67:	0.0876
Query 68:	0.0397
Query 69:	0.5841
Query 70:	0.7585
Query 71:	0.5289
Query 72:	0.6209
Query 73:	0.3647
Query 74:	0.4382
Query 75:	1.0000
Query 76:	0.3285
Query 77:	0.5038
Query 78:	0.4783
Query 79:	0.6911
Query 80:	0.8059
Query 81:	0.9478
Query 82:	0.8236
Query 83:	0.8871
Query 84:	0.3221
Query 85:	0.8195
Query 86:	0.5496
Query 87:	0.5627
Query 88:	0.5915
Query 89:	0.9143
Query 90:	0.3003

Overall statistics
(for 49 queries):

Total number of documents over all queries

Retrieved:	49000
Relevant:	2694
Rel_ret:	2561

Interpolated Recall -
Precision Averages:

at 0.00:	0.8912
at 0.10:	0.8185
at 0.20:	0.7590
at 0.30:	0.6746
at 0.40:	0.6008
at 0.50:	0.5418
at 0.60:	0.4893
at 0.70:	0.3942
at 0.80:	0.3348
at 0.90:	0.2762
at 1.00:	0.1585

Avg. prec. (non-interpolated)
for all rel. documents   0.5302

Precision:

At	5 docs:	0.6616
At	10 docs:	0.6061
At	15 docs:	0.5605
At	20 docs:	0.5153
At	30 docs:	0.4619
At	100 docs:	0.3033
At	200 docs:	0.2013
At	500 docs:	0.0987
At	1000 docs:	0.0523

R-Precision (prec. after R
(=num_rel) docs. retrieved):
Exact: 0.5180

Run BK2SSA1
Recall-Precision Values

Run BK2SSA1
Comparison to median by topic

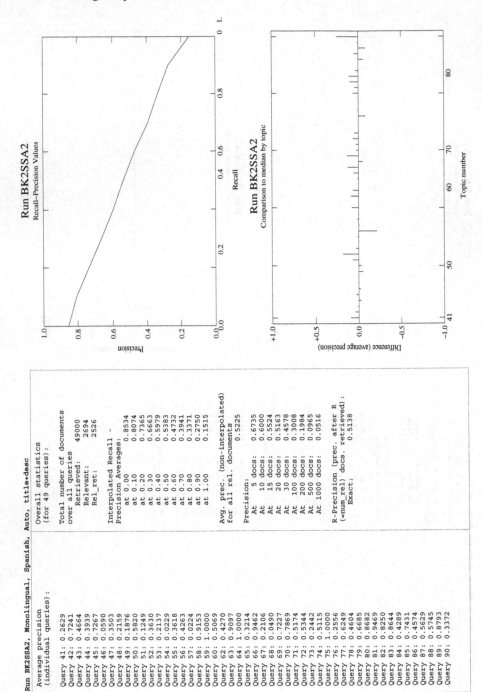

Run BK2SSA2
Recall–Precision Values

Run BK2SSA2
Comparison to median by topic

Run BK2SSA2, Monolingual, Spanish, Auto, title+desc

Average precision
(individual queries):

Query 41:	0.2629
Query 42:	0.7241
Query 43:	0.4664
Query 44:	0.3939
Query 45:	0.7267
Query 46:	0.0590
Query 47:	0.3503
Query 48:	0.2159
Query 49:	0.1876
Query 50:	0.5820
Query 51:	0.1249
Query 52:	0.3630
Query 53:	0.2137
Query 54:	0.0229
Query 55:	0.3618
Query 56:	0.4263
Query 57:	0.0224
Query 58:	0.9153
Query 59:	1.0000
Query 60:	0.5069
Query 62:	0.4270
Query 63:	0.9097
Query 64:	1.0000
Query 65:	0.3214
Query 66:	0.9462
Query 67:	0.2106
Query 68:	0.0490
Query 69:	0.7227
Query 70:	0.7869
Query 71:	0.5174
Query 72:	0.5344
Query 73:	0.2442
Query 74:	0.5115
Query 75:	1.0000
Query 76:	0.2556
Query 77:	0.6249
Query 78:	0.4604
Query 79:	0.6685
Query 80:	0.8682
Query 81:	0.9469
Query 82:	0.8250
Query 83:	0.8644
Query 84:	0.4289
Query 85:	0.7431
Query 86:	0.4574
Query 87:	0.5629
Query 88:	0.5745
Query 89:	0.8793
Query 90:	0.3372

Overall statistics
(for 49 queries):

Total number of documents
over all queries
Retrieved: 49000
Relevant: 2694
Rel_ret: 2526

Interpolated Recall -
Precision Averages:
    at 0.00   0.8534
    at 0.10   0.8074
    at 0.20   0.7365
    at 0.30   0.6663
    at 0.40   0.5979
    at 0.50   0.5383
    at 0.60   0.4732
    at 0.70   0.3941
    at 0.80   0.3371
    at 0.90   0.2750
    at 1.00   0.1515

Avg. prec. (non-interpolated)
for all rel. documents
                0.5225

Precision:
    At   5 docs: 0.6735
    At   10 docs: 0.6000
    At   15 docs: 0.5524
    At   20 docs: 0.5163
    At   30 docs: 0.4578
    At 100 docs: 0.3008
    At 200 docs: 0.1984
    At 500 docs: 0.0965
    At 1000 docs: 0.0516

R-Precision (prec. after R
(=num_rel) docs. retrieved):
    Exact: 0.5138

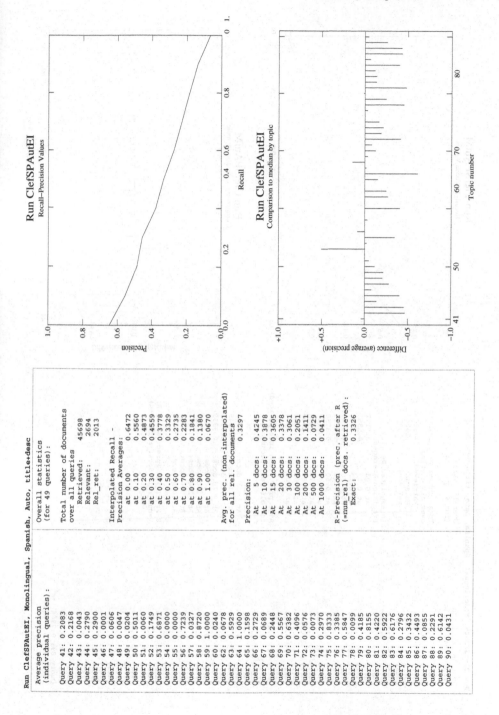

Run ClefSPAutEI
Recall-Precision Values

Run ClefSPAutEI
Comparison to median by topic

Run ClefSPAutEI, Monolingual, Spanish, Auto, title+desc

Average precision
(individual queries):

Query 41:	0.2083
Query 42:	0.2168
Query 43:	0.0043
Query 44:	0.2790
Query 45:	0.2900
Query 46:	0.0001
Query 47:	0.0606
Query 48:	0.0047
Query 49:	0.0204
Query 50:	0.5011
Query 51:	0.0060
Query 52:	0.1749
Query 53:	0.6871
Query 54:	0.0000
Query 55:	0.0000
Query 56:	0.7239
Query 57:	0.0327
Query 58:	0.8720
Query 59:	1.0000
Query 60:	0.0240
Query 61:	0.0678
Query 63:	0.5929
Query 64:	1.0000
Query 65:	0.1598
Query 66:	0.2729
Query 67:	0.0689
Query 68:	0.2448
Query 69:	0.5567
Query 70:	0.6382
Query 71:	0.4096
Query 72:	0.0576
Query 73:	0.0073
Query 74:	0.2970
Query 75:	0.8333
Query 76:	0.3385
Query 77:	0.5847
Query 78:	0.0099
Query 79:	0.4185
Query 80:	0.8155
Query 81:	0.4220
Query 82:	0.5922
Query 83:	0.6176
Query 84:	0.2796
Query 85:	0.3432
Query 86:	0.4493
Query 87:	0.0855
Query 88:	0.2291
Query 89:	0.6142
Query 90:	0.0431

Overall statistics
(for 49 queries):

Total number of documents
over all queries:
    Retrieved: 45698
    Relevant: 2694
    Rel_ret: 2013

Interpolated Recall -
Precision Averages:
    at 0.00   0.6472
    at 0.10   0.5560
    at 0.20   0.4873
    at 0.30   0.4559
    at 0.40   0.3778
    at 0.50   0.3329
    at 0.60   0.2735
    at 0.70   0.2283
    at 0.80   0.1841
    at 0.90   0.1380
    at 1.00   0.0670

Avg. prec. (non-interpolated)
for all rel. documents
                    0.3297

Precision:
    At   5 docs: 0.4245
    At   10 docs: 0.3878
    At   15 docs: 0.3605
    At   20 docs: 0.3378
    At   30 docs: 0.3061
    At 100 docs: 0.2051
    At 200 docs: 0.1411
    At 500 docs: 0.0729
    At 1000 docs: 0.0411

R-Precision (prec. after R
(=num_rel) docs. retrieved):
    Exact: 0.3326

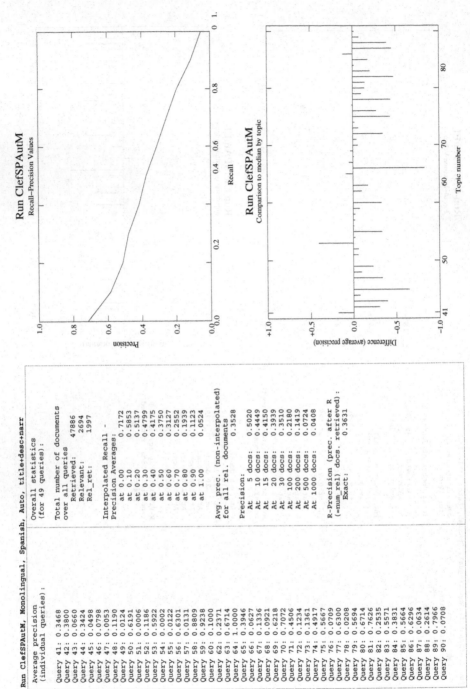

Run ClefSPAutM
Recall-Precision Values

Run ClefSPAutM
Comparison to median by topic

Run ClefSPAutM, Monolingual, Spanish, Auto, title+desc+narr

Average precision
(individual queries):

Query 41:	0.3468
Query 42:	0.3800
Query 43:	0.0660
Query 44:	0.3424
Query 45:	0.0498
Query 46:	0.0798
Query 47:	0.0053
Query 48:	0.1190
Query 49:	0.0124
Query 50:	0.6191
Query 51:	0.0006
Query 52:	0.1186
Query 53:	0.5922
Query 54:	0.0002
Query 55:	0.0122
Query 56:	0.6301
Query 57:	0.0131
Query 58:	0.8809
Query 59:	0.9238
Query 60:	0.1000
Query 62:	0.2371
Query 63:	0.6714
Query 64:	1.0000
Query 65:	0.3946
Query 66:	0.0627
Query 67:	0.1336
Query 68:	0.0921
Query 69:	0.6218
Query 70:	0.7072
Query 71:	0.4506
Query 72:	0.1234
Query 73:	0.1361
Query 74:	0.4917
Query 75:	0.5667
Query 76:	0.0709
Query 77:	0.6300
Query 78:	0.0208
Query 79:	0.5594
Query 80:	0.6714
Query 81:	0.7626
Query 82:	0.2535
Query 83:	0.5571
Query 84:	0.3831
Query 85:	0.5664
Query 86:	0.6296
Query 87:	0.0634
Query 88:	0.2614
Query 89:	0.7966
Query 90:	0.0708

Overall statistics
(for 49 queries):

Total number of documents
over all queries
    Retrieved: 47886
    Relevant: 2694
    Rel_ret: 1997

Interpolated Recall -
Precision Averages:
    at 0.00   0.7172
    at 0.10   0.5853
    at 0.20   0.5137
    at 0.30   0.4799
    at 0.40   0.4175
    at 0.50   0.3750
    at 0.60   0.3127
    at 0.70   0.2552
    at 0.80   0.1939
    at 0.90   0.1123
    at 1.00   0.0524

Avg. prec. (non-interpolated)
for all rel. documents
                     0.3528

Precision:
    At   5 docs: 0.5020
    At   10 docs: 0.4449
    At   15 docs: 0.4150
    At   20 docs: 0.3939
    At   30 docs: 0.3510
    At 100 docs: 0.2180
    At 200 docs: 0.1419
    At 500 docs: 0.0724
    At 1000 docs: 0.0408

R-Precision (prec. after R
(=num_rel) docs. retrieved):
    Exact: 0.3631

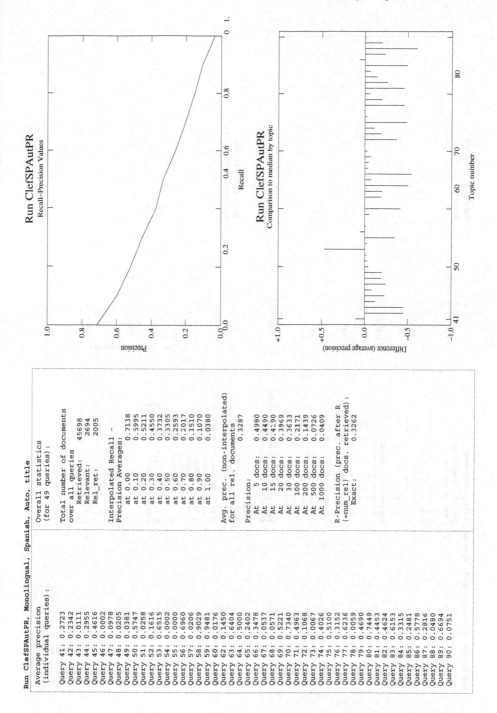

Run ClefSPAutPR
Recall–Precision Values

Run ClefSPAutPR
Comparison to median by topic

Run ClefSPAutPR, Monolingual, Spanish, Auto, title

Average precision
(individual queries):

Query 41:	0.2723
Query 42:	0.2342
Query 43:	0.0111
Query 44:	0.2955
Query 45:	0.4616
Query 46:	0.0002
Query 47:	0.0978
Query 48:	0.0205
Query 49:	0.0381
Query 50:	0.5747
Query 51:	0.0258
Query 52:	0.1616
Query 53:	0.6515
Query 54:	0.0002
Query 55:	0.0000
Query 56:	0.6960
Query 57:	0.0206
Query 58:	0.9029
Query 59:	0.9481
Query 60:	0.0176
Query 62:	0.1450
Query 63:	0.6404
Query 64:	0.5000
Query 65:	0.2402
Query 66:	0.3478
Query 67:	0.0537
Query 68:	0.0571
Query 69:	0.5221
Query 70:	0.7340
Query 71:	0.4963
Query 72:	0.1068
Query 73:	0.0067
Query 74:	0.4026
Query 75:	0.5100
Query 76:	0.3152
Query 77:	0.6236
Query 78:	0.0059
Query 79:	0.4690
Query 80:	0.7449
Query 81:	0.4453
Query 82:	0.4624
Query 83:	0.6153
Query 84:	0.3315
Query 85:	0.2481
Query 86:	0.5778
Query 87:	0.2816
Query 88:	0.0480
Query 89:	0.6694
Query 90:	0.0751

Overall statistics
(for 49 queries):

Total number of documents
over all queries:
Retrieved: 45698
Relevant: 2694
Rel_ret: 2005

Interpolated Recall -
Precision Averages:
at 0.00	0.7138
at 0.10	0.5995
at 0.20	0.5211
at 0.30	0.4550
at 0.40	0.3732
at 0.50	0.3305
at 0.60	0.2593
at 0.70	0.2017
at 0.80	0.1510
at 0.90	0.1070
at 1.00	0.0380

Avg. prec. (non-interpolated)
for all rel. documents
0.3287

Precision:
At 5 docs:	0.4980
At 10 docs:	0.4490
At 15 docs:	0.4290
At 20 docs:	0.3969
At 30 docs:	0.3633
At 100 docs:	0.2171
At 200 docs:	0.1439
At 500 docs:	0.0726
At 1000 docs:	0.0409

R-Precision (prec. after R
(=num_rel) docs. retrieved):
Exact: 0.3262

Run UniNEmoes
Recall–Precision Values

Run UniNEmoes
Comparison to median by topic

Run UniNEmoes, Monolingual, Spanish, Auto, title+desc

Average precision
(individual queries):

Query 41:	0.6211
Query 42:	0.6076
Query 43:	0.5414
Query 44:	0.3438
Query 45:	0.7671
Query 46:	0.1462
Query 47:	0.3919
Query 48:	0.1827
Query 49:	0.2926
Query 50:	0.6250
Query 51:	0.0380
Query 52:	0.5265
Query 53:	0.1347
Query 54:	0.0338
Query 55:	0.5469
Query 56:	0.5562
Query 57:	0.0787
Query 58:	0.9253
Query 59:	0.9481
Query 60:	0.8470
Query 62:	0.4245
Query 63:	0.9467
Query 64:	1.0000
Query 65:	0.3518
Query 66:	0.8909
Query 67:	0.4443
Query 68:	0.1039
Query 69:	0.9103
Query 70:	0.8140
Query 71:	0.5311
Query 72:	0.6586
Query 73:	0.1995
Query 74:	0.7307
Query 75:	1.0000
Query 76:	0.5278
Query 77:	0.7261
Query 78:	0.3575
Query 79:	0.6689
Query 80:	0.7712
Query 81:	0.9498
Query 82:	0.7809
Query 83:	0.8110
Query 84:	0.5443
Query 85:	0.7531
Query 86:	0.5629
Query 87:	0.8057
Query 88:	0.7993
Query 89:	0.9432
Query 90:	0.1571

Overall statistics
(for 49 queries):

Total number of documents
over all queries
Retrieved: 49000
Relevant: 2694
Rel_ret: 2575

Interpolated Recall -
Precision Averages:

at 0.00	0.8985
at 0.10	0.8173
at 0.20	0.7897
at 0.30	0.7176
at 0.40	0.6709
at 0.50	0.6119
at 0.60	0.5507
at 0.70	0.4791
at 0.80	0.4123
at 0.90	0.3032
at 1.00	0.1812

Avg. prec. (non-interpolated)
for all rel. documents   0.5800

Precision:

At 5 docs:	0.6980
At 10 docs:	0.6469
At 15 docs:	0.5973
At 20 docs:	0.5602
At 30 docs:	0.5020
At 100 docs:	0.3173
At 200 docs:	0.2028
At 500 docs:	0.0987
At 1000 docs:	0.0526

R-Precision (prec. after R
(=num rel) docs. retrieved):
Exact: 0.5556

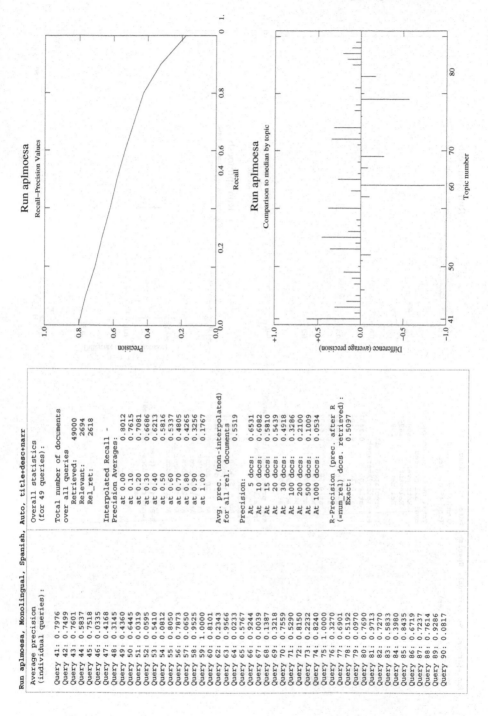

Run aplmoesa
Recall-Precision Values

Precision

Recall

Run aplmoesa
Comparison to median by topic

Difference (average precision)

Topic number

Run aplmoesa, Monolingual, Spanish, Auto, title+desc+narr

Average precision
(individual queries):

Query 41:	0.7976
Query 42:	0.7499
Query 43:	0.7601
Query 44:	0.5837
Query 45:	0.7518
Query 46:	0.0335
Query 47:	0.4168
Query 48:	0.3145
Query 49:	0.4360
Query 50:	0.6445
Query 51:	0.0319
Query 52:	0.0595
Query 53:	0.5410
Query 54:	0.0812
Query 55:	0.8050
Query 56:	0.7873
Query 57:	0.0650
Query 58:	0.9525
Query 59:	1.0000
Query 60:	0.8101
Query 62:	0.2343
Query 63:	0.9566
Query 64:	0.0233
Query 65:	0.5767
Query 66:	0.9244
Query 67:	0.0039
Query 68:	0.1387
Query 69:	0.3218
Query 70:	0.7559
Query 71:	0.5290
Query 72:	0.8150
Query 73:	0.2232
Query 74:	0.8240
Query 75:	1.0000
Query 76:	0.3270
Query 77:	0.6901
Query 78:	0.5192
Query 79:	0.0970
Query 80:	0.7690
Query 81:	0.9713
Query 82:	0.7270
Query 83:	0.5833
Query 84:	0.3980
Query 85:	0.8435
Query 86:	0.6719
Query 87:	0.7237
Query 88:	0.7614
Query 89:	0.9286
Query 90:	0.0817

Overall statistics
(for 49 queries):

Total number of documents
over all queries:
  Retrieved: 49000
  Relevant: 2694
  Rel_ret: 2618

Interpolated Recall -
Precision Averages:
  at 0.00   0.8012
  at 0.10   0.7615
  at 0.20   0.7081
  at 0.30   0.6686
  at 0.40   0.6213
  at 0.50   0.5816
  at 0.60   0.5337
  at 0.70   0.4805
  at 0.80   0.4265
  at 0.90   0.3256
  at 1.00   0.1767
Avg. prec. (non-interpolated)
for all rel. documents
                0.5519

Precision:
  At   5 docs: 0.6531
  At   10 docs: 0.6082
  At   15 docs: 0.5810
  At   20 docs: 0.5439
  At   30 docs: 0.4918
  At 100 docs: 0.3286
  At 200 docs: 0.2100
  At 500 docs: 0.1009
  At 1000 docs: 0.0534

R-Precision (prec. after R
(=num_rel) docs. retrieved):
  Exact: 0.5097

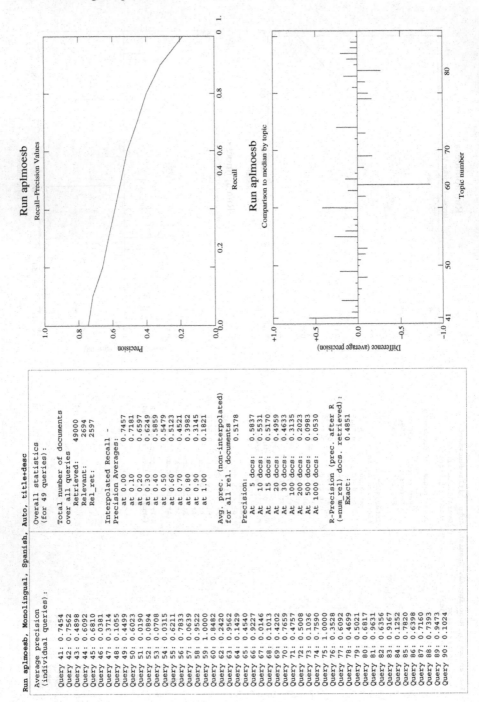

Run aplmoesb
Recall–Precision Values

Run aplmoesb
Comparison to median by topic

Run aplmoesb, Monolingual, Spanish, Auto, title+desc

Average precision
(individual queries):

Query 41:	0.7454
Query 42:	0.7562
Query 43:	0.4898
Query 44:	0.6092
Query 45:	0.6810
Query 46:	0.0381
Query 47:	0.3714
Query 48:	0.1055
Query 49:	0.4499
Query 50:	0.6023
Query 51:	0.0190
Query 52:	0.0894
Query 53:	0.0708
Query 54:	0.0315
Query 55:	0.6211
Query 56:	0.7833
Query 57:	0.0639
Query 58:	0.9522
Query 59:	1.0000
Query 60:	0.8482
Query 62:	0.2420
Query 63:	0.9562
Query 64:	0.1429
Query 65:	0.4540
Query 66:	0.9227
Query 67:	0.0146
Query 68:	0.1013
Query 69:	0.4202
Query 70:	0.7659
Query 71:	0.4757
Query 72:	0.5008
Query 73:	0.1036
Query 74:	0.7590
Query 75:	1.0000
Query 76:	0.3528
Query 77:	0.6092
Query 78:	0.4699
Query 79:	0.5021
Query 80:	0.6817
Query 81:	0.9631
Query 82:	0.6356
Query 83:	0.9167
Query 84:	0.1252
Query 85:	0.7820
Query 86:	0.6398
Query 87:	0.7160
Query 88:	0.7393
Query 89:	0.9473
Query 90:	0.1024

Overall statistics
(for 49 queries):

Total number of documents
over all queries:
　Retrieved:　49000
　Relevant:　2694
　Rel_ret:　2597

Interpolated Recall -
Precision Averages:
at 0.00	0.7457
at 0.10	0.7181
at 0.20	0.6597
at 0.30	0.6249
at 0.40	0.5859
at 0.50	0.5479
at 0.60	0.5123
at 0.70	0.4521
at 0.80	0.3982
at 0.90	0.3145
at 1.00	0.1821

Avg. prec. (non-interpolated)
for all rel. documents
　　　　　　　　　0.5178

Precision:
At 5 docs:	0.5837
At 10 docs:	0.5531
At 15 docs:	0.5170
At 20 docs:	0.4959
At 30 docs:	0.4633
At 100 docs:	0.3135
At 200 docs:	0.2023
At 500 docs:	0.0983
At 1000 docs:	0.0530

R-Precision (prec. after R
(=num_rel) docs. retrieved):
　Exact:　0.4851

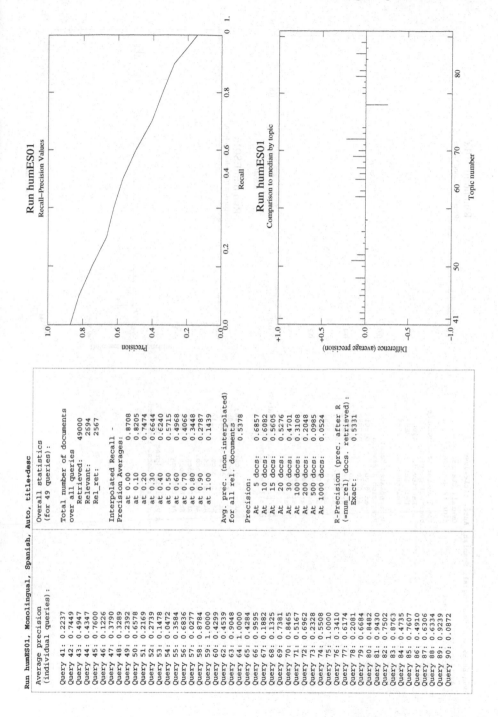

Run humES01
Recall-Precision Values

Run humES01
Comparison to median by topic

Run humES01, Monolingual, Spanish, Auto, title+desc

Average precision
(individual queries):

Query 41:	0.2237
Query 42:	0.7449
Query 43:	0.4947
Query 44:	0.4347
Query 45:	0.7600
Query 46:	0.1226
Query 47:	0.3790
Query 48:	0.3289
Query 49:	0.2392
Query 50:	0.6578
Query 51:	0.2169
Query 52:	0.2739
Query 53:	0.1478
Query 54:	0.0472
Query 55:	0.3584
Query 56:	0.6836
Query 57:	0.0277
Query 58:	0.8784
Query 59:	1.0000
Query 60:	0.4299
Query 62:	0.4539
Query 63:	0.9048
Query 64:	1.0000
Query 65:	0.4284
Query 66:	0.9595
Query 67:	0.1882
Query 68:	0.1325
Query 69:	0.7381
Query 70:	0.8465
Query 71:	0.5167
Query 72:	0.6962
Query 73:	0.2328
Query 74:	0.5508
Query 75:	1.0000
Query 76:	0.3410
Query 77:	0.6174
Query 78:	0.2081
Query 79:	0.6684
Query 80:	0.8482
Query 81:	0.9430
Query 82:	0.7502
Query 83:	0.8763
Query 84:	0.4735
Query 85:	0.7607
Query 86:	0.4910
Query 87:	0.6306
Query 88:	0.6334
Query 89:	0.9239
Query 90:	0.0872

Overall statistics
(for 49 queries):

Total number of documents
over all queries
    Retrieved: 49000
    Relevant: 2694
    Rel_ret: 2567

Interpolated Recall -
Precision Averages:
    at 0.00   0.8708
    at 0.10   0.8205
    at 0.20   0.7474
    at 0.30   0.6644
    at 0.40   0.6240
    at 0.50   0.5715
    at 0.60   0.4968
    at 0.70   0.4066
    at 0.80   0.3448
    at 0.90   0.2787
    at 1.00   0.1439

Avg. prec. (non-interpolated)
for all rel. documents   0.5378

Precision:
    At   5 docs: 0.6857
    At   10 docs: 0.6082
    At   15 docs: 0.5605
    At   20 docs: 0.5276
    At   30 docs: 0.4701
    At 100 docs: 0.3108
    At 200 docs: 0.2048
    At 500 docs: 0.0985
    At 1000 docs: 0.0524

R-Precision (prec. after R
(=num_rel) docs. retrieved):
    Exact: 0.5331

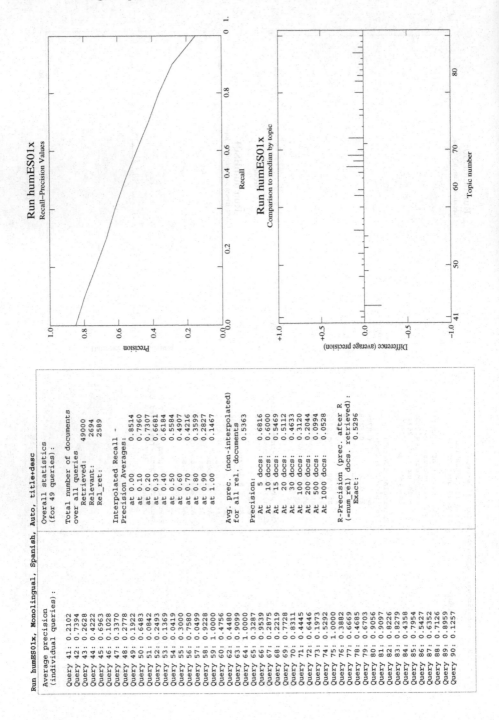

Run humES01x

Recall–Precision Values

Run humES01x

Comparison to median by topic

Run humES01x, Monolingual, Spanish, Auto, title+desc

Average precision
(individual queries):

Query 41:	0.2102
Query 42:	0.7394
Query 43:	0.2628
Query 44:	0.4222
Query 45:	0.6963
Query 46:	0.1028
Query 47:	0.3370
Query 48:	0.2778
Query 49:	0.1922
Query 50:	0.6483
Query 51:	0.0842
Query 52:	0.2493
Query 53:	0.1369
Query 54:	0.0419
Query 55:	0.3000
Query 56:	0.7580
Query 57:	0.0499
Query 58:	0.9228
Query 59:	1.0000
Query 60:	0.4756
Query 62:	0.4480
Query 63:	0.9099
Query 64:	1.0000
Query 65:	0.3287
Query 66:	0.9539
Query 67:	0.2875
Query 68:	0.2219
Query 69:	0.7728
Query 70:	0.8311
Query 71:	0.4445
Query 72:	0.6446
Query 73:	0.1973
Query 74:	0.5292
Query 75:	1.0000
Query 76:	0.3882
Query 77:	0.6669
Query 78:	0.4685
Query 79:	0.6703
Query 80:	0.9056
Query 81:	0.9097
Query 82:	0.8226
Query 83:	0.8279
Query 84:	0.4358
Query 85:	0.7954
Query 86:	0.5427
Query 87:	0.6352
Query 88:	0.7126
Query 89:	0.8959
Query 90:	0.1257

Overall statistics
(for 49 queries):

Total number of documents
over all queries
    Retrieved: 49000
    Relevant: 2694
    Rel_ret: 2589

Interpolated Recall -
Precision Averages:
    at 0.00   0.8514
    at 0.10   0.7960
    at 0.20   0.7307
    at 0.30   0.6681
    at 0.40   0.6184
    at 0.50   0.5584
    at 0.60   0.4907
    at 0.70   0.4216
    at 0.80   0.3599
    at 0.90   0.2827
    at 1.00   0.1467

Avg. prec. (non-interpolated)
for all rel. documents
                   0.5363

Precision:
    At   5 docs: 0.6816
    At   10 docs: 0.6000
    At   15 docs: 0.5469
    At   20 docs: 0.5112
    At   30 docs: 0.4633
    At 100 docs: 0.3120
    At 200 docs: 0.2044
    At 500 docs: 0.0994
    At 1000 docs: 0.0528

R-Precision (prec. after R
(=num_rel) docs. retrieved):
    Exact: 0.5296

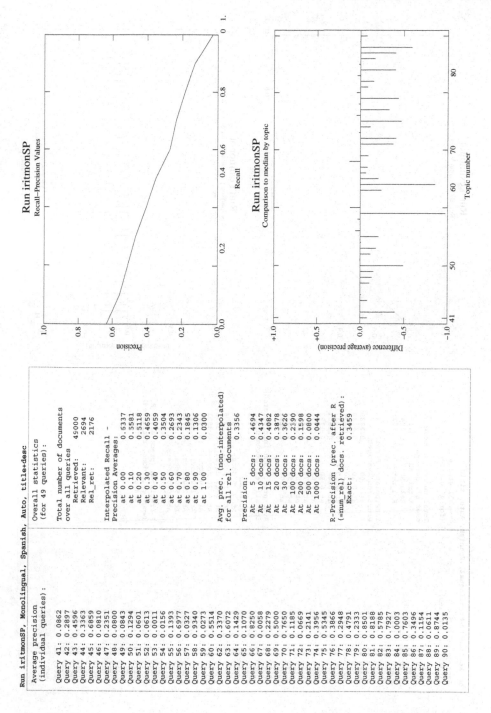

Run iritmonSP
Recall–Precision Values

Run iritmonSP
Comparison to median by topic

Run iritmonSP, Monolingual, Spanish, Auto, title+desc

Average precision
(individual queries):

		Overall statistics (for 49 queries):

Total number of documents
over all queries:

Retrieved:	49000
Relevant:	2694
Rel_ret:	2176

Interpolated Recall -
Precision Averages:

at 0.00	0.5337
at 0.10	0.5581
at 0.20	0.5118
at 0.30	0.4659
at 0.40	0.4059
at 0.50	0.3504
at 0.60	0.2693
at 0.70	0.2343
at 0.80	0.1845
at 0.90	0.1306
at 1.00	0.0300

Avg. prec. (non-interpolated)
for all rel. documents
              0.3356

Precision:

At 5 docs:	0.4694
At 10 docs:	0.4347
At 15 docs:	0.4082
At 20 docs:	0.3878
At 30 docs:	0.3626
At 100 docs:	0.2390
At 200 docs:	0.1598
At 500 docs:	0.0800
At 1000 docs:	0.0444

R-Precision (prec. after R
(=num_rel) docs. retrieved):
    Exact: 0.3459

Query 41:	0.0862
Query 42:	0.2897
Query 43:	0.4596
Query 44:	0.3363
Query 45:	0.6859
Query 46:	0.0810
Query 47:	0.2351
Query 48:	0.0800
Query 49:	0.0843
Query 50:	0.1294
Query 51:	0.0601
Query 52:	0.0613
Query 53:	0.0011
Query 54:	0.0156
Query 55:	0.1393
Query 56:	0.6977
Query 57:	0.0327
Query 58:	0.9340
Query 59:	0.0273
Query 60:	0.5514
Query 62:	0.3370
Query 63:	0.6072
Query 64:	0.1429
Query 65:	0.1070
Query 66:	0.8250
Query 67:	0.0058
Query 68:	0.2279
Query 69:	0.5000
Query 70:	0.7650
Query 71:	0.1185
Query 72:	0.0669
Query 73:	0.2141
Query 74:	0.3956
Query 75:	0.5345
Query 76:	0.3866
Query 77:	0.2948
Query 78:	0.4791
Query 79:	0.2333
Query 80:	0.8501
Query 81:	0.8188
Query 82:	0.5785
Query 83:	0.7927
Query 84:	0.0003
Query 85:	0.7603
Query 86:	0.3496
Query 87:	0.1154
Query 88:	0.0611
Query 89:	0.8744
Query 90:	0.0135

Run kcslmonot
Recall–Precision Values

Run kcslmonot
Comparison to median by topic

Run kcslmonot, Monolingual, Spanish, Auto, title

Average precision
(individual queries):

Query 41:	0.0875
Query 42:	0.1504
Query 43:	0.0001
Query 44:	0.1250
Query 45:	0.4428
Query 46:	0.0257
Query 47:	0.1363
Query 48:	0.0704
Query 49:	0.1174
Query 50:	0.2482
Query 51:	0.0243
Query 52:	0.1787
Query 53:	0.1377
Query 54:	0.0000
Query 55:	0.2143
Query 56:	0.2622
Query 57:	0.0139
Query 58:	0.8919
Query 59:	0.4286
Query 60:	0.0891
Query 62:	0.1739
Query 63:	0.2231
Query 64:	0.0000
Query 65:	0.0709
Query 66:	0.4176
Query 67:	0.0037
Query 68:	0.0298
Query 69:	0.2825
Query 70:	0.5554
Query 71:	0.1553
Query 72:	0.0596
Query 73:	0.1213
Query 74:	0.1818
Query 75:	1.0000
Query 76:	0.4093
Query 77:	0.3365
Query 78:	0.0338
Query 79:	0.3750
Query 80:	0.3628
Query 81:	0.0400
Query 82:	0.1059
Query 83:	0.2519
Query 84:	0.2841
Query 85:	0.2275
Query 86:	0.2380
Query 87:	0.2231
Query 88:	0.5071
Query 89:	0.2620
Query 90:	0.0667

Overall statistics
(for 49 queries):

Total number of documents
over all queries:
Retrieved:	7115
Relevant:	2694
Rel_ret:	872

Interpolated Recall -
Precision Averages:
at 0.00	0.7889
at 0.10	0.6138
at 0.20	0.4296
at 0.30	0.2837
at 0.40	0.1801
at 0.50	0.1182
at 0.60	0.0753
at 0.70	0.0498
at 0.80	0.0365
at 0.90	0.0347
at 1.00	0.0204

Avg. prec. (non-interpolated)
for all rel. documents
0.2172

Precision:
At	5 docs:	0.5510
At	10 docs:	0.4306
At	15 docs:	0.3891
At	20 docs:	0.3551
At	30 docs:	0.3088
At	100 docs:	0.1624
At	200 docs:	0.0882
At	500 docs:	0.0354
At	1000 docs:	0.0178

R-Precision (prec. after R
(=num_rel) docs. retrieved):
Exact:	0.2514

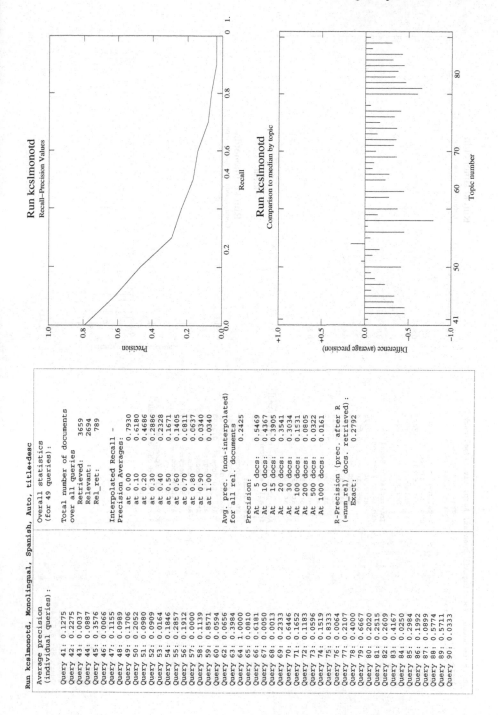

Run kcslmonotd
Recall–Precision Values

Run kcslmonotd
Comparison to median by topic

Run kcslmonotd, Monolingual, Spanish, Auto, title+desc

Average precision
(individual queries):

Query 41:	0.1275
Query 42:	0.2275
Query 43:	0.0037
Query 44:	0.0887
Query 45:	0.3576
Query 46:	0.0066
Query 47:	0.1155
Query 48:	0.0989
Query 49:	0.1706
Query 50:	0.2052
Query 51:	0.0980
Query 52:	0.0909
Query 53:	0.0164
Query 54:	0.1846
Query 55:	0.2857
Query 56:	0.1912
Query 57:	0.0000
Query 58:	0.1139
Query 59:	0.8571
Query 60:	0.0594
Query 62:	0.0656
Query 63:	0.3984
Query 64:	1.0000
Query 65:	0.0810
Query 66:	0.6181
Query 67:	0.0050
Query 68:	0.0013
Query 69:	0.2333
Query 70:	0.6446
Query 71:	0.1652
Query 72:	0.1183
Query 73:	0.0596
Query 74:	0.1519
Query 75:	0.8333
Query 76:	0.0064
Query 77:	0.2107
Query 78:	0.4000
Query 79:	0.6667
Query 80:	0.2020
Query 81:	0.2515
Query 82:	0.2609
Query 83:	0.4167
Query 84:	0.0250
Query 85:	0.2984
Query 86:	0.1992
Query 87:	0.0899
Query 88:	0.5774
Query 89:	0.5711
Query 90:	0.0333

Overall statistics
(for 49 queries):

Total number of documents
over all queries:
Retrieved:	3659
Relevant:	2694
Rel_ret:	789

Interpolated Recall –
Precision Averages:
at 0.00	0.7930
at 0.10	0.6180
at 0.20	0.4686
at 0.30	0.2886
at 0.40	0.2328
at 0.50	0.1671
at 0.60	0.1405
at 0.70	0.0811
at 0.80	0.0637
at 0.90	0.0340
at 1.00	0.0340

Avg. prec. (non-interpolated)
for all rel. documents
                    0.2425

Precision:
At 5 docs:	0.5469
At 10 docs:	0.4367
At 15 docs:	0.3905
At 20 docs:	0.3541
At 30 docs:	0.3034
At 100 docs:	0.1531
At 200 docs:	0.0805
At 500 docs:	0.0322
At 1000 docs:	0.0161

R-Precision (prec. after R
(=num_rel) docs. retrieved):
| Exact: | 0.2792 |

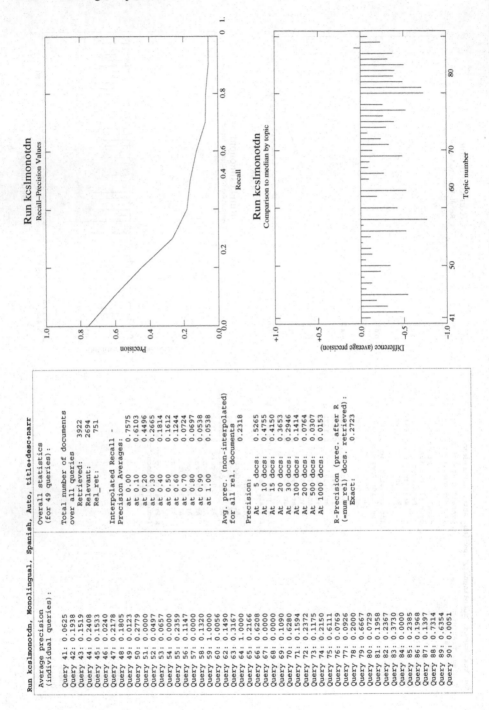

Run kcslmonotdn
Recall-Precision Values

Run kcslmonotdn
Comparison to median by topic

Run kcslmonotdn, Monolingual, Spanish, Auto, title+desc+narr

Average precision
(individual queries):

Query 41:	0.0625
Query 42:	0.1938
Query 43:	0.1519
Query 44:	0.2408
Query 45:	0.1533
Query 46:	0.0240
Query 47:	0.2178
Query 48:	0.1805
Query 49:	0.0123
Query 50:	0.2779
Query 51:	0.0000
Query 52:	0.0497
Query 53:	0.0657
Query 54:	0.0000
Query 55:	0.2359
Query 56:	0.1147
Query 57:	0.0000
Query 58:	0.1320
Query 59:	1.0000
Query 60:	0.0056
Query 62:	0.1490
Query 63:	0.3167
Query 64:	1.0000
Query 65:	0.2166
Query 66:	0.6208
Query 67:	0.0000
Query 68:	0.0000
Query 69:	0.1090
Query 70:	0.6280
Query 71:	0.1594
Query 72:	0.2372
Query 73:	0.1175
Query 74:	0.2150
Query 75:	0.6111
Query 76:	0.0769
Query 77:	0.0926
Query 78:	0.2000
Query 79:	0.6667
Query 80:	0.0729
Query 81:	0.1958
Query 82:	0.2367
Query 83:	0.3730
Query 84:	0.0000
Query 85:	0.2385
Query 86:	0.1968
Query 87:	0.1397
Query 88:	0.7314
Query 89:	0.6354
Query 90:	0.0051

Overall statistics
(for 49 queries):

Total number of documents
over all queries:
Retrieved:	3922
Relevant:	2694
Rel_ret:	751

Interpolated Recall -
Precision Averages:
at 0.00	0.7575
at 0.10	0.6103
at 0.20	0.4496
at 0.30	0.2665
at 0.40	0.1814
at 0.50	0.1612
at 0.60	0.1244
at 0.70	0.0724
at 0.80	0.0697
at 0.90	0.0538
at 1.00	0.0538

Avg. prec. (non-interpolated)
for all rel. documents
0.2318

Precision:
At 5 docs:	0.5265
At 10 docs:	0.4755
At 15 docs:	0.4150
At 20 docs:	0.3653
At 30 docs:	0.2946
At 100 docs:	0.1414
At 200 docs:	0.0764
At 500 docs:	0.0307
At 1000 docs:	0.0153

R-Precision (prec. after R
(=num_rel) docs. retrieved):
Exact: 0.2723

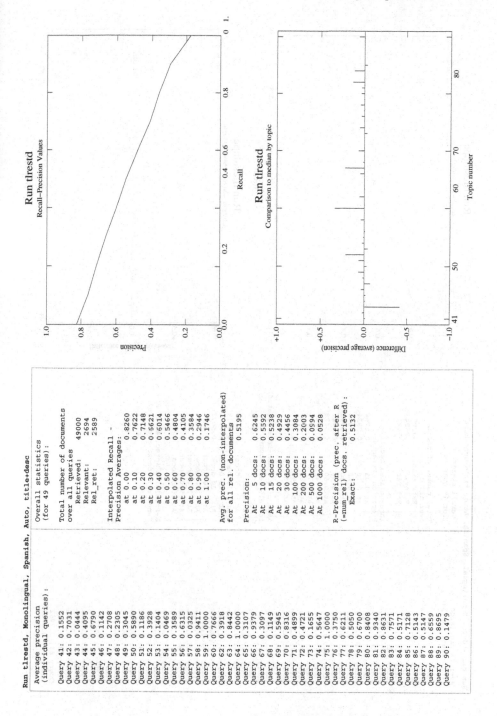

Run tlrestd, Monolingual, Spanish, Auto, title+desc

Average precision
(individual queries):

Query 41:	0.1552
Query 42:	0.7031
Query 43:	0.0444
Query 44:	0.4095
Query 45:	0.6790
Query 46:	0.1142
Query 47:	0.2708
Query 48:	0.2305
Query 49:	0.3045
Query 50:	0.5890
Query 51:	0.1186
Query 52:	0.3928
Query 53:	0.1404
Query 54:	0.0469
Query 55:	0.3589
Query 56:	0.6315
Query 57:	0.0325
Query 58:	0.9411
Query 59:	1.0000
Query 60:	0.7666
Query 62:	0.3918
Query 63:	0.8442
Query 64:	1.0000
Query 65:	0.3107
Query 66:	0.9379
Query 67:	0.3097
Query 68:	0.1149
Query 69:	0.5945
Query 70:	0.8316
Query 71:	0.4899
Query 72:	0.4721
Query 73:	0.1655
Query 74:	0.5647
Query 75:	1.0000
Query 76:	0.3750
Query 77:	0.6211
Query 78:	0.5050
Query 79:	0.6700
Query 80:	0.8408
Query 81:	0.9340
Query 82:	0.8631
Query 83:	0.7571
Query 84:	0.5171
Query 85:	0.7128
Query 86:	0.5143
Query 87:	0.5147
Query 88:	0.6559
Query 89:	0.8695
Query 90:	0.1479

Overall statistics
(for 49 queries):

Total number of documents
over all queries
Retrieved:	49000
Relevant:	2694
Rel_ret:	2589

Interpolated Recall -
Precision Averages:
at 0.00	0.8260
at 0.10	0.7622
at 0.20	0.7148
at 0.30	0.5621
at 0.40	0.6014
at 0.50	0.5466
at 0.60	0.4804
at 0.70	0.4105
at 0.80	0.3584
at 0.90	0.2946
at 1.00	0.1746

Avg. prec. (non-interpolated)
for all rel. documents
                    0.5195

Precision:
At 5 docs:	0.6245
At 10 docs:	0.5592
At 15 docs:	0.5238
At 20 docs:	0.4929
At 30 docs:	0.4456
At 100 docs:	0.3084
At 200 docs:	0.2003
At 500 docs:	0.0594
At 1000 docs:	0.0528

R-Precision (prec. after R
(=num_rel) docs. retrieved):
| Exact: | 0.5132 |

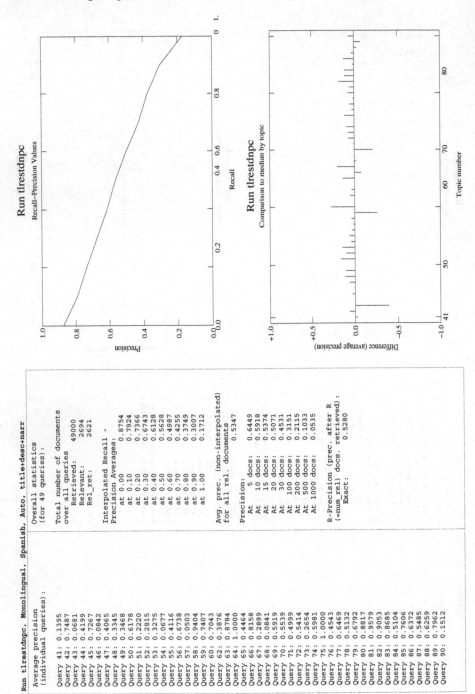

Run tlrestdnpc
Recall–Precision Values

Run tlrestdnpc
Comparison to median by topic

Run tlrestdnpc, Monolingual, Spanish, Auto, title+desc+narr

Average precision
(individual queries):

Query 41:	0.1395
Query 42:	0.7487
Query 43:	0.0681
Query 44:	0.4199
Query 45:	0.7267
Query 46:	0.0842
Query 47:	0.4065
Query 48:	0.3345
Query 49:	0.3468
Query 50:	0.6178
Query 51:	0.2220
Query 52:	0.2815
Query 53:	0.3275
Query 54:	0.0677
Query 55:	0.4116
Query 56:	0.6738
Query 57:	0.0503
Query 58:	0.9404
Query 59:	0.7407
Query 60:	0.7043
Query 62:	0.3876
Query 63:	0.8784
Query 64:	1.0000
Query 65:	0.4464
Query 66:	0.8158
Query 67:	0.2899
Query 68:	0.0841
Query 69:	0.5919
Query 70:	0.5539
Query 71:	0.4999
Query 72:	0.5414
Query 73:	0.2654
Query 74:	0.5981
Query 75:	1.0000
Query 76:	0.4543
Query 77:	0.6469
Query 78:	0.5132
Query 79:	0.6792
Query 80:	0.8817
Query 81:	0.9579
Query 82:	0.9053
Query 83:	0.8685
Query 84:	0.5104
Query 85:	0.7606
Query 86:	0.6372
Query 87:	0.5485
Query 88:	0.6259
Query 89:	0.7962
Query 90:	0.1512

Overall statistics
(for 49 queries):

Total number of documents
over all queries
    Retrieved: 49000
    Relevant: 2694
    Rel_ret: 2621

Interpolated Recall -
Precision Averages:
    at 0.00   0.8754
    at 0.10   0.7924
    at 0.20   0.7366
    at 0.30   0.6743
    at 0.40   0.6128
    at 0.50   0.5628
    at 0.60   0.4987
    at 0.70   0.4255
    at 0.80   0.3749
    at 0.90   0.3007
    at 1.00   0.1712
Avg. prec. (non-interpolated)
for all rel. documents
                 0.5347

Precision:
    At   5 docs: 0.6449
    At   10 docs: 0.5918
    At   15 docs: 0.5374
    At   20 docs: 0.5071
    At   30 docs: 0.4531
    At 100 docs: 0.3151
    At 200 docs: 0.2115
    At 500 docs: 0.1033
    At 1000 docs: 0.0535

R-Precision (prec. after R
(=num_rel) docs. retrieved):
    Exact: 0.5280

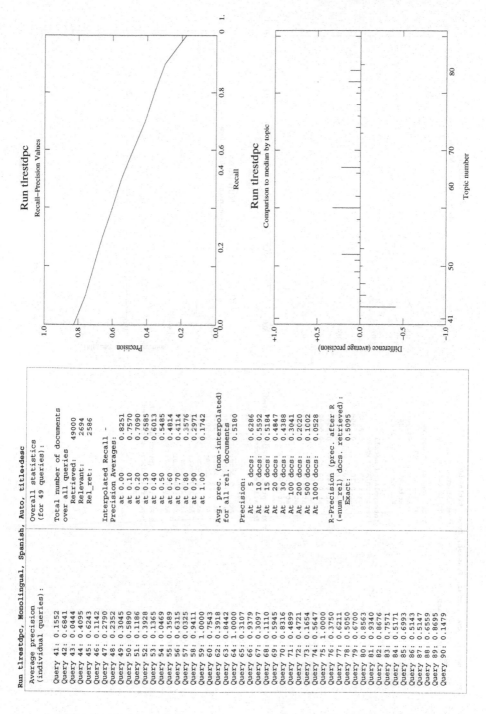

Run tlrestdpc
Recall–Precision Values

Run tlrestdpc
Comparison to median by topic

Run tlrestdpc, Monolingual, Spanish, Auto, title+desc

Average precision
(individual queries):

Query 41:	0.1552
Query 42:	0.6841
Query 43:	0.0444
Query 44:	0.4095
Query 45:	0.6243
Query 46:	0.1142
Query 47:	0.2790
Query 48:	0.2352
Query 49:	0.3045
Query 50:	0.5890
Query 51:	0.1186
Query 52:	0.3928
Query 53:	0.1365
Query 54:	0.0469
Query 55:	0.3589
Query 56:	0.6315
Query 57:	0.0325
Query 58:	0.9411
Query 59:	1.0000
Query 60:	0.7543
Query 62:	0.3918
Query 63:	0.8442
Query 64:	1.0000
Query 65:	0.3107
Query 66:	0.9379
Query 67:	0.3097
Query 68:	0.1110
Query 69:	0.5945
Query 70:	0.8316
Query 71:	0.4899
Query 72:	0.4721
Query 73:	0.1654
Query 74:	0.5647
Query 75:	1.0000
Query 76:	0.3750
Query 77:	0.6211
Query 78:	0.5050
Query 79:	0.6700
Query 80:	0.8563
Query 81:	0.9340
Query 82:	0.8676
Query 83:	0.7571
Query 84:	0.5171
Query 85:	0.6993
Query 86:	0.5143
Query 87:	0.5147
Query 88:	0.6559
Query 89:	0.8695
Query 90:	0.1479

Overall statistics
(for 49 queries):

Total number of documents
over all queries:
Retrieved: 49000
Relevant: 2694
Rel_ret: 2586

Interpolated Recall -
Precision Averages:
at 0.00   0.8251
at 0.10   0.7570
at 0.20   0.7090
at 0.30   0.6585
at 0.40   0.6013
at 0.50   0.5485
at 0.60   0.4814
at 0.70   0.4114
at 0.80   0.3576
at 0.90   0.2971
at 1.00   0.1742

Avg. prec. (non-interpolated)
for all rel. documents   0.5180

Precision:
At   5 docs: 0.6286
At   10 docs: 0.5592
At   15 docs: 0.5184
At   20 docs: 0.4847
At   30 docs: 0.4388
At   100 docs: 0.3041
At   200 docs: 0.2020
At   500 docs: 0.1002
At 1000 docs: 0.0528

R-Precision (prec. after R
(=num_rel) docs. retrieved):
Exact: 0.5095

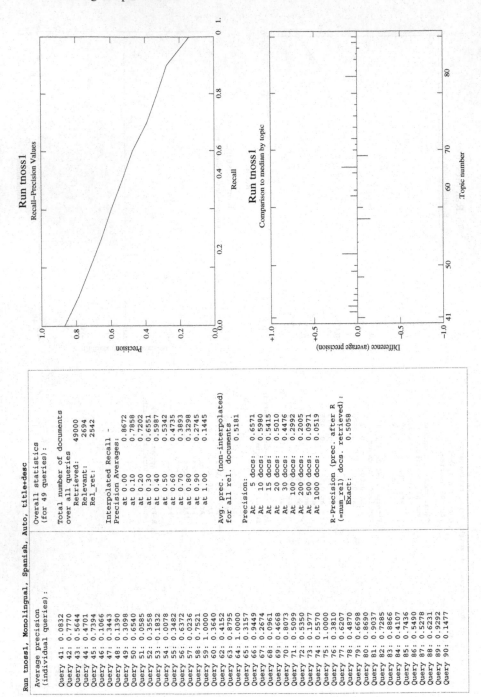

Run tnoss1

Recall-Precision Values

Run tnoss1

Comparison to median by topic

Run tnoss1, Monolingual, Spanish, Auto, title+desc

Average precision
(individual queries):

Query 41:	0.0832
Query 42:	0.7770
Query 43:	0.5644
Query 44:	0.4701
Query 45:	0.7394
Query 46:	0.1066
Query 47:	0.3443
Query 48:	0.1390
Query 49:	0.3098
Query 50:	0.6540
Query 51:	0.0585
Query 52:	0.3558
Query 53:	0.1832
Query 54:	0.0078
Query 55:	0.3482
Query 56:	0.6372
Query 57:	0.0236
Query 58:	0.7521
Query 59:	1.0000
Query 60:	0.3640
Query 62:	0.4152
Query 63:	0.8795
Query 64:	1.0000
Query 65:	0.3157
Query 66:	0.9449
Query 67:	0.2674
Query 68:	0.0961
Query 69:	0.4668
Query 70:	0.8073
Query 71:	0.5099
Query 72:	0.5350
Query 73:	0.1977
Query 74:	0.5570
Query 75:	1.0000
Query 76:	0.3810
Query 77:	0.6207
Query 78:	0.4870
Query 79:	0.6698
Query 80:	0.8690
Query 81:	0.9037
Query 82:	0.7285
Query 83:	0.8866
Query 84:	0.4107
Query 85:	0.7436
Query 86:	0.5490
Query 87:	0.5278
Query 88:	0.6231
Query 89:	0.9292
Query 90:	0.1477

Overall statistics
(for 49 queries):

Total number of documents
over all queries:
Retrieved:	49000
Relevant:	2694
Rel_ret:	2542

Interpolated Recall -
Precision Averages:
at 0.00	0.8672
at 0.10	0.7858
at 0.20	0.7202
at 0.30	0.6551
at 0.40	0.5987
at 0.50	0.5342
at 0.60	0.4735
at 0.70	0.3893
at 0.80	0.3298
at 0.90	0.2745
at 1.00	0.1445

Avg. prec. (non-interpolated)
for all rel. documents
0.5181

Precision:
At	5 docs:	0.6571
At	10 docs:	0.5990
At	15 docs:	0.5415
At	20 docs:	0.5010
At	30 docs:	0.4476
At	100 docs:	0.2992
At	200 docs:	0.2005
At	500 docs:	0.0971
At	1000 docs:	0.0519

R-Precision (prec. after R
(=num rel) docs. retrieved):
Exact:	0.5058

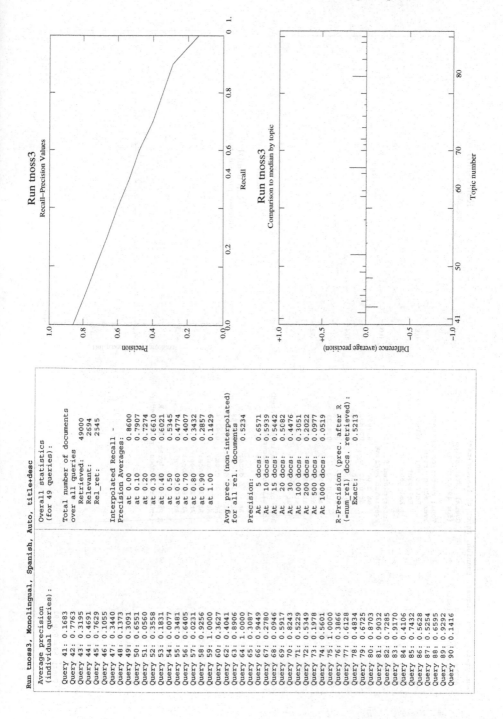

Run tnoss3, Monolingual, Spanish, Auto, title+desc

Average precision
(individual queries):

Query 41:	0.1683
Query 42:	0.7763
Query 43:	0.3195
Query 44:	0.4691
Query 45:	0.7629
Query 46:	0.1055
Query 47:	0.3440
Query 48:	0.1373
Query 49:	0.3091
Query 50:	0.6551
Query 51:	0.0560
Query 52:	0.3558
Query 53:	0.1831
Query 54:	0.0077
Query 55:	0.3481
Query 56:	0.6405
Query 57:	0.0231
Query 58:	0.9256
Query 59:	1.0000
Query 60:	0.3627
Query 62:	0.4041
Query 63:	0.8906
Query 64:	1.0000
Query 65:	0.3087
Query 66:	0.9449
Query 67:	0.2780
Query 68:	0.0946
Query 69:	0.5917
Query 70:	0.8243
Query 71:	0.5229
Query 72:	0.5349
Query 73:	0.1978
Query 74:	0.5601
Query 75:	1.0000
Query 76:	0.3866
Query 77:	0.6128
Query 78:	0.4834
Query 79:	0.6725
Query 80:	0.8703
Query 81:	0.9032
Query 82:	0.7285
Query 83:	0.9170
Query 84:	0.4106
Query 85:	0.7432
Query 86:	0.5628
Query 87:	0.5254
Query 88:	0.6595
Query 89:	0.9292
Query 90:	0.1416

Overall statistics
(for 49 queries):

Total number of documents
over all queries
Retrieved: 49000
Relevant: 2594
Rel_ret: 2545

Interpolated Recall -
Precision Averages:
at 0.00	0.8600
at 0.10	0.7907
at 0.20	0.7274
at 0.30	0.6610
at 0.40	0.6021
at 0.50	0.5345
at 0.60	0.4774
at 0.70	0.4007
at 0.80	0.3432
at 0.90	0.2857
at 1.00	0.1429

Avg. prec. (non-interpolated)
for all rel. documents
0.5234

Precision:
At	5 docs:	0.6571
At	10 docs:	0.5939
At	15 docs:	0.5442
At	20 docs:	0.5082
At	30 docs:	0.4476
At	100 docs:	0.3051
At	200 docs:	0.2022
At	500 docs:	0.0977
At	1000 docs:	0.0519

R-Precision (prec. after R
(=num_rel) docs. retrieved):
Exact: 0.5213

Run tnoss3
Recall-Precision Values

Run tnoss3
Comparison to median by topic

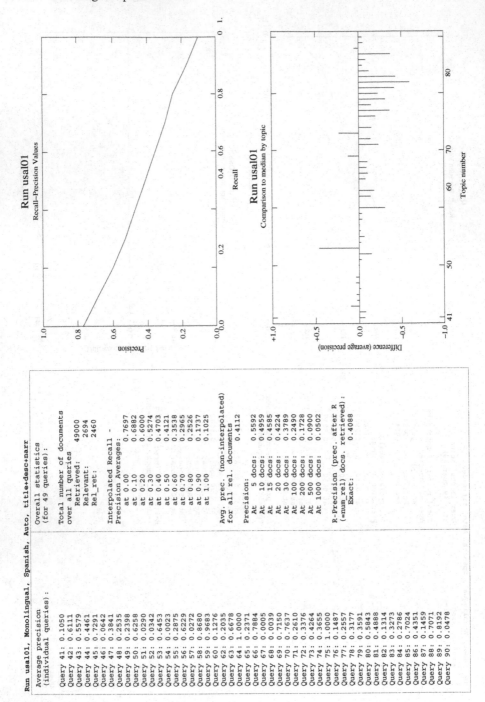

Run usal01
Recall-Precision Values

Run usal01
Comparison to median by topic

Run usal01, Monolingual, Spanish, Auto, title+desc+narr

Average precision
(individual queries):

Query 41:	0.1050
Query 42:	0.6111
Query 43:	0.5579
Query 44:	0.4461
Query 45:	0.7291
Query 46:	0.0642
Query 47:	0.3841
Query 48:	0.2535
Query 49:	0.2398
Query 50:	0.6258
Query 51:	0.0290
Query 52:	0.0342
Query 53:	0.6453
Query 54:	0.0023
Query 55:	0.2875
Query 56:	0.6229
Query 57:	0.0272
Query 58:	0.8680
Query 59:	0.9683
Query 60:	0.1276
Query 62:	0.2035
Query 63:	0.6678
Query 64:	1.0000
Query 65:	0.2371
Query 66:	0.7884
Query 67:	0.0005
Query 68:	0.0039
Query 69:	0.7150
Query 70:	0.7637
Query 71:	0.2610
Query 72:	0.3376
Query 73:	0.4264
Query 74:	0.3655
Query 75:	1.0000
Query 76:	0.1487
Query 77:	0.2557
Query 78:	0.3177
Query 79:	0.3591
Query 80:	0.5843
Query 81:	0.4888
Query 82:	0.1314
Query 83:	0.3273
Query 84:	0.2786
Query 85:	0.7024
Query 86:	0.4351
Query 87:	0.1459
Query 88:	0.7071
Query 89:	0.8192
Query 90:	0.0478

Overall statistics
(for 49 queries):

Total number of documents
over all queries
Retrieved: 49000
Relevant: 2694
Rel_ret: 2460

Interpolated Recall -
Precision Averages:
at 0.00   0.7697
at 0.10   0.6882
at 0.20   0.6000
at 0.30   0.5274
at 0.40   0.4703
at 0.50   0.4121
at 0.60   0.3538
at 0.70   0.2965
at 0.80   0.2526
at 0.90   0.1737
at 1.00   0.1025

Avg. prec. (non-interpolated)
for all rel. documents
                    0.4112

Precision:
At   5 docs: 0.5592
At   10 docs: 0.4959
At   15 docs: 0.4585
At   20 docs: 0.4224
At   30 docs: 0.3789
At 100 docs: 0.2490
At 200 docs: 0.1728
At 500 docs: 0.0900
At 1000 docs: 0.0502

R-Precision (prec. after R
(=num_rel) docs. retrieved):
Exact: 0.4088

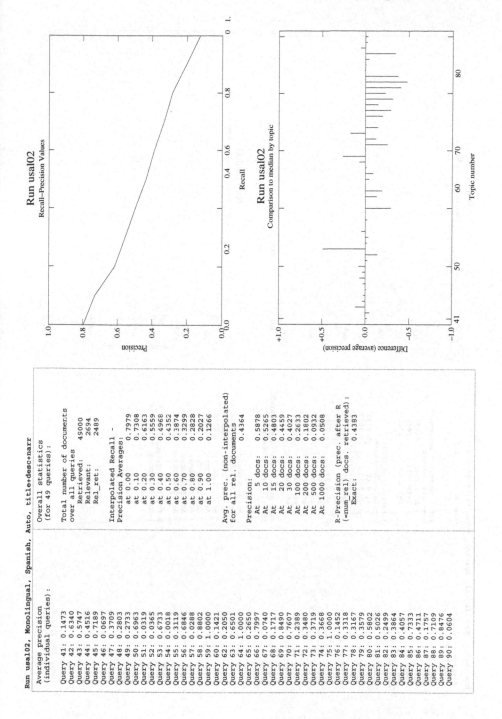

Run usal02

Recall-Precision Values

Precision

1.0

0.8

0.6

0.4

0.2

0.0

0.0   0.2   0.4   0.6   0.8   1.0

Recall

Run usal02

Comparison to median by topic

Difference (average precision)

+1.0

+0.5

0.0

-0.5

-1.0

41   50   60   70   80

Topic number

Run usal02, Monolingual, Spanish, Auto, title+desc+narr

Average precision
(individual queries):

Query 41:	0.1473
Query 42:	0.6340
Query 43:	0.5747
Query 44:	0.4516
Query 45:	0.7189
Query 46:	0.0697
Query 47:	0.3709
Query 48:	0.2803
Query 49:	0.2733
Query 50:	0.6963
Query 51:	0.0319
Query 52:	0.0365
Query 53:	0.6733
Query 54:	0.0018
Query 55:	0.3119
Query 56:	0.6846
Query 57:	0.0288
Query 58:	0.8802
Query 59:	1.0000
Query 60:	0.1421
Query 62:	0.2050
Query 63:	0.6501
Query 64:	1.0000
Query 65:	0.2650
Query 66:	0.7997
Query 67:	0.0740
Query 68:	0.1717
Query 69:	0.8490
Query 70:	0.7607
Query 71:	0.2389
Query 72:	0.3480
Query 73:	0.3719
Query 74:	0.3668
Query 75:	1.0000
Query 76:	0.1452
Query 77:	0.3318
Query 78:	0.3167
Query 79:	0.3579
Query 80:	0.5802
Query 81:	0.5026
Query 82:	0.2499
Query 83:	0.3864
Query 84:	0.4057
Query 85:	0.7333
Query 86:	0.4711
Query 87:	0.1757
Query 88:	0.7109
Query 89:	0.8476
Query 90:	0.0604

Overall statistics
(for 49 queries):

Total number of documents
over all queries
    Retrieved: 49000
    Relevant: 2694
    Rel_ret: 2489

Interpolated Recall -
Precision Averages:
    at 0.00   0.7979
    at 0.10   0.7308
    at 0.20   0.6163
    at 0.30   0.5559
    at 0.40   0.4968
    at 0.50   0.4352
    at 0.60   0.3874
    at 0.70   0.3299
    at 0.80   0.2828
    at 0.90   0.2027
    at 1.00   0.1266

Avg. prec. (non-interpolated)
for all rel. documents
                  0.4364

Precision:
    At   5 docs: 0.5878
    At   10 docs: 0.5265
    At   15 docs: 0.4803
    At   20 docs: 0.4459
    At   30 docs: 0.4027
    At 100 docs: 0.2633
    At 200 docs: 0.1802
    At 500 docs: 0.0932
    At 1000 docs: 0.0508

R-Precision (prec. after R
(=num_rel) docs. retrieved):
    Exact: 0.4383

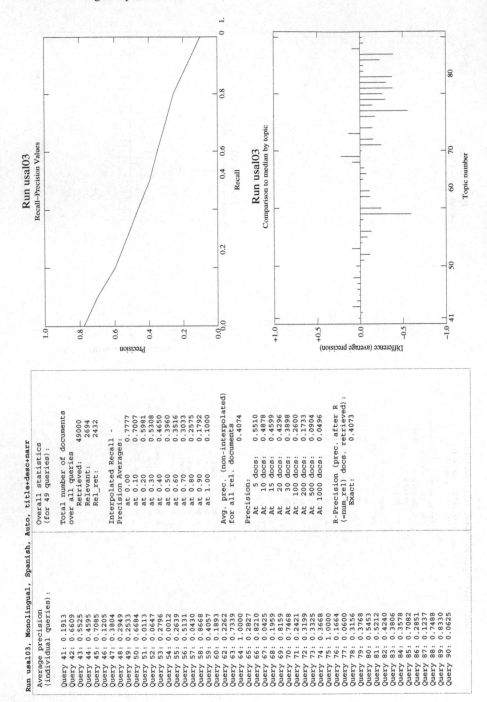

Run usal03
Recall-Precision Values

Run usal03
Comparison to median by topic

Run usal03, Monolingual, Spanish, Auto, title+desc+narr

Average precision
(individual queries):

Query 41:	0.1913	
Query 42:	0.6609	
Query 43:	0.5525	
Query 44:	0.4595	
Query 45:	0.7085	
Query 46:	0.1205	
Query 47:	0.3804	
Query 48:	0.2949	
Query 49:	0.2533	
Query 50:	0.6684	
Query 51:	0.0113	
Query 52:	0.0647	
Query 53:	0.2796	
Query 54:	0.0012	
Query 55:	0.2639	
Query 56:	0.5131	
Query 57:	0.0430	
Query 58:	0.8668	
Query 59:	0.4057	
Query 60:	0.1893	
Query 62:	0.2262	
Query 63:	0.7339	
Query 64:	1.0000	
Query 65:	0.2827	
Query 66:	0.8210	
Query 67:	0.0425	
Query 68:	0.1959	
Query 69:	0.8159	
Query 70:	0.7468	
Query 71:	0.2421	
Query 72:	0.3199	
Query 73:	0.3325	
Query 74:	0.3668	
Query 75:	1.0000	
Query 76:	0.1664	
Query 77:	0.0600	
Query 78:	0.3156	
Query 79:	0.3768	
Query 80:	0.5453	
Query 81:	0.5212	
Query 82:	0.4240	
Query 83:	0.3806	
Query 84:	0.3578	
Query 85:	0.7082	
Query 86:	0.2851	
Query 87:	0.1237	
Query 88:	0.7488	
Query 89:	0.8330	
Query 90:	0.0625	

Overall statistics
(for 49 queries):

Total number of documents
over all queries
    Retrieved: 49000
    Relevant: 2694
    Rel_ret: 2432

Interpolated Recall -
Precision Averages:
    at 0.00   0.7777
    at 0.10   0.7007
    at 0.20   0.5981
    at 0.30   0.5308
    at 0.40   0.4650
    at 0.50   0.3960
    at 0.60   0.3516
    at 0.70   0.3033
    at 0.80   0.2575
    at 0.90   0.1792
    at 1.00   0.1000

Avg. prec. (non-interpolated)
for all rel. documents
                   0.4074

Precision:
    At   5 docs: 0.5510
    At   10 docs: 0.4878
    At   15 docs: 0.4599
    At   20 docs: 0.4296
    At   30 docs: 0.3898
    At 100 docs: 0.2600
    At 200 docs: 0.1733
    At 500 docs: 0.0904
    At 1000 docs: 0.0496

R-Precision (prec. after R
(=num_rel) docs. retrieved):
    Exact: 0.4073

Run BKGRGGA
Recall-Precision Values

Run BKGRGGA
Comparison to median by topic

Run BKGRGGA, GIRT, German, Auto, title+desc+narr

Average precision
(individual queries):

Query 26:	0.6192
Query 27:	0.5836
Query 28:	0.6758
Query 29:	0.1953
Query 30:	0.2740
Query 31:	0.4786
Query 32:	0.4801
Query 33:	0.2026
Query 34:	0.8239
Query 35:	0.3768
Query 36:	0.4766
Query 37:	0.4784
Query 38:	0.6760
Query 39:	0.6233
Query 40:	0.8414
Query 41:	0.0793
Query 42:	0.7934
Query 43:	0.5210
Query 44:	0.3933
Query 45:	0.2636
Query 46:	0.4482
Query 47:	0.2038
Query 48:	0.7722
Query 49:	0.6544
Query 50:	0.5696

Overall statistics
(for 25 queries):

Total number of documents
over all queries:

Retrieved:	25000
Relevant:	1111
Rel_ret:	1054

Interpolated Recall -
Precision Averages:

at 0.00	0.9390
at 0.10	0.3225
at 0.20	0.7501
at 0.30	0.6282
at 0.40	0.5676
at 0.50	0.5166
at 0.60	0.4604
at 0.70	0.4002
at 0.80	0.3038
at 0.90	0.2097
at 1.00	0.0620

Avg. prec. (non-interpolated)
for all rel. documents
0.5302

Precision:

At	5 docs:	0.7040
At	10 docs:	0.6480
At	15 docs:	0.5867
At	20 docs:	0.5460
At	30 docs:	0.5040
At	100 docs:	0.3340
At	200 docs:	0.1680
At	500 docs:	0.0805
At 1000 docs:	0.0422

R-Precision (prec. after R
(=num_rel) docs. retrieved):
Exact: 0.4839

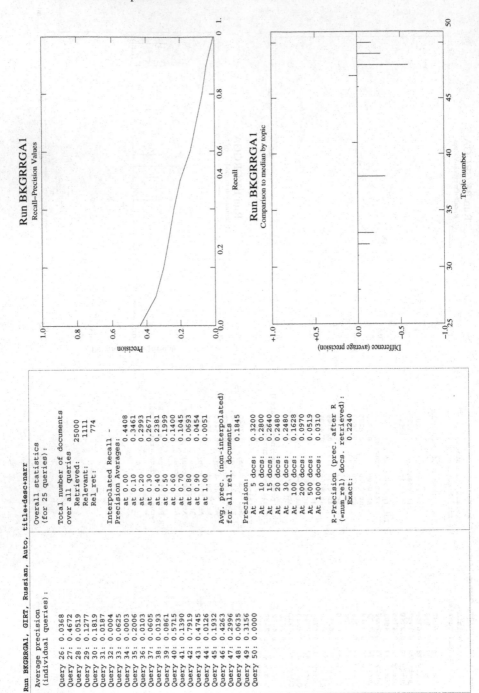

Run BKGRRGA1
Recall–Precision Values

Run BKGRRGA1
Comparison to median by topic

Run BKGRRGA1, GIRT, Russian, Auto, title+desc+narr

Average precision
(individual queries):

Query 26:	0.0368
Query 27:	0.4672
Query 28:	0.0519
Query 29:	0.1277
Query 30:	0.1819
Query 31:	0.0187
Query 32:	0.0004
Query 33:	0.0625
Query 34:	0.0003
Query 35:	0.2006
Query 36:	0.0103
Query 37:	0.0605
Query 38:	0.0193
Query 39:	0.0861
Query 40:	0.5715
Query 41:	0.1390
Query 42:	0.7919
Query 43:	0.4745
Query 44:	0.0126
Query 45:	0.1932
Query 46:	0.4263
Query 47:	0.2996
Query 48:	0.0635
Query 49:	0.3156
Query 50:	0.0000

Overall statistics
(for 25 queries):

Total number of documents
over all queries
　Retrieved:　　25000
　Relevant:　　　1111
　Rel_ret:　　　　774

Interpolated Recall -
Precision Averages:
　at 0.00　0.4408
　at 0.10　0.3461
　at 0.20　0.2993
　at 0.30　0.2671
　at 0.40　0.2381
　at 0.50　0.1999
　at 0.60　0.1400
　at 0.70　0.1045
　at 0.80　0.0693
　at 0.90　0.0454
　at 1.00　0.0051

Avg. prec. (non-interpolated)
for all rel. documents
　　　　　0.1845

Precision:
　At　　5 docs:　0.3200
　At　 10 docs:　0.2800
　At　 15 docs:　0.2640
　At　 20 docs:　0.2480
　At　 30 docs:　0.2480
　At　100 docs:　0.1628
　At　200 docs:　0.0970
　At　500 docs:　0.0519
　At 1000 docs:　0.0310

R-Precision (prec. after R
(=num_rel) docs. retrieved):
　　Exact:　　0.2240

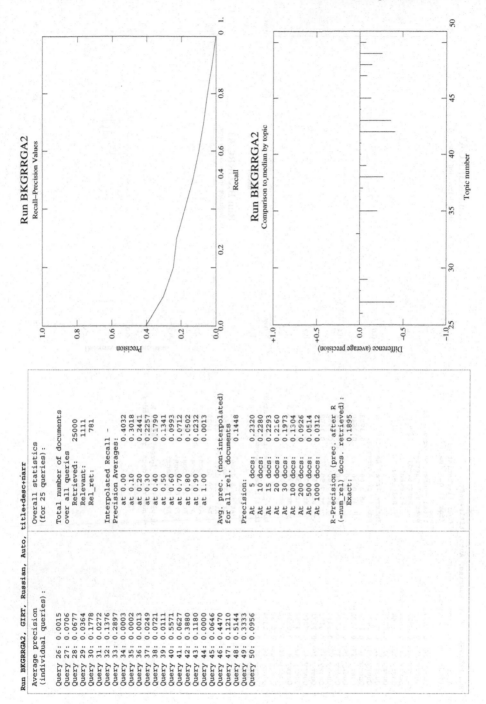

Run BKGRRGA2
Recall-Precision Values

Run BKGRRGA2
Comparison to,median by topic

Run BKGRRGA2, GIRT, Russian, Auto, title+desc+narr

Average precision
(individual queries):

Query 26:	0.0015
Query 27:	0.0706
Query 28:	0.0677
Query 29:	0.0364
Query 30:	0.1778
Query 31:	0.0272
Query 32:	0.1376
Query 33:	0.2897
Query 34:	0.0003
Query 35:	0.0002
Query 36:	0.0013
Query 37:	0.0249
Query 38:	0.0721
Query 39:	0.0111
Query 40:	0.5571
Query 41:	0.0627
Query 42:	0.3880
Query 43:	0.1180
Query 44:	0.0000
Query 45:	0.0646
Query 46:	0.4470
Query 47:	0.1210
Query 48:	0.5144
Query 49:	0.3333
Query 50:	0.0956

Overall statistics
(for 25 queries):

Total number of documents
over all queries
   Retrieved: 25000
   Relevant: 1111
   Rel_ret: 781

Interpolated Recall -
Precision Averages:
   at 0.00   0.4032
   at 0.10   0.3018
   at 0.20   0.2441
   at 0.30   0.2257
   at 0.40   0.1790
   at 0.50   0.1341
   at 0.60   0.0993
   at 0.70   0.0712
   at 0.80   0.0502
   at 0.90   0.0232
   at 1.00   0.0013

Avg. prec. (non-interpolated)
for all rel. documents
   0.1448

Precision:
  At   5 docs: 0.2320
  At 10 docs: 0.2280
  At 15 docs: 0.2293
  At 20 docs: 0.2260
  At 30 docs: 0.1973
  At 100 docs: 0.1304
  At 200 docs: 0.0926
  At 500 docs: 0.0514
  At 1000 docs: 0.0312

R-Precision (prec. after R
(=num_rel) docs. retrieved):
   Exact: 0.1895

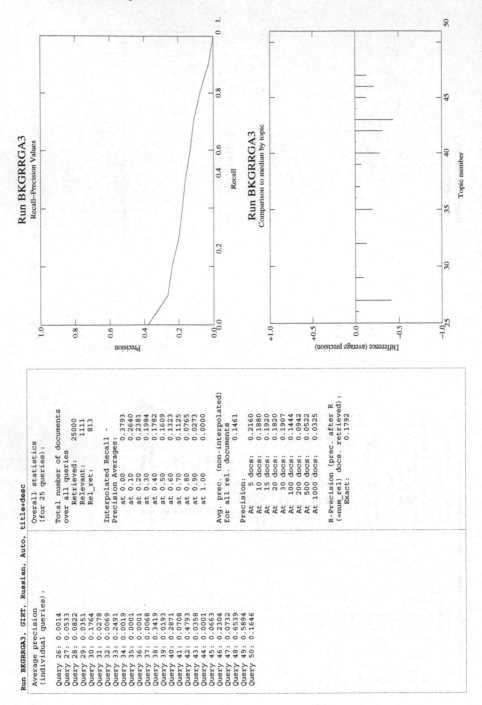

Run BKGRRGA3, GIRT, Russian, Auto, title+desc

Average precision
(individual queries):

Query 26: 0.0014
Query 27: 0.0533
Query 28: 0.0822
Query 29: 0.0351
Query 30: 0.1764
Query 31: 0.0278
Query 32: 0.0069
Query 33: 0.2491
Query 34: 0.0019
Query 35: 0.0001
Query 36: 0.0001
Query 37: 0.0068
Query 38: 0.3419
Query 39: 0.0193
Query 40: 0.2871
Query 41: 0.0708
Query 42: 0.4793
Query 43: 0.0358
Query 44: 0.0001
Query 45: 0.0663
Query 46: 0.2304
Query 47: 0.0732
Query 48: 0.6539
Query 49: 0.5894
Query 50: 0.1646

Overall statistics
(for 25 queries):

Total number of documents
over all queries
    Retrieved: 25000
    Relevant: 1111
    Rel_ret: 813

Interpolated Recall -
Precision Averages:
    at 0.00   0.3793
    at 0.10   0.2640
    at 0.20   0.2381
    at 0.30   0.1984
    at 0.40   0.1782
    at 0.50   0.1609
    at 0.60   0.1323
    at 0.70   0.1125
    at 0.80   0.0765
    at 0.90   0.0273
    at 1.00   0.0000

Avg. prec. (non-interpolated)
for all rel. documents
               0.1461

Precision:
    At   5 docs: 0.2160
    At   10 docs: 0.1880
    At   15 docs: 0.1920
    At   20 docs: 0.1820
    At   30 docs: 0.1907
    At 100 docs: 0.1444
    At 200 docs: 0.0942
    At 500 docs: 0.0522
    At 1000 docs: 0.0325

R-Precision (prec. after R
(=num rel) docs. retrieved):
    Exact: 0.1792

Author Index

Lecture Notes in Computer Science

For information about Vols. 1–2331
please contact your bookseller or Springer-Verlag